COWBOYS
Have Always
Been My Heroes

Other books by Peter Golenbock

DYNASTY

BRONX ZOO

NUMBER 1

BALLS

PERSONAL FOULS

AMERICAN ZOOM

WRIGLEYVILLE

COWBOYS
Have Always Been My Heroes

The Definitive
Oral History of
America's Team

PETER GOLENBOCK

WARNER BOOKS

A Time Warner Company

Warner Books, Inc., 1271 Avenue of the Americas,
New York, NY 10020

 A Time Warner Company

First Printing: August 1997
10 9 8 7 6 5 4 3 2 1

Library of Congress Cataloging-in-Publication Data

Golenbock, Peter, 1946–
    Cowboys have always been my heroes : the definitive oral history
of America's team / Peter Golenbock.
        p.   cm.
    Includes index.
    ISBN 0–446–51950–2
    1. Dallas Cowboys (Football team)—History.   I. Title.
GV956.D3G65   1997
796.332'64'097642812—dc20   96-32361
                                                              CIP

Book design by H. Roberts

Acknowledgments

To Tony Seidl, you old Longhorn you, for taking the ball on this fine idea for a book and running with it to paydirt.

To Rick Wolff of Warner Books, for your patience, encouragement, and friendship. And to Rob McMahon, who was always there for me on the other end of the phone.

To Rich Dalrymple, the director of public relations for the Dallas Cowboys, and his staff—Emily Cruz, Brett Daniels, and Doug Hood—for treating me in a manner exemplary for a public relations staff: openly and with unusual trust. I was allowed unlimited access to whatever material I wished to explore, and many a time I worked late into the night at the Valley Ranch complex with not another employee in the building except the security guard. I sincerely hope the finished product is all that you expected it to be, and more.

To Carlton Stowers, for generously providing me access to his precious telephone book, which got me to my Treasure Island neighbor Maury Youmans, for whom I owe a large debt of gratitude for letting me use his Cowboys-alumni phone and address list. To Steve Sabol and Kathy Davis of NFL Films, for their encouragement and for finding for me the few players who had recently moved or had dropped out of sight.

To some of the most talented newspaper reporters and columnists in

America—the late Steve Perkins, Gary Cartwright, Jim Browder, Sam Blair, Andy Anderson, Frank Luksa, Blackie Sherrod, Bob St. John, Randy Galloway, Gary Myers, Tim Cowlishaw, Jim Dent, Mickey Spagnola, Rick Gooselin, Barry Horn, Mike Fisher, Whitt Canning, Gil Le-Breton, Susie Woodhams, Kevin Blackistone, Rick Cantu, Jim Reeves, Ed Werder, and Skip Bayless—who provided me with reams and reams of juicy research material through their articles, columns, and books. I hope you won't mind my hit-and-run excursion onto your hallowed turf.

To Time-Life veteran Mark Goodman, for explaining college football in Texas when he was a boy. To Kate Agmann, for sharing with me her knowledge of Texas culture and religion, and to Les Leopold, my dear friend, for reminding me about *The Graduate* and the scene where Benjamin is advised to look into "plastics."

To David Solomon, for hours of solid research in the New York Public Library. To the staffs at the St. Petersburg, Tampa, and Dallas libraries for helping me to find tons of important material. To Ken Samelson and Bob Castillo, for your discerning eye. To Carolyn Jack, for all your hard work. And to Alex Gigante, my law school classmate, for your legal advice.

To yesterday's warriors: Margene Atkins, Gene Babb, Rodrigo Barnes, Dick Bielski, Byron Bradfute, Frank Clarke, Fred Cone, Gene Cronin, Buddy Dial, Bob Fry, Pete Gent, John Gonzaga, Cornell Green, Alvin Harper, Thomas Henderson, Calvin Hill, Chuck Howley, Lee Roy Jordan, Steve Kiner, Tom Landry, Eddie LeBaron, Bob Lilly, Ray Mathews, Don McIlhenny, Dick Nolan, Pettis Norman, Jack Patera, Drew Pearson, Don Perkins, Mel Renfro, Tex Schramm, Roger Staubach, Duane Thomas, Jerry Tubbs, and John Wilbur for your time, patience, memories, and encouragement. The greatest joy of these projects is in meeting and getting to know the participants. Thank you all from the bottom of my heart. You men know better than anyone just how difficult it is to be a professional athlete—before, during, and after. My hat is off to you all.

To my wonderful family: Rhonda Sonnenberg, the literary light of the family; Charles Eliot, the light of our lives; and Doris, the dog of our lives, all my love.

And last, but the opposite of least, to Neil and Dawn Reshen, whose generosity and unflagging support made this bucking bronco of a book not just successful, but possible.

Contents

PART I

The Old NFL

The Two Clints

uring the fall of 1958, as America was approaching the end of the tranquil Eisenhower era, Texas oil baron Clint Murchison Sr. and his wife, Virginia, left their 2,000-acre homestead south of downtown Dallas and flew from Love Field to Los Angeles as guests of Californian Ed Pauley, another oil tycoon.

Pauley, a former wildcatter who had literally struck it rich, was one of the owners of the Los Angeles Rams football team, and as their limousine drove them to the massive Coliseum, the L.A. businessman and philanthropist enthusiastically regaled Murchison with stories that conveyed the joy Pauley derived from owning a pro football franchise.

Murchison listened politely. The Dallas oilman, known for his no-nonsense, bottom-line, demeanor, then asked Pauley, "Did the Rams make any money last year?"

"Oh no," said Pauley. "It's just a fun thing."

When Murchison arrived back home, he couldn't wait to tell his rash and foolish son, Clint Jr., who seemed intent on pursuing a quest to blow a large wad of Murchison dough on a pro football franchise for Dallas. Ever since Clint Sr.'s younger son had sought to buy the failing Dallas Texans back in 1952, the old man was constantly irritated at the thought that Clint Jr. wanted to invest in this toy. He couldn't understand why his twenty-nine-year-old offspring, an intellectual with degrees from both Duke and MIT, a man of great wealth and impeccable taste, would want to invest in a small-potatoes business that earned very little money for anyone.

When the father told the son what Ed Pauley had told him, the son was undeterred and unfazed, which was as the father had anticipated; he knew the worst thing you could do was tell the boy either that he was destined for failure or that he shouldn't do something. The father suspected that despite his best advice, Clint Jr. would do the opposite, plunge ahead, unmindful of cost, secure in the knowledge that his instincts had more validity than either logic or the balance sheet.

In this respect the son was no different from his old man. The father, Ethelbert Clinton Murchison, one of the world's richest men, was a true Texas folk hero. Though he had started life with the financial advantages that come with being the son of a well-to-do banker, he earned his niche in Texas history by becoming immensely wealthy the Texas way: mano a mano, down and dirty, dog eat dog, me against you. Like the expert poker player he was, Clint's main pursuit all his life was the Big Score. And if he had to win by dealing from the bottom of the deck, well that was too bad for you. For Clint Murchison, it was no holds barred, and every man for himself.

As a youth Clint Sr. learned about ruthlessness from the Yankee-owned railroads. The citizens of his rural hometown of Athens, located sixty miles southeast of Dallas, had always resented the Texas & Pacific Railroad because the line had passed up their town in favor of going through Dallas, where its citizens had ingratiated themselves with the railroad by buying $100,000 in T&P bonds, and then pressured the state legislature to twist the track toward them. Dallas had grown dramatically. Athens had not.

Murchison, moreover, was aware that the railroad habitually cheated the Athens farmers by fixing freight rates, charging higher rates for farm products than other goods. Clint also saw that the railroad hired the best lawyers, steeling itself against the little guys trying to get a fair deal. In later years, when Murchison was in the oil business, he would remember that the railroads had extracted the last penny from the citizens, and he would ask himself, "If the railroad could do it, why can't I?"

When Clint Sr. was seven, he sold animal pelts to fur traders. He also learned the art of horse and cattle trading, in which the goal is to outwit (read: cheat) the other guy as badly as possible, preying on his ignorance or weakness. In his very first trade, Clint himself was taken when he traded a decent horse and a healthy calf for a handsome horse he didn't know was injured. As he did all his life, Murchison learned from his mistakes and didn't repeat them.

Once he figured out the trading game, Clint Murchison could look a man in the eye and overstate the quality of his steers, at the same time finding imaginative flaws in the opponent's herd. Through his cunning and his charm, as a youth Clint Murchison made more money animal trading than a lot of adults who worked full-time jobs in his Athens hometown.

In 1915 Clint interrupted his practical training when he enrolled in Trinity University, a Christian school in Waxahachie, twenty miles south of Dallas. Clint found college life unbearably tame. He became restless, stifled by the regimentation, bored with the curriculum. His prime activity at Trinity, a school run by Christian brothers, was organizing a floating crap game. When during his freshman year one of the other boys ratted on him, he was told by school authorities that he wouldn't be suspended if he revealed the names of the other participants.

Said Clint years later, "I thought that was a very unethical approach for men operating a Christian school."

He opted to return to Athens to work as a teller in his father's bank, an activity that also proved too mundane. Early in his employ, he quit after an examiner complained that Clint was mixing the nickels with the dimes. He disgustedly told his father he could make more money in a day trading cattle than in a month at the bank.

Soon after leaving the bank, the twenty-year-old Murchison learned that the U.S. Army needed wood. He knew where there was a supply of East Texas pine available, but it needed to be cut. He cut a deal with the army, then hired local Mexican workers for booze and a meager salary. He cleaned up.

During World War I Clint enlisted in the quartermaster corps of the army. While in the service, he took advantage of his trading skills. In Michigan he had his men collect salvage lumber, which he was supposed to burn, but instead sold it for $15,000 for the mess fund. He was loved by his men, though he was almost court-martialed.

When Clint got out of the army in 1918, his close friend Sid Richardson begged him to become his partner in the oil business. Before this time the demand for oil had been limited. Up until the Civil War Americans had used the oil of the sperm whale to light their lamps, and then in 1857 Benjamin Silliman, a chemistry professor at Yale, determined that oil from the ground would work as well. In the summer of 1859 in the hamlet of Titusville, Pennsylvania, oil was struck at the depth of sixty-nine feet.

A cost-conscious Cleveland merchant, John D. Rockefeller, then twenty-one, was attracted to the site, and he determined that it was foolish to invest in oil with prices so unsteady. He did, however, see that there was serious money to be made in the refining process, and by 1865 he was refining more oil than anyone. Rockefeller became immensely wealthy, as did his partner, H. M. Flagler, who would become famous for building the railroad to Miami.

Rockefeller incorporated on January 10, 1870, and his company became Standard Oil of Ohio.

In Texas, oil was first discovered in 1892 outside of Beaumont by a man named Portillo Higgins. The find would be known as Spindletop. Higgins and his chief backer, Anthony Lucas, drilled for ten years without a strike. They asked Standard Oil to back them but Flagler turned them down.

On January 1, 1901, the well exploded with a geyser that gushed oil to the sky, as pools of oil spread across the landscape. Standard Oil's monopoly was broken.

After Spindletop, there were oil strikes across Texas for the next thirty years. Texas, a huge area, was drought-stricken and depressed. Texans who struck oil were few in number, but those who did became very rich. Once oil came in, thousands of male and female quick-buck artists rushed to the area to try to make as much money as possible trading leases or selling provisions, booze, or their bodies to the oil seekers.

With the increased popularity of internal combustion engines for the automobile, gasoline became a valuable commodity. In 1910 there were just over 600,000 cars on the road. By 1920, after Henry Ford had made the family car affordable, there were more than nine million registered vehicles. And all those cars needed gasoline, which was derived from crude oil.

Sid Richardson, Clint Murchison's childhood friend, had been involved in the oil business since 1911, hauling pipes and working on an oil well platform at night, but also trading leases for himself. In 1918, when Richardson was twenty-four, he had made $100,000 buying and selling oil leases. Richardson and Murchison had done a lot of successful horse trading together before Clint's stint in the army, and Richardson figured that Murchison would be a natural trading oil leases. Clint caught on very quickly.

Lease trading, like horse trading, is an art unto itself. If leaseholders sense a well near the property will come in, the value of the leases goes up. If the leaseholder sells and the well comes in, the buyers are winners. If the well comes up dry, the sellers are the big winners. Accurate news is the key to success, and Clint Murchison became skilled at locating the right people to hang around (and pay off) in order to learn the secrets of where oil was about to be found. Late in 1919 he and his partner made $200,000 selling leases just before an oil strike on the Texas-Oklahoma border.

In 1927 Murchison invested in the Hendrick Field near the Texas-New Mexico border. The wells came in, but the oil and natural gas couldn't be shipped. A pipeline was needed, and Clint built it. He then began supplying large cities like Santa Fe and Albuquerque, New Mexico, with natural gas. By 1930 he was supplying forty-three towns in Texas, Oklahoma, New Mexico, Colorado, Wyoming, and Arkansas.

In the spring of 1931 oil was discovered in Woodbine, Texas, and shortly thereafter thirteen miles to the north in Kilgore. The question this time was whether the two finds were connected, whether this was a huge pool of oil or a series of finds. Clint Murchison gambled everything that it was one pool. Early in 1931 Clint drew a circle around the Kilgore strike and told his employees to lease everything they could within the circle. He financed the purchases by offering little up front but a decent return should the wells come in.

"Give them a dollar, two or five, whatever it takes, but give it to them out of a quarter of their oil," ordered Murchison.

Within three years this East Texas oil field was recognized as the largest in the world, a gigantic pool holding more than a billion barrels of oil. To take further financial advantage, Murchison built a pipeline to take the oil west to Tyler, where he would refine it.

Clint built on his fortune using OPM, other people's money. Reasoned Clint, "When you start using your own money, you start thinking you can do anything. Don't do it. Cash makes a man careless." He also taught his sons, "If you are going to owe money, owe more than you can pay, then the lenders can't afford to foreclose." One time when a banker from the Bank of Manhattan wanted to invest in one of Clint's pipelines, he asked how much Clint wanted.

"All the money I can get," he replied.

The bank loaned him more than a million dollars.

After netting profits estimated at between $20 million and $30 million, Clint's next move was to drill his own wells on a large scale. Well drilling is not only an expensive endeavor but it is also extremely risky. Not even Frank, his own brother, thought it prudent. But Clint believed in his instincts, and once again he was proved prescient. Drilling a Kilgore well was as sure a thing as there ever was in the oil business. Of the 29,000 wells sunk into the forty-mile-square oil field, only 555 of them turned up dry. By 1934, when most people couldn't afford $50 for one of Henry Ford's used Model Ts, Clint Murchison was estimated to be worth $50 million.

Murchison added to his wealth by engaging in practices that were forbidden by both federal and state laws. Many Southerners had lost their land and their homes after the Civil War. Their whole way of life had been changed. And it was all because of Abraham Lincoln's government in Washington, D.C., and his damn Yankee soldiers. Then when Northerners invaded their state in order to help the ex-slaves gain the vote, their contempt for outside regulation intensified dramatically. Their lives had been turned upside down once, and Southerners, including most Texans, swore that they would defend their land and their property and their right to do anything they wanted to do without interference of any kind from any government, including the one in Austin, and especially the one in Washington, D.C.

In August 1931 the Texas Oil Commission limited the amount of oil Murchison and the other oil barons could pump. Murchison and hundreds of oilmen refused to follow the rules. Murchison had such contempt for these regulations that as a form of protest he changed the name of his company from Golding-Murchison to the American Liberty Oil Company.

The excess oil was known as "hot oil," and competitors charged that Murchison's company not only sold "hot oil" but that it stole oil from East Texas competitors through the installation of mysterious pipelines with the destinations known only to Liberty Oil Company installers. Murchison was accused of opening hidden refineries in the backwoods, miles from the wells, enabling him to produce excess oil without getting caught. There was a saying, "The American Liberty pipeline was so hot you couldn't sit on it."

If the state enjoined a well for overproducing, Clint would switch the property into the name of another company and keep drilling. There was only one set of rules: Clint's. Murchison's renegade reputation was such that when he later showed up in Washington to argue against federal regulation, he was told that because of his rogue reputation the most helpful thing he could do would be to get back on the plane and go home.

Murchison, though, did not care what others in the industry thought of him. He could recall how the railroads had cheated the farmers of Texas with the help of federal regulation, and he was determined to keep Washington from interfering in his affairs.

To protect their oil investments, the Texas oil barons reached out to men in high political office sympathetic to their cause. Texas Representative Sam Rayburn chaired a House Committee on Interstate and Foreign Commerce to study the question of whether the federal government should step in and cut oil production in order to raise the price. The plan was to make the East Texas pool an oil reserve. Under the plan, the U.S. government was going to issue bonds for the value of the property taken.

Murchison was dead set against such a plan, even though in May of 1933 oil was down to four cents a barrel. Clint's rallying cry was "You are taking away my liberty."

In the end, Murchison's friend, Sam Rayburn, recommended the bill not pass, and it did not. It wasn't until 1935 that the Connolly Hot Oil Act was passed. If you were caught piping hot oil, the government could confiscate it. Only then did the "Hot Oil War" end. The U.S. Supreme Court upheld the validity of the law. Many years later Murchison was still bitter about it.

Clint Murchison for years courted a conservative senator from Wisconsin by the name of Joseph R. McCarthy. During the 1940s the senator would talk to Clint nonstop about the threat of Communist infiltration in America. It was only in the early 1950s, when Senator McCarthy charged that Communists had infiltrated the Truman Administration, that he became famous for it.

At that time Murchison enjoyed watching McCarthy make Truman squirm. "Give 'Em Hell" Harry had vetoed the Congressional Tidelands bill, which would have given Murchison the right to drill as far as ten miles offshore, and Truman had vetoed a bill that would have deregulated the oil and gas industry. Worse, Truman opposed the oil depletion allowance.

(The Texans got even. It was Murchison's friend Sid Richardson who had convinced General Dwight Eisenhower to run for president in 1952, after Eisenhower told him he supported Texan ownership of the Tidelands. Never, ever before had Texas voted Republican, the party of Abraham Lincoln and the hated carpetbaggers, but when Dwight Eisenhower ran under the Republican ticket, Texans voted for him because they saw him more as a war hero than a politician. They felt his choice of party was more a flip of the coin than a choice of philosophies. The oilmen helped swing Texas Ike's way en route to a resounding victory over Democratic candidate Adlai Stevenson.)

Joe McCarthy, who had been a marine, was conservative and combative, both Texas traits. He appealed to the rich Texans, especially H. L. Hunt, Murchison, Sid Richardson, and Hugh Roy Cullen. And they appealed to him. If America was being attacked by subversives, McCarthy wanted the Texans in his foxhole. McCarthy also knew how easily these men could be manipulated. He was aware they had a deep fear that their wealth would disappear as quickly as it had come, and McCarthy, a master manipulator, played heavily on this fear. Often he reminded them that in 1938 Mexican president Lázaro Cárdenas had nationalized all oil properties.

McCarthy also knew these men were staunchly distrustful of the federal government, which had successfully regulated the oil industry under Franklin Roosevelt. Texans would go so far as to refuse to register their cars or line up for a driver's license. He was aware of Texans' intense hatred of the IRS, which was always trying to take their money through infernal income taxes. McCarthy promised he would protect their interests, and he became known as "the third senator from Texas."

Clint Murchison was the Texan closest to McCarthy. He gave him stock tips and contributed millions to his campaign. When Murchison tried to show McCarthy how to make money using other people's money, Murchison was disappointed to discover that McCarthy would take the money, go to Las Vegas, and gamble it away. It soon became apparent that McCarthy was both a drunk and a man of little self-respect. Often McCarthy would get drunk when they played cards, and after he would pass out, they would stuff money in his pants pockets. He may have been a lousy card player, but for a decade his influence was important to them.

In the fall of 1953 McCarthy stepped over the line when he charged the army with harboring Communists. Clint begged McCarthy to document what he was saying and to stop making reckless charges. But by then McCarthy was out of control. He drank heavily, beginning at breakfast. Clint became disgusted. When a drunken McCarthy threw his own wife into a swimming pool one evening, Murchison ordered him to pack his bags and get out. McCarthy was censured after the Army-McCarthy hearings, and a few years later he was dead, but not before he'd caused harm and disillusionment to a lot of people, including Clint. Murchison had deeply believed in McCarthy's brand of Americanism, and he was crushed that the senator had turned out to be a man who couldn't hold his liquor, that his former friend ended up being just another sleazy self-promoter.

Because of his association with Joe McCarthy, Clint Sr. was reputed to be antiblack, anti-Semitic, and antiliberal, like his compatriot H. L.

Hunt, who *was* all of those things. But Clint Murchison was not that way at all. Clint harbored no racial prejudice. And he didn't care enough about religion to be against somebody else's. He only cared about one thing: making money.

Beginning in 1939 Clint Sr. began to diversify, to add properties other than oil and gas to his portfolio. Looking into the future and seeing potential growth of a company proved the key to his unwavering success. Clint demonstrated a genius for searching out companies with untapped growth potential based on trends in America and around the world. Clint saw the future growth of the insurance industry, and that year he and a partner, Toddie Lee Wynne, borrowed a million dollars and bought the Reserve Life Insurance Company of Indianapolis, moving the corporate offices to Dallas the following year.

If the times were a-changing, and a certain company seemed ripe for improved earnings, Murchison would buy it. In the 1940s Clint Sr. saw the potential for curbside convenience stores. His friend Earl Cabell had founded the 7-Eleven stores. When Cabell became mayor of Dallas, he sold 75 percent of the company to Murchison. Clint Sr. wanted to open a chain of these stores all across the country. Cabell didn't have Clint's foresight, and when Cabell said he wasn't interested, Clint Sr. immediately sold out his shares to a third party. As any of us who ever needed a loaf of bread at three in the morning can attest, Clint turned out to be very right, Cabell wrong.

Clint purchased Henry Holt and Company and saw the publisher's profits double as servicemen returning from the war bought millions of its textbooks.

In 1957 Clint Murchison Sr. was listed as one of the richest people in America, along with Vincent Astor, John Hay Whitney, Mrs. Edsel Ford, Doris Duke, the tobacco heir, several DuPonts, and the Rockefeller boys, Nelson, David, John D., Laurence, and Winthrop.

Clint had married young, and in 1921 his wife, Anne, gave birth to a son, John Dabney, and in 1923 to Clint Jr. Two years later a third son, Burk, was born, but he died in April of 1936 of pneumonia. In 1926 Anne died suddenly, leaving Clint Murchison shattered. The boys, raised by servants and nannies, were sickly and frail. When Clint Jr. was eight, he told his grandmother, "I'm just the shyest little boy in the world." As a child Clint Jr. hated the outdoors, much to his father's dismay, preferring to sit at home and read *Popular Mechanics* magazine and the dictionary. On their 2,000-acre farm in South Dallas, where Clint Sr. developed championship race horses the rare times he was home, the boys grew up with the children of servants, seeing few white children and even fewer women.

When neither John nor Clint Jr. showed any interest in the oil business, in the 1940s their father preordained their future by acquiring for them a series of companies under the umbrella of Murchison Brothers— without their knowledge.

At the end of 1949, Papa Murchison popped a surprise on the sons. He presented his two boys with a portfolio of twenty major companies. He wasn't giving them the stock in the companies. He was giving them the companies. Part of the arrangement was that John and Clint Jr. were to be fifty-fifty partners in everything they did.

"Have at it," he told his sons.

The two Murchison boys, very different in personality, were thrown together as a team. John, the more outgoing and social of the two brothers, took to the task with great relish. A Yalie, he was conservative, too deliberate his father thought, but thoughtful and intelligent. John had flown during the war, and he loved to fly and to ski, and when a friend asked him to invest in a new ski area in Vail, Colorado, he did so. In the early 1960s John built a private airport for his fleet of planes and ran it at a profit.

Clint Jr., the other son, was different from both his father and his brother. Clint Jr. was a small, owlish-looking man who assiduously avoided the outdoors, preferring an easy chair and the company of *Popular Mechanics* and scientific journals. His great loves were teaching and mathematical theory. After graduating from Lawrenceville Academy with the highest grade point average in the school's history, he went on to Duke University, where he graduated magna cum laude with a degree in electrical engineering. From there he got his master's degree in mathematics at MIT. He was an A student there as well. Shy and introverted, Clint Jr. believed himself intellectually superior to others, and he could be abrupt to the point of being impolite. He shunned social events, spending most of his time in his office, making deals.

Author Jane Wolfe recalled that one time at a party, a man walked by Clint Jr. and said hello. Clint stared but said nothing.

"Why didn't you speak to him?" asked a friend.

"I saw him yesterday. How often do you have to speak to someone?"

But though he appeared to be an introverted egghead, Clint Jr. had another personality that he could pursue and indulge because he had the money to do so. Behind that sport-jacketed buttoned-down exterior, Clint Jr. was a wild child. His best friend was Bedford Wynne, the son of his dad's former partner, Toddie Lee Wynne. In 1944 Clint Jr.'s dad had dis-covered that Toddie Lee had bought some oil wells without telling him. Clint Sr. was devastated, and he would have nothing more to do with Tod-die Lee. But Clint Jr. admired Bedford for his outgoing personality and for his ability to have a good time, and the two were best buddies for life.

Bedford was a serious partyer and he was more than willing to help Clint Jr. with his extramarital sexual conquests. Clint Jr. may have been shy, but after Bedford would make the introductions for him, Clint Jr. wasn't without his charms. For Clint Jr., "Want to fly to Mexico for the weekend on my private plane?" was a very effective way of starting an af-fair on just the right note.

Clint Jr. loved the less-educated drinking crowd, partied openly with women who weren't his wife, and had as much fun as he could find. His brother John, who was devoted to his family, was often disgusted by his brother's frat-house behavior. But in that the two brothers had been bound to each other in business as lifelong fifty-fifty partners, there wasn't any-thing John could do about it.

His father recognized Clint Jr.'s flaws. In addition to his son's stub-bornness, his father also saw that in business he was a reckless gambler, a man who moved impulsively without giving his decisions much consid-eration. Clint Murchison Sr. saw that his younger son would move from deal to deal, often losing interest in past investments and leaving them un-attended. He also saw that Clint Jr. was also the sort of guy who did little work if his heart wasn't into it.

In 1951 the old man built fifty-two middle-income houses for re-turning servicemen, and he appointed Clint Jr. to go out and sell them, hoping it would make him more gregarious. The son's partner in selling was Robert Thompson, who would become Clint Jr.'s other best friend along with Bedford Wynne, and it wasn't long before Thompson found himself involved in Junior's life procuring women for him. When Clint Sr. saw that his playboy son and his fun-loving buddy weren't going to sell the houses, he hired a go-getter female hat salesperson to do it. Within nine months she had sold all fifty-two houses. Afterward, with Papa Murchison's backing, she started her own construction company, and she became rich as one of the top real estate brokers in America.

Making his employees rich was one of Clint Murchison's hallmarks. One of his credos was "If you've got a good man working for you, make sure he dies rich."

But Clint Jr. was already rich. Money wasn't an incentive. He needed to find a line of work that interested him, and he found it in construction, which gave him an opportunity to use the engineering degree he had earned. He bought the City Construction Company, a Dallas street-paving company, and he hired his buddy Robert Thompson to run it. Clint Jr. soon expanded it into a large pyramid of construction companies. In true Texas fashion, Clint named his company Tecon, for Take On, as in "We'll take on anything."

Clint Jr. through his actions displayed a strong love-hate relationship with his powerful father. He was always demonstrating a willingness to take risks as big as those taken by his father. One time Clint Jr. won a bid to remove shale from a high hill near the Panama Canal. The job was risky because any shale that fell into the canal would have to be dredged out at a high cost. Murchison Sr. advised Junior not to do it. He did it anyway. Tecon accomplished it with no major disaster, and the company earned worldwide recognition.

His father was impressed, but he remained deeply concerned about Clint Jr.'s "take on" philosophy. He saw an ego (or perhaps a lack thereof) that caused his son to boast that he could beat anyone, no matter how big the opponent. In one residential development deal, despite all warnings that he was paying too much for the property and would suffer large losses, Clint Jr. went ahead anyway. He borrowed and lost $500,000.

His father warned him, "You can afford to go broke once, but that's all."

During the early days of the Murchison Brothers partnership, Clint Jr. for the most part kept his riverboat gambling instincts in check, with the exception of an occasional bad deal, and the insistence that he buy a football team for Dallas. His father just could not understand why he was intent on putting serious capital into an investment that was virtually guaranteed to lose money. In 1960 pro football was a *very* marginal business. It was a mom-and-pop operation dependent almost solely on ticket sales. Money from television and radio was peanuts. A new expansion team in Dallas, Papa Murchison knew, promised mediocrity at best for the foreseeable future.

Clint Sr. feared that Clint Jr. was unbalanced; that his boy wanted to spend his valuable money and precious time operating an NFL franchise seemed proof enough.

2

Growing Pains

Clint Murchison Jr.'s passion for football began at Lawrenceville Academy, where he was a halfback on the school team, and even though he was small at 5'7", 130 pounds, he played club football at MIT. When Giles Miller, a Dallas textile mogul, bought the National Football League's financially strapped New York Yanks, moved the team to Dallas in 1952, and renamed it the Dallas Texans, Clint Jr. became an instant fan. He was one of the few thousand who traveled to the Cotton Bowl to see the first home game, the Texans against the New York Giants. To help the struggling franchise, Murchison bought twenty season tickets and gave them out to his friends.

At that game Governor Allen Shivers prematurely proclaimed it a "new era in sports in Texas." The highlight of the dismal game came when Giant defensive back Tom Landry fumbled a punt on his own 22-yard line after he was hit by Texan tackle Jim Lansford. The fumble led to a Texan touchdown. Perhaps 5,000 fans saw the game, a scattering in the cavernous, 75,000-seat Cotton Bowl.

When Miller bought the team he had a vision that pro football would become a national phenomenon. Unfortunately for him, his timing was bad. It was before the age of television, before pro football became a national phenomenon. In 1952 the pros had to depend on local support with little outside revenue. If you couldn't draw fans, you were dead. And the Dallas Texans could not draw fans because the area surrounding Fort Worth and Dallas was *the* hotbed of college football in the nation. The powerful Southwest Conference boasted six Texas schools of note: the University of Texas, Southern Methodist University, Baylor, Rice, Texas Christian University, and Texas A&M. Not to mention Texas Tech, which was later to join the conference.

Each of these Texas colleges had a long, illustrious history. Perhaps the most beloved was SMU, which just after World War II boasted Doak Walker, a hero of the magnitude of such other Texas legends as Sam Houston, William Travis, Jim Bowie, and Davy Crockett. The grip Walker had on the imagination of Texans was that great.

Walker, a single wing tailback, could run, pass, and kick extra points and field goals. He was a one-man wrecking crew, and in addition he embodied all the virtues that Texans admired: he was a good Methodist. His parents were schoolteachers in Dallas. He was handsome. He had even married the campus homecoming queen. And on the football field, he was unstoppable. Doak Walker to Texans was as mythic as the Lone Ranger. In 1948 Walker was *Collier* magazine's choice as the college football Player of the Year.

Succeeding Walker at SMU was another heroic back, Kyle Rote. Perhaps the biggest game in the history of the Southwest Conference occurred in 1949 when SMU met national power Notre Dame. It was a very emotional time because Walker had been injured during his senior year, and he was unable to play against the Irish. Taking his place was Rote, who scored three touchdowns as SMU almost won the game. The next year Rote was an All-America.

Opposing SMU in the late 1940s was another Texas legend, Bobby Layne from the University of Texas. Layne was a pinpoint passer and an astute field general but he was the opposite of Walker in that he loved to drink, was a wild partyer, and he could pepper a sentence with profanity like nobody else. Playing with Layne on that University of Texas team was a back by the name of Tom Landry, who was considered one of the finest defensive players in the college game. Landry was shrewd, always seemed to know where the play was going, and he could hit like a truck.

SMU and Texas were the class teams of the conference, but each of the other colleges also had its stars. TCU never again reached the heights after the heroics of Sammy Baugh and Davey O'Brien in the 1930s, but in the postwar era they developed some great running backs, including the elusive Jim Swink. Texas A&M was a bitter rival of Texas. A&M in the late 1950s would boast one of the hardest running backs in college history, John David Crow. Rice, the MIT of the South, seemed to specialize in developing great ends, including Billy Howton and Buddy Dial. Baylor had a string of fine quarterbacks, the best perhaps in the personage of Adrian Burk.

By 1952, when the New York Yanks moved to Dallas, Doak Walker and Bobby Layne were starring for the Detroit Lions, and Kyle Rote for the New York Giants. Team owner Giles Miller was convinced that Texans would flock to the Cotton Bowl to watch their former college heroes play against his Dallas Texans team.

What Giles Miller didn't understand was that Dallas was not like the industrial cities of the North, where college football was weak. The sometimes-powerful University of Pittsburgh played in Pittsburgh, but what other colleges were near enough to NFL teams to compete with the pro stars? There were Columbia and NYU in New York City, Temple and the University of Pennsylvania in Philadelphia, Northwestern in Chicago, and who played in Detroit, Cleveland, and Green Bay? Nobody. Only on the West Coast did the pros have competition from the great California universities, Stanford, University of California at Berkeley, USC, and UCLA.

Giles Miller just could not get the rabid football fans of the Dallas-Fort Worth area to either switch or add their allegiance to his team. In Texas, where the nearest National Football League franchise was in Washington D.C., pro football had been barely a curiosity, and because the Dallas Texans were a losing team, local interest in them was minimal.

Even though the Dallas Texans had breakaway runner Buddy Young and maniacal defensive wizard Gino Marchetti, it quickly became clear that the Dallas Texans would not draw in Dallas. Neither Young, who was black, nor Marchetti, who was *eye-talian,* had roots in Texas. Perhaps if Walker or Layne had been on the team, Miller might have had a fighting chance, but without a real-live Texas hero to guide them, the turnstiles rarely clicked.

Journalist and author Mark Goodman was twelve when he went to see the Dallas Texans as Giles Miller's guest. "It was sad," said Goodman. "Mr. Miller was doing everything he could to fill the Cotton Bowl, and the place was so empty I remember going to those games and being able to sit anywhere we wanted. Boy, Giles was giving tickets away. The only ones who cared a little about pro football were the kids, 'cause we'd send away for pictures of Otto Graham, but really nobody gave a damn. He lost a lot of money that year."

The Texans' final home game was played against the Los Angeles Rams. Before the game NFL Commissioner Bert Bell warned Rams general manager Tex Schramm, "Don't you leave that office until you get your check." After the game Schramm made certain to pick up the Rams' share of the proceeds in person. Schramm could relax only after the check cleared.

Three-quarters of the way into the season the NFL took over the Dallas Texans, and they were made into a "road" team.

Despite the poor attendance at Texan home games, Clint Murchison Jr. thought he would enjoy owning an NFL franchise, and at the end of the '52 season he asked Bert Bell for a twenty-four-hour grace period so he could study the books before agreeing to take over the team. Bell refused his request. Instead, Bell awarded the franchise to an old friend, Carroll Rosenbloom, who, like Giles Miller, also was in the textile business. Bell gave Rosenbloom a sweetheart of a deal, and the Dallas Texans became the Baltimore Colts.

Undeterred, almost immediately Clint tried and failed to buy a minority interest in the Washington Redskins from Harry Wismer, who at the time was part owner and play-by-play announcer for the Redskins.

Two years later Clint's intention was to buy the San Francisco 49ers and move them to Dallas. Clint had been contacted by Fred Saigh, the former general manager of the St. Louis Cardinals baseball team. Saigh had been barred from baseball after a conviction for income tax evasion, and when Bert Bell told Clint that the league would not accept him as an owner, Murchison dropped out of the deal.

"He brought it to me," Clint told Bell, "and if he can't be a part of it, then I'm not going to go ahead."

Then in 1958 Clint came close to buying the Washington Redskins from George Preston Marshall for $600,000 and moving the team to Dallas. Under the terms of the deal, Marshall would run the team for five years and then step down. At the last moment, Marshall decided he wanted to stay for ten years, not five.

"Tell him to go to hell," said Murchison. "The deal's off."

Clint asked NFL commissioner Bert Bell where he should try next. The Chicago Cardinals might be for sale, Bell told him. Murchison was told to negotiate with Walter Wolfner, a nightclub owner from St. Louis, and his wife, Violet, who was the widow of Charlie Bidwell, the founder of the Cardinals.

At the same time, Lamar Hunt, the son of a rival Texas oil baron, also wanted an NFL franchise for Dallas. Hunt, too, asked Bell how he should go about buying a franchise and bringing it to Dallas. Bell told him the same thing: negotiate with Walter and Violet Wolfner. But like Murchison,

Hunt found the negotiations fruitless. Frustrated, Lamar Hunt decided on a course that would ultimately land Murchison his franchise and lead to Hunt founding the American Football League.

If there was one man even richer than Clint Jr.'s daddy, it was Lamar's daddy, Haroldson Lafayette Hunt, a man who traded oil leases with the best of them. Hunt had started on his road to fortune as a gambler. In a poker game he had won an oil well. That was his start. He then made his megafortune by tricking a sick old man out of his grubstake. The man, Marion Joyner, was seventy when he discovered evidence of oil in the town of Henderson in East Texas. Joyner then leased 4,000 acres to the west of his find. When Joyner went to drill, the existing drill bits were not strong enough to reach the oil he was sure was there, and so in September 1930 he was on the verge of bankruptcy when H. L. Hunt met with him.

Hunt kept Joyner in his hotel room, negotiating with him nonstop in an attempt to badger him into selling his leases for $30,000 and a percentage of the profits worth a maximum of $1.26 million. Hunt was so sure of himself he purchased leases on the eastern side of the find as well. Like Murchison, he bought the leases cheap, with promises of a percentage should the oil come in. Hunt spent all but $106 of the money he had to his name.

When a well close to Joyner's came up dry, Hunt relayed that information to Joyner. What he kept from the old man was that a well close to Woodbine came up saturated in oil. Unaware of the positive news, the nearly destitute Joyner broke down and signed the contract with Hunt, glad to have his $30,000. Two days later a major oil company was finally able to get in touch with Joyner and offered him $3.5 million for leases he no longer owned.

Because the find was so huge, Joyner's deal with Hunt earned him the full $1.26 million, and so Joyner became rich. But Hunt became the richest man in the United States. During World War II, Hunt claimed to hold more oil reserves than all of the Axis nations put together, and that included the huge Romanian reserves at Ploesti. At the time of his death in 1975, Hunt was the nation's only billionaire from Texas.

H. L. Hunt's son, Lamar, loved football as much as Clint Jr. Lamar surely was the richest man ever to play college football (third string at SMU behind Doyle Nix and Raymond Berry). When Lamar Hunt couldn't find an existing franchise to buy for himself, Hunt met several times with NFL commissioner Bert Bell in what appeared to be an attempt to land an expansion team for Dallas. Hunt pumped Bell for information on the financial stability of the league. After it was clear that Hunt intended to start his own league, observers believed that Hunt's meetings with Bell were a spy mission, that his goal had been to glean as much information as he could from Bell about the NFL's finances.

In June of 1959 Lamar Hunt announced the formation of the American Football League. To ensure the league's success, Hunt arranged with the American Broadcasting Company a five-year contract to broadcast its games.

On August 14, 1959, the American Football League was founded in the Conrad Hilton Hotel in Chicago. The new teams were announced: the New York Titans, Houston Oilers, Minneapolis Vikings, Denver Broncos, Los Angeles Chargers, and Dallas Texans. Among the original investors to whom Hunt had sold franchises were Harry Wismer in New York, Bud Adams in Houston, Max Winter in Minneapolis, Bob Howsam in Denver, and Barron Hilton in Los Angeles (who after one year moved to San Diego). Hunt would own the Dallas franchise. There were to be two other franchises, which turned out to be Boston and Buffalo. William Sullivan and Ralph Wilson became owners of those teams.

At the same time, Hunt and Bud Adams continued to meet with George Halas, the chairman of the NFL expansion committee. But Halas had two other candidates for NFL franchises in Dallas and Houston. Clint Murchison Jr. had been pressing Halas for an answer because he needed the time to negotiate a lease with the Cotton Bowl. He also didn't want Lamar Hunt's Texans to get a head start in the battle for the hearts and minds of Texas.

On August 29, 1959, Halas and Pittsburgh Steeler owner Art Rooney called Clint Murchison Jr. to tell him that Dallas would be eligible for membership in the NFL. Craig Cullinan was to get an NFL franchise in Houston, but he first had to get permission to use Rice University's stadium. (He never did get the franchise, which the following year went to Minneapolis.) Murchison was told that he had a franchise subject to the membership of the league voting its approval at the league meeting in January. Whether he would start in '60 or '61 would also be decided at the meeting.

On October 11, 1959, commissioner Bert Bell died watching his beloved Philadelphia Eagles playing at Franklin Field. In a meeting following Bell's funeral, all the league owners except George Preston Marshall of Washington voted to expand. The Redskins were the team of the South, watched by southerners from Florida across to Texas. Marshall had no intention of allowing a new franchise to hurt his television and radio revenues. Nevertheless, the politics of the time was that the league badly needed to expand in order to cut off the legs of the new league. On October 19, 1959, in an effort to scare off investors in the AFL, Halas exaggerated the NFL's intent by announcing that it would admit two teams in 1960 and two more in 1961 and 1962.

Murchison was reluctant to have to compete with another pro football team in the same town, and late in October 1959 he offered a partnership in the NFL Dallas franchise to Lamar Hunt. Hunt, however, told Clint he was committed to his partners in the AFL and could not abandon them without the risk of a lawsuit.

There is always intrigue when wealthy, powerful men fight over territory. Observers wondered what the NFL owners, who had enjoyed their monopoly in pro football until now, would do to counter the upstart AFL. Who would be compromised? Who would be paid off?

On November 22, 1959, at a meeting of the AFL owners, Max Winter, who had told Hunt he would buy the AFL franchise in Minneapolis, shocked the newcomers when he double-crossed them by accepting an offer to own an NFL franchise in Minneapolis. If George Halas had wanted to hurt the new league, giving franchises to Dallas and Minneapolis was the most effective way of doing it. The move crippled the American Football League in the South and kept it out of the Midwest for several years. To replace the Minneapolis franchise, the AFL hastily regrouped and put a weak franchise into small-market Oakland.

When Clint Murchison Jr. was told in August of 1959 that he would be the owner of the new Dallas franchise, he still had to wait five months for the league vote. Murchison saw that Hunt and his Dallas Texans were starting up in 1960, and Murchison realized that if he waited to hire his staff in January, he would not be able to put a team on the field until 1961, putting him at a further disadvantage. Murchison saw he had no choice but to hire a general manager, a coach, and sign a slew of free agents immediately in his effort to show the other owners that he was serious about fielding his new team in 1960. Accordingly, Murchison asked the advice of George Halas, who recommended that Tex Schramm, the former L.A. Rams general manager, run the new team's front office. Schramm then personally hired New York Giant defensive coach Tom Landry as the team's head coach. Because his new team was starting too late to be included in the draft of college senior players, George Halas gave Murchison permission to sign personal service contracts with two college standouts, Don Meredith of Southern Methodist University and running back Don Perkins from the University of New Mexico. If the team was not voted into the league, Meredith and Perkins could then sign with whoever picked them in the upcoming draft.

The drama unfolded in Miami Beach at the annual NFL meeting held in January 1960. Murchison, Schramm, and Landry headed to Florida with the existence of their franchise at stake.

Clint Jr. had flown in a dozen or so of his partying friends and put them up at the swanky Kenilworth Hotel, owned by TV personality Arthur Godfrey. Murchison had expected the meeting to last a day, two at the most. What he hadn't counted on was that the league had to vote on a new commissioner before it could decide the fate of the new team. It would be eleven days before the feuding league owners finally picked a commissioner.

One group of owners—including Wellington Mara of the Giants, Paul Brown of Cleveland, and Daniel Reeves of Los Angeles—wanted Marshall Leahy, who was the attorney for the San Francisco 49ers. The opposing faction, including Art Rooney of Pittsburgh and Carroll Rosenbloom of Baltimore, preferred Austin Gunsel, the league's attorney. One reason they opted for Gunsel was that Leahy said he would move the league headquarters to San Francisco if he was elected. The Rooney group held enough votes to keep Leahy from getting the job. At the same time no matter who else the anti-Leahy contingent recommended, the pro-Leahy contingent voted him down, holding out in the hope that Leahy would prevail. Cleveland owner and coach Paul Brown was asked to run for the job. Brown declined. Don Kellett, the general manager of the Colts, was nominated and defeated. The standoff became an ordeal. For twenty-three ballots over ten days, there was a deadlock.

The next day the pro-Leahy forces finally gave up. As a compromise choice, L.A. Rams majority owner Daniel Reeves nominated his general manager, Alvin "Pete" Rozelle, who was asked to leave the room. Rozelle went across the hall and hung out in the bathroom. To keep his nomination secret, every time a reporter came in the bathroom, Rozelle washed his hands so the reporter wouldn't be suspicious that his name was under nomination.

Rozelle was young, and he had made no enemies. After the deciding vote in his favor, Rozelle was asked to come back into the room. His hands were wet.

"I can honestly say I come to you with clean hands," said the man who would lead the NFL for the next generation.

*   *   *

Once the new commissioner was chosen, the league's next order of business was deciding on whether to give Clint Murchison Jr. an expansion franchise in Dallas.

Going into the meeting Murchison knew that his primary opponent would be George Preston Marshall, who had joined the NFL in 1932 when he bought the Boston Braves. He moved the team—renamed the Redskins in 1933—to Washington after the 1936 season.

Marshall was colorful, controversial, flamboyant, and egocentric. Marshall was an old-timer who believed that the success of the sport of pro football was due to the fact that it typified the tough, aggressive nature of the American people. He liked to say, "Football is no place for soft people."

On Sunday evenings after a Redskin home game, Marshall and his wife, Corinne, a movie star once known as the "Orchid Lady," would go to the Blue Room of the Shoreham Hotel for dinner. Bandleader Barney Brisken and his orchestra would be playing, and when the Marshalls entered the room, the orchestra would segue into "Hail to the Redskins," which Brisken and Corinne had written. Marshall would greet the other guests as though he were royalty.

Marshall was a pioneer in broadcasting his games. In 1942 he hired broadcaster Harry Wismer to do the play-by-play, and his Redskin Network spread throughout the South. Throughout the 1950s the fortunes of the Redskins declined in part because Marshall was quick to fire his coaches and in part because of his stubborn refusal to sign black players. Even after stars such as Jim Brown, Lenny Moore, John Henry Johnson, and Ollie Matson came into the league in the 1950s, Marshall maintained that his fans and viewing audience would boycott if the team signed blacks. Said Wismer, who also was a minority stockholder in the team, "He was wrong, he knew he was wrong, refused to admit it, and blamed all the Redskins failures on everyone but himself."

The pigheaded Marshall, Clint Murchison Jr. knew, would be the one formidable stumbling block to his getting his franchise. It may have been in the interest of the league to expand, but it was not in the interest of George Preston Marshall, who didn't want to give up his southern audience.

But Clint Murchison Jr. was not a man used to losing, and ultimately he got his way. How he did so is cloaked in mystery and intrigue. Part of the story has become folklore. The other part was hidden behind closed doors in the back rooms of Washington, D.C., politicians.

The folklore part of the story has been retold over and over, but nevertheless it says a great deal about Clint Murchison. It speaks of Murchison's power, his preparedness, his willingness to turn every stone in his quest for something he badly wanted.

When George and Corinne Marshall were divorced in the late 1950s, in the settlement Corinne received as her property the rights to "Hail to the Redskins," the fight song she co-wrote with Barney Brisken. In 1959 Brisken asked Corinne if she would sell him her rights, and she did so. Perhaps Murchison put him up to it. It's possible, as Murchison knew the society bandleader. Or perhaps, once Murchison learned that Brisken owned the rights, he knew Brisken could use the $2,500 he shelled out to pay for those rights.

Regardless, Murchison loved to tell the story of how in the fall of 1959 he gave $2,500 to his close friend and Washington lobbyist Bobby Baker to go to Brisken and make the buy.

The month before the vote on the new franchise was to be taken, Murchison called Marshall on the phone before a late-season Redskin game.

"Does the Redskins band intend to play the Redskins fight song?" asked Murchison.

"They sure will," said Marshall.

"The hell they will," said Murchison. "Nobody plays *my* fight song without *my* permission." It was at this point that Murchison told him about his purchase of Marshall's beloved song.

Said Bobby Baker, Murchison's messenger, "You couldn't make that sort of basic boo-boo when engaged in a peeing contest with the Murchisons. Their price for the Redskins' being able to continue to use the song—withdrawal of Marshall's opposition to the Dallas NFL franchise."

Clint Jr. could not be certain Marshall would value his fight song highly enough to give up his dominant position broadcasting his Redskin games across the South, and so Murchison moved against him on another front. This is where the behind-the-scenes dealings come in. He used his influence to get Congress to declare Marshall's Redskins Network a monopoly.

It is ironic that Clint Murchison Jr.—whose father hated big government, hated Franklin Roosevelt for his socialistic policies and for trying to regulate the oil industry, hated the federal government for trying to stop him from pumping "hot oil" during the 1930s—knew *all* the powerful people in Washington. Clint Sr. had spit on Washington. Clint Jr. embraced it.

Once again, the man he used to get the job done was Bobby Baker, who later would get in trouble during the Lyndon Johnson administration for taking payoffs. In 1967 Baker was convicted on eight counts of larceny, fraud, and tax evasion, a conviction he fought until 1971, when he went to prison to serve sixteen months.

Baker was a facilitator. If you wanted something done in Washington, you went to Baker, and he would make an "arrangement" with a senator or representative. To make sure your hands stayed clean, you carried out the arrangement with this middleman, or "aide." After he was caught, Baker's job description changed from facilitator to "bag man."

It wasn't until years later that Baker revealed to author Larry L. King what Murchison had done to assure his getting the Dallas franchise. According to Baker, he delivered $25,000 to the late senator Estes Kefauver, chairman of the senate antimonopoly committee, from "a group of Texans who badly wanted to gain a profitable NFL franchise for Dallas.

"I was approached by [Murchison's] courier whom I knew as a fellow reveler and high-roller in Washington. 'Bobby,' he said over drinks in my office, 'my job and my ass are on the line. I've got to lock up that damn football franchise. I have been told not to leave any stone unturned.'"

The courier was probably Robert Thompson, Murchison's right-hand man and head of Tecon, the holding company for all the Murchison enterprises. At the time of the article in 1973, Thompson was still alive.

Baker said the money was delivered to a member of Kefauver's staff in a committee office in the old Senate Office Building.

According to Baker, George Preston Marshall "was adamantly against sharing the South with a Texas-based team certain to divide regional loyalties at the expense of his pocketbook."

The money, according to Baker, was designed to influence the subcommittee's "finding that . . . Marshall . . . held an illegal monopoly with the so-called Redskins Television Network." The subcommittee did make that ruling against Marshall.

Said Baker, "Marshall's proprietary instinct, wholly robber baron in character, may well have been rejected by an honest subcommittee. But with millions at stake, the Texans took no chances."

When the admission was published in *Playboy* in June of 1973, denials flew. Clint Murchison Jr. denied the story. Pete Rozelle even denied the story, though he wasn't involved.

However, Robert Thompson, who was one of Murchison's closest friends and one of his party companions and who had probably been the courier who brought the money to Baker, *loved* to tell the story of the $25,000 bribe to Kefauver.

"It was why Clint hated George Marshall all those years," Thompson told a friend. "The rivalry the Cowboys had with the Redskins was strictly personal on Clint's part."

At the league meeting a pressured George Preston Marshall went from opposing the entry of the new team into a stall tactic where he asked only that the league wait one year before bringing Dallas into the league.

In response, Tex Schramm, who had been hired as the Dallas general manager, explained to Marshall that the Dallas Texans in the AFL would be starting this coming season. To wait a year would be to give the Texans a one-year start.

"We must have an even start," Schramm told him.

Marshall, outflanked in every direction, finally gave in. Murchison paid the league $550,000—fifty grand for the franchise and half a mil for a roster of washed-up, over the hill, or never-were players who were selected during the meeting.

After the meeting broke up a reporter asked Clint, "Are you prepared to come up with $550,000 cash?"

Murchison considered the huge bar bill rung up by Robert Thompson, Bedford Wynne, and his other partying buddies over the course of the eleven days of the marathon NFL league meeting.

"I better be," he said, "or I won't be able to get out of the hotel."

3

Tex

B y 1960 pro football was becoming a national phenomenon, though it still did not generate the mania engendered by pro baseball, with fans agog over the prospect of Mickey Mantle and Roger Maris batting back-to-back in the New York Yankees lineup for the first time. But America's addiction to television was becoming stronger, and part of the sports fare being televised from Maine to California was NFL football. Some clubs were on TV more than others. At that time each pro football franchise cut its own deal. CBS televised a cluster of teams, including the Giants, the Rams, and both Chicago teams, the Bears and the Cardinals. George Preston Marshall had his own network, which was broadcast across the South. Red Grange and Harry Wismer did the announcing.

Television and pro football together reached their adulthood in December of 1958 when the Baltimore Colts defeated the New York Giants in overtime in the NFL championship, as millions watched enthralled from their barcaloungers as Alan Ameche pranced through the huge hole in the Giant line to end the epic battle. Ameche's dash has been etched indelibly in the memory of everyone in the baby boomer generation who saw it.

CBS, moreover, greatly added to the mystique of professional football when it aired its first important special on the sport, called *The Vio-*

lent World of Sam Huff. Huff, the middle linebacker of the Giants, wore a microphone for this program, and as the cameras focused on him throughout a ballgame, the viewers could hear the crashing of the linemen, and they could see that professional football was, in fact, a very violent game. It was riveting to sit in your living room while listening to the participants barking signals or screaming at the opposition, and when Huff put a hit on one of the big backs you could almost feel the impact in your bones. The National Football League was just beginning to wake up to the promotional potential of television, and *The Violent World of Sam Huff* showed the way.

It is interesting that the man Clint Murchison Jr. chose to be the general manager of his new Dallas team was Tex Schramm, who had been working for CBS since 1957, after a ten-year reign as general manager of the strife-ridden Los Angeles Rams.

Schramm was a very bright, very astute man who was as much a competitor in his own right as any coach or player under his employ. Schramm's philosophy was that there was always an angle to explore, a better way of doing something than anyone else. Like Murchison, there was only one set of rules: his rules. If Schramm needed to accomplish something, he would do it, even if he had to invent a new way of doing things. For instance, when he was with the Rams, he tired of guessing at whether a college prospect had ability or not, and so he invented a ruse that prompted hundreds of unpaid, unknowing scouts to send him information. With this information he was the first to build a scouting system, later copied throughout the league. After he was hired to run the Cowboys, Schramm did everything he could to build a team, even before the league gave him permission to begin. Schramm was a rare combination, a visionary and a businessman as tough as Jimmy Hoffa or, for that matter, Clint Murchison Sr.

Schramm had envisioned great profits to be made televising sports, and at CBS he pushed for the network to televise the 1960 Winter Olympics at a time when other executives thought there would be no interest and no sponsors. Schramm won out, and he was the first to use a central anchor for a sporting broadcast, Walter Cronkite, who previewed the various events. That one idea—an anchorman—changed the face of the way sports was presented on TV.

The programming was a revelation as millions of Americans watched day after day from Squaw Valley as David Jenkins and Carol Heiss each won a gold in figure skating, and the U.S. Olympic hockey team defeated the favored Russians in a game still talked about to this day.

In his three years working for Bill Paley and under Bill MacPhail, the brother of future New York Yankee general manager Lee MacPhail, Schramm was a very well paid member of the CBS brain trust, and during that period he turned down the job of general manager with the Detroit Lions and the Montreal Alouettes in football and the Detroit Pistons in the National Basketball Association. The NBA had even talked about Schramm becoming commissioner.

When Clint Murchison Jr. asked George Halas who he would recommend to run the new team's front office, Halas had one choice: Tex Schramm. This time, Schramm accepted. Though raised in California, he had gone to college in Texas and was comfortable living there. Moreover, this was the challenge of which Tex Schramm had always dreamed: the opportunity to start a team from scratch. This would be Tex Schramm's team. His fingerprints would be all over it, which meant that before long the city of Dallas would have an exciting, competitive football team.

TEX SCHRAMM: "I was born and raised in Southern California, and had attended the University of Texas, and during one summer while I was in school I had worked as an intern in the sports department of the *Los Angeles Times*. After I graduated, I became the sports editor of the *American-Statesman* in Austin.

"My father, who was living out in California, was in the stock brokerage business, and Daniel Reeves, the owner of the Los Angeles Rams, had a stock brokerage company out in Beverly Hills, and my father met one of Reeves's partners, Charlie Jowitz, who mentioned to my dad that Reeves had gotten rid of their publicity man, Max Stiles, because he suspected Max, a longtime newspaperman, of leaking stories to favorite reporters.

"My father told Reeves's friend, 'My son, Tex Schramm, just graduated from college, and he's the sports editor of a newspaper down there in Austin, and he might really be interested in the job.' So the guy went back and told Reeves, Reeves called sports editor Paul Zimmerman at the *Times*, and he apparently gave me a glowing recommendation, so the first thing I knew, I got a phone call. At the time I was covering the Kansas relays for the Austin *American-Statesman*—the University of Texas had a team going up there, and I went from there out to California and interviewed with Reeves, and he offered the job, and I accepted it, and that's how I wound up the PR director with the Rams.

"When I joined the club Reeves was the general manager. When the team moved from Cleveland to Los Angeles, the general manager had been a man by the name of Chile Walsh, and at one time his brother, Adam Walsh, was the coach of the Rams. But when they fired Chile, Reeves didn't hire a general manager. Reeves ran the team, and that was the way it was when I arrived.

"It was never really in my heart to be a publicity man, and so when I came there, I saw that Reeves needed help, and that he was anxious to have somebody willing to work, and so immediately I started getting into scouting and the administration of the team. I started doing everything in the administration end. It's no secret, he's dead, and he's in the Hall of Fame, but Daniel Reeves had a drinking problem. He was a certain type of alcoholic. He'd go great for a while, and then he'd go off. But anyway, I started doing more and more.

"I came in '47, and by '49 I hired a man who was at the *Dallas Morning News* to come out and be the publicity director, and he turned out to be a very famous writer with *Sports Illustrated*, a man by the name of Tex Maule. He came out, and though I kept the title of publicity director, he was now doing most of the publicity work. The people out there called us the co-Texes. Tex Maule, Tex Schramm. He did the publicity, and I got more and more involved in the administration of the team and became the assistant to the president—I always hated that title.

"We won the NFL championship in '51. We had Crazylegs Hirsch, Bob Waterfield, Norm Van Brocklin, Tom Fears, Tank Younger, Glenn Davis. We also got to the championship in '55.

"Back in the early '50s, there was very little scouting. We were the first team to spend money on it.

"In those days very few people fooled with the small schools, and so I got this idea to put out the Tom Harmon Little All-America Team. I thought of it. Tom had played with us on the Rams. I knew him very well, and I convinced him Tom Harmon's Little All-America Team would be a good thing for him. We had stationery printed up, gave them an entry form to nominate the players who should be considered for Tom Harmon's Little All-America Football Team, sent them to all the small schools, and told them to nominate players. They didn't know it, but the return address was us, the Rams! And it was great! We'd get the names of all the linemen who were 6'2" or over, and we'd put those on a list and start scouting them. We had a lot of small-college players with the Rams because of Tom Harmon's Little All-America. That's what we did. That way we got all of the names of all of the players in the small schools!

"Things were fine on the Rams until '54, when Daniel Reeves's partners brought a suit against him to try to take over the club. Fred Levy, one of his best friends, turned on him to give them a majority. Fred had come with him from New York when he moved out to California after moving the team from Cleveland.

"By '57 I was having a lot of trouble. I was supposed to check with one side *and* the other side before I could make any major decision. One side was Reeves, the other side was then a very important man in California by the name of Ed Pauley. You've heard of Pauley Pavilion. He was an oilman, and he was one of the co-owners.

"I got along with both of them fine, but when I called one of them, they'd want to know what the other guy was going to do. Pauley became suspicious that I was more friendly with Reeves, which I was, and so then they decided if there was a major decision to be made, I was to refer it to the commissioner, Bert Bell, and he would make the decision.

"I said, 'You can't run a team that way. You can't have the commissioner, who I know has no interest in us being winners, make decisions for us.' So I left the Rams and went to CBS, where I worked for three years. I had gotten to know my boss at CBS, Bill MacPhail, well because they were doing our television. That was the early days when the Rams were one of the teams that went with CBS. When I was hired by Dallas in October of 1960, the team didn't have any offices, and MacPhail said, 'You stay here as long as you want, and if football doesn't work out, you've got your job.'

"When I started, it was with the assumption we were going to start up the next season. I didn't have much time. I needed to hire a coach. While I was with CBS, I was living in Riverside, Connecticut, which is next to Old Greenwich, and working in New York, so I was very familiar with the Giants. I went to a lot of their games, and I was aware that their defensive team had developed a special esprit de corps. It was the first time the fans related to the defense, and they had been very successful, and apparently they had a great relationship with the defensive coach Tom Landry, so that sounded good, and in the meantime, some people here in Dallas who knew Landry had suggested we look into him, so it was tailor-made, so I went and saw him and was impressed by him.

"The Houston Oilers had also approached him, but he liked the sound of Dallas. It was a gamble for him, because we didn't even have a franchise yet. Right after the Giants lost to Baltimore in the '59 playoffs we brought him down, had a press conference and announced him.

"I honestly didn't care that he had played college ball in Texas. That's not why I picked him. I had been in football for ten years and had five coaches with the Rams. The only thing I was interested in was getting a great football coach, not somebody who sounded good in Texas. Where he went to college didn't make any difference to me.

"I knew we were going to be too late for the upcoming NFL draft, so I started by going after as many free agents as I could sign. The first thing I did, I talked to Daniel Reeves, and for $5,000 he agreed to sell me the scouting reports on all the players who were not drafted. Having set it up and been there, I knew how their books were with all their information. That was found money for him, and he wanted to help.

"I hired Gil Brandt, one of the first ones that I got to go out and sign players. Gil was one of the originals of all the people they have now who are amateur evaluators. I knew he was good because when I was with the Rams, we had used him when we needed some kind of project done. If I needed someone to go see someone, or for someone to find out something, he was the guy we used on that kind of stuff. And I knew he always got it. He had lived in Milwaukee, and one time the College All-Star team was training in Stevens Point in Wisconsin. We weren't allowed to scout them, so we got Gil to go over and see what the hell they were doing, and see what the players looked like. So I knew him. So in '59 I called him up and asked him, 'Do you want to sign some players for me?'

"He said, 'Great, give me the names.' And I gave him seven or eight names and a pile of our made-up player contracts.

"So we started signing free agents, even though we weren't in the league. We had started as the Dallas Steers, but that's not a very good name because you don't want your whole football team being castrated. Then we went to the Dallas Rangers, which was the name of the minor league baseball team that was supposedly moving out of town, and so we were going to use that name, and so the first NFL contracts we printed said Dallas Rangers.

"Anyway, that year Bert Bell, the commissioner, had died, and a guy by the name of Austin Gunsel had been the treasurer of the league, and he was acting as interim commissioner, and I called him up and I said, 'We're getting ready for this season, and we're going to have a franchise. Can you send me some contracts?' He said, 'You're not a member of the league. I can't send you any contracts.'

"I said, 'Oh? Well, okay.'

"And so either I had a contract from when I was with the Rams or I got one from the Giants, but either way I had no trouble getting one, and I sent it down to Dallas, and I asked Bedford Wynne, one of the partners in the team, 'Can you go to a printer and have him duplicate this with exactly the same paper, the same type, the same everything, for the Dallas Rangers?'

"He said, 'I think so. Let me go do it.'

"So we had these NFL Dallas Rangers contracts printed, and you couldn't tell the difference. They looked like the real thing. So I had all the contracts I needed. Next I sat with Bedford Wynne, who was an attorney, and if you can imagine it, we drew up a release for the player to sign in which he acknowledged he was signing with the Rangers, but if Dallas didn't get a franchise, we would have no obligation. And it was amazing. We went out and signed players, and those players didn't give a damn about signing that release."

Signing free agents in the NFL was often a fruitless exercise. These were the players still unattached after each of twelve teams has drafted twenty-five rounds of players. True, it still leaves thousands of college seniors to choose from, but by 1960—thanks largely to the pioneering work of Tex Schramm—teams were drafting more knowledgeably than they had in the past. Schramm realized that for him to find an undrafted college player with a shot at making the team, he had to look for unusual circumstances. One of the free agents he courted was Byron Bradfute, a big lineman who had been thrown out of Abilene Christian University for drinking beer. He had finished his senior year at Southern Mississippi, his reputation sullied as a result. But Tex Schramm was one of those general managers who didn't care as much about Bradfute's scrape with the morality police at Abilene Christian as he did about the big kid's raw talent. Schramm's overriding concern was to build a winning team. Though Bradfute had been ignored by the NFL, he had been drafted in the 17th round by the AFL's Los Angeles Chargers. Schramm wanted the twenty-three-year-old Bradfute. Here was a Beeville, Texas, farm boy, who, Schramm argued, ought to be playing pro ball in Texas.

BYRON BRADFUTE: "I had decided to go to the University of Texas, but one of their coaches made a comment about the lack of importance of studying Bible, and it didn't sit well with me nor my folks. And that year they hired Darrell Royal and went on to win. I had signed a letter of intent with the University of Houston with Bill Meek, who was the coach. He promised he was going to stay there forever and ever and all that. He was going to give scholarships to me and to one of our ends, a good friend named Jerry Ford, but when the time came he never did get his, and so I changed my mind. I had been weighing wanting to be a preacher, and Abilene Christian had offered us both four-year scholarships, and so we went there. And as it turned out, Meek resigned at Houston and went to SMU and coached Don Meredith, and for four years the University of Houston was on hard times. You never know how these things will turn out.

"So I went on to Abilene Christian, and I played two years there and was in my third year, and meanwhile I had begun to run, play a little bit, and I was drinking a little beer. They lifted my scholarship for drinking beer. So I wrote five or six letters, and Southern Mississippi offered me a scholarship, and I played my senior year there. And we played Abilene Christian and beat them! Probably if it hadn't been for Southern, I would never have had the opportunity to play pro ball.

"I had been contacted regularly by the New York Giants and the Green Bay Packers. As late as ten o'clock the night before the draft the Giants were telling me they were going to draft me, but they did not, and I was not drafted in the NFL. The only interest I had from the NFL was from Tex Schramm. The Cowboys weren't even in the league yet. Tex was with CBS-TV, and he would call, and they'd get me out of class and say, 'Tex Schramm with CBS is on the phone for you.' That's when I started telling everybody that they were trying to get me to come to New York to cut country-and-western music songs. I kept getting these letters with CBS-TV on the return address. Tex said he was building a team, and he talked about how excited he was and how much he wanted me to be part of it.

"I had been drafted seventeenth by the Chargers in the AFL, but I signed with Tex. It was Texas. I could identify with it. All my family was in Texas, and by then I was homesick. I had been over in Mississippi, and in December I got my contract in the mail, and they gave me a $500 cash bonus, and that paid for my last semester, which I took at Abilene Christian. I got my degree and graduated with my class.

"The first contract Tex sent me was with the Dallas Rangers. I signed it and sent it back. Then he called me and said I would have to re-sign it because they changed the name. I could see they were a little short on secretaries, because in the new contract they had just marked a line through Dallas Rangers, typed in Dallas Cowboys, and sent it down for me to initial. I initialed it and sent it back to them."

TEX SCHRAMM: "In fact, we signed twenty-six players, including Jake Crouthamel, a running back out of Dartmouth, who is now athletic director at Syracuse, and signing those free agents played a little role in encouraging the league to let us start in '60, because we already had twenty-six players signed, and they thought that was pretty good.

"I can remember we had a scout up trying to sign a free agent, and Paul Brown was trying to sign the same free agent. The guy said, 'I have a contract with the Dallas Rangers.' Paul said, 'What the hell are you talking about? They're not even in the league.' The player showed him the contract. Paul called Gunsel and said, 'What in the hell is going on? I've got somebody out there I'm competing against that isn't in the league!'

"We also went out and we signed two of the top college seniors in the country, Don Meredith and Don Perkins, to personal service contracts. We signed Meredith, and it had the blessing of Halas, who was the guy Clint was using as a contact, and then we signed Perkins in New Mexico, because Murchison was a real close friend with the senator from New Mexico, and I can't remember his name. We actually had this senator who had the responsibility of getting Perkins signed. So we got those two signed.

"The draft was in late November, and when the draft came, Halas got up and said, 'Dallas has signed these two players, so don't draft them.' Halas warned them that these two players had been signed by Dallas."

Don Meredith had become famous by his senior year at SMU. A native of Mount Vernon, in East Texas, Jeff and Hazel's baby boy was an outstanding high school athlete in both football and basketball, a sport in which he once set a single-game scoring record of 52 points in the Dr. Pepper High School tournament in Dallas. At SMU he was a two-time All-America, the holder of the record for career passing accuracy at 61 percent. During his junior year he was named national collegiate Back of the Week four times during a ten-game season. Murchison gave him a guaranteed $150,000 contract to remain in Dallas and not sign with Lamar Hunt and the Dallas Texans in the AFL. Meredith would get the money whether Dallas was accepted into the NFL or not.

Meredith had almost gone to Texas A&M to play for the legendary Bear Bryant, but College Station seemed too provincial a place for his luminescent aura. He wanted to leave his dad's farm and go to the Big City, and so he didn't go to Austin to play for UT, nor did he go to TCU where his brother had been a starting quarterback. Instead, he chose to go to Dallas, the home of SMU, where he began his college career as a linebacker because there were seven quarterbacks in front of him on the depth chart.

By his sophomore year he had moved to the top, and against UT he led SMU to a stunning 19–12 upset. That year he led the nation in passing, operating an offense that depended on his ability to get himself free from tacklers in order to throw long bombs downfield for touchdowns. For the next two years, Meredith starred on a mediocre team, and for those two years he had to listen to loud cheers and raucous boos, because no matter how good he was, to the SMU fans it was rarely good enough. For many, the player he was compared to and found wanting was their beloved Doak Walker.

"They were expecting me to be something I never could be," Meredith mused years later.

When Meredith was offered a personal service contract by Clint Murchison Jr., he jumped at it. He knew that no matter what happened on the football field, he would have a good job in the Murchison organization. Don Meredith didn't know it at the time, but his fans would follow him from SMU into the pro ranks, and whatever ambivalence the fans had for him in college would grow exponentially after he entered the pros.

While Meredith was visible and renowned in Dallas, Don Perkins was unknown. A quiet, unselfish, internal man, Perkins played in obscurity for the University of New Mexico despite College All-Star status. But Tex Schramm and Gil Brandt knew that Don Perkins had the makings of a great NFL running back. He was a great blocker, had toughness, had crazy legs that caused him to dart every which way and made him hard to tackle, and he was explosive. Teammates would race him for ten yards, and no one could beat him.

Perkins served as an inspiration to teammates and also as a teacher, as he unselfishly trained the new kids coming up. Once when rookie running back Walt Garrison asked him why he was helping a man intent on taking his job, Perkins told him, "If you're a better player than I am, then you ought to be playing, because I'll make more money that way. If you're not better than I am, then I should be playing." Don Perkins was a pro's pro.

Perkins, who is black, was a pioneer on the Cowboys. Along with receiver Frank Clarke and defensive back Don Bishop, Perkins came to Dallas in 1960 during the last days of Jim Crow segregation in the South. A stranger in a white-run society, Perkins came to Dallas afraid for his job. He knew his place, kept a low profile, did his job extremely well, and eight years after he came, he left Dallas about as unknown as he had been when he came, still grateful to have been given the opportunity.

At the time he quit, only four other running backs in the NFL had gained more yards than his total of 6,217—Jim Brown, Jim Taylor, Joe Perry, and John Henry Johnson. Don Perkins had played eight years, finished in the top ten in rushing each year, and was named to the Pro Bowl six times. Jackie Robinson had hardly done better in Brooklyn with the Dodgers.

DON PERKINS: "I was born in 1938 in a rural part of the Midwest. I grew up in Waterloo, Iowa, one of eight children. My dad worked in a meat-packing plant.

"Waterloo was segregated. The society was segregated. The whole country. The black population—we were colored at the time—lived on the other side of town. We lived on the side with all the poor white trash. It was Appalachia, and only because I lived in that poor part of town, I ended up going to all-white schools and competing on teams where there were no other blacks.

"I was an exceptional athlete, so I didn't have any problems. I don't remember any problems with coaches or any with students. You always have problems with people when you're not in the majority, but I'm sure my problems were fewer than most, because, after all, I was a super jock, the class president, and lots of other things as well.

"In high school I was an All-State performer. I was a marked man on the field when our team showed up, and we had a good team. Nevertheless, I was not offered a scholarship at the University of Iowa. Iowa State did, but not Iowa. As I said, I went to an all-white high school, and I ended up dating a white classmate. And it was pretty common knowledge at the high school that we were dating.

"One time my coach, George Dutcher, came to me—and I think he meant well at the time, and he said, 'You know, Don, sometimes people on the college admissions committee take a dim view of a black athlete who's dating a white girl. And sometimes it can affect whether they recruit you or not.' And that was about as much as he had to say on that subject. Did it play a factor on Iowa not recruiting me? It probably did. I don't know, and I don't really care.

"The coaching staff from Coe College in Cedar Rapids, Iowa, was taking over the helm at the University of New Mexico, and they were doing a lot of heavy recruiting in the Midwest, and my credentials coming out of high school were good. I don't think the university ever had had much of a football program. We played in the old Skyline Conference in the Rocky Mountain area. I wasn't eligible as a freshman, and when I was a sophomore, we didn't win many games. We got better the last couple of years, won more games than we lost.

"In my senior year I was contacted by New Mexico senator Clinton Anderson, who was somehow connected with the Murchisons. This was before Murchison even had a franchise. But he had some kind of deal with the NFL that his team could sign so many players, and 'If you get a franchise, you can keep these guys. If you don't, they'll get picked by other teams.' Anyway, I signed a personal service contract with the Cowboys. It was no risk. Baltimore drafted me, too.

"Anyway, in those days it was a very low-key thing. Football was hardly even televised in the 1950s. People didn't set out to be pro football players. Not many people knew anything about pro football. It was a job opportunity, and I took it. They gave me a little money up front, and I got to keep it whether I made the team or not. I said, 'Why not?' "

TEX SCHRAMM: "After we signed Meredith and Perkins, I put my guys on Billy Cannon, who was one of the top players that year from LSU, and Billy was ready to sign with us except that he had been drafted by the Rams, and running the Rams then, as general manager, was Pete Rozelle. He wouldn't be named commissioner for another couple of months. And Pete called me and said, 'You sign Billy Cannon, and you might have Billy Cannon, but you might not have a franchise. We have to vote on that.'

"I said, 'Yeah, Pete, don't worry.' And I told our guys, 'Get the hell away from Billy Cannon.' So that is what stopped me. That's why we didn't sign ten of them. Don't rock the boat. But we went ahead and signed all the free agents, and then we went to Miami at the end of January to get the franchise.

"We got the franchise, but the league made it very hard for us to draft any good players from the expansion lists. Some people in the league spoke up and said, 'If we're going to have an expansion team, we got to give them a chance.' Some chance. A little chance. There was some or a little, as it turned out. They did it in such a way that the other teams weren't risking anything by the number of players protected. Everybody could protect twenty-nine of their thirty-three players, a big number, and we could select one from each team. But if we picked one, then they could withdraw one name. So no one gave up very much. I can remember after we picked Buzz Guy, we gave the Giants something for them to leave Don Heinrich on the list.

"We had had an idea what players we were going to get, because we had done as much research as we could do before the time came to go to that meeting. There wasn't a lot of time to do it, but we researched all of the players on the other teams who were likely to be left unprotected, and we knew them all pretty well by the time that they did it. Our problem was that the league only gave us twenty-four hours to make the picks, and we couldn't call the players to see if they would play for us. The other teams didn't want the players not picked to know they had been on the list, 'cause they were afraid it wouldn't be good for morale, so they made us stay in the hotel and make the picks blind. As a result, we picked players from Texas. We figured if we could get L. G. Dupre from the Colts or Don McIlhenny from the Packers, they were better than some of the other guys on the lists, and we knew we wouldn't have any trouble signing them, 'cause they would want to come back to Texas.

"We got three good players out of it. Jerry Tubbs, a linebacker, Jim Doran, an end, and another end, Frank Clarke. We got Tubbs because he had threatened to retire. He was always going to retire with us, too. That was his big bargaining chip. He played eight years, and then he winds up coaching and never getting out of football! We got Doran because he was in his mid-thirties and about ready to retire, and we got Clarke because Paul Brown gave up on him.

"I knew it was going to be a rocky time, because they didn't give us anything in the expansion draft. But I *knew*—there was no doubt in my mind—that it was just a matter of time before we would start winning. I never entered anything with more confidence in my life."

4

The Bombardier

The man Tex Schramm picked to coach his new team was unknown to many football fans. Assistant coaches usually are. But to those who had played with him and for him on the New York Giants, Tom Landry was considered a certified football genius.

Born on September 11, 1924, the son of a bricklayer turned car mechanic, Landry had grown up in Mission, Texas, deep in the Rio Grande Valley, not far from the Mexican border in a valley that boasted unending acres of flowering lemon, orange, and grapefruit trees. When the wind blew, he remembered, "there wasn't a prettier smelling place on earth."

As a child he was shy, a characteristic he never overcame. He didn't say much because he had a speech impediment, but the youngster was responsible and goal-oriented, and so his disability didn't stop him from selling newspapers on the street. His dream as a boy was to become a cowboy.

Landry grew up in a segregated, deeply religious society in which the melting pot consisted of Saturday night dances when the Methodists mingled with the Baptists. In high school, his coach feared the corrupting influence of the opposite sex and warned his boys against letting the girls wear their letter sweaters. As a senior, Landry was class valedictorian and a member of the National Honor Society. He was also a talented back on the football team, and in 1941 he led tiny Mission High School to a 12–0 record, as the team outscored the opposition 322 to 7. In the district championship against Aransas Pass, Landry scored on runs of 4 and 38 yards, and then late in the game he ran through the entire Aransas Pass team for a 76-yard touchdown. The celebration was short-lived, because two days later the Japanese attacked Pearl Harbor.

Landry was courted by SMU, Rice, and Mississippi State, but he went to the University of Texas after a local oilman/alum convinced him that UT produced most of Texas's leaders. As important, UT was close enough to home that his parents could come to the games and watch him play. He accepted a full scholarship at UT.

His intention was to enter the oil business, and he enrolled in engineering. Before entering college in the fall of 1942, he worked the entire summer on the floor of a drilling rig, wrestling with heavy pipes as the driller barked orders, warnings, and threats. It was backbreaking labor, but the $4 an hour wages earned him enough money to last the entire school year.

During his freshman year his older brother Robert was reported missing in action while on a flying mission; it was later disclosed that his plane had exploded in midair. In November Landry enlisted in the Army Air Corps, and in February of 1943 was called to active duty. He sailed in the fall of that year on the *Queen Mary* to England, where he learned to fly B-17 Flying Fortress bombers.

At nineteen, Tom Landry was made a co-pilot, one of the youngest among the American bombing squadrons. The B-17s flew in groups of four in a diamond shape with gunners from each plane protecting the others from air attack. The pilots were trained to follow closely what the lead plane was doing. Survival depended on teamwork. As in football, teamwork was at a premium, but in this case individuality could get you killed.

The return rate of these bombers was low, and several times Landry had close calls. He was under constant attack from a decimated Luftwaffe and German ground guns. Landry's first mission was to destroy the oil fields at Mersburg, Germany. He returned safely. On a later mission all four engines suddenly quit over the Netherlands, which was still in German hands. Everyone was getting ready to bail out when, as a last resort, Landry readjusted the fuel mixture, got the engines going again, and pulled the plane out of a dive. Another time, after hitting a target in Czechoslovakia, he ran out of fuel over France and had to crash-land in a forest. It was a miracle he wasn't killed. The plane's wings were sheared off by trees and the nose was buried all the way to the cockpit, but everyone walked away.

After thirty missions, Tom Landry was discharged in November 1945. He returned to Austin in the spring of 1946 to play football during the final season of coaching legend D. X. Bible, who believed in hard work and preparation and would say things like, "If you pay the premiums, you will get the dividends." Landry's philosophies would later ape Bible's.

Landry had been away from football for four years, but at age twenty-three he felt he could still play. He and another talented Texan named Bobby Layne, who could not have been more different from Landry, competed for the starting quarterback job.

Landry was quiet and a loner. At Texas, Landry would meet his one true love, Alicia Wiggs, and remain true to her for life. Layne, who grew up in Dallas, even as a high schooler was a hard-drinking hell-raiser who enjoyed a good bar fight followed by a good roll in the hay with whatever Texas belle he could get drunk and seduce. In high school Layne did things like get drunk and jump off roofs into swimming pools. Though he was beloved by most of his teammates for his exuberance and his freelance style, Tom Landry looked at Layne's behavior and saw sin—not so much the kind of sin written about in the Bible, though that was part of it, but more the kind of sin Landry personally found most objectionable in an athlete, the sin of unfulfilled potential. To Landry, Layne was undisciplined. He didn't practice hard, and he didn't take the game seriously, and for that Landry most faulted him.

The two men were as different as two men could be. In his autobiography, Landry noted that "I wasn't the first person Bobby thought of when he needed a drinking partner or party company," and admitted the stories he knew about Bobby all came from others. And as great as Layne was, attaining All-America and All-Pro status, Landry's penchant for Coach Bible's standards of hard work and preparation caused Landry to comment that Layne "never trained. And I've often wondered how much greater he might have been if he had."

Layne, who was one year ahead of Landry, in turn would freely express his deep dislike for Landry, making fun of his quarterbacking ability and his straitlaced martinet nature.

As a junior Layne took UT to the 1946 Southwest Conference championship, a season in which Landry played little because of an injury. In 1947 Blair Cherry took over as coach and switched from the single wing to the pro-style T formation. Cherry went so far as to send Layne to

Chicago to study under the Bears' resident genius George Halas and his quarterback star Sid Luckman. Under Cherry, Landry's initial assignment was to back up Layne at quarterback, and to go in for him on defense.

Against Oregon, Landry broke his thumb badly making a tackle, and Cherry moved him to fullback, where he became a star. In one game, Landry outgained North Carolina All-America Charlie "Choo Choo" Justice. In 1947 Layne and Landry took UT to a 10–1 record and a number 4 national ranking. The only loss was a heartbreaking one-pointer to Doak Walker and SMU. Landry has always blamed himself for the loss, citing a play in which instead of gaining a key first down he slipped in the mud before he could take a handoff from Layne. UT then beat famed quarterback Harry Gilmer and Alabama in the Sugar Bowl.

When Landry returned in 1948, the colorful Layne was gone, off to the Chicago Bears on the first leg of what would be an outstanding fifteen-year pro career. In Landry's senior year, UT only went 6-3-1, but it was selected to play in the Orange Bowl against Georgia. Landry led UT to a 41–28 win, running for 117 yards on 17 carries.

In 1949 Landry was drafted by both the New York Yankees in the All-America Football Conference and the New York Giants in the NFL. His long-range plan was to have a career in the oil business, and to that end he enrolled at the University of Houston in order to earn an engineering degree. His need to pay tuition made the money a primary consideration in choosing where to play. The Giants were the more established team, but the Yankees offered him the better deal, a $2,000 bonus and a $7,500-a-year salary, double what some established pro players were making. Landry also signed with the Yankees because—ironically—so many of their players had come from the state of Texas, and he figured he'd feel more at home. The heart of Texas always remained deep within Tom Landry. When he went off to training camp, his wife remained in Houston to give birth to their first child. His reason: If the child ever wanted to run for governor, it could run as a "born and bred" Texan.

In his rookie year with the Yanks, an injury to the starter forced Landry into action as a defensive back against the Cleveland Browns, the best team in the league. Browns quarterback Otto Graham wasted no time picking on the inexperienced kid, as he threw to Dante Lavelli and Mac Speedie for over 200 yards, an AAFC record.

It was during that game that Landry realized that skill, emotion, and even determination were not enough to succeed in the game of pro football. He had gone into the game raw and unknowledgeable. Otto Graham had kept him guessing all game long with his play calling. Landry, who saw defeat as an event akin to death, had not only lost, but he had been humiliated as well, and so he decided that in order to make sure what had happened against the Browns wouldn't happen again, he would have to devise a system that would better prepare him for what he would face on the field.

"The primary lesson learned that day served as the very foundation of my philosophical approach to playing and coaching pro football," said Landry years later. "Any success I ever attained would require the utmost in preparation and knowledge. I couldn't wait and react to my opponent. I had to know what he was going to do before he did it."

He learned another lesson as well: Rookies should practice hard all week and sit on the bench during games. When Tom Landry later became coach, rookies would only start for him if they were truly exceptional or he found himself with no other choice.

At the end of the year, the All-America Football Conference and the National Football League merged and the Yankees folded. In 1950 Landry was signed by the New York Giants as a regional draft choice. His first year with the Giants, Landry was the second-best punter in the league to Frankie Albert, and he played behind halfback Buddy Young. When defensive back Harmon Rowe was injured, Landry took his spot in the secondary as the Giants' left cornerback. Teammates noticed that though he was not fast and not as quick as some backs, Landry always seemed to know where the play was going. Also when he hit, he did so viciously. Landry hit his man like a spike going through a board.

"I had an acute hatred for receivers," said Landry. "If a guy caught a ball against me, I'd try to hit him so hard he wished he hadn't."

But what most impressed teammates and foes alike about Landry was that he hated to lose. He was an angry, sore loser.

Glenn Davis, once Mr. Inside of Army football fame, played halfback for the Los Angeles Rams. Davis says that Landry was one of the meanest competitors ever to play the game.

"I remember one game," said Davis, "I ran a turn-in and caught the ball and Landry stuck me in the back, smeared me. It hurt, and we both knew it. Then a play or so later, I ran a turn-in and go. I passed Landry standing still and caught the pass, and I was heading for the open end of the Coliseum, the one with all the open space beyond the end zone. I could hear Tom chasing me from behind.

"I kept going. I went clear through the end zone and five yards behind it. And Landry tackled me anyway. So I got up and slammed the ball at him. 'Here, if you want it so damn bad.'

"And then he chased me all the way to our bench."

Dick Nolan played in the same backfield with Landry on the Giants, and what he recalled best about Landry the football player was that duality of intellect and assassin.

DICK NOLAN: "He was a tough egg. He'd knock your brains out. I remember when we played the Baltimore Colts, Jim Mutscheller, a tough tight end for the Colts, went out and Johnny Unitas hit him with a pass, and Landry hit him and drove up through him in the air until he had Mutscheller turned upside down. His head was straight down, and his feet were straight up in the air, and Landry was still going through him. Tom was a tough guy, a tough tackler. He was strong, and he was tough. He didn't back down from anybody."

The other habit Landry possessed that impressed others was a raging mania for preparation. After he completed his analytical engineering training in '52, he embarked on a self-study course in which he began breaking football down into its component parts. Before it became fashionable, Landry spent hours a week watching game films of the upcoming opponent. What Landry was looking for was what he called "keys." Using his analytical skill, Landry figured out that when the offense lined up in a certain way, there were a limited number of plays that could be run from that formation.

For instance, from watching films he saw that if the halfbacks were split behind the quarterback, the offense would run either a long trap or an end run, or they would run a counter play.

If they set up with the fullback behind the quarterback and the halfback on the side opposite the tight end, he knew the formation called for the fullback to run the ball.

Once Landry knew where the play was going to go, he could ignore the feints and fakes and the window dressing, and all he had to do was lie in wait at the location he knew the ball was going to be, either on a run or through the air.

He developed his analysis to the point that he could actually anticipate what the offense was going to do by the formation and initial movement of the offensive players. Landry saw that if the opposition sent a halfback on a flare pattern toward the sideline, what the offense wanted was for the linebacker on that side to go with him, thereby leaving a big space in the middle of the field for the wide receiver to run into and catch a pass. If you knew that, Landry figured out, all you had to do was lie in wait where the wide receiver was sure to go. Teammates were amazed that, more often than not, Landry would be in perfect position to flatten the receiver with a jarring tackle or intercept the pass. By 1952 Landry had perfected his system to the point that he made eight interceptions and became an All-Pro defensive back.

From his first season with the Giants, Landry had the respect of his teammates. That year the team was preparing to play the powerful Cleveland Browns, with quarterback Otto Graham and receivers Mac Speedie and Dante Lavelli and the rest of a very powerful offensive team. The week before the Browns had creamed the former NFL champs, the Philadelphia Eagles. To stop Speedie and Lavelli, Giant coach Steve Owen devised what looked like a 6–1 defense, with six linemen, one linebacker, and four backs. The twist Owen was bringing to the Cleveland game was that the 6–1 look was only a disguise designed to confuse the normally unflappable Graham. At the snap of the ball in passing situations, the Giant ends were to drop back into the zones, where the quick and talented receivers usually stopped to catch Graham's pinpoint passes. Speedie and Lavelli would be running into double coverage. The other key to the defense was a heavy rush from the defensive linemen.

After Owen described his new defense, with its different assignments and new pass coverage, he walked out of the room. There was a buzzing, a murmuring of confusion about what everyone was supposed to do. Tom Landry, normally taciturn and slow with words, rose from his chair and went to the blackboard. He had never spoken in front of the team before. But his teammates were aware that Landry, with that engineer's mind, could dissect plans. Moreover, he had the gifted ability to explain hard concepts and make them understandable. When he got to the chalkboard, no one questioned his right to be up there before them. He began drawing the X's and O's that make up the football vocabulary, and by the end of the session the Giant players understood Owen's revolutionary "umbrella defense."

Against the Giants, Otto Graham did not complete a pass in the first half. At halftime Paul Brown, himself a coaching genius, adjusted. He ordered Graham to throw short passes or run wide. But Owen reacted as well, and his ends, Ray Poole and Jim Duncan, kept Graham running for his life, and Landry and Emlen Tunnell came up to make tackle after tackle.

The Giants won the game, 6–0, and later in the season beat the powerful Browns again, 17–13. The Giants finished the season 10–2 but lost to the Browns in a playoff, 8–3. In three games against the Giants' umbrella defense, the Browns had scored but one touchdown.

In '51 the season came down to a game against the Pittsburgh Steelers, led by defensive end Ernie Stautner. After Stautner put Giant quarterbacks Charlie Conerly and Fred Benners in the hospital, Landry had to come in and run the offense. Landry had last been a quarterback in high school. Pressed into duty against the Steelers, Landry had to draw the plays in the dirt. Before the end of the game Stautner broke through, doubled his fist, and smashed Landry in the face through the meager face bar, breaking his nose and knocking him down. As Stautner was returning to his huddle, Landry jumped up and punched him in the back. The Steelers won, 63–7.

The Giants were mediocre in '52, and injuries cost them dearly in '53, as their record fell to 3–9. After the season, Giants owner Tim Mara fired Steve Owen and replaced him with former Giant end Jim Lee Howell. Howell hired a young assistant from West Point by the name of Vince Lombardi to coach the offense. To coach the defense he appointed the twenty-nine-year-old Landry as player-coach.

As a player Landry would never have been presumptive enough to try to formally teach his system to the other defensive players, but as defensive coach, it became his job. He designed a defense he called "the inside 4–3" and "the outside 4–3." It was revolutionary because in the past everyone played man-to-man defense. In the past brute strength had been the requisite. You lined up opposite your man, and you tried to beat the crap out of him, using a forearm or your shoulder or a headslap or grabbing him by the jersey and throwing him off to the side in an attempt to get by him to make the tackle.

To improve, you learned through hard knocks. If you were the defensive end and you stepped upfield and were blindsided by the off guard, you went out there again—if he hadn't destroyed your knee—and learned to keep your eyes open for him. In the past, you learned by getting your brains beaten out. Under Tom Landry's new system, you knew exactly what was coming. There were no surprises.

Landry's defense depended on his players knowing what the other team was going to run and stopping the lanes where the play was expected to go. The defense was also designed in such a way that the defensive linemen would control the offensive players so that no one would get a decent block on the middle linebacker, whose job it was to patrol the center of the field behind the line. Under Landry's system, it was the job of the middle linebacker to fill unclosed holes and tackle the ballcarrier.

When the Giants saw that the play was going to run inside, they would set up in their "inside 4–3." The two defensive tackles would control the lanes to the left and right of the center. The middle linebacker would fill the holes outside both tackles, the place where the ballcarrier was expected to be.

If the offense saw it was bogged down when it tried to run inside, then the opposing coach would set up formations designed to run wide, and Landry's defense would counter with its "outside 4–3." The defensive ends would come back inside head up with the offensive tackles, forcing the ballcarrier to go outside, where the middle linebacker and safety would be waiting for him.

Beginning in 1954 Tom Landry revised the teaching manual when it came to defense. He broke every aspect of the game into its minutest part. His lectures on defensive play were revelations to even the salty veterans, who thought they knew everything.

Landry would ask, "Why does the cornerback line up with his outside foot forward? Why not put the inside foot forward?" Then he would explain in great detail: "Because when you drop with the receiver, you want to stay parallel to the line of scrimmage, and if you put your inside foot forward, you have a tendency to throw your inside foot back, and now if you're running with him sideways and he breaks to the sideline, you can't stop him. You have to stop and regroup and then go after him again."

He would take every player from the line of scrimmage and tell him exactly how to play his position every step of the way, and he'd go over it time and time again until it became second nature.

He would school them like they were in a college engineering class, dissecting every aspect of playing defense. For instance, he would teach the defensive backs every single possible way of playing the position.

He'd explain: "You can play man-to-man looking at the receiver and absolutely nothing else. You key off the receiver, run with the receiver, look at the receiver, concentrate on him all the way, and make yourself strong one way or the other. Or you could take a quick look at the quarterback, key the quarterback and see the receiver from your peripheral vision, and once the receiver passes the 'quick' area where he'll come off the line and stop about three or four yards downfield, then you go right back to the receiver and don't worry about the quarterback, because the receiver will take you to the pattern. If you look at the quarterback, you look for the quick throw, so when he does come with that throw, you're going to be able to pick it off. If you just look at the receiver, and he makes that stop route, all you can do is come back and tackle him."

And on and on. And he did this with the linemen and the linebackers. Any player who wished to earn a Ph.D. in defense needed only to listen and learn.

He also did something else that was new and revolutionary. He made his defensive players watch game films for hours on end. Each player had a book of skeleton sheets, and in conjunction with watching the films they had to meticulously learn each offensive formation and the position they had to adopt in order to counter it. Landry's theory was that if you knew in advance what was coming, you could stop it. His credo was that with foreknowledge, you could take away what the other team was trying to do, thus creating chaos in their backfield, causing rushed passes and fumbles, forcing teams to continually operate in second-and-long situations.

All the Giant players needed, he told them, was faith in his system. To Landry, the system was foolproof. But his system went against everything that the defensive players had been taught over the years—chase the ball, attack the ballcarrier. Players who were used to chasing the ball wherever it went had to hold their ground and wait for the ball to come back to them. For some players, Landry's ability to predict what play the offense would run seemed more like black magic than science. Accepting that his "keys" were accurate predictors took more faith than some had in them.

"What if they don't do that?"

"But they will."

"But what if they won't?"

"There are no 'what ifs,' " Landry would reply.

Since most of the Giant defensive players had played alongside Tom Landry and respected him for his savvy nature and brilliant mind, they were more than willing to follow his lead. He continually preached that using this defense, the Giants could play a perfect football game. For four years beginning in 1956, the Giants played games that proved this was possible.

That year Tom Landry orchestrated the first famous defensive unit in the history of professional football. During the off-season, the Giants traded for two tough-as-nails linemen, Andy Robustelli of the Rams and Dick Modzelewski of the Steelers, and from the draft they added lineman Jim Katcavage and an agile, smart, disciplined, and downright mean ball of fire by the name of Sam Huff.

Huff had been a guard at the University of West Virginia, but when Giant middle linebacker Ray Beck had to cut short his career to attend to his sick father, Landry made Huff the middle linebacker, the centerpiece of his "inside 4–3, outside 4–3," tutoring him day and night until he knew every key, every ramification, every nuance. Under Landry's system, the linemen played off their blocks in such a way that the middle linebacker remained free of interference to make the tackle. Without an effective middle linebacker, his entire system of defense would fail. Landry needed Sam Huff to succeed in order for *him* to succeed.

Everyone else told Landry that Huff was too small to play the position. Everyone else is wrong, Landry said, and he set out to prove it.

Landry had a projector in his apartment in the Concourse Plaza Hotel, down the avenue from Yankee Stadium. Huff also had an apartment there. Landry would call Huff on the phone.

"Sam, what are you doing?"

"Watching television."

"Good, I'm glad you aren't doing anything. Why don't you come up to my room and look at some football films with me? There are some things I want to show you."

Off Huff went to watch game films projected on the Landrys' living room wall. There were times that Landry's relentlessness—and the enormity of the task of cramming Landry's complicated system into his young head—got to Huff, and one time the rookie packed to leave for home, along with his rookie roommate, Don Chandler. It took the bull moose persuasion of Vince Lombardi, who caught them as they were about to depart and told them, "You two might not make this club but nobody runs out on me." They stayed.

For his defensive players Landry designed drills to help them in their quest for perfection. He would take an offensive tackle and a tight end, and match them against a defensive end and a linebacker. And he would teach each player the techniques of the position and then explain to the defensive players how to "double down" on the offensive tackle, and explain what the linebacker should do, and explain what happens if the end hits the linebacker, and explain angle blocks, pinch blocks, straight blocks, influence blocks, until the players knew the game from the heart and lungs out.

If Landry had a flaw, it was his tendency to remain the unrelenting perfectionist. Under his system, the player read the "key," then went to a predetermined spot. If the player wasn't there, no matter what the outcome, Landry would be in his ear to remind him.

One time Frank Gifford, who was then playing defensive back, intercepted a pass and ran it back for a touchdown. Gifford had made a spectacular play, but after it was over Landry told him, "Frank, you were out of position on that play." Perfection may have been his goal, but that same perfection also squeezed some of the fun and spontaneity out of the game.

That perfectionism, however, helped turn the New York Giants into a defensive machine, half of a Giant team that began the modern age of professional football. The eleven members of the defense all became well-known to their adoring fans: Andy Robustelli, Jim Katcavage, Rosey Grier, and Dick Modzelewski up front, with linebackers Sam Huff, Tom Scott, and Cliff Livingston, along with defensive backs Dick Nolan, Jimmy Patton, Lindon Crow, and Dick Lynch.

On offense, Vince Lombardi, an outgoing, bellowing "pretend tough guy," as defensive back Dick Nolan called him, had a different philosophy from the stoical, impersonal Landry. Lombardi's philosophy was to run a half dozen basic plays, but to run them with such precision that no one could stop them, even if the defenders knew in advance what was coming. To get his players to reach the perfection he was looking for, Lombardi cajoled and badgered them, but at the same time hugged them hard and let them know he loved them. Like Landry, Lombardi watched hours of films, dissecting defenses to find flaws, and when he found one, in the game he'd run the same play two, three, four times in a row until eventually the other team would slip, and his offense would be right down your throat. Lombardi created a whirlwind attack behind Charlie Conerly at quarterback, Frank Gifford at halfback, and Alex Webster at fullback.

In the locker room, Landry and Lombardi were close friends, but there *was* a rivalry. Here were two perfectionists who hated to lose even at checkers, and each wanted his unit to conquer whomever it came up against. To that end each demanded from head coach Jim Lee Howell extra practice time. And during games, they would fight for their unit's honor. On fourth-and-one, Landry and Lombardi would stand on either side of Howell and try to influence him. Landry would advise Howell to punt, so his unit could get back out there, while Lombardi would importune him to let his players "go for it."

The competition between defense and offense was immense. Big egos were at work. Howell, who was smart enough to let his two genius assistants run things, was also aware of the rivalry, and he only rarely allowed the first teams to scrimmage. "It got pretty heated," said Nolan. "Boy, talk about hitting. Some people got their brains beat out."

Beginning in the fall of 1956, the New York Giants became the glamour team in the NFL, and these Giant players became heroes and ultimately legends. They were adopted by New Yorkers who formerly had cared only about the Yankees, or the Dodgers, or the baseball Giants, or the basketball Knicks, or the hockey Rangers. The fans appreciated Lombardi's style of play, with glamour boy Frank Gifford capturing the hearts of wives and girlfriends, as well as the male rooters. And when the offense filed off the field, those fans cheered on every play for Sam Huff and his destroyers. In third-down situations Giant fans would chant, "*Deee*-fense. *Deee*-fense." And more often than not, the defense would hold, as the frenzy in the stands would escalate. When they loped off the field, they would be treated to standing ovations.

This recognition for a team's defense was a first, and before the TV camera's see-it-all eyes, across the country millions of fans would watch them and root for them.

In December 1956 the New York Giants played the Chicago Bears for the NFL championship on the frozen turf of Yankee Stadium. Before the game, the Giant players donned sneakers, while the Bears played in metal spikes. Giant speedster Gene Filipski took the opening kickoff and ran it back 53 yards to the Bear five. The rout was on. The Giants led at the half, 34–7.

On defense, during the week the Giant defenders had worked on stopping the Bears' big-play man, receiver Harlon Hill, and against the Giants, Hill did little, along with the rest of the Bears. With an offense drilled by Lombardi, the Giants moved the ball with machinelike precision as the Giants won the championship, 47–7.

The next year the interest in the NFL grew with the start of one of the greatest rivalries in the history of the sport. The rivalry was between Sam Huff of the Giants and a rookie running back drafted out of Syracuse University by the Cleveland Browns. That back, Jim Brown, is still considered the greatest runner in the history of the game. With Brown running the ball for the Browns, Sam Huff's world did indeed become violent. The Giants-Browns games pitting Sam Huff against Jim Brown in the late 1950s became legendary.

In 1957 the Browns won the East, with the Giants second, and in 1958 the Browns led the Giants by one game with one game to go— against each other. The Giants would have to win that game for the right to play the Browns in a playoff game for the Eastern title.

The Giants had to twice stop Jim Brown and the Browns, a difficult task considering that Brown ran for 163 yards a game and scored 14 touchdowns that year.

In the season finale Brown early in the game eluded Huff's grasp and ran for a 65-yard touchdown. After that Huff and the 4–3 defense shut him down. Toward the end of the game the score was tied 10–10. If the game ended in a tie, Cleveland would win the division title.

The Giants had the ball fourth-and-ten with 2:09 left. Because snow was falling and blanketing the field it was hard to see what hash mark the ball was on.

Pat Summerall lined up to kick what turned out to be a 49-yard field goal. It was the longest kick he would ever attempt as a Giant. The snow swirled, making it hard for Summerall to even see the goalposts.

As Charlie Conerly kneeled to clear a spot on the powdery turf, all seemed lost, but in one of those mythical moments, the Giant kicker swung his leg and made the football explode toward the end of the field. As it spun forward among the eddies of snowflakes, the ghostly officials standing under the goalposts signalled the kick good.

The Giants and Browns would go at it in Yankee Stadium in frozen New York City one more time.

For two solid weeks Vince Lombardi had studied the Browns on film. The Brown defense put so much pressure on the quarterback, it was hard to score against them. This time Lombardi opened with a stunning surprise. Quarterback Charlie Conerly handed the ball to Alex Webster, who switched it over to Frank Gifford, who turned upfield untouched and ran down to the Cleveland eight-yard line, where as he was about to be tackled, he lateralled to a trailing Conerly, who scored. Summerall later added a field goal.

For two solid weeks Landry too had studied the Browns on film, and he had spent a lot of time tutoring Huff on how to stop Jim Brown. And in this game Landry's defense came as close as was humanly possible to reaching the perfection he had been seeking. Cleveland, led by Brown, its feared runner, was held to eight yards in *total offense*. The Giants won 10–0. It was the first time a Paul Brown team had been shut out since 1950, when Steve Owen concocted his umbrella defense against the Browns.

After the game Cleveland Browns kicker Lou Groza commented, "There's only one man who could have done this to us . . . Tom Landry. Nobody else."

When Andy Robustelli was given the game ball, he turned it over to Landry. "This doesn't belong to me," said Robustelli. Said head coach Jim Lee Howell, "Tom Landry is the best coach in football."

The 1958 NFL championship against the Baltimore Colts, the best offensive team in the league, is one game everyone who saw it still remembers. This was the game that propelled football into America's consciousness as a spectator sport that had the capability of rivaling baseball.

The Giants led 17–14 late in the game on a touchdown pass from

Charlie Conerly to Frank Gifford. The game would be theirs if they could gain one more first down. But on third-and-four, Frank Gifford took the handoff, headed wide, and cut back inside. Colt defensive end Gino Marchetti stopped him with a crushing tackle just shy of the first-down marker. And worse, Gifford was through for the day with a broken leg. A punt put the Colts back on their own 12.

The Giants knew what Johnny Unitas was going to do, but they couldn't stop him. They tried a desperate measure, double-teaming ends Lenny Moore and Ray Berry. Unitas hit Berry with three passes in a row. In a minute and a half Unitas had taken his team to the Giant 13. That was when Steve Myhra kicked his field goal, tying the game, and leading to a loss that has always rankled Giant fans and Tom Landry. But because of that field goal, the game was sent into overtime and into the annals of history.

In overtime the Giants won the toss and elected to receive. Three plays later, the Giants were inches shy of the first-down marker, and Don Chandler had to punt. Unitas started on his own 20, and despite defensive adjustments of all sorts, the Giants could not stop the march of the Colts. When Alan Ameche bulled over from the two, the Colts were world champions.

In 1959 the Giant defense held twelve opponents to 170 points, remarkable in that the Giants had allowed 49 in one game against the Philadelphia Eagles. In the other eleven games, the defense allowed just 121 points, incredible numbers. Despite the loss of Vince Lombardi, who left the team to become head coach of the Green Bay Packers, the Giants again reached the NFL championship, only to lose again to the Colts. Landry's defense had a rough afternoon against Unitas & Co., and against the Colt line of Marchetti, Don Joyce, Big Daddy Lipscomb, and Artie Donovan, the Giants didn't do much. The final score was 31–16, Colts.

Still, in four years using Landry's defense, the Giants had played in three championship games, winning one, and one year finished second in the Eastern Division.

Landry was primed to leave the Giants after the '59 season. Landry's intention all along after getting his degree in industrial engineering was to go into business. After the '55 season, he had moved to Dallas in the off-season in an attempt to find a career in the real world in which he might find success. But what Landry had not anticipated was that whether he was selling storage tanks for oil fields or insurance or real estate, he floundered because for six months of the year he had to be absent coaching football, and employers didn't want six-month employees.

Tom Landry was at a crossroads in his life. His football salary was only around $12,000 a year, and he either had to find a better-paying job in football or get out of the game and go into business full-time.

Rumors abounded that Jim Lee Howell would quit the Giants and let Landry take over, but no offer was made. Bud Adams of the Houston Oilers contacted Landry about coaching his team but Landry wasn't sure he wanted to coach in an unstable new league and demurred.

It was at this point that Tex Schramm offered Tom Landry the job as head coach of the new NFL franchise in Dallas, where Landry was living. This was a chance to get out from under the shadow of Jim Lee Howell and prove his own worth as a coach. And he could do it in front of his homefolk.

Tom Landry was coming back to Texas.

5

The Expendables

There was one other incentive pushing Tom Landry to take the job as head coach at Dallas: He could build a team from scratch and once again prove the worth of his defensive system, an impossible task, one that appealed to him.

"The idea of such a big challenge intrigued me," Landry said years later.

Rarely in the history of pro sports did a coach have so little with which to begin. Two years later the 1962 New York Mets, managed by Casey Stengel and led by Marvelous Marv Throneberry, would give this Cowboy team a run for its money. Until then, this would be the team that would set the standard for fielding a lineup of retreads, has-beens, and never-wuzes.

The key to success for any pro team is young players, unformed, eager, ready to learn, playing on legs not yet pounded and broken. In pro football the college draft is what makes a good team great, as the youngsters imbue a team with their youth and their enthusiasm, pushing the veterans to play harder, and sometimes pushing them out. It is the natural order of things. But in 1960 the fledgling Dallas Rangers did not get to participate in the college draft, because it was held *before* the NFL officially admitted the team into the league.

Only through the largesse of expansion committee head George Halas were the Rangers able to sign their two young talented college seniors, SMU quarterback Don Meredith and University of New Mexico running back Don Perkins. The rest of the Dallas players would come from a hastily compiled list of fringe players grudgingly given up by the existing NFL teams.

A half dozen of the men plucked from the hasty expansion list were pushing thirty or were older. Coaches of the existing NFL teams risked the least by placing their oldest players on the list. Even if they had been stars and still could perform, it would not be long before it was time for them to retire. If a player on the list was younger than thirty, it was probably because he had been broken and hadn't been the same after he had mended, or because he had never approached his potential and was being discarded.

Making Landry's job even harder was the fact that several veterans he was counting on, like fullback Ed Modzelewski of Cleveland and center Charlie Ane from Detroit, retired rather than report to the expansion Rangers, deciding that moving teams and towns—in essence starting from scratch—was too difficult and not worth the emotional price at that point in their careers.

Of the ones who did report, a few looked forward to coming, were even happy to come to this new team, angry or frustrated as they were about their status on their old teams. A few, as Tex Schramm had surmised, were pleased to come to Dallas because they were Texans coming back to Texas.

What most also had in common was that they had played for outstanding teams, either in college or in the pros, and coming to Dallas, they knew, would be a far different experience.

These men had accumulated dozens of years of experience. They had played for some of the most famous coaches in football history, both in college and the pros, and they had played alongside and against the roughest, toughest hombres and the brightest stars the NFL in the 1950s had to offer.

Tex Schramm knew the players taken on the expansion list would be upset at having to leave their teams to play in a new town for a ragtag ensemble. He also knew that if he could draft players who had played in college in Texas, the likelihood would be that they were less likely to be resentful. It was one of the considerations when he plucked running back Don McIlhenny from the draft list of the Green Bay Packers. As it turned out, Schramm was right about McIlhenny. The hard running back was glad to be coming back to Dallas.

McIlhenny was born and raised in Cleveland. When he entered Southern Methodist University in '52, he was a single wing tailback following in the footsteps of Doak Walker and Kyle Rote. But the heyday of the Mustangs was over, and the team was mediocre. In one game against Kansas, McIlhenny scored four touchdowns. But SMU couldn't beat the big boys like Notre Dame. Still, McIlhenny was named the starting halfback in the College All-Star game, and he played in the Shrine Game and Senior Bowl Game as well.

In '56 he was drafted third by Detroit, the same year the Lions picked Howard "Hopalong" Cassady, the All-America from Ohio State, number one. Nevertheless, Lions coach Buddy Parker started McIlhenny, and he was near the top of the league in rushing until he tore up his knee against San Francisco when Leo Nomellini drove his large body through McIlhenny's extended leg. McIlhenny returned in time for the Western Division Championship Game against the Bears.

Middle linebacker Jack Patera was also happy to be coming to Dallas, because he was getting away from the Chicago Cardinals, a dreary, unorganized team. Patera had been a member of a rising Baltimore Colts team, and he was looking forward to playing on a champion, when during training camp in '58 coach Weeb Ewbank asked him to switch from linebacker to the offensive line. Patera stubbornly refused. And as a result, Ewbank got rid of him. Patera missed being part of one of the most exciting championships in the history of the game, the historic win over the New York Giants in Yankee Stadium in December of 1958. Instead, he was shipped to the gulag in Chicago. Thus, when Patera found himself leaving Chicago via the expansion draft, he was ecstatic. Even playing for an expansion team was better than having to spend another year with the Chicago Cardinals.

Patera was born in Bismarck, North Dakota, but when he was three his family moved to Portland, Oregon. After a fine high school career, he went to the University of Oregon because his girlfriend (now his wife) went there. In his senior year Patera was invited to play in the East-West Shrine Game in San Francisco.

In '55 he was drafted by the Baltimore Colts in the fourth round. Baltimore had not been a winning team, but the rookies gave the team a big boost. Even as a rookie Patera could see that the Colts had some great players.

JACK PATERA: "One of the linemen was Artie Donovan, who was exceptionally quick and very strong but terribly out of shape. When it was time to do exercises, Art would stand on one leg and shake the other, and then switch legs, and he'd be ready to go. That's the truth. He was an amazing person. Dunnie never got down in position before the snap. He'd very lightly touch the ground with one hand, almost like squatting. You could never make a training film out of Art Donovan.

"Artie was funny just because of what he did. His eating habits were obnoxious. He would eat nothing but pizza and hot dogs. We'd have a family-style dinner in the dorm, and Art wouldn't eat. The only time he ate was when they served hot dogs. Otherwise he'd go out after dinner and buy himself beer and pizza and hot dogs and hamburgers.

"I can remember Artie and Buddy Young were roommates, and one night Alex Sandusky shot a groundhog and brought it back and put it in one of their beds. When we had bed check at ten o'clock everybody stood around their room, because they knew what was coming. Both of them came running out, this big white guy and this little black guy, and Art has this high squeaky voice, and he was standing fifty yards outside the dormitory, just berating everybody: 'How could you do that to that poor little animal?'

"On that same line was Gino Marchetti. Gino was all business. He may have looked ragged and tired with his head down, but he had a tremendous desire that brought him to overcome anything. He was just a no-nonsense guy. I remember him saying about us the second or third year I was there, 'The thing about you guys, when you came in it seemed you all were mature and had been here for years.' Coming from Gino, an older person who had been in the Battle of the Bulge, an elderly thirty-year-old, he was saying that our rookie class was acceptable, and that was a great compliment.

"At the other end was Don Joyce, who weighed 300 pounds, and he also had great strength and quickness. Our right tackle was a fellow named Tom Finnin, who was a good football player in his own right, and in '56 he lost his job to Big Daddy Lipscomb, who had been picked up after he was waived by the Rams. Most players were surprised, because no one really felt Big Daddy was that good.

"Big Daddy was a character. Even when he wasn't as good as he became, he thought he was very good. He was pretty pumped up with himself. He had an ego that directed attention to himself.

"Our team captain was Don Shula, a defensive back. He was a fierce competitor and a smart football player. And there is no doubt he was a guy who was in control. The thing I remember most about Shula was one time during halftime I was eating orange slices, and he said, 'Don't eat those. They make you sick.' I had been eating orange slices since high school. I thought to myself, Mind your own business.

"And then in '56 Ewbank made Bill Pellington the captain of the team, and this crushed Shula. Then when Pellington got hurt in our first game, I started calling the defenses, and Shula thought that should be reverting back to him. But Weeb had said he wanted a linebacker to call them. I can remember when Shula left the Colts, the owner, Carroll Rosenbloom, said to the effect, 'He's going to come back and coach for me some day.' Mr. Rosenbloom recognized the effectiveness of Don Shula's mind, so although he wasn't a great player, he was a very, very smart one. He *wanted* to run things.

"Toward the end of training camp in '58 Weeb decided to move Big Daddy back to middle linebacker, and he wanted me to play offensive guard. I told him I didn't want to. I said, 'I'd rather leave here than play offense.'

"Weeb traded me to the Chicago Cardinals, and if there was one team I didn't want to go to, it was the Cardinals. Our strong safety, Bert Rechichar, had been traded there in the off-season, and sometime in training camp the Cardinals had released him, and so the trade was nullified, and Bert was saying, 'You can't imagine what it's like. It's the worst thing you can imagine,' and he went on and on. And when I got to Chicago, everything Bert said was true! It was just awful. The equipment had to be from the 1940s, stuff they were still trying to use. The cliques on the team were obnoxious. The people in management and coaching were inferior types. Everything about it was inferior.

"At the end of the season I wrote a letter asking them to put me in the expansion draft. I figured anything would be better than playing on the Cardinals. I knew nothing about the Dallas organization and I could have cared less. It was just an opportunity to start over again."

Some of the players, including tight end Dick Bielski and guard Bob Fry, didn't particularly want to leave their old teams, but they had the sort of personality not to complain once it occurred. Bielski had been a star fullback for the Philadelphia Eagles until quarterback Norm Van Brocklin came and ordered the coach to move him to tight end. In '59 Bielski found himself on a team headed for glory. But at the end of the season he was perplexed to find that coach Buck Shaw had put him on the expansion list. While the Eagles would win the NFL championship in 1960, he would be toiling for expansion Dallas. To his credit, he didn't bitch and moan. It wasn't Dick Bielski's nature.

Bielski was born on the east side of Baltimore. His high school team won twenty-nine games in a row. One season the team was unscored upon. He was intending to go to the University of Southern California when Jim Tatum, the coach of the University of Maryland, told Bielski's mother, "He will be going to California three thousand miles away, and you're liable never to see him again if he gets hooked up with those wild women in Hollywood." His mother told him, "You're going to Maryland with that nice man, Jim Tatum." And he did just that.

In '51 Bielski played as a freshman. It was the last year of unrestricted spring practice. Tatum held spring practice for six months, from the time the snow melted until final exams! And he held scrimmages on Saturday. On Sunday the players met to watch films. The next year spring practice was cut back to thirty days.

In Bielski's freshman year Maryland went undefeated and went to the Sugar Bowl and beat Tennessee, the number one team in the nation. In '52 they lost their final two games, to Alabama and Ole Miss. In '53 the team was undefeated and again named national champs, and in '54 Maryland had a tie and one loss to UCLA.

In '55 Bielski was drafted in the first round by the Philadelphia Eagles. He got $13,500, including a signing bonus. Like most rookies, he was in awe that he had even been drafted, and the fact that he was selected the number one player in the entire draft puzzled him. When he reported to the Eagles camp, he couldn't believe he was playing alongside so many well-known players.

DICK BIELSKI: "To me players like Bucko Kilroy, Norm Willy, Tom Scott, and Chuck Bednarik were ancient. Bucko was the sort of guy who would take a swing at you in practice and knock you out cold. He was a nasty human being. We had a few of them. Wayne Robinson was that way, Tom Scott, Norm Willy, and damn near the whole Eagle defense. They were nasty, belligerent. They didn't win many games, but you damn sure didn't like a victory over us.

"Chuck Bednarik was one of those imposing guys. He was 6'1", about 230 pounds, built like a weightlifter. He had these tremendous arms and hands, and he was agile and strong as an ox. And very nasty.

"One of the most unbelievable things I remember about my rookie year was in a Saturday afternoon scrimmage in Hershey, Pennsylvania. Bednarik just beat the shit out of me, bloodied my face and forearm, knocked me down and stepped on me, and then the next morning I was in church at the communion rail kneeling next to him as he was taking communion. It just seemed bizarre that here this son of a bitch was kicking my ass the day before, and now I was kneeling beside him taking communion in the church. It was weird, a bizarre situation: here's this gentle soul now receiving communion, and the guy is an animal. He belongs in a cage. If that doesn't tell you what pro football is like, nothing does.

"What made going to the Cowboys hard was that everything was different. The attitude was different. The players were all players from different groups. They all had ideas of how it should be, what shouldn't be. And it was very difficult. It was difficult because you had nothing to lean on, nothing to fall back on, nothing to get your teeth into. Everything was so different."

6

The Disgruntled

If some players were not actively unhappy to be playing in Dallas, practically everyone else on that expansion list was. Most made it abundantly clear they were coming to play for the Dallas Rangers against their will. They were not ready to retire, but this was where the NFL was telling them they had to play. As a result they were having to start over very late in their careers, and they hated the idea. One player, linebacker Jerry Tubbs, was in the opposite situation. He had intended to retire from pro football and take a managerial job with Coca-Cola. When the job didn't materialize he joined the Cowboys because he needed the money.

Tubbs, who was acquired from the San Francisco 49ers, grew up in Breckenridge, Texas, about 135 miles west of Dallas. In three years of high school ball Tubbs's teams lost three games as he led Breckenridge High to state championships in both his junior and senior years. Tubbs wanted to play for a winner in college, and so in 1954 he went to the University of Oklahoma to play for coach Bud Wilkinson, one of the most successful coaches in college history.

Wilkinson was the quintessential coach of the Eisenhower '50s. Bud Wilkinson *was* postwar America.

JERRY TUBBS: "Coach Wilkinson believed in the American Dream, and he believed that people who worked hard, who thought about things, and who were motivated were the ones who became successful. He used to tell the story of how a family went from shirtsleeve to shirtsleeve in three generations, how a man came over from Europe, worked hard, and made a big success of himself, and then his son, who saw how hard it was growing up, he worked and did okay, but then the grandson, he had it easy all his life, and he doesn't learn how to compete, and he lets things slide a little bit, and then he loses it all. He used to preach that you couldn't rest on last year's laurels."

Tubbs played on undefeated national champions his junior and senior years at the University of Oklahoma, and in 1957 he was drafted number one by the Chicago Cardinals—ahead of Syracuse running back Jim Brown. Unfortunately for Tubbs, the Chicago Cardinals were the worst-run team in football. Tubbs himself will tell you the fact that the Cards owner took him over Brown was a strong indication that the organization was in disarray.

JERRY TUBBS: "I knew they were in trouble then. And it was a shock to me to go from the University of Oklahoma, where everything was highly organized, where everything was first class, to go to sign my contract at their offices, which were back in an old dilapidated building in downtown Chicago. You had to go through a hallway to get to owner Walter Woofner's office. Inside, there were tickets all over the place. I thought, This isn't what I had in mind for high-class pro football. And it didn't get much better."

Tubbs signed his rookie year for a $9,000 salary and a $2,000 bonus. After hurting himself in the College All-Star Game against the New York Giants, when he arrived in camp he discovered that *everything* about the Cardinals was disorganized.

Tubbs had played middle linebacker at Oklahoma, but because he only weighed 215 pounds, the coaches forced him to play on the outside. He was given a starting role, and then three-quarters of the way through the season he was cut! After missing just one game, he signed with San Francisco, again playing outside linebacker for coach Frankie Albert. The next year he was able to convince the new coach, Red Hickey, that he should play in the middle, and in '59 the 49ers would have been in the championships if they could have beaten the Baltimore Colts.

Tubbs intended to get out of pro football after '59. He had played to find out if he could, and he discovered he had met the challenge. At the end of the season he went back to Breckenridge, Texas, to teach and coach at his old high school. While he was there, he was contacted by Coca-Cola and offered the job of district manager in a plant in Little Rock, Arkansas. An honorable man, Tubbs told Coke he could not leave at that time because one of the other Breckenridge coaches had left to go to another school, and he didn't want to leave the school with two openings in such a short period of time. Tubbs asked Coke to hold the job for him until the end of the school year. Coke told Tubbs they could not do that, but that if another opening came up, they'd let him know.

When Dallas got its franchise, and each existing club was told to make a list of players for the expansion draft, Red Hickey called Tubbs and asked about his plans. Tubbs told him, "If a job opens up with Coke, I'm going to take it." Hickey was incredulous. "You're going to take a job and *not* play pro football?" "Yes," said Tubbs, "if a job opens up. But if a job doesn't open up, I'd like to play again."

The night the 49ers were making the expansion list, Hickey called Tubbs from the meeting and said, "Now Tubbs, if we keep you on the 49ers, tell me you'll play for us. We can't hold you and then lose you to retirement."

"Coach, I just can't do that."

And so Red Hickey put Jerry Tubbs on the expansion list.

JERRY TUBBS: "There wasn't any ulterior motive. I wasn't trying to get to Dallas. In fact, I really didn't like the idea of playing for Dallas, because I knew they were an expansion team, that they wouldn't do very well. When Tex Schramm called, I told him about the Coke deal. When June came, and Coke still didn't have an opening, I finally signed with the Cowboys."

The players who came to that first Cowboy training camp had several characteristics in common. Most were children of the Depression, brought up by parents who had struggled to clothe and feed them. These players, almost all white, were hardworking, honest, forthright, and self-sufficient. They had had to be. Most of them had come from hard times. Tubbs, the son of a tenant farmer in rural Oklahoma, grew up with a toughness he developed from hard times. Defensive end Gene Cronin had been part of the Grapes of Wrath legacy, a Nebraskan who fled the Dust Bowl and relocated in California, where the father dug ditches and the family lived in a tent. Defensive end John Gonzaga couldn't afford even to go to college, and got his tryout with the pros after working in the steel mills. Fullback Gene Babb, who grew up in and around the oil fields of Texas, lost his father when he was eight, his mother when he was thirteen. Kicker Fred Cone was a parachute jumper in the army during World War II when he started playing football. Part of the ethic of the 1950s was that you were supposed to be rewarded for your long service. These men, rather, had been betrayed, and so men like Gene Cronin of the Detroit Lions, John Gonzaga of the San Francisco 49ers, and end Ray Mathews of the Pittsburgh Steelers never got over having been dumped by their old teams. They hated leaving their friends behind, and brimmed with bitterness over being cut adrift. Cronin and Mathews had played for the hard-drinking maverick Buddy Parker, and each had loved him. Gonzaga had played for Red Hickey, whom he disliked, demanding Hickey send him elsewhere. Hickey sent him to Dallas, which didn't suit Gonzaga either.

When Cronin, Gonzaga, and Mathews came to Dallas, they were met by a coach who ran the team like it was boot camp, ordering their lives on and off the field. The three spent a year in Dallas chafing against Tom Landry's iron rule.

This bitterness would permeate the team and subvert Tom Landry's authority the first few years of their existence, until he could supplant them with younger, more malleable, more talented players.

John Gonzaga had been All-County as a fullback in high school in Northern California, despite working at night as a strander in a rolling mill, catching steel bars with a pair of tongs. It was hazardous, but it was a paycheck. A half dozen California colleges were interested in his coming to play for them, but his family needed him to keep working to support them. When fall came around, instead of going to college he continued in the mill while learning structural engineering in trade school. At twenty-one, he became a structural engineer for the firm that helped build the approaches to the toll plazas of the Richmond-San Rafael Bridge north of San Francisco.

For fun Gonzaga played football on the alumni team of a rival high school, and he so impressed one of the coaches that the coach told Pappy Waldorf, the head scout of the San Francisco 49ers, about him, and when Gonzaga's class graduated, he was asked to try out with the nearby 49ers. Unlike most of the rookies, Gonzaga had to take a large pay cut to play for the team.

JOHN GONZAGA: "I was making $9,000, and my contract was for $5,000. At first the prospect of giving up the money really didn't excite me, but after thinking about it, I said, 'Oh, what the hell.' To get in shape for training camp, I'd get up at four in the morning, run my buns off, get down to the gym at six, pump iron, and hope everything worked out. I didn't consider making the 49ers a challenge as much as I did a commitment. Not too many guys made it without playing college ball. I just made up my mind I was going to do it. I decided I wasn't backing up to anyone or anything."

The 49ers coaching staff at first didn't know where to play him because he didn't have any experience, and so they tried him at both offensive tackle and defensive end, and during the four years he was with the 49ers he played as much offense as defense. In '57 Gonzaga played against the Detroit Lions in the Western Division championship. This was the game that the 49ers were winning 27–7, only to see the Lions come back and upset them.

Of all the expansion players, the one who made the biggest show of disrespect for Tom Landry and his system was offensive end Ray Mathews, who had been plucked from the roster of the Pittsburgh Steelers, where he had caught the passes of Jim Finks and then Bobby Layne. As a player, Mathews felt he had had the number of Tom Landry when the new Dallas head coach was playing defensive back for the Giants, and now that Landry was coach Mathews was not shy about reminding him of the numerous catches he made against him. Mathews was the quintessential freelance end, a hell-raiser like Layne. But with the Cowboys Landry made Mathews, who had been one of Bobby Layne's drinking buddies, run specific routes and heel to his precise system. All year long he bitched and moaned loudly about Landry to teammates, even to the coach's face.

Mathews had starred at Clemson under Frank Howard, a tough southerner. Howard's old saying was, "I come from Balderbend, Alabama, two axle greases from Birmingham, and for you damn Yankees who don't know where Birmingham is, the next train leaves at five." Howard was countrified. He would say, "I came to Clemson riding a tiger, using a rattlesnake for a whip. The tiger was so damn mean, when I went to the bathroom, I'd take a club because he might shit a wildcat." His players loved him.

The team played single wing, using a lot of razzle-dazzle. Mathews played on two undefeated teams at Clemson. In his sophomore year (1948) Clemson beat Missouri 24–23 in the Gator Bowl, and his senior year beat Miami 15–14 in the Orange Bowl.

Mathews was drafted by the Steelers in '51. He played both ways his first four years.

It was not until '55 that players started wearing face masks. Football was tough back then.

RAY MATHEWS: "We were playing the Eagles in Forbes Field. We ran a play, and the Eagles' Bucko Kilroy broke through and chased our quarterback, Jim Finks, back a ways. The play was over, and our guard, Bull Schweder, was getting up and coming back to the huddle, when Bucko, who was walking back to his huddle, decked him! Knocked him out! We said to the officials, 'Aren't you going to call a penalty?' They said, 'The play was dead.' Can you imagine that?

"I hated Bucko Kilroy. Boy, if you didn't call him dirty and mean or swear at him, he didn't like you. He enjoyed it most when people really crucified him. He thought that was the greatest thing since sliced bread.

"I had been with the Steelers since 1951 when they put my name on the expansion list. I didn't think they'd do that. I still don't see why they did, just because I was injured. At Clemson my senior year I had broken my ribs on one side and was out for four weeks. Then against Cleveland in '59 I rebroke them, and I was out the last two games of the season. I don't see why . . . I didn't think. . . . They told me they had put my name on the list figuring Dallas wouldn't take me. Art Rooney personally called me from California and told me that Dallas had taken me. I also talked to Buddy Parker.

"I went to Dallas with a chip on my shoulder. I had played nine years with Pittsburgh, and I was hoping the Cowboys would send me back. But they never did. I did everything I could to get them to trade me, but they kept me for the whole year."

7

Mr. Nice

When Tex Schramm was general manager of the Los Angeles Rams, he was a pioneer in bringing black players into the NFL. Schramm had lived in California, where racial tolerance was at its highest in America in the 1950s, and when he sought players for his Rams team, he didn't exclude blacks as other owners did. Tank Younger was a Rams star, as was Deacon Dan Towler, and later Schramm would introduce to the NFL Gene "Big Daddy" Lipscomb.

In Dallas, Schramm's philosophy remained the same. His problem was that the milieu was different. Dallas was in the Deep South, and like the rest of the Bible Belt, it was a segregated city.

Whites in Texas were fiercely outspoken in their hatred of blacks, but they were not as violent about enforcing the Jim Crow laws as whites from other southern states like Alabama, Mississippi, and Georgia. There were several reasons for this:

1. Texas didn't become a state until 1846, only fifteen years before the Civil War.
2. Most Texas blacks were dirt farmers, not slaves, and so when the slaves were freed, the poor whites in Texas were not threatened by

the elevated status of the slaves as much as poor whites in other states of the Confederacy.

3. Only one small skirmish was fought in Texas during the Civil War, unlike the other states, which were destroyed by the Union Army.

4. During Reconstruction, Texas landholders didn't lose their lands, like many in the other Deep South states.

And as a result, Texas whites didn't have the generations of bitterness against either the North or the Negroes that Alabamans or Mississippians or Georgians had.

Nevertheless, Texas *was* a southern state, and the system of segregation was firmly entrenched. As late as the 1960s, the West Texas town of Stinett would not allow a black to remain in the town after sundown. Trains and automobiles pulling into the East Texas town of Greenville passed a large electrified sign that proudly boasted: "Greenville, Texas: The blackest land, the whitest people." In Mount Vernon, about a hundred miles east of Dallas, doctors' offices had separate waiting rooms for blacks and whites.

The assault on white supremacy began after World War II. Blacks had fought valiantly in the war, and when they returned home, they found they had risked their lives to help preserve a way of life they found abhorrent. Black soldiers who passed through Love Field in Dallas could find neither food nor even a place to go to the bathroom.

After the war Negroes were no longer satisfied with the status quo. Many southern blacks moved into northern cities, hoping for better treatment. In the northern cities they could vote. In the northern cities they could get a better education.

In Texas in 1944 Thurgood Marshall, the chief legal counsel for the NAACP, won a case in the Supreme Court in which the all-white political party system in Texas and the South was declared unconstitutional. He later argued another Supreme Court case that held that the law school at the University of Texas could no longer be all-white.

In 1947 Jackie Robinson proved to all of America that blacks could play baseball alongside and do as well as their white teammates. During spring training in the South, Robinson received many death threats. Considering the depth of feeling by southerners against the notion of equality for blacks, it's remarkable nothing happened to him.

In 1948 came the first real crack in the national consensus against segregation when President Truman backed the recommendations of his

Committee on Civil Rights at the Democratic National Convention calling for equality, not paternalism. Dr. Martin Luther King led the call for equal rights.

Then in 1954 Linda Brown, a black student, was bused out of her white neighborhood to attend a black school in Topeka, Kansas. The NAACP sued. Justice Earl Warren of the U.S. Supreme Court ruled that separate facilities were unequal and something should be done with "all deliberate speed."

The two races were to integrate, said the Court. After the decision opinion polls showed that 80 percent of white southerners opposed desegregation. A quarter felt violence was justified in maintaining the current system. And yet, for the first time, small groups of whites publicly advocated racial equality. In Dallas, a flyer titled "The Worst Horror on Earth" was distributed, stating that after the schools were desegregated, white daughters would come home with black boyfriends.

When the Cowboys came into existence in 1960, Dallas was still rigidly segregated. Negroes could live in one of several overly crowded areas, including South Dallas, the east side of Love Field, Oak Cliff, and the State Street-Thomas Avenue area off Hall Street. The hotels and restaurants were still segregated, and on buses, blacks still had to ride in the back. In 1950 federal regulations outlawed segregation on interstate carriers, primarily trains, though after the law was passed, some of the Texas conductors continued to enforce the segregationist policy. Schools were still segregated. In fact, Dallas was one of the largest cities in the South with a completely segregated school system. Despite *Brown v. Board of Education*, it was only in May of 1960 that the school board moved to end segregation in Dallas, voting to desegregate one grade at a time, a plan rejected by the federal courts.

The mayor, Robert L. "Uncle Bob" Thornton, was a member of the powerful Citizens Council, a group more powerful even than the City Council and made up of twenty-five powerful movers and shakers— mostly bankers. They met monthly to decide what was best for Dallas. Led by Thornton, the Citizens Council was concerned that racial violence, like that in Little Rock and New Orleans, would badly hurt their city's image. Thornton didn't want to see businesses burned. He wanted the problem solved quickly and peaceably. To Thornton it was not a question of morality or equality, because he knew that most of the citizens of the city didn't want it. To Thornton it was a matter of economics, of dollars, and of preserving the city's good name. And so in 1960 the Citizens Council took on the task of integrating the schools and all public facilities peaceably. They would prepare the overall community for its acceptance. They undertook a massive public relations campaign. They formed a bi-racial committee and asked the black members to persuade Negro organizations to do all they could not to foul up the implementation of the plan.

It was during this time that Tex Schramm, the general manager of the Dallas Cowboys, went to the Citizens Council in order to solve his own problem. Among those signed by the Cowboys were Don Perkins and Frank Clarke, black players who needed to be able to eat and sleep with the team.

TEX SCHRAMM: "When we came to Dallas, we had no hotel where any of our black players could stay, nor could any of the visiting players who were black. At that time they had a very good situation in Dallas in which there was a group of businessmen that essentially had the influence in the town and ran things with good intentions. I went to them and said, 'Look it. We got a problem. We've got blacks on our team, and the teams coming in are going to have blacks.' They were very conscious and aware of the circumstances, because they had been working with the Negro leaders to prevent things that had happened in other parts of the South, having nothing to do with football, and so the Ramada Inn on the property of the airport said they would take all the players, but only if none of the other hotels would retaliate. Back in those days, if a hotel took a black in, the other hotels would get the word all around, and so the whites wouldn't go there. They got an agreement from the other hotels, and so that first year we stayed at the Ramada Inn, both the white and the black players. We stayed there after we came back from training camp and the night before games.

"We then moved down to the Sheraton downtown, and that broke the hotel barrier, though Dallas still had a restaurant problem."

Frank Clarke had come to the Dallas Rangers in the expansion draft from the Cleveland Browns. Clarke, twenty-seven, had been signed by the Browns as an offensive end. He had spent his three years with the Browns playing mostly on the special teams, but at 6', 215 pounds, Tex Schramm and Tom Landry liked his size and speed. What they could not know was that the combination of an abusive mother and a rigid system of segregation had caused him to feel scared every moment of his life. Clarke, like the rest of a subservient, oppressed generation of Negroes under orders to "know your place," discovered that the best way to get along was to show the world that he was not a threat to others. He rarely became angry, never raising his voice. He was polite, said "Yes, sir," and "No, sir," and hoped society would find him acceptable. "Humble," is how most of his teammates remembered him.

Despite his popularity at the University of Colorado, Clarke chose to keep to himself and had few friends. Pleasure was not one of the emotions in his makeup. Even when Colorado won the Orange Bowl game his senior year, he could not enjoy the victory. Despite his obvious talent, his coach, a southerner, never gave him a starting role. Clarke felt it was because the coach didn't want a junior college transfer who was black to be his star player. When Clarke was drafted by the Cleveland Browns, the men who started ahead of him were not wanted; only he was. Clarke would not even smile at the irony.

When Clarke arrived in Cleveland, he found that head coach Paul Brown was critical and rarely supportive, and he never felt comfortable as a whipping boy. The Browns' star player, Jim Brown, went out of his way to show his contempt for him. To this day Clarke does not know why.

When he was put on the expansion list, it was with the tag of "unfulfilled promise." Frank Clarke had no guts, it was whispered. When the Browns put him on the expansion list, Clarke was thrilled to have escaped. At age twenty-seven, he was going to get a real opportunity to prove his talent. Unlike most of the players on the expansion list, Clarke was excited about coming to the Dallas Cowboys, happy to be getting a fresh start with a new team.

FRANK CLARKE: "I spent the first eighteen years of my life in a small town in south-central Wisconsin called Beloit. I was born in 1934, and at that time things were pretty dark everywhere. It wasn't unusual to be poor, so we, of course, were poor, but being black and poor made it even more difficult.

"For me what compounded the hard times was my relationship with my parents. My father worked a lot and wasn't around much. My mother was tyrannical. She was extremely hard, and for some reason she was particularly hard on me. She beat me a lot, with switches or anything she could get her hands on. She would attack me verbally and physically, really scared the crap out of me, and she used to tell me not to cry while she was beating me. The threat was, 'If you cry, you're going to get beat harder.' I had nowhere to hide, and I didn't know how to defend myself from this. She did all the things that kept a person from feeling confidence in himself, feel good about himself, and to let his creative talents be born. So a lot of mine were repressed. I've never been able to get a sense of her being pleased with anything—ever.

"Adding to those feelings was the crush of living in a segregated society. God almighty, it was terrible. The school was not segregated, but when I was in the classroom, the way the teachers treated me, I *knew* there was something wrong with me. I got the attitude, 'You're not okay.' I got it at school, I got it at church, I got it everywhere.

"My father had come to Beloit from Alabama, because there was a reputation born that if a black person goes north, he'll be treated better. But like when my father got here, he found the *same* kind of racism as he met in the South. The only thing, it was more subtle. You felt it. You felt it when you went to the store. You felt it as soon as you left your house. You'd be in the company of somebody white, and there was this sense, this attitude of, 'I'm better than you,' which came from the way they looked at you, from the way they talked to you, and from the way they communicated to you if you were doing something they didn't think was okay.

"When I was a kid, I developed a knack for being nice to people. I was nice to everybody. I saw what happened to athletes who were probably better than I was, but didn't get the doors open to them because they had an attitude. They showed their resentment. And I didn't know how to do that. The thing I had learned was, hey, I'm a nice-looking kid, and because of my genes I was able to carry myself, to speak the language, and to just get along. People liked me, animals liked me. So I had doors open to me. I became an attractive young boy to all colors. But only to a certain extent, because I couldn't go home with the white boys and white girls who were attracted to me, and vice versa. And this did a number on my psyche, because I couldn't understand it. I knew I wasn't being accepted for who I was.

"High school was a very satisfying experience because the teachers introduced me to thoughts of going to college. They saw a nice boy who could run fast and catch a football, could hit a baseball, and shoot baskets. The summer between my junior and senior year my coach, Ken Currier, said, 'I think you're going to be offered a scholarship at the University of Wisconsin.' Before that, I had *never* even thought about going to college. Here I was, in the public school system twelve years and never thought about it.

"I was a lousy student. I didn't know how to study. I didn't know how to inquire, because I was so *scared*. So scared nobody could imagine. I was scared out of my wits. People called me 'nice,' said I was 'humble.'

'Frank is humble.' Humble my ass. I was scared shitless, of people, of criticism, of failure. I was afraid of constantly being rejected, like I was at home. And if I got that out in the street, where could a kid run? To me criticism meant I wasn't a good person.

"So the coach said, 'You're going to the university,' and I did. I had had a great athletic career in high school, was All-State, was under no pressure at all. I didn't aspire. It just happened. I won gold medals in the state track meet, and everything I touched was fantastic, and I went off to the University of Wisconsin, and whoa. I went to class and had a good attitude, but I hadn't been prepared for the academic part of it. And when I got out onto the football field, I found, My God, there are guys as big or bigger than I am who can run as fast as I can. That was quite a shock. And for the first time in my life, I didn't know how to compete. I had no encouragement from the coaching staff. I can't even remember who the coach was. I stayed there one semester, and I lost my scholarship. They used my grades as the excuse, but they had decided they didn't want me on the team any more.

"I came home and went to work. I did what guys my age and my color did. I went to work where my father worked, in a factory doing menial labor at the Fairbanks and Morris Company making diesel engines. It was dirty, held no promise, paid little.

"My father was a good man in that I didn't feel scared around him. We didn't connect much. But I was working in the factory about two months, and my dad said to me, 'I don't want you to stay here in this factory.' That's all he said.

"A couple days later I got a call from Johnny Thiel, who was coaching at Trinidad Junior College. He said, 'Frank, I hear you lost your scholarship at Wisconsin. I'd like you to come to Trinidad and play for me.' I said, 'Trinidad, that sounds Caribbean.' He said, 'Are you kidding? No, it's in Colorado.' He said. 'I'll give you a full scholarship.'

"I went, and I loved it. I took my nice-person personality with me, and people were just falling in love with me. The reception I got was wonderful, and of course, with any show of affection, I was like a bear with honey. I was again doing well in sports, especially in football. I ran well, made good moves, and it just came to me. And then Dal Ward, the coach at the University of Colorado, contacted me to play my last two years of eligibility for him.

"I transferred to Colorado without knowing anything about Dal Ward or his style of play, and when I got there I discovered he was a southerner and that he had grown up under Bernie Bierman's coaching philosophy at

Minnesota where they used the single wing. Well, I didn't fit in very well with the single wing offense because they didn't pass much, and I needed to spread out so the quarterback could get that ball to me.

"And because of Dal Ward's southern background, he wasn't going to let a black man come in, one from a junior college no less, and get headlines, although there is no question I could have gotten them. What happened was this: In the two years I was eligible for varsity football at Colorado, the only time Dal Ward used me was in do-or-die situations, and it was uncanny the way I came through. The game would be close, down to the last minutes, and I can still remember feeling embarrassed sitting on the bench when the student body would start to chant, 'We want Clarke. We want Clarke.' He'd send me in the game, and I'd get a first down or score. But he made it real clear to me I wasn't ever going to be a starter for him. He did this up to the last game of the season in '56. We either had to tie or beat Missouri to go to the Orange Bowl representing the Big Eight. Oklahoma couldn't go again. You couldn't go two years in a row.

"We went to Columbia, Missouri, and in the first half I was sitting on the bench. Missouri scored, and just before the half Dal Ward sent me into the game with one play, and boom, it was a touchdown. And the same thing happened in the second half, and those two touchdowns gave us the victory. I had very mixed emotions about it. There was not very much of an expression of joy in my life. I felt something, but whatever it was was so deeply repressed I wasn't able to identify it. I was repressing hurt, repressing bewilderment about my world. There was so much a sense of unworthiness, it was as though there was nothing I could experience that would help me feel worthy of myself.

"We went to the Orange Bowl. One of the things I remember was that there were two black athletes on the team, me and a sophomore guard by the name of John Wooten, who later played with the Cleveland Browns and the Washington Redskins. I had helped recruit him, in fact. John and I were the two black athletes going to segregated Miami Beach.

"I can remember our coach talking to us, saying we were going to the South, that there would be segregation, even with the team, that because he wanted the rest of the players to experience some things they wouldn't otherwise get a chance to do, they were going to things blacks couldn't go to, and so when we got there John and I were afforded an escort who took us to the black side of town. Dal Ward had apparently made the decision to segregate the team rather than put up a fight. He could have said to the team, 'Look, if it weren't for Frank Clarke, we wouldn't be here in the Orange Bowl. I want you guys to decide. If we can't take Frank and John, do we want to go?' But he never did that.

"Another thing I remember just before the Orange Bowl game started, I remember looking into the end zone seats and there were nothing but black faces. It dawned on me, 'My God, they are there because this is the only place they can sit.' I thought, By golly, I really want to show them. I want them to see somebody black really do well and be proud.

"In the game we made history for our school, because Colorado had never won a bowl game before that. I was part of a real solid Colorado performance. Ward didn't use me any more than usual. Just before the half Bud Morely threw me a long pass, and I got pushed out on the one, and Morely ran four quarterback sneaks and didn't score. We were losing 21–0, and we thought that was going to be our doom, but in the second half I blocked a punt and set up a score, and that game we played better as a team than we had ever played [and beat Clemson 27–21].

"After my junior year I was walking across campus, and a friend of mine came up to me and said, 'I just heard your name on the radio. You were drafted by the Cleveland Browns in the fifth round.' I said, 'Get out of here, man.' He said, 'No, really.' I thought it was a joke, but it was really true. I thought, Are they kidding? At Colorado I'm second string. And nobody else is being talked to by the pros. I didn't compute.

"But after the Orange Bowl game, Paul Bixler, who was the end coach for the Cleveland Browns, said to me, 'Good game. We want you to play for us,' and he showed me a contract. I showed it to one of our coaches. I said to him, 'They're offering me $7,500 to play. Does this sound okay to you?' He said, 'Yeah, sounds fine.'

"In the parking lot outside the stadium, Paul Bixler spread the contract across the trunk of a car, and I signed it.

"When I got to the Cleveland Browns, I felt, 'Holy Smokes, this is incredible!' Before I even had on a Cleveland uniform, there was an article in the paper saying, 'Clarke is going to be Dante Lavelli's replacement.' There was no way I could relate to that. Are you kidding? Me? I'm going to replace a legend in the NFL? I haven't even run my first 40-yard sprint.

"Paul Brown was the coach. He was very, very cerebral. We were playing the Rams in the Coliseum in a preseason game, and I was on the field on a third-down play, and I was supposed to block a linebacker, and I didn't come close to blocking him. The guy went in and destroyed the play, and we had to punt. After the play, Paul Brown left the sideline and met me at the hash mark and walked toward the bench with me. He told me, 'We can't use you, son. You're through with the Cleveland Browns.' I called my wife from Los Angeles and told her, 'Well, the inevitable has happened,' but after that I played every day, every practice as though it was going to be my last. I had told my wife I was through, but for some reason I wasn't. He kept me around. It was four weeks before the final cut was made.

"One time Paul Brown had cut a player, and this player had attacked him, so Paul Brown eliminated doing that. What he would do, if he had to cut five players on a certain date, he would announce the names of eight to ten players and order them to be in his office at a certain time, and they would show up, and the secretary would come out of her office and she would hand the players letters, and five of the envelopes had airplane tickets and a note saying, 'Good-bye. Good luck.' And the others would have letters saying, 'You remain a member of the Cleveland Browns. Report to practice Monday.' And my rookie year Paul Brown did that to me three times! It was real hard on the nerves. I can remember the final letter. It said, 'You remain one of our players. You have great potential.' And it had Paul Brown's signature on it.

"I can understand why a coach would want me. I weighed close to 210 pounds, and I was as fast as anyone on the Browns at 40 yards, and it made sense for them to want me around. They kept waiting for something to happen, but the only thing was, their approach was way off in terms of trying to get the fire lit in me. They attacked me. That was too much like what I got at home. And I went to pieces. I was a coward, very intimidated by that. It affected my play a lot.

"Also I had a lot of trouble connecting with the players on the Cleveland Browns. I didn't have the personality to make a lot of friends. I can remember when I was a rookie playing against Philadelphia, I caught a pass and was running, and a defensive back caught me going across the middle, and he grabbed my arms and jerked them, so I lost the ball. And when I came back to the bench I could not believe the undressing I got from Mike McCormack, a tackle for the Browns. He was a teammate. He just lit me up, told me how sorry I was. I couldn't believe this was coming from another player.

"I can remember another time I sat down on the bench, and it turned out to be Walt Michaels's spot, and I thought this guy was going to tear my head off, 'cause I happened to be sitting on the bench that was his reserved place.

"And I had a lot of run-ins with Jim Brown, too. I never knew why. Jim and I roomed together during training camp and the night before ballgames. He used to wake up the Sunday morning in the hotel, and he'd start talking about what kind of day he felt like he was going to have. This kind of confidence used to astound me. I can still see him over in the next bed stretching and saying, 'Aw, man, look out Giants, I feel like 150 yards and two or three touchdowns.' And he'd do it. What he was showing me was a kind of confidence I never had. I accepted everything in a very humble way.

"And in '57, four games into my rookie year—and his rookie year— Jim Brown ran for 235 yards! And the greatest thing about it, it was no fluke. He kept doing it for nine years. But there was something about me he didn't like. My locker would be next to his because his name began with B and mine with C and I can remember he would bump into me, almost in defiance. I don't know what it was. I couldn't figure it out. And I did not know how to hide my sensitivity. It was easily identifiable, and that was used against me. Why wouldn't this guy want to encourage me to bring out my best? I played on the offense. I could be in the game blocking for him. Or maybe I could provide the winning first down. It didn't make any sense. And at the time I was taking a lot of this very, very personally. I was scared of Jim Brown. He was one scary dude, on the field and off the field. I was very timid around him, extremely intimidated by him. That was easy, because I was intimidated by a lot of things.

"And from my perspective, Paul Brown was not so great either. I can remember when we were playing Detroit in the NFL championship in '57, the Lions were killing us. Everything Tobin Rote did was horrendous for us, and the people in Tiger Stadium were going crazy. We were getting soundly defeated, and I had not played a down from scrimmage, and so with a few minutes to go in the game, I walked up to Paul and asked him if I could play. He turned his back and walked away. And those were the kinds of experiences I had with him, so I did not think of him as a legend. For three years with the Browns, I played on the special teams. That's all I ever did. In front of me we had Ray Renfro, Darrell 'Pete' Brewster, and Preston Carpenter. With just a little bit of coaching, I could have easily replaced one of those guys. Ray was in the twilight of his career. But maybe I wasn't coachable. I don't think so, but I don't know.

"In '58 I got to watch those classic Jim Brown–Sam Huff games at the end of the season. We needed to beat the Giants to win the championship. If we lost, there would be a playoff.

"We lost the regular season game in an extremely close, well-played game at Yankee Stadium in a snowstorm. There was a lot of electricity. All I remember about the game was that when Pat Summerall lined up to kick the winning field goal, I didn't feel anything that he was going to make it. There wasn't even a question. It was, 'Hey, man, everything's cool,' and when Summerall hit that ball, it just went for days. It cleared everything. I still can't believe it. And in the playoff game against the Giants, I was nonexistent. I was not in that game at all. Sam Huff and Robustelli, Katcavage, those guys said, 'Hey, we have your number,' and they did. They had a psychological advantage, and they were good enough athletes to make it stick. They held Jim to 24 yards. The Giants had his number.

"Before the expansion list came out, I had a feeling the Browns were going to put my name on it. It made sense. I had been with them for three years, and I hadn't played much. I had heard from one of the coaches that Paul reluctantly put my name in it. He knew that eventually Darrell 'Pete' Brewster and Ray Renfro would be gone, and I was going to wake up one day and realize I was a pretty good athlete.

"But I also knew if I went to Dallas, I would be playing for Tom Landry. He had been an assistant coach with the Giants, but because I was a Brown, I knew he was no ordinary assistant coach. I knew his was the epitome of defensive football in the late '50s. Landry had an energy and an air of pure respect. This was a guy who was going to go places.

"From the Browns, the Cowboys selected Dick Modzelewski, Leroy Bolden, and me. Dick didn't go. He said, 'Nah, nah, I'm through.' Leroy went but his heart wasn't in it. He wasn't the same fired up football player he had been with the Browns. It wasn't as though he wanted to be an original Cowboy. Not at all.

"And so I wasn't sad to leave the Browns, any more than I was sad to leave the University of Colorado. I thought, I'll just move on and do this."

8

Little Eddie

The Cowboys had drafted quarterback Don Meredith, the phenom out of SMU, and Don Heinrich, who with the Giants had mostly been a stalking horse for Charlie Conerly, starting the game, deciphering the defense, and then turning the team over to the more talented quarterback. Tex Schramm and Tom Landry didn't think Heinrich was talented enough to start every day, and they figured that Meredith, just a rookie, wouldn't have a clue for at least a year or two. On June 23, 1960, two weeks before the opening of training camp, Schramm traded a first- and sixth-round choice in the '61 draft to Washington for four-time Pro Bowler Eddie LeBaron, the sawed-off quarterback who had announced his retirement in 1959 after seven seasons with the Redskins. LeBaron, who was known for his magical ball handling, scrambling and passing skills, in the off-seasons had gone to George Washington University School of Law and had passed the Texas and California bars, and he had retired from football to pursue a career in law related to the oil and gas business. Tex Schramm knew that LeBaron had had it with the hapless Redskins, and when Tex called him, the quarterback decided he would return to football, saying he wanted to play for Tom Landry.

LeBaron, who would start at quarterback for the Cowboys during their first three years, was the perfect man for the job. Like Landry, he had been in the service. Unlike most of his teammates, who would resent Landry's newfangled ideas, LeBaron believed in the chain of command, believed in respecting your coach, and was rigid about following orders. If Tom Landry wanted LeBaron to do something, he was going to do it, no questions asked. Like a good soldier, it would be his job to carry out orders and to perform to the best of his ability. At age thirty, LeBaron no longer was a spring chicken, but at one time Eddie had been one of the best, and a shadow of his old self would still be plenty good. The Cowboys were lucky to have him.

EDDIE LeBARON: "My dad was in the farming business, and when I was eight we moved from a sheep ranch in the Alexander Valley in the wine country of Sonoma to a dairy farm in a town near Oakdale, which is at the start of the Sierras near Stockton, California. As a boy I had to do farming things, irrigate, milk cows, shear sheep.

"I started high school when I was 12, because in grammar school we had eighteen kids and eight grades, and after going to first grade, I was the only one in second grade, so they let me skip to the third grade. It was during World War II, and even though I was 12 I got to play on the high school varsity because there weren't enough coaches for a JV. I gained twenty pounds that year, and at age 13 I got to play, even though the rule was you were supposed to be 15. In one year I went from being 12 to being 15! Yes, I was small, but in those days no one was that much bigger. When I was a sophomore I was 5'9", which is what I was in pro football. Even though I was 13, I could punt and throw the ball good, in fact do it better than anyone else. Even though we only had 400 kids in the school, 200 boys, my junior year we won the championship, and the next year we were second. In the years I played, we had eight boys who would go on to start or play second-string at the University of the Pacific.

"My first coach at the University of the Pacific was Amos Alonzo Stagg. He was eighty-six, and I was sixteen. It was a great experience, especially listening to him tell old stories. He could remember what happened when Chicago played Michigan in 1904, but he couldn't remember what happened yesterday. Even so, he was an amazing guy. We had a team of tough old guys who had been in the service, and I can remember on a trip to Arizona and then to Chicago to play Northwestern, he made us sing the school songs—he knew the words to all of them—and at first they were a little embarrassed, but after a while they all got into it, and he would talk to us about how important it was to be part of the school. At eighty-six he still knew his football, though he wasn't highly organized anymore. He still used the spread single wing, threw the ball 30 to 40 times a game. He had flankers and all kinds of trick plays, but we just weren't well organized and we were getting beaten by the teams with the T formation. He retired that year, and then Larry Seimering, his assistant, took over. Seimering was one of the great coaches around, a brilliant coach, and he put in the T. We had a team with great speed, and we did a lot of faking, everything we could to fool the other team. In fact, I probably received more notoriety from one play against San Jose where I fooled the referee with my fake than I did for the good plays. We had a big fullback who was about 235, and I faked to him, and he made a good fake, went downfield about eight or nine yards, and I had gone back and thrown a pass downfield for a touchdown about 65 yards, but the referee saw the fullback get tackled and thought he had the ball, and while the end was running for a touchdown he blew the play dead at that spot. We didn't get the touchdown. And the referee wouldn't change his call.

"My sophomore year we lost one game, my junior year we lost one game, and in '49, my senior year, we were undefeated, scoring 575 points to our opponents' 66. We were ranked number ten in the country. We had been invited to a couple of minor bowls, but we wanted to go to a major bowl, Sugar or Orange, and when we weren't invited, we didn't go anywhere. John Brodie and I were the quarterbacks for the West in the East-West game, and I was the Most Valuable Player, and I played in the Senior Bowl game, the first one they had, and the All-Star game against the Philadelphia Eagles, and we beat them, the first time in a long time the college stars won. We had a great team, Doak Walker, Charlie Justice, Art Weiner, R.C. Owens, who played with Oklahoma. Arch Ward, who invented the game, said we saved it.

"In 1950 I was drafted number one by the San Francisco 49ers in the All-America Conference in a secret draft. Pro ball wasn't big then, and I didn't have any great desire to play pro ball. I was intending to go to graduate school. I had played in the Senior Bowl for Bo McMillin, who was head coach at Detroit, and I told him I didn't want to play, but then I was drafted in the ninth round by the Washington Redskins, and at that time I was called into the Marine Corps. I had been in the reserves when the Korean War broke out. I went to Korea for two years, did some fighting. I got a couple of Purple Hearts, a Bronze Star, and a Letter of Commendation, fought at a place called the Wachung Reservoir. I don't remember much about it other than we were moving up, and a piece of artillery shell hit me and knocked me off a cliff, and I got cut up. It wasn't too bad, and then I got hit by a mortar. In another battle, we were on patrol before we got to a place called Heartbreak Ridge, and then I was at the battle of the Punch Bowl, where we got a bunch of merit badges. But I had a platoon in combat probably longer than most. Because I had been in the service longer than anyone else, I got to make the whiskey run to Japan to bring it back for the regiment.

"There were some vicious players in the NFL back then. Hardy Brown, who played for the 49ers and the Cardinals, was the toughest, meanest guy who ever played the game. He only weighed 195, but he had a shoulder lift that had been taught to him at Tulsa, and he knocked a lot of people out with it. He was the only guy I ever got scared about in the NFL, because he just missed me a couple of times, and those were the days before face masks. I saw him knock people completely out. And it didn't look like he was doing anything.

"Most guys weren't dirty. What would happen, someone would work you over, and one of our tackles or guards, Dick Stanfel, someone like that, would say, 'Leave him alone or we're going to go after you,' and then they'd set him up and hit him in the knees. And people learned.

"In those days if you fell down, you could get up and run again, and so what would happen, defensive players would wait for you to go down, and they'd drop a knee on you when you were down, because it was legal. They finally changed the rule, because quarterbacks and backs were getting killed.

"I retired from the Redskins after the '59 season. It had been a miserable year, and I passed the California bar in '59, and I thought, I might as well practice law rather than play. You didn't make much money in those days. I was making $18,000 my last year with the Redskins. So I retired. This was before I knew there was going to be a Dallas team. George Preston Marshall tried to get me to stay. He offered me more money. But we weren't very good, and I didn't see us getting any better. It's an emotional game, and I just didn't feel like I wanted to play for them any more.

"After I retired, I settled in Midland, Texas. I wanted to be an oil and gas lawyer, and I was offered a position in a law firm. During the time I was studying for the Texas bar, I got a call from Roone Arledge at ABC to be color man for the AFL telecasts. I said, 'Give me a day to think it over,' and fortuitously, the very next day Tex called up and said that the Cowboys would be interested in trading for me. We talked back and forth. I was a great admirer of Landry and also of Tex, because of what he had done with the Rams. I said, 'That sounds interesting.' He said, 'We need someone with experience. We have a new team.'

"I came a week late to training camp. From the beginning Tom put in his offensive system of movement and shifting. He didn't put in something simple. I said to him, 'We could beat some of these teams if you made it a little simpler.' He said, 'That's probably right, but I'm putting in a system to compete with the New York Giants and the Cleveland Browns. When we get the talent, we will beat those teams, but we have to have the system in place to beat them.'

"Tom Landry knew exactly what he was doing. And I bought it. I said, 'That makes sense.' The other vets weren't happy with it, but Tom knew that with his way, one day we were going to beat the big boys."

9

The First Herd

B y the start of training camp, the Dallas Rangers minor league baseball club announced that they were staying in Dallas, and so the new
NFL franchise was forced to pick a new name. With "Texans" taken
by the new American Football League team in Dallas, Tex Schramm opted
for "Cowboys," even though no steer or heifer or dogie had ever trod the
streets of the city. To the west down the highway, sister city Fort Worth
was the cattle town, but not Dallas, which was known for its banks and
skyscrapers more than anything else. But the more appropriate Dallas
Bankers carried little romance, and so Schramm went with the name Cowboys, a sobriquet he knew carried with it all sorts of public relations possibilities.

Throughout the spring and summer of 1960 Tex Schramm and his
sidekick, Gil Brandt, kept their ears to the rumor hotline, scouring NFL
rosters in a search for other disgruntled players like Eddie LeBaron, men
who had feuded with their coaches and quit; or, like Jerry Tubbs, had left
the game because the money wasn't there and other opportunities outside
football had arisen. One such player was Gene Babb, a halfback who had
been demoted at San Francisco by Coach Red Hickey. Rather than accept
his demotion, Babb had quit the 49ers in order to coach football and teach
art at Ranger Junior College in Texas.

Wealthy oil tycoon Clint Murchison Sr. couldn't understand why anyone would want to own a small-potatoes football team. *(from the collection of the Texas/Dallas History and Archive Division, Dallas Public Library)*

In the early 1960s Clint Murchison Jr. *(left)* was the only one in the Dallas franchise who seemed to be enjoying himself. *(from the collection of the Texas/Dallas History and Archive Division, Dallas Public Library)*

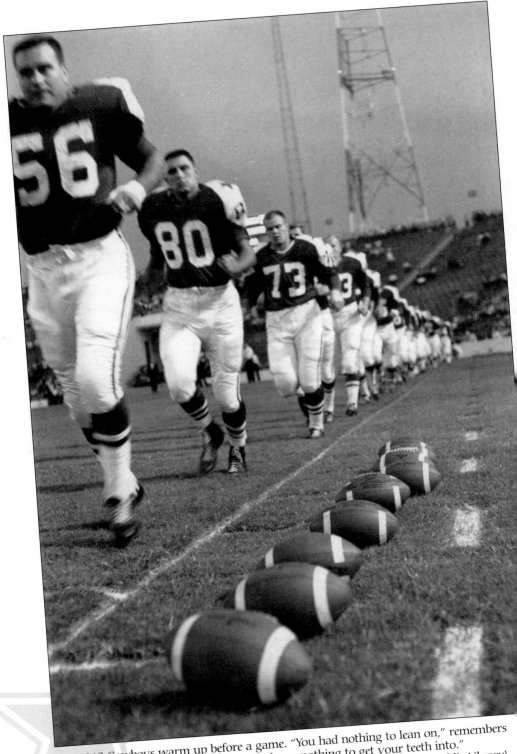

The 1960 Cowboys warm up before a game. "You had nothing to lean on," remembers tight end Dick Bielski, "nothing to fall back on, nothing to get your teeth into." *(from the collection of the Texas/Dallas History and Archive Division, Dallas Public Library)*

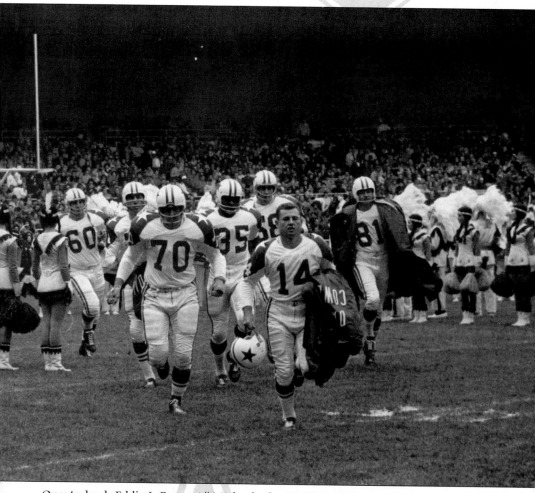

Quarterback Eddie LeBaron (#14) leads the 1961 Cowboys onto the field. Though the team finished 4–9–1, "Tom Landry knew exactly what he was doing," says LeBaron. "The other vets weren't happy with it, but Tom knew that one day we were going to beat the big boys." *(from the collection of the Texas/Dallas History and Archive Division, Dallas Public Library)*

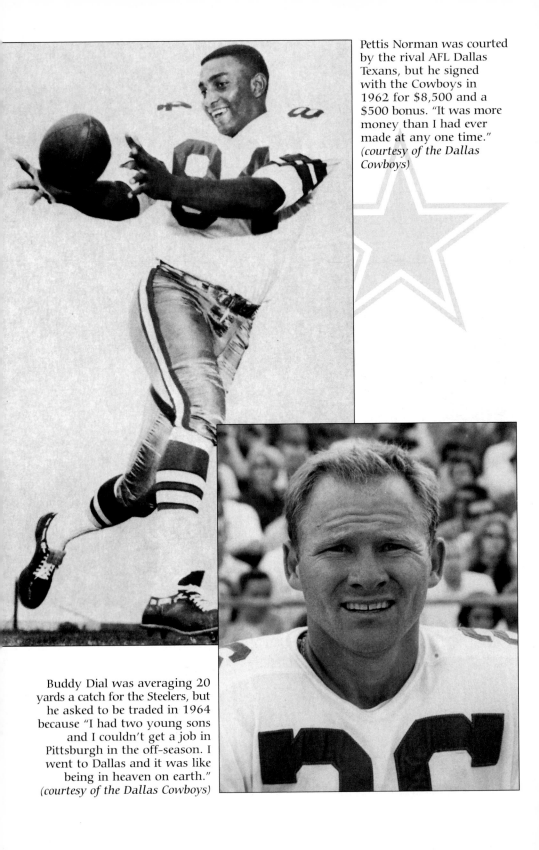

Pettis Norman was courted by the rival AFL Dallas Texans, but he signed with the Cowboys in 1962 for $8,500 and a $500 bonus. "It was more money than I had ever made at any one time." *(courtesy of the Dallas Cowboys)*

Buddy Dial was averaging 20 yards a catch for the Steelers, but he asked to be traded in 1964 because "I had two young sons and I couldn't get a job in Pittsburgh in the off-season. I went to Dallas and it was like being in heaven on earth." *(courtesy of the Dallas Cowboys)*

Maury Youmans came to Dallas from Chicago in 1964 and "couldn't believe how it was like going to Sunday school in comparison to the Bears." *(courtesy of the Dallas Cowboys)*

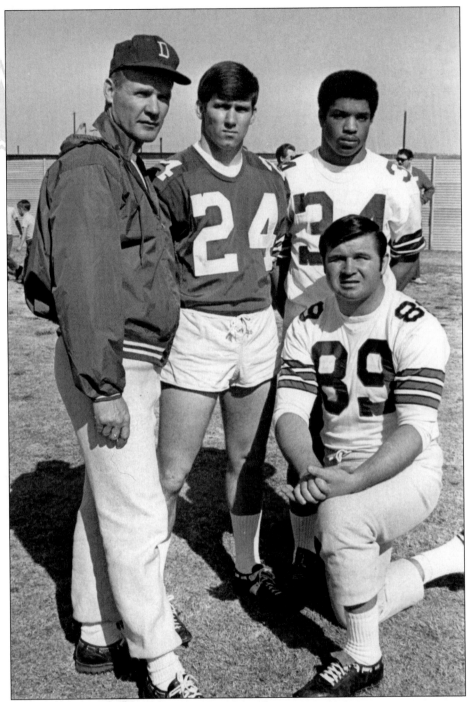

Tom Landry with *(clockwise)* Dennis Homan, Cornell Green, and Mike Ditka. Defensive coordinator Dick Nolan says that "even though it took the players a long time to accept Tom's system, once they did, they virtually became coaches on the field."
(from the collection of the Texas/Dallas History and Archive Division, Dallas Public Library)

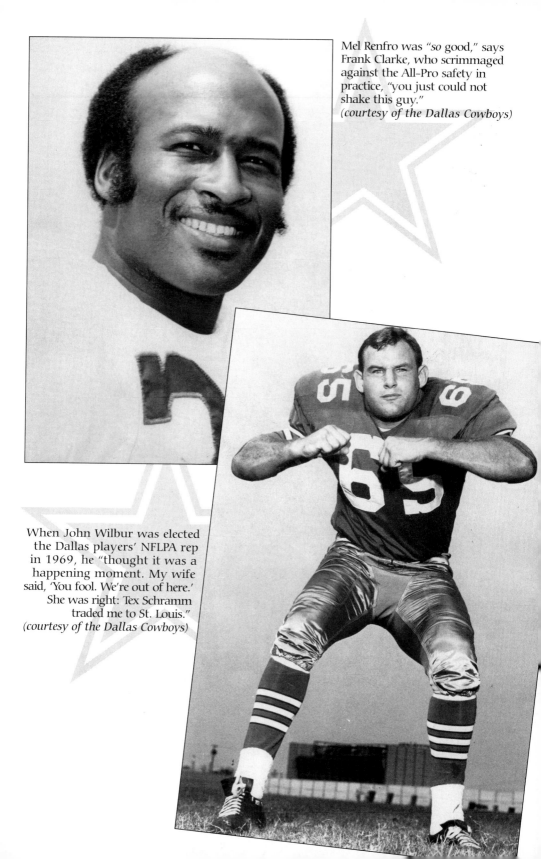

Mel Renfro was "*so good*," says Frank Clarke, who scrimmaged against the All-Pro safety in practice, "you just could not shake this guy."
(courtesy of the Dallas Cowboys)

When John Wilbur was elected the Dallas players' NFLPA rep in 1969, he "thought it was a happening moment. My wife said, 'You fool. We're out of here.' She was right: Tex Schramm traded me to St. Louis."
(courtesy of the Dallas Cowboys)

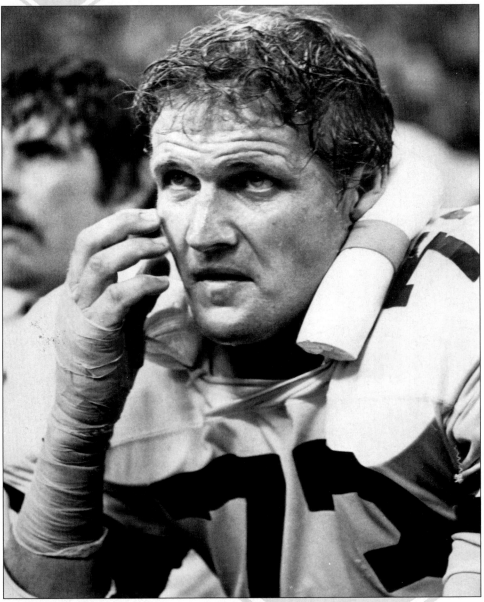

Teammates nicknamed him "Rotten" because he liked to gripe, but
Buddy Dial spoke for many of them when he called Ralph Neely
"the finest offensive lineman I had ever seen."
(courtesy of the Dallas Cowboys)

"Nobody can ever imagine what it's like to stand on the podium and be called one of the world's greatest athletes," Olympic sprinter "Bullet" Bob Hayes told a teammate. "What I do in football, I just do it, but nothing will compare to that."
(from the collection of the Texas/Dallas History and Archive Division, Dallas Public Library)

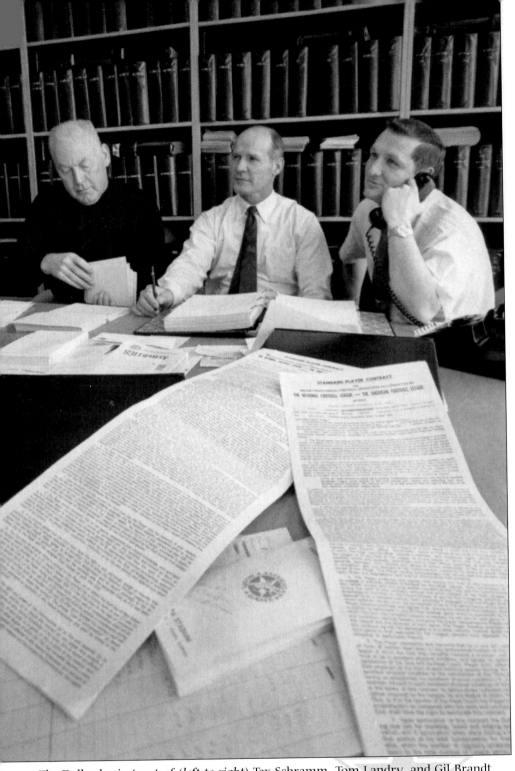

The Dallas brain trust of (*left to right*) Tex Schramm, Tom Landry, and Gil Brandt revolutionized the way the rest of the NFL evaluated college athletes. (*from the collection of the Texas/Dallas History and Archive Division, Dallas Public Library*)

"Dandy" Don Meredith "had such a carefree attitude about life," remembers Walt Garrison, "you just had to love the guy."
(from the collection of the Texas/Dallas History and Archive Division, Dallas Public Library)

Meredith is carried off the field by Frank Clarke (#82) and Jim Boeke. "Don used to play with the kind of pain I wouldn't get out of bed for," says Clarke, "let alone put on a uniform."
(from the collection of the Texas/Dallas History and Archive Division, Dallas Public Library)

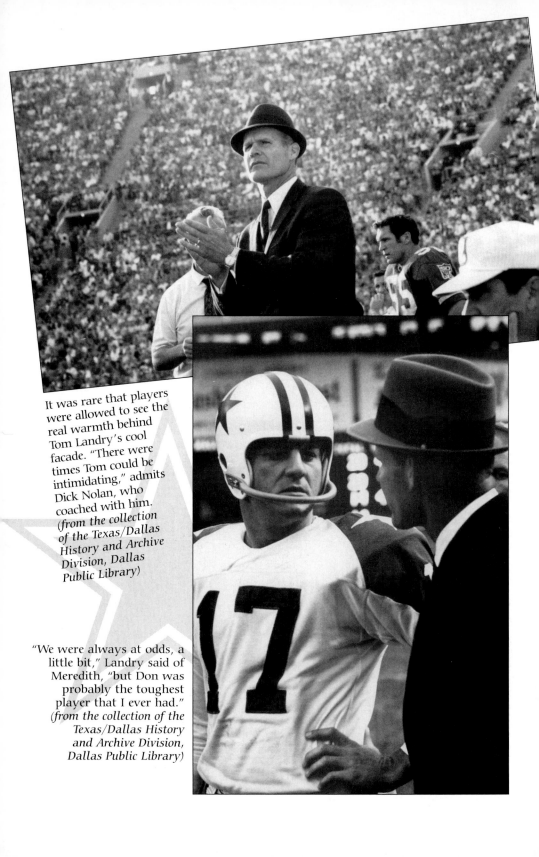

It was rare that players were allowed to see the real warmth behind Tom Landry's cool facade. "There were times Tom could be intimidating," admits Dick Nolan, who coached with him. *(from the collection of the Texas/Dallas History and Archive Division, Dallas Public Library)*

"We were always at odds, a little bit," Landry said of Meredith, "but Don was probably the toughest player that I ever had." *(from the collection of the Texas/Dallas History and Archive Division, Dallas Public Library)*

Lance Rentzel was a gifted receiver on the field but troubled off it. "Somebody has got to talk to him," Pete Gent would urge his teammates. "Lance is going to get busted." *(courtesy of the Dallas Cowboys)*

All-Pro Cornell Green had been a top basketball prospect at Utah State before joining the Cowboys as a defensive back in 1962. Landry usually kept his rookies on the bench, but Green was a starter since his first year in the league—although he limped the first few games because he'd been wearing his hip pads backward. *(courtesy of the Dallas Cowboys)*

Lee Roy Jordan was the backbone of the Dallas defense. In the huddle "we'd look over to the sideline," recalls Mel Renfro, "and our coach would be waving all these defenses. Lee Roy would laugh and say, 'No, we ain't gonna play that. We're gonna kick their butts.' And we'd do it." *(from the collection of the Texas/Dallas History and Archive Division, Dallas Public Library)*

Landry moved All-Pro Frank Clarke from his wide receiver slot to make room for Bob Hayes. "If Tom Landry wanted me to put on a 70s number and play tackle," says Clarke, "I would have done it without a word." *(courtesy of the Dallas Cowboys)*

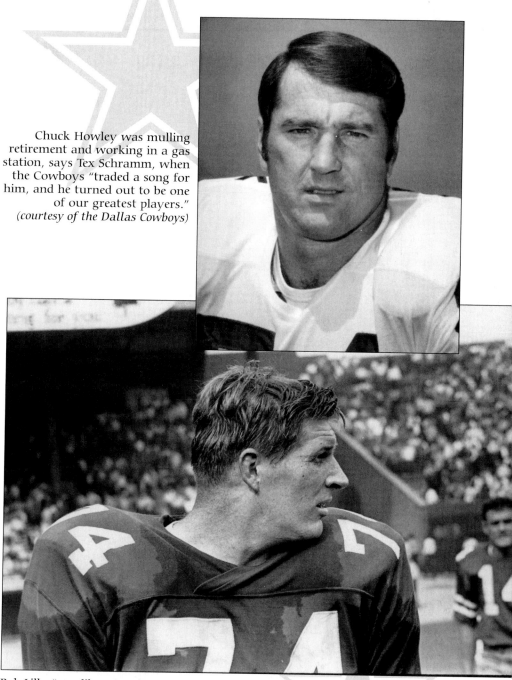

Chuck Howley was mulling retirement and working in a gas station, says Tex Schramm, when the Cowboys "traded a song for him, and he turned out to be one of our greatest players." *(courtesy of the Dallas Cowboys)*

Bob Lilly "was like some damn animal, like a wild lion out on the savannah in Africa," recalls Walt Garrison. "They put him on a football field and he'd just eat people alive." *(from the collection of the Texas/Dallas History and Archive Division, Dallas Public Library)*

Don Perkins never felt he was "good enough to be playing at the professional level," but the six-time All-Pro
was a mainstay of the early Dallas rushing attack.
*(from the collection of the Texas/Dallas History
and Archive Division, Dallas Public Library)*

Babb had signed a contract with the Houston Oilers in the fledgling American Football League. But Tex Schramm had no depth at running back. He had Don McIlhenny and L. G. Dupre, and no backup. Schramm *needed* Babb, who had been in the league since 1957. Babb kept telling Schramm he had already signed a contract, but Schramm would not take no for an answer. Schramm offered him $5,000 a year more than the Oilers were giving him—plus he sent Babb and his new bride off on an all-expenses-paid honeymoon—in part to get him to sign, in part to keep him out of reach of the Oilers prior to training camp. When Gene Babb showed up in Forest Grove, Oregon, for the Cowboys' first training camp, he had become notorious for signing not one, but two contracts. The notoriety, of course, should have gone to Tex Schramm for making Babb the (second) offer he couldn't refuse. What would have made Babb even more notorious to the other players was that Babb, a journeyman, was coming to camp as one of the highest paid players on the roster.

GENE BABB: "I was born in El Paso, Texas, and raised in Odessa. My father lost his life during the war when I was eight. My mother passed away with heart failure five years later. My father's sister and her husband moved in and raised us in our home in West Texas. It was like being granted a second set of parents. We were lucky that everything worked out well. My uncle worked for Jewel Tea, furnishing all the service stations with candy. He also went house to house.

"I grew up in the oil fields of West Texas. I roustabouted on a truck, worked in the oil supply company yard with pipes and blowout protectors. While we were going through high school, we tried to find the hardest job we could find. It usually was in construction or roustabouting. Back then we got an hourly wage of $1.20. And at the time we thought it was a mound of gold."

Babb went to Odessa High. He was a running back until he hurt his knee his senior year and was moved to tight end. Babb could have gone to Oklahoma but instead he wanted to follow in the footsteps of his brother, Fred, who went to Austin College, a Presbyterian church-related college, to go into the ministry.

Austin's head coach, Harry Buffington, was no fool, and when he learned that Babb wanted to play for him instead of Bud Wilkinson, he quickly offered the boy a scholarship. No surprise, Babb started for Austin.

GENE BABB: "When I went to Austin College, I went as a tight end. Franklin Bond was a Little All-America playing in front of me, and he had the flu and had to come out of the first ballgame, and before the half I was thrown a ball over the middle, and I caught it and broke up the field and scored. The first time I touched the ball, I went 87 yards! My brother couldn't believe it!

"Midway through the season our fullback, Billy Bookout, suffered a concussion. Billy had come from Wichita Falls, Texas, where they had won several state championships. He was a castoff from Oklahoma University. He got caught in a panty raid and was dismissed. Buff recruited him, but when he got hurt, he moved me to running back, and that's where I played the remaining three and a half years.

"I was surprised when the 49ers drafted me, though Pappy Waldorf had come by and looked at me. I was pleased, and a little apprehensive. I can remember when Bill 'Tiger' Johnson, who had been an All-Pro center for the 49ers for years, came to see me. Bill didn't wear a face mask, and in his day Bill had had his nose broken three or four times. 'I need for you to sign right here,' he said. I noticed that his nose was sitting under his left eye, and I was kind of wondering whether I should sign or not! But I signed for $6,000. This was back in 1957. That was the same year John Brodie was the number one pick.

"I can remember during our first training camp Brodie and I were walking out of the dorm together heading for breakfast in the dining hall. Well, it just so happened that Ed Henke, who was a great outdoorsman, had been hunting that morning. Our training camp was over at St. Mary's College, and Ed would go into the California hills and hunt deer early in the morning and in the evening after our last meeting of the day. This particular morning Ed had gotten a buck, and he had hung the buck up by its horns in a fork of the tree right outside the dorm on the way to the dining hall, and he was field dressing it. Bob St. Clair was there with him, and just as we came out the door, Brodie and I noticed that St. Clair was holding the deer's heart in his hand. And he ate it! John and I turned around and went right back into the dorm. We decided not to have breakfast!

"It was the year we almost won the conference championship in part because our coach, Red Hickey, developed the Alley Oop pass. Our end, R. C. Owens, had been a basketball player, and he had a great vertical leap, tall, with long arms, and Hickey and Y. A. Tittle worked out a play where Owens would run into the end zone and he'd just jump as high as he could, and Y. A. would throw a floater up to him. R.C. would be a good four feet above the defenders.

"Our quarterback, Y. A. Tittle—Colonel Slick, Y.A., or Yat, as we called him—was like a coach on the field. He was phenomenal. He could pick apart a defense. We didn't have signals, didn't relay in plays. Yat knew. He would call the plays in the huddle. If they were playing a zone, or a certain set, he would come into the huddle and call the individual routes for the receivers. He could read the defense, and also he knew in certain situations what the defense was going to do. He was really something. The first time he ever threw the ball to me, I missed it. We were in San Francisco playing the Cardinals. He called for me to swing out into the flat, and as I turned to look for the ball, he had already released it, and it went right across me. And boy, I didn't want to go back to the huddle. When I returned, all he said was, 'If you'd a looked up, you'd a had a touchdown.' And I'll be darned if he didn't call the same play again, but this time I caught it for a touchdown.

"I would attribute any success we had in '57 to his presence as well as our other great stars, Hugh McElhenny, Joe Perry, Bob St. Clair, Leo Nomellini, and Goose Wilson.

"Hugh was called the King, and when Joe Perry was hurt, I played fullback, and my nickname was Duke, so it was King and Duke. But what Red Hickey did, he moved Hugh out in the slotback as a receiver, where he could also run reverses and run back inside, and he put Perry in as running back, and it was my job to block, and that was the year we led the Lions in the Western Conference championship, only to get blown away in the second half by Tobin Rote and company.

"We weren't nearly as successful in '58, and then in training camp in '59 Red had a defensive end by the name of Smith, and he moved him to fullback, and in one exhibition game I found myself on the third team. We were about three-quarters of the way through camp when I got a call from a friend who had just become president of Ranger Junior College in Ranger, Texas. He offered me a job coaching as an assistant and teaching art. I wasn't happy playing football anymore, and I accepted. I thought, I'll try something else. So I did that, and then in 1960 right after graduation ceremonies at Ranger, I signed a contract with the Houston Oilers, and I got a job working for the city of Houston on a construction job digging drainage ditches.

"About the Fourth of July, my girlfriend—now my wife—and I went to Waco to visit her relatives. We were going to get married, and when we were in Waco I got a call from Vance Jobe saying that Dallas had gotten my rights from the 49ers and that they wanted to sign me, right now. The Dallas training camp had about a week to open. I told him, 'I'm in Waco and I'm fixing to get married.' He said, 'I want to come to Waco and take you and your future bride out to dinner and just talk to you.' I said, 'Mr. Jobe, I signed a contract with the Houston Oilers. And I'm happy.' He said, 'You realize that the Dallas Cowboys have your rights.' I said, 'That's fine, but I signed with Houston.' He said, 'But I want to come down and see you.' I said, 'We'll have dinner with you.'

"So he came down, and we met him at the Black Angus Steak House. We're sitting there eating, and he's visiting with me, and he says, 'Dallas is very interested in you. They want to sign you.' I said, 'I'm happy with what I'm making with Houston. I signed a contract.' (It was for $10,000.) He took out his napkin, and he wrote out, '$15,000.' He said, 'Would you come to Dallas for that amount of money?' I said, 'Well . . . I'll have to think about it.' He said, 'Let me get the phone and call Tex Schramm at camp.' I said, 'You're making it hard on me.' He said, 'Come on with me.' So he got Tex Schramm on the phone, and Tex told me they wanted to sign me, said that Tom Landry had remembered me when I was with the 49ers and he was with the Giants. So I proceeded to tell Tex I had signed with Houston, was happy, that I was fixing to get married, and I was going on my honeymoon.

"He said, 'Well, would you consider coming to us for $15,000?' I said, 'The only way I would do that would be if it was a no-cut contract.' And he said, 'You plan to get married on top of that?' I said, 'Yeah.' He said, 'Put Vance back on the phone.' So I did, and the two of them talked, and Vance and I went back to the table, and he said, 'Okay, here's the deal. I'm going to spend the night. We're going to get you married in the morning. We'll drive to Dallas and my wife will have on deposit a $1,500 signing bonus, and she'll open a bank account, and we'll get all squared away, and we will fly you to the training camp in Forest Grove, Oregon.'

"We agreed. And the next day Gerry and I were married. We drove to Vance Jobe's home in Dallas, and his wife, Anne, bless her heart, she had champagne, and they had the airline tickets for us to go to Denver that night and fly the next morning on to Portland, and then over to Forest Grove to camp. The bank account was opened, the money deposited, we signed the cards, and she had starter checks, and my wife put them in her purse. Anne also had two apartments for us to look at, which we did in the next hour, and we put a deposit down to rent one of them.

"We went to the airport to go on our honeymoon, but the clincher was that Vance Jobe was going with us! We got on the plane and flew to Denver. When we arrived there was a Shriners' Convention, 40,000 Shriners, but Bedford Wynne had influence and managed to get us two rooms on the same floor, and as we got to our door Vance said graciously, 'I'll see you kids in the morning. I'll give you a wake-up call. We have a flight leaving out of here at seven o'clock.'

"We went out, and it took us thirty minutes to cross the street because there were Shriners everywhere. We ate dinner in a candlelit place, had a dance or two, and went to sleep, and it seemed we had just closed our eyes when Vance was banging on the door. We got up and flew to Portland, where Gil Brandt met us at the airport. When we got to Forest Grove, the rookies were still on the field.

"As soon as practice was over, we went to the dorm. Tex came in and said, 'Coach Landry wants to visit with you.' He told me where I fit in his plans, was complimentary. After that, we signed the contract, and Tex said, 'Here's $3,000. You have a reservation over at Ocean Lake, Oregon, at a resort there near the ocean, and here's the keys to the Chevrolet.' It was Wednesday, and he said, 'We need you to be back in camp on Sunday.' So Gerry and I had three days before the start of camp.

"As for the Houston contract, the Cowboys took about three hours deposing me, took my statement, and as it turned out, Houston never contested it. And so I became an original Dallas Cowboy."

The Cowboys' first training camp was on the site of the University of the Pacific in Forest Grove, Oregon. It was in the middle of nowhere, a haul from the nearest big city, Portland. Tom Landry intended to run a boot camp, and Forest Grove was the perfect place to conduct it away from any distractions. The town had one movie theater and one bar. Nearby was a Maraschino cherry factory. The sweet, syrupy aroma permeated the place as the players sweated under blue skies.

Landry opened the first day's practice with a test of stamina the players called the "Landry Mile." Backs and ends had to run a mile in under six minutes. Linemen had to do it in under six and a half. The vets thought the exercise ridiculous.

JOHN GONZAGA: "I hated the Landry Mile. I told Tom Landry, 'If they ever make the field longer than a hundred yards, I'm going to quit.' But he said I had to run the mile anyway. He said, 'I don't have any time for comedians.' So I ran it."

Slowly, but at least he finished. Byron Bradfute, the free agent lineman, passed out before he reached the finish line. Rookie running back Don Perkins was under the assumption that he would get in shape once he came to camp. He arrived fifteen pounds overweight, and when he couldn't run the Landry Mile, he considered quitting right there.

A few of the players, including Frank Clarke, were both physically fit and mentally prepared.

FRANK CLARKE: "I had a big, strong body and pretty good endurance, but halfway through it there was one player, Tom Frankhauser, a defensive back, who was way ahead of me. I knew I could have just finished the thing, but I got a burst of speed and stamina and I really hauled ass, and I ended up passing Frankhauser, winning the Landry Mile, and Tom said to me, 'That showed me a lot of class.' I had never heard praise like that before."

Once Tom Landry began the practice regimen, the players were dismayed to see that it was long and brutal. A lot of the other pro teams saved most of their hitting for the season. Landry had his players hitting in practice all day, every day. The players had to absorb a daily pounding that came from the natural brutality of the game. And when they weren't scrimmaging, Landry had them in one-on-one or two-on-two drills, which could be just as brutal. The regimen was grueling, harder than anything any of these grizzled veterans had ever experienced before. And after a day of pain, there would be long, tedious meetings. If any of the players were anticipating having fun in their off-hours, they were dismayed to learn there were very, very few off-hours. Landry's training camp created strong hostility from some of his players.

Big John Gonzaga, who had come from a winning program in San Francisco, was furious about having to play on an expansion team to begin with. Making his situation worse, he didn't like Landry's impersonal nature, didn't appreciate his autocratic ways ("He even told you when to pray"), and resented Landry's omnipotence. ("Tom's real strength was defense, though Tom wouldn't tell you that. He'd say he knew *everything*.") Gonzaga, moreover, thought all the hitting to be a waste of energy.

JOHN GONZAGA: "It was really unnecessary. We would see guys like Ray Mathews, who had already played ten years in the league, having to do that. They didn't need that kind of crap."

The rookie lineman Byron Bradfute had had nothing to compare to Landry's regimen, and he thought it hard, but like most young rookies he took the attitude he would do whatever he was asked. Bradfute may not have minded Landry's scrimmages, but he did mind a drill designed for the linemen by coach Brad Ecklund.

BYRON BRADFUTE: "He had a little exercise where he took one of those big tackling dummies, put a rope on it, tied it to the crossbar, and let it swing. He'd hold that thing up high and then swing it into you, and you were supposed to hit it with your nose first. That was dumb, really dumb. The older I get, the more I hold that against him."

In addition to the hard, long practices, Landry made the players go to endlessly long meetings, where he introduced his complicated systems. Landry had had little time to build a coaching staff, and had hired three stopgap assistant coaches, offensive line coach Brad Ecklund, who had been coaching in Oregon high schools, backfield coach Babe Demancheck, who had coached under Buddy Parker for the Pittsburgh Steelers, and defensive line coach Tom Dahms, who came from the University of Virginia, but these men did little except make sure the players ran their drills. The teaching was done entirely by Tom Landry, and often players had to sit a long time in their classroom watching game films without commentary or explanation all the while stewing in wait for Landry to arrive for their personal instruction.

DICK BIELSKI: "It was stand around and wait for Tom to do something. I recall sitting in meetings with our offensive coaches, and they would show us films, and not do a thing until Tom got there. Not a play was put in. There was not a bit of coaching until Tom got there to do it. He did everything, because he wanted to make sure the new system was put in right. He taught the offense, and he taught the defense. And when Tom wasn't there, you sat there and watched films for two or three hours with practically no comment whatsoever. And after a while that got to be a bit boring, and you became resentful, because he was not giving us the time we thought we deserved. Here we are, marking time, treading water, waiting for the guy to come in, and there were other things we would have preferred doing. After we spent two or three hours waiting for him to come, well, you feel like stepchildren."

Very quickly the Cowboy training camp became tinged with bitterness on the part of many of the veteran players, angry that their football fortunes had sunk so low.

BOB FRY: "It was like starting over as a rookie. When you played with one club as long as I did, you knew the coaches, knew the trainer, knew the organization. You felt comfortable, and you didn't have to prove yourself every day. Everyone knew you. With the Cowboys, you didn't know anyone. There was a lot of grumbling, players like John Gonzaga, who had played on a winner with San Francisco, L. G. Dupre with Baltimore. The Colts had put L.G. on the expansion list because they didn't think the Cowboys would take older players. What they didn't realize was that they were *all* older players. I could see that so many of the veterans didn't want to be there. In a way, everyone had that feeling. It's like me, thirty years old and going someplace different, doing something different. It isn't like being traded. You get traded because someone wants you. Here, someone wanted to get rid of you. So we had that feeling of having to start over again. It was hard, at our age, to have to prove ourselves all over again."

The players on the defensive line openly rebelled when they were shown Tom Landry's defensive system. They were used to pursuing the ball wherever it went. Under Landry's system, the one he had perfected with the Giants, a lineman was supposed to recognize which formation the offense was using, and glean from it what plays might be run from it. Then, when the ball was snapped and the offensive players began to move, he was then to take his "key" from whatever players he was supposed to "read," and then wait patiently for the play to come to him. Under the system, it was common for a lineman on a running play to take a block and then hold his position, even when the ball was going away from him, because under Landry's system, eventually the ballcarrier would find him. Had the Cowboys drafted members of the Giants' defensive line, perhaps Landry might have had allies. But the Giants had protected their defensive players, and neither offensive guard Buzz Guy nor quarterback Don Heinrich were qualified to tout Landry's defensive acuity to the defensive unit. Not a single other veteran lineman believed that Landry's system could work. Linebacker Jack Patera, who loved and understood Landry's system from the first time he saw it, recalled his teammates' resistance to Landry's way of playing defense.

JACK PATERA: "Tom would tell them, 'If you can just hold your own, we're better off.' But guys would say, 'Why should I just hold my own here if I can make the play?' They didn't understand that part of their job was to not get knocked down so you can make the play or to just create a mess by cutting off offensive players who are supposed to be in pursuit.

Remember, a lot of these players didn't know a whole lot more than their own position. It amazed me how many of these people just didn't know. They entered the situation and criticized it without understanding the overall program."

When he was with the Chicago Cardinals, linebacker Jerry Tubbs had had a sense that Sam Huff and the Giants always knew where their plays were going and that somehow Landry had been responsible. Tubbs was eager to learn Landry's secrets, and he supported his coach from the first.

JERRY TUBBS: "Guys were used to doing things one way. If you tell a defensive tackle who is used to getting to the ball that he has to take a step inside when the ball is going outside, this is against all the things he's done since he began playing the game. And so these older guys didn't like it. You had to have faith in Tom for his system to work. I can remember Gene Cronin and John Gonzaga, defensive linemen, were particularly unhappy."

There was not the universal griping among the members of the offensive unit that there was on the defense. The great irony was that the moaners and groaners on the defense were more talented and more cohesive than the more compliant offensive players like Fred Cone, a halfback and kicker, who for the most part accepted Landry's system but weren't good enough to make it work against the better teams.

FRED CONE: "I respected Tom tremendously. I thought Tom Landry was the finest individual you could ever meet in your life, a top-notch guy and a great football mind.

"Landry was thorough. He talked about our opponent, and then we'd take a test with a pencil and paper. Some players hated to sit in those meetings. They lasted a long time. We'd watch the films over and over. But if you did your homework, you'd know what the other team was doing before they snapped the ball."

BOB FRY: "I don't remember any griping or sniping from the offense. I think Tom is a great person, a wonderful man, and one of the best defensive coaches I've been around. I can remember, though, our great frustration over the inability of the offensive line to stop our quarterback from getting sacked. It was *very* frustrating."

GENE BABB: "I believed in what we were doing. I liked the man, respected him. Tom Landry was one of the most dedicated men I've ever been around in my life. He was very businesslike on the football field. And the man had such a mind on him. He was always two or three plays ahead of where everyone else was.

"He saw everything. He could watch a play start from the line of scrimmage, and after the first two steps, he knew whether it was going to work or not. Especially with the defense, he had a phenomenal mind."

DICK BIELSKI: "I never second-guessed the head coach. I went along with what Tom was doing. I had a good idea of what he was trying to do. I was infatuated with his system. It was a whole new way of playing offensive football. We had basic plays, but we always had the extra dessert, long passing plays for the right situations. Landry's approach on offense was to confuse the other team until he could get better players. I was quite happy with it."

In counterpoint to all of Tom's supporters on the offense was wide receiver Ray Mathews, who was brutally outspoken about the contempt he had for Tom Landry.

FRANK CLARKE: "When Tom Landry said 'Quiet,' Ray would start talking. He showed his disrespect, and everybody saw that. Ray came when he wanted and left when he wanted. Ray was set in his ways, a rebel kind of a guy. Tom in his head knew what he wanted, and Ray said, 'Tom, I've done this my own way, and I'm going to continue doing it my own way.' We didn't take Ray seriously, but this became a challenge and a big frustration for Tom."

DON MCILHENNY: "One time in a meeting Tom criticized Ray. Ray told him, 'Who are you to tell me how to play? When I was with the Steelers, you couldn't cover me. I used to beat you like a stepchild.' "

JACK PATERA: "Ray Mathews called everybody 'Pally.' One day Ray called Tom 'Pally.' Tom said to him, 'If you call me "Pally" again, you're out of here.' Ray said, 'That's what I want, Pally.' "

Landry kept Ray Mathews despite his constant show of disrespect in large part because he had to. The team needed him. With the Steelers Mathews had been a star at split end. The other Cowboy split ends were Jim Doran, who had had a fine career with the Lions but who was reaching the end, and Frank Clarke, who had not yet proven his worth. Three players was not much depth. And Mathews did not roil Landry badly enough for the new coach to get rid of him, though there were others who did, men like Buzz Guy, a former Giant, and Bob Cross of the Rams and the Cardinals. Landry had been forced to cut them for lack of effort as much as lack of respect.

Guy's was perhaps the hardest loss. Offensive linemen were scarce, and Guy was the biggest and fastest of the Cowboy draftees. Landry had known him on the Giants.

BOB FRY: "Tom thought Buzz could be more important on the Cowboys than he had been on the Giants, except that he didn't want to be there."

BYRON BRADFUTE: "Buzz was an Adonis. He was the fastest, most talented offensive lineman. The spot was between him and me, and he would have won it, except that he didn't want to be there."

Guy could be a wildman.

JOHN GONZAGA: "Guy never acted his age. He always acted fourteen. He'd come up with things that you wouldn't believe."

JACK PATERA: "Buzz was a different kind of person. I saw him get hit with a beer bottle right across the forehead, and he just wiped it off. That's all I'm going to say. He just kind of blinked and said, 'You shouldn't have done that.' "

BYRON BRADFUTE: "You know the story in the novel *North Dallas Forty* where this one guy threw the televisions off the motel balcony to see how far he could throw them? That was a true story. That was Buzz Guy. He just pulled them out of the walls and tossed them as far as he could out the window of the motel."

Before the end of training camp, Buzz Guy was gone, and the Cowboys had to make do with the rookie, Bradfute.

Another disruptive player was another big lineman, Bob Cross, whom the players recall most vividly.

JOHN GONZAGA: "He was a small Texas-town type of guy. Cross didn't like anyone who was different. He always thought my name was Gonzalez and that I came from Mexico. He didn't hesitate for a minute to tell anybody how he felt about wetbacks."

FRANK CLARKE: "Someone told me he was a card-carrying member of the Ku Klux Klan. Now I don't know if this was true, but it sure opened my eyes to a lot of strange things that were going on in the world."

Bigotry does not disqualify a player. But taking the coach's twelve-year-old kid on a snipe hunt is not recommended either. And that's what Cross did.

TOM BRAATZ: "Cross gave the boy a pan and a wooden spoon and a gunny sack and told him to go out there and beat on the pan with the spoon and pretty soon he'd have a sackful of snipe. Well, you know how it works. Tom Jr. spent most of the night in the woods, holding that sack and beating on his pan with that wooden spoon.

"A couple of days later Coach Landry got wind of what had happened and Bob Cross got his release."

Tom Landry was well aware of the problems he was facing. He knew how hard it was to teach old dogs some new tricks. He knew that if you take rejects from different teams, every player had his own system, his own way of doing things, and chances were he would not be amenable to change. He also knew how difficult it was going to be to fuse together an offensive unit and a defensive unit with these recycled old dogs. But say one thing about Tom Landry: He was determined to succeed, and he worked those veterans as hard as they ever worked, making them practice three, four hours a day, force-feeding them a system he knew most of them either could not understand or would not stomach.

In his defense, Landry had some disciples from the beginning, including Jack Patera at middle linebacker and Jerry Tubbs at outside linebacker, and on offense split end Frank Clarke.

FRANK CLARKE: "When I arrived in Dallas, Tom came with this 'genius' title. They were calling him a genius, and to me it made sense. He *was* a genius. He was far and above. He had a way of approaching the game of football—the *whole* game—in a way that whatever aspect of the game that Tom Landry put his arm around and embraced, that's what sparkled.

"He told me early on, 'I want you to go downfield, take five steps and then cut at a 60-degree angle, take five more steps, and look for the ball. It will be there.' I had never heard anyone say that before. I would ask him, 'How do you know?' Or, 'What about the people trying to rush the passer? How is the quarterback going to know where I am?' He would say, 'Just do it.' And it was amazing how uncanny this became. I would take the steps he wanted us to take, cut the angle, take more steps, look for the ball, and it was *there*! I'd say to myself, 'Holy smokes. This guy knows everything!' And I would see him do the same thing with the defense, and with the kicking game, and the special teams. And as time went by, more and more guys would remark, 'Who is this guy? How did he get to know so much about the game?' Whenever he was able to impart his confidence, that part of the game just sparkled."

The offensive players weren't nearly as rebellious as the ones on defense, though they had their criticisms, too. When Landry had his linemen all rise up 1-2-3 in synch before the snap count, then get back into their stance before the snap, they thought it "Mickey Mouse nonsense."

DON MCILHENNY: "A lot of guys wondered, 'What the hell are we doing this for?' Looking back, Tom had a reason. We didn't realize he was as smart as he was, and we thought we were a lot smarter than we were."

Though most of the offensive players were not as resistant to Coach Landry's way of doing things as the defenders, that didn't mean they found it easy making his system work. Part of the problem was that Landry, the former Giant defensive coach, looked at everything from the point of view of the defense, and so when he put in the plays, he designated "odd" for left and "even" for right, when almost every other team designated "odd" for right and "even" for left. But Tom was looking at his diagrams from the *defense*'s left and the *defense*'s right, and so he flip-flopped them without considering the consequences. Throughout the year the veteran offensive players would occasionally revert to their ingrained habits, reacting rather than thinking as their brains told them "odd" was right and "even" left. During games veteran linemen would pull the wrong way or backs would head in the opposite direction from the way they were supposed to go on a screen pass, and Landry could never figure out why.

In the beginning Landry kept his offensive playbook simple. The trick plays, the motion would come later. During the exhibition season it was pure vanilla. Landry knew his backs had no speed, saw that his wide receivers had potential, but also realized that his offensive line would not be able to stop the top teams from rushing in and grinding his quarterback into the turf. He was counting on Eddie LeBaron's quickness to keep him from getting killed.

Of the quarterbacks, Eddie LeBaron was square on the coach's side. The former Washington ace had been well aware of Landry's impact when the Redskins had to face the Giants. LeBaron, moreover, was the kind of person to do whatever his coach asked him to do.

EDDIE LEBARON: "I had been an officer in the Marine Corps, and through many years of football had watched the good teams who were well organized, well drilled like the Cleveland Browns and the New York Giants, and you saw what it took. That was my nature. I was prepared to fit into the system."

As for his teammates, LeBaron was respected, both for his great skill and also for his ability to play the game despite his lack of size, which LeBaron insisted was never a factor.

DICK BIELSKI: "LeBaron was a delight. He was a treat. He was a little guy, you pulled for him, you wished him success. He was capable and talented, though undersized, but it never seemed to be a problem for him. He never approached it as a problem. We kind of all accepted him as he was."

The second stringer, New York Giant veteran Don Heinrich, was respected for his worldliness. Having played in New York for so many years, Heinrich was a fixture at such haunts as PJ Clarke's and Downey's, and he would talk about places and restaurants other players had only heard about. Heinrich was also respected for being able to figure out a defense quickly. With the Giants he had opened the game, then after figuring out the defense, would turn it over to the more talented Conerly or Tittle. Heinrich was like a coach on the field.

Heinrich, like LeBaron, generally went along with Landry's system of play. Any reluctance stemmed from the fact he had anticipated being the starting quarterback, until the late arrival of LeBaron. His disappointment at not getting much of a chance to start never abated all season long. The third quarterback, rookie Don Meredith, hated Landry's system, wanting no part of it. At SMU Meredith had spent his career dropping back seven or eight yards and throwing bombs to his receivers. His career completion rate of 61 percent spoke highly of his skill. But Landry was too disciplined a coach to allow what he considered such a haphazard attack, and Meredith was too stubborn to want to do anything different from what had brought him success in high school and college. LeBaron would lecture Meredith on the importance of fitting into the system. Said LeBaron with a chuckle, "He sometimes declined."

Meredith knew he wouldn't have much opportunity to play his first year, and he took a laissez-faire approach to his work. One time in practice Meredith, barking signals, called out the wrong color, indicating the wrong offensive formation.

"It's 'red,'" said backfield coach Babe Demancheck, "not 'purple.'"

Quipped an unrepentant Meredith, "I was close."

The first preseason game in the history of the Dallas Cowboys took place in Seattle against the San Francisco 49ers. Four of the Cowboys' top signees—Don Meredith, running back Don Perkins, lineman Paul Rochester, and running back Jimmy Mooty—were not available for the game. They were in Chicago playing for the College All-Stars against the world champion Baltimore Colts.

Lineman John Gonzaga was playing his old team, and for that reason Landry had made him a captain for the game. When his former teammates asked him how he enjoyed playing on the Cowboys, he replied, "I'll tell you what, guys. Don't let them stars get in your eyes. That's all I can tell you."

The 49ers won that day, 16–10. Most of the game the offense's timing was terrible, but there was one shining moment for the Cowboys when Eddie LeBaron threw a 56-yard touchdown pass to Frank Clarke.

Against the 49ers Gene Cronin suffered a knee injury and had to spend the rest of the preseason in a cast. Also in that game Jack Patera, playing under Landry's system for the first time, learned a valuable lesson.

JACK PATERA: "I had fast become a tremendous disciple of his defense. Against a certain offense, my job was to key the offensive running back, and if he went to his left, I was to step between the left guard and the left tackle. In practice, nothing had ever happened that I couldn't handle, but against San Francisco, Bob St. Clair was the tackle for the 49ers, and after watching the back, I took my step, and the next thing I knew Bob St. Clair, who was 6'8", 275 pounds, hit me so hard I landed almost at the sidelines! It was then I realized there were two parts to his defense: You key the back, and then you look for the tackle coming down on you. That made me study a little bit more, too. I started asking more questions. When we watched the films of the play, Tom and I got a good laugh out of it."

Despite a decent performance by the Cowboys, there was sobering news from the All-Star game in Chicago: Both young Cowboy running backs, Don Perkins and Jim Mooty, had been seriously injured in practice. Perkins had broken the fifth metatarsal in his foot as a junior in college and missed a few games. Doctors had performed surgery on it. At a College All-Star game practice, Perkins planted his foot, and the G forces on the bone proved too great. The bone broke again. He hadn't even been tackled. Perkins would be lost for the entire season, as would Mooty, who had called Schramm to tell him he had torn a leg muscle during drills. When the All-Stars returned in time for the exhibition game in San Antonio against the hapless St. Louis Cardinals, only two of the four top prospects, Don Meredith and Paul Rochester, remained. And Rochester, who would go on to star with the New York Jets in the AFL, would not survive the final cut.

The Cards won by only a touchdown. After the game, at a gathering held in honor of the team, Ray Mathews set his hosts' teeth gnashing when he said that the men at the Alamo, San Antonio's shrine to Texas freedom, had not been heroes but rather cowards. "I talked about them running out the back door of the Alamo," said Mathews, who continually sought to find the magic words that would send him back to his old coach, Buddy Parker, in Pittsburgh.

After the Cardinals game, the Cowboys had to find a new site to continue training camp, and the team traveled to Minnesota, about thirty-five miles south of the Twin Cities to the town of Delafield. After the players settled into the dorms of the St. John's Military Academy, they hated it there.

GENE BABB: "Let me tell you about this place. There were four floors in this dormitory, one of these old stone and marble buildings, ivy going up the walls, and the only bathrooms—toilets and showers—were all the way down in the basement. And it had one of these big belfries on one end, and we had to be in bed with lights out at ten o'clock, and at eleven the bells went off, and the live bats would fly up and down the halls! And that became the sport of the evening. Everybody would lay in their beds, lights out, and you could feel the anticipation in the air, 'cause you laid there with your pillow on top of you, and when the bells chimed at eleven, the bats started flying up and down the halls and in the stairwells. The halls just filled with everybody and their pillows trying to knock down those bats!"

The beds were kid-size, the rooms were as spartan as in a monastery, and Delafield was as inaccessible to the world as Forest Grove. Twice the players hung Tex Schramm's assistant, Gil Brandt, the one they accused of finding St. John's, in effigy.

The third exhibition game was played in Nashville against the Baltimore Colts. The Colts won 14–10. Landry should have gotten a lot of credit from his players for putting together a representative team so quickly, but to the players a loss was a loss. Jack Patera, at middle linebacker, continued to learn the benefits of playing Landry's defensive system. During the game Patera sacked his childhood friend, quarterback George Shaw. The Colts ran a play, and he read his "key," and reacted accordingly. Alex Sandusky, the Colt offensive lineman, was supposed to trap him, but Landry's blueprint had warned Patera that he was coming, and Patera stepped up, avoided him and made the tackle, angering Sandusky, who accused him of "playing the play." Patera laughed. Sandusky didn't know it, but that was the way the Cowboys' defense was designed.

The team traveled to Louisville to play the New York Giants, the defending Eastern Conference champions, in their fourth exhibition game. The temperature on the field reached 120 degrees. "It was the hottest night I ever played," said Patera. The Cowboys gained the first win in their history, albeit in an exhibition game. The score was 14–3. Some of the players wondered whether the Giants were really trying. "I don't know if they gave it to Landry or what," said John Gonzaga. Recalled linebacker Jerry Tubbs, "It was a combination of Landry knowing the Giants, and the Giants not caring."

In that game Eddie LeBaron proved himself to a doubtful Frank Clarke, scrambling and throwing Clarke a 73-yard touchdown pass, and then Don Meredith relieved LeBaron and hit Clarke with a 74-yard touchdown beauty.

FRANK CLARKE: "Eddie LeBaron was short, 5'6", on his tiptoes 5'7", so imagine big guys like Jim Katcavage and Rosey Grier barreling in on little Eddie. He could get the ball over *them*? I figured, No way. I remember running this pass route, a 'quick-in' route is what it's called, and when I looked 'in' for the ball, I couldn't even see the quarterback, so I immediately looked away. As soon as I did, that very second the ball careened off my shoulder pads. I thought, No way, man. *No way* does he get rid of that ball. But Eddie could. He did some tricky things with that ball. So I learned from early on, stay with this guy. In the Giants game, I caught a touchdown pass from LeBaron and one from Meredith. That gave the Cowboys their very first victory."

If the game had a memorable moment, however, it belonged to Don Meredith. Since his return from the All-Star game, the SMU rookie had half-heartedly attempted to learn Tom Landry's complicated system of play calling. Against the Giants, Landry gave Meredith his first opportunity to apply what he had learned. Gene Babb recalled what happened.

GENE BABB: "Don had had to go to the All-Star game, so he hadn't had that much exposure to Landry's system. He came into the huddle, and he said, 'Okay, purple right, 46 lead.' And L. G. Dupre and I were looking at each other. L.G. said, 'Don, that's not the right formation. It's red right, 46 lead.' Don said, 'Okay, whatever, let's just run it.' And we'd line up the way we were supposed to when we got to the line of scrimmage.

"Don was laid-back, very easygoing. He knew the experienced quarterback was going to play, that Don was there to learn, and he was having a great time. He hadn't yet gotten serious, the way Tom wanted him to be."

During the game Meredith's problems multiplied when Sam Huff, the Giant middle linebacker, decided to show the rookie how green he really was. This one time Meredith started his count, and when Huff saw Meredith's offensive formation, he adjusted his defense accordingly, just as Tom Landry had taught him. Meredith then called an audible, and Huff reset his defense to counter. When Meredith realized he was about to send his back right into the heart of the Giant defense, he didn't know what to do about it.

Meredith called, "Four set! . . . uh, red right . . . uh, 22 . . . Ah, shit, son of a bitch, time-out." Huff and the other members of the Giant defense broke out laughing, along with some of the veteran linemen on the Cowboys.

The next exhibition was against the Los Angeles Rams. The game was played in the evening in Pendleton, Oregon. What Gene Babb recalled most vividly was that they had played the game at the rodeo grounds, "on grass that had a lot of fertilizer growing there." The circus had come to town before the NFL, and the elephants, tigers, and bears had left presents behind.

After a 14–14 score at halftime, Rams quarterback Billy Wade ripped the Cowboys apart, 49–14, throwing a touchdown pass to Del Shofner and two to fullback Jon Arnett.

What Jack Patera recalled most vividly was the all-night poker game after the football game.

JACK PATERA: "It started nickel ante, and it got up to pretty big dollars. One of the guys [whom he didn't want to name] was pulling light from the pot. 'I owe $300,' he said, and then after we folded he put the money in his pocket. I looked at him and said, 'I thought you were light. Is that your money?' He said, 'Yes.' I didn't say anything.

"The next time it was a bigger hand, and he was pulling light, and again he put the money in his pocket. This time I counted the pot, and I said, 'Hey, that money goes in the pot.' He said, 'No, it doesn't. It belongs to me.' So I grabbed him, and I took the money out of his pocket, put it all in there, and kicked the table over. It was about five in the morning. Before I walked out I told him, 'I can't believe it, here we're starting the season, and I can't even trust my own teammate.' He only played one year. I didn't like him."

After Tom Landry learned of the incident, he banned the playing of poker by his players.

The final exhibition game was against Vince Lombardi and the Green Bay Packers in Minneapolis. It was only Lombardi's second season with the Pack, but already he had molded it into a powerhouse. The Packers won a close one, 28–23, scoring the winner in the final minutes. Rookie offensive tackle Byron Bradfute recalled that the Packers defense was a little different from what he had been used to in college.

BYRON BRADFUTE: "They didn't run the normal 4–3, and under our blocking formula I thought I was supposed to pass block on the number two man on the line from center. How you start counting is determined by whether the defender is over the center or right behind him or off to the side, and the way I saw it, I was playing right tackle and Willie Davis was playing on my right shoulder, and I thought that Davis was supposed to be the number two man. So that's who I blocked—all day long. And I thought I had one of the best days I ever had.

"But as it turned out, that's not who I was supposed to block. I was supposed to be blocking the *next* guy out, and he had a field day against us! And I can remember Tom Landry showing the game films, and over and over again he kept saying, 'Bradfute . . .' "

Linebacker Jack Patera had his own particular memories of the Packers exhibition.

JACK PATERA: "I remember right in front of the Packer bench some guy running near me on a screen pass. He dropped the ball, and I hit him with an elbow. The Packers all got on me. I remember Lombardi yelling,

'Cheap shot son of a bitch,' or something like that. And then Bart Starr was scrambling, and I flushed him out of the pocket and chased him. He stepped out of bounds, and I dove at him, and I ended up sliding into their bench, and Jimmy Taylor, their fullback, put a knee down, and I slid into it, and he had his helmet off, and he was yelling at me, 'You stupid son of a bitch. We're going to take care of you.' So I turned around and gave him a short jab and punched him in the nose and knocked him over the bench. That brought the bench up, and I ran across to my side.

"The last play of the game the Packers gave me the bootsey, where they snapped the ball, and everybody forgot about hitting anybody but me. They were all on top of me, but there isn't a whole lot they can do. It was nothing. I didn't know who it was at the time, but from the bottom of the pile I reached up and grabbed this guy's jock strap and squeezed it as hard as I could. There was a lot of yelling. They started unpiling, and I just held on, and we got up, and I was holding Fuzzy Thurston. He said, 'You are kind of a tough guy after all, aren't you?' "

There were two full weeks between the end of the exhibition season and the first regular season game, and Tom Landry and Tex Schramm began working harder than ever, inviting to camp players dropped in final cuts from all the other teams.

EDDIE LEBARON: "There were two hundred bodies [actually 193] who tried out that first training camp, and most of them came the last two weeks. It looked like the Greyhound bus station. As teams started cutting players, we had them trooping in and out of there so fast, you couldn't believe it. One day Don Meredith asked me, 'Who's that guy over there?' I said, 'Don, the first thing you learn is never learn their names until the last cut is made. 'Cause you'll feel bad when they get cut.'

"There weren't many who were any good."

Bob Fry remembered the extra work brought on by the influx of bodies.

BOB FRY: "The Cowboys had first pick of the players cut by the other teams, so the week before the first game, we would have two practices. First the forty or fifty guys who they were trying out would practice, and we would practice later."

Landry needed to know if any of the late arrivals could play, so he used his regulars to find out.

JACK PATERA: "Tom was bringing in twenty new guys a day, and he always wanted us to scrimmage them. I don't think I ever scrimmaged so much in my life. It was like playing a game every day. We only had a handful of linebackers, Tom Braatz, Jerry Tubbs, Gene Cronin, and me. Wahoo McDaniel had tried out for middle linebacker, but he wasn't good enough to play. He had a good reputation, but he never did anything. He didn't like to practice. I loved to practice. If I could take three turns, I would take three turns. And if someone else got out of his turn, I'd want his turn. My philosophy was that if a coach never sees a player, he won't know whether he's any better than you are. So I hated to be replaced any time, 'cause if some guy could do something that was outstanding, maybe he might take my job."

No one took Patera's job. And surprise of surprises, Byron Bradfute beat out Paul Rochester, Jerry DeLucca, and Buzz Guy for a starting spot at offensive tackle. Of the eighty or so free agents to pass through the Cowboys training camp, Bradfute and Gary Wisener, an offensive end and defensive back, were the only two free agents to land a spot on the team.

A handful of late arrivals cut from other training camps ended up making the Cowboys final roster. Center had been a serious problem all through the exhibition season, and a rookie, Mike Connelly, was signed despite his relative lack of size after the Los Angeles Rams cut him late in training camp. Among the late arrivals, Tex Schramm also signed defensive back Don Bishop and linebacker Wayne Henson from the Bears, guard Mike Falls from the Packers, and defensive back Bob Bercich from the Giants.

Despite all the bickering and the lack of stability during the exhibition season, with training camp coming to a close, some of the vets approached the coming season with their usual confidence.

JERRY TUBBS: "I went into the season thinking we would win maybe half our games. I was that confident. And we could have if we had had a little luck. And if we'd have been a little better."

Quarterback Eddie LeBaron was equally upbeat.

EDDIE LEBARON: "I thought we were a pretty good football team for just starting out."

10

0-11-1

When rookie halfback Don Perkins broke his foot during training camp, the doctors suggested he wear a special shoe to see if he could run despite the break. By the end of training camp, it was clear he would need an operation, and so Perkins was awaiting surgery in Dallas with his teammates as they were getting ready for the start of the season.

Scouting director Gil Brandt and some of his players, including Don Meredith and Jim Mooty, were heading for lunch and they asked Perkins to come along. Arriving at the Highland Park Cafeteria, they took trays and got in line. When one of the waiters informed Perkins, "Hey, you can't get served here," they all left.

DON PERKINS: "It was the nature of the society. We were very polarized in this country at that time. The black players lived in Oak Cliff on one side of town, the white players lived on another side of town in North Dallas. You saw each other in practice, and then you split. That was it. I don't think what happened was shocking to anybody. How does it feel? Well, I had been called nigger and lots of things in my life by the time I was twenty-two, so this was not the first time I had been told, 'You can't do this. You can't use the bathroom. You can't do that.' Little kids would come up to you to rub their hands across you to see whether your black skin will come off. So there was no new ground broken that day. And after the operation, I was lost for the season, and I went back to Albuquerque. I went back to school, and even though I still got paid by the Cowboys, I also did odd jobs, worked construction."

The other black player, Frank Clarke, also couldn't help but be affected by the segregationist society of Dallas. A northerner from Wisconsin, for the first time he was encountering a situation where he could not stay in hotels or eat at lunch counters.

FRANK CLARKE: "You could walk into a 5-and-10 cent store and see drinking fountains marked 'colored' and 'white.' I had never seen this. It kind of takes your breath away. You go, 'Holy smokes. How far away are we from lynchings?' Though we didn't have any cause to be threatened, I could not divorce myself from the fact we were in Texas.

"Nevertheless, the fact that Dallas was segregated didn't matter to me. When we broke camp, we all stayed together in a hotel as a team until the season actually started. There were no problems there, no segregation there. Then once we made the team, where I could live was limited but I was satisfied with where I lived. Hey, man, the season goes so fast, you don't start messing with other things. My concentration was on playing good football, so where I lived was fine. I wasn't slumming it. And we weren't caught up in any civil rights movement. Our emphasis was on playing football. We just wanted to make the most of it. We were in Dallas to play football. And when the season was over, I went back to my family in Cleveland."

DON PERKINS: "I never even had aspirations of a pro career while I was in college. Even after I signed with the Cowboys, it never occurred to me that I might be around for a long career. I never felt I was good enough to be playing at the professional level. I spent most of my career afraid someone would find me out, suddenly discover that I didn't have any business being where I was."

To the whites on the team, both Frank Clarke and Don Perkins were respected as hard-working and congenial. Both went along in order to get along, and they were awarded high marks for that. It would not be for a couple of years, after Perkins established himself with the Cowboys, and after the civil rights movement began to pick up steam, that he would fight for the right for his son to go to an all-white private school. Black militancy was still a decade away.

For the 1960 Cowboy players, a more immediate source of controversy was the deplorable condition of their practice facility at creaking Burnet Field. In organizing the fledgling team in only a few months' time, Tex Schramm had a lot of scrambling to do. When you start from scratch, sometimes you have to make do and that was certainly the case with Burnett Field. After having to endure monkish facilities at St. John's Military Academy, where they felt like they were in a jail, once they finished the exhibition season and came back to Dallas they had to face the rats and scorpions and uncomfortable conditions that marked their practice facility. For the veterans, it was one more reason to dislike playing for the Cowboys. "We really didn't have a practice facility," said Ray Mathews. "Everything was chaos."

Daily team meetings were held on the second floor of the American Automobile Association building off the North Central Expressway. After the meeting, the coaches and players would get on a bus and drive to antiquated Burnet Field, which had once been the home of a minor league baseball team. The offense would meet in the clubhouse behind first base, and the defense would meet in the clubhouse behind third base.

EDDIE LeBARON: "Burnet Field was in the middle of the Trinity River flood plain. When it would rain, the showers would plug up, and we'd be standing in six inches of water. And when it rained, the field would get flooded, and we'd have to get on a bus and Tom would scout out a park that we could practice in."

DON McILHENNY: "There were rats in pretty nearly every building, including our locker room. The rats would chew the leather shoulder pads at night, and we'd come back the next day and find their teeth marks. When we got to practice, we had to take our shoes and hit them on the ground to shake the scorpions out of them, 'cause they liked the salt, liked to crawl up into moist places.

"The locker rooms were cold. Some of the guys would throw used tape and paper into a barrel and light it. One time we went out onto the field to practice, and we looked back, and smoke was coming out of the stadium locker room. It was sort of fun. The coaches halted practice and began running toward it ready to fight the fire. It did accomplish one thing. It smoked the rats out for the next couple of weeks.

"I can remember one time it had rained so much that we couldn't practice at Burnet Field, and so we got on the bus. We started driving around, hunting for a place to practice. We saw a public park over on Harry Hines Boulevard, over in the industrial district. We jumped out of the bus, went over and practiced. Not a soul showed up. Nobody watched us. I said to my wife not too long ago, 'Can you imagine today if the Dallas Cowboys got on a bus and practiced in a public park? There would be 10,000 people there.'

"I can remember in October of our first year, Don Heinrich and I went to the Texas State Fair as representatives of the Cowboys. They had a booth for us to sign autographs and give pictures away and Cowboys key chains. Hardly anybody stopped by. And if they did, it was to taunt us, because we weren't from the Dallas Texans. We sat out there a couple of hours trying to give away trinkets and pictures, and nobody wanted them."

The opening game of the 1960 season was against Landry's old UT teammate Bobby Layne, plus Ernie Stautner and the rest of the Pittsburgh Steelers in the Cotton Bowl. Twenty thousand spectators (paid and comped), including the 2,100 season ticket holders, took their seats in the huge 70,000-seat arena for the inaugural. To give the event a little extra Texas flavor, Tex Schramm hired Roy Rogers and Dale Evans to ride Trigger and Buttercup around the cavernous bowl before the game. What Schramm, a Californian, didn't realize was that to Texans, Hollywood cowboys made a mockery of the genuine article, and Schramm was mortified when hundreds of Texans amused themselves by pelting an angry Singing Cowboy and his wife with ice cubes from their soda cups.

"I'll never know why," said Schramm, "but it was one of the most embarrassing things to ever happen to me."

The Cowboys opened the game with a run for no gain, then Gene Babb ran for one yard, and on the third play, from his own 15 Eddie LeBaron threw a short turn-in to former Detroit Lion star Jim Doran, who from his position at tight end cut across the middle, captured the pass, got a perfectly timed block from halfback Don McIlhenny, and hightailed it the rest of the way for the first Cowboy touchdown.

EDDIE LEBARON: "I remember the play. It was 'Brown left, X turn in.' Brown calls for the halfback and fullback to be side by side in regular position. 'Brown left' means the flanker goes out on the left side, and the 'X' is the tight end, which was Doran. The play was designed for the halfback to run a little shoot pattern on the right side, and for Doran to go down and turn inside the linebacker. I got it to him, and then he took off."

*　　*　　*

The second time the Cowboys had the football, LeBaron threw a 58-yard pass to Frank Clarke down to the Pittsburgh seven, followed by a touchdown pass to end Fred Dugan. Before Steeler coach Buddy Parker and his star quarterback Bobby Layne could regroup, the Cowboys were ahead 14–0. It was the biggest lead they would have all season long.

For rookie offensive tackle Byron Bradfute, the Steeler game was his inauguration. The Steeler he attempted to stop was Big Daddy Lipscomb, the gargantuan tackle with the vicious disposition.

BYRON BRADFUTE: "Maybe some of the old guys didn't think we could win, but I thought we could win every week. I never will forget, the first words I even remember from Tom Landry, he said, 'The one thing I want you all to remember is that there is only a half step difference between the champions and those who finish on the bottom. And much of that half step is mental.' He convinced me. I really believe most of us thought we could win every time we went out there to play.

"Big Daddy Lipscomb played defensive tackle for the Steelers, and on running plays I blocked down on him a lot. He was big and strong, and Lord a' mercy, he was a talker, just filthy. Steady and filthy. He gave LeBaron a terrible, terrible time. Even after the game I heard Big Daddy say things to LeBaron when his wife was with him. It made LeBaron mad just to think about it. Big Daddy was a *bad* guy."

In addition to Lipscomb, the other Steeler defender the Cowboys had to worry about most was linebacker Ernie Stautner. In that game the responsibility for stopping him fell on tackle Bob Fry.

BOB FRY: "I didn't have success, though I did all right against him. Ernie was a guy who had a super motor. He was short, but he would come at you like gangbusters every time, and he'd come hard. He wasn't a finesse guy. He was a power guy. He had a lot of strength, and boy, when you set up to block him, you had better block him aggressively. You didn't sit back and wait for him to make a move. And the thing about him, he went 110 percent all the time. There was no such thing as going into the fourth quarter and Ernie getting tired. Eventually, he would wear you down. 'Cause it was continuous, continuous, continuous."

Bradfute, Fry, and the rest of the offensive line did well enough that, in all, LeBaron completed 14 of 25 passes for 348 yards. In their inaugural game, the Cowboys scored 28 points. It would not be enough.

For the defenders, the Steeler they had to stop was quarterback Bobby Layne, and on this evening the fledgling defensive unit couldn't do it. Layne threw for four touchdowns, and during the evening he broke the career passing record set by Sammy Baugh. Baugh had managed 22,085 yards passing in fifteen years. This was Layne's thirteenth season, and by the end of the game his total was 22,351. A 58-yard touchdown pass from Layne to Tom "The Bomb" Tracy was the game-winner.

GENE CRONIN: "Bobby Layne wasn't about to lose to us. No way. He usually found a way to win. He'd find a way. I saw him play hurt, bleeding, blood running off him, but he still wouldn't leave the ballgame. It was his *life* to beat you."

JACK PATERA: "We gave up 35 points, but I remember thinking the defense as it was set up was working pretty well. Bobby Layne was always a pleasure for me to play against. He was a fun guy. He'd come out of the huddle and stick his tongue out at you. I remember that game having them close to their goal line and stopping them. We forced them to punt, and we had an opportunity to tie it. But we didn't quite have the personnel to do it."

EDDIE LeBARON: "We weren't bad, but we weren't good enough. We didn't have the killer defense, and we couldn't rush the ball. We had big, strong backs, but we didn't have a big, strong line."

It was in the next game, against the Philadelphia Eagles, that the fate of the Cowboys during their inaugural season would be sealed. The Eagles, led by their exciting quarterback, Norm Van Brocklin, would lose only two games all season long and win the Eastern Conference. Against them, the Cowboys scored 25 points. They should have had 27, except the Eagles blocked two extra points by kicker Fred Cone. Three Eagle interceptions also hurt their effort. These were both games the Cowboys could have won. Perhaps two early victories would have changed the early destiny of the team. But as would happen at least five times this inaugural season, victories turned into losses as a result of a misplay or two.

EDDIE LeBARON: "We had Philadelphia down in the second game, and they were the World Champions that year, and we got beat 27–25. All the Eagles had was a simple zone. They got really deep, and they were so easy to throw against. But I threw to the wrong man a couple of times and was intercepted. That was dumb. We should have won both of those games. We were not a bad football team. But when you don't win games you should win, then people start looking for reasons, and so the players get down. We were a disparate group, guys thrown together. We didn't have that unity experienced teams have going in."

Rookie Byron Bradfute continued his NFL education. The night before the game he and Cowboys line coach Brad Ecklund, who had played at the University of Oregon when Van Brocklin was the quarterback there, went out drinking, came back late, and Bradfute was fined $350. Then in the game the rookie discovered the ramifications of letting one's emotions get the best of you.

BYRON BRADFUTE: "I got into an altercation with Tom Brookshier, took a swing at him with my fist, hit his helmet, and cut my knuckle open. It was bleeding, and I was mad because I had hurt myself more than I had hurt him. The Eagles lined up to punt, and Brookshier lined up as a back to protect the punter from our rush. I was playing defensive right end, and my job was outside containment, but I had nothing in my mind except to go in there and hit him right in the mouth. They had those two-bar face masks, and you could really hurt someone if you could get underneath the bar and hit them in the mouth. And that's all I had on my mind.

"I went tearing in there and focused on him and took a big swing and got a pretty good lick on him, but while I was doing that the punter saw I had left my post, and he ran around my end for about 40 yards! Landry wasn't real happy about that, and the next week while we watched the films, he showed it over and over again. I got semi-even with Brookshier, but it didn't help my career."

One reason the Cowboys had to win early if they were going to win at all is that as a season goes on, injuries take their toll. Against the Eagles, the middle linebacker, Jack Patera, saw that Van Brocklin was going to throw a screen pass, and as he rushed to cover the receiver coming out of the backfield, he was blindsided and clipped behind the knee by one of the Eagle guards. Patera would miss the rest of that game and the next and would return against the Cleveland Browns. That game would be his last.

The Cowboys lost to the Washington Redskins 26–14, and for the third week would play well but not well enough to win. It would be a different story against the powerful Cleveland Browns, who were led on defense by linemen Bob Gain, Floyd Peters, and Jim Marshall. On offense a powerful front line blocked for Jim Brown and Bobby Mitchell, two of the best runners in the history of the NFL. This was to be a big game for Frank Clarke, who had been cast adrift by the Browns. For the others, the challenge of playing against coach Paul Brown and his juggernaut was overwhelming.

DICK BIELSKI: "You watch the film all week, and even though you may not make any comment to anyone else, you say to yourself, 'Boy, this is going to be a *long* Sunday.' You know your chances aren't going to be so good against a team like the Browns, or the Packers, or the Colts, against whom we were completely outclassed. You say to yourself, 'What the hell. They can't kill me, can they?' "

They weren't capable of murder, but the Browns were more than capable of a solid maiming. It was while playing against these Browns that the talented middle linebacker Jack Patera saw his career come to an end.

JACK PATERA: "I played the first half, and on the last play of the half Jimmy Brown ran a sweep to our right, and I got tangled up in a big pileup, and that tore everything in my knee. My foot was jammed up against my hip almost. It was the worst pain I ever felt. It was the one time in my life I said to the trainer, 'Just leave me alone. This hurts so bad it feels good.' I didn't want him to move me for a while. And that was the end of it. I came back the next year, got hurt in the first preseason game, twisted it, and I played the final game of the season, but I had no strength in it. I had to retire."

The loss of Patera would have been far more devastating except for the fact that this was the one position at which the Cowboys had an equally talented backup. At the University of Oklahoma Jerry Tubbs had been an exceptional middle linebacker, but because he only weighed 210 pounds, pro coaches had been hesitant to let him play there. When Patera got hurt, Landry didn't have much choice. When Tubbs begged him to be allowed to return to the middle, the coach reluctantly gave in. He didn't have anybody else. For the next seven years Tubbs starred for the Cowboys as middle linebacker.

GENE BABB: "Jerry was a smart player, had a great mind on him, knew the defenses, and he was a heck of a hitter. He was the ideal guy to play in the middle of Landry's 4–3 defense."

* * *

In his inaugural game at middle linebacker, Tubbs would have the job of keying on and stopping Jim Brown and Bobby Mitchell.

JERRY TUBBS: "Jim Brown was the best runner that ever was. He wasn't the kind of back who would put his shoulder down and go in and deal a terrible blow, unless he was down on the goal line and he wanted to score or it was third-and-one and a critical situation. He was fast and tough to knock off his feet, but he wasn't a punishing runner. He didn't hurt you. But you didn't tackle him either. He had tremendous balance and strength, and he would use you. You'd go in to hit him hard, and it wouldn't do any good. He'd bounce off, use that great balance of his and keep going. Plus he had tremendous speed.

"And what I remember about him, he never said a word, no matter what you did to him. If you hit him as hard as you could, when he was down on the ground, he'd never complain, didn't gripe. He'd get up slowly and just walk back to the huddle, slowly, acting like he was hurt every time. He was telling you, 'You didn't hurt me,' even if he was dying at the time.

"And Bobby Mitchell was the perfect complement to Jim Brown. He was quick and elusive and dangerous. Boy, they had a great offensive team. And the quarterback, Milt Plum, wasn't a great talent, but he did what he had to do with that great complement around him. They started, and for the better part of the '60s beat us pretty bad."

As punishing as was the Browns offensive unit, their defenders were just as devastating. Frank Clarke recalled the verbal abuse he took from his former teammates.

FRANK CLARKE: "I remember the Browns players, especially Bernie Parrish, gave me a hard time. They were screaming things at me, 'You chickenshit,' using energy to try to get me distracted. When I was with the Browns, I had the reputation of being a receiver who heard footsteps. They had been teammates, but they hadn't been friends. They didn't seem to care much about me. They knew if I was going to be effective, I had to keep my cool, so they were doing whatever they could to upset me. Only it wasn't part of my makeup to view that as a form of flattery. I should have said to myself, 'These guys think enough of me to try to get me off my game.' I should have told myself they were just trying to make things even, because with my speed and talent I could beat them one-on-one."

*   *   *

Clarke didn't catch a single pass all day.

For quarterbacks Eddie LeBaron, Don Heinrich, and later Don Meredith, it was a day spent trying to avoid getting killed by the Browns defensive linemen.

EDDIE LEBARON: "Bob Gain was a great football player. He was aggressive and quick, and we'd try to trap him, try all sorts of things to stop him, but we didn't have anyone on the Cowboys who could stop him."

MIKE FALLS: "I was playing [guard] against Bob Gain and he was literally wearing me out, beating my brains out. I've never been so frustrated. Finally, there was a play where Eddie LeBaron was rolling out to pass. Gain was chasing him across the field and finally ran him out of bounds. The whistle had already blown, and there was Gain standing there out of bounds and I still had up a full head of steam. It was the best shot I had all day so I took it. Man, I creamed him. And, of course, got a 15-yard penalty for it. Which wasn't that big a deal, really, since we were already facing third-and-20 anyway."

The final score was Browns 48, Cowboys 7. What followed the next weekend was a heartbreaking 12–10 loss to the St. Louis Cardinals, a game the Cowboys would have won had L. G. Dupre not fumbled toward the end of the game. Then came a 45–7 blowout by the Baltimore Colts, and another blowout, a 38–10 loss to the L.A. Rams in the Cotton Bowl. In this game quarterback Don Meredith made his first start, and the SMU rookie spent much of his effort running from the large Rams defensive linemen.

BYRON BRADFUTE: "I started the day blocking Gene Brito, who was an All-Pro, who was real fast. I had to set back and be on my toes and be ready to go in either direction, react to whatever kind of move he put on you, and I was having a pretty good day against him. And then the Rams substituted for Brito and sent in a backup, John Baker, who was 6'6" and weighed about 290 pounds. Baker had to go over me to get to Meredith, and I didn't even slow him down. I mean, he came over me, and I have never felt so defenseless. I weighed 250 pounds, was reasonably strong, and he went over me like I was a child! I swear, I never even slowed him down. The only way Meredith recognized me was if he laid down on his back and looked up."

* * *

If Landry had any concern for his quarterback, his offensive game plan didn't show it. Some offenses provide a backup blocker if someone gets through. The Cowboys didn't. Landry expected his linemen to keep the brutes out one-on-one. The offensive linemen complained that the defenders got through to the quarterback as much because of Landry's flawed system of blocking as through their lack of talent. It was those flaws, they said, that made it more likely the defenders would get past them and reach the quarterback.

BYRON BRADFUTE: "The first couple of years the only time the offense blocked the defensive ends was on pass plays. And that puts a man at an extreme disadvantage. It gives the defensive end a *terrific* advantage. I'm not trying to say we were all blessed with such great talent, but this was one of the reasons we had so much trouble stopping the defensive ends.

"The defensive end would line up over the offensive tackle. If it was a pass play or draw, we would block. And the defensive end would look for that move. Once we committed ourselves, that end immediately knew what kind of play we were running. So once we started the block, the defensive end would know it was going to be a pass, and he could just go after us wide open. That gave the defensive end an extreme advantage. It was one of the main reasons our quarterbacks were harried."

BOB FRY: "When I went with the Cowboys, we were blocking in a way that we had thrown out with the Rams two years before, because it just wasn't that good. We were still area blocking. If the linebacker would blitz inside, I would pick up the linebacker and the offensive back would pick up the end. Now, what was wrong with that, which Sid Gillman changed on the Rams, say Gino Marchetti or another real good one was the defensive end. The tackle would set up to block him, and then a linebacker might just step inside, fake a rush, and fade back. Well, when the linebacker would fake his charge, the offensive tackle would hesitate, and that little bit of hesitation on his part would allow the end to beat him. And if the back was in motion or was going out on a pass route, there was no one to stop that end. It took a couple of years before we had the back pick up the linebacker no matter what."

From the start, the players on the offensive unit felt a keen respect for Eddie LeBaron, but for Meredith, who obviously had natural talent, they developed a fondness. Dandy Don, as he was called, had a quick wit and engaging personality, and he liked to make jokes as though he didn't have a care in the world. This was his public persona, the one that would most often appear in the newspapers, and as a result the Dallas fans would come to regard Meredith as a happy-go-lucky party boy and a maverick, and when he failed, especially in big games, they would hold that against him. It was not a coincidence that Tom Landry held these very qualities against him as well and would continue to do so Don's entire career.

11

The Righteous and
the Sinners

At first blush, an observer would have assumed that Tom Landry and Don Meredith would have gotten along famously. They were both small-town Texas boys. Tom had come from Mission in the south and Don from Mount Vernon in East Texas. Both had been Texas high school and college football heroes, Landry at UT, Meredith at SMU. But aside from that, they were as different in temperament and approach to the business of life and the game of football as two men could possibly be.

Tom Landry had been a serious young man during his playing days at the University of Texas, but after he accepted Jesus late in 1958 his emphasis on seriousness, clean living, and hard work was magnified to the extent that he had become a prophet trumpeting the Christian ethic.

Landry was one of the few coaches who injected religion into his speeches. A lot of coaches had a minister say a prayer before a game in a ritual much like the playing of the "Star Spangled Banner," but to Landry the Bible, Jesus, and Christianity weren't just for Sunday services. They were a way of life. His religious beliefs were important, and he felt it was appropriate to inject them into his talks to the team. After a game he might recap the game and then take out his Bible. He would say, "I did a lot of things in my life, but my life was empty until a guy in Dallas invited me to go to this prayer group. And after I went to the prayer group and read my Bible, my life changed. I got this job . . ." That was how he presented the Bible: follow Jesus, and you will succeed. And why not? That's exactly what had happened to him. Not long after his conversion, Tex Schramm had offered him a five-year contract at $34,500 a year.

Back in 1958 Tom Landry had been responsible for the great New York Giant defenses, and had been credited for his leadership and acumen. Emotionally, however, he was feeling rudderless and found himself without purpose in life. Part of it was that pro football wasn't paying him very much, a $12,000 salary that he had tried to augment during the off-season. His problem was that employers did not want six-month employees—and each year after football Landry would have to start over again in a new endeavor. It left him frustrated and unsettled.

In the winter of 1958 Landry, born a Methodist, was invited to a Bible study class in the dining room of the Melrose Hotel in Dallas. He sat with forty businessmen as they discussed Jesus' Sermon on the Mount. The session filled him with what he described as "joy," and he embarked on a Bible study program in which he immersed himself in the Scriptures as assiduously as if he were studying an opposing team's offenses. Over a period of months Landry found that the Bible "made sense," and in 1959 his faith outweighed his doubts. That year he committed himself to Christ.

He began to look at life from a Christian fundamentalist perspective. Life became very simple for him. In the Bible, in John 3:16, it says, "I have given you my only living son . . ." Tom Landry gave himself to Christ. For Tom Landry, the Bible became his handbook for life, like a manual for a car. If he wanted to know how to fix his life, he went to the Bible. When he became coach of the Dallas Cowboys he also expected his players to follow its teachings as well as his own.

What Landry read in the Bible was that a person is born into the world a sinner, and then when he accepts Jesus as his savior, his original sin from Adam and sins built up from birth to the time of his acceptance of Christ are washed "white as snow" by the blood of Jesus. He is absolved of all those sins. After he is saved, Jesus then lives in his heart, and if he seeks guidance for any decision or action through prayer, he will be guided by "the still, small voice" of the Holy Spirit.

The problem comes when a person goes against that "still, small voice," when he knows what the right way is according to the Scripture and knowingly strays. Then, according to the Scriptures, that person has "transgressed," and he has to repent. And if he doesn't repent, he suffers the consequences of that transgression. Because he has had access to the Holy Spirit and the Scriptures, whatever happens to him after that as a result of his transgressions is his fault.

Landry, a Methodist, knew his Scriptures and lived by those rules. And when Landry devised his ingenious systems for defense, and his Multiple Offense, he instructed his players with a certainty that his systems would work. Tom Landry became like a pastor to his cleated congregation, a shepherd to his muscular flock. In the Christian tenet there is a chain of command, whether in family or in business or in football. As a good Christian, if you trust that chain of command, if you have that faith, then everything will work out. Tom Landry believed that all his players had to do was listen to him. They didn't have to think. All they had to do was trust him and do what he was telling them to do. The problems came when they would not do that, when they refused to accept his word. It became a terrible frustration for him.

The player who frustrated him the most was his young quarterback, Don Meredith. Meredith had been raised a Methodist, but upon his arrival in Dallas had turned his back on his small-town upbringing. For kids growing up in East Texas, Dallas was Mecca, the Big City, where the lights glowed brightly and life could be lived away from the domination of one's parents and the church. At SMU Meredith enrolled as a divinity student, but once he tried out his newfound freedom, he escaped from what he saw were the twin chains of abstinence and chastity that were tied to his rejection of the more encompassing institution: his religion.

Meredith questioned its tenets. He also rebelled against what he saw as its hypocritical nature. Meredith had seen firsthand that his Christian fundamentalist brethren in the South often projected racist and sexist attitudes. He could not understand how anyone who called himself a Christian could also have such strong hatred for blacks, Mexicans, and Jews. He saw how the southern Christian society used the Scriptures to justify slavery, citing the argument that the Creator had made Negroes to be servants of white men.

After the Civil War, when the rules creating segregation were laid down, these same southerners continued to use the Bible to advance the notion of the inferiority of Negroes, "proving," among other things, that mulattoes had crucified Christ. The great flood was even said to have come about because, during the time of Cain and Abel, there had been a mixing of the blood of Adam with that of a Negro.

For those who used the Bible to defend slavery and the segregationist system after the Civil War, there could be no opposition. Since Christ did not do away with slavery, the argument went, what he didn't change should remain in effect. The segregationists often cited St. Paul's warning to servants to obey their masters. Anyone who didn't believe in slavery was derided as godless.

In this fundamentalist Christian society, it was important that the Negroes act subservient at all times. In 1888 Senator James Eustis of Louisiana argued that Negroes might have the right to appeal the segregationist system were it not that "the unequal relations between the races had been fixed by divine law."

From every pulpit across the South, ministers of the Gospel warned against miscegenation, the mixing of the races, quoting Deuteronomy 22:10–11: "Thou shalt not plow with an ox and an ass together. Thou shalt not wear a garment of divers sorts, as of woolen and linen together"; and Joshua 23:12–13: "Else if you do in any wise go back, and cleave unto the remnant of these nations, even these that remain among you, and make marriages with them, and go in unto them, and they to you: know for a certainty that the Lord your God will no more drive out any of these nations from before you; but they shall be snares and traps unto you, and scourges in your sides, and thorns in your eyes, until you perish from off this good land which the Lord your God has given you."

Don Meredith all his life believed that on the playing field the best eleven players deserved to be out there, regardless of color. But race wasn't the only issue. Don Meredith intended to be the quarterback of his own life. Somebody had to be in charge of it, and he decided it would be himself. Meredith was not the sort of person to give up control of his life to anyone—not to Jesus, and not to Tom Landry. And Don Meredith believed that since you only go around once, a person should have as much fun as he possibly can.

And so, to Tom Landry, Don Meredith was not only a sinner, he was a "rebellious and stiff-necked person," like the Jews, who God was always killing off because of their "rebellious and stiff-necked ways."

Much to Tom Landry's chagrin, Don Meredith—"Jeff and Hazel's baby boy," as he would later call himself—turned out to be the reincarnation of Bobby Layne, Landry's old reprobate teammate. In fact, Meredith, who like Layne drank and partied hard and spent hours in the pursuit of Texas women despite having married the SMU homecoming queen, often paid Layne the highest tribute when he would say, "When I die, I want to come back as Bobby Layne's chauffeur."

If Landry would not forgive Layne, who was a teammate, for his profligacy, his wasting of his natural talent, Landry certainly would not accept this behavior from Meredith, one of his players. It was a tug-of-war between the two that was fought for nine long years.

Unlike Landry, who tried unsuccessfully to get Meredith to leave the party life behind and act serious like an adult, his teammates didn't give a damn about his private life. For most of them, Don's steady, obsessive regimen of hard liquor and women kept them from joining him socially, but they admired him greatly nevertheless. They loved his way of keeping them loose. When the team was getting clobbered, he would sing the words of some country-and-western song, and they would smile. For those players who disliked Tom Landry, but who nevertheless followed his orders because of their fear of him, they rooted for Don Meredith not to bow to the wishes of their martinet coach. Ballplayers play harder for a leader, an independent guy who thinks he knows best, who calls the shots and makes things happen. Everyone knew Don and Landry didn't get along because of the fundamental difference in their personalities. They saw this independent quality in the youngster.

And all his teammates also noticed that Don Meredith, more than anything else, was one tough Texan. Meredith was not mobile in the pocket, a dangerous characteristic when your line is as airy as Swiss cheese. Making the danger even greater for him, often times he chose to stand in there rather than run, hoping he could make something happen at the last moment. Too often the thing that happened was that he would take a severe beating. Still, he kept on getting back up.

BOB FRY: "Meredith was a real Texan, the perfect choice for the Cowboys. Every record he ever bought was cowboy music. Don Meredith was the toughest quarterback I ever played with. Don was unbelievable in the beatings he could take. I saw Don where he stood up, came back to the huddle and couldn't even talk, he got hit so hard. He had gotten the wind knocked out of him. He looked at me and whispered, 'Call the play.' I said, 'I'm going to get someone else in here.' He said, 'No, no, just call a play.' He was a tough, tough kid. That first year he had his ribs separated, his legs hurt, he had pulled muscles, broken ankles, a broken nose, dislocated fingers, and he kept on playing. Talk about a guy who had a lot of toughness. He was as tough as any quarterback I've been around. He was hurt by his party-boy image, but he needed that. It made him feel comfortable. I know that sounds crazy, but it's true. I'll tell you what, when you played with him you were playing against one tough son of a gun."

*   *   *

What his teammates didn't know was that he and his wife, Lynn, had split up, again, and his wife had ended up with custody of his daughter. Meredith's ulcers flared. He suffered terribly from the guilty feelings that the breakup had all been his fault, that he had brought it all upon himself. Meredith saw the brutal beatings he took on the football field each week as his just punishment, something that he felt he deserved.

Meredith would tell a reporter, "In a way I welcomed those beatings after losing a wife and daughter. It felt good."

EDDIE LeBARON: "Don is a very sensitive guy. You'd never think it, but he is. From the beginning Don and his wife were having trouble, and those things really bothered him. He put on this show of bravado, but his outside personality was different from his inside. He was a good guy, and a good leader.

"Don played with as much or more pain than anyone who has played the game. He's tall and thin, and he took a lot of blows. He'd stand in there tough, and he'd get hit, and he'd go out there and play. His way was to stand back in there tough and throw, 'cause that's what he had always done. He was a *tough* guy. He'd say, 'The hell with ya. I'm going to stand here and throw.' And he was long-legged and a real good athlete, could run pretty fast, but he didn't have a lot of quickness. Within the pocket he wasn't real quick. That's where he took more blows than he needed to.

"Don never got credit for that because he had this shoot-'em-up type of thing about him that the writers would write up, and that's all you'd read about. You wouldn't read about the guy who played when he was hurt and played well and kept the team's spirit up."

FRANK CLARKE: "I remember when Don and I first met in training camp. I pulled up in a taxicab and got out of the cab with my bags, and Don Meredith walked out of the dormitory, and he extended his hand, and he said, 'Hi, I'm Don Meredith, SMU.' And I said, 'Hi, Don, I'm Frank Clarke, University of Colorado, Cleveland Browns.' We always felt a closeness. I felt a nice connection. Don and I connected because we were both very sensitive people. That's the part of Don a lot of people didn't see. I don't think he was intentionally trying to hide that part of him. He was unskillful in manifesting that. He didn't know how to let it come out and blossom. My problem was the opposite. I didn't know how to hide my sensitivity. It was easily identified, and people used it against me.

"And I can remember in the early years the offensive line wasn't strong, and as a unit we weren't together. We didn't have confidence. We were just a bunch of guys. Sometimes when I would move into a slot position or play tight end, I had occasion to block linebackers in certain defenses, and sometimes I would go to sleep or totally miss a guy, and the guy would just cream Dandy, really smash him, and I would go back to the huddle, and Don would just look at me like, Frank, you sure let me down on that one. I'd say, 'God, Dandy, I'm sure sorry about that.' But Don wouldn't say anything.

"The highest grade I gave Don Meredith was for courage. Aw, man, I don't know how he did it. He used to play with the kind of pain I wouldn't have even gotten out of bed for, let alone put on a uniform. That first year he had broken bones, ribs, nose, blood everywhere, and he didn't have the strongest body in the world to begin with.

"Don was being asked to do a really awesome task, to know Tom Landry's system like Tom wanted him to. And in the beginning Don fought him. Don liked to drop back and throw the ball. But there was no question that Don knew—*everyone* knew—that if we just stayed with Landry's system, just hung in there long enough, that it was going to pay off. We *knew* that. We had enough of a taste in our mouth for it. Still, what astounded me was how much the quarterbacks were expected to know. I remember thinking, Man, ain't no way they pay these guys enough money."

After the pounding by the Rams, the Cowboys record was 0–7. The next opponent was the Green Bay Packers, led by coach Vince Lombardi and an all-star cast. This was only Lombardi's second season in Green Bay, and already the coach with the big grin and the loud bark was becoming a legend.

JOHN GONZAGA: "Before Lombardi, playing the Packers had been almost like having a day off. You'd show up, get some points, go home, and you didn't even get tired. With Lombardi, it was a different story."

GENE CRONIN: "We had a rough afternoon against the Packers. They had Lombardi, which is a plus for anybody, and they had the people. Before Lombardi came, they had Paul Hornung, Jim Taylor, Bart Starr, Hank Gremminger, but they weren't used the right way. Lombardi came, and he put it all together. His trademark was the Green Bay sweep. It's a play that was in everybody's playbook. Everybody ran it. But Vince Lombardi believed in the running game, and that was his bread-and-butter play, and they worked and worked and worked and worked on that. They lined up in the split formation to the wide side of the field, and you knew it was coming, and they ran it and still made yards because they had some darn good people running it. They had Paul Hornung carrying the ball, and Jim Taylor blocking on the end, and they had two guards, Fuzzy Thurston or Jerry Kramer, out front blocking. On that play Jim Taylor would come after me. He was a tough football player, an excellent blocker."

GENE BABB: "Green Bay had a machine. They really did. They were so methodical, so good at what they did. We practiced all week trying to stop the Green Bay sweep, but if you went one way, they went the other. They had the personnel for it. They were just something else."

Against the Cowboys, Jim Taylor ran for 121 yards and three touchdowns. The Pack dominated, 41–7, for loss number eight. The next game, against the San Francisco 49ers, brought a 26–14 loss on a cold and rainy afternoon in an almost empty Cotton Bowl. The next game was a 17–7 loss to the Chicago Bears, one of the better teams in the league. Don McIlhenny caught a 64-yard touchdown pass from Don Heinrich, and the defense played its best game. After the game McIlhenny went up to Tom Landry and told him that it was the first time he had felt the Cowboys were an NFL team. And yet, despite a fine effort, on the books it amounted to just another loss, the tenth in a row.

If Cowboys owner Clint Murchison was disappointed in his team, he never showed it. For all his millions, Clint was far from the stereotype of the conservative businessman as he was portrayed in business magazines. Clint had been forced into the life of the tycoon businessman by his father, and with his money Clint was determined to have as much fun as any red-blooded tycoon businessman could have. He loved to drink hard, party hard, and more than anything else, loved to have crazy, uninhibited, rowdy fun. He, partner Bedford Wynne, and his right-hand man, Robert Thompson, did the wildest things. Before the Bears game in Chicago, Clint had Larry Karl, the Cowboys PR man, rent a live bear along with an animal trainer. Karl then had the bear brought to the Sheraton Hotel. Murchison's idea was for the bear and a man wearing a cowboy suit to have a mock encounter in the lobby of the hotel at noon before the game. Newspaper photographers came for the photo op. The Cowboy shot the bear, and on cue, it fell over. What followed, the part that didn't get in the papers, was pure Clint Murchison.

The Cowboys owner had the bear driven up the freight elevator to his private party in his penthouse suite. Once there, Murchison and Thompson thought it amusing to give the bear beers. When the bear got drunk it proceeded to use its claws to pull all the curtains off the windows, rip the bedspread to pieces, and then urinate and defecate all over the floor.

The handler then passed out drunk. This was a problem, because by now the bear was out of control. Murchison's cronies rang for an elevator, and when it arrived, they pushed the bear inside. They then reached inside the car and pushed the L button for the lobby.

On the way down two elderly lady teachers from Tulsa, Oklahoma, pushed the button to stop the elevator. They were in Chicago for a convention. When the door opened, there was a huge drunk bear staring at them. Their screams were the last related part of the story, except that Murchison had a large bill to pay to cover the bear's damage.

Murchison, it turned out, was the only one in the Cowboys organization having very much fun at all. For many of the men on the Dallas team, by mid-November 1960, playing football for the Cowboys had become a struggle.

GENE CRONIN: "When you start losing the way we did, you don't know what the hell is going to work. And you have the tendency to blame everybody but yourself. You blame 'the system' or 'the other guy,' but never yourself. It's never your fault. It was like fighting a fifteen-round fight and losing every round. It was no damn fun, but you don't give up. You keep coming out for the next round."

JOHN GONZAGA: "It was frustrating at first, then you think, What the hell, the season is lost. Let's hope to God we all get a little more experience."

BOB FRY: "Our spirits were not that bad, because we knew we were a new club. What made it hard, we also knew we were older, so we wouldn't be there to see the fruits of the improvement. That's what made it hard."

DICK BIELSKI: "The losing became hard. It became a struggle. It becomes all the things that are unpleasant, because you are losing. What it's telling you is you're not good enough.

"It was hard for guys who had come from great situations and were used to winning. I can remember one time L. G. Dupre stood up and looked at all his teammates and said, 'What the fuck is going on?'"

For others, however, the losses were hard to take, but their morale continued to be good.

FRED CONE: "I wasn't demoralized. Jim Doran wasn't. Every game you went out and did the best you could, did everything we could to win."

GENE BABB: "We didn't like losing. We played hard. We were blown away by good teams, against people who had played together a long time, had good personnel who weren't learning a new system.

"With the Cowboys under Tom Landry's system, every week we got a new game plan, a new way to run the same play. Each week the blocking schemes would change, the formations would change. Some became exasperated. The core of the team came closer together."

The next game was to be played in Yankee Stadium against the New York Giants, a powerhouse. The Giant defense starred Andy Robustelli and Sam Huff, and on offense were a number of all-time Giant performers: Frank Gifford, Kyle Rote, and Alex Webster in the backfield. The quarterback, George Shaw, was subbing for an aging, banged-up Charlie Conerly, and that was a break for the Cowboys. But the Giants were still 13-point favorites.

On the flight from Dallas to New York, the team plane flew above the Statue of Liberty. Dick Bielski and Gene Babb called Byron Bradfute, who had only been as far east as Mississippi, to see it.

"What do you think of that?" the rookie Texan was asked.

"It looks just like the Bee County Courthouse," Bradfute replied.

On the bus from Newark Airport into New York, halfback Gene Babb recalled the intensity with which Tom Landry approached the Giant game.

GENE BABB: "We were on the bus the day before the Giant game, and Alicia, Tom's wife, went along on the trip. To give you an idea about Tom's ability to concentrate, we'd landed in Newark, and we were on the bus going to the Manhattan Hotel, and it was a city bus, and you had the long seats up at the front by the door, and Mike Dowdle and I were sitting across from Alicia and Tom, and as we were heading in, Alicia was just talking up a storm. Mike and I were sitting there, and you couldn't help but overhear. She said, 'Maybe this evening we can see so-and-so, and give so-and-so a call, and perhaps have dinner with so-and-so,' mentioning all these people they knew. Mike and I both looked at Tom, and of course Tom had his hat on, and he was looking straight ahead, and I don't know that he heard a word of what Alicia was saying, 'cause we both knew that he was already at the ballgame on Sunday. And that's just the way he was."

When the team arrived in New York, Byron Bradfute noticed a heightened excitement that emanated from the normally sphinxlike Tom Landry. This was his coach's former team, and Tom Landry wanted his new charges to put on a good show.

BYRON BRADFUTE: "Psychologically everybody wanted to beat them because Tom wanted to beat them. I've read where he said it didn't make that much difference, but I don't remember it that way. My perception was that he wanted to beat them real bad."

FRANK CLARKE: "Tom had a different air about him when we were getting ready to play the Giants. It wasn't so much a clamor. It was in his eyes. He would get us quiet, as though he had something to whisper to us, something he knew we would like to hear. And he would egg us to the end of our chair, and then he would say, 'Do you know that if you play well against the Giants, you are playing in front of the whole world? Because that's where the news mecca is, that's where everything starts. If you do well against the Giants, everybody is going to be seeing you and talking about you.' And that used to really get us."

When Tom Landry's name was announced over the public address system before the game, the huge Yankee Stadium crowd gave him a welcoming ovation. And when the Cowboys, led by three touchdowns by L. G. Dupre, two on receptions and one on a five-yard run, played the Giants even, a significant portion of the Giant rooters found themselves cheering the Cowboys.

With the Giants ahead by a touchdown, Giant running back Joe Morrison fumbled and the Cowboys' Bill Herchman recovered. Eddie LeBaron then took the Cowboys down the field, scoring the tying points on a touchdown to split end Billy Howton, who had starred for years in Green Bay and had been acquired from Cleveland. The touchdown gave the Cowboys a 31–31 tie, the team's first nonloss. Some of the players celebrated as though it had been a victory.

EDDIE LeBARON: "We started out the season pretty good, but we didn't win, and then we went to New York. Number one, we had practiced against New York's defense every day, because that was our defense. We knew it pretty well. We knew what they could do. And secondly, Tom had scouted the Giants beautifully. Also, we matched up pretty well against them. They had a great defense, but we just knew how to attack it, because that's what we did every day in practice. They used Tom's patented defense, a man-to-man defense with a free safety. Tom would tell us, 'If this guy steps this way, then it will be . . .' He knew the defense really well, so we could read it.

"We weren't going to run a lot against them, and we had to throw. Against the Giants—this was true even in the years I was with the Redskins—your wide receivers had a tough time, so you had to throw to the halfbacks, tight ends, the fullback in the flat. The tight end was important, and Dick Bielski caught a lot of balls, and the halfback was important, because they covered him with a linebacker, and I was able to hit L.G. for a couple of touchdowns. We were able to take it down the field, and our defense played well.

"I always got inspired playing in Yankee Stadium. I had some of my better games there. It wasn't a loss, so we were happy. Just to look halfway decent was more important than the wins or the losses at the time."

GENE CRONIN: "The Giants were as shocked at tying as we were. This was Gifford and Huff, Conerly and Tittle and Kyle Rote. They had some great players."

JERRY TUBBS: "We felt like we were the champions, though it's sort of silly to feel this good about having tied a game."

FRANK CLARKE: "It was like a victory, man. I loved it. And what I remember, it was so typical of New York fans, they were cheering for us. I suppose part of it had to do with Tom Landry coming from the Giants, and also it was an empathy thing: 'Wow, this might be the only game this team might not lose.' And the fans in New York were loving it. They were seeing a good football game, nothing sloppy. Both teams played really well."

The final game of the 1960 season took place in Detroit against the Lions. The game was played in the snow, and the Cowboys lost 23–14, to finish with a season record of 0–11–1. The game was marked by an uncharacteristic outburst by Tom Landry, who berated officials for allowing Eddie LeBaron to be roughed up by the Lion defenders. It was also a game in which rookie quarterback Don Meredith learned an important lesson.

DON MEREDITH: "Eddie had been playing well and I was dead certain he would go all the way, so the night before ol' Don decides to spend the entire evening introducing himself to the Motor City. That was the first time in my football career I had ever made a complete night of it. But, shoot, I wasn't worried. In fact, by the time the sun came up I wasn't even feeling the cold anymore.

"When I arrived in the clubhouse, Tom Landry told me I was starting against the Lions. I was sitting there with my pads on, my jersey, my socks and shoes, trying to figure out how I was going to make it through the day, when Nate Borden looked down at me and said, 'Boy, you are gonna need a lot of help today.' I told him, 'Hey, man, I'm ready.' Well, he started to laugh his head off and then said, 'Maybe it would be a good idea, then, to put your pants on before we go out. Which I understand we're going to do in just a very few minutes. It's a little cold today.'

"Then at the last minute Landry decided to start LeBaron. Don Heinrich and I sat on the bench smoking cigarettes. LeBaron started the second half, but then got his hand stepped on. They thought something might be broken, but he stayed in the game, as I kept throwing to keep my arm warm. I sat down again. In the fourth quarter Landry told me to warm up again. This time I told him I would not do it.

"I didn't play any football that day but I learned a couple of things. First, I found out that all-night partying is okay if you don't have to play a football game the next day.

"And it was on that afternoon that I first began to realize that Tom and I were going to really have a lot of fun together."

FRANK CLARKE: "The only thing you can say about the season was, 'Hey, who didn't expect this?' So there wasn't even anything to think about. We were glad the season was over with. It was going to be fun to get back to another way of living again. 'Cause even though football was nothing like what it is today, we were under a lot of pressure. It was the pressure that led me into smoking. After my rookie season with the Browns, I was with a friend, and I bought a pack of Salem cigarettes. I had never smoked, and for some reason, after the season I began smoking cigarettes like I had been smoking all my life. I smoked for thirty-one years. A lot of it was a direct response to the pressure we put ourselves through."

GENE CRONIN: "It was no damn fun. But I thought all along that Tom Landry would be successful. He was a dedicated man, smart about a lot of things, not only football. You knew he was going to persevere and succeed."

BYRON BRADFUTE: "We scored a lot of points that first year. A lot of folks do not realize that we came awfully close to beating some folks."

JERRY TUBBS: "We had a team party after the season, a lot of drinking, and Ray Mathews was loud and vocal blasting Tom."

BYRON BRADFUTE: "At the end of the season Ray Mathews made the mistake of telling Landry everything he did wrong, and that was the end of 'Pally.' I bought his car. He still owed $900 on it, and I bought it from him for $800. I gave him the money, he put $100 with it, handed me the title, and went home to Pittsburgh."

GENE BABB: "Those who were disgruntled didn't last long. Tom Landry had a plan and he intended to go a long way with it."

12

Big Bob and Hogmeat

It was hard to imagine that the 0–11–1 Cowboys could improve themselves in the '61 draft considering that they had traded their number one pick to the Washington Redskins to acquire quarterback Eddie LeBaron. But the Cowboys had a general manager of great cunning, a shrewd competitor who could not only ferret out a jewel in a competitor's slag heap, but could also find a way to get around the system and then take advantage. As a result, despite the team's inferior position in the draft, Tex Schramm was able to acquire for the Cowboys two of the finest defensive players in the history of the franchise, twenty-five-year-old linebacker Chuck Howley and twenty-two-year-old rookie defensive lineman Bob Lilly. In his second year with the Cowboys, middle linebacker Jerry Tubbs would have some help, and the defense would improve as it began to grow younger.

Howley, a five-sport letterman at the University of West Virginia, had been the number one draft choice of George Halas and the Chicago Bears in 1958, then in 1959 he tore up his knee and retired to run a service station back home in West Virginia. Don Healy, a defensive tackle who had come to the Cowboys from the Bears in the expansion draft, touted Howley to Tex Schramm. Howley had wanted to come back to football, but he wasn't the sort of guy to pick up the phone and ask George

Halas for a job. As a result, Schramm acquired Howley from the Bears, and Howley played outside linebacker for Dallas from 1961 through 1973.

At 6'4", 235 pounds, Howley, whom his teammates called "Hogmeat," had the agility of a big cat. He could outmuscle, outjump, and outrun just about anyone who came his way. He also had an uncanny instinct for playing defense. Many times Howley would ignore his assignment, roaming not where he was supposed to go but where he was sure the ball or ballcarrier would be. To the amazement of his teammates, most often he would be right, and as a result during his thirteen-year career, the six-time All-Pro often made the big play, blitzing to throw a runner for a loss, backpedalling and roaming to make an interception, or sniffing out the ball and recovering a fumble.

TEX SCHRAMM: "He was working in a gas station, and the Bears weren't that high on him, and we traded a song for him, and he turned out to be one of our greatest players."

CHUCK HOWLEY: "I lettered in five sports at the University of West Virginia. It was just the fact that I enjoyed not going to class. That last period of every day had to be taken up with the sport you were participating in, so I ended up going out for every sport throughout the school year. That's how in reality I became involved in so many sports. I lettered in football, track, swimming, wrestling, and gymnastics. I had participated in gymnastics back home with the YMCA. We did exhibitions at PTA meetings, did the trampoline, the tumbling routines, made it into a show group traveling throughout the state of West Virginia.

"Most tumblers are small and agile. I was big, 6'3", 200 pounds, and it was astounding I could do some of the things I was able to do. When you get bouncing around on a trampoline, you get fairly agile, and my gymnastics skills developed over the years and progressed and enabled me to do many things in football.

"When I went out for gymnastics at the university, the coach remarked, 'What's this big dumb guy going to be able to do?' He found out quickly enough, found out I could compete on the college level. I was also involved in diving in swim competitions. This also related back to the trampoline. I dove from the one-meter board in competition.

"I was a linebacker in college, and I ended up the number one draft choice of the Chicago Bears. I guess I was a little naive. Back when I was playing, I didn't even know what a college draft was. One of the assistant coaches in college, Bob Snyder, came in and said, 'Chuck, you were drafted number one by the Bears.' I said, 'Bob, what is that? I don't know.' He said, 'You're the number one draft choice in the National Football League.' I said, 'That's great, but I don't know anything about the National Football League. I'd like to play, but it's all new to me.'

"Bob and I flew to Chicago, and my first year I got $7,000. Remember, I was the number one draft choice. George Halas told me, 'If you get married'—which I was planning to do in June—'I'll give you $500.' Which he so diligently did.

"I enjoyed Halas. He founded the NFL. He was someone you could really enjoy, a very enthusiastic coach. He had a very strange vocabulary, but he was fair.

"I remember one incident up in Baltimore. We had played an exhibition game and had gotten our tails beaten pretty good up there, something like 52–7. That pony they had got tired running around in a circle after every touchdown. I was staying in Baltimore with one of the Colt players, so after the game we met at midfield, talking about how we'd get together, and I was trying to be cordial, and I guess I had a smile on my face, and the next thing I knew, I heard someone screaming and cussing, and I looked back, and all I heard was, 'I'll teach you to smile.' And I headed for the dressing room. George did not like to lose.

"His assistant coach, Clark Shaughnessy, was in charge of the defense, but it was middle linebacker Bill George's defense. It was blitz, blitz, blitz, and cut the receivers down before they got off the line of scrimmage. It worked very well for us, and we enjoyed it. It was a lot of fun to play that kind of defense.

"I got hurt in '59. I tore up my knee in practice. Clark came over to the sideline and said to Bill, 'I want you to take your defense and make George happy.' In Chicago, it was the offense against the defense. Each unit had a lot of pride. When we scrimmaged, the competition was serious. Back in those days the crackback block was legal. What you did was hit a player when he wasn't looking behind the knee area. A lot of knees got torn up as a result. A linebacker had to watch the wide receiver to make sure he didn't crack back on you. Well, we were scrimmaging, but they were kind of clowning around, not really cracking back, and on this one play, I didn't think he was going to go, so I ran across the line of scrimmage like I was supposed to do, and I hesitated for an instant, and he cracked back on me and tore up my knee. It never did get quite right the rest of the year, so I quit at the end of the '59 season. I had proved to myself I could play professional football, and Chicago gets very cold in the wintertime, so I thought I'd try my hand at business. I went back to Wheeling, West Virginia, and I bought myself a filling station and ran it prior to the Cowboys contacting me in '61.

"One night Don Healy, who had gone to the Cowboys in the expansion draft, called and asked me if I would be interested in playing again. I said, 'Yes. If Dallas ever got my contract, I'd be really interested.' I had been working, and I was wanting to get back into football. When a friend calls and asks a question, you answer him.

"Tex called and said, 'How would you like to play for the Cowboys?' I said, 'I would dearly enjoy it. You are at the bottom, and there is only one way for you to go, and that's up, so I'd like to be part of that.'

"He said, 'If we can get your contract.'

"I said, 'Tex, I believe you already have my contract, or you would not have called me.'

"He said, 'Well, how would you like to fly down here for the weekend?'

"My first contract from Mr. Schramm was $9,000. Which was an improvement. I went to St. Olaf's College, where they had their training camp, and that was the year they drafted Bob Lilly. My position was linebacker, and when I got there I felt I was a starter and so it was my position to lose. I was a first-year Cowboy, and Bob was a rookie, but we looked at each other like we were veterans. And a clique began to develop with us and Jerry Tubbs, Larry Stephens, and Nate Borden. We all kind of fell into our responsibilities.

"There is no doubt that we had a collection of everything. You had older players, who had a tendency to be stuck in their ways. I was still young, and I felt like a rookie, even though I had been in the league three years. With the Bears you tried to let instinct take care of you. With the Cowboys, Tom had a system we didn't know a whole lot about. Tom was trying to preach to us, 'Forget your instincts. Do what I tell you.' And we didn't want to believe that if the ball was going away from us, we shouldn't pursue it. Tom kept telling us to do what the defense told us to do, but it was very difficult building that confidence in his system. Most all defenses up to that time were pursuit defenses.

"In every defense you need containment, and being the corner linebacker, I learned real quick that a lot of times I had to stay at home. There are reverses, bootlegs, option plays that will cause you to become pretty embarrassed, so I had to learn the hard way how to fit into the system. At first I was reacting to instinct, but at the same time I was failing to believe in his defense. We were all failing to believe in the system itself. It took a while. One of the biggest things we learned and admired Coach Landry for: Once you become a believer, you will never do it any other way. You're not supposed to have the advantage on defense. The offense has the advantage because it has the snap count. But under Tom Landry's system, we would get that 'key' from the offensive player, and we would have the advantage back again. And after a while, the defensive linemen, the linebackers, the defensive backs, we all knew where we were going to be. We relied on each other, and we began to see that even if we had three guys coming at us, we were not under attack. If we did what we were supposed to do, we would have the support from either the defensive safety or the defensive end.

"Part of the reason it took us so long to gain confidence in his system was that my first year Tom didn't coach the defense. He had defensive coaches, and I guess you don't pay as much attention to the assistant coaches as you do the head man. When Tom was in meetings you paid attention. It wasn't until Tom started to flip-flop and coach the defense that he began to make believers out of us. What we absorbed with Tom in a meeting was a lot greater, because we didn't want to be embarrassed.

"When I came to camp, they handed us a playbook, a big fat thing two inches thick. Tom did his best to make us as responsible as coaches. He wanted us to know the responsibility of every man around us, and as the years progressed we learned that. I didn't dig in and study it out of the book as was his intention. When I got done with it, my playbook ended up being about ten sheets of paper! What related to me, that's what I concentrated on, and I think most of us did that, because it took so long for it to sink in. If we had been all straight A students—not that we were a bunch of dumb jocks—we'd have picked it up in a month and believed in it.

"Remember, we played football because we have hard heads."

The other new defensive standout, rookie Bob Lilly, had more to do with the later success of the Cowboys than anyone. He was the most physically talented defensive lineman ever to play football, so talented that Tom Landry would design an entire defensive system around him. Lilly's responsibility was to use his speed and quickness to beat his blocker and foil the play. Almost as often as not, he did that. Bob Lilly could foil an opposition's offensive plan all by himself. His teammate Walt Garrison once said of Lilly, "He was like some damn animal, like a wild lion out on the savannah in Africa. Just born that way. They put him on a football field and he'd just eat people alive."

Bob Lilly should never have been available when the Cowboys made their first choice in the second round of the 1961 draft. Lilly, who weighed in at 250 pounds on a 6'6" frame, was one of the quickest large men ever to play the game of football. At Texas Christian University, Lilly gained fame as a defensive lineman who could set up on the line, and at the snap of the ball jump like a flash into the backfield and get to the quarterback in almost the time it took the ball to get there. Schramm was able to get him because Lilly, who came from the small Texas town of Throckmorton, told everyone and anyone who asked him that he would play pro ball only in Texas. In any other era, a club could ignore such a demand, but in 1961 the NFL was competing for players with the American Football League, and Lilly had been drafted by the Dallas Texans. The other NFL teams were afraid that if they drafted Lilly, he would make good on his threat to play only with a Texas team and sign with the AFL. The one hope the NFL had to keep Lilly in the league was if he signed with the one Texas team in the NFL: the Dallas Cowboys. And so when it was Dallas's turn to make its first pick in the second round, the hulking Bob Lilly was still unplucked. Tex Schramm, who very well knew how lucky he was, quickly took this man-child.

Like a lot of players from his generation, Bob Lilly fought his way up from hard times. After a drought baked West Texas for a half decade, in 1956 Lilly's dad was forced to quit the farm and Texas as well, moving the family to find a job near relatives in Pendleton, Oregon. Lilly played his senior year for a Portland high school, then returned to Texas to go to Texas Christian University, where he became an All-America. Because of his insistence on playing pro ball in Texas, he anchored the Cowboys' defensive line for fourteen glorious seasons. Before he was through, Lilly would be rated the finest defensive tackle ever to play the game.

Because Lilly was left-handed, Tom Landry initially placed Lilly at left defensive end, a position ill-suited to his talents. Ends have to run long distances to chase down ballcarriers, and Lilly did not have long-range speed. On many plays, his job was merely to watch and make sure the play did not come back in his direction. Lilly was adequate at end, but uninspired. The first two years of Lilly's career were a nightmare for him. He was so talented that despite playing out of position and despite a hurt knee, two sprained ankles, a broken thumb, a broken wrist, and five broken ribs, his first year he was named to the All-Rookie team. Nevertheless, during practice he would become so frustrated he would start smacking the offensive linemen around. He felt so overmatched that he considered quitting.

BOB LILLY: "I grew up in a small town, Throckmorton, Texas. Starting in the first grade, I was always a head taller than everybody else. I was bigger and I was faster than the little guys. We used to have wars where you put a guy on your shoulder, and you fought each other, and I was always the horse, with a guy sitting on my shoulder. I remember when I was very young, they would tease me, because I was so big. They teased me a lot, called me 'Big Bully,' or 'You big baby,' and then they'd run from me. By the third grade, I could catch them, so they quit calling me names.

"My father had broken his femur as a boy, and back in those days they didn't know how to stretch the leg with weights, so he was crippled, had a big limp, had to put two inches on the sole of his right shoe, so he could never participate, so he promoted me. I took his place, and he was my biggest fan. He loved all sports, and he started taking me when I was eight or nine. That's when I saw TCU play, because his hero was Sammy Baugh, and Sammy Baugh grew up thirty miles from Throckmorton. As a freshman in high school, we had a get-together that we held in the library, and Sammy Baugh came and spoke.

"And so I always dreamed of being a football player. Texas football was a big deal. Back in those days we didn't have television, and everybody would turn out for a high school football game. That was recreation for people. And it was wonderful. We've lost a lot of that. They turn out for Little League, but not for the whole town any more.

"By the eighth grade I was 6'3", weighed 155 pounds. I was pretty skinny. I was better at basketball than football because of my height, but then I began to fill out and by the time I was a sophomore in high school, I weighed 195, and by the time I was a senior I weighed 230 during the football season.

"Throckmorton wasn't too good because we played in the Class 1A division. All the towns had from 2,000 to 3,500 students, and we only had 1,300, which put us at a disadvantage. We'd win six or seven games a year, which wasn't bad. After I left, they went down to B division and went to the finals every year.

"Then my senior year in high school, our family moved to Pendleton, Oregon. We had had a drought in Texas that lasted seven years. It started in '51 and went through '57. My father owned bulldozers and hay balers. I was a hay-baling guy, and my dad had men to run the bulldozers to build cattle ponds and roads and to clear the mesquite, which is a nuisance. But when no one had any money and were starving to death, or when the money had to be spent to feed the cattle, we moved to Oregon, where we had kinfolks, and they found my dad a job. So I played my senior year in Pendleton, which was the equivalent of a 4A school in Texas. I noticed that the competition was a little stiffer, and that the heat wasn't as bad as it was in Texas.

"I really enjoyed my year in Oregon. My senior year I got more scholarship offers in basketball than I did in football, got a lot of offers, many from colleges in that area and as far down as California. But I wanted to go to TCU, because that's where my father had taken me as a child. The drought ended a year after we moved, and my parents went back to Throckmorton in '57. I wanted to be back there with them.

"We had good teams at TCU. We won our conference my first year, tied for it my junior year. My senior year we were 4-4-2. Texas beat us, 5–2. We lost to Arkansas by a point. We had a good team, but it wasn't quite good enough.

"I made All-America my senior year. The real interesting thing for me that year was that the Dallas Cowboys and the Dallas Texans came into existence. I went to Stanford University to play in the East-West Shrine Game. All the scouts were out there. They were trying to sign you to a contract. This was prior to the draft. They had a lot of money to pass around, flashing $100 bills, a lot of money. They were doing this with all the players.

"A lot of players would sign a contract, and then if that team drafted them, it was a valid contract. I told all the teams I wanted to play in Dallas with the Cowboys. I always wanted to play with an NFL team because that's all I ever watched on TV. I knew that Coach Landry was from Texas and had been coaching with Vince Lombardi. I just kind of wanted to play under him. I told all the teams I wanted to play with the Dallas Cowboys. And I said that if I didn't get drafted by the Cowboys, I wanted to play for the Dallas Texans.

"The Cleveland Browns and the Dallas Texans were putting so much pressure on me, I had to hide. I didn't have any money at all, and it was hard to resist the money. E. J. Holub and I roomed together. We were in the dorm working out for the Shrine Game, and the scouts would come and show you two or three thousand bucks. It was yours if you'd sign a precontract. I mean, it was *very* difficult to resist that, but I just knew I wanted to sign with the Dallas Cowboys and didn't want to go anywhere else. That I wanted to stay in Texas was partly because I was a little bit timid. I grew up there in Texas, and I didn't know much about other places. E.J. was also drafted by the Cowboys, but he ended up signing with the Dallas Texans.

"I knew the Cowboys hadn't won a game in '60, but it didn't bother me a lot because I knew they were a new team. I hadn't been in the pros, so I didn't realize how hard it was to build a team from scratch. Landry was pretty lucky the first year 'cause he got Don Meredith and Don Perkins, and my first year we got Chuck Howley. I don't know how we got him, but I do remember he had torn his knee up, ran a service station, and the Cowboys got him from the Bears, and I can recall Chuck had a big scar on his knee.

"So there he was when I arrived for training camp, and Jerry Tubbs was there, and so we had a little bitty nucleus of good football players. Between Tubbs and Howley, they made about 80 percent of the tackles for a couple of years there.

"I went to St. Olaf College in Northfield, Minnesota, for training camp. That was a beautiful campus, except you had to walk down 386 steps—I counted them—to get from the dorm to the playing field, plus I was on the third floor of the dorm.

"When I returned from practice for the College All-Star game, I noticed that some of the older veterans were bitching all the time. They made fun of Landry. They were almost as old as he was, and they made fun of his new system because they had come from other systems, and this hampered his building a team in those early years. We could have done it faster if he had just gotten all new guys. And looking back, I suppose he was getting rid of guys as fast as he could. But the bickering caused us to have doubts about the system, too, just because the veterans had been in other places, and I didn't know. I admired Coach Landry, but I wasn't going to sit down with him on a first-name basis and talk to him. I was in awe of him really. And yet, here were these older players talking about 'rinky-dink' this, and how 'stupid' that was, and that destroys your confidence a little bit.

"We played a 4–3 defense, and I was playing defensive end the first two years. The playbook called for me to 'read' my man, and I had never done that. I had always just reacted. And my first couple years half the time I would run toward the quarterback, and he would bootleg and go the other way, and I'd be standing there as he was throwing a touchdown. Or I'd be rushing in as fast as I could, and they would pull a reverse on me. I finally learned that if somebody was letting me get in real easy, something was wrong, that it was going to be a screen or something tricky.

"Coach Landry wanted me to 'key' the tackle and guard, but I also had to look at the fullback if he was lined up in a certain position. And I couldn't do all that. I just wasn't used to it. It would take a few years before I learned to do those things.

"In some systems, you can be productive in your first or second year.

But under Coach Landry's system, you had to be thinking all the time, and I was never sure what I was doing, and I wasn't real productive. Basically, I was just lost those first two years.

"I can remember early in my career playing against Jim Parker of the Colts. I was 260 pounds, and he worked me over, and I remember thinking, 'If this is pro ball, I don't know if I'm going to make it.' A guy named Charlie Bradshaw from Baylor played for Pittsburgh and worked me over. Roosevelt Brown with the Giants was another one. They were all clean, good football players, but I was very inexperienced, didn't have any kind of pass rush technique, and they just played with me. They would fake me, and I'd start to hit them, and then they'd block down on the guard, and the guard would cross block on me, and I'd be ready to hit the tackle, and all of a sudden I'd get hit from another angle. Or they would set me up for a screen, drag me back, drag me back, and finally I'd get in, and they'd release, and I couldn't stop my momentum, and the ball would zip right over my head. Or they would draw me back, and the quarterback would fake a handoff, and I'd go after the ballcarrier, and the quarterback would roll around me. Did I mention draw plays? Those were the things they'd pull on me.

"Chuck Howley came up with me. He was in his own world. Chuck didn't really say much. He was *very* quiet. But Chuck was so good, he could run with the wide receivers or with the backs. He ran a 9.4 hundred! Chuck was so good he just played on instinct as much as he played within the system. He was *always* in the right place. I mean, Chuck had that sixth sense, and he had a little bit more freedom than Jerry Tubbs, because he was playing on the outside. He could see things. The linebackers could see more than we could on the line. As a lineman, we get a feel from what's going on, from the split of the backs or the way the center is tilted, and I'm sure outside linebackers have the same feel, the sense that 'this guy is fixing to take off on me,' or 'he's going to try to block me,' and sometimes you have to make arbitrary decisions. You just have to make them, and they may not be within the system. It's like Landry used to tell me, 'Bob, I'm going to give you a little more freedom than I do the rest of these guys, but you better make the play.' And I'm sure Howley had the same thing, 'cause he was such a gifted athlete. But Howley played *within* Landry's system. He was not against it by any means. It's just he was so good, he would do things at times that weren't within the realm of our defense.

"I felt sorry for Jerry Tubbs those first couple of years, when we didn't have much. He had two, three guys, especially me, who weren't doing their jobs, and he'd have to cover for all of us, plus his own responsibilities. Jerry helped us as much as he could, and he was hurt himself, playing with a bad back, bad knees, and yet he would make 20 to 30 tackles a game. He was the only one who could catch them. When I'd forget to close off my man, Jerry would give me some fatherly advice. He'd bark at me, 'Lilly, close the trap. You're going to get me killed.' I'd say, 'Jerry, I'm sorry.' And I was. I felt bad.

"My first year I hurt my knee, sprained both ankles, broke my thumb, broke a wrist, and cracked some ribs. They weren't totally broken. The worst thing was my knee. I had never been hurt, and I wouldn't have been hurt then except my own man shoved me. Against Minnesota we were playing on the field where the baseball team also played, and we were going down on a punt return, and I was just fixing to get ready to make the hit when a teammate behind me got hit and ricocheted, and out of a reflex shoved me, and when he did, I went up in the air and I came down on the pitcher's mound, where it was hard, right on the point of my knee, and it tore the cruciates a little bit. The knee swelled up.

"We only had four defensive linemen left, and me. I wasn't supposed to play the next week, but the coach told me I had to play, so they taped my leg stiff and I went out and played. And it was a good lesson. I limped through it, got killed out there, but I played the whole game. And in a couple weeks it quit hurting.

"At the same time my thumb had broken and gone through the skin just a little, and they put it in a cast, and every week I broke it again. My arm was made relatively useless. That was my best arm, the one I used to grab somebody, and then my ribs hurt but they put pads there and it didn't bother me too much.

"And they use novocaine, too. They shoot you to kill the pain. And you went out there, and it would wear off, and that was a problem, but you at least got out there and played.

"Luckily playing defensive end, you don't get hit near as much as you do at tackle or middle linebacker. The tackles and middle linebacker get hit every play, just like a running back. So at defensive end, a lot of times you don't get hit hard. The offensive linemen are just shielding you off plays that are going away, and on those plays you are responsible just to make sure they don't come back on a reverse—things I didn't do very well—but about half the time, you don't get a hard knock. So it wasn't quite as bad as it sounds.

"But most of the time when I got hurt, it was by my own man. It was always my own man who creamed me, because over a few years as a football player you develop a sense of seeing other colors. You just don't pay attention to your own man, and that's usually when you get hurt.

"Coach Landry knew an injury was going to affect the way you played, but he wasn't sympathetic about being hurt. I think part of the reason for that was that we only had 35 players in those early two or three years. There just weren't any replacements, so that's why he wasn't very sympathetic. He always said, 'The mark of a pro is if you can play hurt.' He said, 'Everybody gets hurt. If you can't play hurt, you can't play in the NFL.' So that's really the way it was. You just accepted the pain.

"As I said, the problem my first year was that even though we had some pretty good football players, we weren't all on the same page. A lot of them were playing their old way, and a lot of them like me didn't know what page they were on. All I remember was that the guys were always talking, 'We shouldn't be doing this. We should be doing that.' And then in the game there would be a lot of bitching in the huddle. Tubbs had to shut everybody up, because they were all griping at each other, blaming each other. Half the time they were bitching about me, and I didn't blame them. That was a humbling experience, playing defensive end in pro football without ever having played it before. I just didn't fit. Those two years I hated football. I could not stand being out there at the end. I wanted to be in the middle of things. When you're the end, you're never free to really go out there. You can't pursue, because you're waiting for a fake or a lateral, a rollout, a keeper, a reverse, or a screen play. And so you're always sitting out there, watching. And half the time you don't even get hit. They're just screening you off. I *hated* it, and if I had continued at end, I probably wouldn't have played much longer. In fact, he probably would have gotten rid of me."

Commensurate with the influx of new blood was the excising of some of the old. Kicker Fred Cone, now thirty-four, quit to take a job recruiting for his alma mater, Clemson University. Quarterback Don Heinrich, twenty-eight, unused and frustrated, packed it in. He was replaced in the '62 draft by 6'5" TCU quarterback Sonny Gibbs. LeBaron, quietly sensitive about the many references to his 5'6" height and the constant wonderment that his lack of height should have disqualified him from being able to play in the NFL, was master of ceremonies at a banquet at which the gangly Gibbs was also a guest. While introducing the young quarterback, LeBaron publicly asked him, "Sonny, did it ever occur to you that you're *too tall* to play quarterback in the NFL?" Gibbs, unsure what LeBaron was referring to, said, "Huh?" It got a good laugh. Gibbs never made it with the Cowboys.

Disgruntled lineman Gene Cronin found himself traded to the Washington Redskins. Another lineman, John Gonzaga, reported to training camp at St. Olaf's angry at having to play another season with an expansion team. Then the hot weather, the rain at night, and the mugginess, combined with Tom Landry's killer workouts, finally made him snap.

JOHN GONZAGA: "I thought about it one night, and the next morning at breakfast I went to see Tom Landry and told him he had ten days to get me out of there, because 'I consider myself a Cowboy no longer.'

"After about four days, I asked him if he had anything going for me. He said, 'I was kind of hoping you'd change your mind.' I said, 'I have. I'm not going to wait the ten days. I'm leaving now.' I was going back home to go to work. As far as I was concerned at that point, football was over.

"The Cowboys took me to the airport, and at the airport I was paged. I got to the phone, and it was E. J. Anderson from the Detroit Lions. He told me that he owned me. I enjoyed five years more than I even dreamed I could."

The return to health of halfback Don Perkins caused Landry to make a couple of personnel shifts. Landry informed the incumbent, Don McIlhenny, that to stay on the team he had to gain some weight and play fullback. Two games into the preseason Landry informed him he was too slow to play fullback. "But you're the one who told me to gain the weight," said McIlhenny. No matter. The veteran back was dispatched to the San Francisco 49ers. Another back, Gene Babb, was switched from offense to defense, where he was installed as a linebacker. Another player might have balked. Babb didn't care. He just wanted to play football.

GENE BABB: "Now I'm over there trying to learn the Landry defense, and that's no easy chore. I'd played both ways in college. Back then things were different than they are today. Back then it was 'Yes, sir,' and 'No, sir.' This day in time it's 'Why?' and 'What for?' It's a different outlook. I just wanted to play. I loved to play. The money wasn't the thing. The tail wasn't trying to wag the dog. Since I had played linebacker before, it wasn't a big change for me to move over. They had an opportunity for me, and I took it. I really never ever gave it a second thought."

*   *   *

With such additions as Lilly, Howley, and Don Perkins, the other players felt encouraged because of the injection of talented new blood and because after a full season, they were more organized as a team. But many of the players, especially the veteran defenders, continued to buck the way Landry wanted things done, and there was some consternation when Lilly began fighting with Tom as well.

JERRY TUBBS: "In those early years Lilly really got frustrated. Lilly was a griper. For a lot of years he complained. A lot of players do. Nothing wrong with that if they perform. And boy, was Bob talented. But Bob griped about anything and everybody. Part of it had to do with Tom's system and his relationship with Tom. Lilly knew he had great natural ability, and sometimes he would want to do something different from what Tom wanted him to do. He always liked it in a passing situation when he didn't have to worry about the run. But he'd get frustrated against the run. He'd say to himself, 'I can trap the quarterback.' Lilly *knew* what he could do. But Tom wanted him to hold his ground. And so he felt held back by the system. And this was also true when he was later moved to tackle.

"Bob Lilly was our superstar for so long. They would have two or three guys blocking him. It was unbelievable how he could beat one man every time. He was the best player we've ever had, and we've had some great ones."

If many of the players continued to resist doing what Landry asked of them, there were also a few conversions to his way of thinking. Wide receiver Frank Clarke was one.

FRANK CLARKE: "I had been in the league four years and I still had no idea what was going on. I still had no confidence in myself in being able to visualize myself as a respected pass catcher.

"We were in Fresno, getting ready to play a preseason game against the 49ers. This was the afternoon before a Saturday night game. Tom Landry said, 'Frank, come to my motel room. I want to talk with you.' Of course, when you hear that in preseason you get a little nervous, a lot nervous. Anyway, I swallowed hard three or four times, and I went down to his room. He sat down, and right away I sensed that this would be an okay time.

"He said, 'Frank, as you know, I'm going to handle the offense this year, and I want you to know that you're at a place right now where I want you to make this team, and I think you can be extremely good, but you're going to have to start showing me some things that you haven't been showing me. I want you to do well, but because of where we are timewise, I need to know who I can count on to take me into the regular season. You need to start producing, starting now.'

"That was all he wanted to say. Nothing else. But I knew what he was saying. 'Cause I knew me. I knew I was one of the most frustrating players a coach could ever have, because I had all this physical equipment and it wasn't being used to its fullest, so I knew what he was talking about.

"Well, I went out in that game, and I did some things that just blew me away. I remember a slant across the middle, and when a wide receiver goes across the middle, that's when all those big hungry linebackers wait to decapitate you and tear you up. Well, Meredith threw me a pass that was way high. I had to leave the ground, and when you leave the ground, you have to stretch your arms up in the air, leaving your ribs exposed. When the ball hit my hand, I felt as if three linebackers hit me simultaneously. I really, really felt it. I heard this incredible impact, and to my amazement, I held onto the ball. I still remember hearing one of the defensive players say, 'Damn, he held onto it.' And from then on, there was a difference in the way Tom Landry saw me.

"But that seed was planted in his room in Fresno. Tom was making it clear to me, and it wasn't just me. He was doing this with other players. He was saying, 'I know what I want to do, and I believe you are a player who can help me do it, but I just want you to know that I'm counting on you, and if you don't do the job, you've got to go.'

"And in '61 we started playing football with a different kind of intensity. As early as '61, because this whole thing was starting to take shape. We were starting to believe more in Tom as a leader. 'Maybe this guy knows what he's talking about.' Tom was saying, 'If we're going to play football, why not play to win?' We were waking up to that.

"There was a newness, an intensity that was starting to be ignited in us."

For that rare player who allowed himself to get to know Tom Landry a little better, what he began to see was the warmth behind the cool facade.

GENE BABB: "That second year we were up in Northfield, Minnesota, had our training camp up there, and we're getting ready to break camp and play the Salesmanship Club game against the Green Bay Packers in Dallas. We finished our practice that morning in Minnesota. We went in, and I was hustling everybody through the showers, telling everybody, 'Hurry up, we gotta get to Dallas. My little boy is going to be born.' About that time Tom came wandering through the showers, and he said, 'What did you say?' I said, 'Coach, we gotta get on this plane and get home. My little boy is going to be born.'

"He said, 'You don't want a little boy.'

"I said, 'What do you mean, I don't want a little boy?'

"He said, 'Nah, you want a daddy's baby.'

"I said, 'Come on, Coach, don't give me that.'

"He said, 'You'll know what I mean one of these days.'

"So we arrived in Dallas, and we had a workout, and the night before the Green Bay game the team stayed at the Ramada Inn out by Love Field. Because my wife, Gerry, was pregnant and so close, Tom allowed Gerry to stay with me, got me a room by myself, allowed Gerry to stay out there with me.

"About ten that night, her water broke. So we went to Baylor Hospital, and we were over there all night, and the next morning at 10:31 A.M., on the eleventh of August, my daughter, Tracy, was born.

"Well, about four o'clock that afternoon, they're having the pregame meal. I had waited around to see Gerry and the baby. I got back out to the Ramada just in time to go in and jump on the training table to get my ankles taped, and on the way out there I picked up a box of Dutch Masters cigars.

"I was sitting on the training table getting my ankles taped, when Tom came in. He came over and said, 'Well, what did you have?' I thrust that box of cigars out there, and offered him one, and he picked one up, and they all had 'It's a girl!' on it. And I kind of smiled. I said, 'I had a daddy's baby.'

"So we suited up and went to the stadium. I didn't get to play much that night against Green Bay. Tom knew I had other things on my mind."

The season began against the Pittsburgh Steelers. Don Meredith started, and he was playing well until he threw a pass that Johnny Sample intercepted and ran back 39 yards for a touchdown to give the Steelers a 24–17 lead. When Tom Landry substituted Eddie LeBaron, Meredith joked with a couple of players on the bench, went to sit by himself, and cried.

With 56 seconds left in the game Eddie LeBaron capped a 75-yard drive by throwing a 17-yard touchdown pass to tight end Dick Bielski. Linebacker Jerry Tubbs then intercepted a Bobby Layne pass on the Cowboy 38. There were five seconds left in the game.

LeBaron threw a long pass down the left sideline to Billy Howton, who ran out of bounds on the Pittsburgh 22.

EDDIE LEBARON: "Billy was a *great* end. He wanted the ball *all* the time. The only trouble I had with him was that he'd say, 'I can get behind him,' when he was reaching the age were he wasn't getting behind them nearly as well as he could cut in front of them. But he was still a really good receiver.

"On that play I had to run out of the pocket to the left, and then he broke it off and got behind the corner and underneath the safety, and I threw about a 40-yard pass. He didn't score, but it gave Allen Green the chance to kick a field goal to win it."

One second remained. Green, a graduate of Ole Miss, had missed two field goals and had had a punt blocked that led to a Steeler touchdown. When he came into the game for the final time, the Cotton Bowl crowd roundly booed him.

ALLEN GREEN: "I had definitely not had a good day. Big Daddy Lipscomb had been putting tremendous pressure on me all afternoon, blocking one and forcing me to rush all afternoon. I was getting pretty roundly booed every time I came off the field."

He managed to kick himself into the record books with a straight and true 27-yarder. Tom Landry and his Cowboys had gotten the monkey off their backs.

ALLEN GREEN: "It was a great feeling to come off the field that day knowing I had made a contribution to the first regular-season win in the team's history."

It was to be Green's one and only season with the Cowboys. The second time they played the Steelers, a defender hit him during a punting attempt and chipped his anklebone. Eddie LeBaron had to replace him as punter. In the off-season Green was traded to the Packers.

The second game was against the second expansion team, the Minnesota Vikings, coached by Norm Van Brocklin and led by a young University of Georgia quarterback, Fran Tarkenton. The Cowboys won again, this time by the score of 21–7. The defense was effective, and on offense the star of the game was Don Perkins, who ran for 108 yards on 17 carries. He also caught five passes for 61 yards. From the start, Perkins's impression was a lasting one.

BOB FRY: "Don Perkins was a great football player. Perk was as smart as any back I've been around. He knew his assignments, knew what he had to do, knew how to do it. Ermal Allen, the coach who ran the offense, would ask something, and even though he was only a rookie, Perk would be the one to ask, 'Is this how you want me to pick it up?' Or, 'Do you want me to do it this way?' He was right into it. He picked up Landry's system. So he was a leader among the backs even as a rookie."

DON PERKINS: "When I came to Dallas I can't say that I was overwhelmed by Tom's system. At every level of competition it gets a little more challenging, and as a running back, you have to instinctively find things, and you better find them quick. I don't have a feel for how different or complex his system was. This was my first year playing at that level. You go in, take your shot, and see what happens.

"I thought Tom was very thorough, very patient, a professional. He was not emotional. He didn't feel it was his job to be a cheerleader. He prepared you, and you played. His attitude was, 'I've got my job, you've got yours. Let's go do them.' I thought it was cool. I didn't need anybody to wind me up. I knew what my job was. And my first year, there may have been a whole country believing we couldn't win, and for the most part, we didn't, but I don't think we ever went into a game thinking we could not win. How could I possibly critique what was going on in the offensive or defensive line, or anyplace else? I had enough of a job as a young person trying to hold down a running back slot."

In the third game of '61 Cleveland dominated, 25–7, but the next weekend the Cowboys shut out the expansion Vikings in their second meeting, 28–0, as the defensive line sparkled. In this game Tom Landry inaugurated a system of shuttling quarterbacks in and out, a system that has raised the hackles of his field generals over the years. In this case, his veteran, Eddie LeBaron, the good soldier, accepted the arrangement. The young kid, Don Meredith, hated it.

EDDIE LeBARON: "I thought it was a pretty good deal. I thought the system was very good. And it was interesting. If you were the first- and third-down quarterback, you got to throw a lot. If you were the second-down quarterback, you didn't.

"Normally I was the first-down quarterback, but it varied as time went on. See, if you make a first down on the first play, then the other guy became the first-down quarterback. I remember one game against the Redskins, and the first half I think I went 0 for 7, and then I was 10 for 10 the second half, with real good statistics, but they were completely different because of which down I played.

"What I liked about the system was that when you came off the field, you really got a chance to sit and talk about the next play with Tom. He would say, 'What are they doing when this happens?' You'd say, 'The safety is moving over.' He'd say, 'Let's try this,' or 'Let's try that,' or if you had a good suggestion, he'd say, 'Fine, go ahead.'

"You had time to think about all the ramifications by the time you got back out onto the field. I really liked the system.

"I know Don didn't like it. He was young, and he felt he wanted to be in there all the time. I don't blame him, but . . . all I know was that in one game against the Steelers in which we were alternating, I threw five touchdown passes. It wasn't something you could not have a good day in."

DON MEREDITH: "What I didn't realize then was that all along Tom knew what he wanted. It must have been tough for him, because he received so much criticism the way he did things, but he never altered.

"In '61 I really wasn't impressed with anything. I became rebellious and antagonistic about the whole situation. I really thought Tom was wrong, and it became sort of a personal thing, which is the worst thing which could have happened to me. I wasn't hurting him, just myself."

In the blowout against the Vikings, Don Perkins scored on a short run, and Frank Clarke showed Tom Landry something with touchdown catches of 16 yards from Eddie LeBaron and 52 yards from Don Meredith. Clarke, finally, was beginning to live up to his potential.

EDDIE LeBARON: "When Frank came, he hadn't played a lot at Cleveland. And he had a bum rap on him: They said he couldn't catch the ball across the middle.

"I used to work with him all the time, because he was really a talented guy, and he loved to stay out after and work, catch the ball, and we spent a lot of time together. We practiced a lot, worked out our own routes together. On a pattern I might tell him to run a 'Zig-in,' or a 'Zig-out,' which might be different from a regular pattern. When he first started, he had good soft hands, but he didn't always watch the ball. I think part of any rap he might have had, he just didn't watch the ball closely. As time went on, he really became a great receiver. He was a very durable player. He never got hurt, and he had that great speed, and he was a great guy to work with."

FRANK CLARKE: "I wasn't bothered by Tom's shuttling Eddie and Don in and out. I had faith in whatever Tom wanted to do, and I do think I was in the majority on the offense. My confidence was in him. I found myself surrendering to him, surrendering to this man who had won with the Giants, who was telling us in so many words, 'Guys, if you just listen to me and do it, we're going places.' He was telling us, 'Don't think. Do it.'

"In Christianity, you have to surrender to Jesus. In some way, Landry, who was a devout Christian, was saying to his players, 'In order for us to succeed, you have to surrender to me.' Today my surrender to Jesus is the pillar, the whole basis for my existence now, to surrender to that divine power. And Tom, he exuded his own surrender to Christ. He couldn't say that, but man, he was totally devoted to Him. And a lot of players who had respect for Tom, this is what they saw in him. They saw that this guy was this epitomized example of surrender to Jesus. And here Tom was saying, 'Surrender to me.' And I did.

"And it was not until he got the entire team to surrender to him that we could win a championship. It was at that point we got to where we said, 'Oh yeah, now we know what it's *all* about.' 'We saw the whole picture.' That's when we started winning.

"I still have a lot of respect for everything that Tom did, the way he connected himself with his family, and the way he used his spiritual life to buoy him through a lot of hard times. He really impressed me with his ability as a young man—because he *was* a pretty young man. He seemed to have this plan in his head. They call a person like that a 'visionary.' He was able to *see* something, and also to teach it to us."

After three early wins in '61, the Cowboys' bubble burst with a 31–10 drubbing by the New York Giants before 42,000 fans in the Cotton Bowl. The home crowd was substantial, because Dallas fans believed the team had turned the corner. But the early start had been illusory, and the lopsided loss disappointed a lot of them.

TEX SCHRAMM: "We had won a couple of games, and people got a little interested, and we had 42,000 people, and we got the hell kicked out of us, and the next home game we had 16,000. We hadn't become established."

The Cowboys had toyed with their fans' emotions, not for the last time, as once again Sam Huff toyed with Don Meredith.

FRANK CLARKE: "Sam Huff was playing middle linebacker. What would happen, Meredith would call an audible, and the Giants wouldn't move. And at one point Meredith even looked at Sam Huff, and moved his head, like he was telling Sam, 'You're supposed to move over this way.' He nodded his head toward his right shoulder as if to say, 'Tom Landry told us, Sam, that when you saw this formation, you were going to move over there, so damnit, get over there!' "

After a 43–7 demolition by Sonny Jurgensen and the Philadelphia Eagles, the Cowboys flew to New York where, before 60,000 Giant fans in Yankee Stadium, they defeated an excellent Giant team, 17–16. Once again an Allen Green field goal won it. And after that the game wasn't in hand until Don Healy stopped a final Giant drive by intercepting a Y. A. Tittle pass.

It was a joyous triumph for Tom Landry, who was uncharacteristically whooping and hollering in the locker room after the game. At 4 wins and 3 losses, some players were under the illusion that there was a possibility of making a run at the championship. But in the final seven games, all the Cowboys could accomplish was a tie against a terrible Washington Redskin team. The Giant triumph would be the last win in what would turn out to be a 4–9–1 season. The Cowboys just did not have enough talent.

BOB FRY: "Don Perkins was a good running back, and we had a couple of wide receivers, but you have to have eleven guys to win consistently. It only takes one weak link. When you throw a pass, if just one lineman doesn't block, if you're playing against Deacon Jones or Merlin Olsen . . . it's tough, unless you have people to match them."

Against the Washington Redskins, former Cowboy defensive lineman Gene Cronin proved exactly what Fry was talking about. Tackle Byron Bradfute had torn cartilage during the exhibition season and returned in time to face Washington, who had won just one game in their last 34 exhibition and regular-season games. This game would end in a 28–28 tie. Bradfute, a second-year player, recalled the beating he took from defensive end Gene Cronin.

BYRON BRADFUTE: "In the middle of the season the Cowboys cut Charley Granger and activated me, and so I felt, 'This is a great chance to bring my old high school coach up here,' and so I brought him to Dallas to watch us play the Redskins. That was my first game to be activated, and there was no way I was supposed to play. So I partied a little bit too much the night before with my old high school coach and then went out there to play the Redskins. In the first quarter Bob McCreary got kicked out of the game, and I had to play the rest of the game. An ex-Cowboy named Gene Cronin was playing defensive end for the Redskins, and he had an absolute field day against me. He'd have made All-Pro if he had played against me all season. In fact, that's what he told me. We'd line up, and he'd say, 'Bradfute, I'm going to make All-Pro against you.' And boy, he did, too. In fact, they moved me over to the other side and put Bob Fry on him, and really, I didn't stop him and nobody else did either."

As he did the year before, owner Clint Murchison was the one person in the Cowboys organization having a lot of fun. In '60 he had wreaked havoc on the city of Chicago with his drunken bear. This year Murchison's practical joking had a more personal target: Redskin owner George Preston Marshall. Murchison had a strong and lasting dislike for Marshall for trying to stop him from getting the franchise, and Murchison used every weapon he had, including his friendship with FBI director J. Edgar Hoover, to torture Marshall.

The Cowboy-Redskin game took place in Washington, one week before Christmas, and Marshall was planning a spectacular halftime show that was to include Santa Claus being pulled by a dogsled of twelve huskies, who were to ride around the entire stadium.

Murchison, who was an agnostic, huddled with his drinking buddies Robert Thompson and Bedford Wynne and cooked up a scheme that was downright sacrilegious (if you somehow see Santa Claus as a religious figure).

The night before the game, the three went out to Griffith Stadium and seeded the entire playing field with corn. The next thing they did was buy 5,000 chickens, which they smuggled inside a storeroom in the bowels of the stadium. The plan, brilliant and sick as it was, was to set the chickens loose during the halftime ceremonies so that the sled dogs would abandon their holiday duties, attack the chickens, and there would be an epic bloodbath.

Unfortunately for Murchison, their plan was scuttled when an observant security guard heard the clucking of the chickens from behind the stadium storeroom wall.

Frustrated but undeterred, Murchison, Thompson, and Wynne would go out at night drinking, and in the middle of the night they would call George Preston Marshall on his private line. A groggy Marshall would waken from a sound sleep, pick up the receiver, say hello, and on the other end Murchison would intone, "Cluck, cluck, cluck, cluck, cluck, cluck," until Marshall hung up. Marshall would then call the phone company and get his phone number changed. And every time he changed the number, that's when Murchison would call J. Edgar Hoover and find out his new number. Once again, the phone would ring in Marshall's home, and a gleeful, sodden Murchison again would cluck into the telephone.

Despite the 4–9–1 record in '61, quarterback Eddie LeBaron had a strong feeling that this team was progressing.

EDDIE LEBARON: "We were getting better. Oh yes, you could see it. The defense was getting better. We had Bob Lilly and Chuck Howley. On offense we had Frank Clarke and Don Perkins. We were just getting better people.

"In the next draft we got speed. Cornell Green was going to play tight end when he came up from Michigan State, and they made him a defensive back. Lee Roy Jordan, George Andrie, Dave Edwards, and Mike Gaechter also joined the team on defense. And we added tight end Pettis Norman, who had so much talent. Tex Schramm was starting to put together the nucleus of a very good football team."

13

Pettis and Cornell

When Tex Schramm was running the Los Angeles Rams, he had one overriding drafting philosophy: If you mine where everyone else does, you'll be mediocre like everyone else. As a result, Schramm looked for talent, regardless of color, the size and reputation of the school, or whether an athlete had even played football.

Even though in 1947 Jackie Robinson had proved the ability of black ballplayers to compete alongside whites, in the early 1950s owners and general managers of many sports teams still were reluctant to sign blacks for fear they would drive away their white fans. George Preston Marshall, the owner of the Washington Redskins, flatly refused to sign black players, fearing the appearance of a black player would alienate his southern audience. It wasn't until 1962, with the trade for halfback Bobby Mitchell, that the Redskins finally fielded a black player.

Tex Schramm was acutely aware that his Cowboys were playing in the Bible Belt, but he refused to allow the collective feelings of his Deep South constituents against blacks to affect his chances of winning football games. In the early years with the Cowboys, Schramm thoroughly investigated the black players he signed in an attempt to eliminate malcontents and to determine that the players he hired were smart enough to learn Tom Landry's systems. As the years went on, Schramm saw that to win, a team needed a lot of black players, and he even did away with those tests. For the most part, if Schramm saw a player he thought could help the Cowboys, he would sign him regardless of race. It would not be long before the Cowboys would field more black players than just about any other sports team. According to Schramm, this lack of prejudice had been passed on to him by team owner Dan Reeves, his friend and boss on the Los Angeles Rams.

TEX SCHRAMM: "People have always been more tolerant in California than in a lot of other places around the country. Before I was hired by the Rams, Dan Reeves had drafted the first black player. Reeves had been negotiating for the use of the Los Angeles Coliseum, and he was told it would help his cause if he signed Kenny Washington, a very popular athlete at that time. Kenny had played football with Jackie Robinson at UCLA, and so in 1946 he signed Washington and he also signed Woody Strode, who later became an actor. Washington was a hell of a baseball player. He was better even than Jackie Robinson, but the war came at the wrong time for him, and when he went back to baseball with the Los Angeles Angels, he couldn't make it. He had bad knees. He had ruined them playing football.

"Dan Reeves never got the credit for integrating football the way Branch Rickey did in baseball. Of course, there had been a few black players in the NFL, players like Fritz Pollard, but the last one had played in 1934, and there wasn't another one until Kenny and Woody played for the Rams in '46.

"When I joined the Rams, we signed Tank Younger, the first player signed out of Grambling, and we drafted Dan Towler from William & Mary.

"When I began drafting players with Dallas, I just kept doing what I had been doing, drafting the best players I could find, regardless of color."

Finding great black football players in the 1950s and early 1960s wasn't as easy as it is today. The institution of segregation kept black players from the great southern football schools like the University of Alabama, the University of Georgia, the University of Oklahoma, and all the big Texas schools. The best of the black players either played for those northern schools that were integrated, or they played for the many unpublicized all-black colleges around the country.

During the era of the '50s teams didn't scout in an organized manner. There were no staffs for scouting prospects. Word of mouth, newspaper clippings, and statistics produced draft choices, and aside from the All-Americas and the record-setters, teams often had a miserable time picking competent players.

Tex Schramm realized that if he could get the athletic directors and coaches of hundreds of the small colleges—white and black—from across the nation to do his legwork for him, he would have a significant advantage over the opposition. That's where his brilliantly conceived Tom Harmon All-America Team came into play. Each year these so-called awards honored the best football players from the little-known small schools by publicizing the names of the winners. No one knew who was behind them, but since the legendary University of Michigan and pro quarterback Tom Harmon was the name sponsor, no one thought to question it. Had someone, anyone, investigated, he would have discovered that these "awards" were but a vehicle for Tex Schramm and his Rams football team to learn the identities of the best players at these small schools. It was a drafting ploy that benefited Tex financially, while at the same time heaping lots of glory on Tom Harmon and the honored football players. To this day the coaches and athletic directors who filled out the questionnaire for the Tom Harmon awards never knew their ulterior purpose. More than anything else, this ingenuity in finding players marked the genius of Tex Schramm as he struggled to make the Dallas Cowboys into a competitive football team.

In addition to Schramm's contacts, the Cowboys also had the benefit of having Gil Brandt running the scouting department. Brandt was a real-life Walter Mitty, who as a collegiate at the University of Wisconsin was one of the very first "draftniks." He would write to college sports departments to borrow game films in order to advance his hobby of making a list of the top pro prospects.

After working part-time for Schramm in L.A., Tex hired him in 1960, and it wasn't long before Brandt, who the players said had the heart and mind of a bunko artist, developed a huge network of informants among college coaches, trainers, secretaries, and athletic directors in colleges large and small. If a coach needed a favor, he would go to Brandt. In return, Brandt wanted information. It was Brandt's scouting reports that for many years gave Schramm and Landry the advantage in drafting unknown players in the lower rounds and free agents.

In 1962 a total of thirteen of Tex Schramm's draft picks and free agents made the Dallas Cowboys. The guys who made it in '62 were typical of the Cowboys. The top choice, TCU quarterback Sonny Gibbs, didn't make it. A few picks came from major colleges—defensive tackle Don

Talbert from the University of Texas, offensive tackle John Myers from the University of Washington, and Mike Gaechter from the University of Oregon—but of the thirteen rookies, a remarkably high number were unheralded low draft choices and free agents from colleges few had ever heard of. Among the Cowboys' choices were a defensive end named George Andrie, who hadn't even played his senior year because his college, Marquette, had dropped its football program. There was linebacker Harold Hays from Southern Mississippi; a defensive back, Don Davis, from Southern University; a fullback, Amos Bullocks, from Southern Illinois; and a free agent offensive end named Pettis Norman from a small North Carolina black college, Johnson C. Smith University.

Pettis Norman, unlike black teammates Frank Clarke and Don Perkins, had grown up in the Deep South, subject to all the rules and regulations—and crushing indignities and limitations imposed on him by segregation. Growing up, Norman faced all obstacles with honesty, industriousness, determination, and intelligence. He demonstrated the ability to get knocked down and get back up, traits that would serve him well both on the football field and off. His motto was to never let anyone, or anything, defeat him. In addition, he maintained a moral strength that helped carry him to success; both on the field and off. It was that sense of righteousness which he would use to help change the segregationist climate first on the Cowboys, and later in the city of Dallas itself.

Norman spent his first eleven years in rural Georgia, working with his nine brothers and sisters to help his father sharecrop the land. After his father died, his family moved to Charlotte, North Carolina, but the size of his new school petrified him so that Norman stayed in Georgia for two more years to continue his education in the two-room schoolhouse that he had been accustomed to. When he returned to Charlotte as a seventh-grader, the fourteen-year-old boy played tackle football for the first time in the sandlots. Despite the culture shock of going from sandlot ball to big-time high school football, he made the team his junior year, but didn't start until he was a senior. His intention was to join the Air Force, but he was recruited by the coach of Johnson C. Smith University, which was located near his home in Charlotte, and he developed so fast he was named the team's MVP as a freshman.

Norman was both a sprint star on the track team and was named All-America as an offensive end on the football team, but he was not drafted by an NFL team after the Dallas Texans in the AFL falsely told everyone he had signed with them. When the Texans tried to strong-arm Norman into signing, he became angry and broke off negotiations. He signed with the Cowboys as a free agent, starring as a tight end for Dallas from 1962 through 1970, when he was traded to the San Diego Chargers for split end Lance Alworth.

PETTIS NORMAN: "I was born on January 4, 1939, in Lincolnton, Georgia, about 110 miles outside of Atlanta, 38 miles out of Augusta. I was the youngest of ten kids. All my sisters and brothers grew up on the farm. Though Georgia was strictly segregated, I really was not aware of the social conditions, simply because that's the way it was. You became conditioned to your environment, and as an African-American in that environment for the most part you stayed completely to yourself. You went to separate schools. You walked to school when Anglo kids rode the bus. You saw that most of them had much nicer things than you, but you really didn't dwell on it too much. It was part of your consciousness, but that was, as the book says, as it was 'supposed to be.'

"You also had to watch yourself. We all worked in the fields, and when the crops were laid by, we went to work in the sawmill, which was the other common labor. When it was time to plant the crops, we stopped sawmilling, and came back to plow the fields.

"When I was about nine years old, three years before my father died, it was time for us to go back and plow the fields again. And so my brother didn't report to the sawmill truck and went to start plowing the fields. The gentleman who lived down the street who owned the sawmill and most of the land around there came up to the house. I remember him asking my father, 'Why didn't he catch the sawmill truck?'

"My father said, 'Well, because it's time for him to go plow the fields.' And the gentleman said, 'I want you to have him on that truck tomorrow, or else I'm going to teach him a lesson.'

"My father said to this gentleman, 'I had him and I raised him, and if he needs a whipping, I'll give it to him. Anybody else who tries will have to do it over my dead body.' My father, whose name was Fessor, was a very, very mild-mannered person, very well respected. Today people talk about him as if he just passed away last year, and he passed away in 1951.

"The other thing that happened was there were any number of times in the evening, at nine, ten o'clock at night, we'd look down this old dirt road and see a long procession of car headlights with something burning on the front of it, and when it passed the house, you recognized it as a burning cross. And these people were dressed in white robes, and you could hear them up the highway a few miles from us, making all kinds of noise, having a jamboree.

"When you're nine years old, you don't really understand the essence of it. My parents yelled at us to stay away. To me it was just a spectacle, because I was a young kid. But they never bothered my family, and I don't know of any other families they bothered, even though I heard stories about other young men who were taken out into the fields and whipped at night for any number of reasons.

"The one incident that really served as my point of demarcation, or deportation, made me see and know that there was a difference between folk. I was ten years old, and I used to play with this white boy, one of the grandkids of the store owner and large landowner around there. He and his family lived a block and a half from where we lived, and we used to play together all the time. He was about two years older than I was, but he was a little smaller than I was. He used to come over to my house, and we used to go down to his place, played all kinds of games like hide-and-seek, hopscotch, and I can remember all of a sudden, the little girls, his sisters who we had played with, didn't play with us anymore, but the boys and I continued to play together.

"I had played with this young man as far back as I can remember—we lived, ate together, and grew up together as kids—and ran together. We really were buddies, and this particular day I was down to his house, and it was time for him to go and feed his uncle's dogs. His uncle had several fox dogs, and traditionally when I was down there, he'd say, 'Pettis, come with me,' and we'd jump in the truck, put the food in the back of the pickup truck, and drive it down and feed his uncle's dogs. That was a ritual.

"And so this particular day, he said, 'Pettis, are you going with me to feed the dogs?' I said, 'Yeah.' So we got the food, put it in the back of the truck, got in the cab of the pickup truck, and he said, 'Pettis, what did you say to me when I asked if you were going to feed the dogs?' I can still remember my trying to make sense of the question, and I said, 'Yes.'

"He said, 'We are old enough now where you are going to have to say to me, 'Yes, sir.' And I could see he was dead serious.

"I remember getting out of that pickup truck, thinking to myself, I will never, ever say 'Yes, sir,' to my friend. I got out, hurt, angry, and went to my house. I was so angry, I didn't know what to do. I couldn't wait for the opportunity to get back at him.

"The next day I didn't go down to play with him, and so he came up to my house, where I was sitting on the steps. I can see him coming right now. I had been playing hopscotch. So he came up, and he said, 'Can I play, too?' I said, 'Yes.' And I knew he was going to step on my line and he would be 'out' because he was kind of clumsy, so he never could get through the whole game without stepping on a line. And so he stepped on the line, and that was my cue. I said, 'You stepped on my hopscotch line.' In the past it was no big deal. But that day, it was my fighting call, and I jumped on him for that reason, and even though he was a couple years older, I was as big as he was, and I could handle him. And I beat him up.

"And we literally never spoke again from that day on. Never, ever spoke again. He has since died, but I don't want to name him, because his family still lives there, and they may or may not read this.

"When I was eleven we moved to Charlotte, North Carolina. My father had passed away, and he was the center of the family, the person who knew how to farm, and after he passed away, my brothers farmed for a couple of years, and we could eke out a living, but not as good as what my father did. It was a tough way to live. My mother had a sister who had moved to Charlotte because she had a son and daughters up there, and she wrote my mother to try to get her to come up there. So finally my mother went up to visit her, and she thought, This would be a nice change, and so we packed up and moved to Charlotte.

"Though we lived in the rural area, Charlotte was a city. I was a country boy who found it difficult to make the transition from rural to urban life. I was so petrified at the transition from the rural South to the city, I literally could not go to school in Charlotte. I just could not think of going to school where there were 800 students in a school, 'cause the one I had gone to was two rooms, first through fourth in one room, and fifth through eleventh on the other side. Maybe there were a total of 40 students in that school. There were two teachers. It was a little old shack. Have you seen the movie *Tobacco Road*? Well, that building would make *Tobacco Road* look like a mansion. A pot-bellied stove sat in the middle of the floor. The school was made out of old slabs and had holes in the walls, floors, and ceiling. You had to carry out water from a spring a quarter of a mile away, had to break the firewood for the stove, had to go outside to an outhouse. So that was my setting, and in North Carolina they had running water, bathrooms, classrooms, that were just so foreign to me. I was so petrified going to school in Charlotte that my mother sent me back down to Georgia for fifth and sixth grades, and finally she said, 'You're going to stay up here and go to school.' So the seventh grade is when I started school in Charlotte.

"Charlotte had segregated communities which were clearly defined by railroad tracks and highways, and I went to an all-black school, West

Charlotte Senior High School, a wonderful experience because it was brand-new, recently built, a very nice school. It was very unusual to have such a new facility like that in an African-American neighborhood. I don't know another community that had one at that time.

"It was very segregated, all black teachers, never any contact with white teachers or white principals during my educational journey. Living in Charlotte, I literally didn't see white people from one day to the next. When you did it was downtown, and when you passed white people, it was almost like you were nobody. White people didn't even make eye contact with you. The public facilities were segregated. We needed to go to the back of the bus. You couldn't go into the five-and-dime store to the lunch counter to buy a hamburger or a Coke. You couldn't go to the soda shop to buy one unless it was in your part of town. If you wanted a hamburger downtown, you had to go to that backdoor and get one, and so most black people just avoided that rather than go through that indignation.

"There were a number of students in my high school who went on to college, a number out of my class who *knew* they were going to college, because they came from middle- and upper-middle-income parents, lawyers and doctors, and then there were a large number of students who knew that their educational journey would end in the twelfth grade, if not before. I was one of those. My sisters and brothers did not have a chance to finish high school because they had to work. One of my sisters had been a teacher, but she did not have any formal teacher training, just a lot of common sense. She taught me my first four years in school. So there was not a role model there, except for some reason my mother literally used to whip me in order to make me go to school. She'd say, 'You're going to get an education if I have to kill you.' And later on, when I was in high school, she would always say, 'I really want you to get an education. I want to see one of my kids get a college education.' And I don't know where she got this idea from. She was a housekeeper, a maid if you want to call it that, and perhaps she got it from the people she worked for. But she said that to me more than one time, and frankly I never knew how I would ever do that, because although I was a pretty decent student in high school—I was in what was known as the Junior Boys Honors Club—I didn't have the money. I never really dreamed about going to college. I lived one block from Johnson C. Smith University, and used to go over there and watch football practice through the fence, and always wondered how those boys got to go there and what it took and imagined that was beyond my means, both financially and educationally.

"I was fourteen when I first saw a football. My friends from class would play sandlot tackle football every evening after school, and one day one of my friends asked me to come watch him play, and I sat there on the bank while they played, watching what they were doing, and I would mentally play the game as they were. Sandlot football was *the* game. You'd get the ball and run and be tackled, and if you went out for a pass, somebody might upend you. They knew how to play. They had been playing for years. About two weeks later, I said to my friend, 'I wonder if I could play with you?' He knew I had never played. He said, 'These guys are tough, and they'll get you.' I wasn't afraid. I said, 'I'll get them, too.'

"I had to wait until this one day when they didn't have enough to make out the team. I got to play. There was a big guy on the opposite team who everybody was afraid to tackle, and he'd get the ball and run for a touchdown every time. When I was out there, the first time he ran the ball, I hit him so hard, everybody was stunned. They couldn't believe it. And every time he tried to run, I would tackle him, and so from that day on, they always picked me to play.

"In the tenth grade I went out for organized football, and I met with another bit of culture shock. I really wasn't sure if I could play organized football, 'cause my experience had been limited to the sandlot. I quit, partially because I had a job and I needed to work, but also because I was afraid of being burned, though after I quit I couldn't stand it, because I had quit something I thought I could play, so I went back out the eleventh grade, made the football team, fourth string, played a total of two minutes in two games, and in the twelfth grade played about half the games and then signed up to go into the Air Force right after my senior year.

"I had worked at a service station all through high school, and this day I was inside the service station washing cars when a gentleman drove up in a brand new car. My friend Nate Evans, who worked with me at the service station, went out to wait on him, sold him some gas, and all of a sudden they walked up behind me. This gentleman introduced himself and said, 'I understand you're a pretty good football player.' I looked around, and he was talking to me. I was dumbfounded. Where did he get that?

"I said, 'Are you talking to me?' He said, 'Yes.' I said, 'Oh no, sir.' And he said, 'Nate said you were a pretty good football player. He tells me you are the *best* football player in the state.' Nate had often told me that. He'd say, 'You really are the best player on this team. You ought to be starting,' and he'd give all the traditional reasons why I wasn't—the coaching staff likes someone else more, and so on. And I thought Nate was just blowing smoke. I said to the gentleman, 'Nate's just teasing.' He said, 'What are you going to do after high school?' I said, 'I have already signed up to go into the Air Force, and I'll be leaving in about two weeks for active duty.' He said, 'I'm Eddie McGirt, the new coach at Johnson C. Smith. Would you like to go to school? Have you thought about it?' I said, 'I thought about it, but beyond that I didn't make any plans because I don't have the money and I don't have a scholarship.' He said, 'Do you think you can get out of going to the Air Force? If you can, I would like you to come to Smith and play football, and I'll give you a scholarship.'

"I went down and talked to the recruiter. He was a very nice gentleman, a white gentleman. He had really taken a liking to me, and I explained my good fortune to him, and this gentleman said, 'Let me check. I never had anything like this where after a person signed we released him. Let me see what I can do.' So he checked and called me back to say, 'I have been able to get you released from this commitment. I'm just so happy for you. You're a nice young man. I hate to lose you, but I really want you to take advantage of going to college.' So I got out of that commitment to the Air Force, and I went to Johnson C. Smith.

"My freshman year at Johnson C. Smith I made the team and was chosen Most Valuable Player. I have the trophy. Johnson Smith had not had a winning record in years, but we were 6–2 that year, and we had a winning record every year I was there. I was chosen co-captain or captain three years there, and I made all-conference three years, made Currier All-America, but the main thing was, we had cohesion, a lot of spirit on the team, and we had a lot of good student-athletes who did well in class and did well later on in life. I got my degree in four years, and that was the crowning glory. When I left school four years later, I had my degree.

"In addition to playing football, I also ran track. I could run the 100 in 9.8. In one track meet in South Carolina I got the chance to run against Bob Hayes. I didn't know it, but he was more famous than I knew. He ran a 9.4 hundred that day into a 20-mile-an-hour wind. From that point on everyone began to know who Bob Hayes was.

"In addition to playing sports, I had three jobs. My brother and I borrowed an old panel truck, and I took that truck and developed a cleaning route, worked out a deal with a cleaning service where we shared the revenues. I also worked at the service station while I was in college, and during the off-season when I was out of school and was not working at the service station, I contracted painting. One of my first jobs came after I heard that Smith was putting up some bleachers at the stadium, and I contracted to paint those bleachers.

"During my years at Smith, especially starting my junior year and especially after I was named Currier All-America and MVP my senior year,

I started getting some type of correspondence from the Green Bay Packers, Chicago Bears, Dallas Cowboys, who had a scout in the area, almost every team in the NFL. And several Canadian teams, Montreal, Saskatchewan, and a couple others. I was also contacted by the AFL and courted by the Dallas Texans.

"The AFL had an early, secret draft. They had contacted me and visited with me, and they had indicated that they wanted to draft me. They asked me to sign an agreement that if they drafted me, I would not sign with another team unless and until I gave them the first right of refusal, give them the chance to match their offer. I thought that was an okay deal. They paid me $100 to do that.

"Before the NFL draft, the word got out—on purpose by the Texans—that I had signed a contract. And so when the Cowboys called, Gil Brandt said, 'We wanted to draft you, but you've signed a contract.' I told Gil I hadn't. He said, 'We don't want to waste a draft choice, but if you're not drafted, we want to sign you to a free agent contract.'

"Part of it was they were afraid I had signed a contract, but part of it was, and I didn't know it then, but I do know it now, it was a cheap way of getting me.

"Well, sure enough, right after the NFL draft, Gil Brandt called and said he wanted to come up. I called the Texans and told them the Cowboys had called, and they told me over the phone, 'You can't sign a contract with them, because you've already signed a contract with us.' Which wasn't true. We got into a dispute. I felt they had lied to me and tried to cheat me, and I told them I didn't want to deal with them any more.

"Gil and I went out and had a hamburger. He had 500 $1 bills, and he was flipping through them on the table like they were a pack of cards. He offered me an $8,500 contract, and we agreed, and as a bonus I got those 500 $1 bills.

"Gil Brandt was the consummate salesperson. He made contact with college coaches all over, took them out and bought them a hamburger like he did me, I guess, and they would call him about these players. He had friends in *every* town. In Charlotte there was a gentleman who worked in a bank who was very friendly with the Cowboys, who called him and told him they ought to watch me. And that's how the Cowboys found out. Other teams weren't doing that. They weren't doing anything at all. Absolutely nothing at all. The Cowboys really refined scouting as we know it today. They put together notebooks on players, tested players, really refined the art of scouting and blending players.

"When I signed I was happy, and for a number of reasons. It was more money than I had ever made at any one time. Eight thousand five hundred dollars was more money than my college professors were making at the time. And at that time my mother had had a second stroke. She was an invalid, and we were poor, and she needed medical attention, and so I could use that money to help defray the medical costs. And so I signed with the Cowboys and reported to training camp."

Another free agent signed by Tex Schramm and his sidekick, Gil Brandt, had played no football in college at all. Rather, Cornell Green had played basketball, and with great ability, at Utah State University. It was Schramm's theory that if an athlete had size and enough ability, he could learn to play the game of football. Over the years Schramm would occasionally gamble low draft choices on college hoop stars, including Green, Pete Gent, who starred in basketball at Michigan State University, and Minnesota's Lou Hudson, Kentucky's Pat Riley, and Ohio State's John Havlicek, and he would sign track stars Mike Gaechter from Oregon and Olympic hero Bob Hayes of Florida A&M, losing Olympian Carl Lewis to a professional track career.

TEX SCHRAMM: "If you start an expansion club, and if you're going to be able to compete, you have to do more, spend more money on scouting. We did. We had more people and did more things. One of the things I did was go after great athletes. I especially wanted a star basketball player who fell in the gray area of not being tall enough to make it as a forward in the NBA, and not being quick enough to be a guard. 'Cause you're never going to get the *top* college basketball players. If they played basketball all four years in college, they are not going to come in as a tryout in football. Among the players we drafted over the years were Lou Hudson, Pat Riley, and John Havlicek. They would have made great football players. Unfortunately, they all made it in the NBA.

"Gil Brandt, our scouting director, knew as many basketball coaches as he knew football coaches, and he would ask them, "Who do you see who won't make it in the NBA but who's a hell of an athlete?" That's how we found Cornell Green at Utah State. It's how we found Pete Gent. The ones who made it were the exceptions.

"In other words, we fooled around with a lot of guys, and some of them worked, and some of them didn't. One time I drafted Carl Lewis, who came out of the University of Houston. But Carl was the first one who wanted to make track as a livelihood, and he was good enough to do it. But you have to do something different. If you do the same thing, you're going to be in the same spot they are."

Cornell Green was an All-America hoop star at Utah State who was swayed from playing in the NBA because the Cowboys made him an offer he couldn't refuse. Green, who hadn't played football since high school, originally was going to play tight end, but he was turned into a defensive back by Coach Landry and his defensive coordinator, Dick Nolan, and Pettis Norman was given the tight end job. Tall at 6'4", athletic, fast, and most of all smart, Cornell Green found himself starting for the Cowboys when the '62 season started, despite Coach Landry's intense dislike of having rookies on the field. Green was an All-Pro selection four times (1966, '67, '68, '69) and was named to the Pro Bowl five times. He retired after the 1975 season.

Green, a black player from Southern California, had played on mostly white teams in high school, and in college was one of a handful of black students on the campus of Utah State in Logan, Utah. Green came to Dallas, lived where he was told, but otherwise found he could do pretty much whatever he pleased.

CORNELL GREEN: "I grew up in Richmond, California. My dad was a truck driver. In high school I made all-league in football and All-America in basketball. The most I scored in a basketball game was 46 in a tournament in Greeley, California.

"All the California schools recruited me, and a lot of schools back East. I went to Utah State in Logan, Utah. At that time I had not been out of California. It was just far enough from home to be out of the state, but I wasn't too far where I couldn't come home. I was very happy at Utah State. I enjoyed it. There weren't a whole lot of black people there, but I enjoyed it. My sophomore year our team was rated fifth in the nation. We won some tournaments, and my senior year we were eliminated in the second round of the NCAA tournament by Walt Hazzard and UCLA.

"I was the number two draft choice of the NBA's Chicago Zephyrs, which later became the Washington Bullets. The NBA wasn't paying the money they are now, and at that time the NFL and AFL were at war, and pro football was paying a lot more money than basketball. The 49ers had also shown interest. At one time I talked to one of the 49ers scouts. When the Cowboys offered me a big contract, I took it.

"Gil Brandt took me and a couple of the Utah State football players out to dinner, and we started talking. When he told me the Cowboys were interested in signing me, I thought he was BS-ing me, so I talked to our football coach John Ralston and a couple more coaches up there, and they said they *were* interested, and so they hammered out a contract.

"It wasn't that I thought I could make it. At the time I didn't care if I made it or not. Tex Schramm had offered me a nonrefundable bonus. It was the bonus I was going for. To get it, all I had to do was show up.

"I arrived in training camp in '62, and I'm sure you heard that story about how I had my hip pads on backward, much to everybody's amusement. That story was blown out of proportion so much that even the people involved got changed. The writers had the equipment manager telling me that, and he didn't even know about it. What happened was that I had worn the pads the wrong way for three preseason games, and I was chafed between my legs because the pads were rubbing me raw. I was talking to Dick Nolan, the defensive backfield coach. He said, 'You're limping. What's wrong with you?' And I was telling him about the pads, and he told me I had them on backward. And that was the end of that. It wasn't that everybody saw it and started laughing. Nobody even knew until we told them.

"I hadn't played a bit of football since high school, but as a rookie I started at the corner against the Green Bay Packers. Landry didn't usually start rookies, but back in those days we had some injuries, and he didn't have a lot of choice.

"You have to understand that even though I had never played college football, training camp gave you plenty of time to learn what you needed to know. Before we played the first preseason game, we had two-a-day sessions for a month. Training camp is what separates the players. Training camp is a lot tougher on you than playing during the season. If I could survive training camp, I could play during the season.

"For me, playing defensive back under Tom Landry's system was easy, because back in those days 90 percent of the time it was just 'man' coverage. We didn't have a lot of zones and combinations.

"I was also fortunate to have Dick Nolan as a coach and also as a player playing beside me. He started as a coach, and a couple of guys got hurt, and Dick Nolan ended up a player. He had a bad shoulder, bad wrist, bad everything, bad knees. He was beat to hell. Dick was very helpful, very, very much so. He'd tell me a lot of things to help me get through the game. Back then you didn't learn a lot from the other players. We had a really young team. Everybody was trying to make it for themselves.

"When I started with the Cowboys in '62, Tom Landry was teaching the Flex to the defensive players. You had to read 'keys' and take the key to where you were supposed to go. A lot of the older vets didn't want to do it, because they were used to playing a certain way. But to the younger guys, guys like Bob Lilly, George Andrie, and myself, it didn't matter, because hell, we had never played any other way at all, so it wasn't that big a thing. A bunch of the old guys who had been around and who had played under other systems thought it was stupid, and Tom Landry ended up getting rid of them.

"I didn't have any opinion about the system at all. Since I had never even played college football, I didn't have anything to judge it by. I didn't say to myself, 'I understand your system and I'm buying it.' Rather it was, 'You're the coach, so I'm doing what you want.' It was as simple as that.

"I really didn't encounter any racial problems, nothing, when I came to Dallas, because I was told where to go and where to stay. A lot of things I saw for the first time down here in Texas amazed me. I was from California, and I had never seen a system where people had to live in only a certain section. That was where you had to be in. It had nice houses, very nice homes, but just the idea that you had to stay in a certain section amazed me. I had never seen an all-black college. In my whole high school, grammar school, growing up, I only had one black teacher in California. Here, all the teachers were black in the school.

"In our own way we came down here fighting the system. The system was being fought at *every* turn. We didn't do anything to get our names publicized. We would go and do things against the system knowing there wasn't a whole lot they could do about it because I was a Cowboy, a member of the NFL.

"A lot of white guys from up North didn't understand the system either. Take a guy like Mike Gaechter, who was also a rookie that year. Gaechter and I would go wherever we wanted. We never said, 'We can't go in here.' Or 'I'm not supposed to be in here.' And I don't remember anyone challenging me. Just by my being there I was integrating the city."

When Pettis Norman and Cornell Green reported for training camp, the Cowboys roomed them together. Since 1960, the Cowboys had always roomed black players with black players and white players with white players, consistent with the racial policies of the Deep South. It would be a few years before Pettis Norman would act to change the system of room assignments.

PETTIS NORMAN: "In 1962 I reported to training camp at Marquette, Michigan, on the campus of Northern Michigan University. They sent me a ticket, and I caught that little DC-3, and flew to Chicago, and met these other guys who had gone to Auburn and Georgia Tech and all these big schools I had seen on TV and heard about, and I thought, My God, look at these guys. From Chicago we flew into Marquette, Michigan.

"My focus and all my thoughts were, I'm not going back to Charlotte without making this team. Nothing or nobody will get in my way of making this team. And from that first day when I got there and we got our playbooks, I made sure I understood the playbook and made sure I knew my assignments, and under Coach Landry's system I learned where the plays were going, and then practiced and did well.

"Everything back then was by race. We were separated by race within the dorm. You roomed by race. Cornell Green was my first roommate. I hung out mostly with the black players because of that, though there was very little socializing in Marquette, Michigan. Most times, you stayed in your room studying, keeping to yourself.

"The first practice we had lifted my spirits. After the scrimmage, Coach Landry put the film on, got it all set, and before he turned the camera on, he said, 'If you all want to know how to play football, watch Pettis Norman in this film.' For Coach Landry, that was really a high compliment. I'll never forget that.

"That first year I didn't have a great appreciation for Tom Landry as a coach. I appreciated that he didn't seem to get rattled, and that he didn't berate players if they made mistakes. He didn't try to embarrass the player. Rather he took every situation and tried to make it a teaching situation. He made some bold statements like, 'By 1965 we're going to be a winner,' and it was hard for me to see that based on what I saw.

"Still, there were things that happened during the course of the season that had you begin to build confidence in him. You began to know if you followed his instructions to a T, if you took exactly ten steps, and everyone did his job, chances were you were going to catch the pass and be successful. So you began to develop that kind of respect.

"I started camp as a split end, blocked well in a game, knocked people down on the run, and then one day Tom Landry came up beside me as we were walking to practice and he said, 'I really want to move you to tight end.' I thought to myself, I thought you said I was doing well. Why do you want to move me to tight end? I asked him why he wanted to do that, and he said, 'I want to take advantage of your blocking.' And so he moved me to tight end.

"Eddie LeBaron and Don Meredith were the quarterbacks, and early on they helped me tremendously, especially LeBaron. He was the veteran. He really took me under his wing, and he would stay out with me after practice every day, and would stay out there as long as I wanted to stay out, and he'd throw balls to me. He'd teach me little techniques, how to catch the ball better, how to relax.

"Don Meredith was a happy-go-lucky person, but a nice person as well, and he also worked with me. He was such a young guy, much younger than Eddie. Don was certainly very nice about staying out and working after practice as well, but Eddie just made me feel so comfortable. He would come over and say, 'Do you want to work some extra time today? Anytime you want to work, just let me know.' He was really, really nice, and for a rookie it makes all the difference in the world. See, I grew up on Eddie LeBaron, watching the Washington Redskins in Charlotte, North Carolina. I knew exactly who he was. He had been an idol of mine when I was in high school and college. He was *the* quarterback for the Washington Redskins, a magician. So it was a real pleasure to be on the same team with him.

"At Dallas, too, he *was* a magician. Had Eddie been three or four inches taller, there is just no telling how great he could have been. He was very good as it was, but there is no telling how great he could have been, 'cause he really had the ability to fake the ball and hide it, and threw just a wonderful pass, and although he was only 5'6", he had a way of getting that ball to you.

"We were not a good team in '62. We finished 5–8–1. The main weakness was that the team was still made up of a lot of guys who were castoffs, and they thought of themselves as castoffs. They never thought of themselves as people who were going out to win. They thought of themselves as people who were going to go out and lose games. They were going to stick around as long as they could to make that money. That was over half the team.

"The other half of the team was made up of rookies, because in '62 we had thirteen guys in my rookie class to make the team. Some of us really believed we could win and had a winning attitude, and some of us played a lot during that rookie year, and others played in a support role. So we had a lot of inexperienced players, in addition to the castoffs who thought of themselves that way.

"We could look very good one week, and very bad the next, and you never knew which one was going to show up."

14

Inconsistent D

E ven with this influx of talent, there were glaring holes. The biggest
was on the offensive line, which was hurt badly when tackle Byron
Bradfute suddenly quit before the season began in '62. Tom Landry
had hired as an offensive coach a man by the name of Jim Myers, who had
worked under Bear Bryant at Texas A&M. Myers was the sort of coach
who constantly yelled criticisms at his players, and during the last week
of a rigorous training camp, Bradfute decided he had had it with Myers
and the business of football. Football was paying him $8,000 a year. Out-
side of football, Bradfute knew he could do better and have more fun
doing it.

BYRON BRADFUTE: "During the off-season I had worked for one of Clint
Murchison's companies. Because of football I had plenty of money, but I
was trying to build a career, so I started at a sand and gravel pit with a
shovel in my hand making $1.25 an hour. By the time the off-season was
over, I was making time-and-motion studies and involved in control standards in production and doing marketing as an assistant to the president.
And it was not because I was in football. It was because I was doing the
job. And so I perceived that I had a real good career in front of me with
Clint Murchison's companies. And as it turned out, I wasn't with them

much longer after that, changed companies several times, but the point is that during the off-season my mind was challenged a lot. I was really doing something I had gone to school for, and it was exciting. When I went back to training camp, I had to listen to Myers telling me, 'You dumb son of a bitch,' that kind of stuff, and I kept wondering why I was doing this.

"One night a lot of us couldn't sleep. About five of us, Dickie Moegle, Bob Lilly, Mike Connelly, L. G. Dupre, and I were going to quit. We sat up talking until about three in the morning. It was training camp. It was a low point.

"The next morning I went to Tex Schramm and demanded that he trade me. When Tex said he couldn't guarantee who I'd get traded to, I said, 'Well then, I'll go on home.'

"I've talked to Lilly about it since then. He said, 'The next day it looks different.' And he stuck it out one more day. That's what the others did, stuck it out one more day, and then one day turns into another day, and before long, the season starts and you get paid. So quitting at that point is the dumbest thing you can do, because we were only getting $50 a week during training camp, and only when the season started did we get paid. I was dumb. They were smart, a lot smarter than me.

"I went and told Tom I was leaving. Tom said I hadn't given it enough of a chance. I was at the point of crying, not sure of what I had done when I told one of my better friends on the team, Bill Herchman, about it. His was the first commiseration. He looked up at me and said, 'Since you're quitting, can I have your shoes?'

"So I gave him my shoes and left camp. That kind of put it all in perspective."

To fill Bradfute's offensive tackle spot, Tex Schramm was able to acquire twenty-five-year-old Monte Clark from the San Francisco 49ers. When Clark arrived in camp that Monday, Tex Schramm told him he would start just as soon as he was able to learn the offense. Clark studied every waking moment, hoping he could win a spot in the starting lineup in three or four weeks. Six days after arriving in Dallas, he started.

The other vulnerable spot was defensive back. After the '61 season Dick Nolan had been released by New York Giants coach Allie Sherman, who was dumping a lot of Jim Lee Howell's vets, and Tom Landry immediately asked the thirty-year-old Nolan to join him in Dallas as his defensive coordinator. Coach Landry had been coaching both the offense and defense, and he desperately needed help. Landry knew that Nolan had been a disciple when they were together on the Giants. Landry figured that leaving Nolan to teach the defense would allow him to spend more time teaching the offense.

The day before the opening game of the season against the Washington Redskins, Landry approached Nolan.

"How about playing again?" he asked.

"When do you want me to start?"

"Tomorrow."

"Tom, if you want me to, I'll give it a try. You know I haven't done any conditioning to speak of."

Said Landry, "Dick, I know you. You'll do just fine. By the way, I activated you yesterday."

And so in addition to taking the job of head honcho of defense, he would also have to play corner as part of that defense. Nolan discovered he had a *big* job ahead of him.

DICK NOLAN: "When I went to Dallas in '62 as a coach, we had a bunch of ragnuts, never wazes and never will be's. In '62 there was no defense at all. They had a bunch of dogs. The offense won the games. On defense we were struggling for our lives.

"We were really struggling in those days. The simple fact that I had to come back and play was a pretty good indication of how much we were struggling.

"Part of the problem was that Tom was different, and sometimes because somebody is different than you are, you take a dislike. Tom was a very stoic guy. He kept to himself, distant. I know Tom and Don Meredith had their differences. Don was a very emotional guy, and he wished somewhere along the line that Tom would be a pal or a friend. Don would have liked to have had Tom say, 'Hey, Don, you did a great job,' and pat him on the back. But that was not Tom. He was not that way.

"Perhaps if Tom had had a little more of Vince's personality he might have been better able to motivate his players. I know there were times Tom could be intimidating.

"I can remember Tom and I used to set up quizzes the night before study sessions. We'd tell the players, 'Fold up your books and put everything away.' I'd fire questions at guys. I'd say, 'Okay, Bob Lilly, what happens if we're on our goal line, five yards out, and they have first down, and you're in an inside 4–3, and so-and-so calls a Rita. What are you going to do?' And he'd say, 'I go into a Rita position.' I'd say, 'That's right. What are you going to do?' 'Key to the inside.' Then I'd say, 'What's the force on that side?' He'd say, 'Belt force.'

"Well, when I was running the meeting I would ask Chuck Howley ten questions, and he'd have the answers so fast you wouldn't know what would hit him. But every time I'd bring Landry in there, Tom would ask Howley one question, and he would get so tongue-tied, he couldn't get it out! I'd say to Howley after it was over, 'What the hell is the matter with you? You knew it, but you made me look like a jerk. Why don't you answer? You can give it to me. Why can't you give it to him?' He'd say, 'Geez, I don't know.' I finally told Howley, 'I'll tell Tom to leave you alone.'"

CHUCK HOWLEY: "Dick came in as a coach, and when he became player-coach, Dick played behind me. We had word signals, 'Pistol,' or 'Rifle,' indicating what our coverage responsibilities were, but during the game, Dick would say, 'Forget it. In case you can't hear me, just wave wherever you want me. If you want me on the right, wave right. If you want me on the left, wave to the left.' On the field we got to playing games like that, and it worked out great for us. The thing we appreciated most about Dick was his devotion to the game. When he hit somebody and his bad shoulder would pop out, he'd just run off, get it popped back in and come back onto the field. He never complained, but that *had* to be painful for him. I don't know how many times his shoulder popped out that year.

"Dick was a lot of fun. He was one who communicated well with the players. He was a player, but yet he was a coach. He respected Landry, because he had played so many years with Tom. We liked him as a player, and from a player-coach relationship, Dick shared a good relationship with all the players."

DICK NOLAN: "Even though it took a lot of the players a long time to accept Tom's system, once they did, under Tom's system the players virtually became coaches on the field, linebackers like Chuck Howley and Jerry Tubbs, and later on Dave Edwards and Lee Roy Jordan. They had his system down pat. They knew where everything was, and they'd tell people where everything was. They'd stop the others from making mistakes. They'd be talking to them all the time about what they were going to do, if they were worried the guy was going to do it.

"They knew so much football. Tubbs would call a defense in the huddle, and he'd say, 'It's third-and-eight, and you know what they like to do here.' And he'd remind them, 'Be ready.' He'd remind everybody, and boom, they'd be out of the huddle, ready.

"When it came to teaching, Tom knew how to teach. The players knew he knew his football. No question about that. They never could say he didn't know football. Ask any of them.

"Nevertheless, the first few years some of the players would gripe about Tom's system. Landry was doing a lot of shifting players around, and the players would complain that we should be doing this, should be doing that, and because a lot of people felt it was different, they didn't want to do it, and they talked against it.

"Teaching his defense, there are a lot of things contrary to what a guy wants to do. And what you do, you have to force him into it. You have to push him, make him do, keep working at him, hit him with a piece of pipe if you have to, to get him to do it right. Once they do it right, they say, 'Hey, this is something. This is really good.' Then they like it. See, but you have to push guys that way.

"Even Bob Lilly didn't like it at first. That's what makes it for you as a coach. You get guys who know what you're doing and believe in what you're doing and force the other guys to come into it, and they help you. And the thing is, you have success. See with me, they knew I'd help them, but I wasn't their pal. You can't. You try to be one, and they will bury you."

BOB LILLY: "Tom and Dick were on the same page, they had the same terminology. Tom had coached Dick at the Giants, and Dick was one of his pupils, and it helped a lot because it freed Tom up to spend more time on offense and develop our offense to much greater extent than it was at that time. Also, Jerry Tubbs caught on pretty fast, and Jerry became a player-coach as time went along. I'll tell you, Dick Nolan helped a lot with the basic training of people like Mike Gaechter and Cornell Green, guys who didn't know anything about playing in the secondary. So our secondary was much better, because he was an instant help back there. It was like having a coach on the field, a guy who knew what we were only trying to do, because I don't think any of us had the concept yet as to what we were trying to accomplish under Tom's system. I knew we were trying to win, but I didn't understand the direction we were going exactly.

"Tom wanted the defense to be coordinated, and we weren't. He wanted everyone to pretty well know what everyone else was doing. He gave us keys, told us what to look for, but the problem was that we understood what we were *trying* to do, but we weren't all doing it every play.

A few of us would do it one play, and it would break down somewhere else. I'd make an error, and then it would break down where I was.

"In 1962 we beat the Washington Redskins badly. They didn't score until late in the game. It was one of those freak games where we did a lot of things right, where we were more coordinated, and we were stopping things they had done. There were several turnovers in that game, and George Andrie and Chuck Howley had real good days. Let me say this, too, when you're a very poor team, no one takes you very seriously. That's why we were able to beat the Giants the year before, because they looked at the films, and they just couldn't get very excited about us, so they didn't approach it on the higher intensity level that they would if they had been playing the Green Bay Packers or somebody like that. That's one thing that happened to a lot of those teams that we beat. They would watch our films and see us get beat 40–10, and they just couldn't get up for it. And we were up, because we wanted to beat somebody. That's one reason you see a team one week win big against a good team and then the next week play a mediocre team, and get beat, 'cause they just didn't take it very seriously. It's hard to stay on that high plane. Just a few times can you do that. But that's what happened when we won. We surprised them that we had more ability than they thought, and we were up for the game and they weren't.

"We had talent. We were getting a lot of good talent in those early years. The talent is not that much different from team to team. It's just a matter of whether all of you are going in the same direction. What surprised a lot of teams was that every once in a while we would jell a little bit. We would have a good game. Everyone would be coordinated, and they would be doing the things that we did the best against.

"But I do remember that Washington game, because that was the first time we beat anybody really bad, not that anybody noticed. You went to a Cowboy game, and if it was raining and everybody was underneath the eaves, you couldn't tell that anybody was there. So in Dallas they were just out there writing 'So what?' Because we were very inconsistent."

On December 2, 1962, the Cowboys played one of the finest games ever, shocking the powerful Cleveland Browns, 45–21. Don Meredith had his finest day as a pro, and on defense the Cowboys virtually stopped cold legendary fullback Jim Brown.

CHUCK HOWLEY: "In our third-to-last game against Cleveland in 1962 we held Jim Brown to just 13 yards. Jim Brown was a great athlete. He had power. You knew that when you tackled Jim Brown, you needed a lot of help. So we were keying on Jim all game. We just didn't want him to get started. He was a great breakaway runner, one of those superb runners. If he had a weak point, it was pass protection. We all have our weaknesses, and we felt Jim Brown was a person who didn't like to block on the pass rush, so as linebackers we didn't pay a whole lot of attention to him. He'd set up, and we'd just run by him. Because Jim just didn't want to block. I'm not saying he never did, but it was his weak point. Most of the time they used him in pass patterns rather than in pass protection.

"We'd watch the game films, and Tom would say, 'This guy doesn't like to block, so even if he sets up to block, don't pay too much attention to him.' That didn't mean you weren't going to get popped. But when we studied him in game preparation and saw him set up to block, we could see defenders buzzing right on by him. You could see in the films that if you gave just a little bit, he was not going to come after you."

The next week, in the next-to-last game of the season, the Cowboys were crushed by the St. Louis Cardinals, 52–20. Quarterback Charlie Johnson threw five touchdown passes against the defense, throwing three long bombs in the final minutes.

Defensive consistency was still several seasons away.

15

Clarke Star

On offense the Cowboys could put the points up on the board. The 1962 team, led by backs Don Perkins and Amos Marsh, rushed for 2,040 yards, second only to the Green Bay Packers, and its passing yardage was comparable to the top teams'. Wide receiver Frank Clarke, after years of living under the cloud of his self-doubts, proved in 1962 that he was as good as anyone, that year catching 47 passes for 1,043 yards, and a league-high 14 touchdowns.

FRANK CLARKE: "We beat some teams in '62. We beat the Rams, the Eagles, and against the Pittsburgh Steelers in Pittsburgh, when Eddie LeBaron threw me three touchdown passes. I was *good*. I had some of the best moves that any NFL end had. I could run corner routes, I could run turns. I could run some of the best routes a receiver could ever run, and when you ran them with my speed and size, and my ability to catch the ball, it was really fantastic, really something.

"Eddie LeBaron was a good quarterback, but we didn't have a relationship. I felt an intimidation around Eddie because he came with such a sense of maturity, and I knew subconsciously at least how lacking in that maturity I was. Being around a guy like Eddie was like a little kid being around a father. Everybody liked him and everybody respected him, but I felt for some reason or other, there was no way I could measure up to him.

"But early on I had great confidence in his ability. When he called a route, I knew he was going to get the ball to me. No question about that.

"Eddie was a good quarterback. He knew he could get rid of the ball. He knew where he wanted to put it, and by golly, he put it there. And because of my relationship with Tom, and because of my budding confidence in myself, I was on the receiving end of a lot of his passes. Not very many NFL players can talk about three-touchdown games. But again, it was just something that happened. It was at a point where Eddie's confidence was high and mine was growing.

"The toughest loss that year was by two points to the Pittsburgh Steelers in the Cotton Bowl. We had the ball on our own two-inch line, just barely not touching our goal line. The play came in from the bench for Eddie to throw me a fly pattern. I spread wide to the left, facing Brady Keys, and I just did a number on him, 'cause I was very fast and very deceptive, a tight end playing wide receiver, and they'd relax, 'cause they'd say to themselves, 'He's not going to beat me.' But before they knew it, I was gone, and they didn't catch me. So I was flying, scalding the dog down the sideline, and Eddie laid this ball right in my lap. I caught it and ran like the dickens into the end zone. The play went 99 yards.

"There were not many people in the stands, certainly not more than 20,000 people in the big, cavernous Cotton Bowl, but they were making all kinds of noise. I ran the 100 yards, made the turn, and looked back down the field, and I could see all the players still down there. The defense didn't leave to go to the sideline, and the offense didn't leave either. I thought, Hey, wait a minute. What's going on?

"I walked back down to the other end of the field, and somewhere near the 30- or 40-yard line, Tom Landry was talking to the official. He was livid. Tom was saying, 'You *better* make it good.' And the people started booing. They made more noise than anybody I ever heard. Literally, I had to take off my helmet, because the boos were so loud it was making a funny sound in my head. I thought, Look at all these people going crazy.

"I didn't know the officials had called the play back and gave the Steelers a safety because Andy Cvercko was holding in the end zone. Hell, hardly anybody did. We did not understand that the rule was that if you're caught holding in your own end zone, it's a safety. [The rule is on page 65 of the *Official Rules of Professional Football,* Rule 9, Section 5, Article

2.] Because we were thinking that the whole thing was going to be played under protest.

"To this day people talk about it. Somebody sent me a book of all the crazy things that happened in the NFL. It talked about this play, calling it 'The NFL's only eight-point play.' If someone asks you, 'Can you name an eight-point play in the NFL?' that would be it.

"For me it was one of those never-take-me-out-of-the-record-books chances. And what I remember most was how livid Tom Landry was. Tom Landry showed something that he had never showed any Cowboy fan ever. He met the official on the hash mark, and I can still remember Tom screaming at the referee as he was telling Tom he was going to explain it to him. 'You better explain it, and it better be good.' Tom was screaming.

"Tom, with all his knowledge, didn't know the rule, but it was in the book. That official came out smelling like a rose.

"In '62 I was on the verge of breaking a seventeen-game-in-a-row touchdown record. I had fourteen games in a row with three games to go, and against Washington I got hurt. I got banged up real bad. I was coming down to block the linebacker, and the guy—I do not remember who it was—viciously took his knee and with all of his force, hit me in the thigh, and gave me real bad internal bleeding.

"I was still on the sidelines when the Giants beat us bad, and I had to miss the next game when we lost to the Bears by a point. I watched from the sidelines as Dandy had a great game, threw four touchdown passes. Do you know what else I remember from that game? I remember seeing the Bears' Mike Ditka catch passes and look for people to run over. He was amazing. I never saw any receiver catch the ball and *look* for people and then run over them. He was amazing. Of course, you pay the price when you want that kind of contact. At the end of his career, he could hardly walk. I didn't play again that year until the third-to-last game of the season against the Cleveland Browns."

Don Meredith in that game threw Clarke a two-yard pass for the big end's fourteenth touchdown of the season, tops in the NFL.

The Cowboys appeared to be up and coming.

16

A Season Dies with a President

U nfair as it might be and even though he had a five-year contract, Tom Landry in his own mind believed that if he didn't produce a winner in three years he would be fired. Nineteen sixty-three was the start of his fourth season. He had faced an impossible task building a team from scratch, but he was a keen analyst of situations as well as football strategy, and history had proved over and over that team owners as a group seemed to have less patience than the average fan or hometown beatwriter. When the 1963 season began, Tom Landry figured that every day he lasted on the job would be "gravy."

Despite the ominous noose hanging over him, Landry had reasons for guarded optimism. For one, Clint Murchison, the owner of the team, didn't seem to care whether the team won, nor did he seem to mind that it wasn't drawing very well. Clint loved being part of this team, and he treated his players like they were part of his family. When he asked a player, "How is the wife and family?" he was sincere. At Christmas, he gave gifts to all the players. One year it was TV sets, another year jewelry. But more than the gifts themselves, the players appreciated that Murchison was thinking of them. What was important to Clint Murchison was to be able to walk to the back of the plane after a game and chat quietly with his players, strung out on painkillers or filled with beer to ease the pain as some of them might have been.

In fact, the year before on a flight home from a game the Cowboy plane experienced engine trouble. The pilot made an emergency landing in Memphis and pulled the plane to the gate farthest from the terminal, where a three-man emergency repair crew was waiting in a Jeep. As the players stood up, preparing to deplane, Clint Murchison rose from his seat and hollered, "Look sharp, men! This may be our biggest reception yet."

Tex Schramm, too, showed no impatience with the progress made by the team. Schramm steadfastly maintained that in time the team would be a winner and a top drawer. The team would get a boost beginning this year because it would no longer have to compete head to head against the AFL's Dallas Texans. Lamar Hunt was offered a guarantee of 25,000 season tickets by the municipality of Kansas City, Missouri, and as a going away present Clint Murchison agreed to pay his pal a nice chunk of change for moving out of state. From now on, the Cowboys would be the only Sunday game in town.

As for his own team, Tom Landry was pleased that he was slowly replacing his disgruntled retreads with talented young kids, and in 1963 the Cowboys added another jewel, number one draft choice Lee Roy Jordan, an alligator-quick, tenacious, cussed, Bear Bryant–trained junkyard-dog linebacker to bolster the defense. Bryant once bragged to a reporter, "If the runner is in bounds, Jordan will tackle him."

A two-time All-America at Alabama, Jordan was thought by some to be a risk because at 6'1" and only 200 pounds, he gave away 20 to 30 pounds to some of the beefier linebackers. But despite his apparent lack of size, Jordan had something football fans would talk about during his illustrious fourteen-year career: He tackled you with the force of a sledgehammer crushing a tin can. And in addition to his bone-jarring ferocity, he provided needed leadership. It would be a couple of years before he started for the Cowboys, but once he took over from Jerry Tubbs he became the soul of the defense. "Who's gonna make this tackle?" he would growl in the huddle. During scrimmages, Jordan pushed his teammates, and as a result the Alabama farmboy would be criticized by several offensive players on the Cowboys for being a redneck, but the men on the defensive unit, white and black, found him to be an inspiration. They raved about his intensity and sense of mission. Few in the college or pro game played with the dedication, determination, and love of the game of football that Lee Roy Jordan did.

LEE ROY JORDAN: "I was born April 27, 1941, and I grew up in Excel, a small farm town of about 300 people in south central Alabama. My dad was a farmer. We had beef cattle, cotton, corn, and peanut crops. The farm produced our food. We raised chickens and turkeys, pigs and cattle, and we always had horses around for work and recreation. We did not have money, and this was not a hobby-type deal. No, it was the real thing. That was the way we grew up.

"My kids are shocked when I tell them stories about growing up. We didn't get electricity until I was twelve years old. I had to walk to the outhouse and I had to use a hand pump to pump all the water for the animals and for the family. Since I was the baby of four boys, that became my job a lot of the times.

"I can remember many, many days when I had to walk home two miles from school. If the school bus had run for the afternoon and I had to stay over for basketball or football, the most normal way to get home was to walk, because none of us had vehicles, not even bicycles. I used to ride one of our horses to school a lot and tie him out behind the ag building, and after football practice I'd saddle him up and ride home.

"I started playing football when I was in the sixth grade. Normally the high school didn't have enough guys to have twenty-two people, so when I was in the sixth grade, the coach would get me to play safety, because my brothers were on the team. And back then as soon as you felt you were big enough or tough enough, you could dress for the varsity, and as a seventh-grader I started dressing. Matter of fact, I started on the high school varsity as an eighth-grader, even though I really didn't grow until after my sophomore year. But they saw that I was a pretty tough kid, which came from being a farm kid and growing up the youngest of four boys. I was always having my spats with my brothers, and most of the time I came out on the short end of the stick as far as winning any battles. We were always wrestling, scrapping, but we didn't do anything to hurt the others, because we didn't want the wrath of Dad to be on us. Dad was a tough disciplinarian, a great father, a great Christian who was a tremendous supporter of the church, a deacon in the church, and a leader in our church community.

"I was first noticed by the University of Alabama in my junior year in high school. I played for a very small school—we had the largest class ever to graduate—32 seniors in my class. I played middle linebacker and I also played tailback on offense because we didn't have enough people to come in and out. We dressed from 17 to 20 guys per game, so you couldn't get injured, because we didn't have anybody to replace you. You just had to keep playing. So my junior year we were playing a much larger team, W. S. Neal High School in Bruton, forty miles east of Excel, and they were scouting a fullback who was a senior at this other school. I had an outstanding game, really overshadowed the play of the fullback on the other team, and after the game Jerry Claiborne, who went on to be a great coach at Kentucky and Maryland, came by and talked to me and told me Alabama would be back the next year to scout me consistently. And they *were* there.

"At the time Alabama had been losing for several years, but Coach Bryant had come a year and a half before, and he had his first recruiting class, had recruited some outstanding players, and so they were looking at every guy no matter what size school you were in trying to find guys who fit their program, which called for small, quicker guys than Georgia Tech or Auburn, which had won the national championship in '57 and was the dominant team at this time. Coach Bryant depended on quickness, endurance, and speed to win.

"I can remember the first time I met him. He was an imposing figure. He was 6'4" and about 240 pounds, a big man. We chatted. He wanted to know about my parents, said he wanted to meet them. He stressed how he was going to be responsible for you if you came to the university and played football for him. He was going to insist you do things your mother and dad had already taught you to do, like go to church and be a good citizen and be in class every day. To miss classes there had to be something wrong with you, you really had to be sick enough to go to the hospital. He chatted about the farm because he grew up in a similar rural community, and that's one reason he took a liking to me as much as he did.

"My deal with him was that I respected him so much as a coach, he was like a second father so I sure didn't want to do anything that he would be disappointed in me. As a player I wanted to give every effort, wanted to please him as much as I possibly could by my effort, just doing the best I could on every play. And I think most of us had that feeling about him.

"Coach Bryant had a way of saying the right things to the right people. He individually motivated guys. He knew how to do that better than anyone I ever met in sports. I needed the pat on the back, the stroking, him letting me know what he expected me to do and how well he thought I could play, and I certainly tried never to disappoint him.

"My junior year I was All-America on quite a few selections, and then on most all of them my senior year. I came in third in the Heisman voting, because we had two guys from the South, myself and Jerry Stovall, a great back from LSU, and we split the vote from that part of the country, and Terry Baker from Oregon State, a left-handed quarterback, got it.

"When I was drafted number one by the Cowboys in '63, everyone questioned my size. As a linebacker I was 6'1", 200 pounds. What the heck, you didn't have time to gain weight at Alabama, because Coach Bryant believed in endurance, not size. We worked out all the time, ran cross-country, ran everywhere on the field. You never walked. You never jogged. Hell, you ran from one drill to the next. And in all drills you ran full-speed. He believed the guys who were in the best condition would always win in the fourth quarter because you'd outlast the other team. And he believed that if you had more energy, you would think better because you were not tired, wouldn't make mistakes.

"As a matter of fact, when I weighed in the first time at the Dallas training camp, I weighed 203 pounds, and the trainer said, 'Oh, my God. Man, I thought you were bigger than this.' I said, 'Wellll, maybe I *will* get bigger.' "

With the addition of Jordan some experts were noticing that the Cowboys, at least on paper, were looking very strong. In a *Sports Illustrated* cover story Tex Maule, Tex Schramm's former assistant with the Rams and now the football pundit of America's leading sporting weekly, predicted that the Cowboys would win the Eastern Division of the NFL. It was a prediction that surprised and annoyed just about everyone on the Cowboys.

BOB FRY: "When Tex Maule predicted we'd win the East, I thought maybe he was a little crazy. I don't know where he got that from. I was amazed. It put the pressure on the whole organization."

FRANK CLARKE: "In 1963 Tex Maule predicted that the Cowboys would win the East. Thanks, Tex. We didn't like reading that. It was like, 'Hey, come on, we don't need to hear that.' We were afraid the opposing players would start looking at us in a different way. 'Hey, wait a minute? You mean we have to play these guys harder?' Oh, that was weird to see that.

"We started out in '63 losing six of our first seven games. That's what I mean. Tex Maule didn't do us any favors at all. That was a mean thing to do."

PETTIS NORMAN: "In '63 I wondered if I had been overzealous in my estimation of Tom Landry. It was a hard year, but interestingly, he had told us, 'You might take a dip before taking a step up.' At the time I didn't really understand what he meant. You reflect back, and I recall things the man said, and that they were so prophetic, and sure enough that would be exactly what would happen. Later he'd say, 'You have to learn how to win big games.' Or, 'Keep doing the things I say. Just believe in them, and in our fifth year we're going to win.' And in the last game of the season in the fifth year, we won and became winners. It was amazing!

"In those respects Tom Landry was an *amazing* person. As I look back and learn, I can see that this man knew more about football than all other coaches put together. And he had a way of convincing his players to stick with it, and that was the essence why we eventually won. Even when we faced difficulties, he had faith that we would always come back. To me he was an amazing coach. He was a brilliant football man. He expressed a deep faith in Christ, and I wouldn't have any reason to question that. I saw him do things that were very good, though like all men, he wasn't perfect. I look at him as being a human being who tried to be better than most folk. I didn't understand some of the things he did, like the need for him to shuttle in Frank Clarke and me, but that didn't take away from the fact that I thought he was a great coach."

LEE ROY JORDAN: "When I came to the Cowboys, I had difficulty accepting Tom's system, because it was different from what I had been successful with in the past. You'd say, 'God, I don't know whether this will work or not.' I knew Coach Landry had been very successful putting together this type of defense with the Giants. His concept was to stop the run first and then to put people into passing situations where they *had* to throw the football, third-and-long, long-passing situations, where they didn't have any choice but to pass. I didn't question it. But as a team, it took us a long time to develop the confidence in it, because we didn't have film where Tom could say, 'Hey, let's look at the way we executed it perfectly last year. All you have to do is duplicate this.' We didn't have that, and so we had to put it together one guy at a time. Coach Landry would come in and say, 'This is what we're talking about. On this move, Bob Lilly has done it right, and I want it done this way every time from now on.' So we had to put it together in pieces, and it took a few years to really get it where we had a concept that was totally together, where the coaches all knew it and the players all knew it, and where we could work on repetition where we could repeat it every play."

FRANK CLARKE: "Despite the fact we only won four games that year in '63 the offense was really coming nicely. Don Meredith took over at quarterback for Eddie. By that time my confidence in Tom was so strong that I knew he was doing the thing that would make the team continue to move forward. It had nothing to do with Eddie, nothing to do with Don. It was Tom Landry saying, 'Stay with me you guys. We're going to heaven.'

"My feeling was, if Tom Landry said it, I was happy to do it. Aw, man, yes. Landry was saying, 'I have been testing him, and I like what I see.' And against the 49ers in Kezar Stadium, Don threw for 460 yards, and close to 200 of that was mine. Man, it was fantastic. God, it was wonderful. The 49ers had pretty close to the same yardage. I mean, their offense was pretty potent too. John Brodie was the quarterback, and it was one of those games where the air was filled with passes, and it was wonderful to play so well in that foreign territory, to be so far from Dallas, and to play so well, 'cause we had a rhythm going.

"There was something happening with the club, and to produce like that offensively was really a high thing for us.

"And after that game we upset the Philadelphia Eagles, and Don again was brilliant, and we were practicing, getting ready to play the Browns in Cleveland, when we learned that President Kennedy had been killed."

The Kennedy assassination was the worst in a series of ugly events that prompted outsiders to brand Dallas the "City of Hate." Four days before the 1960 elections, vice presidential candidate Lyndon Johnson and his wife, Lady Bird, came to Dallas for a noon Democratic Party luncheon. Lyndon, a senator from Texas, angered conservative Texans by agreeing to run with Kennedy, who was hated for being Catholic and for being a "nigger lover." The Johnsons were confronted by an angry, screaming crowd of demonstrators who shook insulting signs at them—"Smiling Judas Johnson"; "LBJ Sold Out to Yankee Socialists"—and taunted them as soon as they got out of their car. Lady Bird was genuinely frightened. Some demonstrators spit on them.

The demonstrators were livid that Johnson would join a ticket with a Catholic. W. A. Criswell, pastor of the First Baptist Church of Dallas, in July 1960 declared, "The election of a Catholic as president would mean the end of religious liberty in America." He had also preached against the evils of school integration as contrary to the Bible's teachings. In a sermon Criswell endorsed Richard Nixon.

The *Dallas Morning News*, meanwhile, blasted Kennedy for being a "Socialist" and for his liberal views on civil rights. When *News* publisher E. M. "Ted" Dealey went to a White House luncheon, he infuriated President Kennedy when he told him, "The people in Texas and the Southwest need and want a strong president who would get off Caroline's tricycle and lead the nation from horseback."

On October 26, 1963, United Nations ambassador Adlai Stevenson was invited to town to speak. The John Birch Society, a far right-wing organization opposed to the United Nations as an institution, staged a demonstration during which 1,400 protestors, led by former army General Edwin Walker, blasted Stevenson, the U.N., and Supreme Court Justice Earl Warren, who had ordered desegregation years earlier. Walker told the crowd that the Communists and "the Alger Hiss crowd" were behind the founding of the United Nations.

At that rally Lee Harvey Oswald was there stalking Walker. Six months earlier he had tried to assassinate Walker, shooting at him with a rifle from an alley while he sat in his office working late. Oswald was not as accurate as he would be accused of being later.

The next day Stevenson was scheduled to speak. That morning the Walker group distributed handbills with pictures of John Kennedy with the words: "Wanted for Treason. This man is wanted for treasonous activities against the United States." Among the charges were that he permitted "known Communists" to abound in federal offices.

When Stevenson got up to speak, he was shouted down with a bullhorn. After the speech, as he was getting into his car, one woman hit him on the head with a homemade sign. A college student spat on him. It was all recorded for television's all-seeing eye.

The city leaders were aghast by this incident. Mayor Cabell and dozens of city leaders sent telegrams of apology to Stevenson. In a letter the former presidential candidate recalled the days when the Ku Klux Klan had reigned in the city and made it the "hate capital" of the Southwest. He urged Dallas residents to reject the radical right just as it had ultimately rejected the Klan.

For four days the event rated front-page newspaper coverage. Said the *Dallas Times-Herald*: "We must quit preaching hate. We must stop spreading the believing of the ridiculous stories of suspicion and distrust of our fellow citizens from the seeds of uncontrolled frenzy."

In a few weeks President Kennedy, the primary target of that fury, was coming to Dallas. Because he felt he needed the Dixie vote, Kennedy had sat on the sidelines during the sit-ins and the first freedom rides in 1961 as blacks began to demand the vote, but in 1962 as black students were integrating the state university system in Mississippi, Kennedy sent federal troops. Then after a black demonstration in Birmingham in April of 1963 in which white mobs set upon the protestors with clubs and dogs, Kennedy called Birmingham officials to negotiate a settlement. Public facilities were integrated. When Martin Luther King's motel was bombed, Kennedy sent 3,000 federal troops into position near the city. He ordered the National Guard to protect two students enrolling at the University of Alabama.

On June 11, 1963, Kennedy made a speech on national television. He asked, "Who among us would be content to have the color of his skin changed and stand in his place?"

A few hours later NAACP field director Medgar Evers was shot in the back and killed in the driveway of his home in Jackson, Mississippi. In September 1963, soon after a church in Birmingham was blown up, killing four little girls, Kennedy asked Congress for the most sweeping civil rights bill in American history, a law preventing discrimination at all facilities that served the public. He also came out against school segregation and for voting rights.

By now the southern outrage against Kennedy had increased so much that Adlai Stevenson wondered whether the president should even go to Dallas. So did some of the city's leaders. Stanley Marcus, the owner of Neiman Marcus, the famed department store, told Lyndon Johnson to urge him not to come. Johnson knew Kennedy well. He told Marcus he would be coming, so "go out and raise money."

The Dallas players remember November 22, 1963, because they were all out on the practice field. Even though President and Mrs. Kennedy were to ride down the streets of downtown Dallas, an experience attended by a huge throng that day, Tom Landry refused to allow his players to skip practice—not for the president or for any other reason.

Though a couple of the southern players would say they were glad that Kennedy had died, his death was a cruel blow to most of the players, especially the blacks. To them, Kennedy's death raised an alarm. With Kennedy gone, who in the federal government would care about them, take up their cause? The death of John Kennedy would haunt the Cowboys for the rest of the season and into the next. Like the city of Dallas itself, the team would be associated by the rest of the country with the murder of President John F. Kennedy.

LEE ROY JORDAN: "There were a lot of people in Alabama who respected President Kennedy very much. He might not have been our favorite person, but he was the president of the United States, and we had a great deal of respect for him and the job he was filling and the position he had been put in by the majority of the people in the United States. I respected him highly, and I think the majority of people in the state of Alabama did. I think most people like me thought he was a dynamic young man who was a great leader. I didn't have opinions of who was good or bad. He was the guy who was chosen. To me, to be up there you had to be an outstanding person.

"I was horrified when it happened. I had had a punctured kidney, and I was injured and out for the rest of the year, and I was in my apartment. I got in my car to go to practice to get therapy and turned on the radio, and boom, they were chasing the guy, trying to catch him downtown among the buildings, and it was going on in Dallas right then.

"I sat there in the car for thirty minutes just shocked, totally bewildered that something like this could happen, and was happening in the city of Dallas where I was! It was a shocking, horrifying, unbelievable experience for me, and I think the majority of the people felt the same way, whether you were from Alabama or Dallas, Texas."

CHUCK HOWLEY: "When we heard what had happened, we really didn't believe it. We were as stunned as the rest of the world was. We were very concerned how it would affect us as a team. In fact, we were playing in Cleveland that weekend. They were going to cancel, and then the National Football League decided that they had to go ahead and play those games, and I remember trying to ship a suitcase because Cleveland was close to my hometown in West Virginia. I had taken a suitcase full of Christmas presents home with me on that charter, and I was trying to ship them by Greyhound the rest of the way. And the Greyhound employee saw that I had a Dallas return address on it, and he said, 'I'm not going to do this. You're from Dallas.'

"So the general tendency among people was to blame the people of Dallas for this, and it was a great tragedy, as we all know. In Cleveland we all stayed close to the hotel, stayed closed to each other through that particular weekend, and we played that game, and we got out of town as fast as we could."

BOB LILLY: "On the day President Kennedy was shot, our equipment manager came out and told us, and we didn't want to believe it, but it killed practice. All of our enthusiasm was gone. It was like we wanted to quit and go in and find out if it was real, and to hear that it was almost made you want to throw up. You just wanted to go vomit. And we just couldn't believe it, none of us could.

"That was the worst thing that happened to Dallas. We couldn't believe it happened, and we couldn't believe it happened in Dallas. In fact, most of us were really looking forward to going to his parade that day, but we couldn't go because we had to practice.

"It was devastating, and then we found out we had to play that week, which we did not want to do. No player wanted to. We had to go to Cleveland, and when we arrived there we had to unload the plane, haul our own luggage, because nobody would do it for us.

"And then when we went to the stadium, we didn't know if we were going to get shot or what. They called us everything, murderers, everything, from the stands. Like we had something to do with it. It wasn't much of a game. We were beaten that week. The death of President Kennedy was pretty disheartening. I really think that destroyed our '63 year. I know it did for me, and I think most of us felt the same way. We didn't get over it for weeks. We didn't get over not only our own personal feelings, but the stigma. It affected us, no question about it.

"It was extremely distracting, because we never got over it. We never got over the stigma when we played other teams. But the other thing was, it was too distracting, an ongoing saga of what happened. For weeks, months, in the paper, the media, everywhere you went, people asking you where you were that day, what you were doing, this and that. And we felt kind of disgraced that it had happened in our town. We'd go on the road, and people booed us because of that. It was *very* distracting."

FRANK CLARKE: "I remember we were on the practice field at the North Central Expressway, when a guy named Jimmy Parker, who handled a lot of our publicity, drove up, got out of his car, and when I looked at Jimmy, I knew something was wrong. That whole thing was so otherworldly. Just the idea that someone had killed this man who lit fires for us. He lit fires for this whole country. He was doing some things for the *whole* country.

"We were numb. It was surreal. We couldn't believe it, like 'We are asleep, this is not happening, this is a dream. Kennedy has *not* been killed right here under our noses. There is *no way* this is happening.'

"We went to Cleveland a couple of days later to play the Browns, and we were still numb. I remember being there in Cleveland, and I remember playing the game, but I don't remember *being there*. It was just numbing. Everything was just thrown off, so surreal.

"I wish you could have experienced Cleveland Stadium. I used to play there a lot. It was like, 'Why are we even doing this?' Because some people were saying, 'How could they not cancel the NFL games that week?' It didn't make sense. It *didn't*. It was really weird to play that game. Because we weren't ready to play at all.

"His death affected us. It affected us a lot. There were a lot of people commenting on the fact that we were from Dallas, where our president was killed, almost as if *we* had something to do with it. My goodness, what a numbing thing for our country to go through."

CORNELL GREEN: "John Kennedy affected everybody's life. He meant that as a black man, I would have a chance. We weren't so worried about segregated housing at the time. I didn't care if you lived next door to me or not. It didn't hurt me. I didn't want to live next door to you either. It's just that: Don't discriminate against me in the job field. Don't hold my being black against me when it comes to getting a job. And they were. That was the main thing. That was it. And with Kennedy as president, the feeling among the blacks was that it was ending.

"I was numb for three or four days. It doesn't sink in what magnitude this is going to be. And then after a while, as it goes on, you start thinking about it, what is really happening, what's going to happen, and you think about who did it, and a lot of things. When they made Lyndon Johnson president, I had no idea even who he was, and probably nobody else in the country did either.

"At one time they thought everybody from Texas was responsible for it, really. If you were from Texas, then you heard, 'You son of a bitch, you killed Kennedy.' Even some towns we went into to play football, the Texans were looked at as people who killed Kennedy. But that was just people's own ignorance. It never really affected me one way or the other, 'cause I knew where I was that day and what I was doing. I just was sorry that the man was dead. A great man had died."

PETTIS NORMAN: "Incredibly, it was almost like I had had a premonition about it. Frank Clarke and I were on the field practicing, running pass routes, and we were engaged in conversation. The practice field was right by the trainer's room, and the trainer had a radio out on the back porch of the trainer's room up loud, and we could hear it. They were describing the presidential motorcade while we were running passes.

"A lot of us would have loved to have been there, because President Kennedy represented a whole new concept of a president, a very, very engaging, gregarious young man, everything the presidents before him had not been. He just captivated the country. And I remember saying to Frank Clarke, 'Wouldn't it be something if some nut tried to shoot the president?' And the reason that thought came to my mind was I saw how mean-spirited the people in Dallas had seemed to be toward Kennedy and the Kennedy people. I got a sense when I first came to Dallas that white people, unlike in urban Charlotte and other urban cities I had been to, really wanted to relegate blacks to a lower status. As little as white people in other cities appreciated blacks, it was even less in Dallas. It was a mean-spirited thing I had picked up, and so coupled with these thoughts and my feeling that everybody talked alike and thought alike, 'Wouldn't it be something if one of these nuts with this Texas mentality were to shoot the president?' And within a matter of seconds of saying this to Frank, the trainer ran out and said, 'They just shot the president.'

"Frank and I looked at each other and thought, 'This guy is lying. He heard us talking.' And we said, 'You've got to be kidding me.' 'No, no, listen,' and he turned the radio up loud, and then louder, and we heard it, and we still could not believe it. We stood there and looked at each other, and our mouths just dropped open, and I felt a sense of innocence, of loss at that moment that I could not explain. It was a sense of devastation. I thought, What are we going to do now? They have shot the president.

"The other thing I remember was that when we were sure that President Kennedy had died, some of the players—I won't say their names—they were almost happy that it had occurred. The perception was that Kennedy was doing things for minorities, and I knew that was behind a lot of that strong sentiment against him by whites in Texas at that time. It just reinforced some things that we knew, that we really had people on the team who had such a hatred for our people.

"I felt such outrage. I couldn't help but feel that these people were basically moral cowards, that they could only be brave behind sheets or in large gatherings of folks of their kind. They could never go out on a limb, like the civil rights workers who had to fight against long odds for a chance to be equal.

"When I was a student at Johnson C. Smith University I had partici-pated in one of the first student sit-in demonstrations in Charlotte. My school was the second school to do that, after the North Carolina A&T students who sat-in in the Woolworth coffee shop in Greensboro in 1960. We sat-in in the Woolworth's in Charlotte the very next day.

"I can remember they had dogs and police outside. You walked down the street, and the white people would spit on you and yell, 'Get out of here, nigger, you're not supposed to be here.' We had been schooled not to argue and fight back.

"The point I'm making about that, those people who hated us so much would *never* have put themselves on the line like that. They would have hid behind a sheet and a group. And they hid behind their religion.

"It's funny, if you look at the atrocities of the world, most of them are committed in the name of religion. One thing I have never been able to reconcile is how people do things like that in the name of religion, and still serve God. But I guess that gives them the escape, an out, and maybe that's part of what Voltaire meant when he said, 'If God did not exist, it would be necessary to invent him.' People use God to escape whatever they want to escape, and maybe the only way they can escape the atrocities of their mind is by wrapping it in religion, saying, 'That's the way God intended it.'

"We all have consciences, and somehow I guess that's the way they can do that. But we're not dealing with people who are level thinkers, or righteous thinkers. If you were dealing with the righteous, they would not draw those conclusions from the Bible. You would use the Bible to draw other sorts of conclusions about being kind and gentle and neighborly and loving.

"During the next few days after Kennedy's assassination we were in a dark cloud. It's amazing the thoughts that go through your mind. You just kept waiting and hoping that the stone would be rolled away and all the things you heard about Jesus' resurrection would happen again. And as I watched the procession going to the burial, I remember thinking, 'Resurrection is *not* going to happen. It hasn't happened in nineteen hundred years, and it ain't gonna happen today. They are going to bury him. This is final.' And I just kept wondering how this country would pull out of this. It was almost the first time I had heard of Lyndon Johnson, and frankly, after I learned more about him, I thought, 'We really *are* in trouble.'

"Kennedy's death affected the team the rest of the year. It was *always* in the back of the team's mind, and you could never 100 percent focus on what you were doing. It was like that for most people in Dallas; it was something we could not get out of our minds. It was enough in your subconscious, and so we just went through the season. We were 4–10, nowhere near what we had envisioned."

FRANK CLARKE: "In the final game against St. Louis, a team we had never beaten, we were down by ten points late in the game, but Don led us back to win it on a pass he threw to me. I had never done that before, and I never did it since, been on the receiving end of a game-winning touchdown. That was neat.

"From the huddle, Dandy called for me from the left formation to run a corner route. I was flanked out, spread wide.

"Don called, 'Red left.' The color designates the formation, tells the fullback where to be, tells both halfbacks where to be, and it tells the tight end where to line up. Then he says, 'Wing corner. On two.' He gets up there, and looks at the defense, and calls out some numbers, and those numbers are either dummy or live numbers for an audible.

"If it's a dummy color, we'll just run the play that he's called in the huddle. In this particular case, I went downfield seven or eight yards, and I did a strong slant in, and I looked at the quarterback to catch the ball underneath the defensive back.

"A lot of times the defensive back will guess. He'll say, 'I'm not going to let him catch this sideline route.' So he'll make a move to come up toward the receiver, and as soon as he makes that move, man, somebody as fast and as sharp a mover as I am will plant my right foot and head for the left corner of the end zone.

"And I could do that as well as anybody, 'cause once I saw a defensive back make that commitment, I had him. 'Cause there was no way they were going to turn around and catch me, 'cause I had too much speed and too much strength moving off that angle.

"Don was looking at the same thing I was looking at. He was looking for the defensive back making his commitment, and once he made the commitment, it was just a question of getting me the ball. And in this particular case it was a cornerback by the name of Jimmy Hill. We knew his tendencies. We knew he played off of us pretty strong and that a lot of times he would give you the route underneath, so what I would do, I would run real fast to get to my first inside move real fast—make it look like that was what I was going to do, and that he needed to hurry and commit himself, otherwise I was going to gain 20 yards. So as soon as he committed himself to cover my first inside move, then that's when I would plant my right foot and head toward the left corner of the end zone. Meredith just sweetly landed that baby right in my arms.

"Over the years as he gained more experience, Don got to where he took a lot of the lift out of the ball, but in '62 and '63, he was getting a rise out of the ball—what I mean, he used to throw a lot of passes that took off on the receiver. The ball would look like it was coming to shoulder height, but because of the way he threw it, that baby kept going up, so by the time it got to you, you had to either jump or stretch real high to catch it, and that's okay, but you take away from the receiver's potential by doing that. There aren't many quarterbacks who come into the league who already know how to do that. They have to work at it. By the time he learned and gained the confidence, Don could throw a sweet pass."

*   *   *

The 28–24 win over the Cardinals gave the Cowboys a 4–10 record. Tom Landry's overall record after the four years was 13–38–3. Four of the losses in '63 were by ten or more points, and the Dallas sportswriters, led by the rapier pens of Gary Cartwright and Steve Perkins, called for Landry's firing, if not his lynching. Many of the Cowboy faithful agreed. There were unconfirmed (and untrue) rumors that Oklahoma coach Bud Wilkinson was in the wings to replace him.

DICK NOLAN: "At that time the sportswriters were against Tom because for four years we hadn't won. Ordinarily you don't see a coach go four years and not win something without being gone. He'll be gone in three years if they don't see it. If they get a glimmer, he might get four.

"During the '63 season I was talking to Tom about doing something 'next year,' and he said, 'Gee, Dick. I don't know. There may not be a next year. I have to go down and see Clint Murchison.' "

TOM LANDRY: "I began wondering if it was time again to start thinking about life after football. Maybe God wanted me to be doing something else."

Tom Landry prayed for guidance.

EDDIE LEBARON: "I can remember when everyone was on Tom. The papers were on him badly. I was upset that the reporters didn't realize how good Tom was, and it made me mad that even after they found out, a lot of writers still didn't like him because he didn't have the personality that some of them might like. Tom's reputation was that the Cowboys were a clinical, cold-blooded team that relied on science and skill and not the razzle-dazzle and shoot-'em-up type of guys, and yet the truth was, our offense was very exciting. And no one ever gave him credit for that."

FRANK CLARKE: "Toward the end of the '63 season, there was some talk in the papers that Landry would be fired. But I'm almost certain there were not many players who came close to even thinking that. As a matter of fact, it would have been more in line to give this guy a long-term contract. Oh yeah. That's the way we felt.

"I know for a fact—I was there—there was *nothing* buzzing around through our locker room that had anything at all with Tom being seriously considered for not being there. Not with what he had done. Not with what we were *feeling*. The press didn't know this. They did not feel what we were feeling. It wasn't that they didn't bother to ask. With all due respect, it was more that they didn't know *how* to ask."

PETTIS NORMAN: "After we had finished the '63 season, there was talk among a few of the players, and talk within the community, that Tom Landry would be fired. Most people following the Cowboys concluded that Landry would not be back for the 1964 season, because of the intensity and the breadth of that talk.

"Gary Cartwright, especially, really didn't like Landry, didn't have any respect for his ability to coach. Gary was pretty sharp with his knife. He could cut you up. For whatever reason, he seemed to be able to state his position with a great deal of impunity. Gary did not believe that Landry would ever be a winning coach, that he had seen the best of the years of the Cowboys.

"And so all the news and all the whispers and gossip I was privy to suggested that Tom was not going to be around after the '63 season. Although I had no question about how much football this man knew, everything pointed to the fact he was not going to be able to lead the Cowboys to the Promised Land, and so subconsciously I bought into the theory that there might be a change. And frankly, I thought as much that Tom Landry himself might think about giving it up."

BOB LILLY: "Some of the older players wanted their own coaches to come. Some of them wanted Bear Bryant, and I did hear Bud Wilkinson's name. Everybody had a different opinion on what it took to win, and there was hope among some of the players that Tom would go and we would get another coach.

"If Landry had a weakness, it was in motivation, and that may have been one reason the writers wanted him fired. Because he was always the same: honest and trustworthy and didn't make waves. Tom never said *anything* that made headlines. But look at Tom's record: with just a little more luck we could have *easily* been in seven or eight Super Bowls. Look at his record over the years. We won our division year after year after year and were in the playoffs eighteen out of nineteen years.

"Tom ran it well, for a long time. Tom never got the credit he deserved from the media, but he got it from his opposing coaches. He got it from Joe Gibbs at Washington, he got it from Mike Ditka, Dan Reeves, got it from Bill Parcells, got it from Don Shula."

Fortunately for Coach Landry, only Clint Murchison, not the reporters or the fans, could make the decision on whether to retain him or not. Clint was a guy who was taught by his father to pick the best person to run his outfit, and then let him do his job. He also believed in loyalty, and Tom

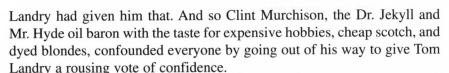

Landry had given him that. And so Clint Murchison, the Dr. Jekyll and Mr. Hyde oil baron with the taste for expensive hobbies, cheap scotch, and dyed blondes, confounded everyone by going out of his way to give Tom Landry a rousing vote of confidence.

Clint Murchison was one of those Texans who refused to let himself be pushed around, not by any two-bit newspaper reporter nor by ignorant fans. Clint never once lost faith in Tom Landry, and neither did Tex Schramm.

Clint Murchison, rather than firing Landry as the throng demanded, instead gave Tom Landry the richest contract in the history of football up to that time, presenting him with a ten-year contract extension, to begin after his present one expired at the end of the 1965 season. The players who believed in Tom Landry's genius understood and agreed.

PETTIS NORMAN: "Out of the clear blue nowhere, Tom got a ten-year contract. This told you something about Clint Murchison. That was done as much out of a deep sense of loyalty and commitment than his foresight into what was going to happen."

DICK NOLAN: "Though it was more than five years before we won, Clint could see. He knew it wasn't a lack of work, 'cause boy, people worked. And they worked and worked.

"Clint Murchison. That's the guy. He said, 'Nobody tells me how to run my football team.' He was a guy who took all the heat, and he told Tom, 'You just keep going, brother. It'll straighten out.' And he had great confidence in him, and of course, Tom did it.

"See, Clint was like Tom, a very intellectual guy, an MIT graduate. But he could see, and maybe, too, it was that he was so wealthy. But he was a super guy, a great guy. He was a guy who said, 'Nobody tells me how to run my football team, and nobody tells me how to run my business.' Of course, everything turned."

BOB LILLY: "Clint Murchison did a very wise thing signing Tom to a ten-year contract, because once Tom signed that contract, then all the players knew where they stood. And at that point was where Coach really started building the team. He got rid of all the bitchers, people who were not for him, and that's what he had to do."

17

Mel and Maury

In selecting future Cowboys in the 1964 draft, the brain trust of Tex Schramm, Gil Brandt, and Tom Landry again showed both guts and ingenuity. Their second-round draft choice was a running back from the University of Oregon by the name of Mel Renfro, a lightning-fast sprinter who had run anchor in college on the world-record setting 4 x 100-yard relay team along with Cowboy defensive back Mike Gaechter. Renfro, called "Suds" by his teammates, would have been a surefire first-round pick, but on the day John F. Kennedy was killed in November 1963, he was so distraught over life's vicissitudes that he punched out a glass mirror and severed tendons in his right hand. Renfro's hand was still a mess at the time of the draft, and so when it was the Cowboys' turn for their second pick, Mel Renfro, who would be an All-Pro performer ten times, was still available.

MEL RENFRO: "I grew up in Portland, Oregon. My dad was a carpet cleaner by trade, and he spent most of his life dong that and odd jobs. We lived in Bannport, the only area in town where blacks were allowed to live. As long as we stayed in our own area, in our own land, as we say, we didn't have any problems. My dad always told me, 'Don't go over there, 'cause that's trouble.' He didn't explain to me what the trouble was. I knew enough to pay attention to my father.

202

"I went to a mostly white grade school and a mostly white high school, and things were kind of easy for me because I was the star. I went through my entire high school career only losing one football game out of thirty-five, and that was in the last game I played. We went to three straight state championships, won two and lost the last one by a point.

"My sophomore and junior years I was a running back, because we had Terry Baker, who later was a Heisman Trophy winner, playing quarterback, and after he graduated I became the quarterback. In one game I scored six touchdowns. I ran back a couple of interceptions for touchdowns, ran a punt back for a touchdown, and scored the others on offense. The score was 69–0.

"I was going to follow Terry to Oregon State, but Len Casanova, the coach at Oregon, spent a lot of time with my parents, and he convinced them Oregon was the place for me to go. My parents made the decision for me, because of Len, who was very personable, and when I went and played for him, he was like another father to me.

"I grew up as an introvert, very quiet and unassuming. My platform was the athletic arena, and that's where I did my thing. Off the field, away from that arena, I was just a quiet, shy little kid. I didn't like to speak, I didn't feel like I was a good student. I had problems concentrating and getting into studies. I was a C and C-minus student, and I felt like I had to work real hard to be that.

"When I learned how to drink alcohol in college, that almost destroyed me, because it gave me that false confidence to be able to speak out and do things I wouldn't ordinarily do if I had not had alcohol in my system. I was a college binge drinker. On weekends we'd go and drink beer. We'd drink until we couldn't drink any more.

"And so, when President Kennedy was assassinated, because I was a shy, sensitive person, it affected me very deeply. I cried. And because of the assassination, our football game was postponed that weekend, and when the game's postponed, what are the guys going to do? At night, we sat around and drank beer. And at that time I was having marital problems. I had a young bride, and we were separated. She was eight months pregnant, and we weren't getting along, so I had a double whammy.

"We were having a little get-together at the apartment, and I had had a little bit too much to drink, and somehow she ended up at the party, and I walked into her room and she was sitting and talking to another fella, and I just totally went berserk. I took a beer bottle and burst it against a wall above their heads. I then went into the bathroom and I banged my right hand against a mirror, and the next thing I knew, I was sitting on the couch bleeding. I would have probably bled to death but my teammates Herman McKenny and H. D. Murphy said, 'Man, you need to go to the hospital.' It wasn't hurting because I had so much alcohol in me, but after seeing all the blood—wrapping the hand didn't stop the bleeding—we went to the emergency room, and they sewed it up.

"The next morning the doctor walked in and he said, 'Mel, you're going to be able to play but not soon. You're going to be able to play, but I'm not sure about your grip.' That's all he said.

"There was a cover-up as to what happened. The rumor went out that I had tried to commit suicide. There were lots of rumors, and it kind of quieted down, and I didn't get to play in the next game because I had severed some nerves. People to this day don't know that I don't have feeling in half of my right hand.

"The day of the NFL draft, I was sitting in a hotel room in downtown Eugene with four or five scouts from around the country. They all had me pegged number one, the first pick. The Cowboys drafted first, and they started calling around to check with my doctor about my hand to see if it was okay. Well, they had a tough time getting ahold of him, and Tex held up the draft. While I was sitting around in the hotel room, people were wondering what was going on with the Cowboys. And when they finally picked, they didn't pick me. They drafted Scott Appleton, a defensive lineman out of Texas, and traded him immediately, and then they spread the rumor that I had cut my hand off, that I wouldn't be able to play pro ball. No question the Cowboys did that. They admitted it. Because they came right back in the second round and picked me up just like that, and so they got two first-round draft choices. They pulled a coup, and everybody else had egg on their faces." ·

TEX SCHRAMM: "We were interested in Mel Renfro but he had cut his hand and severed the nerves or tendons. At that time he didn't have any feeling in three or four of his fingers. The word got around the draft room in Chicago that he'd be who we'd take on the first round.

"Before we made our first pick, we held up the draft several hours. Buddy Parker was offering us a trade for Buddy Dial, and we were spending all that time trying to work out that deal. Everyone else thought we were checking on Renfro. The season wasn't over so we couldn't say anything about the trade because Dial was still playing for Pittsburgh.

"When we drafted [defensive tackle] Scott Appleton on the first round, the word spread that obviously we'd found something wrong with Renfro, so nobody else drafted him on the first round.

"Then when we came back and took Renfro on the second round, everybody screamed they'd been taken."

In football, as in life, there can be funny bounces. Renfro became a defensive gem for the Cowboys. In the deal to acquire Buddy Dial, the best wide receiver in the league at the time, Schramm sent Appleton to the Steelers, who turned up empty-handed when the big tackle signed with the Houston Oilers of the AFL.

On the face of it, the pundits saw the Cowboys as the big winners. But Tex Schramm knew something no one else knew and it would haunt him, but only because he was the sort of person who always wanted his cake and to eat it too: Had the Cowboys not traded for Dial, they were prepared to draft and sign a player they had tucked away in a hotel room in Columbus, Ohio. Had not Buddy Parker popped the Dial idea, said Schramm, "We probably would have drafted him number one because of the doubt with Mel's hand."

That player was star receiver Paul Warfield of Ohio State. Warfield would help defeat the Cowboys in important playoff games as a member of the Cleveland Browns.

When Buddy Dial hurt himself early and did little with the Cowboys, Schramm would mull the "what-ifs" of ending up with a Warfield-Renfro duo. Any misgivings, however, certainly were lessened because in that same draft in '64 Tex Schramm picked in the seventh round a track star and football player from Florida A&M University by the name of Bob Hayes, a future Olympic medalist, and the man who would be branded as the "World's Fastest Human." Because of his commitment to the U.S. Olympic team, Hayes would not be available to the Cowboys until '65, but when he finally arrived he would change the game of pro football with his explosive speed. (In the tenth round in '64 Schramm would gamble and pick a player who wouldn't show up for another *five* years, Navy quarterback, Heisman Trophy winner, *Time* magazine cover boy Roger Staubach.)

But, Tex being Tex, he would always wonder: How many Super Bowls would the Cowboys have won if they had come away with Renfro, Warfield, *and* Hayes in '64?

For Coach Landry, the key addition in '64 was Renfro, who had been an outstanding runner at Oregon. Landry had figured that with his athletic ability, even with a bad hand, the fleet Renfro would make a great defensive back. As it was, Landry felt Renfro was too frail to be a runner in the pros, and after giving him a shot during training camp, Landry decided the risk of his getting hurt running the ball was too great, and he made him his free safety.

As usual, Landry was right, and as a rookie Mel Renfro became the Cowboys' weapon for stopping the other team's fastest receivers. Renfro would be a mainstay of the defense for eleven years. In Cornell Green and Mike Gaechter, the Cowboys had had some solid speed in the corners. With Renfro, they had a rocketman, a center fielder with magical ability who seemed to have a sixth sense to divine where his man was going to go. Hooked into Tom Landry's system, Renfro, a quiet man, was virtually unshakeable. He had a methodical deftness to his movements, so that he always seemed to be in position against his man. And if the pass was completed in front of him, he was a sure tackler, too.

In practice wide receiver Frank Clarke had to scrimmage often against Renfro. He well knew just how great Mel Renfro was.

FRANK CLARKE: "Mel was *so* good. Man, yes, I can tell you about Mel Renfro. He was *incredible*. It was like he knew where you were going. I can only say that he had that sense great defensive backs are born with. You just could not shake this guy.

"We'd scrimmage, and on most defenders I could plant that right foot and go, but I couldn't do that with Mel. He had this hip movement that allowed him to be right there with you no matter what cuts you made, no matter where you moved, no matter what you did. And he had the quickness of a jaguar or one of those cats that has speed *and* quickness, too. This was Mel Renfro, speed and quickness, and no matter what you did, he was there. And it got to be really frustrating, like, 'Mel, God, get off of me!' And you'd realize, this guy is going to be *real* good. It seemed he was *always* in position, and I say to myself that that kind of skill is 'innate,' 'inborn.' This was not something that some coach at Oregon taught him. He was amazing."

On defense, the Cowboys were improving steadily. The front line was anchored by Bob Lilly, who had been moved from defensive left end to defensive right tackle in mid-'63 to take better advantage of his strength and quick bursts, but defensive end George Andrie had been hurt much of '63, and the Cowboys had had to trade for veteran Larry Stephens of the L.A. Rams. The line was still in flux and was a question mark, though the linebacking corps of Jerry Tubbs, Chuck Howley, Dave Edwards, and Lee Roy Jordan was improving every year. In the backfield Green, Gaechter, and Renfro were joined by Jim Ridlon, who had been the other back at Syracuse University along with Jim Brown and who had played for six years with the San Francisco 49ers before being acquired by the Cowboys in 1963. Landry's system was built for Ridlon, who was both athletic and very smart.

JIMMY RIDLON: "In one of our first team meetings Coach Landry looked around the room and asked who had the most NFL experience. He decided I was the man, so he asked me to come to the front of the room and draw up the six basic ways defensive teams run the sweep in pro ball. I had no idea there were so many. It was embarrassing.

"Later that evening Tom came up to me and told me he was sorry he had put me on the spot like that. Then he said, 'Jim, you're going to enjoy playing ball here because you're going to start playing it with your mind as well as your body.'

"By the end of my first season with the Cowboys, I was comfortable with his style of coaching. It was a great experience to learn from him. To be honest, I don't think there were a lot of people in our group who fully understood what he meant by playing the game with the mind. What it boiled down to for me was first the fact that we were going into the game with far more information than players on other teams. We were prepared; knew what we were expected to do. When you've got that kind of information, you've naturally got to be more confident. You play the game without the element of fear getting in the way.

"He didn't want a team going on the field all excited. In his style of play emotions get in the way. What he wanted you to do was use logic, conception, and reaction."

To shore up the defensive line, Landry and Schramm acquired from the Chicago Bears a 260-pound tackle by the name of Maury Youmans, who grew up in the Syracuse area. After a year at prep school, he went to Syracuse University on a scholarship under coach Ben Schwartzwalter, a former paratrooper who had made the D Day jump. Under Schwartzwalter, Youmans learned that his coach valued toughness more than anything. A player could only miss a play if he had a broken leg.

In 1963 Youmans, playing for the Chicago Bears, tore up his knee. In an exhibition game in Washington against the Redskins, he took an outside rush, but the lineman covered his outside. Youmans grabbed his shoulders and planted his left foot to pull him to the inside, but his left knee could not take the pressure. The cartilage went and all the ligaments were torn. Unfortunately for Youmans, the doctor who did the operation allowed him to leave the hospital while he still had a fever and a bad infection. He should have been back in six weeks. He could have returned to play the World Championship game against the Giants, but his leg had atrophied, and his replacement got the game ball in the season finale, so Halas kept him out of the game, won by the Bears, 14–10.

At this point Youmans got a call from the Packers' Jim Ringo, one of his teammates at Syracuse. Ringo said to him, "Maury, the old man [Vince Lombardi] likes the way you play. How would you like to play for the Packers?" Ringo told him that Lombardi was fed up with defensive end Bill Quinlan, who was giving the other tackle, Willie Davis, problems because Davis was getting more publicity than Quinlan could stomach.

Figuring he was going to Green Bay, Youmans asked Halas to trade him.

MAURY YOUMANS: "The next thing I know, I got a call. I was traded to the Dallas Cowboys, which at that time was a disaster. I thought, 'Holy geez.' I was traded for an end named Gary Barnes. He lasted a year in Chicago."

When Youmans arrived at Thousand Oaks in California for training camp in '64, what struck him more than anything was the difference between the rough-and-tough Bears and the more gentlemanly Cowboys.

MAURY YOUMANS: "When I arrived at Thousand Oaks I couldn't believe how it was like going to Sunday school in comparison to the Bears. The Bears were an old-line team, rough-and-tumble guys. One night when I was with the Bears, Doug Atkins, our big defensive end, went out—he loved martinis, and he had quite a few martinis—and late at night he came back, walked into his room, and being a good Tennessee boy, Doug turned up that country music as loud as he could. George Halas was right across the hall. George came in. 'Doug, turn that music down.' The music didn't change, and after three times, you heard, 'Doug, come into my room,' and Doug went into his room, and they talked for a while, and Doug went back to his room and the music maybe came down two decibels, that was about it.

"Rick Casares was a great guy, the salt of the earth, but wild, and Harlan Hill was wild.

"With the Cowboys the players were such *nice* guys; it was more like Sunday school. When they would party on Sunday after a home ballgame, they would party together at a little brewery, in a little room, very quiet, very mild compared to the Bears.

"I can remember after reporting, we had to run a mile in six minutes thirty seconds. I'll never forget. We'd all run as a defensive line. You'd line up. Larry Stephens lined up on the inside, and we ran on the track at Thousand Oaks. We started out, not at a real fast pace, and just before we got to the first curve, you saw Larry's legs wobbling, and Larry would fall over on the grass on the infield, and at this point we were all really ticked off that we had to run that damn mile, and Larry would be laying there. And he laid there the rest of the time.

"The Cowboy practices were a little more difficult than those of the Bears, because the Cowboys would run through ballplayers at that time. In practice you would hit. I remember double sessions, and we would hit with shoulder pads and helmets on. That would be our morning drills. And then in the afternoon we'd scrimmage. Full pads at Thousand Oaks and hitting. So you did a lot of hitting.

"With the Bears you got in shape yourself. You didn't hit much with the Bears. You hit a lot with the Cowboys. My shoulders were so bad there my last year in Dallas that I took Demerol after every ballgame to get to sleep. Both shoulders were gone, just beat up, and that was all from hitting through training camp. I could not roll over either way. Then after Wednesday I'd be fine.

"The Cowboys system was harder to learn because everything on the defense was coordinated. The playbook didn't startle me as much as did the learning process, because all of a sudden you had to know every offensive formation. No longer was it read and react. It became key and react. You read your key and reacted at the same time. Once you learned it, it was a much easier defense to play. Also, you knew where the breakdowns were.

"When I arrived in '64 a lot of the vets *still* didn't understand Tom's system. Tom is a very quiet, almost impersonal individual. He has an engineering personality. That's what he is. But he had a way of convincing you that if you really learned his system and you really all played it, you could play the *perfect* defensive football game. He made me believe that we could play the perfect defense. He would walk away after a ballgame convincing you that, 'Next week, if you work and continue to learn the system, you can do it.' That's how I felt. By '64 we really believed in Tom's defense. And the more you played it, the more you felt comfortable in it, the more you learned it.

"There was some dissension, but the dissension went less against Tom than it was offense against defense. The defense was better, as you probably know, than the offense, so the consequence was that we would blame the offense for the loss, or the offense would say, 'Aw, it's your fault.' That went on more than blaming the coach.

"The defensive players were frustrated and angry at the offense. Keep in mind the way the Cowboys set it up, the offense did everything on its own, and we did everything on our own, so it was almost like we were two teams. So you didn't develop the community that you would normally develop. It would have been smarter, in hindsight, to do that, because you want unity as a team. You naturally pulled for each other, but there was still a certain amount of rationalization—if you were going to blame somebody, if you wanted to rationalize, you were going to blame the other guys, and unfortunately during that period of time, the offense was not as good as the defense."

18

Buddy and Don

The reason the Cowboys appeared to be choirboys compared to the barbarians on other NFL teams was that Tom Landry preferred them that way. Tom Landry was heart-attack serious, and he believed that his players should be as serious about life, football, and family as he was. To Tom Landry the perfect player gave 100 percent during practice or in a game, returned home to his wife and 3.2 tow-headed kids, studied the game films or read the Scriptures in his spare time, and went to church every Sunday. That's what Tom did. That's what he wanted his players to do.

What Tom was constitutionally unable to tolerate were players whose mission in life was to go out and have fun, and if they could make their living playing football, so much the better.

Tom had contempt for such players, because no matter how great they might have been, all he could see was unfulfilled promise, and to Tom Landry that was a sin he could not forgive. Players who laughed on the practice field or who tittered during film sessions or who got rip-roaring drunk at night were just trying to break the grinding tension of pro ball. To Tom Landry, they were creating sacrilege, making a mockery of his chosen profession. Tom handled such players in two ways. If he could re-place them with an equal or better player, he did so as quickly as possible.

If he could not, he would continually lecture that player on the importance of taking the game—and life—seriously.

The first in a growing bush of thorns in Landry's side was a talented kicker by the name of Sam Baker. Sam, a running back at Oregon State, is the top punter in the history of the Cowboys, with a 45.1 average. His longest was 75 yards, a total of 90 yards from where he kicked the ball. He never had one blocked. He was also a field goal and extra point specialist, and in the two years he was with the Cowboys, he led the team in scoring, with 92 points in '62 and 75 points in '63. Despite all that, he was released at the end of '63. Right or wrong, Tom Landry didn't want the carefree, backtalking Baker around any more.

Part of the reason Sam Baker was tossed aside was that neither Landry nor Tex Schramm ever had any respect for kickers, believing them to be easily replaceable. The other part was that Baker continually balked at having to be serious, responsible, focused, and sober, the way Landry wanted his players to be. Baker's resentment of Landry's solemnity and authority caused him to taunt and make fun of the coach, even in front of others.

When Baker reported to the Cowboys in '62, Landry had written out the requirements for his Landry Mile. He gave the time expected for the backs, and the time for the linemen. His instructions did not include the kickers, and Baker tried to argue that he was exempt as a result. When Landry ordered him to run, Baker did so while reading a book. He cut corners, acting like the entire exercise was foolish, and ran the slowest time in Cowboy history.

Another time after a game Baker missed the team plane back to Dallas. When he finally arrived, it was early in the morning. Gil Brandt met him and took him to see Landry. Baker knocked on Tom Landry's door at 4 A.M.

When Landry opened the door, Baker snapped to attention, saluted, and said, "Baker reporting, sir." Landry told him he was fined $1,000 for missing the flight. Another time he showed up for a game in Pittsburgh carrying a potted orange plant and looking quite drunk.

Baker never seemed to say the right thing in front of Landry. One time he made it seem he was laughing at Landry's religious beliefs.

SAM BAKER: "We were in a team meeting one time and Tom was talking about his philosophy of team dedication. He said, 'If I thought it would help this team in some way, I'd climb on top of this building and sing "Glory to God."' Bill Howton was sitting in front of me and said, 'Hallelujah,' and I started laughing. Landry turned just in time to see me crack up and, obviously, thought I was laughing at him."

At another team meeting Landry was lecturing the players that the team would have to exhibit more harmony if the Cowboys were to accomplish anything. To show his willingness to harmonize, Baker responded with a loud, humorous, "Hmmmmmmmmmmmmmm." Some of the players tittered while Landry frowned and burned inside.

By 1964 Baker was gone, replaced by a rookie kicker, Dick Van Raaphorst. At the end of the year Baker and Van Raaphorst had almost identical records, and Landry slept better at night. The levity, however, did not disappear from the Cowboy team. Landry still had to endure the shenanigans of his starting quarterback, Don Meredith, who continued to exhibit his Wild West, drink 'em up, shoot 'em up outlook. To the dismay of the abstemious and monogamous Tom Landry, Don pursued his late-night emulation of Bobby Layne, at times showing up for games hungover and sorry-looking, and there were times when he would sass Landry. Once Meredith said about his coach, "Landry's the kind of guy if he was married to Raquel Welch, he'd want to know if she could cook." Sometimes to show his contempt, Dandy Don even sent the messengers carrying Landry's plays back to the sidelines. The whole time Landry would lecture him and wonder when Don would finally tilt toward adulthood.

PETTIS NORMAN: "Meredith was a happy-go-lucky guy who didn't take himself too seriously, who approached the game of football with a lightheartedness that I had not been used to in college. Don would be on the field, and in the middle of the huddle he'd crack a joke and not remember the play Landry had called and just say, 'Okay, run the last play all over again.' We had that happen a number of times.

"On the other hand, you had Landry, who was a very serious person, tolerating him, and yet he respected Landry to a degree, so it was a divergency that existed. And it was really interesting. As I look back, how would it have been if we didn't have Don on the team? We might have been too serious.

"Landry lectured him about being more serious but he would not do it in front of the team, unless it was, 'Get your head in the game.' And Don could be quite flip with Landry at times, and part of that flippant attitude was when Landry would send a play in and he'd tell a joke and forget the play, and he'd say, 'We'll run the last play, on two.' That was Don's way of being flippant toward Landry. So it was really very interesting, if you consider Landry on one hand, and Don Meredith on the other."

In 1964 Meredith found a "podner" in receiver Buddy Dial, himself a born and bred Texan who had been a huge star at Rice University. Dial was one of them fallen fellas, a Layne Disciple, not a Landry Disciple. He was one of them renegades, and how could the fun-loving Dial have been otherwise in that he had been Layne's primary receiver and running mate in Pittsburgh? Layne and Dial were freelancers, and they had become so close they could almost read each other's minds. They played instinctive football, and there wasn't a better passing combination in all of football. Over the previous four seasons Dial had averaged over 1,000 yards a season catching Layne's passes. In five years, he hadn't missed a single play because of injuries. He was also a guy with a guitar looking for a bar to croon a tune and for honky-tonk women with whom to sing along. When Landry traded for Buddy Dial the receiver, he also got Dial the country-and-western singer. It would not be long before Landry wished he had signed Paul Warfield instead.

When Dial arrived in camp in '64, he made the fatal mistake of being out of shape. Under Buddy Parker and the Steelers, the players had worked their way into playing shape during training camp. In Dallas, the players were supposed to come to camp ready to go full-out from the first day.

Dial wasn't in shape to run the Landry Mile, and he wasn't ready to run the 40-yard dash. Before the end of the first week of training camp during an afternoon scrimmage, practice was coming to an end. Don Meredith wanted another score, and he called a long pass to Dial down the left side. Dial made the long run and then had to jump high and extend himself to catch the ball. As he launched himself upward, he heard and felt the sickening snap of a muscle in his thigh.

Dial practiced another two weeks before the doctors realized that a muscle had pulled off his knee, and he was sent back to Dallas to be operated on. The doctors sewed the muscle back together, but when they reattached it to the knee, they made it too tight, and when he began working out again, the muscle pulled off the hip. In '64 Dial played against the Steelers the third game of the season, but didn't get to play again until the last game, also against Pittsburgh. In between Buddy Dial provided his teammates with a lot of songs and a lot of fun.

BUDDY DIAL: "The last four years in Pittsburgh I averaged 20-something yards per catch, averaged 1,000 yards a season over that period. But at the end of the '63 season I asked Buddy Parker to trade me to Dallas, because I had two young sons, and I found I couldn't get a job in Pittsburgh in the off-season. It was impossible. No one had any respect for the Steelers ballclub, because we never won, and so during my last two years I tried to get a job there but couldn't. I was willing to stay. But I needed to work 'cause we weren't making that much money, and so I went to Parker the last week, and I said, 'I want to raise my kids in Texas, and I'd love to go play in Dallas.' And he cried. He said, 'I have never had a player ask me to trade him. Everybody wants to play for me.' And I said, 'I love to play for you, Buddy, and I love Art Rooney like a father,' and he *was* the greatest sportsman I ever met, but I said, 'I've got two sons, and I can't get a job in Pittsburgh,' and so I went to Dallas, and it was just like being in heaven on earth, except that I didn't contribute.

"The first game I started was in Pittsburgh. We went and played the Steelers, and I had a good day against my old partners. We were behind, and we were on about the 12-yard line, and Meredith wanted to score, and he wanted me to run a square-in across the middle, and he threw the ball a little high, and Clendon Thomas just killed me. I missed several more games with a concussion, but I played in the last game against Pittsburgh in Dallas and had a real good day that day.

"In that game Don was trying to go deep that day, and he got killed. He really did. The Steelers sacked him seven times, and really hurt him badly. Prior to that game in Philadelphia he had gotten his ribs busted. He collapsed on the plane coming back. His lungs collapsed.

"Don had more guts . . . he and Bobby Layne. Layne was kind of the leader of the crazy, drinking fun crowd at the time, and he was the epitome of the fun player. I was a little bit crazy, and of course, playing under Layne, he was God, and as long as I made Bobby happy, it didn't make any difference. While I was in Pittsburgh, I was Bobby's go-to guy, and Bobby loved me. Bobby knew I played the guitar, so he bought me one, and he said, 'I want music. Play.' And everywhere I went I took that dumb guitar, and Layne would call me at two, three in the morning, and he'd say, 'Dial, you ain't gonna believe what I got down here now at the hotel. Come play my favorite song.' And I'd take that stupid guitar down there and sing for him, and he'd have some chick from New York or somewhere. Bobby imported his women. He wouldn't date the Pittsburgh girls. He said they had 'dirty legs.' He said they had coal dust on them around their ankles, called them 'damn dirty legs.' He wanted his women from New York, Detroit, Florida.

"He and Ernie [Stautner] were roommates. Ernie was his bodyguard.

They lived in a house, and old Dickie Moegle was traded to Pittsburgh my second year—he had been in San Francisco freeloading off the 49ers, and he came out to Pittsburgh where there were really hard times, and old Bobby—I didn't drink, and Bobby respected that—said, 'Damnit, if you don't drink with me, you better not drink with anybody else.' So Moegle didn't drink either, but Bobby didn't trust him. So he told Moegle, 'I want you and Dial to meet me in town, and we're going to have dinner.' Bobby went to all these places, and if he liked the band, he liked to take them with him, and he'd pay them, and they'd travel with him, and he'd get in the cabs and the cars, and he ended up at the Hurricane Bar in the Hill District in Pittsburgh, the end of the world, and Bobby was sitting on a barstool next to Ernie, and they were both drunk, and Bobby was talking about how tough Ernie was, and he said, 'He's the toughest son of a bitch who ever lived,' and Bobby took a big draw on his cigarette, and he turned around to Ernie, and Ernie put his tongue out, and Bobby put his cigarette out on Ernie's tongue! He said, 'See what I mean? The toughest son of a bitch who ever lived.'

"Meredith, his senior year at SMU, went to Chicago for the All-America team, and Layne was there on the Pro Bowl All-Pro team, and ole Bobby came back to Pittsburgh after the game in Chicago, and Bobby knew that I lived the Christian life and was active in church, and he had that ole whiskey voice from drinking all that Cutty Sark and smoking them Lucky Strikes, and he came back to practice, and he said, 'Dial, I shot another Christian down!' I said, 'What do you mean?' He said, 'I got Meredith drunk in Chicago.'

"So Meredith just fell in love with Bobby, and Don was so colorful himself. He had all these East Texas sayings. The women just worshiped the ground he walked on. He was genuinely funny, had a great sense of humor, was witty as all get-out. In Pittsburgh I had had a radio and television show, which was kind of fun. I did it with the guy who did the baseball, ole Bob Friend. We had a fun deal there, and I did it about four years in Pittsburgh, and you know, I made $100 a show, but I'd have paid them for the exposure. So when I came to Dallas, Don and I had been partners in college, I going to Rice and him being at SMU, we played against each other, knew each other well, and I said, 'Don, let's do the radio and television show.' He said, 'Yeah, they really need one, don't they?' 'Cause they hadn't won very much. But I sold him on the idea, and we went and got a car dealer as a sponsor, and we had the Dial-Meredith radio show and the Dial-Meredith television show, and I'm telling you, he was the funniest guy I ever saw in my life. We did just really stupid stuff. The Beatles were real popular, and the Steelers came to town, and this was my first year with the Cowboys in Pittsburgh, the last game of the season, and we had Bob Lilly and Jim Colvin and a linebacker, can't remember his name, and we all put wigs on, and had guitars, and we sang a Beatle medley of songs to a Beatle record, and the Steelers thought we were making fun of them, and they wanted to kill us the next day. I think they were trying to kill Meredith and me because we were making fun of them.

"Well, I remember one day we were taping the television show. I had a football. And Meredith had fumbled several times the game before, gotten killed, and somebody sent it in and wanted it autographed, and I had handed it to Meredith, and just as he reached to get it, I knocked it out of his hands, and on TV they couldn't tell I did it, and I made fun of him for fumbling, and it was just slapstick all the time!

"We'd speed the films up and make fun of everybody. It was cute. We had a lot of fun. We got to drive a dumb blue convertible, and we got $100 per radio show, and $100 per TV show. We were really big-time, weren't we?

"Don and I were roommates, and I was a terrible influence on him. I played the guitar, and he loved to sing and drink, and we just stayed in trouble all the time. We almost stayed in jail for three years because of Landry, 'cause he never knew what we were going to do. So Tom finally demanded that Meredith mature a little bit, and they got rid of me due to injury, so Don, he kind of grew up and got serious a little bit, but not all that much.

"I'll tell you, Meredith was, and is, a *very* classy guy. I mean, he is a high-caliber person, a clean guy, and the people got down on him, because he didn't have an offensive line at the time, and he was a free spirit. He'd come to the huddle, and he'd be singing. We'd been in Vegas, seen Dean Martin's show, and Meredith would come back to the huddle singing one of Martin's songs, and he'd call a play, and Danny Reeves—he knew more about the offense than anybody except Landry—and ole Danny Reeves would say, 'Dandy, that ain't the way we call that play.' And ole Don would say, 'Hell, you call it, Danny.' So Don was slapstick, but boy, he played hard. And he practiced hard. But he was a very classy guy, and he still is.

"I'll tell you one thing, nobody got the better of him. No one ever came on top of Meredith, 'cause he was so witty and articulate. He's just a winner.

"The newspaper reporters ate him alive, and you know what, they would kiss up to him, get a good story, and he would have a bad day, and they'd crucify him. But he being a nice guy, he never played that get-even type stuff that a lot of guys played. I remember one time Gary Cartwright wrote a critical article about me, the first time I had been criticized in my career, and I canceled the paper! And I really got some bad publicity when I canceled the paper. Then he wrote a big article about 'Dial Pissed Off, Cancels the Paper.' So I wouldn't take the crap. But Meredith would.

"And, you know, Landry was tough on Don. Don was just a free spirit, and Tom was as serious as the Holocaust every time you saw him. If Tom laughed, his face would break. Don just didn't buy the life-or-death struggle that Tom said we were involved in, and so Tom caused Don to be criticized a lot, because he would cut Meredith up, 'cause Don would mess up. And you know, Roger Staubach was so serious. He was the opposite of Meredith. He paid the price, and he was so successful, and so Don really never got credit. Don brought a lot of class to that ballclub and to that city, and people never gave him credit. I think he got even with them, because he was such a smash on *Monday Night Football*. The people in Hollywood worshiped him. We'd train out in Thousand Oaks, and we'd go to town, to Hollywood, and the people would just fall out wanting to meet Meredith, and the women, I mean they loved him like a god! Who was the other guy, Blackie Sherrod, he was good to Don, because Blackie was a class act. But those other guys, Cartwright and Steve Perkins, aw, they crucified Don, and you know, Cartwright and Perkins they just seemed to see who could get the dirtiest stuff about Meredith, and if it hadn't been for Blackie carrying on a little class act personally, Meredith would have been crucified all the time.

"And as a result, it carried over to the other cities. We'd go up to play in New York or Cleveland or Pittsburgh, and the opposing players respected Don, but the press would treat him like they did in Dallas, because of the influence the Dallas press carried."

On the field the team did not miss Dial, because in '64 Frank Clarke became an All-Pro receiver. Clarke was a bright spot during a 5–8–1 season during which Don Meredith was injured over and over, crashed to the ground by ferocious linemen with little to stop them. During the preseason Meredith tore up his knee, but he didn't sit on the bench. Rather, he played the entire year with a torn cartilage, missing just one game, in what Tom Landry would call "perhaps the most courageous and gutsy season any professional quarterback ever played." Said Landry, "What made it worse was that our line couldn't have protected a healthy quarterback, let alone a hobbling one."

Early in the season, one Dallas writer suggested a new statistic,

"Yardage lost attempting to live." Every week Meredith took a pounding, suffering one injury after another. Despite the pain, he refused to quit.

FRANK CLARKE: "In 1964 the Cowboys traded for two outstanding receivers from other teams in the league, Tommy McDonald and Buddy Dial. Of course, when that happened, it was real clear: People were saying that 'Frank Clarke is expendable. Frank Clarke is gone.' I was taking a look at that, and I was talking to myself in ways I had never done before. I was saying to myself, 'By golly, if I'm going to do the things I'd like to be able to do in this game, I have to do it this year. This is the time to do it.'

"And everything I did from training camp all the way through that '64 season was otherworldly. Things were happening. I became consistent in my blocking. It was almost as though the team itself got a sense of my sincerity in what I was doing. And Dandy was calling on me in third-down situations, and I felt *so* fantastic, so good, because I was answering the challenge. But most of all, I felt as though I was fitting into what I strongly aspired to do, and that was to follow Tom Landry's tutoring. I really wanted to do it for this guy, 'cause I just had a good feeling about *everything* about him. To me he was the same sort of general that a lot of guys thought of George Patton, that they would do anything for him.

"In the third game against the Steelers, the team lost when it couldn't score from inside the ten right at the end of the game. In the final minutes, Don Meredith's knee buckled, and he had to come out of the game. Going into the game, his knee was weak, and I was just amazed he could perform as well as he did with all the injuries he had.

"Dandy had such bad legs. He would look at my legs and then he'd look at his, and his were pretty spindly, *really* spindly, and he'd point to his, grab his calf, and say, 'Thoroughbreds.' He'd look at mine and grab mine and go, 'Clydesdales.'

"He was hurt a lot, and unfortunately, he came to the Cowboys at a time when our offensive line had a lot of holes in it, and I know, because I helped make it porous. It was not intentional. But we had a lot of mental lapses. And the quarterback paid the price. I'm sure they paid him pretty well, but they didn't pay him nearly enough.

"Don was hurt in the Redskin game, and so he didn't play against Green Bay, a game we lost, and when he came back against Philadelphia he was sacked time and time again and got hurt again. Against the Steelers, he went back out, and he was sacked seven or so times, and again he got hurt. It's hard to win when that happens. And except for that Green Bay game, he played in every game."

PETTIS NORMAN: "Oh boy, did Don take a beating. I have pictures of Don where he's taped like a mummy, literally from his ankles up—he had two bad ankles, bad knees, had hip pointers, a cracked rib, his nose broke. He was literally held together by tape, but he played. He had more courage than any one person I can think of.

"Part of it had to do with the fact that you go through stages when you build the team. You can't build it all at one time. Landry was more into building the defense first, and then the running game, because Landry's system produced a lot of yardage and touchdowns. When it came to pass blocking, I'm not sure we had people who could really protect the quarterback like they should. 'Cause the offensive line changed quite often. We'd have a different set of linemen almost every year.

"And yet I never once heard Don get on a lineman for not blocking. He'd just get up and come at it again. He was so valiant, yet he never got any credit for it, not from the press or the fans or in retrospect even from Coach Landry. I'm not defending Landry, but maybe he didn't like Don's flippant attitude, and for whatever reason thought if he was more serious, maybe some of these injuries wouldn't happen, or he would be better, but I'll tell you, Don took more punishment than any five quarterbacks would take in a lifetime."

After the final '64 game, a win, Landry went over to congratulate Meredith, who had to shake with his left hand because he'd injured the right one in the first quarter.

Landry said to him, "You did a fine job in a tough situation this year. We're gonna get you more protection next year."

Said Meredith, "Promise?"

DON MEREDITH: "It wasn't really a matter of courage as much as of determination. Nobody is going to beat me. I knew if I didn't get up they would have beaten me. I couldn't stand the thought of that."

FRANK CLARKE: "In spite of the losses, our momentum was building. We were not a doldrum team. We kept our focus in spite of all of that. I don't know what kind of schedule Tom Landry had us on, but I felt like we were either at it or ahead of it during those times, in spite of those things.

"Not everyone felt the way I did, but when it came to Tom Landry, there were a lot of players who were willing to go along with him, more on the offense than the defense. We knew we had something on offense, and we were just waiting for the defense to catch up. So was Tom. That's why every year they were drafting defensive players. And ironically, most of the bitching by this time came from the defensive guys, and it's funny, because the offense was better than the defense, and yet the defense was always complaining about the offense."

19

Pete

When Tex Schramm sent out a questionnaire to Big Ten basketball coaches and athletic directors asking them to name some college hoopsters who might make it in the NFL, Michigan State's freshman coach Danny Petersen included on his list the University of Indiana's Van Arsdale twin brothers, Tom and Dick, and as an afterthought wrote in the name of Michigan State's top scorer, forward Pete Gent. Petersen figured that the 6'5" Gent had the quickness, agility, and size necessary to play pro football.

When Gil Brandt came to East Lansing, Michigan, to sign Gent, Brandt swore to him that the Cowboys were only bringing in 3 defensive backs. (When Gent got to camp, there were 100 rookies, and 17 of them were defensive backs.)

When he arrived in camp, Tom Landry had little use for Pete Gent. However, the Cowboys' offensive coordinator, Red Hickey, saw in Gent the making of a fine receiver. Hickey liked his soft hands and his aggressiveness, and he kept Landry from cutting the effervescent, free-spirited free agent. Thanks to Red Hickey, Gent became a Cowboy in 1964, and he remained on the team through the 1968 season, long enough to see the highs and lows of the great years of the Don Meredith Cowboys. After Gent retired from football, he wrote a controversial, hard-edged novel,

North Dallas Forty, a book about how a football team takes advantage of its players and treats them like faceless cattle. In the book Gent used all he saw and heard, adding embellishments for dramatic effect. Cowboys owner Clint Murchison, himself a rebel, loved *North Dallas Forty*. Tex Schramm and Tom Landry, who were protective of their image and were portrayed as manipulative, uncaring men, passionately hated it.

Now living with his mother and his son in Bangor, Michigan, in the home where he grew up, Pete Gent is continuing his path as a dropout from society and a novelist. Gent may not have been the greatest player to ever perform for the Cowboys, but certainly he was one of the more observant and entertaining.

PETE GENT: "I had never played football. The NBA had offered me $8,500 a year to play for Baltimore before I met Gil, who took me into this Holiday Inn hotel room, showed me a contract, and refused to turn the light on. The only light in the room was coming through the window. I could sort of see the contract. But I couldn't really. It was the standard NFL contract, but he threw some cash bonuses in there that were bigger than what some of the draft choices got. As long as I made the team I got a bonus, and I ended up making twelve grand my first year, and shit, I was making as much as George Andrie, who had been starting for five years. But I'll never forget, I asked him, 'Could you turn the light on so I could see?'

" 'No. Uh uh.'

" 'I can't even see where to sign.'

" 'Uh uh.'

"As soon as I signed, he turned the light on. I loved Gil. He was always good to me, because I was a big find for him.

"When I got to camp in Thousand Oaks, California, it turned out I couldn't defend worth a damn, but I wasn't going to quit. If I stayed twenty calendar days, I was going to get another $500, so I was trying to stay there to get the $500, 'cause I ain't gonna quit. Training camp was horrible. You are in tears about half the time. You're watching grown men, 6'8", 280-pound men standing in their room who can't take it anymore, crying and throwing their clothes in their luggage.

"The guy who was my roommate my first year got cut relatively early. He was a receiver from Kansas State, and they cut him the first week, so I had a room all to myself, so I could cry by myself.

"There was a suitemate of mine, a running back, a blond-haired guy from the University of North Dakota named Les Josephson who cried all the time. He was a low draft choice in '64. Every day in practice he cried. He would try to leave, and they'd catch him at the bus station and bring him back.

"He hated it. *Hated* it. A lot of guys did. You'd see guys who played five or six years, offensive, defensive linemen in the middle of their room, throwing their clothes in their suitcase, crying. 'I hate this. I'm never going to do this again. I can get a job in the real world.'

"We traded Les Josephson to the Rams for Jim Boeke and Danny Villanueva. The fucker made All-Pro with the Rams his rookie year!

"California Lutheran was this all-aluminum junior college. Literally all the buildings were pole buildings, and to show you how desolate this country was, the football practice field was in a bowl, and one of the hills on the side of the bowl had been the location they had used for Mt. Surabachi in the movie *Sands of Iwo Jima*. And if you walked over that hill, there were all the location sets from *Gunsmoke*. You were just out in the middle of *nowhere*. El Conejo Boulevard, the Rabbit Boulevard, was the main street of the town that had an all-aluminum shopping center, with one movie theater that ran the movie *The Long Ships* with Richard Widmark, all summer long. I saw it six times. I remember exactly where the scar was over his eye.

"You got off Wednesday nights, but you had to be back by midnight. Well, L.A. was 35 miles away. There wasn't even a bar in town. You would drive for miles along those brown hillsides. Most of that property was owned by Bing Crosby and Bob Hope. And I'd look at it and think, 'What are they going to do with this land? There's no water, nothing.' And now it's a city. So you were out there, isolated, not able to go anywhere.

"Early on in the practice, all through rookie camp, about ten days long, I was out there with 100 guys and it seemed like all these guys were college All-Americas. I watched 50 of them disappear, and I thought, 'This is really good,' and then it dawned on me that the veterans hadn't come yet!

"And then in came guys who looked like old men. And once the veterans got there, I knew I had a problem. For a while they moved me into linebacker, which I liked. I liked middle linebacker best of all, because Landry's system was designed that nobody was supposed to block you. If everybody else did his job right, they kept anybody from getting to you, but then of course, your job was to hit some 220-pound back straight on. I could do that. That wasn't hard. Outside linebacker was tough. You had so many different assignments and reads, I could never figure that out. You had to decide on pass coverages and all that stuff.

"They moved me to work on trying to catch punts. See, at the time one of the big stats was running the 40. Well, I had been playing basketball for four years on an offense that ran the fast break every chance it had. My 40 time was around 4.6, and in those days that was pretty good. They always kept that in mind, so they kept moving me around to different positions.

"What eventually happened was totally by accident. I was beginning to get the feeling they were getting ready to send me home, and one day in practice they were running single routes, man-on-man coverage, and they didn't have a whole lot of receivers. They had drafted a bunch of them, but none of them turned out well. We still had ten defensive backs and only had four or five receivers. So Red Hickey, who had obviously heard in one of the coaches' meetings that I was being cut pretty soon anyway, called me over to run routes, just to even things out. And I caught ten balls in a row, including some circus catches. The thing was, it's real easy to catch a football. A football is made to catch. You just catch it and fall down. Try catching a basketball at full speed and having to make up your mind what you have to do in a step and a half. And so the concentration part of it came real easy. All I had to do was get past hearing footsteps. That wasn't difficult either. I had learned that in basketball because you were playing so close to the crowd.

"Immediately Red called me aside, and he said, 'Look, I've had a couple guys who were basketball players.' He mentioned R.C. Owens, for whom he had developed the Alley Oop pass. Red said, 'You have the ability to be a receiver, but you're going to have to work. And I'll stay out with you every day and teach you.' Which he did. And of course, the other thing you know, when the coaches are in a meeting, when they are trying to decide who to cut, you've got a guy who is in your corner, who is arguing for you.

"When I came that year, the receivers were Pettis Norman, who would eventually become an All-Pro tight end, Lee Folkins, who was a good tight end from Washington, and they traded for Tommy McDonald and Buddy Dial at wide receiver, and Frank Clarke. And they were only planning to keep five. Because of Red, they made room for me as the sixth, but Tom Landry didn't plan to play me much. Which he didn't.

"To keep me, they had to cut Sonny Gibbs. Sonny was their number two quarterback, but Sonny was too erratic as a passer. He was a big, 6'8" guy from TCU, a nice guy. He ended up making golf clubs."

From the start Pete Gent and Tom Landry did not see eye to eye. Landry was a member of a postwar generation that venerated conformity, consensus, rules, and regulations. A nice girl was a virgin who didn't smoke cigarettes. Guys wore saddle shoes and sang "Love Letters in the Sand." Dwight and Mamie Eisenhower (and Pat Boone) represented that era of the 1950s, and on TV the favorites were Robert Young and Jane Wyatt in *Father Knows Best* and Ozzie and Harriet Nelson.

Gent, like many who were kids when Elvis Presley came along to excite a generation, saw themselves as rebels against their parents' drab lives. They listened to and were thrilled by Jerry Lee Lewis, Chuck Berry, and The Big Bopper, the Bad Boys of rock and roll, and they began to rebel against their parents' lifestyle. Once in college they questioned the prudery that called for curfews and wanted to know why they couldn't entertain girls in their rooms. In October of 1964 the students at Cal Berkeley erupted in protest over the college policing their moral lives. In January 1965 the free-speech movement began on campuses all over America.

In college, Pete Gent began to question things. A Methodist like Landry, he wondered how a person could love Jesus and still hate his fellow man just because his religion or skin color was different.

Cynicism began to creep into Pete Gent's view of those who were dogmatic about their religion, and he developed doubts about whether there really was a God. That cynicism also caused him to attempt to use religion to his benefit in training camp as a way of influencing Tom Landry to keep him on the 40-man roster.

PETE GENT: "In those days they posted the starting times for the area churches on the bulletin boards. A lot of the guys in those days were Catholic, and they rode together to Mass. Landry was a Methodist, and I was a lapsed Methodist—that's an agnostic. Anyway, when I realized he was a Methodist, I signed up. My theory was, 'I'm going to get this first Sunday punch,' even though church had been distasteful since I was a kid. To me it was stupid. But I figured if I went to church with him, it had to have some effect on him, and maybe that would be enough to make the team.

"It turned out the only Cowboy beside me going to the Methodist church was Landry. So that first Sunday, who do you think was riding in the front seat next to him? Me.

"I never went again. I wasn't going to go twice. 'Cause there could be a God! But this was just football.'"

Once Gent became an offensive player, the teammate he gravitated toward and who gravitated toward him was his quarterback, Don Meredith. It's not hard to see why Don liked Gent, though Gent was a Yankee who had never even played college football. What Gent was was very bright, very witty, and the sort of person willing to go anywhere or do anything Meredith wanted to do. Over the years the two became close, as anyone who read *North Dallas Forty* could see. The two main characters, Shake Tiller and Seth Maxwell, were close, brothers almost. So were Gent and Meredith. Gent would become Meredith's primary confidant and amateur psychologist as the Cowboy quarterback's life would become more and more topsy-turvy as the years went on. And in the battle of wills between Don Meredith and Tom Landry, Gent would always side with his buddy.

PETE GENT: "Meredith's approach to the game was the realization he had to lead the team. Don was the Old NFL, which I still think is right. The quarterback should call the plays from the field. That's where you get your best information. And the other thing was, here was a losing team that would get so depressed and so down on themselves, they needed someone to lead them and keep them feeling up. Don had seen the Cowboys year after year just corkscrew right into the ground as their season went on. So in '64, what I saw was this happy-go-lucky guy on the outside and this very serious guy on the inside. His first marriage had broken up. Don had been a divinity student, for Christ sake, who had turned into a drinker and a womanizer.

"Meredith's parents are Baptist. He actually started school as a divinity student. At SMU he was dating Lynn Chamberg, who was a cheerleader. She was the best-looking girl on campus. He was the best-looking guy. By the end of his sophomore year he was famous. Suddenly with all that fame in Dallas came all these opportunities to do whatever the fuck he wanted. And there was nobody there to stop him. So for two or three years in college, he broke all the rules. And he still had his girlfriend. It was the classic southern attitude: 'There are certain girls you fuck, and other girls you marry.'

"When I started running with Don, he was going to be a country-and-western singer. He had a record out on Reveler Records, 'Them That Ain't Got It Cain't Lose.' In fact, in the off-season, he almost married Mollie Bee, who was a big country-and-western singer back in the '60s. But he was also going with a girl from Fort Worth, Cheryl King, and he married her just before the '65 season began.

"His marriage to his second wife was in trouble from the day they got married. She was pretty flighty, but what Don would do, what a lot of guys would do, he'd say, 'No, I'm not running around. That's bullshit. I'm not doing that. Who are you going to believe, me or your lying eyes?' And he was doing it all the time.

"And Don and I had long talks about that. I'd say, 'What are you doing? Is it fair to give someone the false illusion of what reality is?' She was just out there swimming blind.

"When you go from college to pro football you just become a different person. If you want to stay in football, your whole focus is on the team, and your family comes secondary, plus you are under so much pressure—it's like a cop's life. You're under so much stress, there is so much violence, so many things you just don't want to talk about, that you end up with nothing to talk about at home. Also, the things that the normal people do seem so pointless. Life outside of football moves so slow it's agonizing. In football, the whole theory is that you get things done by running right over somebody immediately. And then you revert into what is 'normal' life, and you're sitting there on a lawn, talking about stuff with this guy who's a salesman.

"And beyond that, Don was changing as a person. He had become a drinker. I'm sure he was a womanizer before I met him. I know he was when I met him in '64. He once told me he always looked for married women, 'cause he didn't want involvement. He just didn't want that emotional involvement. Apparently the first divorce had taken a tremendous emotional toll on him. He had loved her very much, and it had turned out badly. When I came to the Cowboys, he had married and divorced her twice.

"In fact, I met his first wife once. She was working for a congressman in D.C., and I met her at the airport when Don picked up his daughter to come back on the team plane, so he could see her for a while. We were sitting side by side, and Don had her sitting on his lap. I looked over at him, and he had tears in his eyes, and he just pointed at the little girl. He cried the whole trip back.

"Don's life off the field was just one incredible tragedy after another. Horrible bad luck and mistakes and just circumstance. And he *always* blamed himself. He was not a guy who did not take the blame. Don was a guy who beat himself unmercifully. He constantly tortured himself with guilt. He was absolutely guilt-ridden. It wasn't religious guilt. It was personal guilt, deeply felt. And because it wasn't religious guilt, there was no way for him to cleanse himself of it.

"How did he survive? The guy's character was incredible, and I don't think I was the only guy who noticed that. I always noticed that wherever we were, Don Meredith was *the* focus. In football the defense hates the offense, because they think no matter what they do, the offense loses the game. But Meredith was the one guy who nobody on the team ever, ever said a bad word about.

"And Meredith felt—we *all* felt—and I still believe this to be true, it's why the NFL is not as interesting as it used to be, that the quarterback should call the game on the field. If the quarterback can't remember the plays, then why are you paying him all that money?

"Tom Landry's whole theory, on the other hand, was industrial. Football was a machine with replaceable parts. This came as a result of his experiences as a bomber pilot, I presume. He didn't want to know the gunners. He didn't want to know them, because they were probably going to get killed. It was the biggest struggle between Landry and Meredith.

"I sided with Don on that issue. I've been around sports long enough to know that everything is great in theory, but you also have that human factor that elevates you even higher. And if you get that working for you, then you've got everything. And that's what Landry wanted to eliminate. And that was the huge philosophical gap, which you could never cross. And within that huge gap, all sorts of turmoil developed. Landry didn't like Meredith's lifestyle. Meredith would walk out onto the field and he wouldn't be serious enough for Landry. But that whole style that Meredith had adapted was designed to take pressure off the players and keep them believing that if Don was happy and feeling good, then we must be okay.

"Nineteen sixty-four was a disaster because Meredith stayed hurt, his substitute, Billy Lothridge, was hurt, and John Roach, who came from the Packers, never did figure out the offense.

"In '64 we did not have a real good line coach and we did not have a very good line. Jim Myers was the coach. He got better as we got more talent. Until Dave Manders took over, in '64 our starting center was Mike Connelly, who was only 215 pounds. We had a tackle who was only 220. The guards couldn't pull. Don barely got back into the backfield to throw, and the defense was waiting to pounce on him. Of course, he was scrambling to try and throw, while Landry was trying to get him to stay in the pocket, which was insane. There was no pocket. And what happened was, with Sonny Gibbs gone, Meredith got hurt in the exhibition season. He tore up his knee.

"Our punter, Billy Lothridge, had been a quarterback at Georgia Tech, and he took over when Don got hurt. Billy got injured almost immediately. We were down on the goal line, and he was trying to run a play, and he fumbled, and when he bent down to pick up the ball, the defense ran by him and he ran in for the touchdown, but he tore a muscle, so now Billy was hurt.

"At the time Meredith was hurt, there was still time to set the roster, so they brought in John Roach from the Packers, 'cause they wanted a quarterback with some experience. Roach went out there, and although he had all this experience, it was running the Packer offense, which is the absolute opposite of ours literally in every way. In fact, that was Landry's whole theory: His defense was specifically designed to stop Vince Lombardi's offense.

"Landry always was obsessed with Vince Lombardi. They both had been coaches with the Giants. Lombardi got the first head job. Lombardi's theory was this: 'We got six running plays. We got six passing plays. I don't care what you do. You know we're going to run it. We'll tell you. Just try and stop us. 'Cause we're not going to make a mistake.'

"Landry's theory was the opposite: 'We're going to run a lot of different defenses, and multiple offenses with shifting backs. I'll bet you can't guess what we're going to run.' His theory was, you make everything much more complicated, but you get smarter players. He used to give us intelligence tests because they didn't want guys who were dumb, but they were always concerned about guys who were too smart. And I think that came because of me. I heard from Gary Cartwright, who was then the beat reporter for the *Dallas Morning News*, that I was the only guy who ever scored higher on the IQ test than Landry. And you took these personality tests, the Minnesota Multiphasic Personality tests, to find out if you were aggressive and hostile enough. Well, that test was easy to figure out. You always wanted to do the most violent thing, and your answers always tried to show you had to have organization in your life and a willingness to cooperate.

"After the team was set in training camp, Landry would explain his system to the rookies in a long speech he would give. First the trainer would talk to you about how to behave, what you should do. And the equipment man would tell you how to pick up your equipment. The publicity man, Larry Carl, would tell us, 'Boys, remember, this is show business. Your first job if you have an interview is to show up. If you have a photo session, show up.' You got fined if you didn't do it.

"And then Landry would come and speak, and the first thing he would explain was the history of the development of his offense and of modern football, and he would cite the Packers as the prefect example of the opposite of what we did. He'd talk about the simplicity and execution and talent of the Packers. He'd say, 'The Packers are this, and we are the opposite end, but we are willing to give up a few more mistakes, because we're going to beat them on the big play. Ultimately we will break down and give up things and we'll have a few turnovers, but we will get better and better as we execute better and better, as you know the offense more and more, it can't be stopped.'

"When I first came into the league, I can remember Dick Nolan, who was my defensive backfield coach, a great guy, I loved him, a classic Old NFL player, just busted all to shit, smoked Lucky Strikes all day long, always telling me, 'In the NFL, as a defensive back you can't stop the perfectly run pattern. You gotta hope the guy either makes a mistake on his pattern or the quarterback doesn't make the proper throw. Otherwise, you're beat. The best you can hope to be is within a step.' Well, Landry's offense eliminated even that. You were wide open.

"And by the time I was leaving that team, we had it so finely tuned that after he called the play in the huddle, Meredith got to the line, and he could audible off at the line to another play, but if you had a pass pattern called, the receivers were still required as they took off from the line to take the same keys in the secondary. First you looked at the linebacker on your side, watched where he dropped, then you moved your key to the safety to see where he went, and by then, you knew what kind of defense the secondary was in.

"And if you had a sideline call, and they came up in a rolled zone, then you automatically changed your route to a turn-in. And everybody had to know that without it being called. That was second nature. And on every pass play you had all those alternatives, plus in the line, if there were blocking steps, the linemen had to know the same things. The center's job was actually to call out blocking assignments, audible off-blocking assignments. Nobody else in the NFL was doing this at this time. And it was just genius. When you saw it laid out, you realized, 'Good God, this is impossible to stop!'

"As much as Landry and I fought, and we fought like cats, Landry was a fascinating guy. He was a guy who at nineteen years old was flying B-17s over Germany, and then he had to deal with us! We were fighting the Vietnam War, and we'd come drunk and stoned to practice. As a man, as a presence, still to this day, he was the most impressive coach I've ever been around.

"He just knew everything."

20

Bob Lilly and the Flex

Soon after Maury Youmans was traded from the Chicago Bears to the Cowboys in '64, the two teams played in an exhibition. George Allen, who had been one of Youmans's coaches on the Bears, came over to make small talk. "Maury, how's it going?" The big tackle couldn't wait to tell him about Tom Landry's eye-opening defensive system known as the Flex.

"George, this is great," replied Youmans. "You won't believe it. The defense here is so interesting. You know every place you gotta be, where you line up, what you gotta do. It's all coordinated." Youmans told him, "George, I learned more football just in this training camp than I did in the four years with the Bears."

"No kidding," was all Allen said.

After the '64 season was over, Youmans was living in Treasure Island, Florida, where his wife's parents owned the Buccaneer Motel. That winter he received a call from Allen, who was vacationing down the bench in nearby St. Petersburg. He said, "Maury, I'm going to be down your way. Do you mind if we get together?" Youmans, glad to hear from the personable coach, said, "Sure." They met at the Biltmore Motel; Allen was sitting at the bar when Youmans arrived. Allen said, "Maury, I brought a projector along. I'd like to get together with you and go over your defenses."

Youmans was taken aback. Finally, he said, "George, I can't do that. I'm playing for the Cowboys now!"

MAURY YOUMANS: "He wanted to pick my mind. And George ended up the head coach of the Washington Redskins, our archenemy. You can imagine if I had given him all that information!

"That was George. Tom Landry once accused him of having spies, and it was true. George would do anything to win. Well, he learned it from the master, George Halas. There were rumors, and I'll never know if it was true or not, that Halas had microphones in the visiting locker room at Wrigley Field to hear what was going on."

Tom Landry's famed Flex defense made its debut in 1964, when the Cowboys used it on occasion to test whether it would work. In '65 it became a regular part of the defensive system. That year, for the first time, the Dallas defense became effective. In all but three of the fourteen games, the defense held the opposition under 24 points.

DICK NOLAN: "Over the years Tom had watched and studied all the films, noting the formations, and plotting all the plays that were run from those formations. All of a sudden, he saw a master key to it. Those keys told us in advance what the other team was going to run. At the same time, he devised a defense to disguise what *we* were going to do to attack an offense. What Tom came up with was the Flex, a combination of the 4–3 inside and the 4–3 outside defenses. On one side of the line you're playing an inside, and on the other side, you're playing an outside.

"We had been strictly an inside-outside 4–3 team, like the old Giants, and then in '64, we used the Flex as a change-up defense in different spots, just to work our way into it, see what it was all about, to see how it worked.

"In 1965 we went to it big time. Bob Lilly was the key to the defense. He had moved from left end to right tackle, and boy he was quick as a cat. He was so quick off that ball, the center couldn't block back and get him. If the center did try to block back on the line of scrimmage, he'd knock his own guard off trying to pull. That's how quick Bob was. The only way that center could get him was straight down the line of scrimmage. Not on an angle. And the guard would be knocked off. 'Cause Bob was so quick.

"See, Lilly wasn't a sprinter of any kind. He wasn't a great 40-yard guy. But he was so quick for five or ten yards, and brother, once he got his hands on you, he was so strong, too, you couldn't get away. And he'd throw you any way he wanted to.

"Let me try to explain the Flex to you. Let's say the Packers set up in a split backfield. The two backs are split, Paul Hornung behind one tackle, Jimmy Taylor behind the other. What we did, we took our left defensive tackle and put him head-up on the line of scrimmage with their right guard. Now, you take your left defensive end, and you bring him back off the ball by two feet, head-up on their right offensive tackle.

"We then took our right tackle opposite their left guard, and put him *off* the ball. His job was to read the head of the guard. Whichever way the head of the guard went, he was to go with him. And the defensive end on that right side, he plays on the outside shoulder of the left offensive tackle.

"As soon as the Packers set up in a split backfield, under Tom's system of reading the keys you have to anticipate that one or both of those guards will be pulling. In this formation, it was the job of our right tackle, in this case, Bob Lilly, to explode on that guard.

"Let's say the other team tries the old Lombardi sweep. When that guard pulls and that center tries to choke back to get Lilly, he can't get to him quick enough because Lilly can just go around him, and the center will fall on his nose trying to block him. Lilly will be running right behind their guard, and Paul Hornung will be running the ball, and Paul Hornung can't come back, because if he does, he'll be running right back into Lilly, who is running down the line of scrimmage with him.

"So now, when he does that, the right defensive end, who is head-up on the tackle off the ball, he's keying the guard, too. If that guard pulls away, he'll follow him, take it down inside with him, go along the line of scrimmage, so if they try to cut back behind Lilly, who is chasing the guard, Lilly will pick up the guy cutting back that far, and the defensive end will pick up the rest of it.

"And then what you do also, you can give them that Flex look, and all you would play was the normal inside 4–3 and *not* the Flex. The next time you could play the normal outside 4–3 from that look and *not* the Flex. So they didn't know *when* to pull or *who* to pull.

"When the defensive end is head-up on that tackle, he can key the tackle if he wants to, just read his head. If the tackle tries to cut inside of him, cut him off in the pursuit of the play, he'll get by his head. See, if he fires straight out at him, he'll say, 'Fine, I'll straighten you up and control your inside.' If he tries to reach to his outside, he'll say, 'Okay, I'll step into you and control you on the inside by knowing that the play is trying to come there.'

"The only thing that would hurt me as a defensive end off the ball and looking at the tackle is if the tackle sets for a pass, and then they try to run something underneath me. Then I'm in trouble. Because I'm taking the influence of a pass, and I see it as a pass and nothing else. Well, as a defensive end, if that guy did that to me, the first thing I would do would be to go right back to the guard key. Now I don't care what you as the tackle do. You can set back to pass; I won't even look at you because the guard is telling me what's going on. So that's the truer key. But the end was an easier key. He used to be on all fours just like a tackle. He'd be off the ball looking down at the guard.

"And *nobody*, not me, and probably not even you knew what we were doing. [It had to be experienced on the playing field, which is why it took three years for the average player to learn the system.] They didn't know, because we gave them the same look, and they'd say, 'Here's the Flex,' and it wasn't the Flex at all. It was nothing but the inside-outside 4–3. And the next time we'd play the Flex, and they wouldn't be ready for it. That's how we got to control most people.

"And sometimes what we'd do too off that same look, we'd play a regular blitzing defense, the 4–3 storm, where both inside linebackers would be coming hard full-tilt, and you have every gap shut off. So you'd blitz your linebackers. You weren't playing a Flex, but it looked like a Flex."

MAURY YOUMANS: "Larry Stephens had played for Texas when we played them in the Cotton Bowl. Larry was probably one of the brightest ballplayers on that team. He picked up the system better and quicker than anyone else on the Cowboys at that time. Larry had some talent as a football player, but when you ran Landry's system, you didn't have to have all the talent in the world to be a good football player. With the Bears a linebacker might cover an end, but he made the play just on physical ability. With the Cowboys, you covered the end because Tom's system told you to do it before the play ever began. You knew exactly where the play was going to go. As a consequence, Larry became a *really* good football player with the Cowboys.

"None of us were as studious as we should have been, except for maybe Larry, and for Larry it was almost like osmosis. It wasn't that he just sat down and studied, it was that he had a quick mind and picked it up. He's a schoolteacher now. And a really good guy.

"George Andrie was our left end. George Andrie was a terrific player, but he didn't get much credit because it's a little hard when you have a Bob

Lilly on the team. George was as good as any of the defensive ends at that time. He was a hard worker. I don't think he had as much ability as he had heart, and that led him a long way. And he learned Tom's system very well. George made the Pro Bowl a few years, so he did get *some* recognition.

"Bob Lilly, our right tackle, was *the* most agile football player I ever saw. Bob could do kip-ups with pads on. A kip-up is where you lay on your back and kick up onto your feet. He would lay on his back and kick himself up. He was that agile. And he was strong. He had a very good upper body. And he had the right mental attitude for a football player. He was just hard-nosed, not mean, but intense. There was never one tackle who could block him on a pass defense.

"In fact, I guess you know, they designed the Flex defense *for* him. I was playing the right end next to him the year the Flex came in, and what they did was, they put Bob head-up closer on the guard. Instead of having my left shoulder to the left shoulder of the tackle, I had to go head-up on all fours. And the whole object of that was for me to watch the helmet of the tackle. If he closed down, I had to close that hole. Lilly was so quick that when they pulled the guard, he could follow and make the tackle on the halfback. The offense had the sucker play where they would pull the guard and run the halfback up through that hole, so they needed to cover it with the defensive end, and so it was the job of the defensive end to step into that hole. That was my job or Larry's job. We didn't like it because if it turned out to be a pass play, it took our rush away. There is *no way* you're going to get a rush coming around. You don't even have a start on it. First, you're waiting to see what the helmet does, but it was because of Bob's quickness that we could do it."

BOB LILLY: "We were starting to get into Tom's theories more and more, and I call them 'theories' because that's what they were when he came to Dallas. He implemented them slowly. By my third year, that's when we got into the Flex defense.

"The Flex defense was a gap defense. I don't care what defense it was, everyone had a responsibility for a certain gap. A lot of teams back in those days played a gap defense where the men were actually *in* the gaps. They had a defender between center and guard and another one between guard and tackle. The defensive end was out wide, and the linebackers were in the gaps that weren't covered. And therefore the guy in front of you knew exactly what you were going to do.

"But with the Flex, what we tried to do was disguise it, to keep our strategy from the offensive linemen.

"When I first began with the Cowboys, we played what we called the inside-outside 4–3. The linebacker would call it, depending on what formation we had, and that meant we had to step with our right foot if it was an outside 4–3, and we'd be responsible from the head of the guard to the head of the tackle. That was my position. Lee Roy Jordan, our middle linebacker, had responsibilities from the head of the center over to the head of the guard. And so forth and so on. And then if it was an inside 4–3, then I'd step with my left foot. I had inside responsibility, and so did the other tackle, and Lee Roy had to fill either gap between the guard and the tackle. The defensive ends had the gaps on the inside.

"Our goal was to push the play up the middle to Jerry Tubbs or Lee Roy."

LEE ROY JORDAN: "I've seen a lot of good players, and I'm not sure that Bob Lilly still isn't the best one I've ever seen. If Bob Lilly had had the weight program like they have now, I'm not sure Bob would have been controllable. And if he had had a mean streak like some defensive linemen, you would have had to outlaw him. Bob would tackle quarterbacks and lay them down on the ground, where other guys would tackle them and throw them onto the AstroTurf with their 300-pound bodies and maybe break a rib or shoulder or something. But Bob wasn't that way. Bob really didn't try to injure anyone, but his escape from offensive people trying to block him was unbelievable. He was like magic. He was just an unbelievable athlete. His foot coordination, his hand and arm strength were unbelievable, especially for a guy who didn't lift weights.

"We would go back and watch films after games, and he was 'Mr. Amazing.' We'd say, 'Let's run that back. I can't believe Bob Lilly did that.' He would have three guys on him, and he would go through them like there were little doors in between each one of them that they were opening for Bob Lilly. And he did it week after week, year after year.

"A whole generation of great linemen never got written about because they were playing alongside Bob. And I don't really think it bothered the other linemen, because we all got to watch him in person and on film, and we were so amazed. Hell, I know my career lasted as long as it did because I got to play behind him. I might not have lasted five years behind some other defensive line. I was not the main problem. Hell, they had to worry about Bob Lilly first.

"If you were coming across the middle, I did create some problems, but like us, the other team had to set its priorities, and the other team's number one priority was to block Bob Lilly. And then they could say,

'Okay, once we contain Lilly, we have to block the linebackers. You have to keep Jordan from working the Flex if you're going to run on them.' I had a couple holes to fill on the Flex, and if they couldn't get me blocked, there was not going to be a hole for them to run in."

BOB LILLY: "In 1964 we went from the inside-outside 4–3 into the Flex, and I don't know if that was part of Tom's long-term plan, or whether he did it for me, I have no idea, but the Flex defense was identical to what we had been doing, only we brought the defensive end on the short side on the outside shoulder of the offensive tackle. If I were on the weak side, I'd be head-up with the guard, right on the line of scrimmage, whereas the tackle on the other side would be three feet back. George Andrie would be right over the tackle, and instead of being on his outside shoulder, he'd be head-up, three feet back. He would be keying my guard. I also keyed my guard.

"We got to where we could play the inside-outside from the Flex look. I don't know whether Tom designed the Flex defense as something else to do off the inside-outside 4–3, or whether the Flex was the major defense, but we would play our old inside-outside 4–3 to give them a different look.

"Anyway, that's what football is all about, disguising the defense and never letting them know what you're doing."

When Bob Lilly was told that Coach Landry had designed the Flex defense specifically to take advantage of his superior play, the big tackle seemed surprised. "I was never told he designed that for me," he said. "But I loved it, I'll tell you that." Lilly explained why he and the Flex were made for each other.

BOB LILLY: "Back in those days the other teams ran 65 percent of their plays to the right. So I was in wonderful pursuit. I could catch the offensive guard *before* he could get out of his stance. I'd usually grab him by the back of the jersey and let him pull me right into the play.

"Also I had a good inside move for a pass rush, which is the fastest way to get there. I don't know how many traps I had. I know one year I had 18 or 19, but mainly I was able to force that quarterback out of the pocket, and then our other tackle and our two defensive ends could get after him.

"But it was a natural position for me. I *loved* it. I finally felt at home.

"A lot of the other defensive players didn't like Tom's system when he first showed it to them. Most players want to see the ball and react. And the way we had to play defense was totally opposite of that. We had to think first and then react, which is very difficult, because those guys are coming at you full blast.

"But after we learned how to do it, it was easy. That was the thing I didn't realize early on. Once we learned it, we were *always* in the right position. We didn't always make the play, and we sometimes got beat physically, but we were always in the right position, and it was just a matter of whether we were healthy or whether we matched up well that day or whether we were fired up. But many of us lasted a long time in the league because of the fact we played the kind of defense we did. Tom's system was *why* we all played fourteen years. A lot of people talked about the Cowboys not being real aggressive, and that's the reason, that rather than just take off, we had to think before we moved. We had the quality of personnel to do so. If we could have moved and hit, I don't have any doubt we would have gotten a lot of traps—but as it was, we got 61 traps one year, and we were in the 50s a lot, and that was in the top of the league.

"By '65 we were playing pretty consistently good defense, not every game, but if you look at the whole season, we accomplished most of our goals. Dave Edwards didn't start until '64. That's when Jerry Tubbs came up with the idea of switching Dave and Chuck Howley. Dave wasn't quite fast enough to play weakside linebacker [where the assignment was to guard the flanker] so Jerry came up with the idea of switching our linebackers, putting Dave on the strong side [where the assignment was to guard the tight end] and Chuck on the weak side so that no matter how they lined up, Dave played opposite the other team's tight end. And what Dave added was a lot of strength. He could hold a tight end and stand him up when they tried to block him, so they couldn't run around that side. They never could get a clear block, no matter who it was, even Mike Ditka, didn't matter. Dave was strong enough to hold up any of them. He could stand 'em right up on the line of scrimmage: Jackie Smith, Ditka, even John Mackey at Baltimore. They couldn't push him around. So that's what he added. Plus he was a smart football player, never made a mistake. Tom liked that about him.

"Mel Renfro came in '64, and he was an All-Pro. He was the finest cornerback I saw, with maybe the exception of Mel Blount, during my years of watching football. They wouldn't throw at him. They just wouldn't throw because he always intercepted it or knocked it down. And Mel was also a great return man. He had been a running back in college. Mel forced the other team to go all to the other side, and that way we could set up our defenses. Tom was able to create the situation where they had to throw over there, and we had some good cornerbacks, but unfortunately not another one like Mel. Cornell Green was a good cornerback, but he wasn't as fast as Mel either. Charlie Waters was a good one, but he wasn't as fast as Mel.

"Then in '65 we added defensive lineman Jethro Pugh, and before long he became an excellent football player, adding an awful lot to our team. We started playing good defense, because we were consistent. We got beat sometimes and we didn't play well, but ten out of fourteen we played pretty good defensive games. Our statistics were good as far as yards per carry, yards per catch, total offense, total points. We had goals for all those, and we kept pretty much within those goals, which according to Coach Landry, should have won the game, but we weren't winning some of those games because we weren't scoring consistently enough. We might have averaged 25 points, but we'd score 45 points in one game and we'd score 10 in another.

"The problem was our offense was erratic. They would score 50 points one week, and we'd play a good team and get beat. In '64 and '65 on the defense we were judging our offense a little bit, and we shouldn't have, but we did, and it took us until '66 to stop—after we started winning. The few years we bitched about our offense, we created a division in our team. In '63, '64, and '65 we were bitchin', and when we had a bad game, I suspect they were bitching, too.

"I don't know that Tom was aware of it. There again, part of that was that we didn't have enough coaches. We went three years without having even a defensive line coach. We just had an overall defensive coach, Dick Nolan. So we were kind of on our own, and we could get together and bitch all we wanted to. We could bitch and raise hell and all that.

"Through '65 the offensive line was leaky, and Don Meredith was playing on bad legs, and we continued to chirp about the offense. We liked Don. It wasn't personal as much as it was frustrating. It wasn't that we didn't respect him. It's just that we could never seem to get together in a big game. Either we'd let them down, or they'd let us down. It got to where they let us down in the big games more than we let them down. That's what we bitched about. And that's what you can't have. And a lot of that was due to our having a little bit of a porous offensive line, and because of that, Meredith was beat up, hurt a lot. Don played with everything, even broken fingers. He played one time with a broken nose. His nose was *so* big I took a picture of it—his eyes were covered up. We had a lot of respect for his toughness."

21

Varmint

Pete Gent grew up in northern Michigan from the same sort of farming community as many of the other players. His father, a former marine, had been hired out at age twelve to another farmer as a laborer. As an adult he worked on the railroad mail, but in his spare time he was an environmentalist before the term was even coined, walking alone over several hundred acres planting pine seedlings and then hand cultivating them. When he sprayed insecticide, Gent's dad saw the dead birds and realized that in his attempt to make the fields grow, he was killing wildlife.

During the age of Joe McCarthy and the Red Scare in the 1950s, Gent's father, a staunch Republican, would ask, "Why are we afraid of the Communists? If we think Communism is so dangerous, let them try to feed the world for a while and see how good their system is."

It was from his dad that Peter Gent inherited his individuality and a certain disdain for those in seats of authority. When he came to Dallas, he saw discrimination that offended him, and when the war in Vietnam began to heat up, he was one of those who questioned its wisdom.

Of the many influences in his life, though, it was the game of football that changed him most. When he joined the Cowboys, Gent was a mild-mannered, well-behaved kid who didn't drink, didn't smoke, and whose idea of a perfect marriage was Ozzie and Harriet's. He had spent a frustrating first season with the Cowboys, and after passing the law boards, began attending SMU Law School at night with an eye toward a law career. Gent had worked in Chicago for a few months in the advertising firm of Foot, Cone and Belding. A life of middle-class respectability seemed to await. And then, during training camp in '65, Pete Gent roomed with one of the wildest Texans ever to play for the Cowboys, Don Talbert, called Varmint, one of four brothers known as the Varmint Brothers. Gent's life would never be the same again.

PETE GENT: "Most of the '64 season I lived by myself near the Cowboy practice field. I mostly hung around with Dave Manders, his wife, and his two kids and with Frank Clarke and his wife. I didn't know anybody else. I made no other friends. It was stultifying only because I couldn't figure out how to live. I was real lonely, and every time I tried to do something with Billy Lothridge or Don Meredith or any of the partyers, it wasn't any fun, because I didn't drink.

"Before I played football, the way I had always looked at my life, everything was a means of getting somewhere else. I could not adapt that to football. From my flanker position, any time you headed inside, you were going to get hit, so you better hit somebody. The old line was, 'You might as well catch it. They are going to hit you anyway.' They were going to knock the piss out of you. It was brutal. It really was. That's why you couldn't think too far in the future.

"Football was so violent that thinking wasn't encouraged in that atmosphere. Reflection, what the future was going to bring, long-term thinking, you couldn't deal with that in football. You really couldn't think beyond what you were doing that day. If you really thought beyond that day, you'd quit. You'd say to yourself, 'How can I survive doing this?'

"So after my rookie year I realized if I went back into football, I was going to have to do what all those other guys on the team who I liked and liked being around were doing.

"To me, in order to play professional sports, the biggest change is in your head. If you can't make that change, you'll never survive. I can remember coming back from Dallas after the first year thinking, 'I don't know if I ever want to do that again.' I spent the whole off-season saying, 'If I have to become like that, be really mean and hateful . . .' I didn't drink, and I was so upset all the time that drinking was part of it, but you were totally out of the social network if you didn't drink, and there is *nothing* worse than going to a bar with a bunch of ballplayers and being the only guy sober.

"In '65 I ran into Craig Morton, a rookie, and Craig drank vodka gimlets, and I could get those down. You didn't have to drink a lot of those to feel it, and by the third one you didn't care what it tasted like. And I immediately became a drunk, going from not drinking at all to drinking every day.

"I had hurt my knee playing basketball in the off-season. I was getting what they called joint mice, little pieces of cartilage the size of a quarter floating around the joint, and then they'd lock in the joint. That happened in mid-spring, I had it operated on, and then I worked to get ready for camp, and I was in camp the second day, and some more broke off. So I came back to Dallas, and they went in and made a small hole, just did a small incision and got the small piece of cartilage out.

"I stayed in Dallas till the first exhibition game and started working out, and when I got back to camp, I was walking in at around ten o'clock at night, had my suitcase, and standing naked in the hall was Don Talbert, who had been in Vietnam, who I had never met. He went about 6'5", 250 pounds. He'd gone in to do his six months in the reserves, got frozen in the service, and got sent to Vietnam. You think he wasn't pissed? He missed a complete year. He spent it in Saigon as an MP in 1964. He was so mad they had sent him over there.

"I had seen Don the first couple of days but I had yet to meet him, and there he was standing there, and as I walked by him he said, 'Hey, motherfucker, I need a roommate—and you're it!'

"I went down to my room thinking, 'Oh, fuck, I can't say no to this guy.' So I roomed with Don Talbert, and it changed my whole life.

"We lived in this apartment called the Four Seasons, and the only people who lived there were single football players, Dave Edwards, Mike Gaechter, Colin Ridgway, Obert Logan, Talbert, and me, and we lived next to four stewardesses from American Airlines.

"This apartment house had luxury apartments. Dave Edwards had one that had a champagne fountain next to his bed. I don't know how he put in the champagne.

"In Dallas in those days you could not buy liquor over the bar, except in private clubs, and that apartment complex had a private club called the Fifth Season. Talbert was a drinker, and so Don and I went to that club every night after practice. Every night after practice we'd get drunk.

"Talbert and Edwards and all those guys from the South barbecued all the time. Outside the back door of the club Edwards had his barbecue on the deck, and we'd eat and get drunk. It was insane.

"Oh God, Talbert and I did shit like get drunk and play golf in the apartment. We put divots in the carpeting with nine irons. We tried to hit the ball out the door, put it through the window, off the walls, Jesus. It was nuts but oh God, it was really fun.

"Talbert was one of those guys, when he would step into a club, everybody would look at the door and they'd be saying to themselves, 'Oh boy, I hope he doesn't sit down with us!'

"Don had a brother, Diron, who was still at the University of Texas. Diron was also 6'5", about 250 pounds. He later played with the L.A. Rams and the Washington Redskins. Charlie, his older brother, was in law school at the University of Texas, and then the youngest was at the University of Colorado.

"Don would do absolutely anything. He had no fear. There was nothing you could do to scare Don. How were you going to threaten him, kill him? What were you going to threaten him with, to send him back to Vietnam?

"I used to walk down the street with Don and Diron, and they'd say, 'Let's motherfuck these people,' and they would walk up to guys who would be walking with their girls, and Don and Diron would just grab the girl and pick her up and fondle her, grab her breasts, and the women just loved it. Of course, the men hated it. But they couldn't do anything.

"One time we went to the Byron Nelson Golf Classic in Dallas. Talbert came and picked up me and my first wife, who was my girlfriend then, in his new Riviera. I was living in Lahoma in a house off Lemon Avenue, and Talbert and his brother came and picked us up. The Byron Nelson was at the old Preston Trails Golf Course. Preston Trails Road, when it got out to the LBJ Expressway, narrowed down into a two-lane road, and for ten blocks back to the expressway there was a huge traffic jam.

"We were sitting in the backseat of the car when I heard Don say, 'Let's motherfuck these guys.' That could only mean one thing: trouble. Talbert drove on the right shoulder, and at 80 miles an hour he passed everybody, knocking over mailboxes, anything in his way. He was so nuts he didn't care. When we pulled up to the clubhouse my wife just got out of the car and threw up, went to the press tent and stayed there all day.

"We were sitting at the press tent, and this good-looking blond woman walked by, and Don and Diron just grabbed her and laid her out over a table and were just molesting her, putting their hands all over her breasts, and then they gave her their room number at the Royal Coach Inn, past the airport, and I'll be damned if she didn't show up there!

"The thing was, Don Talbert was really smart, too. He knew when to do it. He never ever would do anything out of line in front of your parents. He really respected older people, and certain women. He really had it down. But when he went nuts, boy, everybody got out of the way. When the two of them were together, look out.

"I remember one time Donnie Anderson, who was Diron's friend, had come back from signing his bonus at Green Bay, and he came to the Fifth Season Club and started talking about Green Bay, and Don and Diron started slapping him on top of the head, 'Shut up about that Green Bay shit,' whacking him on the head. Anderson said, 'Okay okay okay okay. I'll be quiet. Just let me hang around with you guys.'

"One night I walked up to the Fifth Season Club after a game, and there was Bobby Layne sitting with the guy who ran the club. There were a lot of interesting guys who went through that bar, Bobby, George Jones. I sat down and started talking to Bobby. I was from Michigan, and I remembered watching him with the Lions. Don Talbert and Don Meredith knew him as a big star at the University of Texas, and a big high school star in Texas. Bobby was like God to Meredith and Talbert. To me he was an interesting guy. Bobby missed his last plane out, and so he decided to spend the night with us. We had an extra bed. All he had in his overnight bag was two changes of underwear and three bottles of Johnny Walker Red, and he would take a big eight-ounce tumbler and fill it to the top. I was finding half-full tumblers around the apartment for a week after he left.

"He came over to the apartment and called everybody he knew on the phone and sang 'Ida Red' to them. He called Ernie Stautner in Pittsburgh, called all the guys he played with in Pittsburgh and Detroit, Harley Sewell, and Yale Lary, called all those guys, and kept calling Don Meredith to come over. Meredith was married then, and the wife was really pissed, so he didn't come.

"We were in the living room/dining room/kitchen area, and Bobby was running off at the mouth about 'what an asshole Landry was' and 'he couldn't play quarterback if he had to.' Landry had played behind Layne at Texas. God, Bobby just hated Landry. He hated that 'God squad' stuff. Layne thought a team needed to drink together to run together. He believed that was real important. And so did Meredith. Layne was Meredith's hero. I suspect that was part of the tension between Landry and Meredith. The easiest thing in the world to see was how hard Meredith tried to model himself after Bobby Layne, to be that kind of leader.

"At the time Bobby Layne's kid was playing for Texas, and all he was doing was kicking, and so Bobby was pissed. Talbert and I were walking behind him, and Talbert said, 'Hey, Bobby, how 'bout them Horns?' Bobby said, 'Fuck the Horns.' And I started laughing, and Talbert, who had also gone to Texas, turned around and smashed me right in the stomach, knocking me flat. He couldn't hit Layne. Who was he going to hit?

"After the '65 season Don and I went to Aspen. I had to have my knee operated on after the season again, so I couldn't ski. We drove all the way from Texas to Michigan to pick up my little brother, who was going to Central Michigan. We dragged him out of bed at midnight, and threw him in the back of the car, and he really didn't wake up until we were in Iowa! 'Where am I?'

"We picked up Paul Talbert, the youngest brother, in Boulder. Then we drove straight to Aspen, where Diron and Charlie Talbert were waiting for us.

"All the way Don Talbert was telling me about this hotel in Aspen Highlands where we were going to stay. 'The owner *really* loves us,' he said. They had been there the year before.

"We were drunk, and we came roaring up the front gate, and as soon as we pulled in the owner came running out of the hotel waving his arms. He said, 'No, no, you *can't* stay here. We *can't* have you in the hotel. Absolutely not.' He said, 'I will give you my condominium out by Ajax.' He gave us a six-bedroom condominium just so we wouldn't come to his hotel!

"We used to go out to Clint Murchison's place to hunt doves, and coming back through Athens, Texas, this one day, it was Talbert, Larry Stephens and Larry's kid—they got Larry Stephens's kid drunk—George Andrie, and Bob Lilly, and as they were coming through Athens, they shot a housepainter! The guy, Billy Ray Jackson, something like that, was up on a ladder painting his house! I named my dog after the guy when they came home and told me the story. They had sprayed him with bird shot from the road!

"He was a little bitty guy, about killed by paint fumes, chasing five giants in a pickup who had shot him with a shotgun. He chased them down in his truck, ran them off the road, caught them, and then threatened them all! None of them would get out of the truck. They were all scared to death of the guy!

"Lilly said the guy was all covered with blood, BBs in his arm, and that Talbert was drunk, saying, 'Hey hey hey, what are you going to do?' The guy kept saying, 'Come on down here, Mouther, I want you.' He was going to take on two thousand pounds of defensive linemen! And they all had guns!

"When they came back and told the story, I was on the floor. I hunted as a kid my whole life. In Michigan the rule was you *never* drank and hunted. I knew a couple guys who drank the night before deer hunting, and I thought that was nuts. But down in Texas, they *all* drank when they hunted. That story in *North Dallas Forty* of being in a duck blind and getting sprayed by shot was a true story. Talbert and Lilly, or somebody else, started shooting at us from across the lake!

"I met Don Meredith through Talbert. Talbert and Meredith had played together in Dallas before Talbert went to Vietnam. When I started running with Meredith, that's when my life *really* changed."

22

Turmoil and Dandy Don

PETTIS NORMAN: "In '65 we had broken training camp and were staying at the Holiday Inn, and it was a Wednesday night off, and we had a get-together. I walked in, one of the last to walk in, and everybody was standing around pretending to have fun but watching for me to come in the door. As I walked in, I saw this group of people in the center of the room. Don Talbert was over there pretending to be dumping some bread into this cage, and tapping on the cage.

"Dave Edwards and Pete Gent came up and started talking to me. As we were talking, I was looking out of the corner of my eyes at Talbert. I asked, 'What is Don doing?' Dave said, 'You're not going to believe what that crazy Don Talbert is doing. He has a wild mongoose.' I said, 'A mongoose?' They said, 'Yeah, a wild mongoose. Come on over and look at it.'

"Dave Edwards and Pete led me over there and I said, 'What are you doing?' Don said, 'I'm trying to feed this mongoose. The crazy thing won't come out and eat.' I said, 'A mongoose? What is a mongoose?'

"He said, 'First of all, they are vicious. A little hairy animal, but very vicious. You don't want to put your hand in the cage or your finger through the wire, because man, it will rip your hand apart.' I said, 'Don, what would you want with a mongoose?' He said, 'I was out hunting, and I saw him and I caught him.' And knowing Don, he would be a guy who would do that with his bare hands.

"I looked into the wooden cage with a little round hole in it, and a hairy tail sticking out of the hole. Don said, 'He won't come out. They are as stubborn as I don't know what.' Don was knocking on the side of the cage, saying, 'Come on out, you mongoose, you lazy so and so.' And as he was beating on the side of the cage I started leaning down closer to see.

"He started rattling the cage, and I was leaning down closer and closer, and I said, 'This thing must be sleeping.' Don said, 'He's just lazy. And he's ornery. He just won't come out.' So I leaned farther, and Don hit a switch for the trap door, and this tail jumped out of the cage at me, and I had a can of beer in my hand, even though I don't drink beer. Someone had given me the beer, but boy, as I saw that tail coming at me, it looked like a lion! I can swear to you that tail had teeth and fangs, and as I saw them coming through the air getting ready to devour me I leaped backward. I mean, I hold the world record for leaping backward from a standstill. I must have leaped 20 feet in the air backward, and as I was leaping, I threw this container of beer at that tail and hit it. I thought I was going to die of a heart attack. It was incredible, and everybody in that place just laughed until they couldn't stand up. I mean, they got me *real* good.

"It really was fun. You had Don Talbert, Don Meredith, Pete Gent, and several others who didn't take themselves too seriously, who approached the game of football with a lightheartedness that I had not been used to in college.

"There were times we could pick up a flippant attitude or statement by Don Meredith, and on the other hand, you had Tom Landry, who was a very serious person coaching this bunch, and tolerating them, and yet they respected Landry to a degree, so it was a divergency that existed among this group of players. And it was really interesting. As I look back, how would it have been if we didn't have them on the team? We might have been too serious. Because out of that we developed a winning mixture. So it was really a very interesting mix, if you consider Tom Landry on one hand, and Don Talbert, Don Meredith, and Pete Gent on the other."

Traditionally, when the coach spoke, a player obeyed without questioning him. But with the cynicism brought by the controversy over the murder of John F. Kennedy, and a growing revolution against race discrimination and the burgeoning Vietnam War, some of the formerly malleable players began to challenge authority. They wanted to know *why* the coach was doing what he was doing. And if it didn't seem right, the player no longer kept silent.

Pete Gent was one of the first to speak up if things didn't make sense, at times angering Tom Landry. This generation war started as a battle between Landry and Gent. By the end of the decade there would be an army of other players just as vocal but more cynical and vicious. This generation gap between coach and players would widen until by the end of the decade it would be the size of the Grand Canyon.

PETE GENT: "The first thing you had to do when you got to training camp was run the Landry Mile. You did it before they gave you your physical, before you did your electrocardiogram, before anything. You had to go out there in 85-degree heat and run a mile in under six minutes if you were a back or end, and under six and a half if you were a lineman. In '65 Bob Lilly held out and came late to camp. Lilly, of course, hadn't worked out in months. We had all been in camp, so the only player to run the mile that day was Lilly. We were all waiting for him to run the mile, and he came out loaded up on Dexadrine. On the third lap he went blind. He had Larry Stephens on one side and George Andrie on the other, running with him around the track. Landry made him finish, and he was blind! He finished the mile, staggered off, and fell into the dummy shed, a small sheet-metal building that was like an oven. While we went on with practice, Lilly was just lying there. After lunch he was still there. And he was our best player.

"The next year Pettis Norman almost went into cardiac arrest. And that was the last time they ran the Landry Mile. It was just nuts. That was still post–World War II era coaches. The game was about meanness and toughness. If you went blind, you ran blind. It didn't make any sense at all."

Another of the players with whom Landry didn't see eye to eye, Don Meredith, began the '65 season getting off on the wrong foot with his coach. For four years Landry had been preaching seriousness and commitment to his quarterback, and in return he was treated to country-and-western songs in the huddle and raucous behavior that seemed to him to belie a lack of maturity. In one preseason scrimmage, a Meredith pass was intercepted by Cornell Green. Meredith took off his helmet, held it high as though he was going to whack him with it, and began chasing Green, who was laughing. Landry didn't find it funny.

Not long after Meredith informed Coach Landry that he "fell in a puddle of water" in his dorm and badly hurt his shoulder and elbow. Landry was not happy or sympathetic.

BUDDY DIAL: "During training camp in '65, Don and I went to town, and we bought a bunch of water guns. They were like machine guns, and we were having a war in the hall, and he slipped on the wet floor, and hurt his arm. Of course, I got blamed for it."

It was the first in a string of injuries that would keep Meredith from being effective for much of the '65 season and that would bring turmoil to the entire team. It's bad enough for a quarterback to have a bad arm, but to Tom Landry this injury was inexcusable because of the way it had happened. There was no question, though, that Meredith had to play at a serious disadvantage.

FRANK CLARKE: "Dandy started the season with a sore arm. We knew Dandy's arm was really painful, and it became a challenge for us: Do we stay with our style of running these routes and know he's going to get the ball to us, or do we make the mistake of getting out there and starting to think about making some kind of compensation so that we can catch the ball or make it easier for him to throw it to us?

"And the answer was, Don't think, just run your routes, because if he's supposed to be there, he'll be there. If he can't do the job, then he *shouldn't* be there. And that was it: No compensation, no compromises. Run your route and keep your concentration. It was something intuitive, something I did on my own.

"The coaches weren't making any big deal out of it, because mentally if you bring these things up, the players start to think about it. It was not anything we talked about, but the intuitive part of us said, 'Pretend Dandy's arm has never been stronger.' But it certainly did pain him."

Backed by only two rookies, Craig Morton of Cal Berkeley and Jerry Rhome of Tulsa, Meredith was *the man*, and Tom Landry was counting on his arm, for this year the team was adding one of the most exciting offensive weapons in the history of the game of football. His name was Bob Hayes, and he was billed as the World's Fastest Human. He could run the 100-yard dash faster than any man alive, which meant that there wasn't a defensive back in any league fast enough to catch him. Before he came to camp the only questions were whether he had the skills to get open and, if he could get open, whether he could catch the ball.

PETE GENT: "Hayes had been in camp several days before me, and when I got there everyone was saying how bad he was. The problem was that he was catching Craig Morton, who only threw at one speed, which was like shooting the ball out of a cannon. In fact, I was the only guy in camp who could catch Craig.

"In fact, I said to several guys, 'I'm going to start here because nobody can catch this kid but me.' Craig literally threw a pass so hard to Bobby Hayes that it split his hand in half between his two middle fingers, and it took seventeen stitches in the webbing to close the split.

"And then Red Hickey started working with Bob, and I would stay out with him, too. Red taught Bob how to cradle the ball, how to handle the ball, and by the end of camp there was no doubt in my mind that he was going to be something special. You don't think there is much difference between a 9.3 sprinter and a 9.1, but when Hayes turned it on, the 9.3 sprinters looked like they had stopped to walk and Hayes had just been shot out of a cannon. And it changed the game. It literally changed the whole game. When Hayes was in there, I *always* had single coverage. They had to put everybody over on Hayes's side.

"And halfback Dan Reeves, who was another rookie in '65, became a key receiver, because we could run him out of the backfield on Hayes's side, and there would be nobody there. Everybody was chasing Hayes."

FRANK CLARKE: "I had made All-Pro in '64. Tommy McDonald and Buddy Dial were real quiet. The talk of the Cowboys and in the league was the rise of Frank Clarke, because I had a sparkling season, played well, blocked well, and I was smart, and everything just happened for me. And so there I was, an All-Pro. It stunned me.

"But the Cowboys knew they had Bob Hayes coming, and Tom Landry knew this guy was going to be great. He *knew* it. And so to make space for Bobby Hayes and to utilize my physical talents and pass-catching ability, he moved me to a slot position, because he was going to give the wide receiver spot where I just made All-Pro to Bobby Hayes—as a rookie.

"That's quite a statement, isn't it? To take an All-Pro and move him to another position and move a rookie in, a guy you've never seen play? Bob hadn't played a down. And this was fine with me.

"If Tom Landry wanted me to put on a '70s number and play tackle, I would have done it without a word. I had surrendered to his tutelage. I knew this guy was incredible. He had a mental approach to the game that astounded me, and I knew how important it was not only to have physical ability but mental ability, and this guy had it, so if he wanted me to go to another position, I didn't question it whatsoever. I knew it was in the best interest of what we all wanted.

"Heh heh heh, Tom knew. He knew, man. Paul Brown used to make the statement, 'If you got a gun, use it.' Brown was referring to Jim Brown. People would ask Paul Brown, 'Why do you give him the ball so often?' Jim was carrying the ball a hundred and sixty million times a game, and Tom Landry knew about Bob Hayes. It was, 'We have to get this guy in the game.' You gotta.

"We had drafted Bobby before the Olympic games in '64, and of course I watched his Olympic performance prior to his coming to the Cowboys. I've seen it so many times, and every time I look at it, I'm in awe. I cannot believe what he did, especially in the 400-meter relay.

"The U.S. was way behind when Hayes got the baton, and he was like a shot. He closed on those guys ahead of him like it was astounding. I thought, 'Wow! Can this guy catch up?' I also thought, 'If there is any way we can get the ball to him, can you imagine what he will do?' He won the 100 meter, too, and got tabbed as the World's Fastest Human. What would that do to most people coming in, with people calling you the World's Fastest Human? It would cause a lot of us to think a little bit, but it just seemed as though Bobby took it all in stride.

"One time I asked him about it. I said, 'Bob, it was so amazing to watch you run in the Olympics and see what you do with that football.' He said, 'Charlie.' My nickname with the black players was 'Charlie.' We called Bob 'Speedo.' Cornell Green was 'Sweet Lips.' And Mel Renfro was 'Suds.' Pettis Norman was 'Birch.' That's his middle name. Pettis Birch Norman. Bobby said, 'Charlie, nobody can ever imagine what it's like to stand on the podium and get a gold medal and be called one of the world's greatest athletes.' He said, 'Once you do that, nothing else can touch it. So what I do in football, I just do it, but nothing will compare to that.'

"It was really fantastic, I loved hearing this. It was as though he was saying, 'Once you've run in the Olympics, you've already done everything possible you can do as an athlete.'

"He was so incredible. I can remember in a game the other team was marching down the field for the winning touchdown. We were on our knees on the sidelines watching, a real tight situation, and Bobby Hayes turned to me, and he said, 'Hey, Charlie, what are you going to do after the game?' Everybody else was chewing on their fingernails. Everyone else had this intensity. Bobby wanted to know what I was going to do after the game! I looked at him and said, 'Man, here we are in this tense situation. Who are you anyway?' It was things like that that made me think, 'This guy is so amazing. So incredible.'

"Bobby played like he was just so loose—it was rooted in his Olympic performance, that once you're on the world stage, all the other stuff pales and there is nothing to get excited about.

"Bobby was so fast nobody dared race him, not even Mel Renfro—as quick and fast as he was. We ran our 40-yard sprints, and of course, Bob always would win, always would have the best times, but we all knew he could run even faster. It was kind of like a joke that we *really* wanted him to open up. 'Come on, man, really show us what you've got.' We *knew* there was a 4.2 in this guy, maybe a 4.1, maybe a 4.0.

"What we wanted was to see what Bobby could do. But we never felt we did. He just ran to win. Forty yards is over in a blink. We would tease him to find out, 'cause we wanted to see. We wanted to be able to say, 'Hey, we had this guy on our team. He ran the 40 in 4.1!' Just to be able to say that. We really didn't think that he would do it, but it would have been really fantastic to see this guy open up.

"It was at least two years since we were the laughingstock of the league. We knew that had changed really quickly. And we were headed toward being one of the top teams in the league, so when Tom said, 'I want you to move to the slot,' I said, 'Fine, okay.'

"I didn't even question it until I started hearing from some close friends who were fans of the Cowboys and until it came out in a couple of sports articles, where sportswriters said things like, 'Well, this smacks of some kind of racism. They take this black player who just made All-Pro and move him,' and I resented that somebody would come to me with this kind of baloney. I thought it sucked, and I still do, thought it was really in poor taste. And I told everyone that. I stood up for Tom."

PETTIS NORMAN: "In the opening game of '65, Coach Landry started Frank Clarke, Bob Hayes, and Buddy Dial instead of me, and I was troubled by that move. I knew from past history that we were a running team, and I knew I could block with the best of tight ends in the league. I knew also that when given the opportunity, I could catch with a good portion of them, because I had done this all through my college career. So I was troubled by that. As much as anything I thought it was done to accommodate the trade for Buddy Dial. Tom was trying to experiment with a passing offense and hoping the run would somehow be adequate. It didn't work out that way. But I was troubled by that move. There was also speculation he did it because Dallas wasn't ready for three black receivers all on the field at the same time. Interestingly, I didn't say it, but I had a lot of teammates who did, a *lot* of African-American teammates who were very vocal about it. They were saying, 'Landry just doesn't want to start three black receivers in this town. This town is not ready for that.' That's what *they* were saying.

"I didn't think about it like that because I guess I just didn't look at it like that. I could never really understand why I was benched, because I had consistently proven myself in every training camp and every other time that I could handle that position. The switch couldn't have been made for speed, because I was the third-fastest guy on the team behind Hayes and Mike Gaechter. Mike was a 9.6 sprinter in college, and I was a 9.7 sprinter, and so we'd just be nip and tuck in the 40-yard dash. When Bob Hayes came, he was even faster. I was always a team player. I would give whatever I had whenever I was out there. So that was a troubled season for me, trying to reconcile that."

The Cowboys won the first two games of the '65 season by the scores of 31–2 over the New York Giants and 27–7 over the Washington Redskins. The buzz was that the Cowboys were the most exciting young team in the NFL.

FRANK CLARKE: "In the fall of '65 we beat the Redskins on three long touchdowns to Bobby. He was starting to get a lot of coverage in the papers, but more important he was also getting a lot of coverage defensively. People were starting to double up on him as best they could.

"We were all quite stunned watching him run. It was really a tribute to Don Meredith how quickly Don got to where he could get Bob Hayes the ball. He didn't underthrow Bob very much, and we were very impressed with how quickly Dandy was able to do that. One of the things that helped, Bob Hayes and Meredith practiced a lot after our regular practice. They spent a lot of time together.

"Bobby was such a joy to watch running routes. He not only had this great way of practicing his moves and working on his moves, practicing as though he didn't have this great speed. He practiced the moves and got the timing down and used his peripheral vision, his way of looking at the whole secondary so he could see if they were rolling into a zone or if the linebackers were going to blitz, because he would have adjustments to make, and it was if he was doing all of this mentally as if he just had normal speed. When he got into a game, it was amazing how quickly he made all these adjustments, and he turned these great moves into getting behind defensive backs. Once he got behind a defensive back, it was *over*.

"Bobby was committed to succeeding. Because of his work ethic and because of his connection with Meredith, he became a dominating player.

"I have every reason to believe that he worked just as hard as Jerry Rice does, and people talk about that a lot. Bobby worked. He sure did. And this is one of the things that rewarded all of us, too, because we *knew* again, more and more and more of us were getting the sense that this is what it was going to take for us to go where we were beginning to see the horizon.

"And so Bobby would work harder, and I would work harder, and Pettis Norman would work harder, and it was not unusual for Tom Landry to tell guys, 'Okay guys, this is enough. Go in.' Offensive guys, and defensive guys would stay out, too, but especially us receivers, he would tell us to go in. 'This is enough.' That was the kind of attitude that was developing with us, because we were getting that sense. He actually said it to me, that 'Okay, this is enough.' In other words, he had dismissed practice, guys had gone in for the shower, and the quarterbacks and receivers would stay out there running routes, and he would say to us, 'That's enough, go in.' "

If Don Meredith could stay healthy, Tom Landry and the Cowboys would finally reach their long-term goals. But the '65 Cowboys had an Achilles' heel, their offensive line. In the season opener the Giants sacked Meredith five times, and against the Redskins he wrenched his back when he was violently thrown to the ground. Added to the elbow injury incurred during training camp, Meredith entered the third game against the St. Louis Cardinals banged up and severely damaged.

BUDDY DIAL: "In '65 we did not have a great line. We were weak at guard and didn't have a real good center—it was a patchwork offensive line, but Don, he had a devil-may-care attitude. He released the ball late, and he loved to go deep. And if he wanted to throw deep, he was going to throw deep. Coach Landry would beg him to get rid of the ball and not take such a beating, but Don, he just was fearless. He knew if he had a little second, he could go deep against anybody. I can remember in our second game against Washington, the Redskins had some veteran ballplayers, really a good defense, and Myron Pottios hit him and hurt him.

"In the next game against St. Louis, Don was throwing late and real high. That was a night game, a Monday night, a weird night, and Don was off. I remember he threw me a turn-in, and Meredith threw it real high, and I went up to catch it, and Larry Wilson, the free safety, a tough hitter, hit me in the ribs, and I broke four ribs and my spine, and they didn't tell me. They doped me up, and I kept playing, but that messed me up pretty good right there."

One of the reasons Landry kept playing Dial was that he didn't have any faith in Pete Gent. Assistant coach Red Hickey kept pleading with Landry to put Gent in, but Landry was adamant. Gent was a rookie—a free agent rookie at that. The dispute added to the unrest.

PETE GENT: "That same year I became a real sore point between Tom and Red Hickey, who felt I should be playing a lot, if not starting. I wasn't playing much at all. I was almost 6'6", and I weighed about 220, but my problem was that Red was a great technician at telling you how to catch the ball, but nobody knew how to show you how to run routes. And the only guy who ran really beautiful routes who would show me was Frank Clarke, but Frank had such a unique running style, it was like he was on roller skates. I kept trying to run like that and couldn't do it. He'd make these fluid cuts. Tommy McDonald and Buddy Dial were no help. Dial was a one-on-one receiver who Bobby Layne had made famous with the Steelers. He never really did well with Dallas, and Tommy McDonald was just such a mean little bastard, he just, God . . . So as a rookie I had nobody to teach me how to run routes, and I was not making the right kind of moves, because I was using basketball fakes."

After starting the season with two big wins and then losing to the St. Louis Cardinals in a game in which the offense in the first half could gain only 47 yards and make but two first downs, Tom Landry shocked the team by benching Don Meredith, citing his inability to hit the open receivers. His teammates, who knew how banged up Meredith was, could scarcely believe it.

FRANK CLARKE: "Dandy played injured against the Cards, and threw some interceptions, didn't play well, and Landry benched him, but Landry never said, 'I'm benching Don Meredith because he's hurt.' It was always, 'I'm benching Don Meredith because he's not performing.'

"It did seem as though this would have been quite a blow to any player's ego, to have been injured and then to be benched not because you're injured but because you're not doing the job. And that was real hard. I'm certain if Dandy spoke frankly about that, he would say that might have been one of the seeds for his retirement at the end of the '68 season. In fact, that probably was *the* seed, because Dandy never overcame that."

PETE GENT: "In '65 Meredith started out well, with two wins in a row, and the third win should have been against St. Louis, but Don Perkins dropped a pass in the end zone. Don was never really a strong receiver, but a great running back. The reason I'm certain it was Don Perkins was that Don made so few mistakes, and I can remember that he was just mortified. And then the next week Tom Landry benched Meredith, which just infuriated Perkins, 'cause he knew it wasn't Meredith's fault. We all did. And Landry went to the quarterback shuffle of Craig Morton and Jerry Rhome.

"That's when I first began to see that I was not going to get along with this guy. Because Tom Landry could sit there and tell you all his numbers, that it was all based on numbers and performance. They literally rated you on a three-point system. On any play you got no points for doing your job, you got a minus one if you didn't do your job, you got a plus one if you did more than your job. And a good score in a game was 17. You had 40 to 45 offensive plays. And they would read your scores out in front of everybody else. That was another thing: Tom thought that everyone should know who was letting them down.

"Right away I began to notice that the guys whose scores didn't seem to jibe with the way they were playing were the guys Tom didn't like. And I found out later your individual coach was supposed to score you, but then Tom would rescore you, and the first game I started and played in, I scored a plus 48, which meant I did more than my job on every play. And two games later I was on the bench. And that had come the same season that they benched Meredith, and by then I saw that Tom was saying one thing, that it was all numbers and performance, but on the other hand, this personal animosity between him and Meredith affected his decisions and his judgment of Meredith."

BUDDY DIAL: "Against the Eagles, Coach Landry alternated Craig Morton and Jerry Rhome. But see, Don was playing under a handicap. He was playing with strange receivers, guys who they had traded for, and they hadn't worked together enough, and the timing was off, and Don got dumped on for the whole damage, and it was *not* his fault. He had me and Tommy McDonald alternating, he had Frank Clarke out of position, he had Pettis Norman at tight end, and Pettis was a good blocker, but not a good receiver as yet. No one gave Don credit. And Landry never backed him. Never.

"Let me tell you something. Don had a *long* memory. He never said anything to the press, but he and I had some long, long, long talks in our room and on the road. It's really personal. I'd rather not violate a trust, because it was critical of the situation.

"See, Don's a country kid from Mount Vernon, Texas. He worshiped his mom and dad. He's just a good country guy, and I mean that with the highest praise possible, and here for the first time in his life he's being criticized, and wrongly so, and he has such honor, he's not going to say, 'Dial is not running good routes; he's hurt.' He's not going to say, 'McDonald is out of shape.' He wouldn't say, 'They are not hitting the holes,' or 'They are not blocking for me.' He was not going to criticize anybody. He was going to take the *whole* blame. And he took it on his shoulders. He'd say, 'Hey, we're losing. I threw the ball bad.' So Landry and the rest of them hung him out to dry.

"There was no one to go to Landry and say, 'This is terrible.' The running back coach was a guy named Ermal Allen, a little hypocrite. He cut up Meredith behind his back and to the press, and Don despised him, but he never would say so. But Allen never defended Don, never said, 'Hey, this guy is hurt, he's playing hurt, he's getting killed, they're hanging him out to dry, the system is not working, the players are not playing, and Meredith is taking the whole blame.' He wouldn't do that.

"But I'll tell you what, Dandy, he didn't forget. He kept a record, because he was that smart. He didn't want to hurt anybody or get even, all he wanted to do was win, and that's a class act. I mean, he could have been vindictive, because he was unjustly crucified for losing, but he just kept it to himself, and he said, 'I want to win.' "

PETTIS NORMAN: "My mind questioned what was going on at the time. I felt that Don had been there, he had taken a beating, he had answered the call, and I thought he was more serious about the game at that point than ever before. I really did not understand his being benched, especially since Craig Morton and Jerry Rhome were rookies who just did not understand the concept of the game. Nothing against them, but they *were* rookies.

"In my mind the team suffered as a result of that, and I could see no legitimate reason for Landry to have done that, except that Don missed some passes, or maybe Landry decided that he wasn't serious enough about the game, and he just made the change. He may have explained it to Don, but he certainly didn't explain it to anyone else, except to say he was going to shuttle in Morton and Rhome.

"When Landry benched Don, Don was *very* hurt. I really think he started thinking about whether he really wanted to play this game, and how much longer did he want to play? It was from that point on. He was *wounded* by that move, and I'm not sure that he ever got over that completely.

"And to give Don his due, you have to be strong to overcome something like that, because you begin to doubt yourself if you're not very careful. It's like a receiver missing two passes and getting benched. It's really hard to overcome that and to a degree I'm sure that's what Don went through as well."

With Don Meredith fuming on the bench, and the two rookies trying to get something going, the Cowboys lost to the Philadelphia Eagles and the Cleveland Browns. Meredith returned in the Cleveland game, but a large Browns lead made it impossible for the Cowboys to catch up.

FRANK CLARKE: "We lost to Cleveland, then lost to Green Bay, our fourth straight loss. Tom kept changing quarterbacks, and it was definitely chaotic. Our constant march to improve was being strongly challenged, in terms of our confidence in ourselves and in our leader, Tom Landry.

"And we looked at some of the things that were happening, too, like Dandy's injury didn't help the situation at all, and we knew problems arise when you have to switch quarterbacks for any reason other than by choice—remember in the late '50s and early '60s when the Giants had Conerly and Tittle, and they sent one quarterback in, and he would set things up, get things warmed up, and then they put in another quarterback, and that was fine, but when you had to do it the way that we did it, because of an injury, and then coupled with the kind of controversy that we couldn't ignore, and the controversy was, 'Is he being benched because he isn't good enough? Why won't Tom make this clear?' These things were playing on our minds, and we couldn't dismiss it right away, and it made a difference. We were beginning to question ourselves, to get our confidence challenged at that time."

The turmoil on the team was becoming so destructive that even the defensive players were beginning to take notice.

BOB LILLY: "The whole year we had this controversy over who was going to be the quarterback and it was very distracting, just like the Kennedy thing in '63. In '65 I remember that was the year Tom began alternating Meredith, Morton, and Rhome. Boy, that was distracting for us. We did *not* like that. In fact, I hated that. We all hated that, because the quarterback never could get in synch, and we knew that as players. Tom had a reason, but I never knew what it was. The coaches don't know what's going on on the field. The quarterback knows how they're rushing, how they're blitzing. You put another quarterback in there, and it might take him a few plays to recognize what's going on. And I just don't think you can do that.

"When Tom did it with LeBaron and Don we didn't mind, because we had such a lousy team it wouldn't have mattered anyway. With Meredith and Morton, it did. We wanted *one* of them in there. We didn't care who. Just somebody. And Meredith was the natural choice, because he *knew*, sensed a lot of things out there that Craig was going to have to develop to know."

Tom Landry decided to start Don Meredith against the Pittsburgh Steelers, a bad team he figured he would beat. But Meredith was only able to complete 12 of his 34 passes for 187 yards, and the Cowboys lost 22–13, the team's fifth straight loss.

After the game, when Tom Landry walked into the locker room after the game, no one looked up. The usually stoic Landry walked to the middle of the room. He began to address the team. His voice seemed to quaver.

He said, "In the six years I have been with the Cowboys, this is the first time I have felt truly ashamed of the team's performance." No one looked up.

After a minute—a silence that seemed eternal—he continued, "Maybe the fault is in the system, with the approach we are . . ." His voice broke, and then he coughed, and then came a slow rivulet of tears down his cheeks. Tom Landry began to cry.

Don Meredith, who admitted later that he had tried very hard but had done poorly because of the pressure he was feeling, stood up and most gallantly apologized to his teammates for not playing better.

"I tried my hardest," he said, "but I'm going to work even harder, and we will start winning again."

The players knew that the fault did not lie on the valiant shoulders of their beat-up quarterback. They were four-square behind Dandy Don. Any resentment they were feeling was being directed at their coach. When he cried in front of them, some were moved more than others. Despite the tears the players who loved Dandy Don could never fully forgive Landry for not being more supportive of their leader.

BOB LILLY: "After we lost to Pittsburgh, Coach Landry told everyone to get out of the locker room except the players and coaches. He told us he came to the Cowboys and had studied football for fifty years in New York, going back to the archives, had devised the Multiple Offense and the Flex defense, and that he thought those were the types of philosophies that were going to carry us for the next twenty years. He wanted to thank all of us for giving him 100 percent, and this and that, and then he broke down and started crying. That touched every one of us. And it seemed like it went on for about an hour, though it was more like two or three minutes. But he was just crying, and he couldn't control it.

"He said, 'I very likely won't be here next year.' And then he just broke down, and boy, that touched us. We were touched. Very deeply. I think it humbled all of us. From that point on we were much more attentive and much more diligent. We saw a real man up there. We had always taken Coach Landry for granted, and this time we saw a real person, and we wanted to fight for him. And we did. And I don't think we planned it that way. I know he didn't. It just happened. And I never saw him cry again."

FRANK CLARKE: "Tom had a way of telling us what he wanted us to do, what he thought that we could do, and if we didn't do it, he had an expression of his where you knew exactly how disappointed he was in you. But when he shed tears after the game in Pittsburgh, that blew me away. We had never, ever seen anything like this before. When I saw him crying, I felt a swallow, one of those swallow things you do because you feel like, 'This guy's tears might be contagious.' And I don't know how many other guys might have felt that too, but there was a quietness of that moment. It's very possible that every one of us might have felt that same way at that time. And we got a sense of what kind of commitment this man was willing to make."

PETTIS NORMAN: "In the game against the Steelers, Don fumbled a couple of times, played inconsistently, and part of that was the confidence factor. He had lost confidence in himself, and the team started wondering, 'Where are we going?' As a whole, Landry's benching him really affected the confidence of the team.

"We lost to the Steelers, a game we should have won. After the game we were just bewildered, because we had lost. We knew something was wrong, though we didn't know what it was, that we were better than that, and we really started questioning whether or not we could win as a unit.

"And to everybody's surprise, when Tom came in, he closed the door to reporters, and got everyone around him, and he said, 'I want to apologize.' 'Cause I lost this game. You all were not ready to play, but it wasn't your fault. It was my fault.' And he cried. And he vowed that that would never happen again, that we would never ever not be ready to play.

"I suspect he meant that so many things had occurred over the last few weeks to give the players a lot of reasons to doubt each other, and to begin to doubt the team. Tom was not settled on anybody. There were a lot of new players being shuffled in, and people didn't know where they stood. So how can you be ready to play if I allow this to happen?

"If you know who your teammates are, if you know they're going to be there day in and day out, you can play to your potential. But if one guy will be in a quarter and another guy another quarter, you can't get a rhythm going, substituting quarterbacks every quarter, shuttling quarterbacks. You have to settle on players and stick with those players, and they are either good enough or they are not good enough.

"He was apologizing for allowing too many things to happen. He was not settled in his own mind about who to play, when to play them. He did not exhibit the kind of confidence in a lot of players that he should have, Meredith included. And so consequently, you can't be prepared as a team when you don't know who's going to start at quarterback, and you don't know who's going to be pulled in what quarter. You don't know who's going to start at tight end or wide receiver or running back. And a team can't prepare like that. And so he was saying, 'It wasn't your fault. It was *my* fault.' He was saying in effect, I have allowed doubt to set in myself and I passed it on to you all, so you couldn't play any better than how you've been playing.

"It was remarkable, because Tom was not the type of person to admit his faults. And I don't remember him doing it again."

BUDDY DIAL: "After the Steelers game, Landry met with the players and talked about how he had failed, and he began to cry. Tom was so sincere, and he meant it, but when Landry started crying, well, it didn't seem real to me. It really didn't. It was not a *real* response, because we had had a lot of emotion, a lot of failure, and for him to start crying at this time, it seemed a little self-serving, especially to the veterans who had been around. To us, he was crying for himself. He really was. He was so dadgum frustrated he was losing. We were playing and running his system, and it wasn't working because he didn't have the players he needed, and we didn't believe in the system, and Meredith was getting killed. And I want to tell you something: Jerry Rhome was not a pro quarterback, and Craig Morton could throw the ball 500 yards in the air, but he'd knock you down one time and throw it late the next. We were *so* uneven.

"I was saying to myself, 'Golly, I wish Coach Landry would let the players run the thing a little more.' He called every goddarn play, and that was causing so much dissension on the ballclub. 'Here comes the play.' And it would come in late. It would be miscalled. And Meredith didn't have time to correct a lot of them, and Dan Reeves had to help him straighten them out, and it was a jungle. I know the players were so frustrated. We felt, 'Gollee, let Don call the play. Let him have a couple plays in a row.' I know all the coaches call the plays now. But it wasn't done then, except for Paul Brown who did it in Cleveland. Brown was so domineering; the guys hated it in Cleveland. And here comes Landry wanting to do it, and it was really not popular at the time. And it drove Meredith crazy, because he had things he wanted to do on the field, and here was Landry. He'd go up to Landry during the game, and he'd say something would work, but what you didn't realize, Tom was three or four plays ahead of you! And it took us a long time to figure that out. What we thought didn't matter, because in his head Landry was running the next series. He was so brilliant, he didn't even know what we just did, because he was three plays ahead of us! And Don couldn't relate to that.

"Landry had tried starting Morton and Rhome in practice, and he would threaten it during the game, but if Don was healthy he really needed to turn it over to Meredith."

During the 1965 season Landry was using his all-important statistics for guidance, and he didn't like what he was seeing. Later Landry would say that the press and fans were justified in their sharp criticism of Meredith and that he had been justified in benching him by citing his completion percentage.

TOM LANDRY: "He had only completed an embarrassing 38 percent of his passes all season. We couldn't possibly win with that kind of performance. I had to go with one or both of the rookies."

It was an assessment with which a number of the players found fault. Pete Gent, for one, found Landry's use of statistics arbitrary and self-serving.

PETE GENT: "Tom Landry finally showed that what he was doing was unmaintainable. You couldn't demand these things and expect them to work. The other thing you couldn't do was lie to yourself. You couldn't say, 'I'm judging everyone on their statistics,' and then play the guys you liked and wanted. Because if you believe that, you better live with that. Because then you could live with your wins and your losses if you really, truly believed what you were doing. But see, he broke down and cried because he believed he had been betrayed, but he couldn't figure out who. Well, he was betraying himself."

The way the players saw it, Tom Landry should have chosen his quarterback and then let him play. In their opinion, his decision to replace Don Meredith with two rookies was foolish from its inception, and in doing so he had doomed the entire ballclub.

For three days Tom Landry mulled over what to do. He truly did not like Don Meredith, not as a player and not as a person, and even perhaps for reasons he himself did not understand. Had he had an acceptable replacement, surely Tom Landry would have junked Dandy Don. But after experimenting with Craig Morton and Jerry Rhome and seeing the team display a bitterness bordering on open resentment, Landry decided that he had to sink or swim with Meredith.

According to his autobiography, Landry tossed and turned for two nights. He prayed for wisdom to make the right decision.

TOM LANDRY: "Finally I called Meredith into my office. He sat down, his face somber, ready for the blow he knew had to be coming. When I looked at him and said, 'Don, I believe in you. You're my starting quarterback the rest of the year,' Don began to cry. Then we both cried."

On November 3, 1965, Tom Landry called a press conference. He told the reporters, "Our offensive team is very young. We have three rookies starting, and Leon Donahue [at guard] is a veteran who has been with us only two months. The only veterans with experience on our offensive team are Jim Boeke, Don Perkins, and Frank Clarke. We need a quarterback to lead us to our potential and that's why I have made my decision. . . . Don Meredith will start the next seven games this season."

Landry continued, "After five straight losses a decision of this nature is difficult, but I had to go with the man I felt everyone on the team had the most confidence in; the man I felt could make the team rise up and play well enough to make up the seven to ten points we've been losing by all season."

Concluded Landry: "I have no doubt Don can win."

It was what his teammates had been saying all along.

PETTIS NORMAN: "It took him three days to finally announce Meredith was the quarterback, and during that time everybody was trying to figure out what he meant by what he said after the Steelers game, and everybody was trying to figure out what was wrong with us. We were better than what we were showing. We should have won several, if not all of those games. Here we were, he had promised us we would be winners, and instead of being winners, instead we were sliding down, and everyone was trying to figure out, 'How low can this bottom get?'

"In small groups the players were criticizing him for experimenting too much, saying, 'Landry has to get set on who's going to quarterback the team, and who's going to play the other positions, and let people play. And he has to stop jerking people out every time they make a mistake.'

"And after he finally announced that Don would be our quarterback, the doubts went away, and we were as good as any team in the league the rest of the way."

BUDDY DIAL: "After the Steelers game, Landry gave the ball to Meredith and let him call the plays. We had been so frustrated. We finally decided it was garbage time, and we had a little freedom to play, and we did pretty well. We won five of our last seven."

FRANK CLARKE: "When Landry finally announced that Don would be our quarterback the rest of the season, we all took a deep breath. Yes, oh God. We felt, of course Don's our quarterback. We knew. And because Dandy wanted this, man. That's why he was having the trouble he was having in the game prior to that. Let the guy know. Tell *him*. Don't just make an announcement and announce that it's Meredith. You knew damn well that was going to turn the trick. And that's what it took. We needed him, and by golly, yes, there was a sigh of relief. And the rest of the way, we played inspired football.

"We were all very much involved in this quarterback controversy. It wasn't just Meredith, it was the whole offense. And when that decision was made, things were just looser. There was an air of lightness we hadn't known in several weeks. Prior to that string of defeats and faux pas, dropped passes and switching quarterbacks, we had been building up to a nice sense of confidence, and then three or four weeks of crazy things put us at the brink of having our confidence destroyed, but as soon as Tom said, 'Don Meredith is my quarterback,' that was over with. We all became Don, and we all got lighter. It was almost as if we could predict that we were going to have a fine close of the season, that we would do well."

In the next game, Don Meredith led the Cowboys to a 39–31 win over the San Francisco 49ers, winning the game with 4:18 remaining on a 34-yard pass to Bullet Bob Hayes, one of two Hayes touchdowns. Hayes also ran back a kickoff 66 yards.

FRANK CLARKE: "When Don came back against the San Francisco 49ers, he had aches and pains. His knee was very weak, and he probably still had trouble with his back, too, but he was relatively healthy. For Meredith, he was relatively strong, and we beat the 49ers and we beat the Steelers, 24–17, and then we played the Browns."

PETTIS NORMAN: "After losing to Cleveland [24–17], in the paper the next day Gary Cartwright of the *Dallas Morning News* really put the knock on Don. [Meredith had thrown two interceptions, including one from the one-yard line for which Cartwright seemingly could not forgive him. Cartwright paraphrased Grantland Rice by writing, "Outlined against a gray November sky, the Four Horsemen rode again Sunday. You know them: Pestilence, death, famine, Meredith."]

"It was devastating to Meredith. It angered a lot of players. It probably was the sour grape that really made the Gary Cartwright Era in Dallas as far as players were concerned, made him a real outsider, because a lot of players felt Gary was someone who would criticize everybody on everything, and who was there just to tear people down. I remember people started talking, saying they didn't want to be around Gary Cartwright any more, and a lot of them avoided him from that point on. Lee Roy Jordan wanted to beat him up. I can remember people cursing Gary Cartwright like he was really a piece of dirt, so it was a good thing he wasn't there at that moment."

LEE ROY JORDAN: "After Cartwright wrote that article about the Four Horsemen, some of the players wanted to beat him to a pulp. I was one of them. Gary deserved it several times and never got it the way he should have."

BUDDY DIAL: "We didn't lose the Cleveland game because of Don Meredith. We lost it because of the coach. You know what happened there? The play came in from the sideline. Meredith had the play he wanted to run, and Landry's play was the opposite of Don's, and the team wanted Don's play. Whose fault was that? It wasn't Meredith's. But Meredith had to do what Landry wanted 'cause Rhome and Morton were on the sideline, and Landry was over there, and he'd have had his head in his helmet.

"On the play from the one-yard line, Don threw to Frank Clarke, it was tipped, and intercepted, and the next day Don was just crucified in the papers by Gary Cartwright. Oh boy, and that hurt so bad, because typical of the situation it wasn't Don's call, it wasn't his play, it wasn't his fault.

"Don and I talked about it. Yeah, he hated 'Poison Pen' Cartwright. He *hated* him. Gary was a wormy little old devil. I mean, he breathed an ill wind. Cartwright killed. He was so negative about everybody, and he really had it in for Meredith. Because Meredith was a class act, and Cartwright was so jealous of him. How can a sportswriter be jealous of an athlete? Meredith was just a class act, and here a bad deal happened that he had no control over, and Cartwright really cut him up and hung him up. Even so, when it came to Cartwright and Landry, Meredith was so restrained in what he would say.

"Unlike Don, my kettle was volatile. I would get angry. I really said some bad things to Tom. I just didn't give a shit, and I would mouth off. I didn't like some of the play calling, though I didn't have any reason to disagree with him, because he knew so much more than anybody else. I give him credit for that. Still you hated to give up all freedom on the field. You didn't have *anything* to say on the field. I know Meredith was so frustrated, that there were things he would have loved to have done, could have done, should have done, but he didn't have the freedom to do it, and he was such a class act that he wouldn't be critical of anyone, despite the restraints placed on him.

"And Don had it so tough off the field. Aw. His first wife was a rich young lady, a beautiful girl, and Don came home one day from practice, and she was gone.

"She was gorgeous and rich and fine, but flaky. It takes a strong person to live with Meredith. He's dangerous. She finally got fed up with it all. Several times. And so they got divorced. And then they remarried. And that deal blew up, and he had problems with his daughter, and it was just one thing after another. And so he never knew where he stood off the field. And he never knew where he stood *on* the field. This guy had a load. But he *never* complained. Never complained."

PETE GENT: "Here's the true story. At the start of the week we got the game plan for Cleveland. We looked at the game plan, and everyone noticed that we had no goal line running game. We argued for two days. We had *no* goal line running plays. Zero. It was all passes. Tom said, 'Look, Cleveland has this defense that bends between the 20s, but then digs in inside the 20, so once you get inside the 20, you gotta throw, because they are just not going to let you run.' And we were saying, 'We have to have a running play. We need some running plays.' Landry said, 'No. Uh-uh.' We argued. I can remember as clear as day the arguments, and he just would not hear of it. 'Absolutely not.'

"And so what happened, Cleveland fumbled almost on the goal line, so it was the first play from scrimmage, and it was about the three, so actually at first it wasn't a bad call. The other thing was, Don had no other call to make. The only other play we could have run that we didn't need to practice would have been a straight wedge play, where you just wedge into the line, but see, against a really good defensive run team like the Browns that play would have been only good at best for a yard, unless somebody fell over and you split the seam and the whole theory with Cleveland was that they never did that. So Meredith was at the worst possible place to have *no* running plays, no options, nothing. So he called the quick slant to Frank. Frank got held at the line, and the ball bounced off his hands and was intercepted. Now, did Landry say, 'There were no running plays'? Did Landry say that we had two days of arguments, that we needed running plays? No. All he said was, 'It was a poorly executed play.' And Gary Cartwright wrote that.

"If anybody knew we didn't have a goal line running offense, it would have been Gary. He had probably been at Don's house for dinner sometime during the week, 'cause Don treated him that way. I talked to him several times during the week, and I always told Gary what was going on. I always told him stuff nobody else got. 'Cause I liked Gary.

"The problem with Gary was that he was at the tail end of that Dan Jenkins-Bud Shrake-Blackie Sherrod era, and Shrake particularly played him. Shrake would egg him on into doing awful things, not just in his column, but in his daily life, incredible shit. Shrake had gone to *Sports Illustrated*, but he was back in Dallas a lot.

"We had a private team meeting without the coaches over Cartwright. They all wanted to kill him, and Meredith kept saying, 'You can't. It's his job. He's just doing his job like we're doing ours.' And Cartwright would be nice to Meredith. I would go up and talk to Gary. I'd say, 'Gary, don't you understand what you're doing? You're killing this

guy, and these guys are going to beat the shit out of you. They hate you.'
He said, 'Oh no, they understand that they're just doing their job and I'm
doing my job.' I said, 'Gary, you don't know anything about football.
You're not doing your job. You're just a flack for the team. If you write
something the club doesn't like about the club, you'll be gone. They won't
let you in the locker room. As long as you just beat up on one or two players, that's fine.' He said, 'No, no, no. They understand that I'm just doing
my job.' And he never got any wiser.

"The players were mad at him. They were furious. They really
wanted to hurt him. I've never known that kind of fury against any reporter. They were going to beat the shit out of him. And after they beat the
shit out of him, they were going to go to Schramm, Landry, and Murchison and demand that Cartwright not be allowed on the team plane.

"And Meredith would stick up for Cartwright. He'd be the *only* guy
on the team to keep these other players from wanting to kill him. And I
never remember another reporter who the players actually wanted to beat
the shit out of. And could have. You think Lee Roy Jordan wouldn't have
beat the shit out of Gary Cartwright? In a heartbeat. But Meredith kept the
team off him. Cartwright doesn't know how many times he came close to
a savage beating. He'd walk back after the game was over and start interviewing somebody, and he doesn't know how close he came to guys dragging him to the back of the plane and just beating the shit out of him. Guys
were still on speed, man. They were half drunk. They wanted to kill him.
Lilly, Lee Roy, Andrie, Ralph Neely. All the offensive linemen were particularly furious because they have a real pride about protecting their
quarterback, and if you're running down their quarterback, that's a reflection on them. I never could make Gary understand it. And I was friends
with him a long time.

"And so I tried to tell Gary that we had team meetings where everybody on the team except Meredith said, 'I don't want that son of a bitch
on the team plane. If he shows up, we're going to kick the shit out of him.'
And Meredith would be the one to say, 'Look, you can't do that.' And it
was Meredith who was taking the brunt of Gary's words, because he was
the easiest target.

"Meredith was such a decent man. We had a team meeting after the
Four Horsemen article, and everyone wanted Gary dead. They wanted to
kill him. And I tried to tell Cartwright that, but he'd say, 'No, they like me.
They have their job, and I have mine.' I said, 'Gary, you think your job is
to cost us our jobs. These guys are pissed.' And Meredith would calm
them all down.

"The other half of it was that because it was Landry who was the one always criticizing Don, none of the other players, except myself, defended Meredith in any of the papers.

"The reason for that was that the worst thing in the world that you could do was be in the paper saying that Landry was wrong or worse, lying. Danny Reeves wanted to be a coach. Danny was young, a kid, and he was very smart, and look where he is. Walt Garrison's remark was, 'I like rodeo better than football, because it has a better class of people.' Walt just didn't get into the politics of it. He did his job and he felt that was enough. And he was a good friend of Don's. Privately Walt would defend Meredith to anybody. But you were taking a *big* risk going public against Landry. But see, for me, I realized that Landry was *never* going to warm up to me. I knew I would never be able to do enough to satisfy him."

The next game was against Sonny Jurgensen and the Washington Redskins. Don Meredith played an excellent game, throwing for 249 yards and two touchdowns, including a 53-yarder to Frank Clarke late in the game that appeared to be the game-winner.

But Jurgensen, who would go on to have a Hall of Fame career, took the Redskins 64 yards for a score in just four plays. Even then Meredith almost pulled it out, losing only when Danny Villanueva missed a 45-yard field goal. When the game was over, some of the players couldn't believe they had lost.

FRANK CLARKE: "It all happened so fast, even though it may have taken three minutes. First of all, as a pro athlete, you don't sense that something bad is going to happen. You think, 'We're going to stop Jurgensen. Our defense is so good, our guys are going to stop him.' And you keep that feeling, until you realize you're taking off your jersey and shoulder pads in the locker room, and you go, 'Hey, they beat us.' You don't even get a chance to think about it during the game. Later on, you say to yourself, 'I can't believe that happened.'

"That was the way we felt, too, especially about our defense. We were feeling really good about the way our defense was playing, 'cause they were really catching up in terms of the offense, and catching up statistically with the best defenses in the league. So when Jurgensen and those guys were moving the ball, we had a sense, 'We're going to stop them. We're going to win.' And then we looked up at the scoreboard, and it was, 'Hey, they got more points than we did.' "

* * *

After the game Don Meredith met his ex-wife at Dulles Airport for the purpose of accompanying his twelve-year-old daughter, Mary Donna, back to Texas. Their rocky relationship had been a constant strain on Meredith, in addition to all that Landry had put him through over the years.

PETER GENT: "Don's ex-wife Lynn was working in Washington as an aide to a congressman, and she came to the airport and brought their daughter so that Don could have her for a week in Dallas. Mary Donna was either going to fly back or her mother was going to come to Texas to visit her family.

"Losing the game was tough, but what was most difficult for Don was the realization that he was spending a lot of his time away from his daughter. During much of the flight she was sitting in his lap.

"I was standing up leaning on the chair in the row in front of Don, and Don kept looking at me and then looking with his eyes at this beautiful little girl, who was curled up in his lap with her head against his shoulder. He was looking at this great tragedy. Here was this little girl he had not been able to provide for in terms of being around as her father, and I think Don felt a great sense of failure at that point, not as much as a football player as his desperate attempt to be a good husband and father.

"And he was looking at her and then looking at me, that's when he began crying. He was crying and saying out loud, 'I am not a loser,' and I always took that to refer to his personal life, about his personal relationship with his daughter and wife more than the fact we had lost the football game. 'Cause Don was just heartbroken about not being able to be with her. My heart just ached for him. In fact, I was engaged at the time, and I remember when I got off the plane, one of the first things that went through my mind was, 'I am never going to get married and get in that situation.' Because you could literally see him being torn in about five different directions. Because Don really liked Lynn, his first wife, but it was just impossible to make that marriage work. They had been the king and queen of the SMU campus, and then he ended up in that madhouse called professional football."

BUDDY DIAL: "All season long Don just carried the whole dadgum load. If we were ahead and we got beat, like when Sonny Jurgensen of the Redskins beat us, that was Meredith's fault, even when they scored on the defense.

"Don was sitting with his daughter in the back of the plane, and finally the pressure got to him. He began sobbing. His off-the-field life was just such a burden to him, and on the field it was also a struggle. And he had wanted to be successful in both places. He really loved his family. He wanted to be a good father, a good husband, a good guy. He really *wanted* to be. And he wanted to win so bad. And he was losing in both places. And it was just a burden for ole Don.

"He was saying, 'I'm not a loser,' and I want to tell you something: He wasn't. And he ain't. What he went through would have killed an ordinary man. I mean, it would have killed three ordinary men to live what Don went through.

"And for him to be a victor and to win at the end just makes you want to respect him that much more."

Of the other players who saw Meredith's pain and heard his words, "I'm not a loser," they thought Meredith was talking in a football context. Their hearts went out to him just the same.

PETTIS NORMAN: "We lost to Washington when Sonny Jurgensen led his team 65 yards at the end of the game. Don had played a great game. It certainly wasn't his fault we had lost, but on the plane after the game, I can remember Meredith sitting with his daughter, and he began to cry, and he started saying things like, 'I'm not a loser.'

"Other players were trying to comfort him and assure him that he was not a loser. He felt really bad about that, because he had not gotten over the wounds of being benched earlier on and of Gary Cartwright's vicious article, and I think what happened, he expected he would be crucified and vilified in the papers the next day, and even maybe benched. He had developed a defeatist attitude, started believing the self-fulfilling prophecy, and he was talking to himself, trying to convince the players, 'I'm not all those things my benching might have suggested, or Gary Cartwright might have suggested.'

"Don was a good friend of mine. I've always considered him a good friend of mine. I was one of those guys who always tried to lift everybody else's spirits. I told Don he was a good quarterback and to hang in there. We all told him we supported him."

It was the lowest moment of Don Meredith's professional life, until the day he finally retired. But it was at this point that Don Meredith proved to himself, and to his critics, that he was not a loser, as he quarterbacked the Cowboys to victory in the final three games of the season despite the continual mauling he endured. Meredith led the Cowboys to a win against the Eagles, despite playing in the fourth quarter with a dislocated finger, and against the St. Louis Cards, he was 16–30 for three touchdowns in the first half alone, finishing the game with 326 yards passing despite getting sacked so hard he did not know his teammates.

BUDDY DIAL: "Against the Cards, he was hit so hard, he couldn't remember his teammates' names, and Landry left him in the game. Landry would send out the plays, but Danny Reeves had to interpret them for Meredith. I'm telling you, it's hard enough to play when your head is on straight, but when you get the crap knocked out of you, it's a little hard to remember who to give the ball to, never mind which team you're playing for."

The Cowboys had a final game against the still-tough New York Giants. A win would give Dallas second place and a spot in the Playoff Bowl in Miami.

Meredith threw two touchdown passes to Bob Hayes and broke the game open in the fourth quarter with a 29-yard touchdown to Buddy Dial, the last TD pass he would ever catch, as the Cowboys won 38–20.

In the last seven games, Meredith had thrown 16 touchdown passes as the Cowboy offense proved itself the equal to any in the league.

PETTIS NORMAN: "We won the final three games of the season, beating New York in the last game of the season. The win enabled us to go to the Playoff Bowl. I was so happy, I didn't know what to do. After the Giant game, I threw my helmet into the air, singing 'Moon Over Miami.'

"It was one of the happiest moments I can think about in pro football. People ask me, 'What was one of the happiest moments you can remember?' and most of them think it was playing in the Super Bowl, but really, truly, beating the Giants that day was one of the happiest moments I can remember, because we became winners. The team had reached a milestone. We were *winners*. We had won as many games as we lost. We were going to go to an extra game. We were going to Miami to play in the Losers Bowl.

"You reach milestones in your lifetime. You have to appreciate the moment when the next step you take represents a *real* milestone in your journey. Beating the Giants was a major milestone in our journey. Whoever couldn't be happy about that just didn't understand its significance. Going to Miami was what was important. It was the fact we had gotten ourselves in a position to go by winning that game by beating another team on their home field to become winners for the first time, to be able to say that we had won as many games as we had lost. We had never been able to say that before."

Some of the veterans felt that going to the Playoff Bowl in Miami against the Baltimore Colts was a waste of a weekend. They called it the "Losers Bowl," and they liked it even less when Tom Landry treated it like the Super Bowl, making the players work hard during the week while the Baltimore Colt players were enjoying themselves in sunny Miami Beach. In the game, the Colts' halfback Tom Matte, filling in for injured quarterbacks Johnny Unitas and Gary Cuozzo, taped the plays to his arm and led Baltimore to a 35–3 win.

DON MEREDITH: "We knew Johnny Unitas wasn't going to play, so we thought it would be a breeze. We forgot Unitas didn't play defense. Their defense killed us."

BUDDY DIAL: "We went to the Playoff Bowl against the Colts. What a disgrace! I think we got $500 for losing. They got $750 for winning. It was just a party time down there, because who wants to play in a Losers Bowl? And Landry was making changes, getting ready for next season, and everybody was going dizzy trying to figure out what was going on, and here we were playing a stupid playoff ballgame against Baltimore, and Meredith and I were playing golf every day, and he was having fun at night, so it wasn't a very good ballgame."

FRANK CLARKE: "That week I had one of the most embarrassing experiences of my life. The Cowboys went to Florida a week or so before the game just to practice down there and be in Florida, get ready for the game. I was standing in the airport and a guy walked up to me, tapped me on the shoulder, and he said, 'Aren't you Frank Clarke? I always wanted to meet you.' I turned around, and it was Raymond Berry of the Colts. And I was stunned, because this guy had been my idol. If ever there was a player who I wanted to emulate, it was Raymond Berry. 'Cause this guy was everything. His moves and his concentration, and his great ability, and I was so dumbfounded. The first thing that went through my head was, 'This is supposed to be the other way around.' I was supposed to be going up to him saying, 'Aren't you Raymond Berry?' But here Raymond Berry was coming up to me, Frank Clarke. I was so blown away by that, I asked him, 'Wow, Raymond Berry, what in the world are you doing in Florida?'

"And when he heard me say that, he somehow sensed that I wasn't kidding. And in this really sweet way, a really understanding way, it was almost as though he was going to go along with it until I woke up, he said, 'We're going to play you all Sunday, Frank.'

"And then I realized what I had said. I was *so* embarrassed. The story typifies the strange air of the whole playoff episode. It may have something to do with the idea of, 'A playoff? Are you kidding?' The only playoff we're supposed to be in is for the NFC championship. Maybe that had something to do with it.

"I don't recall a thing about the game except that we were soundly outplayed. That was easy. The way we were, it would have been easy to soundly trounce us. Of course they were going to walk all over us."

BOB LILLY: "After the '65 regular season, we went to Miami to play the Baltimore Colts in the Playoff Bowl. When we went down I don't think we took the game very seriously. It wasn't an important thing to us. We had finished 7–7. We were just happy to be there. I remember [offensive guard] Ralph Neely and Don Talbert and George Andrie and I drove around in a Cadillac convertible, and we went to the jai alai games, the dog races, went out and ate at a nice restaurant. We didn't have our wives down there, because Tex Schramm wouldn't let us, and I think that we had a resentment toward Tex Schramm starting then. Because we really fought those last seven games to get where we were, and here we were in a playoff game, and the Colts were staying just down the street from us, and Carroll Rosenbloom, the owner of the Colts, took their wives down, paid their way, put them all up, had an open bar where they could go in and have a drink after practice and even sign his name. And the Colt players were telling us how well they were being treated, and here were were, eating as a team, not allowed to bring our wives. It was probably childish for us to feel that way, but that's the way it was. It was a joke among the team that a whole front office of twenty-seven people went down there, and we couldn't even bring our wives.

"One night Don Meredith ended up signing Tex Schramm's name to the checks, and we all got a letter about that in the off-season. We just went down there and had a good time. I honestly don't know why we did that.

"It was the first time we had been in any kind of playoff but it wasn't something we were proud of, particularly, because we didn't have that good a year. But we knew we were going to be a lot better team. We *knew* that."

23

Iconoclasts

When an entire nation turned on the city of Dallas after the Kennedy assassination, its residents looked for something that would give them pride, that would make them forget. The outlet for their depressed emotions was one they had turned to in the past on both the high school and college level: football. But the Cowboys were a team that represented the entire city, and not only were the players young, flashy, and talented, but they were also winning some games. A hundred and twenty thousand fans had flocked to the Cotton Bowl for the first two 1965 home games, only 7,500 less than for the *entire* '64 attendance.

And then on November 21, 1965, a crowd of 76,251 flocked to see the Cowboys host the Cleveland Browns, and even though the Cowboys lost that day, from that day on a horde of fans would make their weekly influx into the city to watch what was arguably the most interesting football team in the NFL. A stoic Tom Landry fascinated everyone, as he stood on the sidelines wearing a suit, topcoat, and a serious hat made of houndstooth, looking to all the world like a humorless stockbroker. But for many of the Dallas fans, Tom Landry represented exactly what they had been raised to believe in: God, hard work, and faith. In his case, the faith had been in himself. For six years the Cowboys had stumbled, and only once, out of public view, had Landry let on that he was questioning himself.

With the resurrection of Don Meredith, however, the crisis passed, and as the 1966 season began with five straight preseason victories, including a win over the Green Bay Packers, that two-year-old prediction by Tex Maule that the Cowboys would win the division title seemed to be coming to pass.

The '66 Cowboys, at least, were a team to be reckoned with. They could score on big plays from anywhere on the field. Don Meredith was the quarterback, Don Perkins had a good year running the ball, and catching Dandy Don's passes was a corps of exciting talent led by Bullet Bob Hayes, the World's Fastest Human, Frank Clarke, Buddy Dial, Pettis Norman, and the unknown former basketball player, free agent Pete Gent.

PETE GENT: "In training camp of '66, I hit my stride. We beat the San Francisco 49ers in an exhibition game after I caught two touchdowns, one a circus catch about 45 yards over Jimmy Johnson, even though he had me step for step. They are reading your eyes so I just pretended like I was running, and then just caught the ball falling into the end zone backward. I ended up with five catches for two touchdowns. And I got coldcocked by Matt Hazeltine. Then when I got back in, Meredith threw an across-the-field pass to me in the open a little high, and it bounced off my hands, and I was fingertipping it, trying to pull it in, but it slowed me up just enough for him to hit me, and I didn't hold on to it, or that would have been a third touchdown, and that would have gone for about 80 yards, so I'd have had close to 200 yards. But the next game I beat Clancy Williams in Los Angeles for a 35-yard touchdown, and then against Detroit in Tulsa I didn't do a whole lot, but we beat them pretty easily. My job when you got against those teams was to catch the early passes until we could open up Hayes.

"By the end of the '66 season Bob Hayes and I were the leading receivers on the team."

On defense the team was greatly bolstered by the addition of defensive line coach Ernie Stautner. Bob Lilly, George Andrie, Lee Roy Jordan, Chuck Howley, Mel Renfro, and Cornell Green were recognized names beginning to play excellently on defense. It took the addition of Stautner to instill the one missing ingredient: ferocity.

DICK NOLAN: "In '65 Tom said to me, 'Let's get a line coach the next year,' and Ernie Stautner had been fired by the Redskins. When Bill Mc-Peak was released as coach, Ernie was out, too, and I got a hold of Ernie, because I knew Ernie was a guy who would work like a horse. He was good and he was smart, and I brought him down to Dallas, and I taught him the Flex defense. So now I had a line coach to do some of it, along with Jerry Tubbs to coach the linebackers, so we were pretty solid.

"Landry let me run the defense, and he ran the offense, and he never bothered me at all. I used to go to his home on Wednesday nights, and we'd sit down there for hours just to go over what I was going to do on defense, and I'd tell him, 'This is why I'm doing it,' and of course, I was schooled by him so much, he knew I was going to be doing just what I did. I put some things in there that worked pretty good. We used them. But the thing was, we almost always ended up rated one or two on defense."

BOB LILLY: "Ernie Stautner came to the team in 1966. I can remember that when Ernie played for the Steelers, Bob Fry, our right tackle on offense, in practice used to tell George Andrie, 'George, all I want you to do is beat me up every day, beat the crap out of me, hit me in the head with your hand, your fist, your forearm, 'cause that's what Ernie Stautner is going to do.' And that's what Ernie did. He just beat him up. Boy, every game Bob was just bloody all over. And Ernie hit Meredith like that a few times, too.

"So we had a lot of respect for Ernie. He had been at Washington for one year to coach, then he came to Dallas. Ernie started computerizing the defenses, computerizing the plays, and so he brought that with him. We had done that a little bit, but he was the one who was responsible for having a good computer program where they had high school coaches who would come over and grade film, take off all the plays of the opposition, write 'em down, and program them in, and they'd have a printout of all the plays they ran, against what defenses, what down and distance, what end of the field, so we knew all that.

"During the game he'd get in our face, right in it. He would try to be nice, and then he'd get carried away, kind of like Mike Ditka. When he became a coach, Ernie was always a gentleman. He never hit anybody, never cursed anybody. He was a good teacher, very patient.

"Ernie helped us a lot. He *really* helped our defensive line because we had been on our own. We worked hard, but you're never going to accomplish as much unless you have somebody pushing you a little harder than you want to go, and we didn't have that. Once we had Ernie in there, he made us study harder, he made us work harder in practice, and he made us much more aware of our job during the game. We weren't doing a bad job during that time, but he put us up another level."

*　　*　　*

Year by year Tom Landry had built this team, taking the best athlete available. For some reason that "best athlete" was usually a defensive player.
In '66 for the first time Landry directed his attention to molding a line that
would keep Don Meredith from his weekly mauling. Landry drafted in the
first round a behemoth guard from Iowa, John Niland, and teamed him
with a second-year man, the 6'5", 257-pound Ralph Neely, a guard from
Oklahoma who had signed with the Cowboys despite also signing with the
Houston Oilers.

Neely was huge and agile, with the hand and foot quickness necessary for pass protection. He also had great strength to block on running
plays. A quirky character, Neely could expound on any topic. At the same
time, he loved to complain. The beer was never cold enough. The sun was
always too hot. Nothing was ever good enough for Neely. His teammates
had a nickname for him: "Rotten." But he could block. He may have been
the finest offensive lineman the Cowboys ever had.

But to keep him, Tex Schramm would have to really pull a rabbit out
of the hat, especially after the U.S. Supreme Court ruled that at the end of
the season Neely would become property of the Oilers.

These hulks, Neely and Niland—who had quirks of his own—were
the final pieces of a puzzle that would lead the Cowboys to the steps of
greatness.

BUDDY DIAL: "In '66 we were strengthened by the addition of a couple of
offensive linemen, Ralph Neely and John Niland. What horses they were,
especially Neely. Neely was the finest offensive lineman I had ever seen,
until he hurt his knee bad later on. You talk about a phenomenal athlete.

"Niland was from Iowa, a typical dumb guard, but number 76 could
play a little football. John talked a lot, and he thought he was smart, but
he was dumber than dirt, you know. He drove people crazy. One night in
Dallas he ran through a neighborhood buck naked, just crazier'n a loon.
Here was an All-Pro guard running buck naked through a neighborhood,
and Don Meredith saw him to be an inspiration. I mean, would you like
to have your life on the line protected by a lineman running naked through
your neighborhood?

"And at tight end Pettis Norman began to play a little more regularly,
and he was a good blocker, and he caught some good balls, too. Pettis was
a really competitive guy. On the field he was mean, a wild animal. But off
the field he was a real kind, gentle person.

"Old Pete Gent was tough. I'm telling you, he got killed. If the ball was anywhere close to Pete, he knew he would catch it. We often wondered who was going to get off the plane and get in the ambulance first, Meredith or Gent. Many times they'd bring the ambulance to the airport and take Meredith or Gent to the hospital. We'd all get off the plane and get in our cars and drive home, and they would take one of them to the hospital."

In addition to Neely and Niland, the Cowboys signed as a free agent another talented offensive lineman, John Wilbur from Stanford University. Wilbur was different from most of the Cowboy players who came before him. His father had not been a struggling farmer, a postman, or a baker. Rather, Wilbur's dad was a well-to-do attorney who raised his son in a Jewish, white-collar suburb of Los Angeles. The boy attended L.A. Ram games with his dad, who had owned season tickets since 1948.

Because his father had attended Stanford Law School, the son always loved Stanford football. As a boy, he could sing all the Stanford songs, including "Join the Band," "The X Cheer," and "The Golden Bear."

In high school Wilbur played baseball, football, volleyball, and participated in water sports including swimming and water polo. A California beach boy, in his spare time he loved to body surf.

After his senior year, the University of California at Berkeley expressed a willingness to give Wilbur a scholarship, but since he didn't need the money, his intention was to play football for Stanford, with or without a scholarship.

After playing in an All-Star game that pitted the top L.A. high school stars against San Diego's counterparts, USC and UCLA also began talking scholarship. He told them he was going to Stanford.

Stanford ultimately took him, but not on an athletic scholarship. Wilbur got a full ride from being an Eagle Scout to play in a woefully weak Stanford program. Wilbur didn't care. His future was law, not football.

His sophomore year John Ralston became head coach, bringing with him some legendary assistants, including Bill Walsh and Dick Vermeil, a Who's Who of future NFL greats.

Wilbur played on good Stanford teams. He never did beat USC or the University of Washington, but he did well enough to be drafted after his junior year as a future prospect by the Kansas City Chiefs in the American Football League. When it came time for the NFL draft, Wilbur was nowhere to be found. Rumors were that he had signed with the AFL, and so he wasn't drafted. When Gil Brandt learned he had *not* signed with the Chiefs, he made Wilbur an offer he could not refuse.

JOHN WILBUR: "At the time of the NFL draft, Bobby Beathard was baby-sitting me and Gary Pettigrew for Kansas City. We didn't realize it, but he hid us away in a hotel so the other side couldn't get ahold of us. We thought we were just getting a free room and booze and food. We weren't reachable, and Beathard started a rumor I was signing with him, and so I didn't get drafted in the NFL.

"After the draft, the Cowboys contacted me, because they were really big on free agents, along with several other NFL teams. My dad handled the negotiations. Kansas City offered a bonus of $1,000, and the Cowboys offered four grand, with a salary of $12,000. That was a lot of money then, about what I owed Stanford, so I took it. Gil Brandt was really good at the PR, sending stuff about the Cowboys to college seniors. They hadn't won yet. They were 7–7. They had a good record of free agents making their team, so I did the deal.

"I had prepared really diligently for training camp. Under a doctor's care I actually took a six-week cycle of steroids, and with heavy weightlifting got my weight up from 220 in college to 250. That was the only time I ever took them.

"When you show up for training camp, first is ten days of rookie camp. Even though it was just a bunch of rookies, I was nearly over-whelmed. Coaching the offensive line was Jim Myers, a drill instructor, an ex-Marine who coached under Bear Bryant, southern trained, and along with me was a hell of a lot of man power as far as the numbers of large-sized people. There were twenty other offensive linemen, including John Niland, the number one draft choice, who was a guard. I was a free agent.

"It was one of the hardest things I ever did in my life, brutal, so competitive, and you never knew where you stood.

"I only found out where I stood when I tried to quit. The veterans had been in for a while, and I just didn't see the percentage in it. I wanted to be a lawyer. I had taken my law and business boards, and I had an opportunity to go to law school, and I was thinking, 'Maybe law school would be better than this.'

"The trainer found out I was in my room, and they called me, and Gil Brandt and Tom Landry and the coaches came up to talk me out of it. My initial impression was that Landry was a really bright guy, a player-oriented guy, someone who cared for the players. They did a good job trying to encourage the young guys. He was a king in his castle, and you kiss his ring but he spread his praise to the guys who counted, either the ones they drafted and were bringing up or the ones like myself who were trying to fight my way up.

"The first thing Brandt asked was, 'Is it the money?' Well, like a fool I said, 'No, it's *not* the money.' I could have had a hell of a raise. But I told them, 'I want to go to law school. I'm tired of football. Blah blah blah.' I made a pretty good case for myself, and they were very positive about me, encouraging, and they raised my spirits, so I went out to afternoon practice.

"I came out kind of late, got into a scrimmage, and I got into a fall-down, knock-down, drag-out fistfight with Lee Roy Jordan. We ran a play, and he hit me late. It was a pull-on pad, helmet-off fight with Lee Roy Jordan. They left us alone so we could slug it out for a while. I always kicked Lee Roy's ass. He rode all the rookies, and he deserved it, shooting his mouth off and hitting late and doing cheap things in practice. When I was a player I hated him, and I hated him when I was with the Redskins, too. He was a dirty, mouthy guy. He was always the redneck of the team and the team snitch. But I'll tell you what, he was a hell of a guy to have on your team. He played hard and was a great team leader. When push comes to shove, Lee Roy was a great player.

"That rookie season I saw real quick that it was the Southern Influence versus the California Influence—I guess you could call it the Whigs from north of the Mason-Dixon line—along with the blacks. And you could see that this did not sit too well with the rednecks.

"Bob Hayes and Pettis were all really tight with the California guys, the radical guys, the hipster guys, the music people, the pot smokers. Did anyone talk about the pot smoking? I won't say everyone smoked pot, because under Texas law it's still fifty years in jail for smoking pot. But I will say it was a prevailing thing at the time. Every college student smoked it, and all of us had been to college, so what did you expect?

"Dallas was not my favorite place. In those days it was the Changing South, but it was a town I didn't want to be in during the off-season. Dallas was in the middle of nowhere, had no ocean, was cold, and everybody spoke southern and said racial things, was prejudiced, and in addition, the night clubs closed early.

"Prejudice was everywhere. Danny Villanueva, our kicker, used to get hate calls, obscene calls, harassing calls all the time in Dallas from fans who hated Mexicans. He was scared to death. He had threats against his family. His being on the team unleashed the racial tensions existing in Dallas at the time.

"The black players had to live in Oak Cliff. That's why Pete Gent called his book *North Dallas Forty*. The blacks lived in South Dallas. I wasn't a civil rights activist, but civil rights activism had been all around me. I had come from Stanford, and we had participated in the Mississippi Project. I was sympathetic to their cause and gave money and time.

"I wasn't into the good old boys of the team. The good old boys were the staff, Landry, Jim Myers, and Ermal Allen, and George Andrie, Bob Lilly, Dave Edwards, Ralph Neely, Chuck Howley, Harold Hays, and Lee Roy, the guys who still live in Dallas, the 'let's go hunting' guys.

"Bob Lilly in *North Dallas Forty* was the guy hunting who was shooting all the birds. Lilly was definitely a classic, and George Andrie, too. He and Andrie were really good friends. The first year Andrie kicked my ass in practice. Those guys were the stereotypical linemen. Lilly and Andrie were just out of hand, really crazy. I had no idea. Pete Gent asked me if I wanted to go hunting with him and Lilly and Andrie. We went on a hunting trip, and they were drinking, and with their guns loaded, they rode around on the hood shooting everything in sight.

"And you had to be really, really careful where you were standing in relation to them. We were staking out a sluice for ducks to land, and we'd be on different points with shotguns, and I just remember the guns going off and hearing pellets hitting leaves at head height right around me. I couldn't believe they weren't shooting into the air. I hit the ground, got all muddy, 'cause they were just wild and dangerous with guns.

"Bob Lilly could be a very mean person. If Lilly were a young guy today, he would probably have a bunch of tattoos on him. Bob was as competitive and mean and nasty a guy you'd ever want, and that's who you want on defense. You want a guy who really gets pissed when he's controlled, a guy who always was a great leader of the defense by example and his motivation and leadership. But he was a nasty guy.

"Off the ballfield he was pretty easygoing, happy-go-lucky. He looks like a mellow Rotarian. And then he'd put his helmet on, and he became tough and hard-nosed and mean and nasty as anyone you've ever seen. His real persona is one of Knight Rider on a Harley Davidson.

"Craig Morton and I were pretty good friends because he went to Cal. We all lived in this Barcelona Apartments in North Dallas, all the bachelor guys. It was a happening area for the women. It was my rookie year, and I always had a bike at Stanford. I was kind of a biker guy, and I borrowed Craig's Scrambler. I had to go find a hill, obviously, and I rode until I found one, and I went up in the dirt, rode around, and I was coming back to Craig's apartment, and I got to Harry Hines Circle, and I hadn't ridden around a circle that much. We don't have circles in California, and so I came into the circle and as I accelerated, a car was coming off the circle going down toward town, and I didn't see it, and he hit me right in front of my ankle on the bike. I flew over the car about 30 or 40 feet, landed on a grassy median strip, did a roll, and I had one little scratch. His bike was totalled.

"I pushed the bike to the side and took a cab to my house, got my car, put the bike in the trunk of my car and took it back to Craig. I said, 'Hey, Craig, I'm sorry about your motorcycle. I'm sure it's better for you that it's destroyed by me than by you. And here's the money for it.' He wouldn't take the money. He said, 'I have insurance.' That was the kind of guy Craig was. A great guy. But I was by the hair of my chinny chin chin from getting terminated physically from football.

"I didn't play much that preseason. I was a scrub. We were playing Cleveland in Cleveland, and Jim Boeke went down with a bad knee, and I played left tackle against Bill Glass. I got beat up so bad, but I somehow survived. I guess it wasn't that embarrassing. I'm sure Meredith knew who was playing left tackle when he was dropping back.

"Bill Glass was supposedly the most religious guy in the league. He was for years an evangelist. He was trying to convert me right there on the line of scrimmage. He had me calling for God, believe me! I was just trying to save Meredith's life. I was asking to be born again right there on the line of scrimmage, with Glass bearing down on me. And Meredith was yelling for God as in 'God damnit.' It was a tough day.

"The left tackle is the hardest position to play on the offensive line. Glass had a sack and I had two holding penalties. I was holding him on every down.

"My rookie year I had a fan club in Dallas, the 'John Wilbur Fan Club.' I was an anachronistic hero, kind of an antihero. The guys made banners, 'Go John Wilbur,' made buttons. They had cards, because they liked my style on special teams, a wedge-buster. That's where I made my reputation when I started out. These guys called and asked me if they could start a fan club. They were always there after a game. It was kind of cool for a rookie to have a fan club. So they had the Most Popular Cowboy contest. On the expressway they had a billboard: Oak Farms Milk, with players' pictures, and a running tally. And the way you voted, you got a milk carton and cut out a ballot and sent it in to them. A big promotion. Whoever's name was on it, you got a vote. So my guys got behind this.

They got this smart idea to go down to the city dumps, and they scrounged everywhere in all the dumps in Dallas for milk cartons, 'cause each one had a ballot on it, and they cut them all out and put my name on them.

"I got a call late in the year, 'You're invited to come down to the Quarterback Club. You're going to win something.' I said okay, and I went down there, and they went through the announcements, and they were announcing that day the winner of the Oak Farms Most Popular Cowboy Contest. Curt Mosher, the PR guy, came up to me, and said, 'Look, we never have a second place for this award, but you're the second-place winner. We have a $1,000 check for you.' First place was a round-trip ticket to Hawaii, to stay at the Kahala Hilton first class for two people.

"They announced: 'The winner of the Most Popular Cowboy is Bob Lilly, and the second-place award goes to John Wilbur.' I got the $1,000 check. I figured what had happened was that I had won, but they couldn't give it to me because I had no name, nobody knew who I was, and there was no PR value to the milk company. So they gave me the second-place award.

"That's the way the Cowboys worked. Unfortunately, the fix was on. And the fix was *always* on. That was a Tex Schramm, Gil Brandt signature. Because of Vietnam a lot of guys were in the reserve. In fact, the way the Cowboys could get rid of guys they wanted to redshirt was to get them in the reserve. Dave McDaniels, a draft choice one year, couldn't play. They didn't know what to do with him. They thought he had potential and wanted to season him, but they didn't want someone else to pick him up, so they put him in the army reserve! They had all kinds of ways to get guys out of the military. There were two or three guys that way. The fix was on. Like the Most Popular Cowboy Contest."

When Tex Schramm signed him, he had been unaware that John Wilbur would be nothing but trouble for the Cowboys, participating in civil rights activities to antiwar protesting to what Schramm considered the worst sin of all: representing the Dallas Cowboys players for the hated players' union.

John Wilbur would play with the Cowboys from 1966 through the 1968 season, when the Cowboys would ship him off to the lowly St. Louis Cardinals. When he refused to go, he was able to get himself sent home, to the L.A. Rams and George Allen. Wilbur insists that he was traded by Schramm only because of his politics. That he became an All-Pro guard for the Washington Redskins likely makes his suspicions plausible.

As the team (and the country) was being populated more and more with what from Tom Landry's perspective seemed to be "radicals," the job of head coach of the Cowboys would become more and more trying. Now he had John Wilbur *and* Pete Gent.

JOHN WILBUR: "Tom Landry did have a sense of humor. He had a *great* sense of humor. When you got him to smile, it would light up a room, because he was usually so taciturn. Pete Gent would try to get him to laugh. He would wisecrack. If Pete had a shot, he'd take it.

"Pete was the team card. I'm sure he's been the guy who has always been disciplined for shooting his mouth off and making jokes his whole life. He added a great deal of continuity and quality to the team experience, and the rednecks didn't like him either. 'Cause he was so atypical for them. He was laughing at everybody, with that sardonic wit. And he added a lot with his sense of humor.

"Landry didn't mind it much the first two years I played. Then he moved Gent from flanker to split end to tight end to traded. Pete worked his way down the line."

When a person is constitutionally unable to give himself over to authority, he becomes tagged a rebel, like James Dean in *Rebel Without a Cause*, or like Marlon Brando in *The Wild One*. Pete Gent, along with John Wilbur and Don Meredith, became part of the Wild Rebel Bunch on the Cowboys. As a football player, Pete Gent would play an integral role in the team's success in '66, fighting for every yard, and he would sacrifice his body to the game he loved to play, but it would be his quick wit and sacrilege that people would remember. Like the time in training camp Gent walked up to a rookie who was reading his playbook. "Don't bother reading it, kid," Gent told him. "Everybody gets killed in the end."

Pete Gent saw himself like the hero in a popular TV series at the time, *The Fugitive*, someone on the run who had to keep one step ahead of management, and that included Tom Landry. At the end of the '65 season the Cowboys sent questionnaires to their players, asking them to make suggestions to the coaching staff. According to the instructions, the responses would be anonymous. Gent didn't believe a word of it.

PETE GENT: "The only way I kept up with Landry, I read a lot of psychology—abnormal psych.

"They knew they were having problems with the coaches, so after the '65 season, they sent out a questionnaire that was supposed to be anonymous. You were supposed to say anything you wanted about any of the coaches.

"I had just gotten through reading how you could send out supposedly anonymous questionnaires, but they could find out who was actually answering by coding the return addresses in pinholes, and not two weeks later here comes this questionnaire from the Cowboys. I held that son of a bitch up to the light, and there are the fucking pinholes!

"I wrote that everybody was wonderful!"

It did not take Tom Landry long to determine that Pete Gent was a "troublemaker." Early in '66 Gent found himself in Dutch with Landry for seemingly contradicting him in the newspapers.

PETE GENT: "In training camp Bob St. John interviewed me for a column in the *Morning News*. He asked me, 'How do you think you're going to do?' I said, 'We're going to win the East. I've been here two years now. I know we're going to win it.' At that time you just played the Eastern teams home and away, and you played just one Western Division team. By my third year, I knew who we had and I knew what the other teams had. And I knew what we had in Don Meredith. That ability to lead is so important, to get other guys to do what has to be done and think like you're thinking. Because instead of having eleven guys going in all different directions, you've got them following the game plan and going in the direction that the quarterback is thinking. And so Meredith would call a play, but he would also remind guys in the huddle what they were doing, and tell them, 'Make certain to make this adjustment,' even though it wasn't in the game plan. And lots of times he would call a play designed to do one thing, and he would do something else off of it. The other thing Don knew, when you are like Landry, you are predictable. Pretty soon, even with all the shifting, you could break his game down by percentages, and so Don was just incredible at coming in at the last minute and changing everything and making those drives we had to have. So when St. John interviewed me, I said, 'We are going to go 10–4, and we will win the East.'

"And then he interviewed Landry, who said he hoped to go 8–6 or 9–5, who said he didn't think we had the talent yet to win it.

"Well, Bob St. John ran the interviews like Landry and I were having a conversation with him at the same time, and when it came out, Landry was just fucking furious. I don't think Landry ever forgave me for that. No. Oh no. And of course, we went 10–3 [actually 10–3–1] and won the East.

"I really didn't do anything, but that wasn't relevant. You have to go back to who Landry was. The guy was a bomber pilot. The tailgunner doesn't call up to the front. And it doesn't even matter if you're right. 'Cause remember, he has to answer to Curtis LeMay, 'Bomb them back to the Stone Age.' And that was the way Tom was. Tom was set in that.

"As the years went on, and I listened to him in later years, he got more and more wisdom and began to realize that he had to change. But in the '60s, when he was confronted with so much change, when society was changing, the war was on, blacks were demanding civil rights, *football players* were demanding civil rights—I was the first football player in the National Football League whose hair came out from beneath his helmet. And it was maybe an inch. My hair was just touching my ears. And it was because I had forgotten to go to the barber. Literally I had just forgotten. And the Cowboys called me in and demanded I cut my hair. That pissed me off so much I never cut my hair again. This was in 1966. And it got to the point where the fans in the Cotton Bowl started calling me a hippie."

The real trouble between Landry and Gent occurred when Landry didn't start him, even though he was producing and playing well. In the past, when Landry started one player over another, no one said a word. Pete Gent wasn't like that. Gent not only felt that Landry was treating him unfairly, he said that to Landry's face and also told it to the world.

PETE GENT: "In '66, I had a great exhibition season, and Meredith and I had a really good rapport. We were running together. He'd been married and divorced, and married again, and I'm married, and now we're two married guys. He married a woman named Cheryl King. Her father was a big trucking executive in Forth Worth. He married her in the off-season after '65. Yes he did, because I got married in June of '66, just before camp, and after I had been in camp for a while—he had met my wife before we got married, although she was at Michigan State and only came down and visited—he sidled up to me, trying to hem and haw around, wanting to know whether I ran around on my wife. I said, 'Well, not really,' but I liked him so much, I loved running around with him, so we went out every night.

"Dick Nolan was in charge of curfew, so we were in L.A. every night. Of course, we'd get drunk, and Meredith would come back and complain that his arm hurt and miss morning practice, and I'd be out there having to run around, dying. But to me it was a classic example of Meredith knowing what worked, particularly dealing with Landry. You had to stay loose, or you just went crazy. So I had a really good exhibition season, then opened the season against New York, and just blew them away.

"I didn't catch the ball, but otherwise I did my job. I blocked. I was an excellent blocker for a flanker, and in those days you could crack back, so I blocked the linebackers a lot. That's why Dan Reeves had such good running stats, because they always ran to the strong side, and I cracked back on whoever showed up first, a linebacker or whoever, and you'd get such a huge pileup, lots of times it would knock down two or three guys. Anyway, in the Minnesota game, we started out slow. Everybody was having trouble, and Minnesota got up on us by a touchdown. He pulled me at the half, put Buddy Dial in, and Dial caught a five yards down-and-in for a touchdown. I've lost my job.

"And this was how you found out you weren't starting from Landry: When you're starting, he tells everybody his assignment. 'Bobby, you're doing this. Pettis, you're going to do this. Danny, you'll be coming out of the backfield.' And then he said, 'And the flanker will be doing this.' Well, as soon as I heard that, I knew that I wasn't the flanker. And sure enough, come the first full workout with the game plan, Dial was the starting flanker.

"I took it to his face. I went to him. I said, 'This is bullshit.' I told him, 'You say the numbers count. Look at my numbers. Look at Buddy Dial's numbers. He drops more than he catches. You got him out there, and he won't block anybody. You got an offense that has a flanker that has to block. Your outside game isn't there if he doesn't block. He hasn't touched a guy in two years. You have me sitting on the bench.'

"So immediately the papers wanted to know why I wasn't starting. And I went public.

"Landry told the paper, 'I never considered that Gent had the job.' He also said, 'I consider that I have two starters.' But I didn't get off the bench."

Pete Gent would not become a factor in the Cowboys' success in '66 until the team hit a mid-season slump and end coach Red Hickey had to bully Tom Landry into giving Gent another chance to play.

24

Success–At Last

In 1966 Tom Landry told his players he was putting more of an emphasis on winning the exhibition games because he wanted to "establish a pattern of winning." He told them, "I want you to get used to feeling the emotions of winning." His players nodded, went out on the field, and won all five preseason games, including their first win ever against Vince Lombardi's Green Bay Packers.

PETE GENT: "The biggest difference in the Cowboys in '66 and the Cowboys I had known in the first couple of years I was playing for them was that now the players were convinced Tom's system was right. When I first joined the team there were a lot of guys on the team who questioned what he was trying to do. There were a lot of personality conflicts between players and coaches, and coaches and players. But Tom Landry stuck to his beliefs and finally won everyone over. You could see the confidence in him growing toward the end of the '65 season. By 1966 he was in charge of the situation.

"I can remember having a long talk with Meredith about it, and at the time I was a little surprised to hear Don defending Landry so strongly. He said, 'Hey, the guy has shown me a lot.' "

FRANK CLARKE: "We were focused on surrendering and following this amazing leader of ours, and sometimes wondering what he might do next. We could look back to see how and why we got where we were, and we just became more and more and more confident in our offensive ability. By this point, Landry's system was ingrained in us.

"And during the exhibition season of '66, for the first time, we were even able to beat the Green Bay Packers.

"What we were looking at, we were hearing it from Tom Landry, we were seeing it in the newspapers, we were seeing it in the results of each practice, each week, each game, each experience of competition with other teams, good teams, and the bottom line was: 'We've got every phase of our game covered.' Our running game was going well. We were blocking well. I mean *everybody*—wide receivers like Bob Hayes, who weighed 180 pounds tops, blocking well from out there, enabling guys to get extra yards. We were sharp. The thing I remember most, we were no longer making the mental errors that we used to that had really hurt us a lot, hurt our confidence and also hurt our ability to be a solid offensive team.

"It made sense that we were winning games, that we were beating the teams that used to beat us, and it was easy to remember—and these are things that are really powerful, but when you think about where we were in 1960—how people used to push us around, that we were a laughing-stock. In the '66 season that gave us a strong impetus to be even stronger, 'cause we knew that those days were over. We saw how we got where we were and that we could be totally responsible for it. Totally responsible. And feel good about it. That was a great feeling to be able to take a look at the complete picture of the Cowboys, from its inception to that '66 season and realize how strong we were, and it was a wonderful, wonderful experience to be a part of that.

"And we became part of a whole great movement. It was in '66 that somebody coined this phrase, 'The Cowboys Are America's Team.' We, too, were tapping into that imagery, and we saw that wherever we went, and this was especially true when we went to New York, people were liking the Cowboys. We could go to Pittsburgh, and they liked us. They may not have wanted us to beat their Steelers, but people liked us."

When Pete Gent came in '64, many Dallas sports fans didn't even know who or what the Cowboys were. But by '66, the Cowboys had indeed become America's darlings.

PETE GENT: "When I was a rookie in '64, I found an apartment directly across from the practice field, where they eventually built the Cowboy Towers. At the time the Cowboys' offices were in a temporary building down the street aways, and across the street, on Mockingbird, by the Central Expressway, was a shopping mall. In it was a TV store run by an acquaintance whose father was the sports information director for SMU.

"I wanted to buy a television so I went down there, and since I never had any money, it seemed to me the way you bought everything was on time, and so I filled out a credit report, and he looked at this, and he said, 'The Dallas Cowboys? What are you, in a rodeo?' Now this guy's father was not only in the sports business, he was only a block away from the practice field and the offices, and he didn't even know who the Cowboys were! People in Dallas didn't know who the Cowboys were. The crowds were 30,000 people, and half of those were black because they were playing in the Cotton Bowl, which is on the black side of town. They were the greatest fans in the world. The end zones were always full.

"In 1964 if you bought an adult ticket, you got five kids in for nothing *and* a free football. Tickets in the end zone were a dollar. An adult ticket was only five or six dollars anywhere. The only time we filled the stadium was when Green Bay came.

"By '66 we were sold out every game. In just two years we went from our not being able to get a seat in a restaurant in Dallas to literally being America's guest. I can remember I was driving back and forth across the country then, and if I wanted to drive 100 miles an hour from Texas to Michigan, I just pulled on my Dallas Cowboys practice shirt. I had a souped-up Ford. A state policeman stopped me in Iowa one time. When I got out, the cop saw I was with the Cowboys, and he said, 'Jesus Christ, we needed a plane to catch you. Slow down.' They knew who I was and let me go.

"But you also saw a change in the players. Ralph Neely, when he came in as a rookie in '65, was a sweet kid. By '66 Neely was cruising around in a Mercedes with a car phone going to his oil wells. And Don Meredith and I just used to laugh about it. You saw all these guys believing that suddenly *they* were different. It didn't dawn on them that what had changed was everybody else. *We* were the same people. And interestingly enough there were only a few guys who really grasped that, guys like Don Perkins, Frank Clarke, and Meredith, the guys you'd expect, and also the really bright thinkers in the offensive and defensive lines, guys like Blaine Nye and Larry Cole, John Wilbur, Leon Donahue, Dave Manders, Jim Colvin, and of course, Bob Lilly, who had an innate brilliance about him."

BOB LILLY: "We scored 52 points against the Giants in the opener. We always played well in the opener. Don threw five touchdown passes, two to Bob Hayes, and we were saying to the offense, 'Save some of those for next week. We understand you only have so many of those in you. You don't want to waste them all in one game.'

"In the second game we beat Fran Tarkenton and the Vikings, 28–17. Fran was the greatest scrambler I ever saw in my life. He made an awful lot of yardage and touchdowns out of scrambling. He was a little bit short for quarterback. I think that's why he had to scramble a lot, because we held our hands up, and he couldn't see over us. But boy, he made you really have to watch your pass rush, because you couldn't really cut loose on him.

"The best way to control his passing was to maintain your lanes, as we called it, and keep him in a pocket. When he started rolling out, that was when he killed you. He was a great quarterback. For his size he was one of the best quarterbacks who ever played.

"I can remember that day it was 90 degrees, and we were exhausted. We called timeout, and Tom sent in one guy as a replacement. All four of us left the field for him to replace us."

Then came romps over the expansion Atlanta Falcons, 47–14, and a 56–7 stomping over the Philadelphia Eagles. After these offensive showings set a team scoring record, Buddy Dial said about Meredith: "Don was so accurate that he could spit in a swinging jug."

The undefeated Cowboys tied the undefeated St. Louis Cards, as defensive back Larry Stallings led the defense against Meredith, who didn't have much time to operate. But this was a new day for the Cowboys, and even the skeptical Don Meredith was beginning to see that Tom Landry was indeed a master, not some quack with weirdo theories, as had been suspected before now.

After the Card game, Meredith told reporters: "When the Cowboys start winning, we're going to win more consistently than any team who ever won in this league. More than Cleveland, more than the Giants, more than Green Bay. And the reason is Tom.

"Tom is right. You get tired of a guy being so right so often. You almost wish he could be wrong some time. The hardest thing about this system is believing Tom every time.

"I used to fight believing Tom. I really rebelled against it. It was immature and I was stupid, but we were losing and I wasn't used to losing.

When every man on this team learns and accepts this about Tom, Dallas will be the world champion."

Pete Gent had sat glued to the bench against both Atlanta and Philadelphia. The next game was against the St. Louis Cardinals. Gent's cause would be hurt further by an outrageous article in the morning paper.

PETE GENT: "We were getting ready to play St. Louis in '66, and we needed to beat them to stay on top. We always practiced at the Cotton Bowl on Saturday before the game, and I had to go down early, because my right leg was so fucked up that I had to get taped and my knee drained. So I was in the shitty Cotton Bowl locker room on the training table when Bob Lilly walked in, and he was just furious. He had the *Dallas Morning News* in his hands, and he whacked me in the back of the head with it and said, 'I hope that son of a bitch kills you, you dumb bastard.' I had no idea what he was talking about.

"I opened the paper, and there was a full-page interview with me about Cardinal defensive back Larry Wilson. I was saying, 'Larry Wilson is uglier than an Idaho winter,' and 'We're going to kick his ass.' Now, one, Larry Wilson was one of the nicer guys in the league. And two, Larry Wilson had a personal tragedy that was beyond belief. He had a child who had been born totally disabled, and it was taking all his money to keep that child alive. So here was this third-year player talking about one of the great defensive safeties of all time, running at the mouth. I couldn't believe it. I had never said any of those words!"

Against the Cardinals, just before the half, the Cowboys were losing. Buddy Dial had not caught a pass, and from the press box Red Hickey began screaming down to Tom Landry to send in Pete Gent. The Cowboys had the ball with less than a minute to go in the half.

PETE GENT: "I caught about a 45-yard post in between Larry Stallings and Abe Woodson and fell on the three. Dan Reeves got in on the next play for a touchdown. We were back in the game. 'Cause you could never blow St. Louis out. They were always tight games. And I caught one other pass in the second half that set up Danny Villanueva to kick the go-ahead field goal, but with hardly any time left in the game, Bob Hayes fumbled a punt, and they moved it down and Jim Bakken tied the game at 10–10. So now, although I played a great game, we didn't win. So now I didn't know what Landry was going to do."

*   *   *

Tom Landry, a thoughtful man, must have agreed that he had been wrong to bench Gent without telling him first, because before the game between Dallas and Cleveland, Tom Landry announced to the players that in the future he would tell a player to his face when he was being benched.

In the newspaper that day Landry also announced that Pete Gent would start at wide receiver for the rest of that season. It was a replay of the Meredith drama the year before, only this time no one much cared one way or the other except Pete Gent.

Adding to the intensity of the next game against the Jim Brown–less Cleveland Browns was the publication of a newspaper article written by Joan Ryan, the wife of Cleveland quarterback Frank Ryan, saying that the Cowboys in general and Don Meredith in particular were "losers." She made this observation in a column in the *Cleveland Plain Dealer* after watching Dallas and St. Louis tie at 10–10.

PETE GENT: "I started against Cleveland, and in that game Don and I went back to our old routine, opening up with quick passes to me, and then the rest of the game I blocked for Don Perkins up the middle. I would come across and generally catch middle linebacker Vince Costello unaware. What Landry did with me was have me cut down my split, and I would just come across the middle and take the middle linebacker on myself. Ask Sam Huff. Sam Huff hates me to this day 'cause it was such an insult for him to be blocked by a wide receiver. And in that Cleveland game we needed a touchdown, and I came across the middle, and I was off-balance so I didn't get down to block Costello, but I got in his way, and Perkins cut off my hip and went in for the touchdown."

Despite Gent's heroics, the Browns won, 30–21. Don Meredith had one of his worst days. He was intercepted four times. Andy Anderson in the *Dallas Press* wrote that the Cowboys had "choked."

Some of the players agreed with Anderson.

FRANK CLARKE: "When we went to Cleveland and lost, they wrote that we choked, and it *was* a choke. When we played Cleveland, for some reason or another, we played them like we didn't know who we were. They had a way of just showing up, and we'd forget who we were, and it *was* a choke. When you write about it, that's *exactly* what it was. It's the only thing you could call it. We panicked when we played Cleveland. I don't know what it was. And it wasn't just me, though I felt it. Cleveland was more than just the team I used to play for and wanted to do well against, and all this other crap.

"But yeah, that was very well put. We could relate to that. It felt like a choke, but you know what else it felt like? I remember this, too, it also felt like it was a wake-up call that we needed to get, that we aren't there yet, and we know what we need to do 'cause we aren't where we want to be.

"We wanted to be NFL champions, not just divisional champions or conference champions, and we weren't there yet, so when we lost to Cleveland, it *was* a choke, but it came at a good time. It was early in the season, and we had time to recover, and also to test our ability to let that go and concentrate on our next opponent.

"Tom Landry had a way of letting us know exactly what broke down to cause this. He would let us know where the breakdowns were, and he would do something else, too, that was really fantastic that helped take our attention off the fact we had lost. He brought an energy to whatever it was that he focused on, and when we saw him focus on something, he took us with him, so during the week he would spend more time on the area where the breakdown was that caused our defeat. And we rode that and forgot about what happened, and we knew we were going to be ready to meet that next challenge, and this is what he was able to do for us. And it was amazing to watch that happen, 'cause he brought a lustre, he brought an uplift, he brought something to what he touched that was really fantastic."

Athletes are very sensitive to what is being written about them, and some of the Cowboy players were furious with the negativism of the Dallas sportswriters. The contempt for the writers by some of the players was intense.

PETE GENT: "It was only our first loss of the year. Even though our record was 4–1–1, the headline in the paper said, 'The Cowboys Choked.' For any of us, reading the paper was never a pleasant experience. I would pick up the paper and see an article and glance through it looking for my name to see if I was in trouble. But I wouldn't sit there and read it. Early on I learned from these guys that they weren't talking about what was happening. It was one of the reasons I got the idea that I ought to write a book. That media view of the game, I know, isn't right. That's also why I have no faith in newspapers. Thirty percent of the people buy the paper for the sports pages, and the sportswriters are not correct about *anything*. All they wrote about was numbers, like in Vietnam the way the correspondents wrote about body counts. And this was going on at the same time. 'Cause I would go speak somewhere, and you'd talk to these people who were getting their information from television and the newspapers, and they had such a totally different idea of what was happening in professional football than what was *really* happening."

After a 52–21 shellacking of the Pittsburgh Steelers, the Cowboys lost their second game, this time to the Philadelphia Eagles, when with 90 seconds left in the game second-year back Dan Reeves, who was running for a touchdown, thought he heard a whistle. Relaxing, he was tackled so hard he fumbled, and it was bye-bye ballgame when the referee ruled he had been hit *before* the whistle. In that game Tommy Brown ran back two kicks—of 90 and 93 yards—for touchdowns. On the latter play John Wilbur threw his knee out trying to tackle Brown. Said Wilbur, "He made me cut so radically, my cartilage tore." Wilbur had to have a knee operation and would be out the rest of the season.

The next game was against the Washington Redskins. It was the game that made believers out of *everybody*. The Cowboys trailed 30–28 with 1:10 left on the clock. They were on their own three-yard line, 97 yards away from victory. And they had no timeouts left in the game.

The first play was a 26-yard rollout pass from Don Meredith to Pete Gent. On the next play the Cowboy QB rolled right for 12 yards and then ran out of bounds. After an incomplete pass, Meredith threw a swing pass to rookie Walt Garrison, good for but a yard. It was third-and-nine with 48 seconds left.

Meredith went back to Gent, who gained 25 yards and ran out of bounds. The lanky QB rolled right for six yards, and when Redskin linebacker John Reger hit him late, another 15 yards was added to the play.

The Cowboys, miraculously, were on the Redskin 12 with fifteen seconds left.

After the roughing penalty the ball was moved to the middle of the field, where Danny Villanueva calmly kicked a 20-yard field goal for the 31–30 victory. Said Villanueva after the game, "What if I'd missed it? I'd have gone home. What would I have said to those guys?"

Said Gent about Meredith, "You can't imagine how much this team loves that guy."

BOB HAYES: "We did love Meredith. We really did. We loved him, because he had taken so much abuse. He would go out there and play for you when he should have been in the hospital, and you've got to like somebody like that. I don't know anybody who didn't think a lot of Don. Don would have been at the very highest level if he hadn't gotten killed and got bad-mouthed so much that he just wanted out."

FRANK CLARKE: "Against Washington we won in the final minutes. Don took us just about the whole length of the field in the Cotton Bowl with no timeouts to win it. The crowd was going berserko. That was so fantastic.

"I know this for a fact: During that drive there were at least six plays that were picture-perfect from what Tom Landry had conceived, put on paper, and we had talked about in our meetings. I can see him now telling Bob Hayes to go down, curl in at 15 yards, and him telling the tight end to run a post or a corner route, which would take this linebacker and this safetyman with him, and it would enable Pete Gent to come underneath and catch the ball, and then flare out to the sideline. This happened for at least five or six plays of that drive.

"Each of us on the field knew that we were doing exactly what we were supposed to do. Those plays were designed to connect, so that we could move with that kind of precision for 97 yards without a timeout. Nobody was making a mistake, and everything was happening absolutely perfectly. Walt Garrison or Gent or Reeves was getting the ball, because the play was *exactly* designed for that person to have the ball. And Landry probably was even getting the extra yardage that he wanted out of each play. 'We need 12 yards on this one? Let's get 13.'

"Danny Villanueva kicked a field goal to win the game, and it was absolutely amazing. Because we all knew that this was the first time the Cowboys had ever moved the ball with that kind of confidence.

"It probably was the most important moment of our Cowboy offensive history. As you know, the teams that win consistently are the teams that move the ball like that. And here we were—in our infancy! 'Cause we were still a young team, in the league just seven years. To have that experience, you say to yourself, 'Oh my goodness, this is fantastic.' "

25

Two Feet Away

The '66 season ended with four wins in five games, including a spectacular 26–14 Thanksgiving Day victory over Frank Ryan, Leroy Kelly, Paul Warfield, and the rest of the Cleveland Browns in front of 80,259 howling, berserk fans in the Cotton Bowl. The players had not forgotten Mrs. Ryan's article. Before the game in the silent locker room Tom Landry told his players, "I have all the confidence in the world you'll win this game." Afterward, Landry would call the win "the biggest game in our history."

FRANK CLARKE: "The Cleveland game on Thanksgiving in '66 was the best football game I personally have ever played. I caught the ball well, blocked well, and I was part of this wonderful offensive movement. We were *so* good that day, and I think for the first time, I got a sense of having *fun*. It was beyond a methodical following directions, following our instincts, following our mentor Landry. It was like, 'Wow, man, maybe we can do this consistently!' And God, that was a fun game.

"We had deserved that 'choke' label against the Browns the first time. But we were able to set that aside in terms of 'Don't lose concentration about who we are and what we're doing here. We're not where we want to be, so yes, when we make a mistake, we're going to learn from it, and we're going to keep moving forward.'

"By the time we came to that week, we had an intensity of purpose. It was a night game, so we practiced late under the lights of the stadium, and I remember during that week that there was an air of confidence around everything that we did, and every movement of our practice. In retrospect, when you saw how we played, it just made total sense. We were ready. All the games we had played in the seven years of being in the league prepared us against Cleveland.

"And it was fun for me, because I had come from Cleveland. These guys *had* given me a hard time, and it was fun to see all of that laid to rest. I knew it was final. It was finally just laid to rest because our offense, aw man, we played so well. The defense did too, but it's easy for me to remember how easily we moved the football. It was the sweetest victory I can ever remember."

A 34–31 loss in the final four seconds to Washington on a field goal by Charlie Gogolak followed by a 17–7 victory over the New York Giants gave the Cowboys a regular-season record of 10–3–1, as they won the Eastern Conference championship for the first time. Under the two-division organization of the time, the Cowboys would play the Green Bay Packers for the NFL championship. The winner of that game would play in the first ever Super Bowl, a game arranged as part of the June 8, 1966, merger agreement between Tex Schramm and Lamar Hunt of the AFL. (As part of the New Era of Good Feeling, Tex Schramm and Bud Adams, the owner of the Houston Oilers, agreed that Dallas would get to keep Ralph Neely. In exchange, the Oilers would get a number one draft choice, and most important to Adams, the Oilers would get to play a string of preseason exhibition games against a team that was now being called "America's Team.")

Getting the opportunity to play the Packers for the title meant tremendous satisfaction for the players, but it was especially so for a player like Frank Clarke, who had been there at the beginning.

FRANK CLARKE: "The NFL title game was against the Green Bay Packers. For Tom and Don and me it meant that hard work, determination, and self-sacrifice had paid off. The Packers had the reputation as being the NFL's best. Their style of play was envious, and it was also well known. They told people: we know that you know what we're going to do, and we're not trying to disguise it—which is the opposite of what the Cowboys did.

"By the time we were playing the Packers in the NFL Championship Game of '66, their reputation was, 'We're going to do it because we're better than you are.' So that in '66 when the Packers came onto the field to play us in the Cotton Bowl, they *knew* that they would win, and we knew that they knew that. The difference was that we *thought* that we could win, but we didn't *know* that we could win. And that was basically the difference in the game."

BUDDY DIAL: "The thing about Green Bay was they were not going to beat themselves, and if you made a mistake, you'd lose.

"I remember during our preparation for the game, Coach Landry had our whole team together. He was up at the blackboard, and Bobby Hayes and Meredith and I were sitting at the back of the room. Hayes was sitting at his desk, and he was leaning back against the wall. And ole Tom turned around to the blackboard, and he said, 'All this year, Bobby, you have been going deep and Dial and Gent have been coming across the middle.' And he said, 'This week for Green Bay, Dial, you, and Gent are going to go deep, and Bobby, you're going to come across the middle,' and from the back of the room we heard Bobby Hayes say, 'Shiiiiiiiiit.' Hell, Landry nearly dropped the chalk. We all fell out of our chairs when Bobby said, 'Shiiiiiiiiit.'

"And in that game he did not run across the middle."

Though it was only nine years since the Giants-Colts championship of 1958, the Packer game was billed as the "Game of the Decade." The Cowboys started poorly. On the opening drive the Pack drove 76 yards, as Bart Starr hit halfback Elijah Pitts for a score, and on the ensuing kickoff Mel Renfro fumbled and Jim Grabowski picked up the ball and ran for a touchdown, making the score 14–0 before the offense had even touched the ball.

LEE ROY JORDAN: "We were trying to do too much defensively in the secondary. Under the game plan we were trying to set up our defenses depending on how wide the split end was set. If Boyd Dowler was eight yards out, we were going to play one defense, and if he was fifteen yards out, we were going to play another defense.

"And the first time the Packers got the ball, Dowler moved from a wide position to a closer position, and I didn't see it, didn't hear the call, and so I played the defense for his original position, and in the spot where I was supposed to be, Elijah Pitts caught a pass for a 17-yard touchdown. If I'd have been playing the right defense, I'd have come his way, but because of my mistake it left a big hole in the area where the halfback was running, and Bart Starr picked it up and hit the right guy, and boom, it was a touchdown. They then came back and returned a [fumbled] kickoff for a touchdown, and we were down 14–0, and our offense had never been on the field.

"We were a very inexperienced team wanting to show we could compete against a Green Bay team that knew they were good and had all the confidence of a veteran team that had been in the playoffs and championships.

"At the end of the game we were throwing at the end zone from five yards away, and that's a great position to be in for a young football team that we were. Had we not made mistakes early, we would have beaten them. But at the time we were just not mature enough to handle them as a defensive football team."

Dallas managed to tie the game at 14–14 before Green Bay scored twice late in the game. In the third quarter Tom Landry began substituting wholesale, prompting some of the players to wonder whether he had given up.

PETE GENT: "I can remember in the championship game of 1966, Landry quit in the third quarter. He started substituting, putting guys in for next year. He had his back to the field looking at guys on the bench, trying to decide what linemen to put in, when Meredith hit Frank Clarke for a 68-yard touchdown to put us within seven."

FRANK CLARKE: "My father was there, my mother was there from Dallas, my brothers and sisters, and I remember catching a 68-yard touchdown pass in that game from Meredith that was really fantastic.

"The play was Red Right motion X post. The offensive formation was Red Right, where I'm at the tight end spot, Pete Gent is the flanker, and Bobby Hayes is the wide receiver. Danny Reeves goes in motion to the left. X is the tight end spot, and what happened was, when Danny Reeves went in motion to the right, Packer linebacker Dave Robinson, who was on my nose, went with the motion man, so it left me uncovered. Now I take off, and I have this wonderful shot at defensive back Tom Brown, I'm looking right at Tom Brown's number, nobody to block me, nobody to mess with me, and I run down, and I make this great inside move, and he goes for it, and then I make another move toward the corner, and he recovers, but as he's recovering, the greatest thing that could happen to an offensive receiver happened: the defensive back fell down. He tripped over his own legs trying to keep up with the offensive move, and that was wonderful, man. You know you have done your job when that happens. So Tom Brown tripped over his own legs trying to keep up with me, and now I break toward the post, and nobody is near me, and Meredith lofted that ball up there fantastically, but the key to the whole play was not this, 'cause I *knew* I could beat Tom Brown, or any defensive back, one-on-one, no question about it; the key to it was what Bob Hayes was doing over on the other side and what Dandy did. Bob Hayes was split wide to the left on Bob Jeter, and he went down, and he did a great sideline route, and then looked like he was going up, and by his going up toward the end zone, like he was running a 'fly' route, this momentarily made Willie Wood, the weak safety, hesitate. By Bob Hayes momentarily running that route, it froze Willie Wood for just a fraction of a second, and that's all it took, because by the time Meredith put that ball in the air, Willie Wood, with his great speed and ability, was not able to come over in time to catch me running this post route. He dove, and he did clip me, and I can still feel his hand on the back of my left heel, but it wasn't enough. I sped into the end zone with the ball.

"And for a second it seemed as though everything was still. I couldn't hear myself breathe. I could hear nothing. And it seemed as though the Cotton Bowl crowd erupted in this thunderous explosion. I ran into the end zone, ran up to the Cotton Bowl wall, and I handed the ball to a man in the stands there. I later found out that this guy was a Green Bay Packer fan, and he knew I was from Beloit, and he sent me a note thanking me for the ball."

PETE GENT: "When Frank Clarke scored, Landry heard everybody cheering, and he turned around, and all the linemen were up in front of him, and he couldn't see what had happened. And personally, I don't think he ever recovered from that. This is now midway through the fourth quarter. He had started substituting guys who hadn't played all year. Like this was a regular season game we were losing."

FRANK CLARKE: "I went back to the bench, and our defense went in the game, and there were four minutes left in the game, and then, fantastically, the Cowboys got the ball back. We held, four downs. Don Chandler punted, and it went off the side of his foot, a lousy kick. And we're saying, 'We're *supposed* to win this game.' So we went into the game, and we had another third down call, and we did the same thing, but here's what we did: Dandy said, 'Red Right motion, X corner.' So instead of going for the goalpost this time, I went to the corner. And everything worked out just fine. Dan Reeves went in motion and Dave Robinson left me uncovered. I ran down, and this time I made a real strong inside move, and Brown went for it, because he figured we were going to hit a quick post this time, and then when I planted and went back toward the corner, he said, 'Oh my God,' and he was close enough to me to grab my arm, break my stride, but the official saw it and threw the flag, but the ball was still very close because of my power to keep going. I still almost got to the ball, which meant if I had caught it, we would have tied the game.

"And that's when we got the ball on the one-yard line. And then on the first play, we fumbled. Dan Reeves ran right into the middle of the Packer line, and he was knocked senseless by Lionel Aldridge, and the next play tackle Jim Boeke jumped before the snap, and that put the ball back on the six.

"Don threw a swing pass to Dan. We didn't know it, but Dan was seeing double, and he dropped the ball.

"On third down Don then threw to Pettis, who got down to the two."

BUDDY DIAL: "After the Boeke penalty, we were pushed back to the six. Meredith had a play he wanted to call, and I remember what it was. He wanted to throw to me coming across from the weak side, 'cause I was open all night doing that. But Landry called another play, and Don hated it. Landry wanted to call a turn-in to Pettis Norman. Well, Meredith tried to throw the turn-in to the tight end, and it was crushed up on that side, and it only got us to the two.

"Don knew what the defense was going to be, but Landry didn't have any confidence in me at that time. Pete was more productive than I was, but Gent was so beat up. It was a weak position at that time, but I remember coming across so open, and oh, mercy, the throw was made to the tight end."

FRANK CLARKE: "The next play is one that I still wonder about to this day. On short-yardage plays anywhere on the field or in goal line situations on the field, I was always the tight end. Bob Hayes would come out of the game. I always played the tight end, and Bob Hayes always came out of the game. In this particular situation we had fourth-and-two with 45 seconds left. The Packers had a seven-point lead. A touchdown and extra point would have tied the game. On this particular play, the tight end was supposed to block linebacker Dave Robinson. For some reason or another—and it stunned me, I couldn't figure it out—Tom Landry sent Bob Hayes *into* the game for me. And it was supposed to be the other way around. I was already on the field, so I was getting ready to line up for that short-yardage play. And I couldn't figure out what was going on. I thought, 'This is unlike Tom to try something different. Not in a situation like this.'

"Perhaps I should have said, 'Excuse me, Coach, for calling timeout, but . . . what's going on? Is this what you want to do?' But I didn't even consider it. Not even close.

"And on that particular play, Bobby Hayes, who had never done this before, had never even practiced doing it, basically he didn't know what to do. Dave Robinson, the big linebacker, just brushed by Bobby like he wasn't even there, and he charged in on Meredith, who was rolling out to the right to throw the pass, and Dave Robinson foiled that. Meredith in desperation threw the ball up in the air, and Tom Brown intercepted it, and that was the game. And I've often wondered, 'Did Tom Landry in his astute way of seeing himself as a coach, did he in that moment want to see that happen, because he knew that if the Cowboys had won that game it would have turned our whole destiny in another way, that it made sense that the Packers would win that game?' 'Cause I was trying to figure out, 'Did he choke? Was it a situation where Tom Landry, the head coach, lost his concentration for the moment?' That might have happened, but I've often toyed with that other idea, that he certainly wasn't trying to lose, that would be impossible to imagine, but did he in some way feel that the destiny of the Packers was that they should win that game, because Tom had a timetable where he was going, and the roadmap showed the Packers winning that game?

"My primary sense tells me that we were so close to beating the heralded Packers. Even though we were seven points down, there was every reason to believe if we had scored that touchdown, we were going to win in overtime. It might have been so overwhelming to him. He had never been in a situation like that before. His former peer, Vince Lombardi, was heralded. The so-respected Packers—he had a chance to beat them, so that he probably could not quite get it together. But why would he have sent Bob Hayes into the game? It just stuns me that he would have done something *so* out of character. How do you explain that?"

PETE GENT: "In '66 I felt that we won because Meredith led. In '66 Landry had no choice. Meredith had him by the balls. Meredith was *the* quarterback in the NFL that year. He was great. Jesus Christ, we scored so many points. And he could throw. The ball was just right there, and it was so soft and so catchable.

"I had been on the sidelines and saw the insanity that could control Landry. The sidelines, if you've ever been down there, is just chaos. It's the worst place in the world to watch the game from. Landry literally could forget the game plan. When I would run plays for him, he would call the wrong plays. Well, in '66 it didn't matter because Meredith was calling the plays, even when Landry would send them in. Lots of times Landry would send in a suggestion, and Meredith would send the player back out to publicly show up Landry. The player would start out, and Meredith would wave him back.

"Against the Packers we were down on the goal line, time running out, first down, 17 seconds to go, and Bob Hayes was in the game even though we were on the goal line. Ordinarily on the goal line Frank Clarke would come in, because your split end always comes down tight, and Hayes could never do that, because he was so light he could never get off the line. The linebackers just grabbed him.

"We had an option play that ran off a fake dive to Don Perkins called 'Fire 93, G pull,' which is the guard. And the theory was that Frank blocked for two counts, allowing Leon Donahue to pull out and get in front of Dave Robinson, Green Bay's linebacker, and then Meredith would pull out behind him, and then Clarke would release inside Robinson, because Robinson wouldn't assume he was rolling. He would plant inside, then break back to the corner. It's an option play. If the defensive halfback doesn't come up and force Meredith, he just runs into the end zone. Because the linebacker is already covered by the guard and the safety was too far back to do anything. If the safety came up, Clarke was open in the back of the end zone.

"We broke the huddle, only Hayes was in for Clarke. I wondered, 'What the hell is Hayes doing out there?' Clarke was supposed to be in there, but no one bothered to tell Clarke to go into the game, and Clarke was not the sort of person to go in on his own. That's the difference between him and me. I would have just gone. There was time after time when I just put my foot down. But that wasn't Frank's makeup.

"Everyone blamed Boeke's jumping offsides for the loss, 'cause NFL Films got such good shots of that. Why did they think that cost us the game? He jumped offsides, and we got a five-yard penalty, but we got the down over, and we got the yardage back. It is hard in any game to isolate a single thing and say it is the reason you lost, but a couple of things come to mind more quickly than Boeke's jumping offsides.

"Really what cost us the game was that Danny got poked in the eye. He was in the huddle, and we couldn't get him to leave. Danny was one of those competitors. He bought that old philosophy that you played whether you were blind or not. Reeves was seeing double. Hayes had gone right to the end zone and taken everybody with him, and Danny was wide open. That ball came at him, and he needed six pairs of hands to catch the ball. And *that's* what cost us the game.

"It's so strange because you see the play from so many different perspectives. You never really remember where you were. Right now I picture that play as though I were Meredith throwing the ball, 'cause the ball hit Danny right in the chest. But see, Tom Landry loved Danny. So Danny wasn't going to go in for any blame. Danny was man enough to accept blame. He didn't try to dodge it. I have heard Danny talk about how he should have taken himself out of the game. He was a kid. He didn't know what to do.

"Then it was a mistake for Landry to have Bob Hayes instead of Frank Clarke in there on that fourth-and-two play at the end of the game. Hayes had never been in on goal line situations before. But because Landry was substituting so much, there was a fuckup in substitutions on that goal line play. Why else would Hayes be in there rather than Clarke? As I said, Landry had started running guys in and out by the third quarter. He pulled me in the third quarter for Buddy Dial, and he started pulling linemen, and he started screwing with the rotations. Things the guys would automatically do, they no longer automatically did. So Clarke stood there waiting for orders, rather than going in like he would normally do.

"I honestly think that the main reason so much attention was dealt to Boeke's mistake was the fact that NFL Films got some really good shots of it. They played that thing over and over; using several different angles. And there was always that deep bass voice of John Facenda dramatically saying how the 'Cowboys' hopes died with that play.'

"They didn't. Shoot, we moved the ball back down to the two. But again, that points out what was right about what Meredith and I believed, that you have to make the decisions on the field. If you've got half your players paralyzed to move because they are afraid of what the coach is going to say, then Frank Clarke is going to stand there on the sideline when he should be in the game, and Danny Reeves is going to stay in the game when he should take himself out.

"And those are your breakdowns. Those are the breakdowns that kill you. Mental breakdowns kill you ten times worse than physical breakdowns. If you make mental mistakes, you're going to lose. Everybody makes physical mistakes. The game is played in your head."

BUDDY DIAL: "After the game, I came off the field, and I walked up to Landry, and they showed that picture before every broadcast of me talking to Landry after the game. Aw, I can't say what I called him. Aw, I was so bad. I called him an ill-advised name. I had a little single-bar face mask, and I was right in his face. It was very embarrassing for me when they replayed that. But we wanted to win so bad. You never saw so many guys cry after a ballgame as we did after that one.

"I blamed Landry for making the wrong call. But he had no reason to have confidence in me. In my heart I wanted the chance to catch it. But everybody did at that point. I didn't justify the ball being thrown to me. I had not been that significant that year. And I really wonder, because that was the type of play I had made all my life. And it was thrown to the other side. And essentially, that was the end of my playing career.

"I know, when watching the film, how wide open I was, because I split out way wide to the left, and came across, and they went strongside, and golly . . . But it was very frustrating for Meredith and the guys who really deserved to win. I hadn't done anything for the team, but Don really deserved to win that night. But we were real close, running a strong side play, and aw, we should have won that game. Don would have had the satisfaction of winning a championship and going to the first Super Bowl.

"We should have won it. The defense played brilliantly. And the offense had a good day, too. That should have been the beginning of the Cowboys' victory seasons, right there, but we broke down and got beat. If we had won that game, Don would have been the winner he wanted to be, and it would have allowed him to stay at his own choice. But because we lost, there was so much pressure on him. The next year Roger Staubach was behind him, and he did not want to go through another LeBaron/Morton/Rhome episode, and before long he quit."

FRANK CLARKE: "It was at the end of this game that I was beginning to take stock about 'What in the world is all this about?' Like 'Whoa.' And I remember going into the locker room after we played that game, and it was like a wake, like somebody had died. And I could *not* relate to that. I didn't say it to anybody, but here I was thinking, 'Wow, this is *not right*.'

This is really weird. We had had a fine season. We had reached many of our goals. We had even surpassed some of them. And here we had just played one of the best teams in the history of the sport. There had been no NFL playoff game quite like that since 1958, and we had every reason to be proud and pleased with how we had done. It was the last game of the season, we weren't getting ready for another game, and we should have been thrilled.

"I wondered, 'Why are we feeling like this? This does not make sense.' And that's when I started saying to myself, 'Maybe I'm just not cut out for this. Maybe I don't have what it takes.' And I really began to question, 'What the heck is really going on here?' And it was at that point where I felt that, 'Am I looking at a flaw in a coaching philosophy? Is this going to help us, or is this going to tear us down?' 'Cause I felt as if the coaching leadership at that point should have praised us. It would have been a great spot for one of the coaches to say something about the wonderful season we had just had, and that winning or losing that game at that point didn't have anything paramount to do with what we had accomplished. And it wasn't there, and it really took something out of me, and one of the reasons I was feeling that way was because I had just played maybe the finest offensive game I had ever played in terms of producing. I caught four or five passes in that game, and they were either third-down plays or touchdown plays. And I blocked well, and all in all, our offense was coming through, and it was just a great game.

"I didn't express this to anyone, because it didn't seem as though the other guys felt that way. I wondered, 'Why was our Cotton Bowl locker room so damn dismal after that game?' It just did not make any sense at all. So I doubt very many guys were feeling the way I was. If more guys felt that way, it probably would have had a way of manifesting itself, a way of lifting the doldrums of that place.

"And in the papers, Landry *wasn't* praising us. He was saying, 'We blew it.' That's when I began to question something that I had never questioned before. It was, 'Maybe I don't know what this guy sees. Maybe I don't see what he sees.' How could this be the feeling, especially at the end of this fine season? My God.

"I don't know, Tom might have seen his faux pas for leaving Hayes in for me on that key play. He might have been feeling so responsible that he couldn't bring himself to say what he might have otherwise said to his team after such a great season. 'Cause it did not make sense, did not click that we should feel the way we were feeling after such an outstanding season.

"It was so weird. 'Tom, what's missing here?' Something is missing. And we looked to him. I know I did. I thought about it. But after that experience I knew I was playing one game at a time. I knew that I wasn't going to be there, and even if I was there, I wasn't going to be there, because I didn't know what it was going to take. I got a sense of it, what it took to be on an NFL team, on a Landry team, as close to the brink of champion as we were. And I saw I didn't fit in there."

26

Lance on the Flank

PETE GENT: "In '65 we had been sitting in a meeting at our old practice field, the first one of the regular season. It was raining, a miserable day, and Al Ward, the assistant general manager, a really nice guy, came in and announced, 'We have word that Lyndon Johnson has plans to accelerate the war in Vietnam, and the draft lists are going to go way up. So any of you guys aren't in a reserve unit, get in one.'

"Ward said that football was no longer going to be a safe haven and that they were holding guard unit spots for everybody. And this was before anybody had seen a word in public print.

"John Hannah, the president of Michigan State, was a friend of mine, and so my first year with the Cowboys the college carried me as a student, so I still had a 2-S deferment. Even though I was living in Texas. The draft board I was under was twelve hundred miles away in Paw Paw, Michigan, and their high school was in the same conference as my high school, and they hated me and my brothers. We always kicked their ass. So it wasn't long before they found out I was in Texas playing football and the next year, '66, I didn't get away with a 2-S deferment, so on Al Ward's instructions, I decided I better get into a guard unit.

"My board in Michigan waited six months and then called me up for a physical, which I failed, and they did that every six months from 1965 to the spring of 1967. So I had taken four physicals down there, flunked them all, and by May of '67 the trip to the mailbox had become a literal nightmare. Finally one day, I walked to the box, and I saw another letter from Selective Service, and I thought, 'Aw fuck,' another physical, another trip through that nightmare. But instead, it was a letter telling me I had been inducted, that I had to report to Fort Wayne on July 13, which was two days before training camp was to start.

"In February, I was desperate. I couldn't get any help. No one would help me. I didn't know what to do. So I went to the Cowboys and I said, 'You have to help me.' Tex Schramm said, 'Don't worry, we'll help you.' And immediately Tex traded for Lance Rentzel.

"I imagine the Rentzel trade was already in the works, but it sure was strange. 'Yeah, we'll help ya.' "

Gent had reason to be worried. The weekly casualty rate for American servicemen in Vietnam was reaching an alarming level. In April of 1967, heavyweight champion Muhammad Ali, formerly Cassius Clay, refused to go based on religious grounds, and he was stripped of his title. Officially, we were winning the war. Said General Westmoreland, "We are winning slowly but steadily." No one who faced induction cared much whether we were winning or not.

Pete Gent got his deferment only after fate intervened. He became drinking buddies with a lawyer who represented the Buick dealership that sponsored his five-minute weekly radio show. The lawyer, who had fought in World Wars I and II, was a retired inspector general, and he wrote letters appealing Gent's draft status to every Democratic representative from Texas. In July of 1966, two days before Gent was to begin down the path leading to Vietnam, Texas senator Lloyd Bentsen stopped his induction and got Lewis Hershey, the head of the Selective Service, to order a medical deferment for Gent and to write him an apology. (About that time Gent's brother was also inducted, but he never served because on the way to the induction the Detroit riots forced police to turn back their bus. Their papers got lost in the bureaucracy, and none of the people on the bus were ever called.)

Gent's body may have been saved from shrapnel wounds, but his days with the Cowboys appeared numbered with the arrival of Lance Rentzel in '67. In Rentzel the Cowboys were getting a talented kick and punt return specialist who had the speed to become an excellent receiver. Rentzel had suffered in Minnesota from not getting along with Minnesota

Viking coach Norm Van Brocklin. Like Gent, Rentzel was an odd mix of intelligence and jockness. His mom had wanted him to go to Princeton, but Rentzel instead went to Bud Wilkinson's football factory at the University of Oklahoma, where he played with one of the most famous football crazies in American sports, the uncontrollable Joe Don Looney. Also on that Sooner team was Cowboy tackle Ralph Neely, who himself gained notoriety for signing contracts with two pro teams while in school.

As a sophomore Rentzel was told by Bud Wilkinson that there wasn't enough room for him on the flight to Dallas and if he wanted to suit up for the Texas game he would have to drive. Against Texas he caught his first two passes, one for 38 yards, and on the next play for 47 yards and a touchdown.

His junior year he started at halfback. That year he returned a punt 72 yards for a touchdown. The day after President Kennedy was killed he fumbled four times, and OU lost to Nebraska, 29–20, costing the team the national championship.

During the off-season Rentzel took steroids to gain weight, and when he returned as a senior he weighed 215. Against Maryland, he caught a pass and ran 90 yards. In ten weeks, he became famous as a college star. There was a league war, and so the NFL held a secret draft. Rentzel was a second-round draft choice of the Vikings. He was also drafted by the Buffalo Bills, and because they didn't want to lose him to the Bills, the Vikings signed him *before* the bowl game.

When Ralph Neely was caught signing early, they asked Rentzel if he had signed, too. He said he had, and OU cancelled his scholarship and kicked him off the team. Rentzel ripped up the Viking contract. Coach Norm Van Brocklin talked him out of it. They had him sign another one.

Rentzel's attraction toward the opposite sex brought him his share of negative publicity. Before the Senior Bowl in Mobile, Rentzel was attacked in the bed of a beautiful German Fräulein by her pissed-off boyfriend. The police had to be called.

Rentzel played two years as a Viking, playing mostly on special teams, running back punts and kickoffs. On May 2, 1967, the Vikings traded Rentzel to the Cowboys. No mention was made of his prior problems in any of the articles in the Dallas papers.

PETE GENT: "When Lance came to camp in '67, he was there to take my job. I knew that. And by this time I had enough experience, had seen all the tricks you could play on a guy. I had seen that if you can't beat a guy on the field, you fuck with his head. Already the rumors were around about him. So I figured I would take his head away from him. We'd get out on the field, and we'd start running pass routes, and I just wouldn't let him ever run when he wanted to.

"You'd line up and take turns, and I would always make him run with the second- or third- or fourth- and fifth-string quarterbacks so he couldn't get any timing with Meredith. I just pushed him out of the way and stepped in front of him. I was just dominating him. And he was a real sweet kid.

"He was already having problems, because guys like Lee Roy Jordan knew all about Minnesota, so they were already calling him a 'fag,' which he wasn't. That wasn't his problem.

"And so even when he was playing for Minnesota, everybody *knew* he was an exhibitionist. Van Brocklin, the Vikings coach, would call him a 'flasher' in team meetings. So that was an open secret when he came to the Cowboys, although nobody talked about it. He and Ralph Neely had played together in college at Oklahoma, and Ralph knew, but everybody went into denial except guys like Lee Roy, who were so cruel to him. Lee Roy thought being an exhibitionist was the same thing as being a fag and a child molester, and treated him accordingly, so there was all that pressure on Lance, plus the pressure to perform, which comes with playing the game.

"And here I was, just fucking with him, just playing with his head. He was a big, tough, muscular kid. He didn't take any shit. And maybe he couldn't have kicked my ass, but he would have hurt me.

"One day when I tried to do it he turned to me with the saddest eyes, and they just welled up with tears, and he said, 'Why are you so mean to me? I didn't do anything to you.' And I stepped back and I thought, 'My God, I'm doing the very thing that I resent guys like Lee Roy Jordan doing. Look what I have become.' And after that, we became friends."

When Rentzel came to the Cowboys, he became the regular flanker and Gent became a backup, which only made the outspoken Gent more biting and sarcastic in his jibes at Landry and what he perceived to be the coach's humorless approach to what he felt should have been a fun game.

One time after Bob Hayes was injured during a game in Pittsburgh, on the return flight Landry decided he'd move Gent from flanker to the other side, split end, where he'd start against Philadelphia in Hayes's spot. Landry walked to the back of the plane and told Gent.

Said Landry, "Pete, you'll be moving to the other side this week. So get ready."

"You mean, Coach, that I'm going to play for Philadelphia?"
Landry inhaled deeply and walked back up the aisle.

In the second preseason game Don Meredith cracked two ribs, and against San Francisco, Craig Morton came in and won the game. Morton played outstandingly the rest of the preseason. Instantly there rang a chorus that Morton should be the number one quarterback.

FRANK CLARKE: "Don got hurt, cracked two ribs in the second preseason game, so then Craig Morton came in and won, and immediately the fans started calling for Morton to be the quarterback. I don't know why. What did those people want from Don? When you hear about some of the things that go on in our great Southwest . . . The fans were saying they wanted him traded, and don't you know, Don was deeply hurt.

"Dandy used to come over to our house. He loved our kids, and our kids adored him. He was so wonderful. And my wife loved him a lot. His sensitivity was as clear as the nose on my face, and if you've looked at any photographs, I got this nice schnozzle, it's nice and round and obvious, and I can just remember how much that hurt him. And hurt us, too. Those of us who knew and loved him, we felt Don's hurt. We were as much a part of it as he was. No separation. If they were hurting him, they were hurting us. We all felt it. And that was terrible.

"That gave us an idea of what we were up against, what it takes to be involved in this game, and to be committed to it, and not only to be committed to it to play, but to be committed to it to be part of a guy who wants *nothing else* out of it but to win, who won't settle for anything less than a Super Bowl championship. And it became very obvious that's what Tom Landry was all about."

In addition to fans calling for Meredith's benching, trade rumors persisted. Gent blamed Tom Landry for allowing them to spread.

PETE GENT: "In '67, in the preseason, there were all these trade rumors, which I never believed, because Clint Murchison never would trade Don, he was too close to him, but there was a strong call from the fans to trade him. And again, this all came from Tom Landry. A lot of it was a result of Landry's inability to control Meredith.

"Landry wanted to control Meredith, and when he couldn't, whenever anything went wrong, Tom allowed the blame to fall on Meredith, rather than ever shouldering it himself.

"Tom *never* could stand Don's independence. He was looking for a quarterback who would do absolutely everything he said, so Tom could run it. It was like being the lead pilot in the bomber group. Everybody followed him. And he just assumed that that's the way you carried it out on the football field. The problem was, the best information you get is in the huddle. It doesn't matter what your game plan says, if your left tackle has a bad ankle, and he can't control the guy over him, it doesn't matter how well you've planned if he can't move that guy, and he's going to tell you that in the huddle. Or for some reason if they are playing a different defense than what you've expected all week, the first guys to find that out are the guys on the field. You can't make those adjustments on the sidelines until halftime, when the coaches get down from the press box and go over their stats, and say, 'They are not doing what we expected.' And all the guys in the huddle go, 'Big fucking surprise. We knew that from the first play.'

"Meredith was so complex. There were so many nooks and crannies in Meredith's personality. We spent a lot of time together over the period of '65, '66, and '67. I'll tell you exactly what happened to us in '67. We began to decline. Our production went down, and we ended up with a 9–5 season, though still got to the Ice Bowl.

"Two things happened in '67. After a USO tour to Vietnam, about five in the morning Don came right from the airport to my house, which was only two blocks away. He sat on the bed and we were smoking dope, and he said, 'You know, I've been thinking. I think Tom may be right.' He said he had been thinking and he decided he was going to cooperate with Landry. Don was even going to let Tom call the plays.

"The moment Don said that, I said, 'Uh-uh. If you do that, you're dead. Because he's going to see that as a weakness. And once he sees that he's got you, you're fucked. He'll continue to lay the blame at your feet like he did in '65, and early '66, and you're going to be right back where you were in '65.'

"I can't tell how much of my judgment was also colored by the fact that I knew if Meredith did that, I was dead. Part of the way I played totally depended on Meredith being at quarterback. I argued and argued, because I knew, 'Here's trouble for me.' I really was arguing from a selfish viewpoint. But also, I really believed in Don. Because the ability to control stars is a great talent, and Meredith had that. And to see him suddenly give that up so easily, to try to go along to get along, I said, 'Don, remember what you went through to get this. You don't just give this up. He won't respect that. Why would you allow yourself to be in his hip pocket? That's what he wants.'

"But Don gave in to Tom, and the season showed it.

"And the second thing that happened, we got to training camp, and Landry started talking about 'better production out of the flanker.' And I knew I was screwed. But the thing was, to get better production out of the flanker, he changed what had worked for us so brilliantly, which was to get the ball to Bob Hayes. Bob Hayes had been the top receiver for two years. This was another issue over which I argued with Landry. I remember the arguments. We got to camp, and Lance Rentzel was there as a wide receiver, and he was playing flanker with me, and Tom said, 'Our job this year is to get more production out of the flanker.' I had caught 35 passes for 3 or 4 touchdowns. But catching touchdowns wasn't my job. That was Bob Hayes's job. He had caught 14 touchdowns. My job was third downs. Of the 35 passes to me, 31 were on third down. But Landry looked at his numbers, and in my mind, it was, 'Tom has finally figured out a way that the numbers don't come out too good for me. And so now we're going to interpret these numbers into: Gent had a bad season.' And there was no doubt Lance Rentzel was a great athlete. I was doomed when he got there. It didn't help that I had busted my back early in the '67 season against the Giants, but I could see him coming. I could feel him breathing down my neck. The problem with Lance was, for every five great plays he would make, he would make one catastrophic mistake that would cost you the game. So I felt my role was to catch third-down passes, and that Lance and I ultimately would be splitting time, 'cause Tom had to be careful how he used Lance, unless Landry just absolutely hated me.

"Under Landry's new system, you still had the options, still had to change your routes, but Meredith was under strict orders that whenever they went into a roll zone against Hayes, he was automatically to come to the strong side. No questions asked. You just immediately came off of Hayes.

"Landry brought to the defense the theory that everyone has to work as a coordinated team, and when he coached the Giants' defense he made Sam Huff famous, not because Sam Huff was such a great linebacker in the same way Ray Nitschke or Joe Schmidt were, but Landry's defense was designed so that you never got to the middle linebacker. He was the guy who made all the tackles. Your linemen were supposed to take one step, control the area, and then the middle linebacker was to fill, and he was always there to make the tackle. My rookie year I played some middle linebacker and was just stunned at how much easier it was to play middle linebacker than to play cornerback. It was much less violent. At cornerback, you got killed. Jesus. But middle linebacker, all you had to do was keep your calls clear and watch where the holes opened up. So that was the mentality he took from defense, and then he moved it over to offense, and he thought the same thing would work in offense. But he was making the assumption that the defense was going to do what his defense did, and the defenses we came up against didn't always do that. And so when you coach offense from a defensive standpoint, which particularly showed in '67, he had literally outcoached himself.

"Well, I was the first one to say, 'Wait a minute. If you don't throw to Hayes any time he's double-covered, that means the coverage works.' And I spoke up because I knew it was my job on the line. They weren't going to throw 65 balls to me. My job was third downs. I was fast for 30 yards, and then my stride broke, 'cause I was used to running on a basketball floor.

"In '67, Bob Hayes was not the same player and by mid-season the defense knew what we were doing. The defense would just *show* double coverage. Because these other guys aren't dumb. You show them three game films and Hayes *never* gets the ball into double coverage—'Well, then, we'll just give them the double coverage look, and after the quarterback turns, we'll slide the free safety back into the middle.' And suddenly what looked like an open post route to the flanker, you have two men to beat now.

"In '67 this totally destroyed Hayes's output. And the input went to the other side, which was the flanker, Rentzel and I, but mostly Rentzel. I think Rentzel set a game record for receptions, but if you take the number of touchdown catches he made and factor in how many touchdowns he scored, the output—give those same number of catches to Hayes, and you get three times more touchdowns.

"Hayes had forced the changing of defense in the NFL. They literally had to design defenses to try to stop him. Landry always thought from a defensive standpoint, so he finally thought someone was going to outsmart his offense, and what he did was think, 'I'm going to be a jump ahead of them, and outsmart them,' but what he basically did was immediately any time they double-teamed Hayes, the double team would work, because he gave up trying to get the ball to Hayes.

"Meredith could put that ball in there when he was on. And Hayes could catch in a crowd. He was not afraid. I've seen him lots of time catch the ball with two or three guys around him, and after he caught the ball, none of them ever touched him. And he would turn a 5-yard catch into a

65-yard touchdown. If you threw to the other side, that never happened. Rentzel would make 12 to 18 yards, I would make 10 or 15. We weren't going to go 60, 70 yards for a touchdown like Bob did.

"The arguments lasted most of training camp. Hayes was furious, and Meredith was angry, because it took away some of his freedom back at quarterback. 'If you don't do as I say . . .' It meant Landry was going to be pissed at what his choices were.

"Part of it goes back to the brilliance of Landry's system. You have all these adjustments. Well, give Hayes an adjustment. He had an adjustment he was supposed to do on double coverage anyway. You could still get the ball to him. He just curled in on double coverage. But despite that, Landry decided that automatically, when he was double-covered, automatically you don't go to Hayes. If you look at his statistics, they plummeted.

"Meredith would still try to get the ball to him, but as the season went on, Hayes just got more and more upset, and of course, when Hayes wasn't getting the ball and Hayes wasn't breaking for touchdowns, suddenly we weren't the team we were in '66. Landry wasn't going to tell the press: 'Well, I changed the offense.' He said, 'poor execution,' or 'We're not getting the kind of play out of the quarterback we want.' The guy was as disingenuous as you wanted to get. I guess that's what made me so angry about him. One side of him I really respected, and then there was this other side that was just so dishonest, and so disingenuous that it made me furious. Most of it seemed to fall on Don Meredith, and I liked Meredith, and what fell on me—a lot I drew on myself, but I also felt it was my job to protect my quarterback, even if I had to protect him from the coach."

It was to be a year in which Meredith would need a lot of protection—from his coach, the Dallas fans, and from defensive behemoths intent on breaking his bones. His agony began in the very first exhibition game against Green Bay at home when he was booed during the introductions. In the next game Ernie Ladd of the Houston Oilers grabbed him with 41 seconds to go in the game and KOed him with a body slam and broke his nose. Against San Francisco his ribs hurt, and they were reinjured against Baltimore in the second quarter of the final exhibition game. Meredith escaped further damage in the season opener in a big win against the Cleveland Browns, and he was relatively unscathed against the New York Giants, though Pete Gent was seriously injured when middle linebacker Vince Costello kneed him hard in the back, cracking several ribs. After a loss to the Rams, Meredith led the Cowboys to a stirring win over the Washington Redskins when he completed a 36-yard touchdown pass to

Dan Reeves with only ten seconds left in the game. A few plays earlier Redskin linebacker Chris Hanburger had broken Meredith in half when he crashed through and mashed the Cowboy quarterback into the ground.

After the game a reporter asked Landry why he hadn't noticed that Meredith was woozy and why he hadn't taken him out of the game. Standing near his quarterback, Landry said sarcastically, "Well, I can't tell the difference."

On Sunday and Monday night Meredith had trouble sleeping. On Tuesday he went to the Presbyterian Hospital in Dallas, where doctors found fluid in his lungs. As a result of Hanburger's hit, Meredith had suffered a partially collapsed lung. He lost twenty pounds and would miss the next three games.

PETE GENT: "If you look at the clips of that Washington game, Meredith was getting hit by two and three guys all the time. He was getting sandwiched between two defensive linemen continually—somebody had to help him to his feet after each play—and when in that last drive he punctured a lung, he still got up.

"On fourth down, Meredith hit Dan Reeves down the sidelines, and Dan ran in for the winning touchdown with 10 seconds left in the game.

"Two days later Don was in the hospital, having his lung pumped up. I snuck into the hospital, had to sneak by the desk, and got to see him. They were pumping his lung back up, and he was just in agony, crying. After they finished, we talked for about five or ten minutes, and then I went to the practice field.

"When you got to the practice field, the first thing you did was get dressed and taped, and then you went to the team meeting. You have a general meeting, and then you break up into groups. Before looking at the films, Landry would make general statements, comments, and at this meeting he never said anything about Meredith being in the hospital with a punctured lung. And then during the films he tore Don apart.

"For me that was the last fucking straw with that guy. I wanted out of there. I knew I was only going to play if they needed me, and the minute they didn't need me, I was gone. And I knew that it didn't matter how well I did. I could call Tom an asshole to his face, and he wasn't going to trade me until he had somebody to play my spot, and the moment he had somebody to play my spot, I was gone. And so from then on, that was my attitude toward Tom Landry, and the rest of the organization going all the way up to Tex Schramm."

27

Agony

With Don Meredith out with a collapsed lung, quarterback Craig Morton filled in and showed skill, winning games against the New Orleans Saints and the Pittsburgh Steelers before losing to the Philadelphia Eagles. Meredith announced he would return against the Atlanta Falcons, promising the offense would score 35 points against the second-year team; the final score was 37–7. Meredith hit running back Dan Reeves six times for 114 yards and two touchdowns. In that game Reeves, playing in his third year, scored four times, a club record. With Tom Landry's new strategy at work, only one pass went to a wide receiver all game long; Bob Hayes caught it for 34 yards.

At the end of the game Meredith told reporters, "Don't let this get around, but we are going to win the whole thing."

In the next game Meredith led the Cowboys to a 27–10 win over the New Orleans Saints before 83,437 unruly drunks and drunkettes in the Sugar Bowl. The highlight of the game was a 56-yard touchdown run on a reverse by Frank Clarke, who most of the season was playing part-time, coming in at tight end in short-yardage situations to take advantage of his superior blocking. This scintillating run indirectly led to Clarke's decision to retire at the end of the season.

FRANK CLARKE: "I had a good game against the Saints. On an end around Dandy gave this great reverse to me, and I went untouched, unscathed, at scalded-dog speed, 56 yards for a touchdown, and that was enough for our victory. That came at a good time, too, because we were losing to an upstart team that we should have beaten easily.

"After the game we went back to Dallas, and on Monday the television reporter, Vern Lundquist, called me and said, 'Meet me downtown. I want to do an interview with you.' I said, 'Sure.' So we were talking about the game and my career, now in its eleventh year, and he asked me, 'Frank, do you think you might play two or three more years?' And that sounded very reasonable. I wasn't slowing down. I said, 'No, Vern, it's possible that this could be my last season.' And then we went on to talk about other things.

"The next morning in the *Dallas Morning News*, the headline said, 'Frank Clarke Announces His Retirement from Pro Football.' I said to myself, 'Aw, you guys did it again. Aw, man.' So that was the way it came out.

"Neither Tom Landry nor Tex Schramm said anything to me, and I didn't say anything either, didn't go to Tex Schramm and say, 'Let's set the record straight.' I didn't tell them exactly what happened. I don't know why I didn't. One of the reasons I didn't, I guess, was fate, that I really *was* supposed to retire. That's the only answer I could have to why I didn't go to them at that time."

Meanwhile, throughout the season the battle raged between Tom Landry and Pete Gent, who never stopped trying to get his job back after Landry gave it to Lance Rentzel. The anarchistic Gent went so far as to put himself into ballgames behind the coach's back.

PETE GENT: "I figured he wouldn't notice. If I put myself in the game ten times, he would catch me four, and then he'd send the guy back in and glare at me when I came off. And that would be it.

"We had quite a thing going. I'm the only guy he would ever call into his office to tell me I was going on to the bench. He'd call me in the first of the week, have a long talk with me. We literally had meetings every week or so."

Gent was tough and he was persistent. It took a broken back suffered the third game of the season against the Giants to keep him out of the lineup, and even then it was not for long.

PETE GENT: "Against the Giants I caught a ball in the dirt over the middle. I didn't want to get up. I knew the moment I did, somebody was going to kill me. I had gotten the first-down yardage, so I just laid there. Well, Vince Costello, the Giant middle linebacker, rather than touch me, decided he would jump about six yards through the air and bury both knees into my lower back, and from the waist down I was paralyzed. I had no feeling. My left leg drew up, for some reason, was pulled up. My knee was up in the air and my foot was on the ground, and it was just dead. There was no feeling. I could not feel my leg. I couldn't lift it or get it to straighten out. And my right leg was just burning like fire, and then on the left side I had absolutely no feeling. And the trainers and team doctor came out, and I said, 'I've broken my back.' And they said, 'No, no, you haven't.' I said, 'I *have* broken my back. I can't feel anything in my left leg. I can't move it.' They said, 'Move your left leg.' I said, 'I can't move my leg. It doesn't move. I've tried.' 'Move your leg.' 'I can't do it.' So they just lifted me up by the shoulders and dragged me off the field at the 18-yard line and laid me facedown on the sideline and left me there. They went back to the bench.

"And this was in the first quarter. It took me until halftime to get to the bench, about 20 yards. I crawled back to the bench, and I said, 'I have to go in. I'm hurting.' I was on my feet, but I hurt so bad I couldn't stand. I kept falling. So I got up and I was almost to the tunnel when halftime broke, so when the team ran over, a couple guys helped me into the locker room, where they laid me down on the training table and then called an ambulance, took me to the hospital, X-rayed my back, and I had fractured vertebrae in the lumbar region of the spine.

"The doctors didn't give a shit. They literally did not care. It was a bad injury. What the Cowboys wanted to do was waive me through, but the Falcons and the Giants kept trying to pick me up, so they had to put me on injured reserve, kept me out thirty days, but I was back out trying to run the next week. And it hurt so bad. And what I didn't realize was that I had truly paralyzed some muscles. I had lost muscles from the mid-lumbar down to my hip, and to this day I have no feeling there, and so to run, I had to learn to throw my left leg. I couldn't run in the normal fashion. I had to throw the leg, and that's how I learned to run, and so I was really ready to play by playoff time. I was running at a pretty good rate again, and I was taking a lot of painkillers.

"They tried to play me the next week, shot my back full of novocaine, and I got halfway through the warm-ups against the Rams, and so then they put me on injured reserve, and then against the Cleveland

Browns in the conference championship playoff game I got in for one play and I broke my leg.

"Tom put me in for Hayes for one play. One play! I was to crack back, and we were going to run to the weak side, so I was in for Hayes, who had just run a fly route and wanted out. So he signaled me, and since I was in, we decided to run a quick pitch to Walt Garrison to the weak side, and I was to crack back on whoever showed up first. It was the cornerback. While I was blocking him, the safety went at Garrison, and my recollection is that Garrison spun him off and swung him around, and he hit me right above the ankle with the heel of the shoe. Well, I thought I had just been kicked, so I pushed off that leg to keep blocking, and my foot turned around backward. And I went down and I looked at it, and at first I thought I just knocked my shoe off. And then I looked at my foot, and uh uh, I'll never forget it, the official came by, and I grabbed him by the pant leg and I pointed down to my foot, and I said, 'I've broken my leg,' and he said, 'Well, do you want to call a timeout?' And I looked at him for a minute, and I said, 'I can't. I'm not the captain.' He said, 'Oh, okay,' and walked away. And I laid there for what seemed like an hour. It hadn't hurt yet, but I knew it was coming. And finally, Craig Morton, who was standing over me, called timeout.

"I was in a hip-length cast for thirteen weeks after that. I can remember looking down, remembering my shoe had been knocked off, because it was backward at such an odd position, and then I saw my foot was in it! My ankle was so messed up I had to be in a hip-length cast. They had to operate that night, put two screws in it. All the ligaments were torn out."

Gent was through for '67; his friend Don Meredith, meanwhile, had continued to suffer from one injury after another. In a win against Philadelphia in the second-to-last game of the season, Don broke his nose, and just before halftime in the finale in a loss to the San Francisco 49ers, linebacker Stan Hindman threw him to the ground with an armhold with such brute force that he lay on the ground holding his left knee, writhing in pain. Meredith did not return the rest of the contest and there was concern he would not be able to perform in the playoffs.

Finishing at 9–5, the Cowboys had won their division the second year in a row, but this year they would have to defeat *two* teams to reach the NFL finals. Because of the merger with the AFL and expansion there were now four divisions, and the first opponent was the champion of the new Century Division, the Cleveland Browns, led by Frank Ryan, Paul

Warfield, and Co. Only four days before the game the Cowboys grieved for Bob Lilly after his seven-week-old daughter, Carmen, died suddenly in her crib.

BOB LILLY: "That was so sad. I'm the one who found my daughter. She was already . . . Earlier in the morning I had heard her. It was pretty early when I went up, around seven. I assumed everything was fine. We had all our kids upstairs. There were three others. Anyway, she had already turned blue and was starting to get kind of hard. I screamed, and that's when my wife went up, and she screamed. It was sad; it was tough. Then we had to do the funeral and get ready to play, and it was very difficult.

"My teammates were very supportive. We had a big funeral. Everybody was there from the Cowboys. Then they did an autopsy, and it was really terrible. It was crib death. Her lungs had filled up. It was one of those deals.

"Practicing was my only way of getting relief, and I wouldn't have missed that game for anything. But it was very sad. It was one of those times. It ended up helping to destroy my marriage. I married again a couple of years later. It just happened, one of the things in life that happens. It's like the Kennedy weekend. It's hard to remember. I just went out there against Cleveland and played as hard as I could."

The Cleveland playoff game was a crowning achievement for both Bob Lilly—who had one of his greatest days, sacking Frank Ryan three times and batting down two passes—and for Don Meredith, who discarded his specially made face protector, wrapped his aching knees, and played an almost flawless ballgame, going 10 for 12 for 212 yards and two touchdowns, including an 86-yarder to Bob Hayes. The Cowboys won this Big One, 52–14, in front of 70,786 screaming Texans in the Cotton Bowl. Before he left the field, Meredith shook hands with each of his offensive linemen.

On defense the line of Willie Townes, Jethro Pugh, Bob Lilly, and George Andrie stopped Leroy Kelly and the Browns running game. Defensive back Cornell Green stymied Browns star receiver Gary Collins and ran an interception back 60 yards for a touchdown.

CORNELL GREEN: "In '67 we played the Browns in the first round of the playoffs, and Don Meredith had one hell of a game. We weren't on the field a lot. The defense was very seldom on the field. I remember every time Meredith got the ball, he would walk them right down the field and score. And then you'd get a punt, and here he comes again, walking them right down the field.

"The offense makes it easier for the defense. If you have your offense putting points on people, that determines what they can do to you. If we *know* they have to pass to catch us, it makes it easier playing defense. In other words, a strong offense makes our job easier because as long as our offense is holding the ball, the other team can't get on the field to score against us. And that's exactly what happened that day."

The Cowboys for a second year in a row were one game from playing in a Super Bowl. To get there they would once again have to defeat Vince Lombardi's Green Bay Packers.

JOHN WILBUR: "Vince Lombardi was a monkey on Tom Landry's back. He had been an old teammate on the New York Giants. I expect if you look deeply into his history, you'll find that Lombardi was always the monkey on Landry's back. Lombardi wanted the players to do what he wanted them to do, to depend on him, and at the right time come together, and history shows they did. And in the end Landry didn't. Landry never did conquer Lombardi's world. Lombardi always outsmarted him."

CHUCK HOWLEY: "Vince Lombardi was one of the great coaches of all time. I admired the man, the way he coached. I believed in the philosophy that if you do something wrong, you get your butt chewed up. And Lombardi really showed us all throughout his coaching career that this was the type of coach he was. He got right in the middle of you, and you didn't want any part of it.

"Tom wasn't that way. Tom was very quiet in the early years. He believed, and eventually he got us to believe, in his system. But in his own way, you knew when you did something wrong. So Vince had his way, and Tom had his way. I felt Tom was his equal, but if I had the choice of the two, I would much rather know where I stand and have my butt chewed royally by a Lombardi than get a look from Landry."

28

The Ice Bowl

This game, played in frozen Wisconsin on the coldest December 31 in Green Bay history, would forever be known to those who played in it as the Ice Bowl.

FRANK CLARKE: "We arrived in Green Bay on Saturday. We landed in Appleton, Wisconsin. It was a wonderful day. Practice was great, the sun was shining, it was beautiful, 35 degrees, the field was fine. God, we were *high*. We just *knew* we were going to play well. When we met the Packers the year before, we *thought* we could win. This time we *knew* we were going to win that game. No doubt whatsoever. We didn't have an ounce of doubt that we were going to play well and win.

"But in that part of Wisconsin in December, anything can happen. It could snow. It could be zero degrees for days. Sunday morning, the day of the game, the operator called us. We got that wake-up call, just so we'd be in rhythm. I still remember answering the phone. The operator said, 'Good morning, boys. It's seven-thirty in the morning. It's thirteen degrees below zero.'

"I said, 'I beg your pardon. Thirteen degrees *below zero*?' Ow, God. We weren't prepared for that, so it was demoralizing. I just was not ready for that. It was almost like, 'Are the heavens against us again? What is this? How could this be to go from such a fantastic day?'

"In just a few hours the field was totally frozen, and not only that, the winds were due to pick up. So we not only had very cold weather, but added cold with the wind blowing. It was so bad people risked really getting hurt playing in that kind of weather. But there was no way the game was going to be postponed, absolutely none, so consequently the game went on."

BOB LILLY: "Everyone says there are some things in your life you never forget, and one was when our president was shot, and another was the Ice Bowl. I may have forgotten a lot of other things, but I will never forget the Ice Bowl.

"Lombardi had installed a system of pipes underneath the ground that were warmed by water going through them, and the day before the game we went to the stadium to work out. The field *was* in good shape, though just a little bit damp. You could wear real cleats. The turf was pretty good, and temperature was nice, the wind wasn't blowing, just a pretty day, and when we warmed up we didn't even feel the cold at all so we were all happy.

"We all knew a cold front was coming, but it wasn't supposed to get there until after the game, sometime the next night. So we weren't concerned about that.

"We had our meetings. We were in great spirits. We were finally relatively healthy. The Packers were beat up pretty bad. We hadn't had a great year, but we had become better and better as the year went on.

"The next morning George Andrie, my roommate, got up, and went to Mass at about six-thirty or seven, and he came back about seven-thirty. I was up, watching TV. He came in and didn't say a word. We were in a Holiday Inn. He got a glass of water, and threw the water on the plate-glass window. Half the water froze before it got down to the windowsill. He said, 'Bob, it's cold. It's already ten below, and there's about a 35-mile-an-hour wind out. It's supposed to be twenty below by game time.'

"We were pretty somber at breakfast. We went on out to the field, got dressed, and as we were going to go out and warm up, he said, 'You and I are going to have to be leaders out there today. I grew up in this weather,' and he talked me into not wearing any longhandles or any warm-up jacket, because we were going to show these guys that it wasn't that bad.

"And so I walked out that door, and when I did, I said to myself, 'You fool, you fool.' I looked at George, and I said, 'Don't ever ask me to do anything like this again.' I like froze to death. I had icicles hanging out my nose about four inches. And I was absolutely freezing. I just barely got through warm-ups.

"We went back into the locker room, and I put on everything I had. I got my longhandles out, put Saran Wrap on my feet, put an extra pair of socks on. Ernie Stautner wouldn't let us wear gloves. Ernie said, 'Men don't wear gloves in this league.' We went back out and every guy on Green Bay had gloves on, and as a result we all got frostbite. I didn't get much, but we all got frostbite. And we about froze to death.

"I remember the first play vividly. The referee blew his whistle, and it froze on his lip. He pulled part of his lip off, and the blood froze down his chin. After that, they wore Vaseline.

"That was the beginning of the game, and as it went on the conditions got worse. The field wasn't totally frozen when we started, but by the first quarter I had already taken my cleats off and put on my soccer shoes. We were starting to slide around. I was really having a field day then because Gale Gillingham had on his cleats, and he was trying to figure out what was going on, because I was getting around him so fast. So he put on his soccer shoes, and by the time the end of the game came, we were on a solid sheet of ice, all the way from the 20-yard line in."

LEE ROY JORDAN: "In my mind we were a better football team than Green Bay that day. We were a pretty darn good football team at that time but the conditions eliminated a lot of our offense. We were a speed team. We depended on Bob Hayes and Lance Rentzel, and to win those guys had to make big plays, and I don't know if Bob caught a pass all day. He had his hands down his shorts trying to keep them warm, and hell, it *was* cold. I went out there at the start of the game to show them how to be tough. In warm-ups and the first series I didn't wear any gloves, because Ernie Stautner wouldn't let the linemen wear gloves, and I was one of the leaders on defense, and I wasn't supposed to do anything to show the guys I was a pansy. But about the second series I went to the equipment manager, and I said, 'Where are the gloves? I don't care what it shows. I want a pair. I'll be a pansy if you want me to. I got to have some gloves. My hands are killing me!' "

FRANK CLARKE: "Midway through the second quarter, a few minutes before the end of the half, I was lined up in my tight end spot, and I ran down this frozen field—you can't imagine what it's like to play on concrete in cleats—so many of the things you did well and easily were totally negated. Hell, you were just trying to stand up, just trying to stay on your feet, let alone throw a block or make a catch.

"I ran a play where I threw a block at a safetyman, Tom Brown or Willie Wood, and I was walking back to the huddle, and I got about two feet away from Ray Nitschke, and he turned, and he started screaming at me, 'Get away from me, you *son of a bitch. I'll break your fucking neck.*' And I looked and he had white froth in the corners of his mouth, and I could see this glare through his face mask. It was like Nitschke was going to literally rip me apart merely because I was so close to him.

"Willie Davis came over, and he put both his hands on my shoulders, and he turned me away from Ray, and he said, 'Don't worry about it, man. Just go on back to the huddle.' This was Willie Davis, his own teammate.

"I thought, 'What in the world is with this guy? He is really strange.' I had never heard about Nitschke doing this. I had played against him before. But there was something about him that day. Man, he was weird."

The Packers led at the half 14–10 on two Bart Starr touchdowns to their little-noticed big play man, Boyd Dowler. The Cowboys scored on a fumble recovery and seven-yard run by George Andrie and a Danny Villanueva field goal, as the conditions stifled the Dallas passing offense. Bob Hayes spent much of the game with his frozen hands buried deep in his pants.

PETE GENT: "Had I not been injured, the Ice Bowl is one game I would have played, because I knew Bob Hayes couldn't play in that cold. The nature of his hands were that he had no moisture in them. His hands were extremely dry, and that cold just split his hands open. A lot of the guys got frostbite real bad, and it still bothers them to this day."

Of the receivers only Lance Rentzel was effective, and when in the fourth quarter he caught a 50-yard bomb from halfback Dan Reeves over a slipping and sliding Packer defense, the Cowboys took a 17–14 lead.

FRANK CLARKE: "We played admirably, under those conditions and meeting the challenge as we did, leading in the game up until the end like that.

"I remember catching a couple of passes in the game, but basically what I liked was the way our offense did keep moving. We didn't just fall flat under those conditions. Most people thought that because of the weather the Packers had the advantage, but we knew that was bullshit, because *nobody* had any advantage. The Packers didn't practice in that kind of weather. It wasn't as though they were used to it. In fact, they probably had as many guys as we did from the South, and there is no way they could be used to that. They never played in it before.

"I can't begin to tell you how cold it was. There was *nothing* warm about me. Nothing. Our hands couldn't get warm. They had these hot air blowers that seemed to blow hot air on you but you had to be standing right in front to get any sense of beginning to warm up, and the second you stepped away from it, you were cold again."

With the Cowboys ahead 17–14, the Packers took over on their own 31-yard line with 4:50 left. The last ten times the Packers had the ball, the most they could advance was 14 yards. It appeared that there was no way Bart Starr could move the ball under such adverse conditions and that the Cowboys would fulfill their destiny and get into Super Bowl II.

JOHN WILBUR: "I was counting on my trip to the Super Bowl."

Pete Gent, doped up and in pain from his injuries, was watching the game on television in his hospital room.

PETE GENT: "I was lying on my hospital bed, watching the game on TV, because I was in a hip-line cast. Reeves had hit Rentzel with a touchdown pass, and I was so excited because I knew there was no way anybody could move the length of that field unless there was some major fuckup, some *huge* fuckup, and Landry made it.

"The Packers got the ball, 70 yards to go, 40 below zero, throwing into a 40-mile-an-hour wind, and what did Landry do? He went into a pre-vent defense! And all they did was throw under it and run. It was just nuts. As soon as that team came out, and I saw where those linebackers were playing, I just cried. All day long I was saving up my pain pills and my shots, and when I saw him put that defense in, I called the nurse and said, 'I'm going to need another shot.'

"*Again* Landry lost the game. He lost the '66 title game *and* the Ice Bowl. I mean, what coach puts his team in a prevent defense against the Green Bay Packers when it's forty below, they are throwing into a 40-mile-an-hour wind, and they have two minutes to score, and it's an ice rink? What team goes into a fucking prevent defense? They are not going to throw a post pattern on you. The worst thing in the world they can do is try to throw deep. They are going to try to throw under you. They are going to try to throw flares and screens. They are *not* going to throw deep. And Landry had his linebackers ten, fifteen yards deep.

"We still almost stopped them. Almost stopped them. But when I saw that defense, I just cried. They hit their backs out of the backfield underneath, and those poor linebackers were running on ice. As I watched, I literally cried. I knew we were lost. I knew we were fucking done."

The final drive was Packer quarterback Bart Starr at his best. He threw short passes under the coverage to backs Donny Anderson and Chuck Mercein, and he had a little help from the officials.

CORNELL GREEN: "They had some lucky plays, and then the ref made them a big call, pass interference on Dave Edwards. That was a big play, and I say that was the worst call I've seen in history. It was *really* a bad call. I was standing right by him. Bart Starr passed to Donny Anderson, and Donny Anderson had Dave beat, and Dave was running trying to catch him, and the ball hit Dave in the back of the helmet, hit him in the head, and the ref called pass interference, saying Dave face-guarded him, and Dave was just trying to catch him. Anderson was three yards ahead of Dave, and Bart Starr just threw a bad pass. And the referee called a penalty and gave them a first down. That would have been a *fourth* down. That was the game.

"I started yelling, complaining, and the ref told me, 'It was face-guarding.' You can call it anyway you want, but the only way you can face-guard, you have to put your hands up in the air and wave them. If the ball hits you in the back of the helmet, you're just running. That ain't no face-guarding. That was just a bad pass."

JOHN WILBUR: "It was tough watching that final drive. We got them to third down, and boom, they'd run a play and get a first down. It took them four or five minutes to get to the 11-yard line, and then they ran a sucker play, and Lilly had the right to go, and Andrie was supposed to cover up for him, but George didn't close down behind him. He stood there, and Chuck Mercein, led by Donny Anderson, got a long gain. It was a big play. Chuck Howley let him get open, missed a tackle, and then Andrie missed the hole on the sucker play, which is to take a sweep and run inside."

FRANK CLARKE: "I was watching a guy named Chuck Mercein be heroic. It was the only time I can remember being in a game when I felt pissed off. I thought, 'This is not right.' Our great linebackers, Chuck Howley, Dave Edwards, and Lee Roy Jordan—there were none better—went for Chuck Mercein to stop him at the line of scrimmage, just routine tackles, and Chuck Mercein, for heaven's sake, a guy who had been around, been with four or five different teams, all of a sudden he's making it look like he's the star of the NFL championship?

"Edwards and Howley would slip on the frozen field, and Mercein would make enough yardage to make a first down. This was the way they moved the ball down there. Remember how they got the ball down there? It was not great football. It was *lucky* football, which was what I hated, and what I was feeling pissed off about. I was thinking, 'The best team is not going to win this game, the luckiest team is.' For the first time in a game, I was feeling, 'God, this is not right. Who's against us?'

"As this was happening, I was sitting next to Danny Villanueva. He was sitting to my left in a shelterlike dugout, shielding some of the wind from us, but not much. We were all damn cold, and when the Packers were moving the ball I became aware of Danny—the only way I can describe it, this must be what a guy goes through in the process of having a nervous breakdown. He was going bananas. His legs were shaking up and down real fast, and he was saying things like, 'Hold 'em. We gotta hold 'em. We gotta hold 'em. We gotta hold 'em.' He was watching that game and viewing it from a place that was so foreign to me in terms of, 'Wow, is this what it takes? Is this the kind of attitude and approach to this game that Tom Landry wants?' That no matter how you play, it's not going to be good enough, that the only thing that matters is winning? 'Cause I'd never experienced a guy going through that kind of a reaction. It was really powerful. You couldn't help but notice it.

"And I said to myself, 'I'm not up for this, folks.' I felt as if I was too detached from this game, or from *any* game that I've ever been involved in, the game of husband, the game of father, the game of employee, or the game of college. I've always been too detached from it to get to this point where I think this stuff is *that* important."

CHUCK HOWLEY: "They were running but two plays on us, an option deal, and I remember vividly my frustration that if we defensed one, they hit the other. The offense had the advantage because as a linebacker I had to help my defensive halfback on a down-and-in pattern, which he couldn't cover when he had to cut. I'd get back to take away the down-and-in, and they'd throw a little circle pass, which was my responsibility. I wasn't able to get back as quick. And I was faced with having to make an open-field tackle, which I did about half the time, because on a frozen field, you have one shot, and it better be the right one.

"So it was a frustrating game for us, and for myself individually. We lost that game on a quarterback sneak, and that's what makes the game of football so great."

The Packers had the ball fourth down and six inches to go at the goal line. There were thirteen seconds left in the game. Green Bay had no timeouts. In their prior two plays, back Donny Anderson made plunges from the one, but each time was stopped by the dogged Dallas defense.

Bart Starr was at a loss what to do. If another running play failed, the game would be over. Nevertheless, Starr decided he would call his own number and run a quarterback sneak. He figured the defense would be keying on the backs. The play called for center Ken Bowman and guard Jerry Kramer to double-team defensive tackle Jethro Pugh, and Starr would follow right behind. At the snap, the Cowboys' Willie Townes submarined tackle Forrest Gregg, and with Bowman and Kramer driving forward on the slick ice, Starr squeezed between them. The six inches would be the difference between victory and defeat.

BOB LILLY: "Right before that last play, I was trying to dig a hole for traction, but I didn't have any success. That's when I wished I had had my cleats on.

"I knew Starr was going to run up the middle. They had just tried a play around the outside and fell. I am pretty sure I told Jethro and Lee Roy that they were going to come up the middle. In fact I told Jethro, 'We ought to call timeout and get a screwdriver out there and dig a couple of holes.' Because we were on a sheet of ice. I don't know why I didn't do that. I should have. It's one thing I'll always wish I had done. But I did think about it. I had the presence of mind to think about it. 'Cause I didn't think there was any way we could stop them if they put two men on you. You're just on ice, and you can't get under them, because they just scoot along. And that's what happened to Jethro. I don't know where I ended up. I've seen the picture of that play. I must have been underneath. Because I never have seen myself."

JETHRO PUGH: "It was like standing in a pot of ice. My feet were so numb, a bucket of ice. I said to Bob Lilly, 'We've got to call a timeout to get an ice pick.' We had to dig holes for our feet. But we didn't know if we could. I tried scraping the ice, but I couldn't feel my feet. My hands were in my pants. I didn't have gloves on because the coaches didn't want us to hurt ourselves in the pass rush. I was sliding back because I was standing on ice.

"We played the percentages. Bart Starr didn't like quarterback sneaks. He was going to call the play to Donny Anderson.

"But Kenny Bowman and Jerry Kramer double-teamed me for the quarterback sneak. Kramer moved before the snap. He was offsides. And Bowman threw an even better block from the other side.

"It was like a gunfight. Somebody pulls the trigger first, and it's too late to do anything."

CHUCK HOWLEY: "When we lined up, we knew we had to stop the run. We felt it was going to be some kind of a power play, and we had to gap them. We were keying the fullback, Jim Taylor. It didn't happen, and they got the surge off the line of scrimmage, and that's all you need on a quarterback sneak, 'cause the ball was on the one-inch line. All he had to do was get the momentum. We would have had to collapse the offensive line, which would have been hard to do because they had the snap count. But we knew it was going to be the last play.

"I was laying on Bart Starr's back as he went across. He kind of went off to the side, and I was able to knife the gap, but my momentum was going down the line, and as he penetrated behind Thurston and Kramer, to make the tackle I had to lay on the runner.

"I thought it was a gutsy play. It was a great game."

LEE ROY JORDAN: "On the final play I was lined up over the fullback. I was watching the fullback, Jim Taylor, closer than I should have been. I should have been watching Starr closer. When the ball was snapped, I took a jab step the wrong way. I don't know where I could have made the tackle if I'd have known he was going to run a quarterback sneak and gone straight for him, because there were a lot of people between me and Bart Starr.

"About seven years later we were riding on the bus to a game, and Coach Landry turned to me and said, 'Why did you take a step to the left when Bart Starr scored up there in Green Bay?' I said, 'Coach, are you still worried about that play?' Seven years later he still thought I could have won the game."

JERRY TUBBS: "I thought that [the QB sneak] was a dumb play on Lombardi's part. Here they were, if he doesn't make it, they lose the game.

They should have kicked a field goal. But maybe they thought they couldn't kick a field goal. But if they thought they were better than we were, why didn't they kick a field goal and play it off and then go on to win the game? I thought he was gambling too much. Turned out well, didn't it?"

CORNELL GREEN: "I was on the line of scrimmage right by where Starr snuck over for the winning score. They made it out to be such a big play, a big deal, and said what a great block Jerry Kramer made, but he didn't do a damn thing. Hell, Jethro and Bob Lilly were standing on ice. All you had to do was push them, and they'd slip down. And they knew the snap count, so they were going to get off first. Our guys got to catch your blows when you push them, and they did, and Bart Starr just walked in. They talked about 'great blocks' and all that. Wasn't nothing great about nothing. None of the blocks. But Jerry Kramer wrote a book on it, and made a fortune, and I guarantee, hell, I could have blocked Jethro, or anybody else on that line that day, 'cause we hadn't played in the end zone, and it was just ice. You ever stand on ice and have somebody push you? That's what it came down to.

"When Starr scored, there was no time left, and that was it. At the end of the game, nobody said anything. Everyone just got dressed and left. There weren't any speeches or talks or anything."

WALT GARRISON: "A quarterback sneak by Bart Starr is just not the smart play. So that's what they do and he scores to win the game. And Jerry Kramer writes a book called *Instant Replay* about how he made the key block on Jethro Pugh and it turns out to be the best-selling football book of all time and it makes Kramer famous and a million dollars. And we lost another heartbreaker.

"If Bart Starr doesn't score, if Jethro Pugh stuffs Kramer, then Jethro could have written the best-seller. If, if, if.

"But like Meredith used to say, 'If ifs and buts were candies and nuts, we'd all have a Merry Christmas.' "

PETE GENT: "I had taken something like five Dilaudid, and the nurse came in with some more Demerol. As soon as that game was over, I just wanted to go to sleep. I knocked myself out. I didn't want to think about it. That was just horrid."

BOB LILLY: "I remember after the game we took a shower, and the water temperature was around 60, but it felt hot. The water wouldn't get hot, but it felt hot, and the happiest feeling in my entire life was when we climbed up that stairway in the tail of that 727 and got on that warm airplane, and when we left the ground, I thanked the Lord that we were out of there.

"After the game my lungs were in bad shape. I used to smoke cigars a lot. I inhaled them, and I smoked a few cigarettes. After that game I quit all smoking. And my lungs have never been the same since that game, ever, because of the cold. I don't know what did it. I can't be in a room with smoke. I can't stand the diesel fuel from trucks. Exhaust or anything of that nature gives me asthma or some sort of an allergy immediately."

On the airplane Don Meredith took the loss so hard that he talked with Tom Landry about retiring. Landry told him he was being too hard on himself, that the conditions had been "dreadful." Chuck Howley overheard Don. Reporter Steve Perkins overheard Howley.

CHUCK HOWLEY: "As we were flying back on the plane, I was in the front of the plane with Phil Clark, and we were sitting there talking, and we were all kind of despondent from losing the ballgame, and I said to Phil, 'Hell, Don's going to retire, and I'm thinking about retiring,' and Steve Perkins of the *Herald* heard me and wrote a story about Don retiring. It came out in the headlines, 'Meredith Retires.'

"Don called me up on the phone, and he said, 'Chuck, what the hell is going on, baby? What do you mean I'm going to retire? I got all these damn endorsements. I have my phone ringing off the hook.' Don was pretty well pissed. I can't blame him. Here's a sportswriter who takes something out of context and makes a story out of it. I mean, after a game you're despondent, the players are talking off the cuff laying back in their seats, you're making all kinds of statements, and to me it's a little bit irresponsible when a sportswriter such as Steve Perkins takes something like that out of context and makes a story out of it.

"I apologized to Don. That's the only thing I could do. I said, 'Hell, Don, I made a comment. Yeah, I said you're going to retire. You made the same kind of statement. We all made crazy statements after that game. We were all kind of down, and we were making statements.' I said to Don, 'For someone to come out and write an article like that based on hearsay, that's not the right thing to do.'

"Within a week, Don put the story to rest.

"Controversy sells newspapers, and for someone who's a sportswriter presenting his views is different than a player giving his views. To me, the player is more qualified to give his views than a sportswriter.

What experience does a sportswriter have other than following the sport itself? Yes, he has an opinion. The media has that unique position. And yes, after we lost, we got a lot of criticism and so did Don."

Because of the conditions that day Don Meredith would not recover from the pneumonia he had contracted until February. Five Cowboys—George Andrie, Jethro Pugh, Mel Renfro, Willie Townes, and Dick Daniels— would be treated for frostbite.

The Cowboys had fought valiantly against a legendary football team, with field conditions adverse to their style of play. They had come within six inches of winning.

None of this had mattered either to Tom Landry or to the press or fans. All that mattered to them was that the Cowboys had lost. In the streets, at restaurants, at parties the talk was how the Cowboys had "choked." For some of the players, the response to the loss was far worse emotionally than the loss itself.

PETE GENT: "After that game the press turned on us with a vengeance. They said we couldn't win the big game. Well, what else are you going to say? Landry was not going to say, 'Boy, what a stupid thing I did to run a prevent defense, when they are running in the face of a 40-mile-an-hour gale and the wind chill is around 50 below zero.'

"So now it was: The Cowboys can't win the big one."

LANCE RENTZEL: "All of this created problems—serious problems. We heard it so often, a part of us wondered if it were true, and once that set in, once that cancer started to work, the whole organization began to contend with its image. This resulted in the so-called self-fulfilling prophecy."

FRANK CLARKE: "When we got back to the clubhouse after the game, the mood in the clubhouse was worse than it had been the year before. Double times worse. It was *more* gloomy, *more* down, *more* negative. Again, I felt, 'Whoa, no way this is . . . this is not . . . I just . . .' It just felt so weird that this would be going on with grown men.

"Two years in a row, man, we had done something that hundreds and hundreds and hundreds and hundreds of athletes would have given their pinkys for, just to be a part of that. And here we were, after back-to-back stellar seasons, very reputable, very enviable years in which we had challenged the world's great Vince Lombardi–led Packers, and we feel like this? This did not make any sense at all.

"And there was a part of me that said, 'Maybe I *should* get out of this. Maybe I'm not meant to be a part of this.'

"At the end of the season I got involved in doing radio and television. And I was doing a pretty good job, and when it came close for the pre-season to start, I started to say, 'Maybe one more year.'

"I called Tom Landry and said I wanted to talk to him about the '68 season, and he encouraged me *not* to come back. He didn't say, 'Don't come back.' But he had always let me know where I stood with his plans. It was almost as if he sensed and he knew that I didn't have the kind of energy that he needed to get to the Super Bowl. And he was right. I did not have it, and there was no way I wanted to manufacture it.

"After our meeting I immediately felt down, depressed, because I had wanted him to say, 'You deserve to come back for one more chance. We think we're going there, and there is no reason why we can't see ourselves as Super Bowl contenders, and you're the kind of player who's helped us get here, and we want you around for one more year.'

"But he just listened to what I had to say. But the other thing, too, that was a downer for me, not one of my friends or anybody else on the team said anything like, 'Charlie, we want you to come back.' It was as if everybody had accepted that fact that once they saw that newspaper article about me retiring, that was it. They knew just by my personality if Frank says that's what he wants to do, he's gonna do it, and that's it. But it did hurt. There was a part of that that really hurt me, that I would go out that way."

For some of the other players, the criticism was justified. They had not won it all. They had not gone to the Super Bowl, and so the following year there would be only one thing to do: work even harder.

CHUCK HOWLEY: "After the Ice Bowl loss, Tom announced that the next year he wanted everyone to work harder. If you don't achieve what you're trying to achieve, there is only one way to achieve it, and that is to work harder. Even today, I say to myself, 'If I had worked harder, I could have been a better player.' I can look back and think, 'Yes, we had goals for ourselves.' Tom taught us how to do that. He was a great goal-setter. He saw these were the things we could pull out within ourselves that we didn't know were there. These were the words that were frowned upon: 'We need to work harder.' But he was right. We hadn't won. We may have been 12–2, but Tom wanted a world championship.

"Because we had come so close, after that it was expected. And when you make it to the top, they are not content unless they repeat. The fans are the same way.

"In the early years all the Dallas fans wanted was a winner. Maybe that's human nature. Fans want to support a winner, not a loser. In the early years, they all wanted to be associated with a winner. It took us eleven years to do it.

"A fan does not look at it in the reality or the context. If you ask anyone who buys an NFL team if he'd be satisfied to go to the Super Bowl in ten years, he'd take you up on the deal. But the fan says, 'I'm only concerned with *now* and what you're doing *this* season. I'm only interested in the Cowboys so long as they're winners.' "

29

Uncivil War

Nine thousand American boys were killed in Vietnam in 1967, and that summer there were bad riots in cities across America. In the fall, antiwar activists looked for someone to oppose Lyndon Johnson. In January of 1968, the Vietcong mounted the Tet offensive, overrunning Saigon and more than a hundred other cities and leaving Americans to wonder whether Vietnam was worth the price. The myth of American invincibility was shattered, and Johnson's popularity sank.

And then on March 16, 1968, Robert Kennedy, the younger brother of the slain president, antiwar and pro civil rights, announced his candidacy for president. Two weeks later, President Johnson announced he would not run for renomination. Though vice president Hubert Humphrey announced he would run in Johnson's place, it seemed that most of the nation was embracing Kennedy, and it certainly appeared he would soon inhabit the White House.

For Cowboy guard John Wilbur, it was an exciting period because Robert Kennedy seemed like someone who would champion the cause of those who, like Wilbur, staunchly opposed the Vietnam war.

JOHN WILBUR: "It was a period of social unrest, a period of time of change in Texas, a period of time of experimentation with drugs. It was a period of time of social unrest and activity and death and war and music. I can remember Don Meredith and Pete Gent and I went to a Rolling Stones concert. We had front-row seats at the SMU auditorium. I recall the three of us and our wives standing on the chairs in the front row just rocking to the Rolling Stones.

"I met Robert Kennedy during his campaign in '68. I had met John Kennedy, and we all idolized him. I'd followed Bobby's path and what he had been doing, and I liked the Kennedys' philosophy. They were willing to stand up against any wrong. Later when I was traded to Washington I worked with Ethel Kennedy to raise money for her charities, and I became socially involved with the whole family. Ethel is a very dynamic woman who has done a wonderful job raising her kids. I am very close to them, and I will always be a Democrat and always be a Kennedy person.

"And so in '68 when Bobby's campaign asked for help getting out the votes in the black community in Los Angeles, I got involved with a group of athletes including Cornell Green, Bob Hayes, Rosey Grier, and Rafer Johnson.

"I would have been with him when he was killed in Los Angeles but I had to go to training camp. And when Bobby was killed, I backed off from politics until '72, when I went to work for George McGovern."

On April 4, 1968, Martin Luther King Jr. was assassinated. Riots swept through over a hundred American cities. On June 5, Robert Kennedy narrowly defeated Minnesota senator Eugene McCarthy in California, leaving him as the only antiwar candidate capable of defeating the mainstream Hubert Humphrey. That night he was murdered. This time there were no riots, only a pall of sadness. With the deaths of Dr. King and Robert Kennedy, the optimism of the sixties had come to an end.

JOHN WILBUR: "On the team in 1968 you had your conservative southern elements, and there's no question many times we heard the word *nigger* among our white teammates—I won't say who, but there was a racist element on the team, and a racist element in the management and on the coaching staff.

"And on the other side was that radical element, the antiwar guys, all the guys who stood up for Mel Renfro when he was denied housing in North Dallas, Pete Gent, myself, Pettis Norman, and Bob Hayes. Bob really didn't come out publicly, but in private. Don Perkins, Cornell Green, Rayfield Wright, Jethro Pugh, and Mel Renfro were also people who were not going to put up with the racism that existed in Dallas at that time, and constantly would talk about it, bring it to our attention. We were young men searching for perfection both in our football team and our lives and in our society. Some mirrored the elements of the society they came from, and others were looking for a better world."

PETTIS NORMAN: "When Martin Luther King and Robert Kennedy were killed, Dallas did not have protests at that time. Dallas was a very laid-back city. It had the reputation that things were 'okay here' between the black and white communities, when they weren't really. It was stuff on top of stuff piled up under a lot of different rugs. The old traditional way of solving problems at the time was, whenever there were questions, the Dallas Tri-racial Committee would come together to discuss that issue. At one time I was on that committee. And the main purpose of that was to keep down any notion of protest or march. It was an organization that talked through the problem, and then the communities went back to try to keep down any type of disturbance that might erupt.

"As a result of that, the black community in Dallas suffered a great deal. I have always said that there was a legacy that came from the general who came two and a half years late to announce to Texans that the slaves had been freed, and that legacy carried over through the sixties and the seventies, and even to some degree up until a few years ago, when Dallas started experiencing a lot of growth from outside, from African-Americans and other people who moved in from outside, to begin to introduce some new thoughts in the process.

"But it was a city that prided itself on being quiet, and on not causing a disturbance. And during that time, Martin Luther King was not welcomed here by the head of the black ministers' group. Because it was thought that he would come in and start up trouble. The white community said that Martin Luther King was a troublemaker, so the black ministers asked him not to come to Dallas.

"King was the person I had looked up to for a long, long time. I had been involved in the same kind of issues he was involved in. I knew him through all the things I saw and read and believed in, which were the things he preached and lived and practiced. He was really a major hero, as far as I was concerned. When Robert Kennedy died a couple months later, I was in a state of disbelief, but it was far worse when Martin Luther King was killed. It was the feeling of 'Who can pick up the mantle and lead this movement?' It had come a long way, but it was very much incomplete, and I knew that. I just did not see anyone on the horizon who could galvanize people and pull them together to march toward some form of equality. And so there was a tremendous void, a sense of almost hopelessness for just a little while.

"I somehow realized that we could not live in a state of hopelessness, and each one of us had to do what we could wherever we were to change things. In essence, we could be as effective, if not more effective, if enough of us picked up the mantle and did our own little piece. And so that's what I attempted to do as an individual, and tried to encourage others to do as well. And a lot of other folks had the same notion. That was my feeling with Martin.

"And even now when I think about him and see his speeches, especially that last one the night before he was killed, I have flashbacks to that time, and I still feel that tremendous void that I felt in me at that time. No one has really stepped forward to fill that void. A lot of people have contributed on a major level, but not to the extent that Martin did.

"And when Bobby Kennedy was killed, I was watching TV. I just sat there in total disbelief, and once again, it was another symbol of hope gone. It seemed like the light had flickered out for a brief moment. And I was thinking that this would be the fate of anyone who steps out and really becomes an advocate for change. And so it was a moment of disbelief and a moment of sadness, a moment of hopelessness, and then you realize you must move beyond that point.

"In 1965 I went to Tex and told him it was time to stop the living arrangements of the players by race. I said, 'We need to do something about the way we assign roommates. We need to stop assigning roommates by color, but by last names. We play together, we eat together, and it's time to take the next step.' He said, 'Let me think about it,' and he called me and Dave Manders, and he said, 'We want you two to room together.' And we did in training camp. Got along fine. Dave was a great roommate. We had fun together. We liked each other, and what we showed, regardless of color, you had the same concerns: You wanted to make the team, you wanted to make money, you had a family back home you loved, you wrote letters, you called at night on the phone. We shared the phone. We had respect for each other. We showered together, and no black or white rubbed off in the shower. We were two human beings who just happened to have slightly different hues of skin.

"And after that training camp, that was the last time players were assigned by race. Because we broke training camp, and during the season we were assigned roommates by last names. And it worked out fine. I don't know of any incidents. There were probably incidents where players had different personalities and requested some other roommate, but for the most part, I don't know of any major blowup.

"But I can tell you that when Dave and I roomed together, that opened the team's eyes. And when it happened with the whole team, it began to open eyes of other guys on the team who had ideas about what would happen if the races came together. It was interesting to watch individuals grow even beyond football, and how people gained a much greater appreciation for people, no matter what color they are.

"Dave Manders and I call each other 'roomie' right now. We still see each other. After my first wife died, I got remarried, and he came to the wedding.

"The Cowboys really had some influence on a lot of things in Dallas. Though the black players lived in South Dallas and the white players in the north, a lot of guys would get together and socialize in the mid-'60s, have aftergame parties, and a few guys would visit each other's homes. Some white guys didn't like it when that happened. But that's what happened. People began to know about the team staying together, eating together as a team, and it became much more acceptable. It gave the white community a chance to relate to the African-American community better, on a whole different level, from kind of a hero-worshiping type level. Little kids would wait after the game to get my autograph, just like they would anybody else's. And so all of this began to subliminally have an effect on the city."

When Mel Renfro moved to Dallas in 1966 from Portland, Oregon, he immediately encountered the kind of segregation experienced by all blacks at that time.

MEL RENFRO: "I wasn't in Dallas three days when I got a dose of Jim Crow. It was borderline Oak Cliff, South Dallas, where there were a lot of white businesses. There was a white restaurant and a black restaurant right next door. It looked like the white restaurant was a little nicer, so I walked in there to have breakfast. I was refused service. I was told, 'We don't serve coloreds here. You go eat next door.' I said, 'I didn't order a color. I ordered breakfast.' That didn't stand too well with them. And I went next door and had a great breakfast.

"I learned my lesson. I remembered what my dad said, 'If they don't want you, get away from it. Don't rock the boat, because you'll get hurt.' So I started looking for places where I knew I'd be accepted. Mostly black restaurants. Very few times would I go to North Dallas or a white area unless it was a team thing, or somewhere where we knew we could go."

For two years Renfro sought to live in North Dallas, closer to where the Cowboys practiced, and time after time was rebuffed. In 1968 Lyndon Johnson signed the Civil Rights Act, which made discrimination on the basis of race illegal, and that year Mel decided he no longer would be silent about his having to suffer the indignities of being denied housing. Against the wishes of Tex Schramm and the Cowboys, Mel Renfro sued to be allowed to live where he wanted.

MEL RENFRO: "It's funny, because when I moved to Dallas as a rookie in '64, the first place I drove to was the Cowboy office, and they directed me to an apartment complex in South Dallas where four or five other black ballplayers were living. It was just automatic. It was okay. It wasn't a slum. It was the Cedar Crest Apartments, one of the nicer apartments for blacks in that area. But just to automatically say, 'This is where you go . . .'

"I remember going into the Cowboys, and they wrote me a map. 'Go down Central South 75 and go through town and hit Corinth Street and go up Corinth, turn left here and here you are. That's going to be your home, buddy.'

"I can remember when the team would go to an area where there was segregation, Tom Landry used to say, 'Fellas, we know what's going on here. We don't particularly agree with it, but that's the way it is, so we have to do what we can so we don't create unnecessary problems.'

"And sometimes we would joke about it. I'll never forget Willie Townes. He called Coach Landry 'Presbyterian Tom.' We'd say, 'There goes Presbyterian Tom again.' Here's a guy who was supposed to be a Christian, and yet he's condoning segregation. He's saying, 'This stuff is happening, and though we may not agree with it, we'll ignore it and stay in our lane.' I'm still a very sensitive person to things like that. But the way I was brought up, my dad told me, 'Just get away from it. Don't challenge it.' But still, you have to be a man. Be a man. And after being denied housing three or four times, the fifth time I said, 'I'm not going to stand for this.'

"I would find an apartment or duplex that had a For Rent or For Lease sign on it, and I'd go up, and immediately it was not available. Several times when we'd call on the phone and we'd get there, it was always leased or it wasn't available. I understood what it was and I didn't want the problem of fighting it. I'd just go on to the next thing. But then, in 1968 when my wife and I went and looked at a duplex, and there were ads in the paper and For Lease signs, and we actually went in and talked to the people, and they actually said there were three or four units available, and did we want to sign up?

"We said no, because the rent was kind of high. At that time $375 a month was a little more than we wanted to pay. I had a game that weekend, so I flew to Philadelphia, and she went home. And while I was in Philadelphia I told my wife, 'Aw, what the heck. You only live once. We want to live in a nice place out near the practice field. Go back in and make the deal.' So she went in, and from the time we had been there, all the signs had been pulled out of the ground and there were no more units for lease, just for sale, and I was so livid I could hardly play the game.

"I discussed this with my teammates, just told them what happened, and it was really no surprise to anybody that that had happened, because they were experiencing the same thing.

"But Oscar Massi, a state senator in Dallas, had heard about what happened, and he contacted me and said, 'Mel, you want to fight this?' I said, 'You bet I do.' He said, 'I'll represent you for free.' So we sat down and talked about it, and we took it to federal court, and when the Cowboys found out I was taking it to court, Tex Schramm called me in front and center. For thirty-five, forty minutes he said, 'Mel, you can't do this. You just can't do this.' I said, 'Tex, this is not the first time. This is the fifth time this has happened. And I can't handle it any more.'

"He said, 'Mel, you can't do this. This is going to hurt you.'

"I said, 'I've been hurt by being denied housing.'

"I found out later, Tex was afraid of the white hierarchy in Dallas, the real estate industry. I guess the real estate industry had been putting pressure on him to have me not do this. Because it drastically changed the laws.

"When he realized I was going to do it, he jumped up behind his desk, got between me and the door, and he just said, 'If you're going to do it, I'm with you all the way.' I had gotten my own lawyer, but the Cowboys later claimed they had hired the attorney to represent me, which they did not.

"I went in to court, and these real estate people actually thought they were going to win. They fought this thing and spent a lot of money. We were in court a long time testifying.

"I said, 'It's the simple truth. I went in to lease the place and they denied me. Why did they deny me? Because I was black.' And this guy, a big builder, he knew if he lost, then that would open the doors for other blacks to move into places that they didn't want them.

"Actually, I got a lot of good letters, a lot of good phone calls from people saying, 'We're glad you're doing this, because they're not messing with us any more. Now we can get a place to live and not be denied.' Then on the other side of the coin the hate mail came. It was ugly. I told my wife one time, 'Don't ever open a letter that looks strange that has no return address on it.' It scared her to death. And what I did, I took a couple of them and put them on the bulletin board at the practice field, and they weren't up five minutes before someone took them down. Never found out who. But they came off in a hurry.

"I thought I was going to lose, because of the way they were presenting their case. I was saying to myself, 'What's going on here?' They were asking these stupid questions for me to answer. It was to the point, 'If you did and if that hadn't happened and this . . .' And I'd say, 'No, it was none of that. It was cut-and-dry.' You know how lawyers are, they work the questions so if you answer it, you're going to incriminate yourself or sound bad. Many times I refused to answer the question, and the judge would say, 'No, he doesn't have to answer that question.'

"The judge was Sara Hughes. She was very sympathetic. She knew what was going on, but she had to act like a judge. It was a very difficult thing for me to experience.

"And after I won, the owner of the complex said, 'Take your pick. You can move into any one you want to.' But I didn't because of all the negative publicity and the hate mail that came in. Because the public knew where it was. I said, 'There is no way I'm going to subject my family to people knowing where I live. There are some racist idiots out there that were saying and writing some nasty things.' I said, 'If they take the time to write a nasty letter like this, they could do anything.' And my daughter was a little baby. My boys were three and four. I said, 'No way.' And so I didn't move in there. I moved into an apartment complex in the North Side about a half a mile from that complex.

"After all the publicity behind it, the doors really opened up in the housing industry. I know that was so because of the many letters I got from people including from mixed couples who were also having problems.

"The black ballplayers were elated, because it opened the doors. And it put a spotlight on the problem. It was right at that time that Dr. King and Bobby Kennedy were assassinated. And that was some ugly stuff. That tore me apart. That *really* tore me apart. I stayed drunk for a week after the King thing, and I got real militant, and had an attitude, and of course, the Cowboys didn't like that. I was the premier player, myself and Bob Lilly and maybe one other, and they couldn't do anything to me, although they sure wanted to. They fixed me by not paying me any money. That was the way they got to me."

30

Jordan versus Gent

A most brutal internal war was waged between Lee Roy Jordan and Pete Gent. The two did not get along on any level. Jordan, like Landry, believed a player should practice as hard as he played, giving 100 percent at all times. Gent believed in having fun in practice, and even in games.

Jordan, a product of the Deep South, preferred country-and-western music to rock and roll and, like America's conservative bedrock, firmly believed drug users should be thrown in jail and unpatriotic antiwar protestors should be thrown out of America. On the issue of integration, Jordan had one test: If a man dedicated himself to the game, he wanted him for a teammate though not necessarily as a friend. His black teammates understood Lee Roy's rural Alabama background, and even if he did say the "n" word every once in a while, the great majority of the Cowboys—black and white—understood it was because of his upbringing and forgave him, at the same time admiring him for his dedication and what he meant to the success of the team.

Because Lee Roy Jordan believed it important to play as viciously in practice as he did in games, a whole generation of Cowboy offensive players held Jordan's ferocious nature against him, and a few took his hard hits personally. Several, including Pete Gent, John Wilbur, and Bob Hayes—

all offensive players—castigated him as a "redneck racist." In his own defense, Jordan says he never, ever acted prejudicially toward his black teammates.

LEE ROY JORDAN: "Hell, I don't know what 'redneck' is. If that's being from the South, I'm a redneck. But if that means I didn't respect Bob Hayes as a person just because of his color, I have to question that, because I judge every guy as an individual, no matter what color he is. Show me a guy who won't compete hard to win, and I won't like him. I don't care what color he is. You show me a guy who competes hard to win every play, I'll love him because that's what I'm all about."

Several black teammates concurred.

PETTIS NORMAN: "I've always had a lot of respect for Lee Roy Jordan. He has changed a lot. I've always had a lot of respect for him, especially for his playing ability and his approach to the game. And he always treated me very, very nicely. Never, never was there one incident when he wasn't very nice. In Dallas, a lot of people changed over the years, and Lee Roy was one among many."

MEL RENFRO: "I had some differences with a couple of the players. I knew they didn't like blacks, and they kind of let me know it. Ralph Neely was one. See, Ralph Neely's a friend. I like Ralph, but behind closed doors, he was a little different. Neely didn't really ever say much, but I knew he was kinda that way.

"And Harold Hays was the other one. Harold even to this day apologizes to me. We were at a Tom Landry function in '95, and he came up and said, 'Mel, you know, I just feel so bad about all that stuff I had in me back in those days.' He admits it. Back in those days he would come up to me right in my face and say, 'I come from the South. This is the way I am. I don't like y'all. I got to play with you, but I don't like you, and I don't want you around me or my wife 'cause that's just the way I am.'

"I never got that from Lee Roy. I knew who Lee Roy was and where he came from, but Lee Roy always treated me with a great deal of respect. Lee Roy was in it to win and he was in it to knock heads. He was in it to beat up on his opponent, and he did that as good as anybody I'd ever seen, including Tommy Nobis and the guy from Chicago, Dick Butkus. Pound for pound, Lee Roy was as good as they could go and as good as they could be. He was a team leader. Many times he'd get in that huddle, and he'd say, 'Man, they are not going to score. They just ain't gonna score. We ain't gonna let them score.' And you'd look over to the sideline, and our defensive coach Ernie Stautner would be over there waving all these defenses, and Lee Roy would laugh and say, 'No, we ain't gonna play that. We are gonna play 31 Safety Zone. We're gonna kick their butts.' And we'd do it. And man, Lee Roy was tough as nails, and he was the guy who would always come up and talk to you, and he'd pat you on the back and you know, Lee Roy was a real good friend to me, and we've always been that way, and I've never known him any other way than to be a good team-mate and a good friend.

"Pete Gent and John Wilbur probably saw the side of him we didn't see. Because they were white. He probably sat around with a group of his buddies, and they passed some words around that weren't so nice about black people, and I'm sure Pete heard that and John heard that, but like I said, none of that 'Down with the niggers' talk came across when I was with him, not like it did with some of the other players that were not so friendly. I know who Lee Roy was, where he came from, how he grew up, but as far as his treatment toward me, that was gold."

CORNELL GREEN: "I didn't think Lee Roy was a racist, and I was as close to him as anybody. I thought Lee Roy was a gung ho, ready to play, want to play, want to win type of guy, and though I didn't know that much about his personal life, on the field I thought he was ready, he wanted it, he would be there, a hard hitter, ready to play. Yah."

LEE ROY JORDAN: "They've been in the huddle with me and they know how important it is to win, and they know that because we stuck together and believed we could do things that we got a lot of things done."

Gent, who was often the target and victim of Jordan's viciousness during scrimmages, does not remember it that way.

PETE GENT: "I hated the guy. Oh, I hated him. He was a racist, sorry bastard. I have absolutely no respect for him as a man. In those days I didn't live in that great a neighborhood, but where some of the blacks lived was far worse. When we went on the road Dickie Daniels and Mike Johnson were afraid to leave their personal belongings in their apartments where they lived, 'cause it was in the paper they were out of town, so they would load up their stereos, TVs, and radios in their cars and drive over to my house and park them in my driveway, because we had firemen next door

354 ★ PETER GOLENBOCK

so there was always somebody watching the house. At the time the blacks still had problems finding hotels. I remember the first time we went to New Orleans in '66, we stayed at the airport hotel, 'cause no hotel downtown would take us. It was horrible. Those guys had such a tough time. They had to try and act like it wasn't happening.

"It was well known that Lee Roy and I didn't like each other. Alabama governor George Wallace was often our favorite subject. I would tell him to his face what a racist asshole Wallace was. In practice drills, Lee Roy would clothesline me half the time. But Lee Roy was a great player. He was tougher than shit, but I hated him for his racism. Most of the receivers were black—Frank Clarke was one of my best friends—and Lee Roy hated that.

"Interestingly enough, the outside linebacker who played behind Chuck Howley, Harold Hays, who was white, came from Hattiesburg, Mississippi. Lee Roy and I had gotten into a fight at some point on the field during a scrimmage, and I remember I was in the shower alone with Harold after a particularly ugly incident with Lee Roy. I don't remember which ugly incident it was, we had so many, and physically I always came out on the short end. Harold and I were in business together, and Harold was sitting there with me, and I said, 'That guy is not a fucking human being. That's bullshit. I don't care if he's your friend or not, Harold. Fuck that.'

"And Harold said, 'You know, Pete, what you've got to try and understand is, when I go home to Mississippi I still have to tell my grandfather we have separate showers for the whites and the blacks. We're in Dallas. We're still in the South here. You come from the North. You've got to understand where Lee Roy is coming from. Lee Roy isn't going to change.'

"As he aged, though, Lee Roy did change, as Dallas changed. If Lee Roy was going to make it in business he was going to have to deal with black people."

Between the southern conservatives and the northern liberals, there was no common ground. Even the team was split in its choice of recreational drugs. For the good old boys, whiskey was the standby. The Protestant ethic was to "Just say no" to drugs, but never to Jack Daniel's. The creed of the sixties antiwar, antiestablishment was that so long as no one got hurt, it didn't matter what you put into your body. As long as it felt good, "Just say yes." It was the Pleasure Principle, and drugs—first marijuana, the drug of the Flower Children, then the hallucinogen LSD, and then the addictive, destructive cocaine—played a large role in it.

The counterculture smoked grass because it felt good and it was fun. Dopers made fun of the nine-to-five corporate execs and their housewives who stayed home and took Valium. Eldridge Cleaver, the head of the Black Panthers, claimed that blacks needed marijuana as a bolster against onslaughts on their manhood by whites. It was the Straights versus the Heads, Us versus Them.

In 1968 the national youth mania was smoking marijuana. In the age of Aquarius and Free Love, it was everywhere, including among those Cowboys who did not feel cowed by Texas's fifty-year sentence for getting caught smoking it, or by cultural and religious inhibitions. And just because the good old boys shunned pot because it was illegal, that didn't mean there weren't substitutes. The potheads on the team found it amusing and hypocritical that their straitlaced brethren sought their kicks in pot-substitutes such as amyl nitrate and speed.

JOHN WILBUR: "Just about everyone was smoking pot at that time, though I would not say the southern redneck contingency of the Cowboys were experimenters. But one thing they did experiment with was amyl nitrate. You used to be able to buy it in the drugstores. So we'd go to the beer bars, the cowboy bars, and these amyl nitrates would get you high for thirty seconds. You'd giggle. It was the redneck way of getting high. We'd snort amyl nitrate to get high and laugh and get light-headed and drink beer. It sounds like a country-and-western song. 'Mama don't let your children grow up to be Cowboys snorting amyl nitrate in cowboy bars.'

"The euphemism was: We were all experimenting with the fruit of the times, whatever the fruit of the times would be: amyl nitrate, mescaline, speed, pot.

"This period was precocaine. There was *a lot* of speed. In fact the team used to dispense it. I was a rookie, and I was in the locker room before the game, and there were these little white boxes in everybody's locker, and I was wondering, 'What's going on? What the heck is that?' I asked one of the older guys, 'What's that?' 'Dexamil.' 'What does it do?' 'It makes you feel good. It's a performance enhancer.' So I said, 'I want some of that, too.' So I got on the list. They were pretty good about not letting the new guys do it. It was just for the old guys. I was kind of into the beer and the speed. The precocaine era. The speed generation. Beer and speed. Beer and speed. And amyl nitrate."

* * *

To those steeped in the Texas culture who had not strayed from biblical ways, marijuana was seen as the Devil's weed. Pot smokers were viewed as fiends as exemplified in the movie *Reefer Madness*. When Lee Roy Jordan somehow learned that Pete Gent was smoking marijuana with Don Meredith and other teammates, Jordan was horrified. He was convinced that Gent was an evil influence on Meredith and the team, and he did what he could to get Gent off the team, including an attempt to maim him during practice.

LEE ROY JORDAN: "Pete was a basketball player in college, and he didn't like contact, and I can understand that from some people. But I didn't think Pete was real committed to football and committed to winning. And I thought Pete wasn't a good character to be a part of the team because Pete experimented with anything that came along, and I think he was a guy who was helpful in exposing some other people to those kind of things, helping them to experiment with them, because he had them available.

"I didn't respect that, and I didn't like that because I thought it was detrimental to our football team. And basically that's it. I like everybody who has a real interest and commitment to helping us win. I respect *anyone* with that commitment. I don't care who you are.

"The [drug] thing *really* angered me and in practice I probably attacked him more than I should have—no, let me take that back, I don't think I could have. If I could have made him quit the team, I felt like we would have been better off. Because I felt like Pete was a bad influence as far as work ethic. I don't think he had a work ethic as far as really wanting to win and having it a major thought in his mind every day in practice and after practice and the next day when he came back.

"I would get on Pete for playing his music loud in the clubhouse. If I thought it was interrupting my concentration, or someone else's, I would, because I didn't think he was going to help us that much anyway. It's kind of like what Don Meredith said after the movie [*North Dallas Forty*]. He said, 'If I had known Pete had been that damn good, I'd have thrown him a lot more passes.' That's the way I felt about Pete. If he had been as good as he felt he was, shit, he'd a caught a lot more balls."

PETE GENT: "Lee Roy turned me in to league security as a guy who was passing out drugs on the team. I wasn't doing that. He knew that Meredith would come to my house, and that Don and I were smoking dope together. When we smoked it on the team plane one time, everybody thought the plane was on fire. They didn't know what the smell was. That was the closest they came to catching us smoking it. We were in back of the team plane, and Don went into the bathroom and smoked half a joint, and I went into the bathroom and smoked the rest, and the stewardess came back and said, 'Jesus, what's that smell?' They thought the plane was on fire. We were sitting there praying, 'I hope it is on fire.'

"So Lee Roy turned me in to league security. In the off-season after the '67 season and all during '68 they followed me. They had guys on me for one whole season.

"I can remember one time a neighbor told me, 'Pete, now don't look, but there is somebody sitting in our parking lot with binoculars.'

"I went out the back door, got in my car and came around and pulled next to this car, and there was a woman with a baby in the front seat, and she had a pair of binoculars, looked like a German tank commander. She was watching my house. I said, 'What are you doing?' And she looked over at me, and her jaw dropped. I said, 'Why are you watching my house?' I had already gotten her license number. She said, 'I'm not,' and she dropped the binoculars and roared off. I gave my lawyer—the guy who got me out of the draft—the license number, and he called me back the next day and he said, 'I don't get this. This license number traces to a judge in Oak Cliff.'

"One time I was driving along, and I looked back and here are these two guys following me, and I said to my wife, 'We are being followed, looks like by two cops.' She said, 'No, you are paranoid.' I said, 'Watch,' and I made a U-turn, and these guys made a U-turn right behind me in front of a patrol car and hit a parked car. The patrol car's lights went on, he walked to that car, and in less than a minute he turned them loose, and they came right after me. And they just kept following me. We were on our way to Casa Dominguez to eat, and when we came out, there they were, parked across the street.

"And then I was getting calls from guys who went home in the off-season like Leon Donahue, who called from San Jose. Leon used to come to my house a lot. Leon said, 'I just had two guys from league security here, and they wanted to know what you are doing.' He said, 'One, they know there are a lot of black guys over at your house, and two, somebody has told them you are doing drugs.' And about that point, Meredith got real paranoid. I went to see him, and he sort of got all over me about my behavior, saying it was me leading him on. I said, 'Look, Don, I never ran your life. I ain't running it now.' Don said, 'I just think you better be careful.' Then I knew the word had come down.

"I found out it was Lee Roy from Bob Thompson, who ran Tecon for Clint Murchison. Lee Roy did it out of a conviction that I was destroying the team because I was introducing recreational drugs, as opposed to the amphetamines and steroids everybody was taking. Everybody thought it was much better to drink a fifth of whiskey before a game than to smoke two joints and go to sleep. Remember, I was in Dallas, a very conservative place.

"I was seen by Landry and particularly by guys like Lee Roy as the bad influence on Meredith. Whereas the way I looked at it, when I came to that club, they were losing, and when I left, they were winning.

"What I found so fascinating was that the southerners on one side and the northerners and blacks on the other didn't agree on anything, had nothing in common, didn't get along at all. There was no unity—until we stepped on the field. I always marvelled at it, too. In *North Dallas Forty*, all through the book and movie, all week long Elliott and Joe Bob would fight, but right before, during, and after the game, they would have a moment of communion where Joe Bob would actually tell him he did well, and then it would be over, and the next week the fighting would start, and it would be the same battle all week long, until the next game.

"It was a constant. It's still amazing to look back at, to see what we would go through each week, and then how the day of the game we were all so focused on what we had to do, and how we counted on each other, black, white, redneck, limousine liberal, whatever you were, you were focused to win that game, because that's who you were. You were football players. If you didn't do that, everything you did during the week was useless. You were meaningless. To me, that explains everybody's behavior, from Don Perkins to mine to Lee Roy's. We all understood at one level that we were football players. That's all we were. Practices were tough enough, because your job would be on the line every day in practice. But on Sunday, your *life* was on the line. You fucked up on Sunday, your life could be over. If you were no longer a football player, you were no longer anything. 'Cause you'd been doing it for so long. It was the only thing you had in your identity."

31

Trials and Tribulations

CORNELL GREEN: "In '68 we started 7–1, and then after we lost to the Giants 27–21, you'd have thought we were the worst team in football. But that was Tom Landry's deal: Even when we won, Tom Landry would go to the media, and you'd think we'd lost. After every game. I have no idea why. Tom had trouble saying we played a good game. He had a *problem* with that. For his whole career, you could beat someone 52–0, and he'd find something wrong with it. And he could do it for two and a half hours! When he did that, though, I kind of cut him off. I didn't even listen half the time. You'd get in the habit of not even listening. Let him ramble on."

PETE GENT: "I must tell you a certain part of what Tom Landry was doing there was some sheer genius. But there was another part of it that was just blind foolishness, and dishonesty, and that's what you kept seeing in the press. That's where the dishonesty showed up, because we were 7 and 2. Yet the press was saying, 'We're terrible.' How could we not be a good team? Who was telling them that? I wasn't telling them that. Who was telling them, 'We're terrible?' It had to be Landry. He was already preparing the ground for his landing."

* * *

After the loss to the Giants, the Cowboys did not fulfill Tom Landry's dire prophecy and sink further, but rather rebounded with a 44–24 shellacking of the Washington Redskins, a game in which Don Meredith passed for 295 yards. In that game Meredith suffered a torn ligament in his leg, and he had to sit out the 34–3 mauling of the Chicago Bears as Craig Morton led the team on offense while Bob Lilly, Chuck Howley, and the rest of the defense held the Bears to a lone field goal.

The next game was a rematch against Washington in the Cotton Bowl, a 29–20 victory, and during the game, which was televised nationally, the Dallas fans spent much of the game booing Don Meredith—despite the 9–2 record and his success in the game. Fueled by Tom Landry's criticisms and the many negative stories written in the Dallas papers over the years, the relentless booing of the fans let Meredith know that they did not approve of him. Meredith was so upset after the game that he refused to talk to reporters. A few days after the game Don and his wife went into a Dallas restaurant, and some men at the bar recognized him and began booing. They continued to do so until Don and his wife, embarrassed, left. The team won the rest of its regular season games, but Don Meredith would never forget the insults.

PETE GENT: "We had pulled back together, and we didn't lose again. We won twelve games. And yet, in a game in the Cotton Bowl against the Redskins, Meredith was getting booed by the fans. We quit introducing the starting lineups on offense, 'cause they would boo Meredith.

"Don and I talked a lot about why he wasn't getting the respect he deserved. I was always harping on what I thought it was. We couldn't agree. We were now slowly moving into separate camps. Mine was, 'You fucked up. You handed back control. You never should have given that up.' And he would say, 'It's not that.'

"Because of the injuries I suffered, I had lost my starting job to Lance Rentzel, and so because I was no longer a starter, and no longer potentially ever going to be a starter, Don now looked at me more like a guy who was a complainer and a malingerer, which really irritated me, because I played hurt all the time.

"About that point is when Lance married Joey Heatherton. I'm convinced he married Joey Heatherton because it was the Cowboys' way of solving his problem, by getting him publicly married to a sex symbol and who continually, when he would go to practice, would take off for L.A.

And Lance would try to get my wife or Meredith's wife to stay with her, so she wouldn't run off.

"I remember we went out to dinner one time with Lance and Joey and a choreographer in Fort Worth, a guy who was wearing more makeup than Joey, and Joey looked ratty, dirt under her nails. She was loud and obnoxious.

"We went out one night to a diner, and she was so bad that we just laid the money on the table and left. I said, 'Come on, Lance. We gotta get the fuck out of here.' My wife went outside. I said to Lance, 'Grab her and let's go.'

"We got out into the parking lot, and Lance was so upset he walked over and threw up. Joey was driving him crazy."

Meredith led the team to a 28–7 win over the Pittsburgh Steelers, a home game in which Craig Morton was booed in the fourth quarter. In the final, meaningless game against the Giants in New York, Meredith needed only to play an average game to win the NFL passing title.

The night before the game Meredith and some teammates attended a party thrown by author and former Detroit Lion quarterback-for-a-day, George Plimpton, the paper Lion. Meredith drank heavily, and during the game he played listlessly, without fire. It was windy that day, but that was only part of the reason for Meredith's 1–9 day, a performance that cost him the passing title. Halfway through the second quarter Meredith told Tom Landry he "didn't have a feel for the game." Landry replaced him with Craig Morton, who saved the day for a 28–10 win over the Giants.

During the Giant game it had snowed, and when the players filed onto the Braniff 727 at the airport, the wings were covered with white. It was a flight that the players remembered for their fright as much as for Don Meredith's cool.

PETE GENT: "We were taking off, and Don Meredith was sitting in front of me. They gave us two beers, and we would smuggle whiskey in. Don said, 'I'm going to drink my first beer before we take off. I'll save the second one for later.' I was playing my record player, smoking a cigar, finishing my beer.

"We started down the runway, and we heard this tremendous *bang*. Everyone just sat up straight in their seats. The plane shut down, and we skidded to the end of the runway. I could hear guys whimpering in the back of the plane. Dan Reeves's face was down.

"The pilot came on and said, 'Aaaaaaa, we think we just had a little snow that blew through the engine. We're going to try it again.' And I can remember George Andrie and other guys broke into tears.

"Meredith turned to me and said, 'I think I'll have my second beer now. I don't want to waste it.'

"So I put the Beatles white album back on, and somebody in the back yelled, 'Gent, you motherfucker, shut off that record player.'

"I said, 'Fuck you. If I'm going to die, I'm going to do it listening to the Beatles.' And we took off.

"The only guys who had any humor about it were Meredith and Walt Garrison, who looked back at me and gave me this wry grin that he always had. Garrison always looked at playing football as punishment. He always said, 'I'd rather be in the rodeo because I meet a nicer brand of people.' I loved Walt. He was a wonderful guy with a great sense of humor."

WALT GARRISON: "One night me and Meredith went out drinking. He started the night with four $100 bills in his wallet. As the night progressed he bought about everybody he saw a beer and he went through the whole wad. All $400—which was a hell of a lot of money back then.

" 'God darn, Meredith,' I said, 'how can you afford to blow all that dough?'

" 'Whadda ya mean?' he said. 'I just made $400.'

" 'How do you figure that?'

" 'Hell, I had $800 worth of fun.'

"Don had such a carefree attitude about life, you just had to love the guy. We're at the back of the plane. I'm on the aisle. Joe Don is sittin' there drinkin' him a beer, smokin' a cigarette.

"It was snowing like shit and this sonuvabitch takes off and the whole plane shudders. It sounded like a bomb went off. *Boom!* They tried climbing again and *boom!*

"We'd been sitting on the ground for about two hours while they de-iced the plane three or four times and, in the meantime, Lilly musta drank a case of beer. So Lilly was ripped. Lilly stands up in the aisle and says, 'We've all had it, baby. It's alllll over.' And he's still chugging his beer.

"The plane is flying at about a 45-degree angle because they can't get its ass in the air, and all Lilly's beer cans start rolling down the aisle. One of the stewardesses comes skidding down the aisle on her hands and knees. The beer cans are flying by her and she's screaming, 'We're in trouble. We're in trouble.'

" 'Oh no.'

"Everyone is scared to piss. Pete Gent yells, 'Joe Don, Joe Don, we're gonna crash.'

"But Meredith is still sitting there and, finally, he takes a long drag on his cigarette and a big swig of beer and he says, 'Well, it's been a good un, ain't it?'

"Now that's cool.

"I'm thinkin', 'It's been a good one? What the hell are you talking about? We're gonna die.'

"But Meredith never even blinked. He just kept sipping his beer. He could have cared less if that plane went down. He didn't actually care. And everybody knew he wasn't bullshitting either."

The plane, of course, didn't crash, and the Cowboys began their march to the title with a game against the Cleveland Browns, a team they had clobbered 52–14 in '67 and had beaten 28–7 in late September. After beating the Browns in what was supposed to be a formality, the Cowboys were to play the winner of the Colts-Vikings game for the right to go to Super Bowl III. The Cowboys were heavily favored. No one thought the Browns would win.

Against the Browns in Cleveland in mud up to the players' ankles, the Cowboys played tentatively. The score was 10–10 at the half. The first play of the second half was a pass from Don Meredith in the left flat to Bob Hayes, but Brown linebacker Dale Lindsey, who was not supposed to be there according to Meredith's "keys," batted it up, intercepted it, and ran 27 yards for a touchdown.

On the next possession Meredith threw a pass that hit Lance Rentzel. The ball should have been caught, but Rentzel let the ball bounce off his hands, and a surprised defensive back named Ben Davis intercepted. On the next play Leroy Kelly ran 35 yards for a touchdown.

The game was but two minutes into the third quarter when Tom Landry panicked. He replaced Don Meredith with Craig Morton, and Meredith did not go back into the game again. He sat on the bench, his head buried between his knees, hurt and depressed, as the Cowboys lost, 31–20. Meredith had played for the Cowboys for nine seasons, but through that whole time Landry had never placed his faith in his country-and-western-song-singing quarterback. In '68 Meredith may have given himself to Landry, but against the Browns, Landry made it clear that the surrender was not mutual. When Landry pulled his star prematurely, he ended all chances the Cowboys had of going to the Super Bowl. During the final minutes of the game, Tex Schramm walked over to Meredith on the sidelines and threw his arms around him. The two men cried.

PETE GENT: "Landry was trying to run this offense all week, and it wasn't working. It wasn't even working in drills. So we got to Cleveland, and I had to go down to the locker room early to get shot up and taped. I always liked to go down early anyway. I didn't like to hang around the hotel. I liked to be in the locker room. And I had a portable record player, and I had on the Beatles white album, and I was laying on a bunch of equipment bags, smoking a long, thin cigar, listening to 'Rocky Raccoon,' when this reporter for the *New York Times* walked in. Then he walked into the Browns' locker room, and there was Leroy Kelly all wired up, ready to play right then.

"And after we lost, the lead paragraph in the *New York Times* was: 'Perhaps the best example of why Cleveland beat Dallas was when I walked through the locker rooms. Pete Gent of the Cowboys was smoking a cigar, listening to the Beatles, while Leroy Kelly was intensely studying his playbook. . . .' That went up on the fucking wall in the Cowboy offices. You know where my fucking history went down.

"I can remember running in that mud in Cleveland, and it was awful. I remember the mud was so heavy, your feet weighed 20 pounds. It was tied at the half, and then suddenly they scored on the defense twice. It was in Municipal Stadium in that awful fucking mud. Your shoes would weigh fifty pounds after being out in that mud. Dale Lindsey scored on an interception that should have been caught, and after Lance fumbled one, Leroy Kelly went one-on-one with Chuck Howley deep for a touchdown.

"Early in the third quarter Landry benched Don and put Craig Morton in the game. He said, 'I did this to have an effect on the team.'

"And it *did* have an effect on the team. It cost us the game. The idea of replacing your quarterback to have an effect on the team is just nuts. Who pulls your starting quarterback in the third period of a playoff game when you're only one or two touchdowns behind? Particularly when you're a team that's as explosive as we were? He had quit. He was planning for next season. Game over.

"The thing about anyone criticizing Tom Landry is, how can you attack God, Mom, and apple pie? The guy was a war hero, a legitimate war hero. So at what point do you start criticizing him? And the press finally started criticizing him at exactly the wrong time. At the end of his career they said, 'The game has passed him by.' And that's not what happened.

That's not why the Cowboys collapsed. They collapsed because the Murchison Brothers collapsed and died. It had nothing to do with Landry.

"The only guy who *ever* had an effect on the Cowboys by being put into the game was Roger Staubach. Otherwise, every time Tom ever replaced a starting quarterback with a backup quarterback, he lost. And Craig was probably the worst guy to ever put in, because Craig suffered from the same problem that coaches cited for why they never liked to let black guys play quarterback—'cause they always felt that black guys at quarterback would always throw long. That was their theory, like in basketball where they say the black guys never give up the ball. Well, that was the way Craig was. He'd get in and call three long passes, rather than try to work his way down the field.

"And so we lost that game when we might have won if Tom hadn't panicked."

JOHN WILBUR: "Why did we lose to Cleveland? I don't know why. We had beaten them 28–7 earlier in the year. They had a good team. We were playing in their backyard. It was a wet field. We couldn't get anything going. We got behind the eight ball, they made a couple of good plays, and now we're playing catch-up, still couldn't get anything going. I tried to do my job. I had to block Walter Johnson. He was tough, a hard player to play against. I had an okay game. But we couldn't run on them.

"This was a very dicey game. It was in Cleveland, colder than shit. Obviously, we weren't prepared. We didn't play good offense, and not too good on defense either.

"After that game, Blaine Nye said, 'It's not whether you win or lose, but who gets the blame.' He didn't invent that comment. Obviously, Landry and the coaching staff blamed Meredith.

"Landry took Don out of the game in the third period. We all liked Dandy. We wanted Dandy in there. It didn't help for Landry to do that. We did what we were told, but it's a matter of confidence. I was always a Dandy fan. He took us there. He should have stayed in there. Obviously, it was a desperate act for Landry to do that. And as it turned out, it was the *wrong* thing to do. Of course, had it gone the other way, it would have been the right thing to do. I don't think Landry really cared what Dandy felt about it. Dandy *never* felt that Landry was really 100 percent behind him. I don't know if that made him a better player or not. After that game he decided he wasn't going to put up with it any more.

"After the game we were all wondering where the hell Don was when he got off the team plane and took that trip to New York. I was a little surprised. I wondered, 'Where is he?' "

PETE GENT: "After losing the Cleveland playoff game, Meredith and I jumped the team plane and went to New York.

"Our team plane was a 727, and we walked in through the tail. We were sitting there. Meredith and I were on opposite sides of the aisle in the back, and he lit up a joint, handed it to me, and I didn't know what to do, because now guys knew what it was, so I put it out. He looked at me and said, 'Let's get the fuck out of here.' And he grabbed his bag and jumped up, and I got up and we walked out the tail of the plane.

"When we walked into the Cleveland Airport, we were walking by all the gates, and Don said, 'Let's find the first flight out of here. I don't care whether it goes to L.A. or New York. Let's just find one.' We were walking along, and there was a flight to New York, and it was going to leave in 25 minutes, and when we walked over, there was Frank Gifford who had broadcast the game for CBS. We sat down and started talking with him. And we went to New York with Frank.

"We sat in the last row of the first-class section of the plane to New York. Meredith was on the window, I was on the aisle, and by accident we ended up sitting next to Gifford. Giant owner Wellington Mara's wife was on the other window seat.

"We sat down, and Don lit up another joint, handed it to me. I puffed and handed it back to Meredith, and then he handed it over to Gifford, who looked at it and immediately put it out in his drink! I looked at Frank and just shrugged my shoulders as if to say, 'The guy's on a death trip.'

"We ended up at Gifford's house for a couple of days. Frank took us out to see where his puppy was buried. It was a schnauzer pup that Don had given him, and it had died. Roy Clark had this record out, 'Yesterday, When I Was Young,' and it was on the record player, and Frank laid his head against the speaker of the record player and began to cry. When I went by, he looked up and said, 'This is my song.' I looked at him and said to myself, 'Life after football is going to be really tough!' He lived in this beautiful house in Westchester. I thought, 'He's got everything, and he's crying about not being out on the football field getting the shit kicked out of him.'

"Frank said, 'I'd give anything in the world to trade places with you.' I said, 'Frank, you are so fucking dumb. I'd give anything in the world to trade places with you!'

"When Frank was first with CBS, he would ditch the crew and come stay with me when they were in Dallas, but I've noticed lately he's just been leaping into these personal attacks against me. When the video of the 75-year anniversary of football came out, he was asked what he thought of it and he said, 'They didn't have me in very long. They had Pete Gent and Al Davis, two rebels and guys who caused all that trouble.'

"The first nine pages of Frank's book launched off in an attack on me, saying I wasn't a loyal friend of Don Meredith like he was. It was so far out of context. He's going back to *North Dallas Forty* and assuming that character Seth Maxwell is Meredith 100 percent. What I find interesting, Meredith was offered that part for the movie, and Don was at Elaine's one night talking with Bud Shrake, Gifford, and several others, and Don said, 'I just don't want others to think that's me.' And Gifford said, 'Well, it *is* you.' That was fifteen years ago. And now Frank's attitude is that I somehow ruined Don's reputation.

"After our stay with Frank, the thing I remember, after we flew back to Dallas, Meredith immediately went back to Landry and apologized. I didn't. I just went back to my house. Fuck him. The season was over.

"Landry hadn't known we were gone until they were almost in Dallas, and some of the writers came back and said, 'Meredith and Gent left.' Of course, it became all my fault."

The loss to the Browns did not end the '68 season. The Cowboys had to travel to Miami to play the Vikings, losers to the Colts in the other divisional playoff. Once in Florida, Don Meredith's life would take a darker, sadder turn.

JOHN WILBUR: "Don played very well in the Losers Bowl game in Miami against Minnesota. We won 17–13. Don was voted the MVP of the game. That was a great game. We had a good time down there. It was a lot of fun. We went to the Jockey Club, had a good time. No curfew. We stayed right on the beach. Good fun. Don probably knew it was his last game. It was the 'last hurrah' for everybody, 'cause at the end of that year everybody got traded or quit."

Two players who quit were Don Perkins and Don Meredith. Perkins had played nine seasons and no longer wished to absorb the physical punishment. Meredith, who came with Perkins that first season of 1960, also quit to end the punishment, but the pain that did in Dandy Don was mostly mental. For eight years Don Meredith had tried to develop a friendship with his coach, but failed. From the time Meredith took over as starting quarterback Tom Landry had allowed him to shoulder all the negative criticism from both the press and fans. Finally, after the vitriol from sportswriters after the Cleveland debacle, Don Meredith decided he had had enough.

LEE ROY JORDAN: "You can accept criticism—all of us got a lot of it through the years, but it was one of those deals where no one—not Tex Schramm, not Tom Landry—ever really took the blame for anything that happened. The players always had to take the blame for the losses. If Tom had a bad game plan or if he called a bad play, it was always the players' fault. It was the defense or the secondary, the linebackers or linemen, or it was the quarterback and the receivers. It was, 'They lost the game. Don threw an interception. We had this guy open. Don missed him.' That was just Tom. And a lot of guys never accepted that, and I think it still bothers Don.

"Tom could have shared the responsibility for the losses much better. To me, if a player performed poorly, it was still Tom's responsibility. 'Cause he didn't prepare him right. But the players always got singled out as the ones, and it is amazing how much pressure the press can put on players, especially when the responsibility needed to be shared in a lot of other places. Early on it *was* shared, because there was a time when there was even talk of firing Tom, and that's when Clint gave him a ten-year extension and took the pressure off him, but it didn't take it off us. I don't know why Tom was that way. We develop patterns and personalities and most of the time we stayed with it and went with it. But a lot of people have a problem saying, 'It was my fault. I'll take responsibility because I didn't take care of it. I should have done a better job.' And I really feel that Coach Landry should have taken more of a role in it, to say, 'Hey, maybe it was my fault. Maybe I didn't have the right game plan, and maybe I didn't have my players prepared well enough, maybe I didn't motivate them well enough.' Because ultimately it's his job to do all those things, and if it didn't happen, to me it wasn't just Don Meredith's fault, or my fault, it was someone else's fault, too. It wasn't just our fault.

"But Tom never did that all through his career, and that's one thing that was hard for me to understand coming from Coach Bryant's program, because Coach Bryant always took criticism outwardly, and he always took responsibility for the team making mistakes, because he knew he didn't have to play the next week, and he was a lot more mature and a lot older than we were. He knew that criticism would affect us a lot more than him.

"But Coach Landry never took any blame, and he let the players take *all* of it, and at that time Don Meredith took the criticism for the entire team not being successful, and that's the reason he retired. He didn't have the offensive line the great quarterbacks who were successful had, like Terry Bradshaw at Pittsburgh and Bob Griese at Miami. Many times it definitely wasn't Don's fault, because Don did a lot of great things for our football team, won a lot of games that we probably should have lost, could have lost real easy were it not for unbelievable performances by him.

"Don and Tom were so different. Tom felt that he couldn't manage people and make decisions on who got cut and who stayed with the team if he got to be personally involved or close to people. Also Tom had a hard time visiting with people when he wasn't talking about steps in a defense, movement on the Flex defense, halfbacks running a route. He was shy. And really sometimes he seemed cold, because he would be thinking about something else, and you'd see him in the hall, and Tom might not even speak to you. He might not do that for a week! And all of a sudden you're thinking, 'Gosh, the coach is mad at me or doesn't like me,' and it wasn't that. Tom was thinking about something in football. He wasn't thinking, 'Here's one of my players. I really should speak to him to let him know I know he's alive.' Early in my career it really bothered me, but once I got to know him, it was, 'Hey, this is Coach Landry. He really doesn't talk to anyone.' And probably the guys it hurt the most were the quarterbacks who really felt like as much time as they spent with him, there should have been some kind of personal relationship there.

"We all would say, 'We should have a little relationship with him,' but we also accepted and understood, 'Hey, that's Tom.' At the same time you always said, 'God, I wish I had gotten to know Coach Landry better.'

"I know it hurt Don Meredith, and that was one reason Don retired as early as he did."

At the time there were also comments made by Coach Landry that Don was retiring because of "personal" reasons. For Don Meredith, bombarded with constant criticism, playing football had lost its appeal. At age thirty, Don Meredith, one of the most valiant, exciting, memorable athletes to ever play the game of professional football, quit prematurely. The constant criticism wasn't bad enough. Family burdens made continuing impossible.

PETE GENT: "When we were in Florida, Meredith's wife was pregnant, and in late June their daughter Heather was born with birth defects. And they didn't know what had caused it.

"Don felt tremendous guilt. He blamed his wild life and all the sleeping around that he did. He was sure that played a part in what happened to the baby.

"The baby was badly retarded. She was institutionalized within a year. When I was living in Wimberly, Texas, in the early '80s, she had been at the Brown School for retarded kids in San Marcos at least ten years. Cheryl brought her over to visit us. She was blind and almost deaf. It was a horrible, horrible story. Talk about trouble on top of trouble. Don just had tragedy after tragedy. Two weeks after the baby was born, Don told Landry he was retiring. He was only thirty.

"Don came by my house right after he did it, and he said, 'I've decided to do this, but I thought Tom would try to talk me out of it.' But Tom never did. So it seems possible that Landry intended to replace Meredith after that year anyway, and so Meredith retiring just made his decision easier.

"Landry said that the reason he didn't stop him was that Don was having personal problems and that the personal problems were so great, the best thing for Don was to quit. But Don had had personal problems from day one. Don *always* had personal problems. Meredith's personal problems were monumental from the first day I ever met him.

"And after he retired Don just went on a binge of self-destruction. He literally was trying to kill himself."

32

Self-Destruction

I n April of 1969 Tex Schramm sent Pete Gent a form letter: "Dear Player. We are not required to renew your contract, but we're making you an offer of 10 percent off your salary . . ." Insulted, Gent sent back a form letter of his own: "Dear General Manager. Here's what I want, and if you don't give it to me, don't bother me."

The next month Tom Landry ended his feud with Gent when he called the receiver into his office for the purpose of informing him he was being placed on waivers. Normally a waived player learns his fate in the papers in the transactions columns of his local newspaper, but Landry apparently just wanted to tell Gent in person, just to see the look on his face.

"I think you've made a mistake," said Gent.

With Frank Gifford's help, Gent was given a shot with the New York Giants. His tenure was short. He saw coach Allie Sherman as incompetent, hated Fran Tarkenton, whom he called "one of the worst people in the world I ever met," and after he called Giant owner Wellington Mara "crazy," his football career came to a sudden end, and he returned to Dallas to live as a civilian.

After Don Meredith retired, Dandy Don turned his back on football and gave his full attention to the stock brokerage business. It took Meredith about a year to lose just about everything he had. Down to his last grubstake, Meredith headed for Baja California with Pete Gent. It was a wonder either came back alive.

PETE GENT: "Oh God, Don was just so self-destructive. Don really had a death wish. He always wanted someone to accompany him, and I always was stupid enough to go along. Of course, he was tougher than I was. His whole theory was, 'When I die, then I'll stop.' But if I died, that was God's signal for him to slow down!

"In '69 he and his wife and I and my wife were invited to go to the Baja Peninsula in Mexico as the guests of Jantzen, the swimwear company that had a sports advisory board with Don and Jerry West and Larry Mahan, the rodeo cowboy. They put their pictures in *Sport* magazine. It was the exact opposite of the *Sports Illustrated* swimsuit edition.

"Don had gone broke in the stock brokerage business. He had a thousand dollars left. Before we left for Mexico, Don's father found the $1,000 in cash, and he thought Don had gotten it from me because I was dealing dope! Aw, his parents hated me!

"A few years earlier I had made a complete ass out of myself at his parents' house. Don had asked me to drive him all the way to Mount Vernon. When we finally got to the town, Don was so drunk he couldn't find his house. It was about nine o'clock at night, and it was dark. So we drove to the Mount Vernon High School, and he got out of the car and walked home from the high school, because that was the only way he could find his way home. I drove along behind him as he walked.

"I was already drunk when I got in the car, and on the way there I drank two more bottles of wine, and Jesus Christ, when we pulled up in front of the house, we fell out of my car, kicking the wine bottles and the empty beer cans and all that shit right out onto his parents' front lawn. This was a Saturday night. I sat at the table, and I didn't want to eat, and then I started eating black-eyed peas right out of the bowl with my hands! It was pretty bad.

"The next day was Sunday. Don's parents were Christian people, and on Sunday everybody was driving by their house, and there laying all across the front yard were all these wine and beer bottles. They were just furious.

"When we got to Mexico, Don left the $1,000 cash in the room, and when he got back, someone had stolen it. That's how his luck was going.

"We were staying in Cabo San Lucas on the coast. Literally there was nothing there, one hotel and a dirt airstrip. The next hotel was forty miles away. We went out fishing one day on a boat with a guy from a fishing magazine who wanted to get pictures of Meredith. I was riding along, and what they told you was, 'Don't swim in the bay.' Because they cut bait in the bay, and the bay was full of sharks. We were out on the boat, and it was just gorgeous on the Baja Peninsula, and so we came in to the shore, about two hundred yards out, and Meredith, who was not a strong swimmer to start with, said, 'Let's swim to shore.' I said, 'Don, Don, sharks, sharks. They said there were sharks here. We shouldn't swim.' He said, 'Boy, sometimes I just wonder about your manhood.' And then he dove in. Ten seconds after he dove in, a big shark swam under the boat, and I was thinking, 'Oh, God, he's going down any minute.' But Don swam right to shore. Nothing got him.

"David Haliburton, who owned a big oil company, showed up in his 60-foot yacht. We went out on Haliburton's boat, and he was just a complete ass, what you'd expect an Oklahoma oil man to be. He had two motorbikes on his boat. Meredith said, 'Come on. We want to borrow them.' Haliburton said, 'Now Don, don't be damaging them.' So we took them out, and we drove to the other motel, forty miles across the desert. There was nobody there, a couple of maids, nothing open, we couldn't get any drinks, and so we drove back until we saw this tin-sided, tin-roofed shanty, a cantina that had seven or eight Mexican workers all wearing machetes. We went in there, and Meredith had four or five beers, got drunk, and he started talking pidgin Spanish, insulting these Mexican guys. The first thing these guys did was move all the way down to the other end of the room so they didn't have to kill us. The bartender came over and said, 'Please, please, I don't want no trouble in here.' And I was trying to shut him up, too. Don was just saying all sorts of shit. '*Chinga de madre.*' And these guys were about ready to kill us. The bartender hustled us outside, and now Meredith was pissed at me.

"He said, 'Gutless bastard, we could have whipped all their asses.' And he jumped on that motorbike and it was getting dark, and he took off down the road, opened it flat out. I got on my bike, putt-putt-putting along, until I came up over this hill, and there was Don's bike just scattered across the desert. I didn't see him anywhere.

"I looked off into this ravine, and there he was, down about twenty yards. He had landed on the only sand on the Baja Peninsula. The rest of it was just rock. He had dislocated his shoulder and had a spiral fracture of his right arm.

"We were out there in the desert twenty miles from the hotel, and it was getting dark, and I didn't know what to do. I said, 'Don, I'm going to have to go back to the hotel to get help.' Just about then a truckload of

Mexicans came out of nowhere, and they picked him up and put him in the back and took him to the hotel.

"I got Meredith back to the room, and I went down and found two doctors, who were dead drunk. It was fortunate they were there, because the guy who ran the hotel said that two weeks before, a girl had sunburned her eyeballs, and the only medication they had to give her was sleeping pills. And the nearest X-ray machine was sixty miles away in a dentist's office.

"The two doctors saw his shoulder was dislocated, and they popped it back in in the normal fashion, pulled and jerked, without any idea that he had a spiral fracture of the arm, and then they shot him full of morphine, and went back to the party.

"About two hours later they came back, and they were *really* drunk, and they said, 'Look, we don't want him waking us up in the middle of the night for another shot of morphine when we got hangovers. So we're going to give it to him now.' Well, they overdosed him. He went crazy, screaming and yelling, reliving his past. So my wife and I just sat up with him all night, making sure he never fell into a deep sleep, because he'd never have woken up.

"The next day the models came in, and one of the models was Jo Ann Pflug. Don and Jo Ann had this thing before she found Jesus, and so when she got there, he was taped up with electrician's duct tape. His arm was taped to his chest, and as soon as he saw her, he took the duct tape off to screw her somewhere, and his shoulder fell out of joint, and at that point I said, 'I've had it. I'm leaving. Somebody is going to die here, and I'm going to get blamed.'

"Before Don fell off the bike and wrecked his shoulder, Don and the Cowboys were talking serious about his coming back in 1970. They were not happy with the team they had, and Don had gone broke in the brokerage business. So he was thinking about making a comeback, until he took the header off the bike, until he went and dislocated his shoulder and ended up with a spiral fracture of his throwing arm."

Don Meredith did not stay out of the limelight long. He became a TV star, an entertainer loved by millions of football fans when he fashioned a second career as one of the stars of ABC's *Monday Night Football* with Howard Cosell and Frank Gifford. Don was a natural, singing songs the way he had in the Cowboys' huddle and just being his own natural self.

Pete Gent, who had been discarded by the game because he angered management with his logic and humor, has never gotten over it, which is true of so many former professional athletes. After football, Gent channeled his energy into writing books, including three highly acclaimed novels, *North Dallas Forty, The Franchise,* and *North Dallas After Forty.* All three are remarkably fine works that reveal the inner workings of the game and the thoughts and emotions of the players in plots devised from the mind of one cynical, angry, beaten, and semitough human being.

Because of *North Dallas Forty,* Don Meredith and Pete Gent will be forever connected through their characters Seth Maxwell and Phil Elliott, played by film stars Mac Davis and Nick Nolte. They were the wild ones, painting the entire team with that image. Most teammates will point out that after reading *North Dallas Forty,* they did not recognize much of what went on, and that is because many of the players stayed home with their wives, while the two of them ran roughshod over Texas and the NFL.

Their retirement after the 1968 season marked the end of the Old NFL. Those who followed would be just as talented, or more so, but none would be as colorful, as salaries would soar and briefcases would replace lunch pails, and investments in stocks and bonds and fancy restaurants would replace the dog track and the ponies.

Meredith and Gent stayed friends after football, though their friendship faded after the release of the movie version of *North Dallas Forty.* Part of the reason was that Meredith had made peace with his past, and Gent still had not. Nevertheless, Gent has never lost his affection for his old running mate.

PETE GENT: "When *Monday Night Football* first was offered to him, he almost didn't take it. He was out of football, and we were sitting in his house on Prescott Road, and he had just gone broke, and he told me about the offer. He said, 'They are thinking about doing a game on Monday night on ABC.' He said, 'I'd be one of the announcers, but I think I'd rather be on CBS on the weekends with Frank Gifford.' I said, 'Don, on Monday night you're going to be the only game on. You're not going to be one of six games. If you're good, you're going to make a fortune.'

"He hemmed and hawed with ABC, never signed a contract, and the thing was such a hugh success, and so when they got around to trying to resign him, he had them. And he was on a *long* time.

"My wife and I lived near the airport, and Don would come by the house, and I'd drive him to the airport, and he'd leave his car in my driveway. Around that time his son Michael lived with my wife and me off and on.

"I can remember one time Don came back from a game in Philadel-

376 ★ PETER GOLENBOCK

phia. He told me during the game Howard Cosell got drunk and threw up into Gifford and Meredith's boots. He said Howard had to leave the game at halftime.

"I haven't seen Don in a long time. Several things happened between us. When *North Dallas Forty* first came out, I came in to Dallas on a book tour for four or five days, and he came back into town to do a Cowboy game on Monday night, so he left me a message at one of the bookstores that 'Seth Maxwell called,' and he left a phone number. I called him, and we planned to go to the game together. At the same time Bob Rafelson was still thinking about doing the movie, and so Rafelson met me that Monday, and we were going to go to that game, too, but I got so fucked up, I was so tired and so drunk and so doped up, that when I got to the stadium, I just hallucinated. I kept seeing Texas Stadium as a big transmitter to God.

"I can still remember, Bob Rafelson wore these real peculiar sunglasses. They looked like welding goggles. He was a peculiar guy, and I could still see him standing there in the parking lot, just stiff, with his head down, talking out of the side of his mouth, saying, 'Pete, quit jumping over the cars.'

"I had tickets to sit in the box of the McClendons, the guy who owned a local radio station. Thank God I didn't get up there. I had a press pass. I had a regular ticket. I had every kind of pass there was, and what happened, I tried to go in through an exit and they arrested me for public drunkenness. It was horrible but it could have been a lot worse. It could have been made public. Apparently it took eight or nine Burns guards to hold me down. In Texas, when the cops grab you, they are supposed to take you to a psychiatrist, and if he can't figure out what's wrong with you, you go to Terrell, the state mental institution, for three days, no questions asked.

"When I finally came to in this jail, I realized, 'I'm in deep shit.' I was laying there half undressed in the cell, and I kept looking over, watching the cops going back and forth, and finally one looked over at the other cop sitting on a desk, and he sort of shrugged, and the cop sitting on the desk said, 'That's old Pete Gent.'

"And then Don Meredith walked in in a yellow ABC blazer, and I thought, 'This is a dream. I'm dreaming all this. This can't be happening.' I figured I would walk right through the bars. I actually felt I could disassemble and reassemble my molecules to the other side of the bars. And I got right to the bars, and I thought, 'Here comes the hard part.' And I hit those bars, and I realized, 'I'm in here. This isn't a fucking dream. I'm in jail.'

"And then the Dallas cops came to transfer me and take me to Baylor Hospital to a psychiatrist, and they got the cuffs on me behind my back and got me in the police car, and they wanted to know why I fought those security guards the way I did. They said, 'Why did you do that?'

"I said, 'Hey, that's not a fair question. It's like me asking why you're a cop.' I said, 'Come on, if I have to see the psychiatrist, it's not fair to keep me handcuffed. What's he going to think when he sees me with handcuffs on? He's going to think I'm nuts. You gotta give me at least an even chance.'

"So the cop reached down to uncuff me, and he said, 'Okay, but if you make one false move, I'm going to beat the shit out of you.'

"They let me walk in without cuffs on, and I sat in front of this psychiatrist. I kept focusing on his hands. He had a Baylor class ring on his hand, and I kept thinking, 'If I can't fool a guy from Baylor, I deserve to go to Terrell.' Christ. It was horrible. Everything they said I did, I had done.

"I had turned out to be exactly what Tom Landry said I would be: someone who should never be let out on his own.

"Don was pretty pissed at me that night. But we stayed in pretty close contact for several years after that. Then the book came out, and they actually asked him to play that character, Seth Maxwell. He dealt with that, and everything was fine. The book didn't seem to bother him. He was sort of glad to see it. But when it came out as a movie, his attitude changed about it. But I never felt we weren't friends. I felt like it was one of those things: He decided to move to Santa Fe. And after a really messy divorce, I left Texas and moved back home to Bangor, Michigan, with my son, Carter.

"My second wife was from North Fort Worth. She was a pretty progressive person, or I couldn't have dealt with her. Still, everybody in her family said 'nigger' and voted for George Wallace. She thought they were all crazy, until the divorce came. Suddenly they all became geniuses and needed to have my property! And they got it. Wiped me fucking out.

"By the time I met Don, he had so many demons in his life, and he tried so hard to deal with them, and I always felt Don did pretty well. I don't know if I'd have done everything exactly the way he did it, but look at the end result, look at where he is today, compared to where he could be. He is not somewhere gagging on his own blood. He's sitting up in the mountains in Santa Fe.

"Jerry Jones and his PR guys have tracked down all the old Cowboys, got their phone numbers, and mailed them out to the rest of us. All Meredith gave was a post office box and a fax number. I intended to buy a box of crayons and fax him an obscene picture, and write on it, 'Remember her, Don?'

"I was talking to Frank Clarke, and the first thing he asked me was, 'Have you talked to Don?' I said, 'Not in ten years.' Don just drifted away. Don is just drifting, slipsliding away. Apparently Frank has tried to get a hold of him, a lot of guys, but he won't respond. A fax number? Give me a break.

"Why is this guy this way? Does this mean he never meant any of that stuff? Is he afraid we're going to find out? We saw his nightmares. We *all* had our nightmares. But we never thought any less of him."

Don Meredith is in hiding. It's as though he's in the NFL witness protection program. He doesn't list an address, only a post office box. He refuses to give a phone number, only a number to fax him. When his former teammates fax, they say he doesn't respond. He avoids most football functions. He has become football's equivalent of Joe DiMaggio, the Yankee Clipper, who makes ceremonial appearances but fiercely protects his privacy. Why Meredith is so reclusive seems a mystery. As Pete Gent asked, "Why is this guy this way?"

Innocently I began my correspondence with Don Meredith by sending him a letter—by fax—asking for an interview. Nothing. I sent a second request, and this time he called me. I told him how much his input would mean to the book, because he was such an important part of it, but he made it clear he would not talk to me about his Cowboy days. I asked if he would talk about his childhood. His voice hardened, and he let me know in no uncertain terms that he would not answer any questions—period.

For a time after football Don Meredith was a Hollywood star. He had the lead in the TV drama series *Police Story*, and while working in L.A. he met his present wife, Susan, who had been married to a prominent actor. Today, she is not only his wife but his business manager as well.

Some actors protect their privacy and are rarely written about because their agents and managers work hard to control what is written about them. This is apparently what happened with Don Meredith. My friends at NFL Films told me that when Don agreed to an interview, Susan insisted on seeing every question before he could go on camera. That's control.

After I wrote the final draft, I sent Don several of the early chapters and requested comments. Athletes for the most part love to talk about their lives. This was especially true of the Dallas football players, who loved the game and each other with a ferocity I hadn't seen before. Meredith's refusal to take part in this project with his teammates was puzzling to me, much as his refusal to participate in Cowboy events had been to his team-mates. But of one thing I was certain: I was getting the Hollywood freeze-out. One of Don's handlers and spin doctors, in this case his wife, was putting me on notice to watch my back. At this point, I was frustrated and a little bit angry myself, because my experience is that those who refuse to be interviewed are always the first to holler that your account of them is awry when the book comes out. I again asked his wife if Don would be willing to talk about any of this. Again she said he would not. She was not friendly.

I decided to fly out to Santa Fe to learn more about Don Meredith's life. Santa Fe is one of this country's most spectacular locales. It is a jewel of a city built in a valley below the towering Sangre de Cristo Mountains in north-central New Mexico. For two days I visited shops and asked townspeople if they knew him. Most said, "I've seen him around. He used to play football." None were friends of his. Most were of the opinion he was retired, like many residents of the posh adobe city with its trendy art galleries and nouvelle New Mexican cuisine. None knew his address. A reporter on the sports staff of the *Santa Fe New Mexican* knew only that he lived somewhere off the Old Santa Fe Trail. The reporter reiterated Meredith's desire for privacy, relaying to me an account of how he had once tried to interview him as part of a benign piece he had done. He said he had called Meredith's attorney several times to try to arrange a meeting. "I never got anywhere," he said.

I drove past the main square of the city and started up the Old Santa Fe Trail toward the shrub-covered mountains. To the right the high desert spread out for miles, with adobe houses randomly dotting the landscape. Dozens of dirt paths cut off to either side of the trail, many made unnavigable by heavy steel gates, others disappearing from view into the brush. I marveled that the former Cowboy from small-town Texas was living in this land steeped in the culture of the Pueblo, Hopi, and the Navaho. It also seemed a long way from L.A.

After riding aimlessly through the dusty, hot desert on this narrow road with its romantic name, I turned around and drove back toward the city. I saw a sign that read "Museums," and drove to the Museum of In-ternational Folk Art, one of the many historic treasures of Santa Fe. After being overwhelmed by the number and quality of the toys and dolls on display, I sat in a museum alcove on a bench staring out at the desert. "If you want to hide, this is as good a place as any," I thought to myself. A security guard came by. I asked him—as I had asked dozens of others—if he knew where Don Meredith lived. Surprisingly, he said he did.

I drove to the spot down a dusty unpaved road off the Old Santa Fe Trail. If the guard's directions were correct the Merediths live in a large, beautiful adobe home dotted with indigenous trees and cacti with a spectacular view of the pink and purple mountains. They are living in paradise, though one desperately in need of reliable central air conditioning.

I went to knock on the door. There was no answer. The blowing of the desert wind was the only sound. Was this in fact his house? There were other houses in the neighborhood, but I was loath to start canvassing the area. If it was Don Meredith's house, he remained a ghost, invisible, just as he wants it. Still, I was sorry Don didn't answer. It would have been my opportunity to tell him how much I admired him as a quarterback and as a commentator on *Monday Night Football*. And you know what, he wasn't bad in *Police Story* either.

I flew home, thinking of how this boy from Mount Vernon had become a national icon, both in the NFL and as a fixture for football fans on TV. And yet so much about Don Meredith seems shrouded in mystery. He remains, for his fans as well as for his teammates, a towering, if reluctant, hero.

PART II

The New NFL

33

The New Order

With the unexpected retirement of Don Meredith and the forced dismissal of his sidekick, Pete Gent, the law-and-order leadership of Tom Landry regained control of the hearts and minds of the Cowboys, a shift that was reflected nationally with the election in the fall of 1968 of Richard Nixon and his vice president, Spiro Agnew. It would be a strange few years, filled with wonder and horror. A black man, Charles Evers, would be elected mayor in a southern town, Fayette, Mississippi. Neil Armstrong would step on the moon. But Mary Jo Kopechne would drown in Senator Edward Kennedy's automobile after a drunken night of partying, and a week later on the other coast Charles Manson's followers would brutally murder Sharon Tate and four others. A week after that Woodstock drew a throng of hippie music lovers, which was followed by news of the My Lai Massacre of 567 old men, women, and children by American soldiers in a faraway Vietnamese village.

It was a time for seriousness, reexamination of purpose. With Gent gone, Lee Roy Jordan could go back to beating up on the opposition and Cowboy management could call a halt to the narc patrols, though drugs would surface as an issue in another year and continue to be a serious problem throughout the coked-up '70s.

With Meredith gone, Tom Landry would no longer have to fight with his quarterback over play calling. The clash of lifestyles between the Puritanical coach and his sinning quarterback, however, would continue as Dandy Don's heir apparent, Craig Morton, a left-wing California intellectual who loved to read, was a rock and rolling night owl in his own right. Walt Garrison, the stocky fullback from the Texas country-and-western, bull-roping rodeo mold, was impressed with Morton's stamina.

WALT GARRISON: "Craig Morton, like Don Meredith before him, was a party animal. In fact, he was the *whole zoo*. Meredith was not the kind of guy who would give you the impression that football was the most important thing in his life. He wasn't going to push himself to work hard to be the best. He let his natural talents do his work for him, and if that wasn't going to be enough, to hell with it. To Meredith football and life were separate. And he sure wasn't going to let football interfere with his pursuit of all the world had to offer in the way of life, libation, and the pursuit of women.

"Morton was like Meredith. Football was not his whole life. He was more dedicated than Meredith but that wasn't saying a lot.

"Craig was famous for his partying. That boy could rock and roll, let me tell you. He spent money like it was fertilizer and he had a couple thousand head of cattle. And boy, he had some good-looking girlfriends. I don't know any of their names but he'd come to a party and he always had somebody shiny with him. But hell, he didn't have a wife or family and he was the quarterback for the Dallas Cowboys, which was glamorous as hell and he had a big contract, so why not enjoy it?

"Morton proved he was a great athlete. You'd have to be great to stay out as many nights as he did and do all the crazy stuff he did and still make practice. The guy was phenomenal."

If Morton provided the nightlife, a gimpy-legged tight end with the disposition of a snorting bull by the name of Mike Ditka added rowdiness. Getting Ditka, a future Hall of Famer with a reputation for bloodlust, was Tom Landry's idea. A few days after the '69 season, Tom Landry called Ditka, who had feuded with coach Joe Kuharich in Philadelphia while spending much of his season with the Eagles drinking heavily. Ditka was thinking about retiring, even though he still had a year left on his contract.

Landry told him, "We don't even know if you can play anymore, but we're going to bring you down and take a look at you and see if you can play a few more years." Ditka had always hated the Cowboys because of their arrogance and their goody-two-shoes image, but he had despised Kuharich more, and he agreed to come if Landry could swing a trade for him. Just prior to the '69 season the Cowboys shipped Dave McDaniels, a second-round draft choice who turned out to be one of Gil Brandt's mistakes, to Philadelphia in exchange for the eight-year veteran.

Ditka created headlines a week before the '69 season began when he was involved in an early-morning accident after a night on the town. He weighed 235, and because of his fat jowls halfback Walt Garrison started calling him "Monk," short for "Chipmunk." Garrison, who enjoyed watching a good train wreck, was fascinated by the unpredictable Ditka.

WALT GARRISON: "When Ditka joined the Cowboys, defensive backs Charlie Waters and Cliff Harris used to taunt Ditka. 'Ya, Mike, you got some great moves.' And they'd swivel their heads back and forth indicating the extent of Ditka's moves.

"In practice Charlie and Cliff would cover Monk like paint. They'd be all over him because he couldn't beat them deep and they knew it. So they didn't have to be honest.

"Ditka would try his damndest when he was running his routes to get those two little bastards up close enough so he could give them a forearm to the chops. Right before he made his cut, he'd try to cream our cornerbacks.

"That was Ditka.

"Ditka got his teeth knocked out in an auto accident the year he joined us. He flipped his car up over on top of a parked car. Went through the windshield and broke his jaw.

"The dentist told Ditka, 'We can wire your teeth shut but you can't play tomorrow. Or we can pull them.'

"Ditka says, 'Pull the sonofabitches.'

"Well, as it turned out, they had to wire his jaw shut anyhow because it was broke. But he played all the same. You could hear him out on the field breathing through his teeth. 'Hiss-haw, hiss-haw, hiss-haw.' Sounded like a rabid hound. And you could hear that mad dog Ditka cussin' even with his mouth wired shut. 'God da otherrucker.'

"Man, that Ditka was mean. He walked into a restaurant one night, walked over to a table with some chairs stacked on it, and just raked them all off with his big ole forearm and motioned for us to come on over and sit down.

"Nobody said a word. I know why, too. Ditka had the foulest temper of any man I've ever met. It was so bad people used to like to get him mad to see what he'd do because he could lose control in a slim second and anything could happen. That was the fun of it—the element of surprise.

"Ya, Ditka was a madman. He had a terrible temper when he played cards. A bad card player who hates to lose with a terrible temper. He'd throw chairs across the room.

"Why did they let him play? Because before he got mad, he'd lose all his money. He was so competitive he'd stick with lousy cards, and everyone knew it. It was like having your own automated handy teller.

"[Dan] Reeves and [Dave] Manders played Landry and Ditka in tennis one evening at training camp over at the apartments at Cal Lutheran and there's a lot of young couples there with kids. Everything's real nice and sociable until Ditka gets behind. Then Mike starts up. 'Shit! How did I miss that goddamn shot! I hate this fucking game!' At the top of his lungs with mothers scattering trying to get their kids out of earshot. They might as well have moved them to Arizona as loud as Ditka was cussin.' 'Goddamn sonsabitches!'

"The whole time Landry never said a word. Finally, Ditka misses a shot, slams his racket down, smashes it all to hell and throws what's left of it at the net. Well, the damn thing goes *under* the net and skips along the court and hits Landry in the ankles. Tom's hopping around hurting like hell and he looks over at Reeves and says, 'Boy, you can get hurt playing this game.' "

With the retirement of Don Perkins, their indestructible back, the Cowboys were looking to Garrison to be one of the starters in the backfield. Garrison, who grew up in Lewisville, Texas, was the perfect Tom Landry ballplayer, an overachiever who worked as hard as he could to do as well as he could. As a high school boy Garrison had worked in the local peanut mill from midnight to eight every Friday and Saturday night to help make ends meet. The man who owned the nut factory was the brother of the governor of New Mexico, and as a favor to Garrison's dad he helped the kid get a scholarship at Oklahoma State. Garrison starred at fullback on a bad team that made history his senior year, when OSU beat the mighty Oklahoma Sooners of Bud Wilkinson in a stunning upset, 17–16.

Garrison signed as a free agent with the Cowboys in '66, sat on the bench for three years, and with Perkins's departure, was finally getting his chance. In Texas, Garrison became a crowd favorite because not only was he a Cowboy but he was also a cowboy, who knew how to rope a bull and ride a bucking bronco, and he actually performed and did well in rodeos. He *was* Texas. He dipped snuff, and his commercials for Skoal and

Copenhagen made him nationally famous. The other thing he did was whittle, though one time it nearly cost him a finger. This was one tough son of a gun Texan.

WALT GARRISON: "One time before a game Bob Lilly brought in a hunting knife for me to sharpen. So I put a hell of an edge on that puppy. Then I decided I'd whittle a little bit. I had a block of wood I carried with me and a couple of pocket knives. I wanted to cut a chunk off that block, so I thought, 'Man, Lilly's knife looks ideal.' Only thing was, it was so sharp it went right through that wood and cut my index finger down to the bone. The whole finger was just hanging there. Blood was gushing out all over the place. It was making such a mess, I had to pull a wastebasket over and let it bleed in there. And I like to fill the damn basket up.

"Charlie Waters was rooming with me then and he threw up, freaked out, and fainted all at the same time. Then he started screaming, 'Walt, you cut your finger off! You cut your finger off!'

"Charlie called down for the team doctor, but, of course, he was out eatin'. So I told Charlie to go down to the trainers' room and get me some tape while I held my finger together. A few minutes later Charlie came back with the tape and I taped the finger back on. Then I got a big bucket of ice and stuck my finger in it and went to sleep.

"Only Charlie couldn't sleep a wink all night. 'You pissed me off so bad that night,' he said. 'You were sound asleep with your hand in that bucket of ice and I stayed up all night. I thought you were gonna bleed to death, so I kept checking to see if the ice bucket was filling up with blood.'

"The next morning I went out to the stadium and the doctor sewed me up. He put nineteen stitches in my finger right before the game. And I told him, 'Don't tell Tom.'

" 'OK, but just don't fumble.'

"I ended up having a great day. I caught seven passes, one of them in the end zone for a TD, and gained 120 yards on the ground. And Charlie played the worst game of his career.

"And all because I needed something to relax."

The other penciled-in backfield starter in '69 was another veteran, Dan Reeves, but because the versatile back needed surgery and was on the downside of his career, the Cowboys in '69 chose as their number one draft choice a surprise pick, a bruising running back by the name of Calvin Hill. The surprise was that Hill had attended Yale University, an Ivy

League school not known for turning out pro football players. (Cowboy fans bristle when reminded that Chuck Mercein, who helped the Packers win the Ice Bowl in '67, went to Yale.) When the pick was announced, Cowboy fans were incensed. What were Tex Schramm and Gil Brandt doing drafting a player from the lowly Ivy League? But in Hill the Cowboys were getting an intelligent, thoughtful man, just the type of player Tom Landry enjoyed working with. But they were also getting an idealist, a divinity student concerned with right and wrong, good and evil, justice and mercy. And this was one player not afraid to speak out on issues such as Vietnam, racial equality, and players' salaries, much to the Cowboys' chagrin.

CALVIN HILL: "I was born in Baltimore, but in the ninth grade I went on a Schenley Wholesaler's Foundation Scholarship to Riverdale, a boarding school in New York City. It was a boarding school at that time, so I lived in the dormitory.

"I was identified because my doctor's son had gone to that school, and he was chatting one day with the headmaster, who said, 'We have this scholarship program, and it would be an opportunity to bring different kinds of people to Riverdale.' Riverdale was founded as an international school, and the idea of getting different people, which you call diversity now, was one that the founder of the school, Frank Hackett, believed in very strongly, and John Jones, the second headmaster, who was headmaster when I was there, also believed in it and was always looking for ways to bring different kinds of people to Riverdale, and so he talked to my doctor, and my doctor recommended me, and made them aware of me and me aware of the scholarship, and I applied for it and I got it.

"My father was a construction worker who had not gotten an education, but he believed in education. When the opportunity arose for me to try to get a scholarship, he was excited about it.

"Going to Riverdale was a tremendous culture shock. I had grown up in a section of Baltimore that was all black. Although I had competed in sports against whites and others, I had never lived around them. I can remember going home for the first time that Thanksgiving after two months at Riverdale, and telling my friends who wanted to know what it was like, wowing them with stories.

"In my world everybody was Christian, so when I met a Jewish friend of mine—the school was predominantly Jewish, 60 percent of the kids were Jewish—they celebrated the Jewish holidays, and I had never been around these holidays, and we had matzoh. I remember the first time we had matzoh, we served it at school, and I thought they had gotten a deal on saltines with no salt. I had never heard of agnostics and atheists, and to find out someone was an agnostic or atheist, I couldn't fathom that. And to find out there were so many differences. I didn't realize. I had never focused on it. In my world you were either white or black. It was a tremendous culture shock for me.

"And it's funny, but at Riverdale, while I was made aware of the differences, they weren't things that in the context of that community were viewed as being divisive. And so, I've often talked to other black kids who went to Riverdale when I was there, and we've often remarked or thought in some respects Riverdale may have ruined it for us, because at Riverdale we could see the possibilities. It was an ideal world, and people accepted you for who you were, and what you brought to the table, and in that sense, perhaps it was ahead of its time.

"I would probably not have played football had I not gone to Riverdale. I had never played organized football before I came to Riverdale. In fact, the first time I ever practiced was the first time I ever put on a uniform, and Paul Zimmerman, who went on to become the football writer for *Sports Illustrated*, was the beat writer for the *World Telegram and Sun*, and he was covering a practice at Riverdale, and I put my thigh pads on the wrong way, and he corrected me and told me how to put my uniform on, but by my senior year I actually was a *Parade* magazine All-America.

"When it came time to look at colleges, in 1968 you drew a line across the northern border of Maryland across the country, and you couldn't look south of that line. The year before I got out, the University of Maryland had taken its first two black football players. A couple years prior to that Navy had its first black player. So you didn't look in the South. A lot of the schools that recruited my son Grant never talked to me. My headmaster at one point wanted me to think about going to Georgia Tech. I figured football was tough enough without having your own team not liking you, too.

"I actually wanted to go to a Big Ten school, but the peer pressure at Riverdale was that if you were able to get into an Ivy League school, you certainly availed yourself of that opportunity, and so I went to Yale, which in some ways was very similar to Riverdale. Bigger to be sure. Very competitive academically. I tell people it took me two or three weeks to find someone I was smarter than. I made sure I saw that person at least once a day!

"It was very competitive football. While we weren't on the same tier as your Big Ten schools like Penn State, we weren't far below them. One of the things that attracted me to Yale was my visit in '64 to the Dartmouth game, and they had 68,000 people at the Yale Bowl. The years I was there, Dartmouth, Harvard, or Princeton were always games you could assume they would sell out or close to it.

"We had good teams. Dartmouth was the other very good team. We were league champs. Our freshman team was undefeated, and then my last two years we were 18–1–1. We tied the last game I played against Harvard, a 29–29 tie. We were ahead 29–13 with a minute and a half to go, and we had the ball. The roof caved in.

"I was a member of the Black Student Alliance at Yale. We were one of the first black student groups in the country. We petitioned for African-American studies, and Yale hired a historian from Tennessee State, Arne Bontemps, and as a result African-American studies gained a great deal of legitimacy at Yale's campus. I was also a member of the Deacons at the student chapel under William Sloane Coffin, who became as much a mentor of mine as anybody.

"I was more involved in the civil rights movement than in the antiwar movement. I had done some picketing back in Baltimore for equal opportunity, and through the chapel and the Black Student Alliance, we did tutoring in various communities in New Haven. I became a mentor for a bunch of kids in New Haven. We agitated for relevant courses. And Yale was good in that respect. [President] Kingman Brewster was ahead of the learning curve in many ways.

"At that juncture if I had any heroes it was Martin Luther King and Coffin. They as much as anyone made me think about going to divinity school after college. When King was assassinated . . . first there was the John Kennedy assassination, and then the King assassination, and then the next Kennedy assassination, and afterward when you were able to reflect on where Malcolm X was moving, not so much when he died, but with the publishing of his autobiography, those four things were a loss of innocence. The night King was killed, I remember thinking, there was a frustration, a certain loss of hope, and I think that's what the '60s represented—so much hope. I can remember marching on Washington in August 1963, and there was so much hope on that day, and by the end of the decade three of the very important people who comprised that hope, who brought that hope, were dead. They were all assassinated. You go in a lot of black houses now, and typically they will have a picture of Jesus Christ, and they will have a picture of King and one or two of the Kennedys. At least from my generation or our parents', that was the extinguishing of people who we felt were in our corner.

"And I can remember the night King was killed. It was strange, just like the first Kennedy assassination. You heard he was shot, and then you said, 'It can't be,' and then they said, 'He's dead.' That didn't happen. You only read about those things happening. It happened perhaps in Austria, and it certainly happened in the 1800s, but it didn't happen in the United States. And then you suddenly became aware that it does happen. Bill Bradley talks about the 'civil society,' and the civil society that didn't happen.

"In 1969 I went from Connecticut during the civil rights era and the anti-Vietnam era to Dallas, which was much more conservative. But that was much the same as going from Baltimore to Riverdale. That was going into a different culture.

"What I saw was a place that was more conservative. On a personal level, I had assumed for example, that most people, white and black, saw Martin Luther King as a responsible, nonviolent figure, and I realized that some people in Dallas didn't see him that way. They saw him as a rabble-rouser. And it was an interesting perspective for me, because while on the one hand, I was coming from Yale, I was also a Dallas Cowboy and I was in Perkins Divinity School at SMU, where I was a little more to the left than the prevailing theology in a lot of churches in Dallas. Perkins was very progressive, and I was able to find like-minded people, but I was accustomed to *everyone* being where I was, and in some respects I was a little different."

Though Tom Landry was skeptical a player from Yale could start at halfback, he was counting on the 6' 4", 225-pound Bulldog to play somewhere, perhaps linebacker or tight end, and during training camp Landry had the quiet rookie practice at those positions as well.

CALVIN HILL: "Nineteen sixty-nine was an interesting year for the Dallas Cowboys, because after the '68 season three things happened that they really had not planned on. For one, Don Meredith retired, so they knew they had to get a new quarterback, but they still had two-thirds of the backfield intact with Don Perkins and Dan Reeves, and so they drafted me, and after that Don Perkins retired and then Reeves wasn't able to come back, and so the question was, 'Would Dan be able to come back from his latest knee surgery?' And if he did, probably I would have played another position.

"At first they weren't quite sure where they were going to play me, and I went off to the College All-Star game, and when I got back, Craig Baynham, who had taken Danny's place the year before and was the second running back, got hurt, and so in the second exhibition game against the 49ers I got to start at running back, primarily because no one else was able to play. And I did a lot better than anybody expected.

"I had just been back for a week or so. Typically in the training camp before the vets come in, they spend the first week with the rookies spoonfeeding them, and then when the vets come in, they put things in very quickly. The vets pretty much know what's going on anyhow. So you have to try to understand what they are putting in, but they are doing it at such a quick pace that you can very easily get lost, and what happened, I had a wonderful coach, a man named Ermal Allen. He was just an unbelievable coach and understood the game. Ermal had a great ability to analyze the game and to break it down, and he ultimately got involved in research and development. There was nobody better. But Ermal was also kind of cynical, and he was honest, and sometimes he hit the wrong nerve, but my sense with Ermal was that beyond the cynicism was a lot of truth. I got along very well with him, because I listened to him and I tried to learn from him, and I learned a lot from him.

"In spite of the force-feeding, I didn't know half the time whether I was getting a pitch or whether I was getting a handoff so that first exhibition game I was uncomfortable. Despite that, in football there's a certain level where you are instinctive. When you're a running back, and you have the ball, you know people are trying to hit you so you try to avoid them as much as possible. I wasn't completely out to lunch."

JOHN WILBUR: "In 1969 Calvin Hill was a rookie. That was a pretty good choice by the Cowboys. Calvin was an inspiration. I'll never forget his first exhibition game. Calvin had just come back from the All-Star game, and they completely changed practice around so that he could get work in for the San Francisco game. He came in, and for one week we had what they called 'Calvin Hill drills,' drills just for him. He was the only running back. He'd run the plays, and the coaches would explain them to him. And we'd run another play. And we did this every day for four, five days. He would get daily coaching, and it would be a ballet for Calvin Hill in practice.

"The game came, and we were playing the 49ers at Kezar Stadium, and Calvin went out and ran for 106 yards. After the game he was sitting next to me on the team bus, and Calvin said to me, 'God, John, I don't think I did very well. I did terrible. I played one of the worst games I ever had in my life. I blew this play, and I blew that assignment.' Little did he know it was the start of a brilliant career, and he had played a wonderful game."

PETTIS NORMAN: "Because of Calvin's size, most people could not envision him as a running back, including the opposition, and we were just taken aback by his athleticism and the fact he could run and jump over people and the way he'd just give his body up, and he was just a breath of fresh air for the Cowboys, to whom he brought another dimension. Because our running attack prior to that had been very successful, Don Perkins off tackle as a fullback, but Calvin could do the sweeps, the traps, he could leap; he just brought another dimension to our offense.

"Everybody liked him. He was very well-liked by everybody. Calvin and I spent a lot of time together. He's a very intelligent person and could be with anybody in any group and feel at ease with them. I developed a deep respect and liking for Calvin. Calvin was Calvin, and he was not going to change for anyone—i.e., the way he dressed. Calvin came with an idea that dressing was not important. He didn't care what anyone else wore. Calvin was not going to spend his money on clothes that were going to wear out anyway. He was like that. He had strong convictions, and I admired him for sticking with those convictions. On road trips he would always wear a coat and tie. But people would accuse him of getting his clothes out of a Goodwill bag. He was just a guy who did not care about wearing the latest fashions. Image to Calvin was not important at all. He had a lot more to him than just image. He had some very strong beliefs about life and God and man and relationships. We would have some very serious conversations."

JOHN WILBUR: "We were playing Washington in '69, and it was the day of the big antiwar demonstration, and Calvin and I went down there and got tear-gassed. We were antiwar, the other side of the team. The young, active, smarter guys, more worldly, wider read, were against the war. The black guys were against the war. Some guys had gone to Vietnam to boost morale during the off-season. There were guys who were in active duty. The southern guys had their opinion, but there wasn't a lot of talk about it in the locker room. We were all on the same team. Everyone had a different way of dealing with it."

During the six years he was a Cowboy, Calvin was outspoken on the issues that were important to him, and he made Cowboy management nervous.

CORNELL GREEN: "Calvin made a big impression, because he was the closest thing to Jim Brown I've seen. People don't realize that Calvin was

6' 4", weighed 235 pounds. Calvin could fall forward for five yards. He could get yards without even passing the line of scrimmage. I just thought he was a great back.

"There were people at the top of the Cowboys organization who didn't like him, people were just thinking he was going to change the status quo too much, or he was going to ask for too much money."

Those "people" would be right on both counts. With the coming of Calvin Hill and a bumper crop of young, politically savvy black men, Tex Schramm and Tom Landry would have to justify their actions and learn to get along with these players for the next decade. Over time, and after making several mistakes in the way he handled rebellious stars, Tom Landry would learn that he would have to adapt to them, not the other way around. As the sixties came to a close, so did the era of the silent, grateful, hat-in-hand football player. In the future these players would demand fairness, rationality in decisions, and above all, respect. Or else.

34

Roger

It must have been fate, because there is no other way to explain how Roger Staubach ended up becoming the symbol of the Dallas Cowboys in the 1970s. Staubach began his pro career in 1969, and before his retirement a decade later, he would be known as Captain America, the leader of America's Team. He would quarterback the Cowboys to four Super Bowls and be hailed as one of the great players of his generation.

He had been drafted in the tenth round his junior year at Navy all the way back in 1964 by Tex Schramm and Gil Brandt, and after five long years—in sports a lifetime—he was finally free from the Navy to begin his pro football career. Tom Landry had been willing to wait. Landry, after all, himself missed four years while flying bombers in World War II, and then returned to the University of Texas. And Landry knew Staubach had been someone special, a Heisman Trophy winner his senior year at Navy, a naval officer, a man dedicated to whatever he attempted. In '68 Staubach had spent his two-week leave attending Landry's Quarterback School, and Landry had been impressed with the fine shape he was in and with his work-hard attitude. Whether he was a skilled-enough passer, that was another issue.

But for Roger Staubach to become the Cowboys' quarterback, a series of events had to transpire, and eerily, these events all took place. The

first came in June 1969 when third-string quarterback Jerry Rhome demanded to be traded and was granted his request. The next came a month
later when Don Meredith unexpectedly retired. Without that one event, it
is doubtful Staubach would ever have remained a Cowboy, for he would
have been backing up *two* veteran quarterbacks, Meredith and Craig Morton, and either the twenty-seven-year-old would have rotted on the bench,
or, more likely, he would have demanded to be traded. But with Don
Meredith in retirement, Staubach came to camp accepting his backup role.
For the first year, anyway.

When Staubach reported in the summer of 1969, to most outsiders he
began as a curiosity. It didn't seem conceivable that he would ever play in
the NFL, never mind take Craig Morton's job. But those people didn't
know what made Roger Staubach tick. All his life Staubach had started
low on depth charts and had worked his way up to fame and glory. Frank
Merriwell was a fictional character who usually won the game in the final
moments by doing something implausibly heroic. But he had nothing on
Roger Staubach.

ROGER STAUBACH: "I grew up in Cincinnati. I was an only child, and my
parents lived their Catholic faith, and so I grew up in a Catholic grade
school, like back in the good old days, with nuns that beat a lot of sense
into my head. I feel the nuns had a great influence on me. I had a very positive experience as far as my faith and my education, and it carried on
through high school. I went to Purcell High School, an all-boys Catholic
school, and I would have gone to a Catholic college, like Notre Dame, but
it wasn't meant to be.

"I played football, basketball, and baseball at Purcell. I also played
baseball in summer leagues. I played against Pete Rose. He was on a team
called S&H Green Stamps and he went to Western Hills High School. I
was highly rated, along with some others like Eddie Brinkman, who went
to the same high school as Pete. Pete wasn't at a high level at that time,
but he developed. Pete was kind of a scrawny kid in high school, but he
had these intangibles, and he continued to develop. He got better, stronger.

"In football I played tight end and defensive back as a freshman, and
my sophomore year our coach, Jim McCarthy, switched me to quarterback. In my junior year I broke my hand so I played only at defensive
halfback. So my senior year was the first year I really played quarterback.

"We were a running team. We had a T formation offense, so we
didn't throw very much. I threw the ball maybe five or six times a game.

I didn't think that was going to be that exciting, but that switch changed my life.

"I had this instinct for running. I improvised, and I ran. No one really knew about my arm. I had a real strong arm from baseball, but no one knew if I was going to be a passing quarterback.

"I signed a tender that if I went to any Big Ten school, I'd go to Purdue. Ohio State had recruited me, and also Northwestern and Michigan, and the quarterback coach at Purdue, Bob DeMoss, felt I had the arm, saw that I was tall, saw my running abilities and saw my baseball arm, so he wanted to groom me as a college quarterback, so I really liked him. I was very close to going to Purdue, but it was one of those things in life where you're not sure, and I was torn between going there and going to the Naval Academy, which was also talking to me.

"I would have gone to Notre Dame, but they never recruited me. When you're in Cincinnati and you're a Catholic kid, Notre Dame is a big deal. I could have gone there. But they didn't contact me until June after I played in a North-South high school All-Star game. The head coach's nephew was the quarterback, and he kept moving me around, so in that All-Star game I played weak safety, wide receiver, and in the fourth quarter I played quarterback. The college scouts were watching, and after that game Notre Dame offered me a scholarship, but it was too late. I was committed to go to the Naval Academy.

"I actually went off to junior college first, to New Mexico Military Institute. I had high grades, but to get to Navy you had to get a 500 in the SATs in both English and math, and in English I had a 480. I had 600-something in math. I only took them once, and I didn't want to take them again. I just said, 'Forget about Navy.' I wasn't sure what I wanted to do.

"They then sent this coach from the New Mexico Military Academy to see me. All the service academies had an arrangement with New Mexico Military. I didn't want to go to prep school because I didn't want to waste a year. I didn't think I had to prep for anything, but the coach talked about the school, said the Navy foundation would fund my scholarship, and it turned out to be one of the real blessings in life. Academically it was just a fantastic school and it was like a redshirt year for me athletically. If I would have gone straight to the Naval Academy with only a year of high school football under my belt, I think it would have been difficult. I don't know what would have happened. And going to New Mexico really helped me develop militarily. I struggled to adapt, not that I was undisciplined, but I got a few demerits. Shining your shoes and doing a lot of stuff like that just didn't seem important, though it really was. It was part of the system, and you had to live with the system, and I had to adapt to that. And that helped me also. And in football we played a very tough junior college schedule.

"When I entered Navy, I really didn't know what my plans were. I knew I wanted to get a good education. The navy would have to sell me on a career, and that's what they do. A lot of kids go there with the dream of being a career marine or naval officer, and they don't do it. And a lot of them with no plans all of a sudden say, 'This is my life.' I didn't really know. I went to Navy because I knew I'd get a good education and also because Navy said I could play both baseball and football. At Navy, you're regimented. You don't have a lot of time to goof off, and I thought it was important if I was going to play sports in college that I just didn't want to skate through. That was fortuitous for me to be thinking that way. I might have spent too much time at sports and not on academics, but at Navy they really made you study.

"As a plebe I had a very good football season. My sophomore year we had two senior quarterbacks, a sophomore quarterback, and a junior quarterback, so on the depth chart I was fifth team going into varsity practice. Our coach, Wayne Hardin, knew about me, and he was counting on me for maybe my junior or senior year, but one of the seniors got hurt and then the sophomore lost a kidney in practice, so now I was third team, though it didn't seem that what I did was going to be very important.

"The senior quarterback, Ron Clemek, was very good. He had had a good junior year, and Bruce Able, the junior quarterback, was good, had a great arm. I was very worried. I was working my tail off.

"We got off to a tough start, lost to Penn State and Minnesota, and I played a little bit at the end of those games. The team was struggling. Our next game was against Cornell, which hopefully was going to be an easier game, but Ron got off to a shaky start, and Coach Hardin put Bruce in, and he had a bad series, so Wayne was ticked off, and so he threw me in there, and we went in and scored, and we won something like 41–7, and so the next week I started against Boston College, and after the first series he took me out. Ron came in, and he didn't do much, and [Coach Hardin] put me back in, and I never came out again. We ended up beating Boston College.

"I was a scrambling quarterback, and our team needed that. Ron was a great passer, but we didn't have the protection, so I ended up doing a lot of scrambling and making things happen, and that was it. I stayed in the rest of the time.

"One of our really outstanding games was outplaying Southern Cal out in California when they were national champions. We lost 13–7, but we were inside the five-yard line at the end of the game when one of our players fumbled on first down on the goal line. It would have been one of the great upsets. I ran for a lot of yards, and so we had this momentum going into the Army game, and we had a great game against Army. We beat Army when they had Paul Dietzel and his Chinese Bandits.

"Wayne Hardin was a very creative coach, a very smart offensive coach, a great X and O guy. Offensively he was great. We always came up with something to take advantage of a team's defense. He taught me a lot about reading defenses. I had a quarterback coach named Doug Scovall, who was with the Eagles a few years ago when he passed away, a great guy, really helped me out. So I had good coaching at Navy and really developed as a quarterback. I continued to develop as a passer.

"In college I ran a lot, and people thought, 'Well, he's a runner.' But if I was just a runner, I never would have made it. In college I had a high percentage of completions. I was a passer, too. But that scrambling confused people. The scouts were wondering, 'Is Roger a scrambling quarterback or is he a passer?' At Navy we had a pro offense. It wasn't a running offense. Wayne would rather have his quarterback drop back and throw the football. He was worried about injuries the same way Landry was later, though in college it's not as bad. And I was not like that. I was different. If I was in trouble I ran. So Wayne adapted to me, because he was like Landry. They knew I wanted to win and they put up with it.

"I was drafted by the Cowboys as a junior in 1964. I was eligible because I had spent a year in junior college. No one thought I would ever play pro ball. I had another year at the Naval Academy and then four years of military service. But Tex Schramm and Gil Brandt saw I was eligible, and so the Cowboys drafted me in the tenth round, and Kansas City did the same thing in a later round.

"I almost signed with the Chiefs. Lamar Hunt came to see me in Annapolis. He designed a contract that would pay me a bonus of $10,000, pay me $500 a month while I was in the Navy, and if I left the Navy, I'd get a contract for a certain amount.

"I called Paul Borden, a Navy legal officer, and I said, 'Paul, can I do this? This is more money than I'm making in the Navy.'

"Paul checked it out, and he said, 'There's no obligation to leave the service. The Navy has no problem with it.' I thought, 'Gee, this is a windfall for me.' So I mentioned it to Dan Petersen, an assistant basketball coach at Navy. Danny, who was close to Gil Brandt, had led the Cowboys to Pete Gent, and Dan said, 'You ought to talk to the Cowboys about it.'

So I mentioned it to Captain Borden, and he called and talked to Gil Brandt, and Gil said, 'Yeah, we want to talk to him.' The next weekend the Cowboys were playing Philadelphia, so Captain Borden flew up there and met with Gil and Tex while Clint Murchison was in the room, and he called me and said that the Cowboys would do the same deal. I said, 'Fine.' 'Cause at the time they were in the NFL, not the AFL, and they had drafted me higher than Kansas City, so I called Lamar Hunt back and said, 'I appreciate everything, but . . .' He said, 'We'd like to negotiate a better deal.' I said, 'That isn't the issue.' I didn't want to get into a bidding war. I just wanted to get it behind me, and I felt Dallas was the right thing, so I signed with Dallas. If you think about it, the $500 a month is almost ludicrous today.

"When it came time for my selection, my choices were to be a line officer in the staff corps, to fly, or be an officer on a ship, to become a Marine, or to go into the supply corps. When I entered Annapolis, it was discovered that though my vision was perfect, at a distance, certain dark colors look alike to me. Dark green and black look the same to me, and as a result it prevented me from being a line officer. They didn't want to train someone to go into a staff corps and be disqualified from flying. The Marines wanted me, and I thought very strongly about that because, though being in the supply corps was a great responsibility, at the Academy if you're gung ho, you want the navy line or the marine corps or flying. The civil engineering corps or the supply corps is less prestigious. So at the last minute I was thinking of the Marines. The Marines are special. They are great, dedicated, but the Marines wanted to be Marines from the time they entered as plebes, and that wasn't me. I didn't feel like I was one of them. So when I went in for my selection, I still wasn't sure what I was going to do, and I decided to stay in the Navy, and so I went into the supply corps. I had a lot of responsibility in Vietnam. Later I learned a lot at Pensacola. I had a big job at the Pensacola Air Station. It helped me as a businessman.

"I volunteered to go to Vietnam. The choices I had were to go out to sea for a couple years or if I went to Vietnam, I'd go for one year and then be on shore duty. At the time my wife, Mary Ann, was pregnant. We had just had a little girl. Vietnam meant I'd get home sooner. And Vietnam had this aura about it that you felt you wanted to participate. Even though I wasn't going to be out there fighting, I was still in a big, big support role. In fact, in an article in *Stars and Stripes* I said I felt guilty I wasn't doing enough in Vietnam, and everybody in the supply corps got ticked off at me. But I didn't mean it in a negative way. When you're a competitor, and

COWBOYS HAVE ALWAYS BEEN MY HEROES ★ 401

you're not out in the middle of things . . . and because my classmates were out there fighting, and I was behind the scenes supporting . . . that was my job.

"The danger was mortar attacks, and at times they threw hand grenades into the officers' club at Danang, and a couple of officers were killed. I used to go there all the time. But it was like being in New York, where you can get hit by a car. Statistically I wasn't in danger.

"I spent my year in Chu Lai, which was south of Danang. We were surrounded by Marines. We had the Marine air wings there. Ordinarily the Marines went in, fought, and didn't stay. Vietnam was the first time the Marines stayed. We supported the Marines and I-corps, which was the northern part of Vietnam from Quang Na all the way to Dong Ah. I was in charge of all the ships that came in there and loaded all the ammunition supplies. I was the officer in charge of logistics. I had 110 sailors working for me. We had these big cranes, forklifts going in and off-loading the ships. It was a lot of responsibility. We brought all the ammunition supplies off the ships and delivered them to the various compounds, which were almost all Marine.

"I had close friends killed in Vietnam, classmates. Tommy Holden, a guard on our football team, was killed. Mike Grammar, a guy in my company. Go to the Vietnam Memorial. If you ever want to be at one of the most emotional places, go there and see all those names. They were all human beings once.

"The trouble with the Vietnam War was that the people who went over there fought because they were told to do it by their country. It wasn't a popular war, and when they came home they were treated like second-class citizens. Robert McNamara, the secretary of defense, was too worried about world opinion rather than American lives. I have never had any respect for him and his baloney and his escalation policies. He can say whatever he wants to say. I started reading his book, and it just made me sick. The decisions that were made did not take into consideration what you have to do in a war. They didn't cut off logistics! We should have mined Hai Phong harbor in 1965. We didn't. Why? 'Cause we might blow up a Russian ship? That's where the Russian ships were bringing in the weapons that were killing our guys. That kind of mentality is a disgrace to this country, and hopefully it will never happen again. If you're going to send people to war, you have to do everything you can to protect them. Even when George Bush went in to the Persian Gulf, he said, 'We're not going to have our hands tied behind our backs like in Vietnam.' All of a sudden you realize what really took place there. You realize our secretary of defense was making decisions that were more concerned with politics than they were about American lives. And that's the tragedy of the war, because a lot of guys died and a lot are still suffering from that war, guys who deserve to be hugged by somebody and told, 'Hey, thanks for going over there.'

"In 1968 I was running the supply arm of the Pensacola Naval Base, and I took a two-week leave and went to my first Cowboys training camp. I had two weeks with the rookies and a very short time with the veterans.

"I was playing for the Pensacola Goshawks after hours. Two months before I was scheduled to arrive, I developed tendinitis in my throwing shoulder. It was serious, because I had never had any trouble with it before. I would go out and throw, and the next day it would be sore as could be. And I was really worried about it. I could not have gone to training camp the way my shoulder was. But I got one shot of cortisone in that shoulder, and I had two very good weeks of training camp.

"I impressed them that I was in good shape, and Landry gave me a playbook, and I was allowed to keep it, which was a real vote of confidence. When I went back to Pensacola, I made up my mind for sure I was going to get out of the navy and play football, and in the spring of '69 I went back to training camp. I was there with Don Meredith and Craig Morton. Jerry Rhome did not go. They were in the middle of trading him.

"And Don Meredith was great to me. He was a fun guy. He was a player's player. They liked him a lot.

"He invited me over to his house for dinner. He was happy-go-lucky, had a good time, but he was one of these guys who could figure out how to get the job done. So here I was thinking, here's Don Meredith, and here was Craig Morton, who was himself getting a little frustrated because he was going into his fifth year, and he was playing behind Don.

"Craig Morton was a very nice person. Craig is one of the finest. He'd give you the shirt off his back. He was a heck of a football player. But people sometimes took advantage of Craig, used him. People got him into some bad investments.

"Craig was one of those guys who was just a good guy. 'Let's go out and have a good time.' He wanted to please everybody. And I think Craig's discipline was affected by that.

"I got along with him. But I knew my age was a factor, and I wanted to play, whether it was in Dallas or someplace else.

"Don and Morton were close, good friends, but Craig was starting to sense, 'Hey, my time has got to come,' and I don't know what would have happened if Meredith had stayed. There's a chance Morton would have been traded, and I would have played behind Don. Who knows what would have happened? Don was a great football player who took the punishment to build Dallas to a winning team. Here was Don Meredith, who had built Dallas to a winning team, but because they didn't win it all, he was getting some criticism. And then, when he retired, everyone said, 'Gee, Don Meredith was really a great player.'

"Don Meredith would have taken Dallas to some Super Bowl victories in the 1970s. Don Meredith was a very good quarterback, and he had the confidence of the team. Some of the players may have questioned Don's discipline at times as far as his fun, but when it came time to play, Don played hurt and he played tough. I think if he would have stayed in Dallas, I would have left. 'Cause I was going to be a starter in the NFL. I would never, ever have allowed myself to be relegated to a backup role for my whole career. I couldn't have handled it. Don would have been very difficult to unseat. Because Landry would not have replaced Don Meredith.

"I remember when the Cowboys PR guy called me and told me Meredith had retired, I was excited. Because even though I had had a real good camp the year before, I didn't know if I was going to make the team. They probably would have kept the three of us. But I wanted to play. I was thinking, 'Gee, I'm twenty-seven, I've got *two* veteran quarterbacks in front of me.' Don was only thirty years old. Now at least I knew that I would definitely be the number two quarterback. I figured I'd spend the first year learning the NFL. But I was thinking that long-term I didn't know where I'd be."

35

The Depths

When Roger Staubach joined the Cowboys, he didn't fit into either of the two camps. He was at odds with the liberals on the team in that he had been in Vietnam, understood why America was fighting there, and defended the policy; and he did not fit into the conservative group of southern hellions in that he was married and square, went to the movies instead of the bars, wasn't hesitant about socializing with the black players, and was such a nose-to-the-grindstone religious straight-arrow that he made the Jim Beam crowd uneasy.

WALT GARRISON: "When Roger Staubach joined the Cowboys in 1969 as a twenty-seven-year-old rookie, nobody figured he'd do much of anything. Yeah, he'd been the Heisman Trophy winner at the Naval Academy. But that was way back in 1963. The Cowboys had drafted him in the tenth round of the 1965 draft on a longshot that in five years, when Roger's tour of duty was up, he'd be both willing and able to play in the NFL.

"But Roger Staubach, of course, was a different kind of person than your normal Homo sapiens. He'd be out on a destroyer in the Gulf of Tonkin or some ungodly place for nine months at a time and then he'd take his leave and come to training camp and work out! That's how sick he was. We'd see him out there sweating his ass off through two-a-days and we'd say, 'What in the hell is he doin' here? He can't even play for three, four more years.'

"The guy had been off serving his country for eleven months and he gets three weeks off and he's out there every day working his butt off. Training camp is exactly like going to boot camp all over again. In fact, I've been to both boot camp and training camp and I'd rather go to boot camp. But Roger'd be out there with us every year.

"Roger Staubach was the epitome of what Landry thought a quarterback should be. He was the most dedicated guy you'll ever be around. If somebody did 100 situps, Roger was going to do 101. If somebody ran a mile in 6 minutes, Roger would do it in 5:59. If somebody threw the ball 60 yards, he was going to throw it 61.

"Landry felt that when you've got a guy as dedicated as Roger was, it was very easy to get the other players to go that extra mile to win. Because your leader was out there doing it. Besides that, Roger was a good Christian, went in and served his country, and had a great wife and kids.

"Landry thought he'd died and gone to heaven.

"Now you've got to admire that kind of dedication. The principles Roger stood for, he wouldn't waver from. If a guy won't compromise his beliefs, no matter what they are, you gotta respect him.

"Roger is not a hypocrite. He doesn't say, 'Hey, you oughta do this.' And then he does something else. Roger just says, 'This is what I do.' He doesn't try to tell you what you oughta do. He ain't a bit phony.

"One thing about Roger Staubach. I've always respected him. I always will. I don't want to spend a lot of time with him but I sure do respect his ass.

"See, Roger just wasn't given to having a good time. He's against having fun. It's in his genes or something. Anything that's fun, you're not supposed to do it. That is the way he feels.

"One time somebody said, 'Boy, wouldn't you love to have your kid grow up to be more like Roger Staubach?'

"And Meredith said, 'No way. I'd want my kid to have more fun.'

"That's the way I feel about Roger. I could never figure out why he couldn't loosen up and have more fun."

Garrison and the other good old boys made fun of Staubach's prudishness. Staubach didn't smoke, drink, or run around at night, and the others would prey on his naivete.

During training camp in 1969, Roger noticed that a very sexy young woman was watching practice. She had on tight shorts and a thin blouse.

She was dating one of the players on the team, and after practice, the player called Staubach over and said, "Roger, you're a Catholic, so I'd like you to meet Sister Teresa."

Roger was very polite and respectful.

"I knew I'd never seen a nun who looked like that," Staubach said later, "but I kept thinking, maybe she really was. I fell for it. The girl told me she was on leave from a convent. I went around the entire camp thinking she was a nun. Every time I'd see her, I'd say, 'Hello, Sister Teresa.' Can you imagine how those guys were laughing at me?"

One time Walt Garrison had Roger try snuff, only he didn't tell him he had to spit it out. During a team meeting Staubach threw up twice, and he was sick for two days, missing practice. He didn't forgive himself, or Garrison.

Yet another time during practice, not long after Walt and his wife had their first son, Roger said to Garrison, "I don't know, gosh darn, my wife and I have had four kids and they've all been girls. And the first one you have is a boy. How did you do it, Walt?"

And Garrison said, "Well, I really can't explain it, Roger. But I'll tell you what, if you bring Mary Ann by the house I'll try and getcha one."

According to Garrison, Roger "was pissed off at me for five years about that crack."

Said Garrison, "Seemed innocent enough to me. Just trying to help out a friend any way I could."

When Staubach joined the team in 1969, right away there was a quarterback controversy. Morton had played behind Meredith and had five years of schooling in the Landry system. Staubach was just an untested rookie. Each could be effective in his own way. Roger had an uncanny ability to scramble that left defenses with their tongues hanging out. But Morton was a disciplined veteran who knew the advantages of staying in the pocket and sharing the load. The offensive players wanted Morton.

WALT GARRISON: "The team was split. The defense liked Roger because he made things happen. But the offensive guys loved Craig. We thought he was a better quarterback. He knew the offense better than Roger. He could read defenses better. He had a better feel for the game and a better arm. And Roger hadn't played professional football for very long, whereas Morton had been playing for six or seven years.

"Morton was more regimented in the Landry system. When Staubach first came up, if things didn't go his way he scrambled. He ran everywhere. And Landry didn't like that. And neither did the offense. The offense had confidence that it could score with Landry's system and the players it had. When Staubach took off on one of his runs, it was Roger against the world. Throw out Dallas's Multiple Offense, throw out Speed Inc., throw out Bob Hayes the fastest man in the world, throw out the best blocking line in the business. Ya, and throw out 'I'll get ya four yards' Garrison. It was Roger versus the NFL."

If Staubach had one advantage over Morton, it was that he worked harder. In fact, Staubach worked harder than Sisyphus, the mythical figure who every day had to push that big rock up the steep hill, only to see it roll back down at the end of the day. Perhaps part of Morton's laissez-faire attitude was that he had sat behind Don Meredith so long, he was not able to immediately readjust his thinking to his new, more important role.

PETTIS NORMAN: "I viewed Craig as a young guy who had come out of college, a number one draft choice, a good-looking guy, women ran after him, and he did not appear to be that serious about football. But Craig's interest was the same as a lot of other young players who had money and looks: play the field for a while. And all of sudden he was handed this job. Craig did not expect to have the job that year, to be quite honest with you. And all of a sudden he had to make the transition, and I don't know this for a fact, but I suspect he found it hard to make the transition from bachelor who was staying out all times at night, a second-string guy, to a guy who now has the mantle and had to lead this team. That's a pretty tough assignment for a young guy to come in without any preparation, any expectation of being in that position.

"He would have had a better shot at greatness had he taken over in an orderly transition. *Nobody* expected Meredith to retire. Meredith was very young. Thirty years old. Other quarterbacks were going until they were thirty-five, thirty-eight years old. Nobody expected Don to retire, and it was a shock. I know it was a shock to Craig. So instead of Craig going to training camp and being the number two guy, all of a sudden he is the number one guy. 'Here's the ball. Get out there. This team is expected to win.'

"We had been to the championship game for two years, and we were expected to win, and that was a tremendous assignment for a young guy who did not have a decent apprenticeship."

* * *

In the end Morton's departure from Dallas had nothing to do with his attitude. It had everything to do with his lack of mobility and his bad luck to be playing alongside Staubach, a competitor who pursued his job with pitbullish ferocity. To keep Landry from replacing him, Morton would have had to avoid injury and win the Super Bowl. In the third game of the '69 season, against the Philadelphia Eagles, Morton was outstanding. He was 15 for 20 and threw for 239 yards, including touchdown passes to Lance Rentzel, Dan Reeves, and Mike Ditka. That's how good Morton would have been had he remained healthy. But Morton was a gutsy pocket passer who stood his ground to pass, even when defensive commandoes were about to lower the boom. And Tom Landry's offenses did not feature protecting the quarterback as a priority. Morton was injured first during the exhibition season and then against Atlanta in the fourth game of the season, giving rookie Roger Staubach his first opportunity to play.

ROGER STAUBACH: "In '69, Craig's first injury, which wasn't serious, was his finger in the Jets game. He messed it up, so I got to finish the game. I came in and pulled a comeback. It was one of those stories, though it was just an exhibition game. But I was all excited. Here I was, given a chance.

"The next week we played the Baltimore Colts, who had a really good team, and I ran like a wild man that day. I ran for over 100 yards. I did not have a good passing game. I threw four interceptions, though some of those interceptions were kind of iffy . . . one was tipped. But all of a sudden the Baltimore Colt players, like Bubba Smith, were saying, 'I hope we don't have to play this guy again.' 'Cause it was a hot night, and I was running all over the place. The fans liked it. But Landry was sitting there saying, 'Geez, what have I got here?'

"In the season opener we played the St. Louis Cardinals, and Morton couldn't play, and Landry's comments in the paper were, 'We're starting this rookie quarterback.' It *was* an unusual deal, a rookie quarterback starting. For him it was really amazing. But I was a little bit older than the usual rookie. Landry said, 'I don't know what's going to happen with Roger.' In other words, I can't predict what he's going to do. And after practice he would stay out with me. We'd work on, 'Hey, this is what you need to see. Larry Wilson is the weak safety. We're going to run this post pattern to Lance Rentzel, and you pump Wilson, and I promise you if you keep looking at Wilson and pump to the other side, if you don't look at Rentzel . . .'

"He gave me a lot of coaching points, and sure enough, the first time we ran that play, Rentzel ran a turn-in, and Bob Hayes did a hook, and I pumped to the hook, and Wilson took two steps forward, Rentzel ran a post and beat the cornerback, and we hit a 60-yard touchdown. It was my first touchdown. It was the most exciting feeling I ever had as a player.

"The rest of the game went very well. I ran well, didn't throw any interceptions. I hit Denny Homan on a long pass that he should have scored on, but a guy caught him from behind. And after that we played the Saints the next week, and Craig came back and had a really good game, and then in Atlanta, he got hurt badly. Morton scrambled out of the pocket, and Claude Humphrey tackled him, and Craig suffered a partial separation of his shoulder. We were playing the Eagles the next week, and he wasn't supposed to play—I practiced the whole week— but in the pregame warm-ups he said, 'I can go.' So he started and had a great game. Craig threw four touchdown passes, but as the year went on his arm started to become a problem."

CALVIN HILL: "Until Craig got hurt, he was the leading passer in the league. Craig was playing at a very high confidence level, and though he had had one knee operation prior to my coming there, physically he was in great shape.

"I remember when he first came into training camp, to me he looked like a million dollars. He was a vet, he had a cannon for an arm, and he knew all the keys. And I got along fine with him. I was a rookie, so he spent little time with me but he was helpful to try to make sure I knew what I was doing.

"Craig and Roger were in the same class but Roger had been away for four years in the navy, so again, so much of the Cowboys' system was understanding, and Craig had understood it, and Roger was trying to play catch-up, and it was difficult."

PETTIS NORMAN: "To give Craig the credit he is due, in the first five games of '69 Craig completed 71 percent of his passes, led the league in passing. And then after he was hurt by Claude Humphrey, he never recovered from that. After Humphrey hit him, one of the things I noticed about Craig was that the motion of his arm was a little bit different from that point on. He would do more slinging than passing, and it was a subconscious thing, his protecting that injury. The ball would sail a lot, and not have as tight a spiral as before.

"It was a real tragedy. In my own mind I always wondered how good Craig could have been. 'Cause he certainly had the tools to do it. I've always wondered, even as I watched him in New York and Denver, had he not been injured, had he not had to alter slightly his throwing motion, how good could Craig have been?

"And even though Craig went to two Super Bowls, he has never been given the credit he deserves, and that is due to expectations. People really expected Craig to be a Hall of Fame quarterback. They thought he had the tools to be a Hall of Famer. But most people do not remember that Craig got hurt and never quite fully recovered from that injury."

Craig Morton's quandary was that after his shoulder injury against Atlanta, he should have undergone an operation. But Morton had waited four long years to become the Cowboys' starting quarterback, and when the doctors told him he could play despite the injury, he opted to go on, pain or no.

On his return, Morton threw very well. He kept playing, too, even while the shoulder kept getting worse. Toward the end of the season he lost the feel for throwing the ball. His passes had little on them.

Using the running ability of Rookie of the Year Calvin Hill, who broke the Cowboy single-game rushing record with 138 yards in his second game, and that of Walt Garrison behind an outstanding offensive line of Ralph Neely, Tony Liscio, Rayfield Wright, John Niland, John Wilbur, and centers Dave Manders and Malcolm Walker, and throwing 12 touchdowns to Lance Rentzel, the wounded but still effective Craig Morton in his first year as the new Cowboy quarterback skillfully led his team to an 11–2–1 record. In '69 the Cowboys lost badly only to Cleveland and by a single point to the Los Angeles Rams in a game marked by the absence due to injury of Hill, Neely, and Jethro Pugh. Hill, who finished the season with 942 yards—second in the league only to Gale Sayers—had fractured his foot in mid-November against Washington and was slowed the final three games. The injured foot would keep him from the vaunted 1,000-yard mark and plague him for the rest of his career.

Craig Morton should have been lionized in Dallas. He was talented and gutsy. His offense was tops in the NFL, quite a feat for a first-year quarterback. Instead he was vilified after the Cowboys were blown out in the conference championship playoff game by the Cleveland Browns, 38–14, in the Cotton Bowl. The game began on an ominous note, when a Brown punt accidentally touched Cowboy lineman Rayfield Wright. The Browns recovered, and the rout was on. In the first half Morton completed just three passes, and Hill and Garrison ran for just 22 yards on seven carries as Cleveland took a 17–0 lead behind the passing of Bill Nelson to Paul Warfield. After Morton threw a pass that was intercepted by Walt Sumner and run back 88 yards for a touchdown, Landry put Staubach into the game in the fourth quarter to mop up.

In the Cowboys locker room following the game and in the papers afterward, the players' criticism was not directed toward their quarterback as much as it was toward Tom Landry, who as part of the defensive game plan had switched Mel Renfro and Otto Brown from safety to cornerback depending on the situation in an attempt to keep Cleveland from isolating Warfield on Brown.

CORNELL GREEN: "Tom Landry had Otto Brown and Mel Renfro switching back and forth between safety and cornerback 'cause Tom thought he could hide a weakness that way. Otto was the weakness, and with Paul Warfield, you knew Cleveland was going after Otto. I was playing the other corner, and Gary Collins was the other end, and they thought me and him would be a wash, so he left that alone, and went the other way, directly at Otto, and so in certain formations, he put Mel out there and put Otto at safety, and on certain formations he switched back, and I have no idea what that was for, because I thought it was stupid. And Cleveland proved it was stupid."

The other criticism felt by the players was that because of Landry's changes in the game plan only days before the game, the confidence of some of his players on both defense and offense had been shaken.

LEE ROY JORDAN: "I felt Tom was one of the smartest men I've ever known in football. Tom could put together the best defensive game plan in pro football, and he could also put together the best offensive game plan. Tom had some problems at times about being so brilliant that he could go back and find things that would bother him two days before the game and change some things about the game plan, which I really felt was a real negative to us, on offense *and* defense. Once you work on something two or three days and feel like 'This is our best plan, let's go with it. It's going to work for us,' then you have to let football players take care of the little things that happen during the course of the game, those one-play deals or an occasional play.

"For the Cleveland playoff game in '69 he changed the game plan right before the game, and that just confused everybody, and everybody had a lack of confidence in what we were doing, because we hadn't had the time to get any repetitions on the field with it. In big games you can study too much for your own good. To me, you need to have all your planning done by Friday, and not go back and look for anything Friday night and Saturday that might encourage you to change your opinion.

"But Tom still would go back and look and look at films and try to find a way to improve your chances, and sometimes what he found was something that really was a minor thing, and maybe make some changes that really confused the players rather than helping them prevent a play from happening to them.

"And so going into the Cleveland game, we were not well-prepared emotionally. Changing game plans close to game day caused us to doubt ourselves, and in his pep talks before the game and during halftime Coach Landry had some doubts about us being able to beat that Cleveland team. And it came through to the team that he doubted we could win. In the locker room just prior to the second half, Coach Landry let slip that he had doubts the Cowboys would win the game.

"We were a good football team. We were as good as or better than the Browns were any time we stepped on the field, but after halftime Coach Landry was making his 'get ready' speech for the game, and all of a sudden it slipped out that he didn't know whether we could win the game, but 'Let's go play them a good game.' I looked at the face of every guy around me there and I could see the shock on every guy who was sitting there, because all of a sudden they felt, 'Coach doesn't believe we can win. He doesn't believe in us as a unit.'

"So it was really a shocking thing, and I know it slipped out, but you have to say, 'It was in his mind or it wouldn't have been on his lips.'

"It was a shocking deal, and we went back out, and in the fourth quarter they intercepted a pass against Craig and ran it in for a touchdown, which is the worst thing in the world that can happen to you as a football team."

PETTIS NORMAN: "In the papers the next day everyone was blaming Tom Landry, saying his time had passed, which was very typical. Even though coaches must take the blame when the team isn't prepared to get beat like that, I never thought it was time for Landry to step down. He was winning a lot of games every year.

"After the game Craig took a beating in the press, because that's where it is: The quarterback gets all the glory and all the blame, unless there's a situation where someone else makes a boo-boo, a fumble. You can't second-guess yourself when you're on the field. You have to do it by instinct, and when you start searching because you haven't practiced something enough and aren't sure, you can get beat 38–14 very easily by a team that is your equal or even less.

"In the locker room after a game in which we had expected so much of ourselves, it was just total devastation. I took losses as hard as anybody. I would be the last person to leave the locker room, just because I would sit there trying to replay the game in my mind to figure out how it could have gone the way it did, realizing that you don't have another chance to redeem yourself. This time it was not a home-and-home situation. This was it. We lost, and we were going home. A lot of things would run through my mind on a day like that. It was a low point."

ROGER STAUBACH: "To me, Landry's low point was after that playoff loss to Cleveland my rookie year in 1969. We were getting ready to board a flight to Miami for the Playoff Bowl. People were crying for his scalp and he looked like a beaten man that day. We had a meeting at Love Field before taking off, and he was the lowest I've ever seen him. He was ashen. He'd had it and he was down."

After the Browns beat the Cowboys in the 1969 championships, Don Meredith called Landry at home and told him he wanted to drop by to talk to him. "The first and last time I was at his house," said Meredith. Meredith was deeply concerned about his coach's emotional well-being and advised Landry to retire.

DON MEREDITH: "I listened to some of the game on the radio, and it had to be the worst game I ever heard. It was kind of sad for such a dedicated, disciplined man to wind up in such a situation. We used to be at odds on a lot of things but we learned to respect one another for different reasons. We're not exactly identical personalities.

"Here was a man who devoted ten years to this year. His philosophy was challenged and all but destroyed. He had taken a torpedo in the hull and was drifting.

"Tom asked me, 'What can I do?' And I told him to hang it up, forget it, get out. Obviously he didn't follow my advice. He is such a fine man . . . it was kind of sad for such a dedicated, disciplined man to wind up in such a situation."

At the Playoff Bowl in Miami the defensive players staged a rebellion of sorts. They had lost confidence in the Flex defense, and they petitioned Landry to allow them to play defense the way they wanted to play, by just using their natural instincts rather than reading keys and moving as those keys dictated. Landry allowed the defense to line up in a 4–3 and play any way they wanted.

They lost to the Rams, 31–0. End of rebellion.

36

Cracking Down

t a Fellowship of Christian Athletes banquet in Atlanta in late June of 1968, Tom Landry gave a speech just a short time after both the Martin Luther King and Robert Kennedy assassinations. In that speech he didn't address the root cause of the civil disobedience bubbling up in America. Rather, in speaking about the changes in society, he concentrated on what he saw as a loss of the Puritan ethic, with too many people not working hard for what they got. Too many people, he noted, were coming to expect something for nothing. His solution: finding Christ.

"The hearts of men must change," he said. "Only Christ can change men so drastically."

In his speech he described how athletes had changed through the years. He said, "I am starting my twentieth year in professional football and I have seen a change in the athlete coming into pro ball. In 1949 all the athletes were a product of the Depression years and World War II. Coaches could treat them any way they wanted and the athletes would respond because to them success was important. The alternatives they had seen had not been attractive.

"In the mid-fifties, the athletes entering pro football were the products of the postwar era—plenty of everything—and we observed more independence, and motivation became an important factor. Job opportunities were plentiful in other lines of work.

"In the sixties, I have seen the decay so prevalent in other areas of American life start to take its toll on the athlete. Competitiveness is being eroded; the will to win and determination to be the best are not so important anymore. There are easier ways to get by. Now is the time we must reestablish a competitive spirit in America that has made it the greatest nation on earth with the highest standard of living."

Later in his speech he said, "If you love your neighbor as much as you love yourself, you will not want to hurt or cheat him, or kill him or steal from him. If we would all do that, it would take care of everything else. But until that happens, we need a value that may be the most pressing at the moment. That is discipline."

He told those in the audience to either play by the rules or suffer the consequences. He cited Police Chief William Parker of Los Angeles, who had said, "I don't care what color they are or what cause they represent. They're breaking the law and there's only one place for them, in jail."

Concluded Landry, "It is high time we define clearly the rules for playing the game in the USA. And it is high time we had the intestinal fortitude to make them stick."

The lines were drawn. It was "My way or the highway." Whether Tom Landry could stick to his guns and continue to win would be a continuing drama throughout the 1970s, as a cast of talented but troublesome players Landry considered "rebels and misfits" would come and go through the Cowboy locker-room door.

One of the first of these rebels to come to the Cowboys was a talented linebacker by the name of Steve Kiner. The Cowboys drafted Kiner in the third round in 1970 after a solid career at the University of Tennessee. The Cowboys were impressed that Kiner was a hitter. What they didn't know about him was that he was an enigma by Texas standards: the son of a career army officer, he was fervently antiwar; a root-for-the-underdog guy, he had befriended black teammates in both high school and college; and he loved to smoke dope. Football and marijuana were his two loves. He loved to play hard and off the field he loved to get high. When Kiner reported to the Cowboys for rookie training camp, he told the media, "Chuck Howley is getting old, and I'm here to take his job." The vets noticed, and on the night the rookies were made to get up and sing, Kiner was made to sing "Happy Birthday" to Howley.

During training camp Kiner's roommates were the Cowboys' number one draft choice, Duane Thomas, a talented running back from West

Texas State, and Margene Adkins, a superfast, talented pass receiver who had left college early to play in the Canadian League. Adkins was a second-round draft choice. What made the arrangement unusual on the Cowboys was that Kiner was white, and Thomas and Adkins black.

STEVE KINER: "I was born June 12, 1947, in Sandstone, Minnesota, about a hundred miles north of St. Paul. I was a military brat. We lived there until I was five, and then we went to Germany for three years, and we came back to Sandstone for a little while, then moved to Fort Riley, Junction, Kansas, where I lived for three years.

"When my dad was seventeen years old, he was captured at Corregidor. He was in the Bataan Death March. After the peace treaty was signed he was still in prison six months. When they finally got him out, he weighed eighty-eight pounds.

"And he was in Korea, too.

"I enjoyed the life, I thought it was great to see all these places, to move around. Only when I got older did I realize there were some kids who had known each other all their lives, and I didn't have any friends like that.

"My dad retired from the army in '62, and we moved to Tampa, Florida. I went to Hillsborough High School in Tampa. I graduated in 1966. I hadn't been introduced to pot in high school. I was aware of it. But at that time it was 'Stay away from it.' You heard the same warnings you hear about it now. And I did.

"Hillsborough was the first high school in the state of Florida to integrate. We had three black students, two girls and one guy in the high school, and the one guy was a football player. His name was Joe Mitchell, the first black football player in an all-white school in the state of Florida. He was a wide receiver. He started for us. And he could run. He came over from Middleton High School in Tampa.

"I was sort of like his surrogate brother. Because I had grown up in the military, I'd played football, basketball, and baseball on the base with blacks, and to me they were just some other kids. But in this school, there were some rednecks on the football team, who were talking like, 'We're going to shoot the son of a bitch.' I just told them, 'Don't, because if you mess with him, you're going to have to answer to me. You're going to have to fight with me.' And they pretty much left him alone. It was an easy transition for Joe in that respect. It helped him to be on the football team."

Kiner's dream was to go to the University of Alabama and play for Bear Bryant, but his father wanted to be able to see him play and ordered him to go to a Florida school. He wanted to go to Florida State, but University of Florida head coach Ray Graves convinced his father that he would benefit more in life from going to Florida. "They just blew a bunch of smoke up my dad's ass," says Kiner. As part of his incentive to go to Florida, he was given a cushy job tending the grounds and pool of a rich University of Florida alum who lived in Tampa. But Kiner got in a shouting match with the alum's snooty daughter, and the angered alum got Ray Graves to revoke Kiner's scholarship offer. The rival SEC coaches knew of Kiner's summary dismissal before Kiner did.

STEVE KINER: "The fight happened on a Saturday, and on Monday I was out on the Hillsborough High football field when Vince Gibson, a coach at the University of Tennessee, walked out to talk to me. He said, 'How are you doing, Steve?' I said, 'Fine.' He said, 'I was watching you run. You look good.' Sort of pepping me up. And then he said, 'How would you like to come up to Tennessee?'

"I said, 'What do you mean?' He said, 'Come up and look at the campus.' I said, 'Well, Coach, I already signed with Florida.' And when I said that, he looked at me real serious-like and said, 'Oh, you don't know.'

" 'I don't know what?'

"He said, 'Well, Florida released you from your scholarship.' Which I didn't know Florida could do. And Coach Gibson already knew, because Florida had sent the information out to the schools in the conference.

"I was real upset. I said, 'I'm not interested in going to Tennessee.' I went home and told my dad, figuring he could straighten it all out. My dad went absolutely nuts. He called Ray Graves, but Graves wouldn't even call him back. And so my dad and I talked about it, and he said, 'I guess you better go up to Tennessee and see what they have to say.'

"So off I went to the University of Tennessee, and when I went up there, I loved it. It was fabulous. The university is in Knoxville, right at the foot of the Smokey Mountains. It's gorgeous, simply gorgeous. I was caught by the mystique of Tennessee's history. Here was a stadium people had been playing football in in the 1800s. Hey, this place has been here a long time. Their program already had some national recognition by that time. I felt, 'Man, I need to be at this place. Something good is going on here.'

"The way Coach Dickey did it back then, it was a war of attrition. They would sign everyone they could to keep them from going to other schools, and then they would run everybody off that didn't want to stay, and the ones who were run off couldn't transfer to another school in the conference, that wasn't allowed, so they would have to go to Troy State or Middle Tennessee State. Of the hundred of us in my freshman class, only twenty-two of us were there when we were seniors.

"One reason I was successful in football was because I could run. I was a white guy—I mean, I still am a white guy, although some people have questioned that at times, but I could run. When I was in high school, I ran a 4.5 40. That was a good time back then.

"And the other reason I was successful was I could follow a chain of command. For me, there was no if, ands, or buts. What the coach said to do, I did it. And I did it to the best of my ability as quickly as I could do it. Coaches love that shit. Where other kids who didn't grow up with that strictness didn't go along so readily. I mean, I saw guys who had more athletic ability than I did, but they couldn't make themselves do anything.

"The country was changing while I was in college. We were the first school in the South to integrate its football team. Not to integrate the student body, but the first to actually sign a black football player. Actually we signed two of them, Albert Davis, out of Alcoa, Tennessee, and then we signed another kid, Lester McLain out of Nashville, and the reason they signed Lester was so that Albert would have a roommate, because Albert was supposed to be the heir apparent to Jimmy Brown. Albert had broken all of Jimmy Brown's high school rushing records. Albert was an absolute phenom. The coaches called me over to watch the films of him in high school. 'Come over and look at this kid,' and I thought, My God. Albert was 6'1" 240 pounds. He was a load. But evidently, the coaches or somebody took an entrance test for him, and they found out about it so Albert wound up going to Tennessee A&I, but Lester passed all the entrance stuff, so all of a sudden we had one black football player. Lester played for us a lot, and he was a good football player and a good kid.

"And when Lester came to Tennessee, I made it my job to look after him. No one designated that responsibility to me, but I had gone through that transition in Tampa with Joe Williams, and Tampa was metropolitan compared to Knoxville, Tennessee, where at that time you were in the heart of the Ku Klux Klan.

"I didn't witness any overt racism toward Lester, just subtle stuff. A line got drawn. Some people decided they could no longer be my friend. I was fine with them up until that point, but then they decided, 'There is something wrong with this guy.' I didn't mind really. I was doing what was right, and my friends had always transitioned from the military. I would be in a place for three years, and then all of a sudden, I was gone. So I was always very open to making new friends, and if somebody went by the wayside, so be it. I wasn't real politically minded.

"And I was getting some of my needs met, nurturing, trying to help Lester out. I wasn't going to let anything bad happen to Lester. And he and I became pals. You'd have to ask Lester this, but I would venture to say that I was sort of a mentor to him. There were no blacks around, and my door was open and my hand was out for Lester, and he would come and talk with me.

"And as far as the social changes, I remember Martin Luther King getting shot in Memphis in '68. And it's part of my pathology, but I disassociate from stuff when it stirs up feelings. I don't like to get angry or upset, so I will push it away from me. And then a couple months later I can remember being upset about Bobby Kennedy being shot. And I kept thinking, 'How does this happen?' I kept wanting an explanation.

"All that happened in '68. The one person I remember very vividly was William Kunstler, the attorney for the Chicago Seven, a real radical. This guy was the first exposure I had to radical thinking. As you might imagine, my dad was not a very radical thinker, even though my dad opposed the Vietnam War. He said Vietnam was a bunch of shit. That's one reason my dad retired from the military. And he had some real strong convictions about the military, though I can't ever remember a politician that he thought anything of. Right after we escalated the war in '65 and '66, he told me how distrustful he was of what they were doing.

"At this time there were guys I was going to high school with, who all of a sudden were going off to war. I was asking him about this. I said, 'Dad, there's a war going on.' He said, 'You need to stay the hell away from that place. If you have to go to Canada, you need to go to Canada.' That was pretty clear thinking to me. He saw that, and there were not a whole lot of other people who saw it that way. As straight as he was, he was advocating that the Vietnam War was wrong, and he *knew* it was wrong.

"In 1968 there was a big antiwar movement. Bill Kunstler came and talked about burning down the ROTC building. I was thinking, 'This guy is nuts.' In the fall there were demonstrations and marches, and all of a sudden Kent State happened. I saw it on TV, and it was like, 'Oh shit. I can't believe the national guard killed students.' It was like something had gone terribly wrong. I was mad at Nixon, livid that they sent troops in there.

"Back then I knew there were different sides, like Alabama and Tennessee, but we both believed in the same things, right? Now all of a sudden a whole element of society didn't believe in what I believed in.

"After Kent State, the Students for a Democratic Society at Tennessee burned the ROTC building, right across from my dormitory, and they wanted to burn the administration building.

"They had a huge rally, maybe five or ten thousand kids. I went. They said they were going to take the administration building. When they asked me if I was with them, I said, 'No, I'm not with you.' They told me to get out.

"The next morning when the administration building opened, we watched the students go in there to take it over. About fifteen minutes later, five school buses and paddy wagons pulled up, and these guys went in and started dragging people out. They were grabbing the girls by the hair and busting them in the head with billy clubs. They were beating the living shit out of those kids, just beating them. And they dragged them all off to jail.

"I was disgusted they would hit these people, especially the girls. It was awful.

"At Tennessee I was very content. I felt I owed a large debt to the coaches. After all, they were my mentors, and they had helped my dream come true. And I had a real good career at Tennessee. We beat Alabama three years in a row. One of the highlights was during my senior year, we beat them 45–14, and as I was walking off the field, Bear Bryant came over and walked with me. I have a picture of him and me walking off the field together. He was real complimentary, and I remember saying to him, 'I don't understand what's the matter with you guys. You don't play like an Alabama team any more. I don't understand it.' It was a complete blowout. And he said, 'Yeah, I don't understand it either, Steve. I'm going to get it straightened out.' I just had a tremendous amount of respect for him.

"The three years I played at Tennessee we won two Southeast Conference championships and played in three major bowls. In '67, my sophomore year, we were number two in the country. We played Oklahoma, who was number three, in the Orange Bowl. Southern Cal was number one, and they played in the Rose Bowl.

"I was named Sophomore of the Year in the Southeast Conference, and now I'm playing in the Orange Bowl. Two years before that I was in high school. We lost the game on a missed field goal with 27 seconds left, about a 30-yarder. I was just caught up in it. The Orange Bowl felt like a carnival, a big show going on with all these side shows. Our team stayed at the Fountainbleu, which at the time was still a prestigious hotel. At that point I was real caught up in the camaraderie, being with all these guys.

"I was living my dreams. I wanted to be a football star, and by God, I *was* a football star.

"During the Cowboys training camp I moved in with Duane Thomas and Margene Adkins, who are black. I can honestly say there were no other white players on the team that were comfortable in that situation. And so I moved right in, and that drew the lines right there.

"Duane was the number one pick, and Duane and I became best of friends. I'm not trying to sound cosmic or anything, but Duane and I were sort of drawn together. It's hard to explain, but I felt real comfortable and he felt real comfortable, and we liked each other. Duane was a very gentle, pleasant guy, and he had a charisma, an aura about him, whether it was because he was the first-round pick or because he was Duane Thomas, I don't know, but beside the fact he was an incredible athlete, he was a likable person. He wasn't at all like—and this is going to be stereotypical—he wasn't at all like what you would imagine a black athlete—that's not fair to say either—'cause I was thinking of some of the negative stereotypes. Well, he wasn't the typical ghetto kid. He was smart and thoughtful and sensitive, and I just liked him. Another reason we became friends, I liked to smoke reefer. Pot. And he used to like to smoke pot, so we'd smoke pot together. We did that all during camp.

"The only thing I knew about Duane was pretty much that something had happened to his parents, they had died when he was young, and that he had been raised by a family member in L.A. and then he had gone to West Texas State to play football, and where the hell West Texas State was, I had no earthly idea. It was in Canyon, Texas. I remember asking him, 'How the hell did you survive in Canyon, Texas, for four years?' Evidently he would go back to L.A. when there were breaks, just did what he had to do. Football was his only avenue up.

"At West Texas State he played on the same team with Mercury Morris and Rocky Thompson. Can you imagine that? Those three were all there at one time. All three had enormous talent.

"Duane never said anything bad about anyone that I know of. He respected the fact that Calvin Hill was the number one tailback, and he never said anything about his playing time. He never in fact talked about anything he did on the football field. Never. He never discussed it. Calvin would discuss it. Calvin was a great athlete in his own right. He had a lot of talent. I think he played out of position. Maybe a wide receiver. They tried him at tight end once. Calvin was an above-average running back. I don't know. It's hard to say. You want to optimize their talent, and I don't know that they did that with him at tailback. For one thing, Duane was a lot tougher mentally and physically than Calvin. Calvin, when he'd get hurt in the game, everybody would know it. You could bust Duane's ribs, do anything to him, and you wouldn't know it. He was like Jimmy Brown. He would not show any effect. He was just tough, mentally tough. Maybe because he had grown up the way he grew up. I saw him one game that year rush for 180 yards against San Francisco in a playoff game in a driving rainstorm, and I don't think he got more than four yards on any carry. He would just bang it. And he just kept pounding. To me, in my mind, and I played with Earl Campbell—I played nine years; it only says eight in the NFL guide, but I played nine—I never saw anybody who played the game any better than Duane did. I've never seen a guy take a football and do any more with it than what he did. He was like Earl Campbell in that respect, but he was bigger than Earl. He was almost 6' 3" and he weighed 225 pounds, and you'd swear he only weighed 190. He didn't look that big, and he didn't look that fast either, but he was a state champion in the 110-yard hurdles in Texas. He could run. Jesus God, he could run.

"Tom Landry's camp was a reflection of Tom. Tom was an engineer, and he expected accountability. That was a transition for me, like, 'I'm supposed to be a man now. I'm no longer a kid. I'm out of college. This is a job, and I'm a man.' It was 'I'm going to hold you accountable because you are a man, and this is what I expect you to do.' And he was very meticulous.

"I had never played for anyone except the coaches I had at Tennessee, and I could play the game, but when I got there and you opened the Dallas Cowboy playbook, it told you exactly what you were supposed to do. Like when you open up a normal playbook, it has, 'You line up over the tight end, and if the tight end blocks down, then you close down to the inside, look for the trapping guard or the fullback kicking you out . . .' Well, in Tom Landry's playbook, it was like, 'When the tight end blocks down, if he blocks inside, you step with your left foot one step and then step with your right foot a backup step and then step first again with your left foot, and then you step again with your right foot, and then you step with your left foot.' He actually had every step you took! It was broken down into the finest of detail. 'And if you do it this way, you'll be able to execute.' And that was the key to his success, and everybody understood that, because he certainly wasn't an inspirational-type motivator, like George Allen. He wasn't a bouncy, rah-rah, get-fired-up kind of guy. He was real sober all the time. *All* the time. He was as sober as a preacher.

"The only time I ever heard him make a quip or even attempt any humor was this one day, a fog choker. It was pouring down rain in Dallas. This was after we had broken camp, and I pulled into the parking lot, and there were no parking places left except the head coach's spot. And I pulled in and parked and went inside. And later on Tom came in and he was soaking wet, *soaking* wet, and Ralph Neely and Mike Ditka turned around to me and said, 'Oh man, your ass is grass. He's going to eat you for lunch. You're dead.' And I was numbed out again, and he got up there and he was wringing wet, and he said, 'I would like to know who parked his car in my parking place.' And I raised my hand and I said, 'Coach, I did. It's raining really hard out there. It was the only place left.' And he said, 'I really like a man who lives dangerously.' And everyone went, Ho ho ho, and that was it. That was as humorous as he ever got. That was the only funny thing I ever heard him say."

MEL RENFRO: "Steve Kiner was *very* different. He was a different kind of animal. As we saw it, Steve was a rebel without a cause. He was a guy coming out of Woodstock, the type of guy who let it all hang out, no inhibitions, just do what you want to do, feel free, antiestablishment, be your own man, all those things. A terrific athlete, had great football ability, and a good person, a good soul. But of a different mind-set, like a flower child.

"Steve was not arrogant at all. He was just a free spirit. He was a drug guy but he was a good guy, a good person, and I got along well with Steve even though I didn't know drugs, never knew drugs. Oh, I had tried marijuana once or twice. I sat in on a session or two with that stuff, and it about killed me. So that was the end of that. I couldn't handle that. But he was into it, boy. I didn't know what it was all about. And the little taste I got of it scared me so bad, I ran and never looked back.

"As far as Steve's relationship with Tom Landry, it was like oil and water. The organization and Tom did not like that type of personality. He was too independent. It went against the grain. He was an early Thomas Henderson, and by the time Thomas got there, they were going to have to accept the fact that they were going to get players like that, that were totally of their own independence."

Margene Adkins, the third roommate of the Kiner-Thomas-Adkins triumvirate, was independent in his own way. Margene was a freelancer. He believed his athletic ability would take him as far as he wanted to go, and never mind the way a play was supposed to be run. "Just get me the ball." Margene had been a true pro all his life. After a stellar high school career, Adkins would have gone straight to the pros if he could have, but under the agreement the NFL had with the NCAA at the time, he was forced to wait to play NFL football until after his college class graduated. So after first attending Henderson Junior College, and after accepting a solid cash-and-gifts offer from Wichita State University, he instead went legit in the Canadian League, where he starred for the Ottawa Roughriders, leading the team to two Grey Cup championships. He was playing in Canada when the plane carrying the Wichita State football team crashed and burned, killing everyone on board.

MARGENE ADKINS: "I never got an opportunity to start for the Cowboys. Who started was supposed to be based on the exhibition season. What was so cold about it, I had a better exhibition season than any wide receiver. But I never got the opportunity to start. Exactly why, I'm going to let that alone. I'd prefer to let that go. Let me just say this: During the year of 1970, two weeks before I was drafted, I was called to preach by Jesus. For thirteen years I would not preach, and a lot of things that happened during that time were because I did not accept my ministry, and that's one reason why a lot of things went on that weren't to my advantage. I'm going to let a lot of it go."

Adkins played two years with the Cowboys. Because he lacked the discipline required by Tom Landry, he failed to break into the starting lineup.

STEVE KINER: "That Margene never got an opportunity had something to do with Landry's approach. You have to understand, Landry drew up his offense the same way as the defense. He would tell you exactly what steps to take on a pass route. It didn't matter if you could catch the ball. If you didn't put your right foot out first when you started your pattern, if you started off with your left foot and then wound up catching the ball, you did it wrong. It was a complicated system, and I can imagine that Margene didn't work the system the way you needed to work the system in order to get playing time.

"But he certainly had a ton of ability. He had as much or more ability than Bob Hayes had. Margene was fast and he had good hands, but Bob had a career, and Margene didn't, even though Margene was more agile than Bob, had more control of his body. And why not line up with Bob on one side and Margene on the other? Why do you line up with Dennis Homan? It looked to me in all honesty that Dennis was afraid all the time when he was on the field. He looked like he was scared to death. And you can't play that game and be scared. You can't do it. You don't last, and he didn't. Physically he was fast. Dennis could run, but he was fragile, and he didn't like to go across the middle, and he wouldn't fight with people for the ball, wasn't aggressive. The only thing he could do was run and catch the ball, and he did that at Alabama. But he looked scared to me all the time.

"And so Dennis played and Margene didn't, and it made sense only in the respect that Landry had a system, and he felt that if you could plug into the system by following the steps, you could play for him. And Dennis must have learned the system real well, so he looked good to Landry. But to the guys who were out there playing the game, it was, 'Look at that guy, man. What's Dennis doing out there?' Margene was fast and very coordinated, but he didn't have a career at Dallas."

MEL RENFRO: "Margene had great athletic ability, could run, jump, catch, but couldn't follow directions. Could *not* follow directions. If Tom said take two steps to the left and one to the right, he couldn't do it. He just could *not* do it, and I don't know if that is dyslexic. I remember we had a receiver named Sim Stokes who was the same way. I remember watching Coach Landry try to get Sim to run a route a particular way, and he did it five times, and Sim never came close. But a tremendous athlete. And Margene was that way. Just couldn't follow directions."

Following directions became very important to Tom Landry following the defeat at the hands of Cleveland in playoff games in both 1968 and 1969. After the first Cleveland debacle, Landry announced to the players that he wanted even more dedication, more seriousness, more hard work.

LANCE RENTZEL: "The impact of our playoff defeats hung over everything and everyone. Tom Landry had an idea that maybe there was too much kidding around at practices, that the team was not serious or dedicated enough, causing us to fail in crucial situations. He made it clear he wanted everything to be strictly business, that if everyone was completely dedicated to football for the entire season, we'd win it all."

After the '69 Cleveland loss, Landry felt that to help the team get to the Super Bowl, he needed to involve his players. Landry's way wasn't individual meetings but rather a player survey. Every player was mailed a meticulously written long questionnaire about each and every aspect of life as a Cowboy. Landry wanted the players to help him change procedures to get the team into the Super Bowl.

ROGER STAUBACH: "At the end of the '69 season Landry sent out a lengthy questionnaire to all the players. He's a control-type person, and he was that way to the end, but he wanted more input into what to do. He was trying to send a message to say, 'I can't do it all myself.' And it was taken in the right vein. He wanted to know a lot of things, everything about the system, our opinion of the coaches. Ermal Allen, who I thought was a very good coach, was moved from backfield coach. Jim Myers, the line coach, became the offensive coordinator. The one thing we didn't have for a long time, which I would have liked, was a quarterback coach. Ray Renfro used to help me as a coach, but he was a receiver. Landry would spend time with the quarterbacks, but during the game he was worried about the defense, and I'd come off the field and be talking to the other players, but it wasn't the same as talking to a quarterback coach. Later Dan Reeves became that. I would have loved to have Dan involved earlier in my career.

"Landry made some discipline changes on the field at Thousand Oaks. He increased discipline by doing a lot of little things. You couldn't lay your helmet down on the ground, for instance. You had to hold it. We made some changes how practice was run, changing the routine. We changed from Tuesday to Monday to watch films and had Tuesdays off."

CORNELL GREEN: "In the questionnaire I told him he should play the younger guys in preseason more. For my whole career I played every preseason game the whole damn game, and I just thought the time to see who to keep on your team, to play the backups, the young guys, was during the preseason. And then you'll know how good they are. That was the only thing I wrote on it.

"Tom said that was one of the things most of the older guys said, to play the young guys in the preseason."

The survey led to substantive changes for the 1970 season. Landry decreed that there would be less reliance on the big plays, the bombs to Bob Hayes and Lance Rentzel, and instead there'd be a greater reliance on the running game, with running back Calvin Hill as the focus. He moved Ermal Allen from backfield coach to scout, gave assistant coaching responsibilities to Dan Reeves—who continued playing as an all-purpose back until 1972—decreed that there be a year-round training program, and most important, that seriousness of purpose be put at a premium. The key to the 1970 season, he said, would be discipline.

Work harder. Play by the rules. Be disciplined. These were Tom Landry's solutions for his Cowboys, and for the nation. But as Landry turned up the pressure on his players, not all of them had the emotional makeup to withstand his relentless whip. Beginning in 1970, the Dallas Cowboys would reach the Super Bowl five times during the decade, but the price exacted would be that over the years a number of the Cowboy players would crack under the terrible strain.

37

Bitterness

While Tom Landry was tightening his screws on the players, demanding loyalty and dedication, the Cowboys coach revealed the true nature of pro football when he made Duane Thomas the number one draft choice in the 1970 draft, using the twenty-third pick to select the talented West Texas State running back. Never mind that the Cowboy backfield already had Calvin Hill, who had been Rookie of the Year in 1969 and had finished second in the league in rushing. Landry had even told Hill that in '70 his role would be expanded, that he would be the focus of the Cowboy attack, and so when the Cowboys selected Thomas, Hill was angry and confused.

After twenty-two other teams passed on Thomas and he was still available, Tex Schramm and Tom Landry realized that here was a runner with too much talent to ignore, never mind whatever promises they had made to Hill. Thomas was 6' 2", 220 pounds, ran a 4.6 in the 40, and was bright and agile and a hard worker.

The Cowboys' computer rated Thomas the third-best athlete in the entire draft. The only reason he had lasted so long was the "attitude" question. Thomas had at times sworn at his college coach. Large black men who talk back in anger tend to offend, if not scare, so Thomas was penalized for his fire and was passed up for less talented but more pliant athletes.

When Red Hickey, a Cowboy assistant, told Landry that he rated Thomas the best running back in the country, the coach chose to judge Thomas on his talent and to worry about having to discipline him once he arrived in camp.

"Does that mean," said Landry, "that he's better than Calvin Hill?"

"If he comes here, Tom," said Hickey, "he'll be your halfback."

"Hmmmmmmmmm."

"Tom, I'm telling you, if Thomas is still there when our pick comes, take him, if you think you can handle him."

"You say he's better than Calvin?" said Landry.

"Yes, he'll be your halfback."

"Then, Red, I think I'll try to handle him."

So much for Tom Landry's concern for Calvin Hill's bright future.

Meanwhile, Tex Schramm, the team president and financial czar, a man who was in the habit of questioning a player's loyalty as soon as that player wanted 10¢ more than Schramm was offering, reveled at his ability to abuse his players at the bargaining table. Like George Weiss of the New York Yankees, Schramm felt the honor of playing for the home team was of far more importance than making a good living, so year after year he negotiated low salaries against overmatched players, outbargaining even those players who dared to bring in agents in an era before free agency. Schramm could and did tell a player "Take it or leave it." He could do this because a player had no choice but to negotiate with him if he wanted to play, and he knew full well that if he waited the player out, the siren song of training camp would be too strong for any of his red-blooded gladiators, that not playing would be far worse than playing for a low salary. What made it worse, as part of his negotiation technique, Tex was quick to let the player know that if he didn't like the offer, he could be replaced in a heartbeat. Tex was effective, but the bitter taste would always remain.

Around 1970 the combination of Landry's added demands and Schramm's stubborn refusal to bring salaries up to league standards began to create a groundswell of bitterness among the Cowboys players. For the first time, many of the veterans were beginning to question Schramm's loyalty to them, starting to feel strongly that they were being treated *unfairly*, that the Cowboys were growing rich, that Tex was growing rich and Tom Landry was growing rich, while they were being doled out crumbs.

PETE GENT: "I was out of football when I ran into Calvin Hill at a banquet in Denton, Texas. I was the master of ceremonies. They were giving Mickey Mantle an award, and Calvin an award for being Rookie of the

Year. Mickey and I both were drunk. Calvin was all natty and looking great. About halfway through dinner Mickey and I sobered up so we could talk to the other people. I asked Calvin what he was going to do. He was playing for $25,000. He said, 'I signed a three-year contract.'

"Well, what he signed were three one-year contracts, and the second two years were not guaranteed. They'd sign him the next year only if *they* wanted him. Calvin Hill fell for Tex's promises. And he was from Yale!

"I said, 'Tell me what you signed.' He said, 'It's a three-year contract.' I said, 'Was it a three-year contract, Calvin, or was it three one-year contracts?' He said, 'Well, isn't that a three-year contract?' I said, 'How many contracts do you have with Tex's signature on them?' And he said, 'He said he'd tear it up if I had a good year.'

"I said, 'Yeah, sure, that's why he had you sign it.'

"He said, 'I'm going back and renegotiate. Tex told me he'd renegotiate.' And they had already drafted Duane Thomas.

"I said, 'Calvin, Jesus Christ, you went to Yale!' And it was the most incredible thing. I made more money than most guys who were All-Pro. I was crazy. I wasn't stupid."

DUANE THOMAS: "It was all about control. Control and power. They had Dave Manders, who played center for us, one of the greatest centers, who should be in the Hall of Fame, begging for a living wage. Blaine Nye, Rayfield Wright, Jethro Pugh, John Niland, Walt Garrison, a lot of them were angry. I couldn't believe my rookie year I was making more money than Jethro Pugh. He was a five-year pro earning $16,000. Rayfield Wright was making less than that. He was one of the greatest hitters. I mean, this boy could deliver!

"The Cowboys had black players on the team who would tell you they were making $65,000, and in actuality it was a three- or four-year contract. I couldn't believe I was making more money than Jethro Pugh. And they were telling me I had a future?"

STEVE KINER: "In 1970 I was drafted in the third round by the Cowboys. I got an agent to do the negotiations. That was a joke. I picked a guy, a really nice guy, much too nice a guy to be an agent, one of the few decent attorneys I ever met in my life. I know there are a lot of decent attorneys out there, but I haven't been fortunate enough to run into a lot of them, but anyway, I ran into him. The guy was out in Phoenix. He had me come out to Phoenix. He was real nice, and he went in, and he negotiated and negotiated with Tex, and we were getting real close to camp, and he told me,

'Steve, I'm sorry, but they won't offer any more but what they offered when we first started this.'

"I said, 'Well, shit, what do you mean they won't offer any more?' He said, 'They just won't come up at all.' I said, 'What should I do?' He said, 'You probably ought to sign for what they are offering. I'm not going to charge you anything, because I didn't get you any more money.' So he didn't.

"I signed for a $5,000 bonus and a $20,000 contract.

"And truthfully, Gil Brandt and Tex Schramm, their whole thing was about dollars and cents. It was like if they could sign somebody cheap, they took pride in the fact they were the stingiest, lowest-paying outfit in the league and still had the best football team. They *prided* themselves on that. They had all the success and these resources at their disposal, but they didn't use any of it. The way they did it, they would reward you for longevity, if you hung with them and rode it out.

"When a guy like Bob Lilly is not happy, that's ludicrous. To me, Bob Lilly was everything I wanted to be. Of all the people who were on that defense, he was the one I thought played the game the way it was supposed to be played. He was the Big Dog. And I wanted to be like that. Not that I had the ability.

"When I was there in '70, a bunch of the players were complaining about the salaries, and they had a right to complain, because the Cowboys were stingy, except with their select few, with Morton, Lee Roy, Chuck Howley, some of the white offensive linemen. I knew there was something wrong when the guy was negotiating for me, he wasn't trying to get me the world. He was trying to get me another five grand, and they kept balking, and then the next year, when I asked Landry to trade me, and he traded me to New England, I got Bob Woolf as my agent, and he got me $35,000. He got me a $15,000 raise, and I hadn't even played on a regular basis with the Cowboys! What Tex and Gil were doing was riding the mystique, the aura of the Cowboys. It was like they were trying to create that college atmosphere, but it was a big puff of smoke is what it was, because in reality they were laughing all the way to the bank. And all they had to do was give each guy an extra ten grand a year and everybody would have been a happy camper. And then, God only knows what might have happened."

LEE ROY JORDAN: "Most of us were unhappy with the money we were making. The Cowboys were making a fortune, and with Tex, we all weren't making any money. It was a problem for us to accept why we were winning and doing as well as we were, while we were the second-lowest-paid team in the league."

MEL RENFRO: "Most of the players that I played with in those years had been there a long time, five, six, seven years. A lot of them had started in the early '60s, and they had had a measure of success, a good measure of success, and we were hearing that other teams and other players were making *good* money. We were hearing this from the opposing players. The word was getting out that there were some guys out there making *good* money, and they didn't have half the success the Dallas Cowboys were having. We were America's Team and we were winning, and winning big.

"I heard that Larry Wilson of the Cards was making almost $100,000. And Mel Renfro was making $35,000. And Mel Renfro had the same credentials as Larry Wilson. And when I asked Tex's assistant, Bob Ward, about that, he said, 'Well, Mel, the Cardinals pay differently than we do.' That didn't make any sense. The guy had called me in, because Tex turned me over to him, and he said, 'Mel, what do you want?' I said, 'Here's what I want, $35,000, $45,000, $55,000. Three years.'

"He repeated, 'Well, Mel, what do you want?' Like he hadn't heard me. I said, 'Well, it's right there in front of you.' He just sat there and stared. He said, 'When you're ready to negotiate, come back and see me.' I never talked to him again.

"So by 1970 the word was getting around that there were players out there making good money, and we were not. None of us, and so we voted to go on strike."

The players' association began negotiating with the owners' negotiating committee in the spring of 1970. The head of the negotiating committee was Tex Schramm. The Football Players Association didn't fare any better than the individual Cowboy players. Schramm played hardball, as usual. One of his first moves was to show the other players what happened when a player chose to take the post of Cowboy player representative. John Wilbur had taken the job. Tex acted swiftly.

JOHN WILBUR: "In 1969 I got elected player rep. I thought that was a big honor. Turned out that I was involved with the players' association as a negotiator of the collective bargaining agreement. I showed up at the meetings for the players. Tex Schramm was on the other side.

"I was always for the union, an activist. We were trying to get preseason pay, pension benefits, free agency. We switched from John Gordy and Mal Kennedy to Ed Garvey, Gene Upshaw, Bertelson, and I was the treasurer of the players' association after that. Schramm didn't like it at all. When I was elected player rep, he went, 'Oh shit, it's Wilbur.' Tex got rid of me because I was a rabble-rouser.

"Obviously, they had something else in mind, too. They were going to move Tony Liscio from guard to tackle, and put Ralph Neely at guard, and Ralph went in there and played a couple games, didn't do that well, he was better at tackle, and they put Blaine Nye in at guard, and Blaine started his career. I had recruited Blaine at Stanford. And he took my job on the Cowboys.

"When I was elected player rep, I thought it was a happening moment. My wife said, 'You fool. We're out of here.' And she was right. Tex Schramm traded me to St. Louis, I'm pretty sure, because I was the player rep."

The players went on strike July 30, 1970. The vets voted to stay out, and they did not go to Thousand Oaks but stayed in Dallas and worked out at SMU.

CORNELL GREEN: "The players struck during training camp in '70. I thought the strike was BS anyway. I went to the meeting, and I told them I was going to cross the line. I didn't, but I was going to, because of one reason: You do not *threaten* to strike. You don't ever *threaten* to strike, because you give them too much time to make amends and prepare for it.

"I told them what they should have done: 'Let's all go to camp, get all the rookies cut, wait till the first league game with all the TVs on that Sunday, with all the TV cameras there, doing the pregame shows, leave. Now let me see what you're going to do.' That's the way you do things. If you aren't going to do things that way, forget it. 'Cause you're not doing it right. Don't sit around in the middle of the summer and say, 'We'll strike.' All they have to do is get more players in there.

"The baseball players did it the right way striking just before the World Series. That told the owners they were serious about it. If you strike, you don't tell anybody in advance, because once management figures it out, they'll get replacement players. You don't ever tell them what you're going to do.

"So I was going to break it anyway my own damn self. I thought it was stupid."

Green turned out to be right about that. On August 2, after just three days, there was a settlement. As Tex Schramm gloated, the players got little for their efforts, and everyone went back to work, still grumbling about their low salaries.

38

Monday Night Humiliation

At the start of training camp in '70, Tom Landry informed all the players that no job was safe, that he was establishing minimum performance levels, and that if a player, no matter who he was, didn't meet those levels, he would lose his starting job. Bob Hayes, who for five years had set Cowboy pass-catching records and was the leading touchdown catcher in the NFL, was one of the first to lose his job under the new regimen. Hayes, the fastest athlete in the NFL, was the sort of player who used the training camp to get in shape. Landry had mandated an off-season training program, and Hayes had rarely shown up for it. Landry wanted his players in shape beginning the first day of training. Landry also reiterated that his intention was to mount a running game very much like the old Vince Lombardi Green Bay offense and keep away from the bombs. Hayes, feeling persecuted, was furious at the way he was being treated and sulked, making his situation even tougher.

PETTIS NORMAN: "We had been close a couple years and had fallen back after we had been in championship games against Green Bay. I suspect that Landry examined the team and felt that if we were going to be champions, we had to step it up a notch. You can't have players not carrying out their assignments to the fullest, even when they are not involved in the play. Coach Landry was a stickler about everybody carrying out their assignments. Tom's thing was, 'You never know when the play is going to break, and you can throw the key block, and if you're loafing, your man might be the one to make the tackle on a run.' And so that was it as much as anything, and it probably was to set an example to any other players who would look at Bob Hayes and say, 'If Bob can do it, I can do it too.'

"And Bob was very free-spirited, let me tell you. And as I think about Bob then and even now, Bob had an insecurity that people did not read. I think Bob was a lot more insecure than he made out to be. And he covered it up by the things he did and said. I think he may have learned to run fast because he could outrun some of the feelings of insecurity, and as a friend of Bob's who personally liked him, I think he did things to cover up some of the insecurities he may have felt as a kid growing up.

"Bob could be boastful, kind of loud at times, and he liked being the center of attention. Ofttimes that's a cover for a lot of other things, and quite often a cover for insecurity, and those things were part of what made him different. A lot of folks didn't bother to penetrate, to look at him close enough. They just laughed at a lot of things he did. And maybe some of the things that happened later in life would suggest there was some validity to that analysis."

When Landry benched him, Bob Hayes was contemptuous. The outspoken Hayes was certain he was being punished not because of any deficiency in his play, but because he had entered the season playing out his option and had publicly complained about Tex Schramm's low salaries.

There were a lot of headlines, and also charges of racism, because Dennis Homan, a slower white guy from Alabama, was the one who took Bullet Bob's job. Said Hayes, "That was the big thing. He never had anything to say to the blacks on the team so it made for a kind of uptight situation."

It was then, according to Bob Hayes, that he began to get the phone calls. At first they were sympathetic, and then they turned angry, with threats of violence to Hayes's tormentors.

"We're Cowboy fans, and we're going to get even with Tom Landry for you. We're going to bomb his house. And if that doesn't work, we'll put a bomb in his car. Maybe we'll even bomb Tex Schramm's house while we're at it."

Hayes says he tried to reason with the callers to get them not to do it. "It's only a contract dispute," he told them.

"You're either with us or against us," the caller said, "and if you're not with us, we're going to kidnap your wife or maybe your daughter."

Hayes said he asked the caller if he would take money to leave him alone. He said he would. Hayes said he had $200 in cash. The caller told him where to leave it at a spot on the playground near the William Brownmiller Elementary School.

"I was convinced they were violent people," said Hayes, who didn't tell the story until a year later. "I was afraid of what they might do if I went to the police or the FBI."

In addition to keeping Bob Hayes on the bench in the opener, Tom Landry also benched Craig Morton and offensive lineman Ralph Neely for not reaching performance levels. Landry was miffed that Morton had not returned from his shoulder operation in better shape. Staubach started the first two games because of the soreness in Morton's shoulder.

ROGER STAUBACH: "Craig had his shoulder operated on, but during the off-season Craig didn't discipline himself, and when he came to training camp he was still having trouble with his shoulder. He hadn't gotten his shoulder back, so when he started throwing, his elbow started bothering him, and as a result I started the opener in a win against the Eagles and then the next game against the Giants.

"At halftime against the Giants we were losing, and I knew when we were walking up the tunnel he was going to take me out, so I said, 'Hey coach, I don't want to come out losing. Just give me a chance in the second half.' I wanted to make up for the first half. And I think I changed his mind right there. And so I played the second half, and we ended up beating the Giants. But I knew Landry was ready and waiting to get Morton in there.

"The next week we played the St. Louis Cardinals, and though Craig was getting healthy again, I started the game, and actually hit Lance Rentzel in the end zone for a touchdown, but he dropped the ball. I was in a groove, and then I threw an interception to Larry Wilson, and as soon as I threw that interception, I *knew* he was going to take me out. I wanted to keep playing until I *really* screwed up, but Craig came in. Craig was the veteran. And so all I got to play was the first quarter. And I was *very* disappointed. It was a tough deal. I didn't say anything."

The Cowboys lost the Cards game, 20–7, and after an impressive display by the defense in a 13–0 win over the Atlanta Falcons, Craig Morton was battered in a 54–13 shellacking by the Minnesota Vikings. During the trip to New York City several weeks earlier, Morton had picked a fight with a guy in a bar, and when he stepped outside, Mafia thugs had beaten him badly. After the Vikings mugging, Morton's body would be in bad shape the rest of the year. That Morton took the Cowboys as far as he did was certainly a credit to his experience, his guts, and his talent.

ROGER STAUBACH: "The next game was against the Vikings, and I had a bursitis problem. The Friday before the game it swelled up, and they drained it and advised me not to play on Sunday. We were getting murdered, and I went in, and I did play part of the game, and went into the hospital after that because they were afraid of my getting a staph infection. When the team plane landed, they took me to Baylor Hospital. So I didn't even dress for the Kansas City game, and Craig had a good game, beat the Chiefs, and Duane Thomas had a big game, ran for more than 100 yards.

"We beat the Eagles on three long touchdowns by Craig, and then lost to the Giants at the very end of the game, when Fran Tarkenton scrambled and threw a touchdown pass.

"And then on Monday night on national TV we got beat 38–0 by St. Louis. I came in at the very end of that game. Craig was having trouble with his arm. It was the beginning of some problems for him. People in the stands were yelling for Don Meredith, who was up in the TV booth, so I was feeling horrible."

STEVE KINER: "I played the whole damn game. I remember St. Louis had a fullback named Sid Smith. He was about 6' 2", weighed about 270. And they had a tailback who lined up behind him named MacArthur Lane, and they would run out of the I. And they would block down, and here came Sid, and Jesus, it looked like a runaway train. They ran all over me! Ran up the field and down the field.

"And after the game, Landry cried. When I say he was crying, there were tears running down his cheeks. He didn't sound like he was crying. He didn't whimper. As tears ran down his cheeks he said that he was real disappointed in the team, because at the beginning of the year he had felt that we had a chance to go to the Super Bowl and here it was with five games left, and we were 5–4. I remember him saying he was sorry he hadn't done a better coaching job, that he had let us down, and basically he said it didn't look like we were going to make it to the playoffs this year, that we had pissed away our opportunity.

"As a younger player, I just had a tremendous amount of respect for him. I had never seen a head coach take the blame for anything. And here was this guy standing up and apologizing in front of all these other guys with tears running in his eyes. I was impressed that 'This guy really is human, that he really does want to win as badly as I want to win.'"

ROGER STAUBACH: "Coach Landry came in the locker room, and pretty much said he didn't think we could win."

MEL RENFRO: "I don't think we played that poorly. But because it was Monday night and the spotlight was on us, and the score was 38–0, it *was* bad, but man-to-man, we didn't really play that poorly even though the scoreboard made it look like we did. But I think because of the embarrassment and the way we lost and our won–lost record, Tom felt he had to put the season on the shelf. He felt we just couldn't come back from that. Because Tom was a statistics numbers guy, and the statistics and numbers said, 'Hey, you guys, it's over.'"

After the game, after the reporters had left, Bob Lilly told his teammates, "Aw, we got 'em right where we want 'em now. We'll trick-fuck 'em." The line became the battle cry for the season.

Lilly told the entire team to forget about Landry. "He doesn't win games, we do," he said.

"Hell with him," said another player. Then Lee Roy Jordan spoke.

LEE ROY JORDAN: "After the game the big thing is we had a team meeting. Just the players. We got together and I said, 'Hey guys, there is no one pulling for us but us, the guys right here in this room. Hell, the coaches aren't pulling for us. They've already given up. Most of the wives have given up. We know damn well the press has been against us forever so they're not pulling for us. And most of the fans are not excited about us anymore.' I said, 'Guys, it's going to happen right here in this room or it's not going to happen.' Several of us talked. We said, 'We are going to do it *for us*, not for somebody else, not for the coaches or the fans or Tex or anyone else.' We were going to do it for *us.*"

CHUCK HOWLEY: "We threw up our hands and said, 'The hell with the coaches.' We were getting our asses ridden pretty hard, and we got so damn disgusted for being second-guessed on the field, and as a result of worrying so much about being second-guessed, we were getting our asses kicked. We said, 'The hell with this. Let's go play ball.' And then we started to win.

"We had so much turmoil between the coaches and the players that we finally said, 'We don't give a shit. We're going to listen, and if it works, fine, but we're going to do what we need to do to win a ballgame.'

"We rebelled against the coaches within our group. It wasn't openly. We said, 'Goddamn, this is what's working for us.' And we got out there and started playing games, Lilly, Lee Roy, me, and those games were working for us. That year we started having fun.

"During practice we got those touch football games going, and it was *us*. We were relaxed, and that's where we needed Don Meredith. He was no longer there, but that's who we needed.

"We knew we had a better team than we were showing. Our failure to perform was evident on the field. We needed to get in a different frame of mind. Meeting as a team and talking as a team, we all in our own way began to operate in a different manner.

"We were looking for a way to tell the coaches, 'Get off my back.' The players pretty well rebelled. We said, 'Let's play for the players.' We weren't forgetting what the coaches were doing, but we played with the attitude in our own minds that we were going to accomplish it, but not the way they wanted it done. It wasn't like us taking over the coaching staff. We took an attitude, 'Whatever was frustrating us, we were going to put it out of our minds.' We were going to take and play whatever worked for us out there and use that.

"Landry was talking like we were going to lose the rest of the games, and that was one of the things that was bugging most of the players. The coaches were despondent, and we were getting it run down our throats, and we began to resent the feeling."

PETTIS NORMAN: "A lot of things affected us in 1970. There was the strike, a change in running backs, in the quarterback, in an emphasis on the running game. We were not cohesive as a team in the first nine games. After we lost to the Cardinals 38–0, our record was still 5–4. I remember saying to several teammates in the locker room that night, 'If we win the rest of the games, we'll have ten victories.' And I remember saying, 'I would take that record any day and let the Cardinals shoot at me.' My point is, that's a tough record to beat. 'We can win the last five games. Give me that record today, and I'll let the Cardinals shoot at us, and I'll bet the money on it that we'll be okay. We can't do anything about the past, but we can do something about the future, so let's go out and play.'

"And I remember thinking, 'The coaches shouldn't give up on us. And we shouldn't give up on ourselves.' And maybe that was the reason I made my statement, and Lilly made his statement, and other fellows made statements. 'Let's win the next five games, and you give me 10 and 4, and I'll let anybody shoot at us. Let's play one game at a time.' And that was a response to the coach's low expectations."

ROGER STAUBACH: "There are a couple schools of thought about that. One was that after that the players took over, and that really got us going again. I don't look at it that the coaches gave up on us.

"The thing that disturbed me was that Craig was definitely having problems, and here I was, ready to go. I thought I was going to get a chance to start after that St. Louis game, and then Landry said, 'Craig Morton is going to be my quarterback.' That's what disturbed me."

CHUCK HOWLEY: "In the next game against Washington, we were losing 7–3, and I recovered a fumble and ran it close to the goal line, and Duane Thomas scored, and we ended up beating them big.

"And we made football fun again. We started winning ballgames. Because we had the talent. We had the ability. But something had caused us to lose the edge. And we found that edge back again."

LEE ROY JORDAN: "After that meeting the intensity changed. We got after each other. The next day in practice we were competing against the offense, and they were competing against us, hard.

"See, what happens to every team after they start losing is loss of intensity. They lose intensity on the practice field. When you don't practice intense against yourself, you don't play intense against somebody else. Shit, it just won't happen. You just don't have that level. You can't turn it on Sunday at 2:50 when the game starts at 3 o'clock. You've got to have it build up to that level every day during the week, every week, or you don't have it.

"And by golly, we beat Washington. It wasn't a real great game, but we played hard, won the game, and then we went to Green Bay and held them to three points, and now all of a sudden everyone is getting excited about us again. The coaches got to coaching real heavy again. And my attitude was, 'Hey, guys, we're going to use what we think works for us, and if we don't think it works, I'm not going to call it.' And that's what we did. We talked about game plans with the coaches, and we were much more involved in expressing our feelings about what we were doing in the game plans. Guys got to where they believed certain things would work, and when something else came out and we didn't believe in it, we told Coach Landry, 'The guys don't think this is a good idea. The guys feel like we're trying to do too much, and we should be doing more letting the athletes take care of it.'

"And in a lot of cases Tom was receptive. He understood and made alterations in the game plan. I have to give him credit for that.

"That was Herb Adderley's first year. We got Herb from Green Bay, and we had Herb and Mel at the corners, and Cornell at one safety and either Charlie Waters or Cliff Harris, who were rookies. That was a heck of a defensive football team."

MEL RENFRO: "What Tom did, he stopped being critical, he stopped being long-winded, he shortened the practices, he shortened the meetings. He pretty much said, 'The season's over. Let's just salvage what we can.' And the pressure was off of everybody. Totally off. And the guys just said, 'Hey, let's just go out and have fun.' And you know what happened after that? Because no one was worried about losing or dropping a pass or fumbling the ball or getting Tom's rage in those Monday morning sessions, nobody worried about that so they got loose and played football.

"Football is a game. It's a game I grew up playing. It was my safe haven, and it was fun and it's a game, and that's the way it has to be. If you change it from being fun and it's not fun, you're not going to perform. You're not going to see a bunch of kids out in the park playing if they're not having fun. They are going to do something else. It's a game. You've got to enjoy it, but the professionalism has put so much emphasis on winning and nowadays they put it on the *way* you perform, the *way* you win. If you look good, then we can sell it. We can create a product and sell it and make money. That's why there is so much in-your-face jiving. They have made it a carnival. Everyone is looking to be on the highlight film. It's a circus.

"And so what we did, we started winning, and we started winning effectively, and then it started getting the coach's attention that we were playing well, so he started increasing the meeting times, started getting serious again. Bob Lilly said, 'Tom just can't let us have fun. He just wants to screw it up.'

"And then Tom backed off. And we won five in a row."

39

Rentzel's Compulsion

hen Tom Landry inaugurated his Spartan nose-to-the-grindstone training camp in '70 and switched the offensive emphasis from long passes to four-yards-and-a-cloud-of-dust, the confidence of some of the players, especially Bob Hayes and Lance Rentzel, sagged dramatically. With the humiliating 38–0 loss to St. Louis, the shaky Cowboys suddenly appeared washed up. Before they had been chokers. Now they were bums. When several of the players went to a restaurant following the debacle, patrons got up and left.

BOB LILLY: "There were many fans who were cordial and nice, but still, the impact of the media when it's negative toward someone, it affects them not just in the newspaper, but it affects your fans and their mentality, their idea of you. So when the media is on you and you go places in Dallas, you're not really welcome. It was really bad, and that happened a lot.

"It happened after we lost to St. Louis 38–0 in 1970. I was playing defensive end again because Larry Cole was hurt. We had a lousy game. We played hard. It wasn't like we weren't trying, but they just beat the crap out of us.

"Well, the next day or two, several of us went out to eat, George Andrie and Lee Roy and Ralph Neely and me at a restaurant on the North

Side of Dallas. And we sat down, and I noticed these people were into eating, and when we sat down they all got up and left! They wouldn't even look at us. I was thinking, 'I didn't realize how bad it is.' They didn't even want to be in the same area in the restaurant with us!'"

One player feeling the pressure of defeat was Lance Rentzel, the Cowboys' glamour-boy wide receiver. In addition, Rentzel's marriage to Joey Heatherton was on the rocks and the supper club he had started was failing. On November 19, 1970, Lance Rentzel got into his car, drove to a local Catholic girls school and waited for the little girls to play on the playground. When he found a ten-year-old who appealed to him, he walked over to her, opened his raincoat, and revealed to her the fact he wasn't wearing any clothes underneath, in addition showing her something she had probably never seen before. The little girl not only gave a description of the blond flasher to one of the teachers, but she was also able to give the make and model of the car, which quickly led police to the identity of its owner.

This was a ritual Rentzel had been playing out for years. He was a classic flasher; psychiatrists call the disorder exhibitionism. Pressures build, and the only way an exhibitionist can reduce them is to expose himself to a young girl. Rentzel had done it in Minnesota, and he continued his flashing with the Cowboys. Several of the players knew about his disorder.

Since coming to the Cowboys in 1967, Rentzel had exposed himself enough times that Tex Schramm and Tom Landry certainly knew about his problem. But instead of getting Rentzel psychological help, they continued to keep their little secret under wraps, hoping Rentzel would play out his career without his problem becoming public.

PETE GENT: "I watched what was happening to him. My lawyer knew that he had been busted in Dallas before it actually became public. And when I was with the team, I kept going to the guys on the team who claimed to be his friends, guys like Ralph Neely and Don Meredith, and I would say, 'Lance is going to get busted. Somebody has got to talk to him.' And they kept saying, 'Come on. I don't want to hear that. You're just pissed because he's got your job.'

"When Lance did it to a girl who was the daughter of a Highland Park lawyer who they couldn't buy off, Lance was fucked. They treated it in the papers like a presidential assassination.

"At the time the story broke Meredith and I were both off the team.

When it came on the network news we were down in Laredo at Meredith's ranch. We didn't have a phone where we were, so we got in my car, and I drove all night back to Dallas and called Lance.

"He was married to Joey Heatherton at the time. She was in Vegas, and he couldn't find her. I called, and he picked up the phone, and I said, 'Lance, Don and I just got back in town.' He said 'Oh, God, you're the first person to call.'

"I said, 'Lance, you better come over. Don's here.' "

MEL RENFRO: "You talk about some strange stuff. You know, I found out Lance left Minnesota because he was having problems. I remember I was sitting in a meeting one day, and the coach said, 'Lance has something to say to the team.' I thought, 'Maybe he's going to give us a pep talk,' because it was Saturday before the Green Bay game. And he started talking about something he was apologizing for. And even after he apologized, I still didn't know what was going on.

"Margene Adkins was sitting next to me, and I said, 'Margene, what's the deal here?' Margene said, 'Lance was caught flipping his thing at some girl.'

"I said, 'Whaaaaat?'

"And ironically, before that Pete Gent had said to me, 'You know, Lance is going to get in trouble. Lance is going to go to jail.' And he didn't elaborate. I said, 'Pete, what the heck are you talking about?' But he didn't answer, and when Margene said, 'Lance was caught flipping his thing,' it came back to me. I thought, 'That's what Pete was talking about.' Even so, Rentzel never did go to jail. He was given probation.

"A lot of things happened around the Cowboys, where I said, 'If that had been me, I'd have gone to jail. But this guy did it, and nothing happened. Mike Ditka got into a car accident drunk at four in the morning and knocked four of his teeth out, and to the Cowboys it was just an unfortunate accident. I couldn't believe it. If that had been me, I know I'd have been shamed, embarrassed, thrown off the team."

PETTIS NORMAN: "Lance getting in trouble was a tremendous distraction. The man was very popular. We all liked him and really regretted what had happened with him as well as with the young girl. It was a tragedy as far as I was concerned, and a lot of people were hurt as a result of that.

"I remember talking to Lance, expressing my sorrow. Because I recognized that that was some type of illness in him, and just regretted that he was ill like that. And I wished him luck. And at the same time I remember feeling very sorry for the little girl."

Lance Rentzel's teammates voted for him to remain on the team and play, but Tex Schramm and Tom Landry overruled them. In meeting with the players Rentzel told his teammates, "No matter how bad things get, I won't ever quit. Ever. It may take me a while, but I'll be back. So long."

Rentzel thought he was going to be suspended for a couple of weeks. But Schramm traded him to Los Angeles, ending the possibility of his return. As soon as he was gone, the Cowboys returned to the task at hand.

STEVE KINER: "When Lance was arrested, I was surprised by the reaction of the older players. I was like, 'Whoa, this guy really has a problem.' And then it was, 'Ah well, we'll put it behind us.' That was just sort of a bump along the road."

40

The Mountaintop

When the Cowboys were manhandled 54–13 by the Vikings in Minnesota in the fifth game of the 1970 season, there wasn't much to cheer about. Craig Morton had been viciously tackled and had the ligaments of his right knee dangerously stretched. Roger Staubach had replaced him, despite an infected right elbow. Calvin Hill was suffering from a serious back injury and Walt Garrison, the bulldog running back, had also been injured, so the Cowboy offense was looking impotent and helpless. But when Duane Thomas entered the game, the rookie running back immediately impressed everyone with his moves and his ability to bounce off tacklers and keep on going, the way Jim Brown had once done. The rookie ran for 79 yards and he showed an ability Brown never had, catching five passes for 45 yards.

Tom Landry was impressed, and against the Super Bowl champion Kansas City Chiefs he carried 20 times for 134 yards, including a 47-yard touchdown. On the play Thomas bounced off defenders, got into the clear, and outraced the defensive backs for an exhilarating touchdown run.

Calvin Hill returned and played two games under the handicap of his injuries, and after the 38–0 beating at the hands of the Cardinals, Tom Landry announced that Thomas would start in Hill's place. In the following game against Washington, Thomas ran for 104 yards on 18 carries and scored three touchdowns. On his final touchdown run, Thomas seemed to be stopped, but he spun completely around, broke free, and ran ahead of his pursuers down the sideline. Cards defensive back Pat Fischer sought to derail him at the last second, but Thomas brushed him off like an elephant flicking a flea, and he went in to score.

To prove it was no fluke, two weeks later in a rematch in the Cotton Bowl, Thomas was again outstanding. Though he didn't score, he gained 102 yards in the first half in helping the Cowboys to defeat the Redskins 34–0.

MEL RENFRO: "Duane was such a talent, tremendous, the next Jim Brown, really. Duane was smooth. He seemed to know where the hole was. He wasn't a power runner, although he was strong and he could break tackles and elude, but he was just like a big antelope, just those giant powerful steps, and the way he'd weave in and out, and just a magnificent specimen. I just loved to see him run. He was such a complement to everybody else. We had a power running game. He was a guy who could run inside, outside, catch the ball, break tackles, go the distance. You got something when you got a guy like that. He had deceptive speed. He could run away from linebackers and defensive backs."

PETTIS NORMAN: "Duane was one of the most gifted runners that I've seen. I remember watching the film of him, 'cause that was the only time I could really see him on the field, and watched how he moved, and how he would slide in and out, something I had never seen with a running back there before, and just thinking that 'This guy could be supernatural if he really wanted to.'"

But with his ascension to star status, his teammates noticed that Duane Thomas was becoming more and more withdrawn from the rest of the team. Duane was complaining about his contract, and they were wondering whether his dissatisfaction with his contract had something to do with the way he was behaving or whether it was something else.

DUANE THOMAS: "When I came to the Cowboys no player was more committed to Dallas than I was, let me tell you. Other guys were telling me I didn't have to play so hard just because I was the number one draft choice. I didn't know that you have one year given to you. I was going at it like it was do or die, because I wanted to see whether I wanted to play ball or not. 'Cause I had offers from other companies. Levi Strauss wanted me to work in their corporate offices in San Francisco. So I was seeing whether I wanted to play football or whether I wanted to go into the business world.

"I always was a team player. If I saw a guy who was doing something wrong and I could encourage him, I would do it. I went to Pettis Norman, who they had thinking he couldn't catch the ball. I said, 'Pettis, your hands are larger than mine. If I can catch the ball, you can.' I was more than willing to share with him. One time Walt Garrison came over to me and said, 'God damn, I don't know how you run like that.' I said, 'It's easy. I pay attention. All I do is watch the defensive people all the way through. 'Cause the defense is always wrong. They are guessing where I'm going. I *know* where I'm going.'

"I would always volunteer my help, 'cause I was brought up to believe in teamwork, that that was what football was really all about. That's why I chose football as a career, as a form of expression, to give and share my points of view in terms of the team, family, and race relations.

"I came to the Cowboys with idealism and integrity, but their computer couldn't tell them that. And if it wasn't on the computer, then it was an error. And they were never at fault. It was always *your* fault. 'Cause their attitude was, 'We are the perfect beings.' You can be that in your head, that's fine, but in reality it didn't hold true.

"My problems started with my agent, who was embezzling money from me. I had gotten him through Mercury Morris, my teammate in college at West Texas State. Merc was going through changes, so he didn't tell me about this boy, who stole ten grand from me. The agent would tell me he was paying bills, and he'd send me statements that the bill had been paid, and the bill hadn't been paid. He said he was paying estimated quarterly taxes, and then the IRS called me up and said, 'You owe us ten thousand dollars.' I said, 'What?' They said, 'Your taxes.' I called him up, and he started ducking and dodging, and the IRS was on me very strongly, so I had to call a friend of mine who worked for Levi Strauss, and I said, 'George, I need ten grand.' He said, 'How quickly do you need it?' I said, 'Yesterday.' He said, 'I'll wire it to you.' And he did. Imagine someone giving you ten grand in 1970. I paid him back every penny. I never did get my money back from that agent. He got away with it. But it shattered my trust. I didn't know who to trust now. I hired another agent, but he never got anything done either.

"I went to Tex Schramm. I had large debts. I was supporting relatives, an ex-wife, and I was hurting financially because my agent had not only made a terrible deal but had stolen much of it from me. I asked Tex to help. You know what he said in his actions? This was his response: 'Okay, Duane, drop your pants, and we're going to stick it to you now.'

"You know, money was an issue, but it was more about principle and honesty. They were taking advantage of the idea that I played more for the love of the game than anything. On an amateur level you are doing it for the love. The word 'amateur' comes from the Latin *amatore* or 'lover.' It's one who loves what he is doing. But Dallas—and when I say Dallas, I mean Tex Schramm and his boys, the decision-makers, the administrators—took advantage of my love of the game. Because skyline caps were making more money than I was. One time I went to tip a skyline cap at the airport, and he told me to keep the money. He said, 'Duane, I make more money than you.'

"How could it not upset me?"

PETTIS NORMAN: "When Duane came to the team he was a very pleasant young man, very quiet, not a person who was really outgoing with everybody. He would talk to a very few people, but he was always very pleasant. I was one of those he would come around and engage in conversation. On the field during practice or during the game he would come up and say something like, 'Boy, you really can block.' Duane was a very nice young man.

"Somewhere, during the course of that year, there was talk about his contract. I remember hearing about the bonus that he signed, and I remember thinking, 'This is really not a good contract for your number one draft choice.' But that was it, and as the year progressed, Duane seemed to have a change in personality, in that he was more withdrawn even from what he had been, though he would still talk to me some."

MARGENE ADKINS: "Duane was always the quiet-type guy. I would sit behind him in the team meetings all the time. He was funny to me. One time we had a meeting. Dan Reeves, the assistant backfield coach, would always come in and he'd call everybody's name, and so this day he said, 'Adkins,' and I raised my hand or said, 'Uh huh,' and Reeves said, 'Duane.' He waited. 'Duane?' Duane never said anything.

"So the next day everybody was waiting to see what was going to happen. Reeves was determined that Duane was going to answer him. So he called the names, 'Adkins, Staubach,' and he came to Duane. He said, 'Duane.' Louder he said, 'Duane?' And what happened, Duane said, 'Why are you asking my name? You see me sitting here.' Which Duane was right to a certain extent, but Dan Reeves was right, too, because he was calling your name."

MEL RENFRO: "Instead of bringing himself along real slowly financially, Duane wanted everything at once, and nobody was going to do that. He made demands, and he wouldn't take anything else. I didn't say anything to him because I was a softy anyway, and I didn't want to get into the man's business with him. I wish I could have said to him, 'Duane, take half and get the other half later. Don't just demand the whole thing.' 'Cause I went through it. Here I was making $40,000 and I was asking for $100,000 and I would have settled for $65,000, but they gave me $50,000, based on what they wanted to give me. And they wouldn't trade me, wouldn't do anything with me, and they wouldn't pay me. You could only get a little bit of it.

"Tex wasn't going to pay him. Tex never paid anybody but Roger. Tex just wasn't going to pay him, come hell or high water, and Duane wasn't going to take anything less than what he wanted.

"I saw him a time or two, and he talked crazy. Duane was talking so crazy, I wondered, 'What's wrong with this guy?' He was doing a TV interview, and his words were like, 'Hey, now you know this is where it's at, and I'm cool with this, and I'm going all the way there, and nobody can do this for me, and I'm here, and I'm going to do it, and hey, man, you know . . .' And I thought, 'This brother ain't saying nothing. Is he on something?' "

STEVE KINER: "Midway through our rookie year I began to see that something was not right with Duane. What happened was, Duane started taking LSD. I didn't see any adverse effects on the field at all. I didn't see any adverse effects when he socialized or interacted, but all of a sudden he started talking about the money that they had screwed him out of. The Cowboys had given him a $20,000 bonus, and a three-year contract at $20,000, $22,000, and $24,000, and he was pissed about that because I had gotten the same contract, except I only got a $5,000 bonus.

"He was pissed at management, and when you start talking about the generals, then I get real squirmish, and I would have long talks with him about the way he was going about getting more money: He was voicing his opinion in the media, and they just took it and ran with it. I told him, 'This is going nowhere, Duane. There are ways to do this that are productive, and the way you're going about this is not productive, it's counterproductive.'

"That's the only place I saw the LSD affect him. It took a toll on his ability to process information. He talked to me a lot, and I had the sense that some of the things he was saying were just totally off the wall, from left field. That he wasn't processing the information he was taking in, wasn't coming up with logical conclusions. When you tried to talk facts with him, it didn't come out right. His logic didn't seem to follow a normal sequence. And you couldn't reason with him. You could reason with him in other areas, but not in that area, and I don't know whether it was because of the LSD or because of the fact that he had always had to fend for himself, and so in the end he was not going to trust anything but his own judgment."

LEE ROY JORDAN: "I think what ruined Duane was his relationship with Steve Kiner. Steve introduced him to things that would destroy your brain cells. The way I felt about Pete Gent, I felt even more so about Steve, because I thought Steve Kiner was a real talent. But hell, Steve was a drug user in Tennessee when he was up there as a player. Then he got Duane to go on a trip to the Islands somewhere for a month, and I don't know what they experimented with, but Kiner got over it quicker than Duane did. But it took both of them some years before they got back where they could communicate, talk reasonably well with people."

MEL RENFRO: "Duane was a strange bird. He wasn't only strange to the management and to the white players, he also was strange to most of the black players.

"His head was a little messed up to start with, but when Tex did to him what he did to him, the kid just totally flipped, and I think a lot of the reason for that was the drugs. I didn't realize the amount and the use, because when we came up, there was a pep pill here and a bennie there and an aspirin here was about all we got. These guys went into acid! I remember one morning Duane was out early in the morning counting blades of grass! At six-thirty in the morning! I said, 'Whoa.' I said, 'Poor Duane. Poor Duane.' He just spaced out. It had to be the drugs.

"But he was still an athlete. He could still perform. He could still do the job."

Duane Thomas carried the offense on his back through a rough part of the schedule, keeping the Cowboys winning until Tom Landry's Flex defense, which was ridiculed and abandoned by his own team at the end of the '69 season, turned impregnable.

Beginning with the Cowboys' 16–3 win over the Green Bay Packers, the defense—led by Bob Lilly, George Andrie, Pat Toomay, and Jethro Pugh on the line, and Lee Roy Jordan, Dave Edwards, and Chuck Howley at linebacker, with an All-Star defensive backfield of Mel Renfro, Cornell Green, Herb Adderley, and two rookies, Charlie Waters and Cliff Harris—went on a record-setting touchdownless streak. In the final four games of the regular season, the defense did not give up a touchdown against Green Bay (16–3), Washington (34–0), Cleveland (6–2), and Houston (52–10; the touchdown was scored by the Oiler defense after a fumble recovery).

Acquiring All-Pro veteran cornerback Herb Adderley from the Green Bay Packers had been a master stroke on Tex Schramm's part.

CORNELL GREEN: "Tom Landry came to me when they were going to trade for Herb Adderley and he said, 'You or Herb is going to have to move to safety.' He said he thought with our defense it would be easier for me to move than Herb. I said, 'Fine with me.' And so Herb and Mel and I gave us three guys who could play man-to-man in any combination, and we had Charlie Waters and Cliff Harris, two rookies, who we could put in at free safety, where they didn't have to lock up in man. We were a tough defensive team. All of a sudden, we were a *real* good defensive team. You had three guys who could lock up on any receiver in the league. And the kids, they would hit you. They might be in the wrong spot, but they would be going full speed. They'd be *all* the way wrong, never half wrong."

When Adderley came to the team, he saw that many of the players were cowed by Tom Landry's second-guessing during film sessions. Scornful, he convinced the defensive players that if they could ignore the criticism and play their game, they could win it all.

MEL RENFRO: "Everyone felt miserable because they were concerned about the Monday film sessions. Herb got my attention when he said, 'It doesn't have to be this way.' He came in like he had been there forever and said, 'Get off your butts and stop crying in your soup. Let's get out and kick some butt.'

"His leadership hit pretty quick. When he started talking, guys started standing at attention. Their antennae went up. Almost immediately. His presence, just the way he carried himself, the way he talked, he always talked with confidence. Herb was so fiery and he had such confidence. He had come up under those Lombardi days where winning wasn't everything, it was the *only* thing. And that's what he instilled in us. 'Guys, you can win, and you're gonna win. *We're* gonna win.' And that was all there was to it.

"He was always a team guy. It wasn't that he bridged a gap between black and white. It was a *team* thing. There was *no* color there. He said, 'Guys, the only way we're going to do it is to come together. White, green, red, all blacks, all whites, all reds, we have to come together as a team and do it.'

"What Herb did, he instilled within us the belief that we could win and win big. I remember one time we lost a game, and Herb got upset. He said, 'You guys are a bunch of miserable losers.' He put it right in our face. We had lost a game, and everyone was sitting around with their heads between their legs, and he said, 'You guys are a bunch of miserable losers, and you don't have to be losers.'

"Herb was always upbeat, always positive. 'Brother Fro, we're gonna get them, Brother Fro. We're gonna do it.'"

The Cleveland game was especially meaningful for the Cowboys. The Browns had kept them from the Super Bowl the past two years. The Cleveland defense was as tough as anyone's. The question was: Could the Cowboys defense keep the Browns from scoring?

PETTIS NORMAN: "It was very cold a lot of times we played Cleveland. I seem to recall balls that were sailing over people's heads because of the cold and the wind, which was not uncommon. It was a miserable day. The field was wet, it was cold, and the wind was blowing. It was a day fit for pigs."

MEL RENFRO: "We beat the Browns 6–2 in the freezing wind in Cleveland. That was a milestone, and I remember it like it was yesterday. Jethro Pugh, Dave Edwards, Lee Roy, everybody was just muddy and dirty and we just rose to the occasion. Here was Lee Roy cursing and screaming in the huddle, 'They're not going to score. They are not going to score. We're gonna stop them,' and we did. That day, Lee Roy was incredible.

"It was just like an angel was there and was protecting us and moving us and making us do the things that we did, 'cause it was like something that was divine.

"I can remember a third- or fourth-down play on our two- or three-yard line. If they had scored, they would have beaten us. Leroy Kelly was carrying the ball, and I happened to be in on the play as one of the tacklers. It was on the weak side, so Jethro was there. We just came up, rose to the occasion, and stopped them on fourth down. That was the game.

"We had lost in that Cleveland Stadium so many times, when we were the better team. To be able to win and win like that, when we were down, down near the Dog Pound in that old, ugly end zone near the cheap seats, with the fans on our back, the wind was blowing, it was cold. All the things John Madden talks about that makes football football, that's what happened down there at that end of the field that afternoon.

"You've heard of Doomsday. That's what they called us, the Doomsday defense. Three downs and out. The defense was much more known than the offense, and so it was the Doomsday. We literally put a hurt on people."

In the final outing, against Houston, Craig Morton had his finest game, hitting 13 of 17 passes for 349 yards and *five* touchdowns. Bob Hayes, finally returning to Tom Landry's good graces after sitting out the first five games, caught four touchdown passes—from 38, 38, 15, and 59 yards out. Had Landry not benched him, Hayes would surely have been the Pro Bowl wide receiver. Duane Thomas carried 17 times for 115 yards. The silent rookie finished the season with a very credible 803 yards rushing.

PETTIS NORMAN: "In the final game we beat the Oilers 52–10, and Craig threw five touchdown passes, including four to Bob Hayes. Bob should be in the Cowboys' Ring of Honor, and he isn't. This notion of people judging other people by so many other standards that really don't apply to athleticism is wrong. If the guy was good, he's just good, and Bob was a guy who really transformed football with his speed, beating double coverage, and really was a major factor in the Cowboys' success. A *major* factor.

"Without Bob Hayes at that time, the Cowboys would have been an ordinary good team, not really exciting, 'cause nobody else could cause defenses to do what he caused, and he beat them. You have a lot of pompous, pious people making judgments on people that should be giving him his due and putting him up in the Ring of Honor, and these very same people shouldn't throw stones, and it kind of makes me sick. It really does. Somebody ought to have enough guts to step up to the plate and say: 'Let's put this guy in the Ring of Honor where he deserves to be for what he did for this team.' And whatever he did in terms of cocaine, he went to jail, he paid a price, and that has nothing to do with his football credentials. Babe Ruth was an alcoholic. Did we keep him out? Yet

Ruth is remembered as the greatest sports hero of all times, and so, I question us sometimes as human beings."

ROGER STAUBACH: "The way we started to win in '70 was a ferocious defense. Other than the one game against the Houston Oilers, where Craig and Bob Hayes had a fantastic game, we went into the playoffs really with a defensive team. Because of Craig's injury, his confidence was shot. *Sports Illustrated* ran a story that ours was a team without a quarterback. I was thinking, 'I'm the backup quarterback. This is really absurd.' I was *very* confident I could play and perform. Though we had other players who were upset, I wasn't complaining, but once we hit the field our guys played hard, and that last stretch our defense really got some momentum, but from my perspective with our great running game we should *never* have lost that Super Bowl against Baltimore."

The Cowboys finished the 1970 regular season with a record of 10–4, including five straight wins following the 38–0 clobbering at the hands of St. Louis and the deportation of Lance Rentzel. The first playoff game was against the Detroit Lions. Duane Thomas ran the ball 30 times for 135 yards. A disabled Morton could complete only 4 of 18. The Cowboys scored on a safety and a field goal. The Lions were shut out, 5–0, as the Cowboy defense extended its no-touchdown streak to 21 quarters. Any time during the game the Lions could have won with a touchdown, but they never got one. The Cowboy players weren't worried.

PETTIS NORMAN: "The score was very low, but I always felt we would win the game. We just seemed to be able to move the ball any time we wanted to. We just couldn't score. That part was frustrating. Normally when you get into a game like that, you start thinking, 'We are really blowing some opportunities.' I can remember I never had that feeling that we weren't going to win the game."

LEE ROY JORDAN: "We shut out the Lions 5–0 in the Cotton Bowl. We definitely believed defensively we were going to win the game no matter what. We weren't separating ourselves from the offense; in fact, we were pulling together as much as we ever had as a team. But our deal was, 'If you score a lot of points that's okay, but if you don't, we're going to hold them to whatever it takes to win.' We were going to make plays to give the offense the opportunity to score whatever we needed, whether it was field position or turnovers—whatever was needed.

"I would be in the huddle and call the defense, and I would say, 'Who's going to make the play? Who's it going to be? Who's going to make it this time?' And always someone would come through. I remember Larry Cole sacked them for a two-yard loss on a running play in a crucial situation. It was amazing how contagious it was. Every guy believed he was going to be the one to make the play.

"The Lions had an excellent football team, but I'll tell you what: We had a tremendous belief and confidence in ourselves because we felt we had come back from some extreme doldrums, that we had really been deep in the hole after that St. Louis game. Everyone had quit on us, and all of a sudden we were a team that had reached down and got some extra intestinal fortitude and desire to be the best we could be as a team."

Late in the game on fourth down Bill Munson threw a long pass to Earl McCullouch. Charlie Waters went for the interception instead of trying to knock down the ball. He missed the ball, and the Lions had a first down on the Cowboys 29. There were 54 seconds left.

MEL RENFRO: "You talk about a challenge, that last drive. They kept picking at me, throwing those ten-yard sidelines to the wide receiver, Earl McCullouch, a sprinter from California. Because of his speed, they were throwing some pinpoint passes always to the outside. Back in those days we were man-to-man. We had to cover inside-outside. And they just moved down the field gradually, moving down, moving down. They completed three against me, and then they threw a deep post pattern and Charlie Waters was there for the interception. I was running along saying, 'This is it. We got it.' But Charlie misplayed it, and Earl caught the ball. And so they were down inside our 30, and people were on the sidelines praying. The crowd was in a frenzy. They completed another sideline, about 12 yards. But that was okay. I said to myself, 'If they keep doing that, I'm going to get one.'

"They were between the 15- and 20-yard line. Munson threw it down and in, and he actually made a bad throw. He had been throwing so many outside routes, he wasn't real sharp on his inside route, so he led Earl a little too much, and he overthrew it. It may have hit Earl in the hands, but it went up in the air. I never remember seeing the ball. I remember feeling it hit my hand. And I just pulled it in around the 11. I was tackled, and then came the elation that the game was over, even though there were a few seconds left.

"I remember going to the sideline and hearing the accolades, 'Way to go, Mel. Way to go, Mel.' I was sitting there by myself, because everyone else was up near the field, just having a good time, celebrating. I just went over and sat down. I thanked the Lord Almighty for letting it happen. And I remember Lee Roy coming over, and D. D. Lewis coming over.

"People talk about my most exciting game in my career. Well, I would say it was that Detroit game, and then the San Francisco game, and then Super Bowl V."

The NFC Championship Game was against the San Francisco 49ers, a team that could rarely beat the Cowboys, despite a solid team and a successful coach in Dick Nolan, who had taken Landry's Flex to the Bay Area and duplicated his friend's success with it.

Against the 49ers, Landry made an offensive game plan designed to establish his powerful running game. If Morton was to pass, it was to be short, to the backs. Since the Cowboys' 6–2 win over Cleveland, there was not a doubt in anyone's mind that the Cowboys would win the game.

PETTIS NORMAN: "Dick Nolan ran the same defense as we did, and I think that made it easier for us, because we had to run against our own defense for a long time in scrimmages. And I felt very confident against the 49ers. The whole team did. I felt we would beat the 49ers. I thought we were better than the 49ers."

With the score tied 3–3 in the third quarter, Cowboy linebacker Lee Roy Jordan made a spectacular diving interception of a John Brodie pass. When he was tackled, the Cowboys had the ball on the 49er 13. From there Duane Thomas ran it in, the key run in a game in which he ran for 143 tough yards.

Walt Garrison gained 71 yards rushing and caught some key passes. He had come into the game suffering from muscle spasms in his back and a sprained ligament in his knee. By game's end, he had sustained a sprained right ankle and a fractured right clavicle. He had to be carried to the locker room when it was over. His teammates were amazed the gritty back was still alive.

In the third quarter Mel Renfro made another key interception, and Lee Roy Jordan grabbed his second of the game in the final period. Though San Francisco finally scored against the Cowboy defense, stopping the streak at twenty-three quarters, no one on the defense complained, because for the first time in Cowboy history, Dallas was going to the Super Bowl.

LEE ROY JORDAN: "In the NFC championship we held the 49ers to 10 points. I knew from the films that John Brodie keyed on the middle linebacker and the safeties, that he would take a read on the middle linebacker the first step or two to get his direction of the defense. Well, every time we played San Francisco, I spent much of my time starting one way at the snap of the ball and then dropping the other way. I'd give him a false move on the first two steps, then pivot and go back the other way. 'Cause after he would read the middle linebacker on the first couple of steps, then he would read our safeties or his receivers.

"Late in the game they were on about their 20-yard line coming out, and a passing situation came up, and I started to my right, and John set up and threw back to my left. I had pivoted and come back the other way, and I intercepted the ball and carried it back to the 13-yard line, and Duane Thomas scored shortly thereafter.

"And in the fourth quarter I intercepted another one near the sidelines. John and I get together every once in a while and talk about how good he was to me. 'Cause it seemed like every game I played him, I made an interception or two off of him."

MEL RENFRO: "John Brodie and Gene Washington were the offensive weapons. They stood between us and the Super Bowl. It was a defensive struggle, blood and guts right up the middle. There was a lot of hard hitting. Lee Roy played an absolutely perfect game. He intercepted two passes and made great plays. We shut them down. They couldn't throw the ball.

"Late in the third quarter Brodie was trying to go deep to Gene Washington, and I intercepted it and brought it back for a few yards, which broke their backs. We put the stamp on it, and talk about the locker room after that game! That was it. There wasn't any better feeling after being Next Year's Champion four, five, six years, and finally getting there. Like Tom Landry said in the locker room, 'You don't know what we've gone through. You don't know how good this feels.'

"Because we had finally gotten to the mountaintop."

41

Almost Super

D uane Thomas stole the headlines before Super Bowl V against the Colts in Miami. When asked, "Is this the ultimate game?" Thomas answered, "Well, they're playing it next year, aren't they?" The line was repeated from coast to coast. The national media didn't know what to make of the Dallas rookie.

The same could be said of his teammates. The morning of the game Craig Morton was walking along the beach by the hotel where the team was staying when he noticed Duane.

CRAIG MORTON: "I saw Duane sitting there on the curb with his head down. He looked zonked. I don't know what he was on, but it scared the hell out of me. I mean, here was a guy who was supposed to be my main man this afternoon. Well, he got back to the hotel, and before the kickoff he gave me this big wink, so I knew he was all right, I guess."

The players discovered that getting to the Super Bowl for the first time was the *real* prize, that the emotion of playing the game would not match that of the game that got them there.

PETTIS NORMAN: "The 49er championship game was better from an emotional standpoint than the Super Bowl. First of all, there was a two-week lag time. To me, you lose some edge when you wait like that and then you try to get it back. We went to the Orange Bowl in Miami, and the atmosphere was not quite real. It was really kind of boring. You get tired of going through thousands of interviews, posing for pictures, this and that. You were all of a sudden thrown into this unnatural setting on which everything was superimposed.

"It was like picture day when you break training camp. That's a dreadful day 'cause you get dressed, stand around, have pictures taken, stand around some more, take more pictures. It was a day you wanted to get out of the way. And the Super Bowl was like a week of that. So it was kind of a drag. You had to be here at this time and there at that time, be here for this interview, there for that photo, and then it was game time.

"And I kept waiting to get as high for that game as I did the 49er game, and I never did feel the oomph of the Super Bowl. The emotion never came. And I think it was because of moving into so many unnatural settings. We did not get involved in going to the parties, so we never got caught up in the atmosphere, and you just kind of got to the point where you said, 'I'll be glad when this is over with.' That's how it was with me, and normally it doesn't take much to get me up for a game.

"The game itself, as it turned out, was not real. So many things happened to us, tipped passes that weren't tipped, and fumbles that we recovered and other folks got, and interceptions at the last minute, and you look back and say, 'This game was as unreal as the week leading up to it.' It was like a picture show."

LEE ROY JORDAN: "To this day I can't understand how it was that we lost to the Baltimore Colts. We certainly gave it away. We made lots of mistakes.

"Their first touchdown was on a tipped ball. But that doesn't matter because we should have won the ballgame several times later."

The Cowboys had gone ahead 6–0 on two Mike Clark field goals. Then in the second quarter Colt quarterback Johnny Unitas—who would later be knocked out of the game following a hard hit by George Andrie and relieved by Earl Morrall—called a pass play designed to go to receiver Eddie Hinton. Unitas's pass hit Hinton's hand, whizzed past Mel Renfro, who was guarding him, and landed in the arms of Colts tight end John Mackey, who ran for a 75-yard touchdown while Cowboy back Charlie Waters, who should have been covering him, was complaining to the officials.

Renfro ran up to one of the officials to tell him that Hinton had tipped the ball, that the touchdown to Mackey should not be allowed, because at that time two receivers could not legally touch the ball one after the other.

The referee told Renfro to "shut up."

MEL RENFRO: "The refs said the ball touched me. Which it could have, I suppose. But I had no sensation of touching the ball. That was my right hand, the hand that was messed up when I punched the mirror back at Oregon. That was the hand I have no feeling in those three fingers. If it hit me, it had to have gone off the finger next to the thumb. I have no feeling in that finger, and if it hit my finger, that's the finger that it hit. But still, when I look at where the game was at that time, it had no consequence. And actually, it wasn't my fault. I was going up to intercept the ball. And it went over my head. My guy was covered.

"The Colt who caught the ball was the tight end, John Mackey, who was the responsibility ultimately of the free safety, Charlie Waters. And he was jumping up and down worrying about the double tip when he should have been tackling John Mackey.

"Even after I returned two punts for TDs in the Pro Bowl and was named the Most Valuable Player, the thing that was uppermost in everybody's mind was the tipped pass. It ate at me for a long time. Because of the question, 'Did you touch that ball?' Well, so what? Right after the game I answered the question. I said, 'I may have touched it, but I had no sensation of touching it.' That's exactly what I said. For the rest of my life, I get the question, 'Did you touch that ball?' I say, 'If you had been listening after the game when I told them, I had no sensation of touching it. I may have. I never said I didn't touch it. Never once did I say I didn't touch it.'

"And I will say this: I know Mr. Murchison is not with us anymore, but one time Mr. Murchison stopped me in the hallway, one of the rare times I had ever seen him other than on the field or in the locker room, and he said, 'Why did you lose that Super Bowl for us?' He was talking about the tipped pass in Super Bowl V. It totally blew my mind. I'm thinking, 'For the owner of the team to say that to me with some sincerity, what are they talking about at those meetings? What is the brass talking about to lead this man to think I lost the Super Bowl?' That play had *nothing* to do with the outcome of the game. At the time we were still tied in the ballgame. This was the second quarter. And Craig Morton threw two fourth-quarter interceptions, one off the hands of Dan Reeves, to lose the game, and Clint Murchison asks me, 'Why did you lose that game?'"

After Mackey's catch was ruled a touchdown, the Cowboys blocked the extra point try, then, following Tom Landry's game plan calling for short passes to the backs, went ahead 13–6 on a seven-yard pass from Craig Morton to Duane Thomas.

The Cowboys kicked off to open the second half, and Colt Jim Duncan fumbled and lost the ball on the Colt 31. In five plays, the Cowboys drove to the two, from where Morton handed off to Duane Thomas for what appeared to be the clinching touchdown.

It was the crucial play of the game—and perhaps the most questionable call by an official in the history of the Super Bowl. As Thomas was crossing the goal line, the Cowboys' John Niland heard one official say, "He's over, he's over," just as Colt linebacker Mike Curtis hooked the ball loose. The ball bounced back across the thick white stripe, and Cowboy center Dave Manders fell on it inches from the goal line.

"It rolled right under me, and I fell on it," Manders said.

With Manders clutching the ball, Colt lineman Billy Ray Smith began yelling, "Our ball, our ball," pointing in the other direction. Referee Jack Fette was so moved by Smith's acting skill that he signaled that the Colts had recovered. Nearby, Manders was cradling the ball.

Manders got up and handed the ball to the ref with a big smile on his face. When the referees gave the ball to Baltimore, Landry couldn't believe it. It was enough to send the normally placid coach running down the sideline under his trademark hat, screaming at the officials.

There isn't a single Cowboy to this day who can understand how the Colts ended up with the ball. You can still hear the bewilderment in their voices.

JOHN NILAND: "I know [Manders] recovered it. I was right there on the ground next to him. There was no way it should have been Baltimore's ball. Some official just came running in from out in left field and made the call. That was the turning point of the game. If we had made the touchdown we would have been up 20–6 and it would have been almost impossible for Baltimore to come back. I couldn't believe it when I heard the call. I still can't."

In 1980 Niland was eating in a Dallas restaurant, when he looked across the room and saw Billy Ray Smith.

JOHN NILAND: "I looked across the room and there was Billy Ray Smith having dinner. I yelled over to him, 'Hey, Billy Ray, you still wearing my ring?' He knew exactly what I was talking about. He raised his hand and showed me his Super Bowl ring."

With the Colts playing the run as the game went on, Craig Morton tested his injured wing and came up short. Two second-half interceptions, both on balls that bounced off the hands of receivers, "proved" to the pundits that the Cowboys truly were a "team without a quarterback," as *Sports Illustrated* had so cruelly commented. Defensive players were saying that Tom Landry should have played Roger Staubach in his place, and their opinion was strengthened when they learned that Morton had sought help from a hypnotist prior to the big game.

MEL RENFRO: "Besides the couple of officiating things, Craig threw two interceptions in the fourth quarter. I was saying, 'Just run the ball.' He had already given them the tying touchdown with one interception. If you just don't throw an interception, we win the game. And if you have to throw an interception, throw it down at their end of the field, not at our end.

"You know when I got really angry at Craig? On the bus ride back to the hotel. My wife and I were sitting there crying our eyes out, and I looked back, and he was back there goosing his girlfriend and laughing. I mean, he was sitting two seats back, and they are laughing, goosing each other. And my wife and I were sitting there crying our eyes out. That's when I got angry at Craig."

LEE ROY JORDAN: "Late in the game with the score tied, 13–13, Morton threw to Danny [Reeves] and the ball hit off his fingers and into the arms of Mike Curtis, who ran the ball down to our 28 with about a minute left in the game. And then number 80, I can't remember his name [Jim O'Brien], he kicked that field goal, and that may be the only one he ever kicked to win a game. A year or two later he was out of the league.

"And after the ball went through the uprights and we lost, Bob Lilly threw his helmet about three hundred feet in the air, and when it hit the ground it splattered into pieces. Pieces just flew everywhere. I can't believe he threw it that high in the air.

"But we were all so disappointed and devastated because we knew we should have won the football game a number of times. Earl Morrall came in and made some big plays, but not nearly enough to win had we not made some mistakes ourselves."

PETTIS NORMAN: "To be honest, I really hated when we lost that Super Bowl. I know we should have won the game. We should have won that game without any hesitation. I just didn't brood over it as much as I did the two Green Bay games in '66 and '67. And maybe it was the false surroundings, the constant distractions leading up to it. You hardly had a chance to focus on the game.

"It's always interesting to speculate 'what if?' One of the interesting things to speculate about is what if we had won that game. One scenario is that Craig stays and Roger leaves. How can you replace a guy who wins a Super Bowl? With anybody, even if he messes up the first half of the season, how would you justify replacing that guy? You'd have a team that would literally eat a coach alive if he did that.

"And who knows where the Cowboys would have gone had that happened. Would they have won two or three more Super Bowls during that decade? It's wild when you think about it. That one game was *the* pivotal game in Cowboy history."

Super Bowl V was, in fact, the beginning of the end for Craig Morton, who had been sufficiently skilled to take the Cowboys to the threshold of the mountaintop. Three tipped passes had beaten him, however, and they would ultimately grease the skids for his replacement by Roger Staubach, who would lead the Cowboys through the rest of the decade. After too many years quarterbacking a mediocre New York Giant team, Craig Morton would lead the Denver Broncos against the Cowboys in Super Bowl XII. But Morton would get little credit for that feat either. In pro football, it seems, going to the dance just isn't good enough.

ROGER STAUBACH: "Against Baltimore, all we had to do was have a halfway good passing game.

"And after that game, that was the lowest I ever felt. Because before that Landry had said to me, 'It takes four years to become a starting quarterback.' Plus I wasn't young anymore. I didn't know where I was going. If I couldn't play in a game and really help the team with Craig injured, what was I going to do when the guy was healthy? After the game I felt that was possibly going to be it for me in Dallas.

"We were flying back to Dallas, and Tom Landry came back and sat with me for a few minutes. I was sitting with my wife, and he said, 'You *will* get your opportunity to be a starting quarterback this coming season.' And when he said that, I was rejuvenated, and I had a great off-season, worked hard, and in '71 Craig came back in great shape, and we competed for the job."

At the end of Super Bowl V, Lee Roy Jordan was saying, "I'm not taking any shit about this game. We'll be back. We've got good personnel, we're playing the defense . . . all we need is a little better passing game. We will be back."

Lee Roy was right, but not before another rocky season of Sturm und Drang as the combination of drugs and an intransigent Tex Schramm would cause their enfant terrible, Duane Thomas, to become so alienated and act so strangely that neither Tom Landry nor any of his concerned teammates knew what to do about it.

42

Duane versus the Plastic Man

By 1971 everyone was familiar with the stern figure of Tom Landry standing on the sideline, staring impassively at the action, his felt hat and cloth coat defining for a nation a successful, serious corporate leader. In the clubhouse, behind closed doors, Landry was that way with his players, whom he kept on edge with his brutal post-game reviews in an attempt to squeeze every ounce of effort from them. By 1971, even though the Dallas Cowboys were a formidable football team that had gone to the Super Bowl, no one on his team was very happy playing football. It was that year that Duane Thomas put in words what many on the team were thinking when he called Tom Landry a "plastic man."

MEL RENFRO: "Tom Landry was a brilliant coach, a brilliant general on the field and in the classroom. We all know his stoic presence on the field and in the media, and he was also that way with the players. There was no warmth or real friendship that was developed between the players and Coach Tom, and we preferred it that way. Because of his personality. He just wasn't a fun person to be around. You did your job for him, you listened to him, you paid attention because you knew what he told you was the right thing to do. He was a brilliant coach.

"Tom was a true coach. That was his life. Twenty-four [hours] and seven [days] of football. That's what he lived for. And I admired him because he had a talent for getting players to do what they were supposed to do. He was a psychologist of sorts. He was very stern. He demanded you perform to a certain level, the level of your ability. If you didn't, you would be reprimanded behind closed doors.

"I remember on several occasions I graded much higher than many of the other players, but was not given any kind of reward for that grading because I wasn't grading to my potential. I was just graded above the others. And I didn't understand that for a long time. 'Mel, with your talent you need to grade 92 plus every time. If you grade 88 or 90, I'm not going to praise you. But here were other guys grading 75 and 80, I'm going to praise them, because their level is below that.'

"I said to myself, 'I graded 93, and this guy graded 85, and he's talking about how great he played.' I said, 'What's wrong here? He doesn't like me or something.' It was Jerry Tubbs who alerted me to it. Not directly, but in what he was saying. He said, 'Mel, we expect so much out of you because you're a great player, and if you don't grade 95 or better, you had a poor game.'

"Back in those days we were all on edge about our own performance. Each one of us was concerned as to how Coach Landry saw our ability. He might praise a guy or cut him down. We were busy worrying about ourselves."

LEE ROY JORDAN: "We always said that Coach Landry, when he reviewed the films, he 'chewed ass by the numbers.' He would have a legal pad full of notes on who made mistakes and who played poorly, and if one guy had a bad game and made fifty mistakes, Coach Landry would cover every one of them. He would criticize that guy's every mistake. And when he got through, sometimes that guy was devastated.

"Blaine Nye once said, 'It's not who wins the game but who gets the blame.' And yeah, that was right. The offensive linemen took a lot of raps for it. Blaine Nye, Dave Manders, John Niland, those guys took their share of hard beatings from Tom.

"Some guys had to go throw up before going into meetings to watch films because they knew they were going to be singled out numerous times during the course of the game for their problems or lack of success during the game. It was somebody every week."

MARGENE ADKINS: "Let me say this: Duane at this time, he took a stand by himself. But one man could not break the system. He didn't have enough blacks standing with him at that particular time, because when he called Tom Landry a 'plastic man,' at that time he was right. See, we'd be having a meeting, and say we'd have lunch break, we'd be in there laying on the floor or eating or playing cards, and we'd see Tom come through, and when he walked through, you could see he wanted to stop and hold a conversation with you, but he was the type of man, he could not do it. He never could hold a conversation with us, wasn't talking to any of us. And another thing about Tom Landry which we all knew: Tom was one intelligent coach, one of the greatest ever, and see where Tom made his mistake, he wanted to coach *everything*. Like on film day, he went over special teams, went over offense, went over defense. He did it all. And he didn't give his other coaches a chance to do anything. That was his problem, and I heard he broke over the years, that later on through the years he began to talk to his men, black and white."

As the country was becoming more corporate, more bottom-line driven, the pursuit of happiness was no longer what America was all about. By the early 1970s commerce was becoming king, as shopping malls began to proliferate along endless ribbons of highways littered with fast-food stands on either side. McDonald's had started in California in the '50s, and by the '70s, those double arches were dotting the landscape everywhere, killing mom-and-pop luncheonettes. America was becoming more and more impersonal. You could drive your car to a prescribed spot, talk into a clown face, order from a preset menu, and drive out with a Big Mac, a pouch of fries, and a large coke. It was organized and quick, and Ronald McDonald was a friendly enough corporate spokesman to make you forget that food was unhealthy in its saturated fat and sugar content. But it got you on your way with a full tummy, and it certainly tasted good. People bought it, in huge quantities, and that was all that mattered. McDonald's was celebrated for its success, and the fat content of its food be damned.

The change to a big business economy benefited a lot of people. Corporate executives of moderate means became rich. CEOs became fabulously wealthy. But there was a downside. To get rich, to climb that ladder, a lot of somebodies had to provide the footing. General Motors could make a lot more money assembling its cars in Mexico. For this to happen, the workers in Flint, Michigan, had to lose their jobs and go on welfare for the rest of the their lives because there were no replacement jobs available to them. So be it. And if you were black and poor, watching powerful men becoming moguls at your expense made the bitterness worse and the emotional equilibrium more difficult.

In 1971 Clint Murchison moved the Cowboys home games from the venerable, dilapidated Cotton Bowl to his magnificent new arena, Texas Stadium, located in the Dallas suburb of Irving. Murchison had wanted city money to build a new stadium downtown, but then Mayor Erik Johnsson, one of the founders of Texas Instruments, told Murchison that city money would only be made available to refurbish the Cotton Bowl.

In late 1966 Murchison shocked the city fathers when he announced he had paid $1 for 90 acres across in Irving, seven miles from downtown, and was building a new stadium there.

A horrified Johnsson asked Murchison, "If you take the Cowboys out of [the Cotton Bowl], what are you suggesting we put there instead?"

Said Murchison archly, "What about an electronics plant?"

The stadium cost $25 million. It was built without any public funds. Fans paid $18 million in bonds. Murchison picked up the rest. Suites, many of which were sold to corporations, cost $50,000, in addition to the seat prices (12 tickets at $1,296 each). Fans sitting between the 30-yard lines had to buy a block of four seats plus four $250 bonds in addition to the price of the tickets. The first-year cost: $4,272. If they didn't want to lose the bond money fans had to buy their seats for thirty-two years. The blue-collar, black, and Spanish fans who had come to see the Cowboys in the Cotton Bowl long before they became fashionable complained that they could no longer afford to go to Cowboy games. Replied an unrepentant Murchison, "If we discriminated against them, we discriminated against them, but no more than all America discriminates against people who don't have money to buy everything they want."

Murchison built a cathedral, with a large oval hole in the roof so the fans would stay dry when it rained on the field. At a dinner party a woman asked Clint, "Why did you leave that great big hole in the roof of your stadium?"

He told her, "So that God can see His team play."

Most of the players disliked the move, because the Cotton Bowl had a grass field and Texas Stadium had a much harder, more injury-prone artificial surface. Others were unhappy because from now on only the well-to-do could get in to see the Cowboys play.

CORNELL GREEN: "In '71 we moved to Texas Stadium. I was sorry to leave the Cotton Bowl. I liked the crowd better there. They were rowdy. I liked all the beer drinkers, the loud people. And when we moved to Texas Stadium, a lot of those fans couldn't even go anymore. At Texas Stadium, it was more like a country club. And at Texas Stadium they put in Astro-Turf [actually Texas Turf], and that was the next bad thing. Football was becoming more corporate. People started wearing minks to the game. Yup. They'd get fully dressed. No more jeans and T-shirts."

MEL RENFRO: "I loved the Cotton Bowl. *Loved* it. My only feeling about Texas Stadium was that we *had* to go. I didn't want to go, but we had to go. It was very disappointing to me because it eliminated a lot of black Americans from attending the games. It eliminated the crowd that we used to have with the excitement and the noise. It was just different, like you were playing in your living room. It was a bunch of rich people who you couldn't get excited about anything. It was just a totally different atmosphere. I didn't like the move at all."

Tex Schramm insisted that the Dallas Cowboys be run according to the same strict guidelines as any other well-run corporation. Tex wanted his players hardworking and obedient. He wanted "team players," which he defined as players who worked like dogs and didn't complain about the hosing they were taking in the salary department. Schramm didn't like "troublemakers," and if they could be replaced, he got rid of them. On Mother's Day in May of 1971 tight end Pettis Norman, a Cowboy pillar since 1962, led a march and boycott with about a hundred blacks along Main Street in downtown Dallas. The group was protesting that the Citizens Charter Association, the town leaders who controlled such appointments, had double-crossed the black community by not appointing a local black businessman the mayor pro tempore, after promising to do so. Norman, the first black ever to be made an officer of a bank in Dallas, in a speech accused the group of affronting all African-Americans in the city.

At the news conference after the march, the first question a reporter asked Norman was, "How is it going to feel to be traded to Kansas City?" Replied Norman, "If that's what it takes to be a man, then Kansas City here I come."

Pettis Norman was traded less than a month later—not to Kansas City but to San Diego—for wide receiver Lance Alworth. Though Coach Landry swore to Norman that he was traded not because of his political views but because San Diego wouldn't give up Alworth unless he was in the deal, the black community suspected otherwise and was furious at Tex

Schramm and the Cowboys. They saw the Norman trade as retaliation for his making waves in a city where the Cowboys sought support from the government and the city's white powerbrokers.

The morning after the announcement of the Norman trade, black citizens congregated at the bank where Norman was working, threatening to march to the Cowboys office building and burn it down. Norman went on television to ask for calm.

As smart and powerful as any business executive, Tex Schramm kept an iron hand over the Cowboys, especially their pursestrings, keeping to his budget as though he and not the Murchisons were the owner of the team. During the 1960s, when the NFL was beginning to grow, the Dallas players knew they were getting peanuts to play but didn't resent it because no one else seemed to be making all that much either, but as the TV contracts swelled and television was beginning to generate substantial ad dollars, players on other teams (especially the Washington Redskins, where George Allen felt it important to pay his players generously) began making six figures while even the Cowboy stars were making half that. With the start of the players' association, the Cowboy players began comparing notes with players from other teams, and they discovered that the Cowboys were among the worst-paying teams in football.

Tex Schramm would not pay his players a fair wage, but there was nothing they could do about it, not yet anyway, and with might making right, Tex would chisel them down financially while at the same time fueling a PR machine that was making them nationally famous. Many players settled for the fame, figuring that their renown would lead to a secure financial future after football. Sadly, most would be very wrong about that.

If you were uncomfortable with the changes in society brought by the coming of the Big Business Age or if you found yourself the victim of corporate ruthlessness, it could literally drive you crazy. If you believed in Flower Power, believed that if you loved your neighbor everything would work out fine, or if you believed in equality as promised in the Bill of Rights, or if you believed in the goodness of your fellow man, the reality of Corporate America was a rude awakening. Making money had little to do with morality or equality or love. Move it or lose it. It was lead, follow, or get out of the way.

The result was a new generation of disillusioned young people shrouded in a blanket of either hopelessness or anger heretofore unseen in American life.

Among the younger blacks, as segregation evaporated but opportunities remained scarce, anger rose dramatically. A small group of militants called the Black Panthers scared the pants off J. Edgar Hoover and the white power structure. They wanted real equality and they wanted it immediately. Their slogan of "Black Power" made everyone jumpy. At Cornell University a group of black students were photographed carrying large guns on campus. Malcolm X, Bobby Seale, Stokely Carmichael, and other young, angry blacks talked about "war against whitey." Malcolm X's group of Muslims, antiwhite-talking men with names foreign to American ears, made it sound like there was going to be a race war in the near future if the "honkies" didn't watch out.

These were the two social forces—the rise in corporate America and the visibility of the Black Power movement—that came into play when in the summer of 1971 Duane Thomas complained that the Cowboys had saddled him with a bad contract and then in bad faith refused to renegotiate it. He called Tom Landry a "plastic man, no man at all," and said that Gil Brandt was a liar. He called Tex Schramm "sick, demented, and dishonest," to which Schramm replied, "two out of three ain't bad." When Schramm made it clear he would not give in to his demands, an angry Thomas told Landry he wanted to be traded.

In addition to releasing antiblack sentiment within the white community of Dallas, Thomas also let loose a torrent of anti–Dallas Cowboy sentiment from all across the rest of the country, mostly from the counterculture, the huge swell of younger anti–Vietnam, anti–Richard Nixon, anti–Jim Crow football fans. Young fans from all the other NFL cities for years had resented the button-down Tom Landry and his glamour team. In 1971 Duane Thomas had spelled out *why* they had hated Landry and his team. It was because Landry was "plastic" and his team corporate. For the rest of his life, to his detractors Tom Landry would be known as the "Plastic Man."

And for the rest of his life, Duane Thomas would be remembered as being "that crazy nigger who refused to talk to the press," though sometimes his more racist critics would replace "crazy" with "dumb."

But the funny thing about stereotypes is that they don't always match the person attached to them. In this case up until the time that the pressures of playing pro football got to him, Duane Thomas was a person any mother would have been proud to call her son. Besides his immense talent, Duane Thomas was very intelligent. He spoke eloquently. He was observant.

In the journal he kept his first season he wrote how impressed he was with the camaraderie of the Cowboys' defensive stars and with the men who blocked for him on the offensive line.

"When I saw Bob Lilly and Jethro Pugh, my two favorite defensive linemen, working in such unison with Lee Roy Jordan, I said, 'Look at what they have going together.' I said 'Look at what we have . . . a championship team,' even though some people didn't realize it. Cornell Green, the brilliance of his play was thrilling. . . . Blaine Nye, Dave Manders, Rayfield Wright, John Niland, impeccable at the point of attack.

"I was so thankful to be surrounded by such men on the field. The team was like an orchestra. It was so beautiful to watch the flow of execution on that team, consistently unstoppable, the scoreboard going like a pinball machine."

This was not the musing of an uneducated street urchin. Here was a young man who appreciated his teammates and wasn't afraid to say so. Here was a *team* player. He was *thrilled* to be a Cowboy. He worked hard. He was soft-spoken. He was polite. And he was trusting.

He believed in family values. Though his mom died when he was a junior in college and his dad died a year later, he never forgot his duty to his younger brothers. When brother Bertrand got in a car accident and lost three fingers, Duane paid his bills. When brother Franklin had kidney trouble and needed expensive medical care, Duane was there for him, too.

Duane had married his high school sweetheart and had two children, but once he entered West Texas State on scholarship, he discovered that under NCAA rules he could get only room, board, and $15 a month for laundry. Several times he tried to leave school to go to work to earn money, but the coaches always sat him down and persuaded him to keep at it. All his young life he had trusted his coaches, because he had had no one else to rely on. At West Texas State, his coach, Joe Kerbel, had been a mentor and a father figure.

When he was named the Cowboys' number one draft choice, the twenty-one-year-old Thomas figured his money worries would be over. When he was first drafted, Tom Landry, superscout Gil Brandt, and president Tex Schramm all hustled him, assuring him that he could place his well-being in their hands.

CALVIN HILL: "In terms of Duane, or a Bob Hayes, who wound up in prison, the sad thing is that I don't think Tom ever understood how much they depended on him."

PETE GENT: "Duane had a coach who treated him like a son, and Landry acted like that when Duane first met him, so Duane thought that's what he was going to get. And what he got was the last years of the plastic man. And it was those years, that awful strain and that failure of being able to deal with Duane that made Landry reexamine himself. You can laugh off a guy like me. But you can't after you've totally blown Duane and the Rookie of the Year in Calvin Hill.

"Tom made Duane absolutely crazy. And I don't think Duane ever recovered. In later years he called me and wanted to become friends, but I could tell by talking to him that he was emotionally crippled. At the end he was trying to be what he thought would make Landry happy, and that was certainly the last guy in the world I wanted to be with. And I liked Duane, he was a nice guy, and I wished the best for him, but I don't think he ever recovered from it. None of us did."

The string of events leading to Duane Thomas's famed "Plastic Man" appellation began a couple of months after Super Bowl V in the winter of 1971, when Thomas charged that the year before his agent and Tex Schramm had sold him down the river by agreeing to a lousy contract. Thomas felt betrayed. He had trusted his agent, giving him power of attorney. He had trusted Gil Brandt, who had put his arm around Thomas's shoulder and said, "Don't worry. We'll take care of you." He had trusted Schramm. He was also upset that Schramm wouldn't pay off on the clause in the contract that called for him to receive a bonus for gaining 1,000 yards. Thomas, who finished with 862 yards, argued that the only reason he came up short was that Tom Landry hadn't played him very much early in the season.

Thomas told Schramm that his $20,000 salary wasn't enough to live on, that he owed the IRS $10,000, that he had an ex-wife with two kids who was demanding alimony, and that he couldn't live on the money he was making.

Schramm looked him in the eyes and told him no.

"But you renegotiated Rayfield Wright's contract," Thomas told him.

"Sorry, son."

Thomas was haunted by what he saw as the unfairness of the situation.

"I saw no appreciation from them—for my hard work, my dedication and my sincerity. All of this was being exploited." Thomas was not wrong, and he knew he wasn't wrong. When Tex Schramm told him he was stuck with his bad deal, all Thomas could think about was the unfairness of his situation. He became fixated on Schramm's rejection of his plea to pay him what he felt he deserved after helping to take the team to the Super Bowl.

"I figured they didn't dig me," said Thomas. "I wasn't the stereotype passing type of nigger who comes in and says, 'Please, Mr. White Man, do this for me.'"

In March, Thomas told CBS television he was retiring. He said that the Cowboys would not have gone to the Super Bowl without him, and said it was he who the fans came to see, not Schramm, and he said publicly what he had told Schramm: he wanted his fair share.

When the articles in the paper the next few days and weeks came out four-square against him, Thomas sank into a deep depression. Not only did the reporters take Schramm's side, but they called Thomas "cocky" and "greedy."

Thomas did not report to training camp, and Schramm waited him out, fully expecting him to give in. He finally arrived in July with a man wearing a dashiki, Ali Ha Ka Kabir (nee Mansfield Collins) and demanded that Kabir be given a tryout. Schramm refused his request. Thomas called a press conference and again requested a trade. It was at this press conference that he blasted Landry, Brandt, and Schramm.

CALVIN HILL: "There was a rumor going around camp that Duane and the Muslims were going to kidnap Tex. Next morning Tex had four or five guards around him. It was wild."

On July 31, 1971, Tex Schramm and Tom Landry thought they had rid themselves of their Duane-Thomas-the-Uppity-Nigger headache when they traded their star back to the New England Patriots along with lineman Halvor Hagen and wide receiver Honor Jackson, for Carl Garrett and a number one draft choice.

Garrett immediately put his foot in his mouth by saying how glad he was to come to Dallas and to get away from the Patriots' leaky offensive line.

Schramm and Landry figured the tandem of Calvin Hill and Garrett had the ability to return them to the Super Bowl. A bitter Thomas angered a lot of his teammates when he told the press that the Cowboys would never make it back there without him. Others felt it was best for Thomas to be playing in a new environment.

CORNELL GREEN: "I thought when they traded Duane to New England it might be the best thing for him. It hurt me to see what he was going through, but the only problem, when you tried to talk to him, he wouldn't listen. He *didn't* listen. I don't have time. I had two kids of my own to raise."

When Thomas reported to the Patriots, he clashed with coach John Mazur. A month before the Thomas trade, the Cowboys had sent Steve Kiner to the New England graveyard. Kiner had been infuriated when Landry coaxed Chuck Howley out of retirement and gave him the linebacking job Kiner thought he deserved. When Kiner was sent to the Patriots, he was in a position to observe what happened between Duane Thomas and the Pats.

STEVE KINER: "I competed with D. D. Lewis the whole camp the second year, the whole preseason in '71, to see who was going start at outside linebacker. If I didn't start, I figured I would have been hot on D.D.'s tail. And then Chuck Howley came out of retirement. And Landry didn't say, 'He's going to have to earn his position.' He just gave him the job back. So I went in and told Landry, 'I don't think that's fair,' and he said, 'I'm not interested in what you think is fair.' I said, 'You need to trade me.' He traded me that afternoon! I was history.

"I went to New England, and then when Howley came out of retirement, D.D. sat on the bench a long time before he got to play. I wasn't interested in sitting there. I probably should have sat there. But I chose not to. Yeah, that was probably one of the unsmart things I did, one of the not-so-smart things, to go from Dallas to New England.

"What Duane said about Landry being plastic and Tex dishonest and Gil a liar was true, but you don't say those kind of things. You just *can't* say that. What does it do for you? How does it benefit you? I talked with Duane about that for six months during the season and even longer than that, because after the '70 season Duane and I went out to L.A. and lived together.

"We lived off of Hollywood Boulevard. I stayed out there three months, but I left before the summer was over, because it was just too much for me, too much of everything. Too much drugs, too much women, too much craziness.

"It was crazy, reckless fun. We'd go to a restaurant and just start throwing plates around and tipping tables over, just crazy, just bizarre, not trying to hurt anybody, but making a big commotion, being crazy. Then running out laughing, then getting high again.

"I was seeing everything, yeah. I saw guns, and I was seeing more cocaine than I knew was on the face of the earth. If you put that in, my wife will kick my ass. Everybody says to me, 'Oh, these crazy football players.' And I used to tell them, 'Hey, this is just a microcosm of the whole society. We're not any different than anybody else.'

"'Cause by that time everybody that I knew, and you're talking about the crowd I ran around with, was into cocaine. *Everybody* was driving their own train. And that's the craziness I had to step out of. I sat down and talked with Duane. I said, 'Look, you guys handle this stuff a lot better than I do. I got to get out of here. I'm going right off the wall.' And I was. That's a vicious drug. It ravaged my brain. It took me a long time to recover from it.

"And so that winter I just quit. I left L.A., and that was it. I hung it up. They didn't have any Cocaine Anonymous, and they didn't have any rehab or anything. And I just quit, and what happened, after I went up to New England, I just had a real tough time. I had a good year on the field, but I had a rough time off the field, just trying to adjust to not being high all the time. And then the next year the Pats traded me to Washington, and George Allen helped me a lot. He extended a hand and said, 'What's the problem?' And I told him what the problem was. 'I'm burned-out on cocaine.' So he got me some help. George was the finest of all the people I encountered. He was there for the players. He filled that role.

"Landry and Tex, they turned a blind eye. They didn't intervene. They didn't value any of these people as human beings. They didn't say, 'This person needs a little help here. We need to show a little kindness.'

"You need a leader who is going to help you out. I thought George Allen was a remarkable human being, and he was so hokey, corny. He'd cheat, but we allow that in our society. That's the American way. George wasn't doing anything nobody else was doing.

"I had been in New England for about a week or two, when their coach, John Mazur, called me in and said, 'Steve, I'm thinking about trading Carl for Duane. Can you tell me about Duane?' I said, 'The guy is phenomenal. He's the best damn running back in the league.' They made the trade, and after Duane was in New England about three days, Mazur was just beside himself. 'I thought you told me this guy was all right.' I said, 'He's not all right; he's a great running back. You just gotta handle him differently.' And John couldn't. Duane just blew him away.

"John wanted Duane to get in a three-point stance, and he wouldn't. All he could do was line up with his hands on his knees. He could not run out of a three-point stance. If John had said, 'Hey, Duane, here's $1,500, I need you to get in a three-point stance,' that would have worked. And see, that's where Duane had lost perspective of everything. Here's what it was about: He thought he had positioned himself where he could make all these demands, and what he found out was that he couldn't.

"Duane got a lot of misinformation from the older, militant black players in the league, militant in the sense that they were disgruntled, and he would listen to them, and he felt he was going to make a difference. I could see Duane was looking at the world differently than I was. I was looking at, 'He's cutting his nose off to spite his face.' And I begged him not to do that. I told him, 'This is just not good for you.' But he couldn't hear any of that. It was a real hard position to be in.

"Duane was as good as any running back that's ever played in the league, or had ever come into the league. And you can take that to the bank. And you can ask any of the Cowboy players, and if any of them say that's not the truth, they are lying through their teeth. All Duane wanted was for the Cowboys to renegotiate his contract. If they had torn that up and given him $30,000, $40,000, and $50,000, he'd have been happier than a pig in shit. For a crummy ten grand, Tex Schramm cost the Cowboys a couple of Super Bowls and threw this guy's career away. And not just his career. As far as I'm concerned, threw his whole life out the window. And that's the tragedy of the sport. When you turn around, they are going to say, 'Well, he's a man. He's an adult. It was his responsibility.' But we were just kids."

After Duane Thomas spent five tumultuous days in New England, the Pats called Tex Schramm and demanded that the trade be canceled.

"They [the Patriots] told me to leave—face-to-face—just like that. So I came home," said Thomas.

Tex didn't want Thomas back, but NFL commissioner Pete Rozelle voided the trade and forced his return to Dallas, where he would lead the Cowboys to another trip to the Super Bowl. A sheepish Garrett had to return to the Pats and their porous offensive line.

Thomas was put on the inactive list and missed the first three games of the '71 season. He returned to action on a Monday night against the New York Giants, and he played on the special teams as though possessed. In the first half on one play he tackled his former college teammate, Rocky Thompson, forcing a fumble. On two other kickoffs he also made tackles on the fleet Thompson.

On the fourth play of the second half, Calvin Hill was injured, and Thomas went into the game. Despite having missed the entire training camp, Thomas looked as though he hadn't missed a beat, running 60 yards on 9 carries.

MEL RENFRO: "When Duane starred against the Giants after missing all of training camp, I wasn't surprised. 'Cause he was a talent. Just like Jim Brown. Jim Brown could have walked on any field at any time and kicked everybody's butt, and Duane, who was a tremendous athletic specimen, was potentially that way."

After the game Thomas, still angry that the Dallas media had taken Tex's side against him, announced his refusal to talk to the press. Said Thomas, "There is nothing to say when you're working." For the rest of the season, their articles about his refusal to talk to them made him sound petty, childish, and flaky, which further fueled Thomas's resentment against the newspaper reporters in particular and the white society in general.

In addition to becoming a celebrity, Thomas had also become a marked man. It bothered him terribly when strangers would stare at him, like he was a curiosity or a freak in a circus sideshow.

"Everyone used to look at me strangelike," said Thomas. "I'd be doing something and they'd act like they were hypnotized. I know I hadn't told them anything and neither did anyone know anything about me. I thought I was in the twilight zone."

But those teammates who respected hard work and dedication to the game of football overlooked the sideshow and saw a football player who stayed in shape, studied the game plan, and gave his all on the field.

LEE ROY JORDAN: "Duane Thomas and I got along perfect. I loved Duane Thomas. I respected him when he went into the deal about not talking. I told him, 'Duane, you have chosen the right thing. You have chosen to concentrate on football. And if you can't handle all these other things, I admire you the priority you have taken in committing to football.' "

What hurt Duane Thomas worse than anything was the double standard that he saw on the Cowboys in the way he was being treated. He saw that when Mike Ditka got drunk and crashed his car at four in the morning, when John Niland got drunk and brawled with cops, and when Lance Rentzel got busted, the media ran one story and dropped it like it had never happened. But here was Duane Thomas whose crime was not talking to the newspaper writers, and he couldn't believe it when the media made a bigger stink about that than any of those other, to him more serious, incidents. The reason, said Thomas, was because the white press excused the behavior of the white players, but not his, because he was black.

"It was accepted as just a bunch of good ol' boys having fun. No big deal."

Thomas bristled at the stereotype of the lazy, unexcited black athlete being placed on him.

"People accuse me of not being excited for games. Well, compared to them [his good old boy teammates] I wasn't excited, because I wasn't using all them damn bennies they were taking. How many times did I see guys hung over for the games . . . in the fourth quarter they were breathing heavy in the huddle, and I was just getting started."

Said Thomas to journalist Howie Evans, "The thing that bothers me is the unjust attitudes many football people have toward black athletes. It's something I find not only in pro football but in life in general. It's the way they talk to us, the way they look at us, and what they really think of us. There are a lot of black players who are afraid to speak out on the grievances they have, and the injustices they know are being inflicted upon them."

The bottom line was that Duane Thomas couldn't stand not being respected and appreciated in a town where he had just helped its team win the prize sought since 1960: the Super Bowl. Said Duane's brother Bertrand sometime later, "The people of Dallas don't want to recognize my brother's ability, and he can do so much for the Cowboys."

Thomas's black teammates saw how the press used Duane's anger against him, how the reporters kept the flow of stories about him coming. They wanted to stop it, but they were powerless to do so. And then when he refused to talk in his own attempt to end the controversy, the stories took on a life of their own: silent Duane, the crazy Cowboy. His teammates could only shake their heads.

PETTIS NORMAN: "Almost before you knew it, there was a full-blown feud, which was being fueled by the press that was playing both sides against each other, and Duane got caught up in that, and not knowing how to get out of it, he became a victim of it, too, to a certain extent.

"He expressed the anger he felt over the contract and how he felt he had been treated. The press would goad him on and pull things out of him and then blow it up, and it would work against him. It was a catch-22 situation he found himself in.

"And when he made that decision he was not going to talk to anybody—the press here especially, with the mentality it has—it paints

African-American players in a whole different light, and it did then, and Duane gave them the fodder to feed on.

"Other players could have been angry and not gotten what Duane got. And to the extent I saw incidents in which the press treated African-American players five times worse than what it did had it been someone else. The press continually went after Duane, when they should have recognized that this was a twenty-one-year-old kid who really didn't know his way around this ballpark, and instead of us doing it the way we're doing it, let's try to get to another level and make some sense of it. Let's try to understand things from Duane's standpoint, instead of making fun of a lot of the things he said. These writers were adults. They were grown men who had been out there for a long time. Duane was just a kid. But it never happened. They just continually wrote about the negative Duane, and the public got to the point where they thought Duane was a demon, and Duane was not a demon at all. But they never wrote the good things about Duane. To them, he was just an angry football player who signed a contract and didn't want to live with his contract. But they never got beyond that to say that this was an interesting young man who made a lot of sense when you sat down and talked to him."

Thomas defended his decision not to talk to the press: "I didn't feel like talking so I didn't talk. If I read the Constitution right, it gives me the freedom to do as I please. There's no stipulation that says if you play football you have to talk. I don't get paid for talking. I get paid to play football.

"I am the symbol of the ghetto. I had to make my choices at an earlier age than guys with better opportunities. I don't want a computer judging my mentality, yet I am tested and rated. I am judged on how I communicate, not on how I perform. I got into pro football looking for a brighter day, yet the brighter day never came."

When Tom Landry told a reporter Duane had to change his attitude, Thomas called Landry "unfair and dishonest."

"There is nothing wrong with my attitude," he said. "My attitude is a winning attitude. I have felt that my attitude coincided with the goal of the team." He added, "I never go around and complain about him [Landry] not talking."

Frustrated and bitter that he had to play under a system that he hated in a town where he felt unwanted and unappreciated after a daily pounding in the press, Thomas even cut off most of his own teammates.

CORNELL GREEN: "Me and Duane got along great. One year he wouldn't talk to nobody on the team. I talked to him every day. See, a reporter thinks just because Duane doesn't talk to him, he ain't talking to nobody. Hell, I talked to him every day. I was over at his house three and four times. I had no problem with Duane, and if he didn't want to talk to reporters, that was his business. People were getting upset, and I told Duane he was also getting a lot of bad advice. He did some stupid things. He could have owned this town. That's why I told him, 'Man, you're getting some *bad* advice. Take the money and run.' But he wouldn't take my advice. 'I'll do it my way,' he said. I said, 'You can do what you want.'

"His agent was Abner Haynes, and he had a good contract the first year. The only thing, it was heavy on the bonus end. Also, he had family members to support, plus he had all them old high school buddies who had financial problems asking him for money, and see, you get some bad advice. Abner got him a good contract, but Abner can't walk around with the man, dishing out his money for him. So you can always blame someone else: 'Abner didn't get me a good contract,' or 'The Cowboys screwed me.' He was happy with it when he signed it. Then he became bitter about it because he took some bad advice. You talk to Duane now, and he'll admit that he screwed it up.

"Duane was one of the best running backs you've ever seen. But there wasn't any way to keep him from going off the way he went off. Nothing. There ain't nothing you can do about it. He took bad advice. He was going to do what he was going to do. And there's nothing you can do about it. It was a shame."

MEL RENFRO: "When Duane came back from New England, he just clammed up. He wouldn't talk to anybody. He wouldn't say a word. And I lockered right next to the guy. I remember one time, the guy hadn't said anything all year, and all of a sudden he said, 'Fro, how you doing? How are the kids?' Totally freaked me out! I said, 'Duane, the kids are fine.' He said, 'Good.' And he didn't say another word for two weeks.

"For a long time Duane was an introvert. He went within himself for a long, long time, and then after he retired he flipped over to the other side. He came out, and he was too much the other way. People started getting tired of him talking so much. It was like, 'Duane, chill.'"

MIKE DITKA: "Duane Thomas was a big factor in us winning. He was a good football player. He was a good all-round receiver, runner, blocker. He was a fluid runner who never took a real hard hit. He was like Jim

Brown. He knew how to give and go, slip and slide, and all that stuff. He was an excellent blocker, which people didn't know about. Dan Reeves worked with him and said, 'That guy is really smart.' He knew the full-back and halfback spots. He had to know both because Walt Garrison got hurt and Duane had to go to fullback with Calvin Hill at halfback. But it was just uncomfortable to be around him, no fun.

"Once we were playing the Giants in Yankee Stadium. I always made a habit of going up and wishing everybody good luck before a game. I went up to him and just patted him on the back and said 'Good luck.' He didn't acknowledge it. I went on my way. We played the game. The following Tuesday, I was sitting beside my locker reading the paper in Dallas before practice and he came up to me and said, 'Hey man, don't ever hit me on the back before a game. It breaks my concentration.'

"I said, 'Hey Duane. Go fuck yourself.'

"That was our conversation."

WALT GARRISON: "People always asked me, 'How did you and Duane get along?' Well, I liked Duane. I always liked him. I liked him when he was weird. I didn't give a damn if he ever talked because he played. And I don't say that even about a lot of guys who did talk.

"One time Duane scored a touchdown against San Francisco in a playoff game in Texas Stadium. They called an audible at the goal line and Duane went to the wrong side of the formation. I told him, 'Duane, other side.' He moved over. They pitched out to him and he scored a TD.

"A writer asked me after the game, 'Did you line up in the wrong spot?' And I said, 'Yes.'

"They found out later that I lied to them and they came back. 'Why didn't you tell us Thomas was lined up in the wrong spot?'

" 'Because y'all been on his ass all year.'

"Hey, I liked the guy."

Ironically, the Duane Thomas situation put Tom Landry in a lose-if-I-do, lose-if-I-don't situation. Thomas was disruptive, but he was a great performer. During practice Thomas at times refused to run in simulation of the opposing team, making the vets mad at both him and Tom Landry, who didn't call him on it. The good old boys on the team—and the majority of Dallas rooters—saw Landry as the good guy in the drama for going out of his way to turn the other cheek when Duane was being disruptive.

WALT GARRISON: "When it came time for the defense to practice, he'd refuse to run. We'd all run on the dummy teams to simulate the opponent's offense. If you had three backs, you'd run every third play. But Duane wouldn't do it, which put an extra load on me and the other running backs. And that pissed us off.

"I got my ass chewed out in practice one day because it was Duane's turn to run a dummy play and he was off dicking around as usual. 'What the hell's wrong with Thomas?' I yelled.

"Landry jumped all over me, then he said, 'It's your turn to run. Get in there.' Oh, that went over big with the rest of the veterans.

"The worst part of it was that Landry let him get away with it. Anybody else would have gotten the boot. You don't want to practice? Goodbye. But not Duane Thomas. Landry left him alone. So while the rest of us kicked butt during practice, Duane stood over on the sidelines chewing gum. And Landry didn't say shit.

"I think Landry looked at Duane as his one big failure. He wanted to get Duane back on the right track. Tom wanted to save him, wanted to give him a chance to get back to being a human being again.

"But it didn't work.

"That's when Landry really lost the respect of the veteran players. Because all of a sudden we now had a double standard.

"Ironically, Landry's failure with Duane showed the strength of his character. It showed how much he really did care about his players.

"If Landry was truly like his image—cold, calculating, humorless, and unemotional—he would have cut Thomas without a second thought."

MIKE DITKA: "The worst anguish Tom ever went through was with Duane Thomas. I've never seen a man suffer in trying to do what he thought was best for a football team, for the individual, and for everybody concerned. It was very agonizing and tough for Tom, but he did it. We won a Super Bowl, but it was pure hell dealing with the way Thomas treated everybody. He treated his teammates no differently than he treated the press or he treated Tom or he treated everybody. He was just a real insensitive person, but he was very mixed up at the time. When you're dealing with what he was dealing with, you've got problems. Duane is basically a good guy.

"Landry never really bent the rules for Thomas, but I think he bent himself a little bit. He tried to keep the rules standard for everyone. Duane was on time for meetings, but he never talked. He never had a conversation with anybody. I don't even know that he ever talked to the coaches, really. He never answered roll call. He would be in the room, but he never said, 'Here.' Things like that. I think Tom made some concessions in that area. He did it because he thought it was best for the football team. After he did it, I'm not sure he believed he could ever make those concessions again with anybody."

WALT GARRISON: "Duane ran us right into the Super Bowl that year and it just about destroyed the team. A Super Bowl is supposed to bring everybody together and here we were holding up the Super Bowl trophy and everybody is pissed off."

All because Tex Schramm stupidly, stubbornly, refused to pay Duane Thomas what he deserved.

43

Roger Takes the Helm

ROGER STAUBACH: "In '71 Craig came back in great shape so that season we competed for the starting quarterback job. We were 6–0 in the preseason, and that was when Landry announced at the start of the season, 'We'll have *two* starting quarterbacks.'

"I was going to start against Buffalo in the first game, but I broke a vessel in my leg against Kansas City in the last exhibition game, so he started Craig. [Calvin Hill scored four touchdowns, and Morton was 10–14 for 220 yards and two touchdowns in a 49–37 win.] Landry said we were going to alternate, so I started the next weekend in Philadelphia.

"On the third play of the game, I threw a pass that was intercepted by Bill Bradley. On the play this guy Mel Tom knocked me out from behind, a dirty shot. [The 260-pound Tom was fined $1,500 after delivering a forearm blow to the side of Staubach's head.] All of a sudden I was over at the sideline, and I was so woozy I didn't know what was going on.

"Craig came in, and we won 42–7, so Coach Landry said, 'I'm going to keep the momentum going,' so he started Craig against Washington, and we lost the Redskins game [20–16], so he started me against the Giants in the Cotton Bowl.

"We were winning 13–6 at halftime. I didn't have a great first half, but we were winning. And Landry took me out, which for me was the end of it. I went crazy.

"I said to him that I needed to be traded, to get out of here. Of course, Landry was a phenomenal coach and we had a great career together, but I don't think he totally understood me as far as someone who could handle pressure and problems. Maybe I wasn't having a good first half, but we were still winning. That was the worst thing he could have done to me. It was what I had said to him the year before, that when I started a game, I wanted to finish what I started. Taking a quarterback out in the middle of the game is the ultimate insult. [A 48-yard Morton to Bob Hayes touchdown pass beat the Giants 20–13. Duane Thomas and Calvin Hill played side-by-side for three plays when Hill was injured. After missing all of training camp, all the preseason games, and the first three regular season games, Thomas carried nine times for 60 yards!]

"We played the next week against the Saints. Craig started, and we were losing 14–0, and he put me in in the second half, and we had a chance to pull it out. We scored twice, came back to 17–14, but we fumbled a punt, and we didn't get the ball back. [The Cowboys lost 24–14.]

"Our record at that point was 3–2, and then we played the New England Patriots in Texas Stadium, the first game we ever played there, and I started that game and had a real good game. [In a 44–21 win, Staubach threw two touchdowns to Bob Hayes and ran for a third. Duane Thomas scored on a 56-yard run the fourth play of the game.]

"So now the next day Landry announces in the team meeting, 'We're going to have two quarterbacks alternate plays.'

"I was sitting there, and I looked over at Morton, and he was looking at me, and I couldn't believe it. This was the most ridiculous thing I ever heard of in my life. But Tom believed in his system. He believed if he had two robots, it would work. What he was really saying was that he felt it didn't matter what player he was inserting into his system, if you did what he wanted you to do, you'd win.

"He didn't understand the emotion and the other human aspects, I don't think, of the notion that a person can make a difference, especially over a long season, and it may be in critical games. You just can't send a guy in there and say, 'Hey, mechanically, if he can throw a football, if you do what I tell you to do you'll win . . .' 'Cause a quarterback is a leader, somebody who can bring emotion among other players.

"So the team was now thinking, 'Well, we have *two* quarterbacks.' It was a divided team, and that is never good.

"We alternated in the Chicago Bears game. Landry called the plays and sent them in with us, and as the game went on, we had phenomenal yardage, something like 480 yards, but we didn't score much. We had this really erratic game. We lost 23–19, so now we were 4 and 3, kind of like the year before, and he played Craig at the end of the Chicago game, left him in for the two-minute drill, and I was thinking, 'It's the same deal, the same decision.' I'm figuring, 'Craig's going to be the quarterback again this year.' To me that was going to be the end."

After the loss to the Bears, the Cowboys at 4–3 were two full games behind the Washington Redskins at 6–1, and the media once again was declaring the Cowboys dead. Moreover, Tom Landry was taking a beating in the papers and from his players for his insistence that under his Multiple Offense system it didn't matter who was playing quarterback, that even if he alternated quarterbacks, the team should win.

The next day during a national telecast of *Monday Night Football*, former quarterback Don Meredith, who had never publicly criticized Landry before, told his audience, "It's Landry's responsibility as the head coach to pick a quarterback. Now after all this time he still has no idea which one is the best. Then get another coach.

"I'm somewhat disappointed but I'm sure not nearly as disappointed as Morton and Staubach, not to mention the other 38 players who are involved in this wishy-washy decision."

Meredith, of course, knew of which he spoke.

LEE ROY JORDAN: "We weren't happy when Tom decided to alternate quarterbacks. The quarterbacks weren't happy and neither were the rest of their teammates.

"There were so many times what with Craig's bad shoulder, he didn't have control of the football. Sometimes the ball would go exactly where he wanted it to, and sometimes it would sail on him and sometimes it would go in the dirt. He didn't have the control he had in '69.

"Tom really admired the way Craig Morton read defenses. He read them a lot better than Roger. Roger had the tendency to look at one receiver and then pull the ball down and run. That wasn't the passing game that Tom really had in mind, so it was really a forced situation that pushed Tom into putting Roger in there.

"Roger wasn't a true passer. He was a true runner who learned to pass later in his life, and became a great one, but it wasn't his true calling to throw a football. To go back and fake a pass and run, that was his true instinct.

"The defensive players liked Roger, because we knew how much trouble a scrambling-type quarterback can cause you. It really puts a lot of pressure on the defensive linemen, wears them out and confuses the secondary because they don't know whether to stay with their receiver or come back up and try to stop the quarterback running game. They chase a guy as he sets up, and then they have to chase him 30 yards upfield. Do that five or six times, and those guys are weary, much more so than with a pocket quarterback like Craig.

"The big thing with the players, it really didn't matter to us *who* started, but let's pick one and stay with him. 'He's our guy. He's the one who's going to do it for us from here on.' Because alternating players makes it seem like you don't have confidence in anyone. It's like, 'We'll try this and maybe one of them will get lucky.' That's the way the team looked at it. So we just wanted to have a permanent guy in there, to use his talents whatever they are and we'll win with him and it'll work for us eventually."

MEL RENFRO: "Our preference was Roger. We knew that Craig was more experienced and Roger was an upstart, but we saw what Roger could do at certain times with his scrambling ability. We knew he had a lot to learn. We said to ourselves, 'Just make a decision and go with it.'

"We did not say these things publicly. We were not allowed to. There was one thing we found out about Coach Landry: Don't open your mouth, even if he asks you. You don't want it to come back and slap you in the face. Yeah, that happened a few times. He'd say, 'Air your grievances and there won't be anything said about it. We just want to know how you feel.' And so we did, and it wasn't long when those grievances started slapping us in the face. So we said, 'We'll know better next time. When they ask us to air our grievances, we'll say everything he wants to hear, not what we want to say.' "

Making matters worse, the next day Ralph "Rotten" Neely (he got his nickname from teammates because he was constantly complaining that things were rotten), the All-Pro offensive tackle, broke his leg. And on that day it was thought that George Andrie, the fine defensive end, had suffered a heart attack.

Neely's teammates told Tom Landry that he had been out riding horses, that his horse had been spooked by a rattlesnake, reared, and dumped Neely to the ground, breaking his leg. That was the cover story. What really happened was that the good old boys were out raising Cain, riding their motorcycles over rough terrain, and Neely took a mean tumble that put him out of action the rest of the season.

WALT GARRISON: "A group of the Cowboys started riding motorcycles. On Mondays after the game, we'd usually go out to Grapevine Lake and ride out in the dirt all day. Mike Ditka was with the Cowboys then and he bought a 125cc. Dave Edwards had a 125. Me and Lilly and Cliff Harris and Dan Reeves had one. And, of course, that meant Ralph had to have one, too.

"Rotten couldn't ride worth a damn. He kept falling off all day. But that didn't make any difference. His bike had to be bigger and better than everybody else's. So Ralph went out and bought a Husqvarna 400, an absolute man-eating monster. Comes with a chain and a whip.

"Anyway, we'd been out riding all day and we're packing up to go home, and off in the distance I could see Cliff coming in and his eyes are as big as silver dollars. And I thought, 'Oh, shit, what happened?'

"Cliff and Rotten had been riding together and Ralph says, 'Cliff, let's jump some hills.'

"And Cliff was thinking, 'Christ, Ralph, you can barely ride. And now you want to jump hills?' Plus, he knew Ralph had a herd of ponies under him like to scare the shit outta Cochise. But he figured, 'Ah, what the hell.'

"There was a grass field out where they were riding and at the end of it was a hill that went up at a nice pitch. Nothing too scary. So Cliff gunned his 125 and went right up the hill and waited for Ralph there.

"Ralph guns his monster and gets about halfway up and falls over. So he gets up cussing. 'Damn motorcycle ain't worth a shit. They don't make nothing worth a damn anymore.'

"Good ole Rotten.

"So Ralph goes back down and tries again, only this time he really cranks that puppy up full throttle. Here comes Ralph *eeeee,* thumb, *eeeeee,* thumb, *eeeeeeee,* about 60 or 70 mph and he climbs right up to the top . . . and keeps right on going. He shoots into the air about twenty feet.

"Ralph's legs are real long and instead of putting them on the footrest, he used to ride with them dangling along the ground. Well, he lands on his back and starts rolling down the hill with those big ol' legs going every whichaway. When he finally stops he looks back up at Cliff and says real calmly, 'Ah, Cliff, I think I hurt my foot. Look at it, would you?'

"And sure enough his leg was pointing up the hill and his foot was pointing down. He'd broken it in three places, dislocated his ankle, and tore a bunch of ligaments. Out for the season.

"They throw Rotten in the back of Ditka's truck with the muddy old bikes and every time they'd go over a bump Neely would scream. But nobody gave a damn about Neely's pain. All they kept saying to him all the way home was, 'Don't tell Landry we were riding motorcycles. Let's tell him we were riding horses. Ya, we were riding along and a snake bit Ralph's horse.'

"So they take him over to the hospital and that night there was a team party. When I got there, somebody comes running up to me and says, 'Did you hear what happened?'

"'Hell, I was with him when it happened.'

"'You were there when George Andrie had his heart attack?'

"'What? Andrie had a heart attack?'

"'Ya.'

"'Didn't you hear about Neely?' I asked.

"'No.'

"'He broke his leg.'

"'How'd he do it?'

"'He stepped off a curb and it snapped.'

"'No shit.'

"Turned out Andrie never did have a heart attack. It was just indigestion. But it sure helped take Landry's mind off Neely's foot and how he did it. The funny thing was there was seven of us Cowboys all happy as hell that George was dying of heart failure. Just as long as Landry didn't find out we'd been riding motorcycles.

"Who says you don't get close with your teammates?"

That evening Roger Staubach was feeling discouraged and lost. He was moping around when assistant coach Ray Renfro took him aside. "Please don't tell anyone I'm telling you this," Renfro told him in a whisper, "because it could cost me my job. You're not supposed to know this, but you will be starting this week."

44

Super

When Tom Landry informed Roger Staubach that he would be the team's starting quarterback for the rest of the '71 season, Staubach told him, "I won't let you down, Coach." And he didn't. Though Staubach had started only eleven games prior to Landry giving him the job, the Cowboys didn't lose another game the rest of the season as the Navy Heisman winner completed 60 percent of his passes (126 of 211, 15 TDs) and ran 41 times for 343 yards, an average of 8 yards a carry. Staubach directed a punishing ground attack and augmented it by hitting the fleet Bob Hayes for 8 touchdowns, as Bullet Bob led the league with an average of 24 yards a catch.

All the while, Tom Landry was in a constant battle with Staubach, who insisted that he be allowed to call his own plays. Despite the perception that Landry and Staubach were close friends in that they both were deeply religious, nothing could have been further from the truth. Staubach and Landry argued incessantly, and over the years Landry would be forced to accept the reality that Roger at times would countermand his play calling and go off on his own.

MARGENE ADKINS: "At meetings, Staubach and Tom had a few problems. Staubach wanted to do this, and Tom wanted to do that. In games, Tom

Landry would want to call a play and Staubach wouldn't like it. Staubach wanted to call his own plays. So Tom'd send a play in, and Staubach might not have liked the play, and what Staubach would do, he would audible that play, but it always worked, and so by it working Tom couldn't say anything. It wasn't to the point where they got angry, where Staubach wanted to run the team and Tom Landry wanted to. It was just a little problem there."

The combination of Tom Landry and Roger Staubach proved to be one of the most successful in league history. Tom Landry would design the game plan, and he would call the plays, but Tom also came to see that if the team was in trouble late in the game, Roger Staubach would figure out a way to pull them out of it. As quarterback of the team through the 1970s, Roger Staubach pulled their toes out of the fire twenty-three times. Landry never stopped begging Staubach not to run with the ball, and Staubach never heeded his advice. But over the years the two developed a deep respect and understanding of each other, as Roger Staubach would take the Cowboys to three Super Bowls and come within an eyelash of getting there several other times.

ROGER STAUBACH: "The beginning of our momentum in '71 came in my first game against the St. Louis Cardinals. We beat them 16 to 13. It was a great game. And St. Louis was a good team at that time.

"We were still emotionally drained as a team. We weren't quite ready. We gained a lot of yardage, there were a lot of close calls, and we should have scored more points. But I personally had a good game running and throwing. Mike Ditka caught a touchdown pass.

"We really started to take off, both offensively *and* defensively. Calvin Hill, Duane, and Walt Garrison were playing very well. Lance Alworth and I started to get on the same page. Bob Hayes got going, and our tight ends, Billy Truax and Ditka, were playing well, so we got on a roll and we started beating teams pretty good.

"We beat the Eagles while Washington was losing to the Bears, putting us only a half game behind them, and then in Washington we shut out the Redskins, 13–0, in a tough game, to take the lead. I called a pass play to Alworth, but when I saw the left side was open, I ran myself the 29 yards to score. The press asked Tom if he had designed that play for me. I guess they didn't know Landry.

"We beat the Rams Thanksgiving Day 28–21. That was a tough one, too. Duane ran for the winning touchdown. In that game I threw a 51-yarder to Bob Hayes and a shorter one to Lance Alworth.

"After we beat the Jets, 52–10, in a game in which Duane scored a touchdown and Calvin three, we went to Yankee Stadium to play the Giants. Duane and Calvin were great again, and Bob Hayes had his best day. He caught two long touchdowns. One of my big thrills was throwing an 85-yard touchdown pass to Bob over Spider Lockhart. I was a big baseball fan, so throwing a long touchdown pass in Yankee Stadium was *great*. But Bob could do that.

"Hayes was phenomenal. Today I don't think anybody could beat him. To get the ball to Bob, you had to get it up quicker, get it in the air so he could run under it, and he made a lot of great catches like that, where he was behind the defensive back. Bob was fantastic. He could break games. Bob had had big years with Meredith, phenomenal years. He had a couple of great years with me, and he could have had a few more if he would have disciplined himself personally. But Bob was having personal problems. He was dependent, an alcoholic. In a dependency situation, you become undisciplined. It affects a lot of players who don't even realize it. They get themselves involved in the pills and the alcohol. There was no physical reason Bob couldn't have continued to play, but it was only a year after that when the Cowboys sent him to San Francisco. I wish I could have played more years with him.

"We won the final game of the season against the St. Louis Cards to win the division title. Duane Thomas scored four touchdowns. Duane was so great.

"Going up to Minnesota for the first playoff game, we had this momentum going. We just played a good game. It was a key game, because the Vikings were pretty unbeatable in Minnesota, and I was fortunate that cold weather just didn't bother me a whole lot. The good thing about it, the weather really wasn't a factor in the game. Fortunately, it wasn't windy.

"We won the game, 20–12. After Duane scored a touchdown, I hit Bob with a pass for a nine-yard touchdown. On defense, we played a great game. We intercepted four passes and recovered a fumble.

"The NFC championship against the San Francisco 49ers was a tough game. They had John Brodie at quarterback, and they were a very good team. Our offense moved the ball a lot, but we didn't do much. We had one big series. on a long scramble where I really could have been trapped in our own end zone, I threw the ball out to Dan Reeves, who limped down the right sideline and set up Duane's touchdown to put the game away, 14–3.

"It was just a very solid game. Our defense was outstanding. The big play in that game was George Andrie intercepting a screen pass near the goal line."

LEE ROY JORDAN: "John Brodie was the quarterback, and the running backs were Ken Willard and Vic Washington, damn good running backs, outstanding runners. They had an outstanding receiving corps, Gene Washington and tight end Ted Kwalick, an outstanding football player, a great receiver and great blocker. Dave [Edwards] had to handle him, and all the linebackers worked on him, along with Cornell Green, our strong safety.

"Our preparation for the game was so good. Once we became confident that we could control certain things, we just knew it wasn't going to be any problem. Like we decided, 'We're going to stop the running game,' and in that game we stopped them. And after stopping the running game, we then had to concentrate on the receivers, and stopped Gene Washington, their number one receiver. And we were able to do that do. We were able to dominate them. Bob Lilly spent the whole game on top of Brodie.

"I intercepted one of Brodie's passes early in the game, near the sideline. A few years ago I ran into John in a senior golf tournament here, and he said, 'Man, what in the hell were you doing way over there on the sideline? There is no way you're going to go over there and catch a ball.'

"I said, 'I don't know why I was there. There must have been some reason in the backfield that made me feel I knew where the ball was going.' But there's where I ended up, and I made the interception, and it set us up with good field position.

"That was special. So was George Andrie's tipping a ball on a screen pass to Ken Willard, catching it and lumbering down to the one. Calvin Hill scored to give us our first points."

MEL RENFRO: "As we celebrated after the game, you had to give credit to the defense. Give credit where credit was due. We held them to three points. George Andrie intercepted a pass to give us a touchdown. We could have beaten anyone with that defense. The Doomsday defense. And it wasn't just that year or the year before, it was the same guys playing together, Bob Lilly, George Andrie, Cornell, Lee Roy, Dave Edwards, I. We were all there, Doomsday, playing together."

In the clubhouse after the game, Duane Thomas angered the San Francisco reporters when he told them, "Man, don't ever try to interview me after a game."

They trooped over to ask Landry what his running back's problem was.

"I don't know if I can enlighten you." He added, "Thomas acts like he is not part of the team, but he *is* part of the team. We've never asked him why he doesn't talk to reporters or sign autographs. The team wants to understand him."

At the time he was traded to New England, he had boasted that the Cowboys would never win the Super Bowl without him. Said AP sportswriter Denne Freeman, "In a mysterious way, maybe he was right."

The team traveled to New Orleans to play the Miami Dolphins in Super Bowl VI. Miami featured quarterback Bob Griese and their outstanding running backs Larry Csonka and Jim Kiick, along with the sensational pass catcher Paul Warfield. Don Shula was the coach.

Ten days before the big game, Duane Thomas set tongues wagging when he was absent for a Thursday practice amid rumors he would skip the Super Bowl if his salary demands were not met. Tex Schramm insisted that his contract would be renegotiated *after* the game.

Thomas refused to tell Landry or anyone else why he had skipped practice except to say, "Personal reasons." Landry told reporters, "He just would not talk about it at all. Football really isn't important to his life. He told me, 'My job is football and I will do my job.' He just doesn't think anything else enters into it."

Concluded Landry, "He didn't specifically say, 'I will play in the Super Bowl,' but you have to assume he will, because he's here."

In the Cowboy locker room before the game, the players didn't feel any of the doubts that they had had against Baltimore in Super Bowl V the year before.

CHUCK HOWLEY: "It was a totally different feeling going back the second time. The trauma all year long was that we should have won the year before. We didn't win, and we felt we *had* to go back. The way we looked at it, we had X amount of games to go through in order to repeat and do what we didn't do the year before. That's the way the Cowboys looked at it. We did what we had to do and went back to the Super Bowl.

"It was an inner feeling. How come we lost the first one and won the second one? What did you feel going into the first one that was different going into the second? I can't put a finger on it. We all went to the first one saying, 'We're going to win it.' But you had a little guy in the back of your head that's saying, 'Do you *really* think you can?' That's the one negative you don't want. The second time around, there was no little guy in the back of my head. The second one we didn't worry about losing. There was *no* doubt in my mind. I don't think there was doubt in anyone's mind who was going to win. We were going to show up, play, and the game was going to be history; we were going to win. Nobody had doubt. Everything was so positive going into the game.

"The week we spent down there, you just felt it within you. Nobody questioned the fact that we were going to win. It wasn't cockiness, it was a feel. I just knew there was no doubt we were going to win that ballgame.

"We had control all the way. It wasn't lopsided, but we had total control. We knew it from the first kickoff, right through to the end. And we finally achieved what everybody in the NFL tries to achieve, and that's to have that Super Bowl ring. It's what we all strive for."

MEL RENFRO: "Against the Dolphins, Tom used the KISS theory: Keep It Simple, Stupid. He let us play football. We knew we had to eliminate Warfield. We had good talent at linebacker, so we could control their tight end, which allowed us to double their wide receivers. And Bob Lilly and the rest of them were all over Bob Griese all day. That was the key to defense.

"There were no outstanding plays to speak of. Not really. When you play defense like we played defense, everybody contributes, and everybody plays well. You have to with the coordination of the defense. Everybody has to do his job. So we were a team that day. We totally dominated, a lot of three downs and out. We won 24–3, and it should have been 31–3 but Calvin fumbled on the three-yard line at the end of the game.

"The offense played so well. Between Walt Garrison and Calvin Hill and Duane Thomas, it just doesn't get any better than that. You've got Lance Alworth and Mike Ditka catching key passes. It was a total team effort. And Roger was the quarterback. He was the man. Roger scrambling and picking up the key plays. Roger was such a tremendous individual. He has never changed. My kids grew up with his kids and to this day that's the first thing he'll ask, 'How are the kids?' And they are all grown. Roger is a great person."

LEE ROY JORDAN: "Tom worked hard studying the film, analyzing the routes Miami took, and they came up with a defense they thought we could play on both sides of the field. It was designed to shut out Paul Warfield on one side and their tight end, Marv Fleming, who used to play with Green Bay, on the other. When they set up, we would take away their favored routes from both sides and have an opportunity to intercept the ball.

"We worked on it, worked on it, and by game time we absolutely went in with the confidence that, 'Hey, this is *the* thing,' and this time Coach Landry made no changes. He was confident from the beginning, all the way through the preparation, and in the game we executed the defenses.

"We also got Larry Csonka to fumble a couple times, something he had not done in the previous year or two. And Bob Lilly, George Andrie, Pat Toomay, and the guys put a lot of pressure on Bob Griese. I remember on one play they trapped him 30 yards downfield. He ran one way, and we had three guys, Bob, Larry Cole, and another guy, chasing him, and he turned one way and couldn't get away, and so he turned back the other way, and he ended up 30 yards downfield.

"When we won that Super Bowl it was certainly a great thrill, but for us, it was more a lifting of a heavy burden that we had been bearing since 1966, when we lost that first Green Bay game. So many of us after the game were so happy to have that lifted off of us, the victory itself wasn't that big. It was almost anticlimactic—it was more important to get the bridesmaid-but-never-a-bride tag removed from us.

"I talked to a lot of guys after the game. Instead of being on an emotional high, everyone was just, 'Hey, man, I'm so relieved, so happy, so delighted. We're Super Bowl champions, and nobody is going to be able to take that away.' Because until that final whistle, we were still in a position to have those negative articles written about us—by this time the job had been passed on by Gary Cartwright to other guys who liked to write plenty of negative stuff about us."

CORNELL GREEN: "Our whole game was to stop the running game and Paul Warfield. If they were going to beat us, they were going to beat us with Twilley and Fleming. They weren't going to beat us with Warfield, Kiick, or Csonka, or Mercury Morris. We geared up for Mercury, and Mercury Morris did not play in that whole game, and that was a blessing. 'Cause Chuck Howley could catch Kiick. If Mercury got in the game, that was going to be tough.

"I have no idea why Shula didn't play Mercury more. I don't know what Mercury did to piss Shula off. I wish I did.

"When it was over, I just said, 'Fine, we won one.' And I ran off the field. A lot of people started carrying Landry around. I didn't have time for that. I was getting out of there and getting to the locker room. So I didn't hang around to celebrate.

"It was, 'We finally did it.' That's it."

45

Duane Thomas's Legacy

he star in the victory over the Miami Dolphins in Super Bowl VI clearly was Duane Thomas, who after pissing everybody off on the planet including his coach, his teammates, the press, and the fans, defied every convention when he thumbed his nose at the sports world's displeasure by playing spectacularly. The silent Thomas, whom contemptuous sportswriters had dubbed the Sphinx, carried the ball 19 times in Super Bowl VI for 95 yards against a tough Dolphin defensive unit led by linebacker Nick Buoniconti.

But Thomas was not given the MVP award (or the Corvette that went with it) because the editors of *Sport* magazine needed to find somebody who they knew would smile and say "Thank you" in the locker room on national TV after the game. In looking for a more suitable recipient, *Sport* editor Larry Klein saw that Roger Staubach had played his usual fine game, completing 12 of 19 passes for 119 yards and two touchdowns, and he made the presentation to a sheepish Staubach, who knew that Duane should have been the one to get the prize.

ROGER STAUBACH: "Duane would have gotten the MVP if he would have talked to the press. Down in New Orleans, Duane hadn't talked to anybody. That's the only reason he didn't get the award. They were looking for someone else to give it to, and they gave it to me."

Thomas had led the Dallas Cowboys to not one, but *two* Super Bowl appearances, and despite his achievements, the snubs and negative comments hadn't stopped. On the field, Thomas was King; off the field, he was an object of scorn and derision. And what made the situation especially unbearable to the running back was the fact that it was far too late to do anything about it. After the victory over the Dolphins, Duane Thomas skipped the team celebration. He went back to his hotel room, lay on the bed, and stared at the ceiling.

Said Thomas years later, "I was upset that the season was over. I didn't ever want to stop playing. I didn't want to come off the field and deal with the outside world."

Two weeks after the Super Bowl, Duane Thomas and his younger brother Bertrand were driving from Dallas to the West Coast, where, Tex Schramm believed, Thomas had been involved with drug use the winter before. Schramm had asked Thomas not to return to Los Angeles, but Thomas had refused. Though Schramm has denied any involvement in the incident, what followed makes sense only in the context of an attempt by Schramm to keep Thomas from reaching L.A.

Duane and his brother had not gotten very far before they were arrested in Greenville, Texas, for possessing one marijuana joint. The two arresting policemen said they'd stopped the brothers because a white Pontiac like the one they were driving had been reported stolen.

The police report said one of the policemen smelled the odor of marijuana and found two matchboxes of marijuana.

According to Thomas, the police searched the car without a warrant, then planted the drugs he was accused of possessing. According to Thomas, the judge told him if he didn't hire a particular defense attorney, he would "sentence him to life."

"The whole thing was scripted," said Thomas. "It had to have been set up."

Pete Gent, who lived in Dallas after his retirement and remained friends with both executives and players on the Cowboys, felt that the Cowboys had "been behind the whole episode."

PETE GENT: "Ask yourself, 'What was Duane doing in Greenville, Texas, with dope on him?' Duane wasn't stupid. Greenville literally had a sign over the Main Street that said, 'The Blackest Land, the Whitest People.' So what was he doing up there with marijuana on him? I'm not saying he didn't do drugs. I'm saying, 'What would he be doing *there* doing drugs?'

"It had to be a setup, because he didn't do any time for it. You have to remember at that time in Texas, the average time served—not sentenced, but served—for first-time possession was nine years in Huntsville. At approximately that same time, they sentenced a guy in Houston to thirty years for the possession of one joint. Duane got probation. So obviously, this wasn't an accidental deal when they got him. Someone wanted to give him a warning shot across his bow."

DUANE THOMAS: "Dan Reeves said, 'Everything turned bad when Duane went to California. He met some wrong people out there.' I told Dan, 'I met some wrong people in Dallas, and would you believe, you're one of them.' "

The bust cost Thomas—and the Cowboys—dearly. Thomas pleaded guilty to drug possession and was given five years probation, and it took him sixteen years to clear his name. All that time Thomas was denied work in many fields because of his conviction. He received a pardon from Governor Mark White, who waited almost four years to sign it, for fear his opponent would crucify him in the next election. After White lost that election, he finally signed it in 1988.

If Thomas was feeling unloved and persecuted by the Cowboys and the state of Texas *before* his arrest, after the incident in Greenville he became even more removed and hostile. When training camp began in the summer of '72, his teammates saw that his alienation was worsening. His behavior would continue to be more erratic than in the past.

ROGER STAUBACH: "In '72 we went to training camp a few days early, and Duane had this guy on the plane who took his seat. We got out to Thousand Oaks, got off the plane, and they met us there. 'Where's Duane?' The guy sitting in his place said he was going to try out for the Cowboys. 'Cause Duane told him to.

"So we had a little passing drill, and this guy was out there. It was the weirdest thing I ever saw. He was out there running routes in sweatpants and combat boots. Around Duane, everyone walked on eggshells, so here we were at camp and everyone was putting up with this because Duane had sent this guy out here! We were throwing the ball, and this guy was catching passes. It didn't look like he could play, but he wasn't ridiculous either. And then Ray Renfro, our receiver coach, came over. He said, 'Who is that?' I said, 'That's Duane's friend.' 'Well, where's Duane?' I said, 'We don't know where Duane is.'

"Then Gil Brandt came out there, and he wanted to know the same thing, and we told him we didn't know where Duane was, and Gil said, 'Get that guy the hell off the field,' and we never saw him again.

"And that was the beginning, because Duane came to camp and was totally reclusive. You had no idea why. I was totally naive about drugs, so I didn't see it. I didn't know. I was even involved in a youth home in Dallas. We were putting these kids in this facility, and 90 percent of them had drug problems, and we didn't know.

"Duane looked the same. You would not believe this guy could have been using drugs the way he looked physically, but *something* was affecting his mind, whether it was drugs or the bitterness he had about his contract. Whatever it was, he could not deal with anything, period.

"In practice one time I threw him a pass, threw it a little behind him, and he barked, 'Throw the ball to me.' He'd make comments like that, but he'd be doing everything he was supposed to be doing, working hard. I was thinking, 'God, I have to make sure to throw the ball just perfect to Duane.' And another time Dan Reeves, who was coaching the backs, asked Duane to switch from halfback to fullback. He knew both positions. Duane was unbelievable at fullback, but he didn't like to play it, and this day Duane said, 'No, I'm going to stay at tailback.'

"I said, 'Hey Duane, why don't you do what Dan says?'

"He said, 'You shut up. You don't interfere.' I got along with Duane, but that did tick me off when he said that. So it was definitely going downhill. You could feel it. You wanted to stop it, but it was snowballing, and it probably was drugs, because he was someone you could not reason with anymore.

"It got to a point where one day he was not out at practice. He was up in his room, and I went up to see him. He said he was a vegetarian, and he wasn't eating. Ray Renfro took some food up there, and I went up there and knocked on his door, and I brought him some food, too.

"I said, 'Do you want to talk?' He said, 'Yeah.' So I started to talk to him. He wouldn't talk back. I said, 'You're not answering.' He said, 'I like to listen to you.' So for forty-five minutes I talked about life and the team and how much we needed him. And he didn't say a word. He just listened to me.

"Because we were the Super Bowl champs, we played in the college All-Star game. Duane didn't run out onto the field with the team. He was leaning up against the goalposts, just leaning. And then when we came back from the game and resumed practicing at Thousand Oaks, he actually refused to go out to practice. The next thing I knew, the Cowboys shipped him off to San Diego."

The Cowboys traded him to San Diego for two young talents, wide receiver Billy Parks and running back Mike Montgomery.

ROGER STAUBACH: "When we played in San Diego, during the National Anthem Duane wouldn't stand. He sat on the Chargers bench, which is a stupid thing to do with all the navy people out there. Then in the pregame warm-up, he just stood there with his hands on his knees. I said to [Charger quarterback] John Hadl, 'Johnny, are you having a little trouble with Duane?' He said, 'Oh, my God. I don't know what to do.' I said, 'You're just like all of us. We were on eggshells with the guy.' So they just let him do what he wanted to. There he was, in the middle of their warm-ups down by the end zone, standing with his hands on his knees."

Duane Thomas never got into a game with San Diego. In 1973 and 1974 he played for Washington's George Allen, the coach of lost causes, backing up Larry Brown. In 1975 he went to the World Football League, playing in Hawaii. In '76, he called Landry and asked for another chance. Landry agreed, but by then he had lost his speed and missed much of training camp with a hamstring pull. In '76 Thomas's anger was gone, and he worked hard and was as affable as anyone. His teammates rooted hard for him to make it, but the great talent had been spent. At the end of preseason he was cut.

PETE GENT: "I once interviewed Duane when he was with the Redskins, and he was a psychopath. He couldn't even talk. We sat in the hotel room and didn't even turn the lights on, and he said, 'I'm just trying to get through today.'

"Four or five years later, Duane called me several times, wanting to talk *business*. He said he thought he had been wrong and Landry and Schramm had been right, that he had been a bad boy. And it was heartbreaking to see that. When he called me, I didn't know what to say to him. My feeling was, 'I've been running on thin ice since 1969. The two of us don't need to get side by side and both go under.' "

Duane Thomas's legacy is a reflection of how people felt about him when he played with the Cowboys. The executives, Tom Landry, and

Tex Schramm, and many of his white teammates saw him as trouble. There was no acknowledgment that he had brought the Cowboys two Super Bowl appearances, that he was a key player who had made them a potful of money. Their bottom line, rather, was that Duane had been disruptive, had brought chaos to their order, and so they were glad he was gone.

Most of his black teammates saw Duane Thomas as a hero, a man who had refused to accept shabby treatment and who had fought back and lost. To them, Duane Thomas was a martyr to their cause, much like the Reverend Martin Luther King, Jr.

In 1981 Cowboy defensive back Everson Walls told Thomas, "You have paved the way for a lot of us."

Like Don Meredith, Duane Thomas was not an easy man to locate. I had heard he was living in Dallas, or California, or Hawaii, and even his brother Franklin, the contact for NFL Films, said he didn't have Duane's phone number. But in the summer of 1996 Duane called Pete Gent, who happened to mention the call, and Gent was gracious enough to give me the number of Thomas's Del Mar, California, home. In a lengthy conversation, Duane Thomas proved the thoughtful, idealistic soul the men close to him had said he was. Still stung by all that had happened to him many years earlier, Thomas says he continues to work toward forgiveness and understanding.

DUANE THOMAS: "I was ready to go to camp in '73, and Dallas told me that I was traded to San Diego. But Dallas knew I wasn't going to talk to the media, so they said what they wanted to say, said things about me that I only learned about later. They could say anything they wanted, because they knew I wouldn't say anything. They talked about my not being willing to practice, of my showing up late. The whole time I was there, I was late for one practice, and that happened because of the time change. No one was more punctual than I was. No one loved the game more than I did. But looking back, I could not have done a single thing differently. And I don't regret anything I've done. I didn't commit murder. I led them to two Super Bowls. But in the end it was a matter of ego. It's like a situation with my son and my brother. My brother wanted to hire my oldest boy, but he didn't want to pay him what the job demanded. My brother wasn't even willing to say to him something like, 'I'll give you the bare minimum, but if you show you can do the work and your effort is strong, then I'll pay you accordingly.'

"My son got all upset about it. I told him it was all about ego, that you have to realize who you're dealing with, whether it's your brother, your mama, or daddy—it doesn't matter who it is, you have to learn to separate yourself from these attachments that will prevent you from growing psychologically, emotionally, spiritually, and in some cases educationally. My son is a young boy, and I explained this to him, and he realized he couldn't work for someone like that. So you pull away from it. I realized I couldn't work for the Dallas Cowboys. I also realized they knew I had the ability to expose them. I use the analogy of Dallas being the Garden of Eden. I was the one who had eaten from the Forbidden Fruit, which means I had consciousness, and because I had this consciousness, then I was ostracized from the Garden. I was stripped of my prestige and thrown out of the Garden forever. Forever.

"I still talk to young players, and I share with them some of my experiences and let them know. I tell them, 'You have to be fully prepared.' They say, 'How do you know when you're fully prepared?' I tell them, 'The whole thing is, you have to have a supporting team, meaning you have to have people who care about you whether you play football or not. You need people who just want to see you do well and be well so you can be a productive citizen in society and make a contribution and to make the world a better place.' I always thought that sports was about building character. Because sports is only a very small segment of one's life.

"But these are things the general public doesn't measure. All they measure by is what the media is telling them. Dallas controlled the media at that time. At that time the media was like the military. Nothing was sent out without Dallas okaying it. Do you think the *Morning News* was going to write what I said or write what Dallas said? Who was paying them more money? They are always going to edit. That's why I said I wasn't going to say anything more, because the point was, every time I said something, it was interpreted the way they wanted it to be.

"And when I decided not to talk anymore, they turned on me. Dallas knew that would happen. That was the whole thing, to put me in a no-win situation, and to demonstrate to others who were even thinking about it: If you do like Duane, this is what we'll do to you.

"I often wonder whether I would have risen to the heights I reached had Dallas not been the way they were. What I do know about me is that I am self-motivated. And I also know I could have done more. It's not wishful thinking or regret in any sense of the word, it's just an attitude that I have as to who I am.

"The same way today I am always asking myself, 'How can I do more for my family? And what can I do to get my kids to carry the same banner?' Just because the requirement is X to get an A grade, I tell my kids to go beyond. Because an A at one school might be a C somewhere else, and you always want to do your very best.

"I wonder whether I have covered all the ground I should with my kids. I tell them, 'It is about the truth. To make yourself a better person and more independent, there are things that have to be done. And it's all about being an active member. Because people will honor you only after you have done for so many others. And then you will understand the statement that it is better to give than to receive.' So to me it was about giving, though being in Dallas it seemed the more I gave, the less people respected me and appreciated it. Because I was doing everything I could, saying, 'This is what it takes to be a champion.' And that took its toll on me in terms of my sitting back and saying, 'Was it all worth it?'

"We had the opportunity to do things and demonstrate a unity that we should have displayed during those years in the '70s. I could see that what was keeping us from the Super Bowl were forces just coming into play, integration and the Vietnam War, which caused a lot of controversy. And that integration happened first in Pittsburgh, with both the Pirates and the Steelers. It was even the Pirates' theme song, 'We Are Family.'

"And I was so disappointed we never became a family like that. Steve Kiner and I were the pioneers. Lee Roy Jordan asked Kiner, 'What are you doing rooming with a nigger?' And Kiner was all upset about it. He came to me, and I said, 'What nigger are you rooming with?' I said, 'They won't come and tell me that.'

"And interestingly enough, I have a lot of respect for Lee Roy Jordan, even after all that went down. Several years after I left the Cowboys, the Cowboys started doing to him some of the things they had done to me, and he called me up and said, 'Duane, I want to have lunch with you.' I thought, 'Hot damn, Lee Roy Jordan wants to have lunch with me? Is this a Klan meeting or what?' I felt like telling him, 'I don't like barbecue.' So I met with him, and he said, 'Duane, when you were on the team I was against everything you said and did.' I said, 'Yeah.' He said, 'But now that some things have happened to me, I'm beginning to see what you were talking about.'

"I mean I was just stunned. But I was happy. Because at the point I was going through in my ordeal, I kept saying to myself, 'People will come around eventually.' It's like what Martin Luther King Jr. said,

'We're not going to make it to the mountain in droves. It will be one by one.'

"We could have easily won three or four more Super Bowls. In '73 Washington represented the NFC. If I had played, we would have been there. And believe me, had I played, Miami would not have been undefeated.

"I'm not angry. I realize I have to go on. What happened, happened, and I know it won't happen again. But if that's the price to pay for the betterment of my kids, it's a small price. I know players who have paid an even greater price, and that was the spirit I was moving in, getting strength from the guys who had played before me: Curtis McClinton, Abner Haynes, Lenny Moore, Jim Brown, and Bobby Mitchell, all who suffered from being pioneers.

"Every now and then I think about what actually happened in terms of how they took advantage of me. Since that point, I've been working on forgiveness. Because it was not only where the Cowboys were but where Dallas, the town itself, was, when you look at it in terms of where football has evolved in terms of [racial] consciousness.

"I'm pleased that guys today are able to be themselves, especially black players who are being accepted more in terms of their individual personalities, as opposed to saying that African-Americans should act just one particular way, which makes it easier for the white counterpart to cope. To me, the Cowboys were the leaders in epitomizing that one role model. Dallas has had some unbelievable talent to come through there, but under the Landry regime there was just no way for a black player to reach the same heights as a Roger Staubach. It was not designed for it.

"After that situation in Dallas, everything was ruined for me. I couldn't get a black taxi in South Dallas. I went out and started meeting people who I knew in Dallas. I knew initially when I'd meet people, they'd be in awe, and once I sat down and started talking to them one-on-one, they'd be saying, 'Duane doesn't match the image of him that was portrayed in the media.'

"After a while I became involved with the Northwest Mutual Life Insurance Company. The company had great self-development programs, which I pursued, and I also pursued courses and subject matter that interested me when I was in college but couldn't [get into] because of sports.

"I'm done with insurance, and today I work in the field of import-export, which enables me to travel all over Europe and to Africa. I met

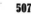

my wife in Los Angeles in '87, and she has been one of the best things to ever happen to me.

"When I left I told them they couldn't win the Super Bowl without me, and that infuriated them. Who does he think he is? But I was right, and they didn't like that either. They didn't like a lot of what I had to say."

46

Craig Fills In

Before the 1972 season, Craig Morton asked Tom Landry for the opportunity to win back his starting quarterback job. But Landry had made up his mind that Roger Staubach would be his man, and rumors floated about that Morton would either ask for a trade or retire. He did neither, waiting patiently for his chance. During the winter Morton had disavowed his fast-track life and joined the oxymoronic Lovers Lane Episcopal Church in Dallas. Observers wondered how long Morton, even having been born again, would be willing to sit on the bench.

The question became moot when in the third exhibition game against the Los Angeles Rams, Staubach suffered the worst injury of his career, a badly separated shoulder delivered by middle linebacker Marlin Mc-Keever.

ROGER STAUBACH: "I separated my shoulder in an exhibition game against the Rams, and that whole season was screwed up.

"The injury was my fault. I was running down near the goal line, and typical, I tried to get a few yards more. I turned to cut back inside just as McKeever was coming at me, and I hit him full force with my right shoulder. Back then I had these little quarterback shoulder pads, and my shoulder was separated severely. I knew I was in bad shape.

"As I lay on the ground I was thinking, 'I wish I could get up for one more play and drop back in the pocket and get hurt in the pocket.' Because I knew everybody was going to criticize me for getting hurt running. Which happened. And that was really the only injury I ever had running. After that, I ran just as much. So I wasn't really injury-prone, except for the concussions which later became a problem. But that separated shoulder was the only serious injury I had with the Cowboys.

"McKeever didn't do anything wrong. In fact, he sent me flowers in the hospital. He was getting sentimental in his old age."

The '72 season had yet to begin, and the Cowboys were facing a long campaign without their two top stars, Duane Thomas for good and Roger Staubach for eight to twelve weeks. It was during this season that the incredible Cowboy depth made itself felt, as the team, haunted by the ghost of Duane Thomas, got to within one game of their third straight Super Bowl.

Craig Morton, who had been a good soldier in '71 as he sat on the bench behind Staubach, got the job back. Said Landry, "Craig Morton is a great quarterback. That's what I tried to tell everybody last year even after he lost his job to Roger. Now that he has the chance to prove what I've been saying, I don't think there's any question how he'll do."

Calvin Hill, who had spent two years of frustration nursing injuries and playing behind Thomas, returned as a starter and became the first Cowboy to gain over 1,000 yards.

ROGER STAUBACH: "Craig took over and played very well. Craig was a heck of a quarterback. And Calvin was a heck of a player, too. Calvin had some injuries, but boy, he was a good runner, even though Calvin really took a backseat to Duane for a couple of years. Calvin played very well when he played."

Other new players provided excellent talent and also a diversity in personalities. With President Richard Nixon still in office and the youth culture still squarely against him, the arguments between the liberal players and the conservatives became heated. In June of 1972 E. Howard Hunt, Gordon Liddy, and three others were arrested for breaking into the Watergate Hotel, and as the scandal widened, players like talented receiver Billy Parks and Calvin Hill, who were fiercely antiwar, spoke out often and loudly against the Nixon regime. Jean Fugett, a twenty-year-old receiver drafted out of little Amherst College, also spoke out against the war, racism, and Richard Nixon. All were sorely disappointed when Nixon defeated Democratic candidate Senator George McGovern in a landslide. Roger Staubach had been to Vietnam, and he continued to stoutly defend America's right to be there, but what surprised some teammates was his siding with the blacks on the racial issue. His black teammates saw that Staubach wasn't on the sidelines when it came to civil rights. Through the years he actually spoke up and supported them, earning him the eternal gratitude of many of his teammates.

ROGER STAUBACH: "I had a pretty good foundation with my parents. When I was young, we lived in a little town called Silverton, Ohio, right outside Cincinnati, and a lot of black families were starting to move in, and there was a big to do, the old myth, 'Our property values are going to go down,' all the old baloney, and my mother just went ballistic and was very, very upset. She said, 'How can we talk that way as people who are supposedly Christian?' And so I saw the hypocrisy in the North, too, people who said they weren't racists, but really were. It was, 'As long as you stay in your place, we can deal with you.' In the South you're brought up with some myths. I can remember when I was with the navy stationed in Athens, Georgia, for six months, at supply school before I went to Vietnam. I would be at parties where people would talk about 'The reason the blacks aren't as smart as the whites is that their brain is smaller.' I said, 'That is just ridiculous.' And everyone in that apartment complex heard me. It was these myths. The idea the black athlete was lazy, wasn't good enough. That's a bunch of crap. But people are taught that, and it becomes a sickness, and you have to rid yourself of it by experimenting, by getting to really know these people, know what they went through.

"In fact, in the '60s when black players came to Dallas, they couldn't live in certain hotels, could only live in the black section of town, could only eat in certain restaurants. That's a self-esteem issue. I used to ask myself, 'What does that do to your self-esteem to have to say I'm not good enough to go into a restaurant?' It's something that really bothered me. Mel Renfro did a lot to give blacks greater access to housing and got a lot of flack for that, and I kind of got upset about it. I said, 'Mel's right. The city's wrong.' He tried to lease an apartment, and then when they saw him, they wouldn't. So I knew from the South there's a different kind of racism. 'My best friend is black, sure, as long as he doesn't live in my neighborhood and doesn't marry my sister.' The other players knew I was a crusader on this issue.

"I would be in a room with Cornell Green and Mel Renfro, and we'd be talking, and they were fantastic to be able to keep the bitterness down. They were competitors, and they were treated poorly. Even today, we have a form of racism that is just as serious as in the past, because people's expectations are greater than they've been before, and deservingly so. Back in those days it was more prevalent and more obvious.

"It was over Vietnam that I had most of the arguments. We had a few fellas who were against Vietnam. Billy Parks was really antiwar. Parks loved to get into political arguments, loved to bait me. He and I would be in the locker room, and we'd have knock-down dragouts, but they were healthy. We got along very well.

"I remember in '72 Mel Laird, the secretary of defense, came to a game. The Cowboys were honoring him, and Billy almost decided not to play. We were in the tunnel going out to the field, and he just went ballistic. He said, 'I can't believe this. I'm not going to . . .' He said he would not play. And he was serious. He was really rabid. Billy beat to his own drummer. But he did play."

One of the players defending Nixon, the war, and the old South was Lee Roy Jordan. He recalled the ideological battles.

LEE ROY JORDAN: "I felt Richard Nixon was the best opportunity at the time. I've never been a Party person, where I'm a Democrat or Republican. I've voted for the person who would do the best job for the country or the state. I see people who vote Democrat no matter whether it's a poor candidate, has moral problems, and he says, 'I have to vote for him. I'm a Democrat.' Me, I don't believe in that. I'm going to vote for whoever is the best candidate in any position, and a lot of times I split my deal up when I go vote the state and local, depending on who I think the best person is.

"At the time I didn't have a lot of confidence in George McGovern. I really didn't like a lot of his philosophies.

"We had some players on the team who didn't agree with me, and I can name Calvin Hill, Pat Toomay, Billy Parks, and Jean Fugett who I would think would be very ultra, ultra liberal types of people.

"Pat was a very free-thinking, writer-type of guy who—I don't know what to say about him. He was a good pass rusher on third down. Let me say that about him. That's what I say about Pat. He was definitely a character. He was long-haired, hippie-looking, and Pat didn't have a real work ethic. He thought this deal ought to be done without any work being put into it. Pat didn't like that hittin' too much. He was great on the outside pass rush because you didn't get hit much out there. So he didn't play the run a lot for us, but Pat . . . shoot, I admire Pat and think a lot of him, but we sure had some differences of opinion on work and football and politics and a lot of other things.

"Jean Fugett was a bright, smart guy, as he went on to be the president of the Beatrice Food Company, had a great career there. After his friend died, he became president of it. Beatrice Food is one of the largest companies in the country. It's some story about Jean and what he's done and where he is right now.

"Jean was outspoken about racial equality, and in certain areas, being from the South, I was appalled at some of the problems we had early on, with the inability to stay in certain hotels and eat in certain restaurants in some of the cities where we went early in our career, that was . . . I think that was a terrible thing. But that's the way the country was at that time."

Though ideologically split in '72, on the field the Cowboys showed a strong united front immediately, defeating Philadelphia with a touchdown run by Calvin Hill and a passing offense featuring passes from Craig Morton to Bob Hayes, Lance Alworth, and Ron Sellers, who had come from New England for a draft choice. Alworth, who had starred for San Diego for a decade, came to the Cowboys with a career record of 83 touchdown catches, second only to the legendary Don Hutson, who topped the list with 99. Against the Eagles, Alworth caught a touchdown and won the next game against the New York Giants with a 13-yard touchdown reception. Green Bay won the next game on a field goal, but the Cowboys came back to Texas Stadium to defeat a tough Pittsburgh Steeler team, 17–13. The defense didn't give up a single touchdown, though Mel Blount scored on a fumble return, one of five Cowboy turnovers. Dallas won on a 55-yard halfback pass from Calvin Hill to Ron Sellers.

The Cowboy fans gave Craig Morton a terrible booing during each home game. By the end of the season, the booing was becoming a crescendo.

Said Morton sadly, "I don't understand it, and really I don't know what to say about it. I'm not going to let it get me down. I'm not going to let it have a detrimental effect. Hell, I think I'm a bigger man than that. But certainly I hear it . . . a deaf man could hear those people."

Craig had his best games on the road. In the fourth game, in Baltimore, he was superb, completing 21 of 30 passes for 279 yards and two touchdowns in a 21–0 win. The Cowboy defense put on a clinic, as Jethro Pugh time and again harassed Colt quarterback Johnny Unitas, sacking him four times.

LEE ROY JORDAN: "We were not great early in the year, but after the fifth or sixth game, the defense came on and really was consistent. We got a tremendous streak going in the latter part of the year. At that time we played the run extremely well. I don't think anyone played the run as well as we did. We forced people into passing situations. I can remember in one game we shut out the Colts, sacking John Unitas four times. John was a great passer and even at this point in his career was still very competitive. John Mackey and Willie Richardson and other targets of John's were outstanding receivers, and we respected them but we also felt like we could pass rush their football team, that we could beat their offensive line with Jethro and Lilly and George Andrie and Larry Cole at left end. We felt like we could pass rush them most of the time and put a lot of pressure on John."

The rest of the season went without a hitch, as Craig Morton did his job beautifully, executing Tom Landry's game plans, directing Calvin Hill and Walt Garrison in a punishing rushing attack, and passing to his receivers Hayes, Alworth, and Sellers for fifteen touchdowns. He finished seventh in the league in passing but would have been third had it not been for twenty-one interceptions.

Under his leadership, the Cowboys finished the regular season 10–4, second in the division behind their archrivals, the 11–3 Washington Redskins. Calvin Hill finished the season with 1,036 yards, a Cowboy record. In just four years, Hill had rushed for 3,023 yards, third-best in Cowboy history. But 1972 was a tough year for Bob Hayes, who did not catch a touchdown pass all season long.

Craig Morton came down with pneumonia the week before the final game with the New York Giants, a game in which the Cowboys looked so listless in a 23–3 loss that Tom Landry played a rehabilitated Roger Staubach in the final quarter. For the opening playoff game against the San Francisco 49ers, who'd given the Cowboys their worst regular season beating, 31–10, once again the controversy blazed: Who should start, Morton, who had led the team all year long, or Staubach?

Landry, as expected, went with Morton. He had been the general all season long. It certainly wasn't Morton's fault that Vic Washington ran back the opening kickoff 97 yards, but then on the next series Morton fumbled, lost the ball on the 15, and the 49ers scored again. With just seventeen seconds gone, the Cowboys trailed 14–0. Their season appeared to be over. A Morton interception led to a third score, and then Calvin Hill fumbled a handoff on the one to give San Francisco another easy score.

The Cowboys were trailing 28–3 when Morton threw a touchdown to Lance Alworth. Another Cowboy field goal left the Cowboys trailing 28–13 at the end of the third quarter. Morton launched a 50 yarder into the end zone to Bob Hayes, but Hayes could not hold on to the ball and it fell away.

A desperate Tom Landry decided to try Roger Staubach and see what he could do.

ROGER STAUBACH: "We had had a good season, but there was something not right. We weren't in synch all the time. And so we went out and played San Francisco, and they ran a kickoff back for a touchdown, and it just looked like it was their day. It was one of those weird deals in the fourth quarter—I don't think anyone really believed we had a chance at all. By the middle of the fourth quarter many of the 49er fans were gone. Half the stadium was empty, and their players, Dave Wilcox, all those guys, were saying to us, 'Now you guys know what it's like to lose in the playoffs.'

"And then we had a long drive. Calvin Hill had some really good runs, and we had some passes, and we kicked a field goal to make it 28–16 with eight minutes left. We could win the game with two scores. But it was still a long-shot deal.

"And then we got the ball back, and they got a little conservative. Billy Parks made some great catches, and then he caught a post for a touchdown with a minute and a half left. When Billy scored, everyone was thinking, 'There's hope.'

"The score was 28–23, 49ers. So now we had to get the onside kick. The onside kick is still one of those long shots. But Toni Fritsch kicked it with his other foot, and their guy was surprised, and the ball hit him in the chest, and Mel Renfro recovered it. Had we not gotten it, we would not have won.

"We started close to midfield. Parks was on a roll, so I was going to try to get the ball to Billy. The first play, I dropped back and ran for 20 yards. And then the next one I was figuring we could beat them on a corner, so we ran a corner, and sure enough Billy caught it going out of bounds around the ten or 12.

"Landry then sent in an 83 pass, a sideline, and as I was breaking the huddle, Ron Sellers said to me, 'I can get open.' I said, 'Hey, Ron, if you get open, I'm going to look for you.' Ron was not the main receiver on the play. I was going to try to throw a sideline to Parks.

"I broke the huddle, and as soon as I took the snap, I saw man-to-man coverage, so I went to Sellers, and he caught the hall in the end zone. Boom, a shock! We won the game 30–28 with only 58 seconds on the clock. I still see the film of Larry Cole rolling on the ground. And Wilcox threw his helmet fifty feet in the air.

"It was one of those comebacks where you almost don't deserve it. It was one you figure was not going to happen. It just didn't seem like it should have happened. But it all went right. As for me, I was feeling healthy again. When I got into the game, I was thinking, 'This is my only chance to look good.' Because I wanted to come back the next year and be the starting quarterback. I didn't know we'd score 17 points to win the game! So it all just turned out well. And it killed the 49ers. I don't think they recovered from it. Dick Nolan told me, 'That just killed us.' That was the third year in a row we beat the 49ers in the playoffs.

LEE ROY JORDAN: "Craig did an outstanding job for us in 1972, but in the playoffs against the 49ers, we were behind, and Tom decided to bring Roger in for Craig. Roger came in late in the game and pulled the game out.

"And then we made the mistake of starting Roger the next week against the Washington Redskins. Roger hadn't played all year, and Craig had been playing—I still believe, hey, if we play and if Craig is not moving the team, bring Roger in. But I don't think Roger was sharp enough to go an entire game. His deal was, he had nothing to lose coming into the San Francisco game, throw hell out of it. If he's intercepted, we're not going to get beat any worse. Against the 49ers he didn't have to start out 0–0 and see what he could have made of it. He was in a position where no matter what he did, it would have been thought of as, 'It was a good effort because we were behind anyway,' and if he had thrown an interception, it would have been, 'Well, we had to do that trying to catch up.'

"When you start out even and you're concerned, 'Hey, if I make a mistake, then I might get my team beat,' then that's a little different pressure. And I feel we should have stayed with Craig and watched him the first half to three quarters, see where we were in the game. If we're not winning, hey, put Roger in and let him do what he will. But Craig had led us all year and had us in the playoffs and had played pretty darn well, let me tell you.

"Roger was rusty, and a lot of us were a little surprised at that move to start him against the Redskins. Even though it had been a great comeback by Roger. When you're even and going into starting a game, you have a lot more throws to make and a lot more opportunities for bad things to happen, misreads that can come about."

Most of the players wanted Craig Morton to start against Washington in the game for the NFC championship. In the two regular season games against the Redskins, Morton had posted 54 points. Craig, moreover, had always had success against the Redskins. And finally, the offense was used to playing with Craig. They had been together all season long.

But Tom Landry had been moved by Staubach's performance against the 49ers. He was hoping Staubach would once again show the form that had allowed the Cowboys to catch lightning in a bottle.

ROGER STAUBACH: "There was a controversy who should play quarterback in the Washington game. I really thought I deserved to start, though if Coach Landry had started Craig I wouldn't have been upset. I hadn't played that much that year, so I was looking forward to the next season to get my job back.

"The real unfortunate thing was that I got a real horrible case of the flu the week before the game, so I didn't even practice during the week. I was seeing the doctor, and I was feeling horrible. During the game I had to run a lot, and I really felt miserable. But the reason we lost was that they shut down our running game. We had beaten them in Texas Stadium earlier in the season when we had run for 200 yards. In this game, they had our running game stopped. I mean, I was our leading rusher. Calvin Hill was stopped for 30 yards. Walt Garrison, too. I was running bootlegs, and in the passing game we didn't hit any big plays. We really didn't do anything.

"The Redskins just killed us. We lost 26–3. And after the game Diron Talbert made a statement that he was glad that I started the game, which really . . . I *know* he didn't wish I started the game. But Talbert was baiting me, and that became something that really goaded me the rest of my playing career. You know, we never lost another [key] game to the Redskins for the next seven years.

"So Talbert really got to me. First of all, I was feeling bad enough that we lost. I know when I have a bad game, and I *didn't* have a bad game that day. We just didn't do anything. We got behind so quick, and they completed these big passes. Billy Kilmer threw two long touchdowns to Charley Taylor.

"We kept trying to run the ball. And then we couldn't run. And as a quarterback I didn't throw. I don't think we threw enough. And we had this new formation of receivers, and we had a lot of confusion there. Landry put in a new system for that game, four wide receivers, and I don't think Billy Parks paid a whole lot of attention to what he was supposed to do that game. For some reason he didn't have the same enthusiasm for that game that he did in San Francisco the week before.

"When Billy was out there, he played hard, but football wasn't his deal. He could take it or leave it, and I think it really hurt us in that playoff game against the Redskins in '72. He was a player, but because of his not making football a priority, they traded him.

"It was just the Redskins' day. It was their time. But it was close at halftime. Toni Fritsch missed a real easy field goal right before the half. So it was a tough loss."

47

A Study in Black and White

At the start of the 1973 season, there was a great deal of uncertainty. Some of it had to do with changes in the coaching staff. Four assistants—Sid Gillman, Ray Renfro, Bobby Franklin, and a bitter Dan Reeves—left for other jobs. Reeves was angry with the way Landry had "coddled" Duane Thomas in '71, then became even angrier when Landry let Sid Gillman run the offense and not him. Reeves left football entirely for a year and went into real estate. In early July offensive coach Ermal Allen suffered a heart attack and had to be replaced.

Adding to the turnover, Chuck Howley again retired, this time for good, George Andrie retired because of back spasms, the Cowboys forced Herb Adderley to retire, and Lance Alworth, unhappy with an uninspired passing game and stuck with having to block for the Cowboy backs for two years, also quit. Tex Schramm shrugged, saying rookie Billy Joe DuPree would take his place. Moreover, Schramm traded Ron Sellers to the Miami Dolphins for the fleet Otto Stowe, who had become dissatisfied sitting on the bench behind Paul Warfield. The last of the '60s pass-catching corps, Bob Hayes, would soon find the Cowboys trying to force him out, too, as Tom Landry attempted to replace him with Golden Richards, the speedy rookie with the great name from the University of Hawaii.

For the players who remained there was a lot of turmoil over money. Players were so frustrated with Tex Schramm's stubborn stinginess they went to the press with their unhappiness. Craig Morton, Mel Renfro, Bob Lilly, and Lee Roy Jordan led the chorus. Morton was just as bitter, moreover, about not starting the NFC Championship Game against the Redskins. "It wasn't explained, and I don't think it ever can," he said. His contract had a slew of incentive clauses in it, and Morton knew if he had to sit behind Staubach, he would be penalized both ways, and he wanted his contract reworked. Schramm said no. He walked out of camp in mid-July. "If I'm going to be used like a yo-yo" he said, "I should be financially rewarded for it."

When Morton was absent a week, Staubach was assured he would be the starter in '73. When Morton finally returned, little was written or said about him.

Center Dave Manders wanted a no-trade clause in his contract, and when Schramm said no, Manders said he wanted $5,000 instead. Again Schramm refused. "I'll take $2,500." Schramm said no. "I'll give it to charity." "No." So Manders retired in disgust. Schramm was convinced Manders would come back by the end of training camp, but this time Tex was wrong. Manders sat out as the Cowboys time and again during the exhibition season watched his replacements bungle too many long snaps for punts and extra point and field goal attempts. First rookie Jim Arneson rolled a snap past backup quarterback Jack Concannon on an extra point in a one-point loss to the Oakland Raiders. Then against the Miami Dolphins Arneson cost them three points, as one bad snap ruined an extra point and another rolled through the end zone for a safety.

Schramm decided he needed Dave Manders, and he gave the veteran center a token raise to come back. His return was made public at a surprise birthday party for Clint Murchison. A friend of Murchison's asked Manders to dress up in a tux and hide inside a big birthday cake. Out popped Manders. After Manders returned, the long-snap problem ended.

The one and only player ever to win big against Tex Schramm was Lee Roy Jordan. As was his practice, in '73 Tex stalled Jordan about his contract until it was time for training camp, then held to his $50,000 offer. Jordan wanted $100,000, which was the going price, what other teams were paying for middle linebackers not even as good as Jordan. Dick Butkus was making close to $150,000 from the Bears.

Jordan waited until Schramm and Landry had cut the last backup linebacker, then he held a press conference and said he would hold out until he got his money. Jordan's tactic left the Cowboys with only Dave

Edwards, D. D. Lewis, and a rookie linebacker from Rice University, Rodrigo Barnes. Landry, who hated to start rookies, was horrified. Schramm, who hated to be outsmarted, had no choice but to give Jordan much of what he was asking. And because Jordan had outwitted him, Tex Schramm kept Lee Roy Jordan from being named to the Cowboys' hallowed Ring of Honor. Only after Schramm was dismissed in 1988 did Jordan get his deserved honor a year later.

LEE ROY JORDAN: "Tex always tried to wait until about June to negotiate my contracts. He would say, 'We can't get anything done. Come on to training camp, and we'll talk about it out there.' And you'd get out there and have to start two-a-day practice, and you're beat, tired, and dead, and you're still wondering, 'I haven't got a contract. Nobody's talking to me. Tex hasn't said boo.' Then you say, 'Tex, I'd like to get something done.' He'd say, 'Well, let's meet tomorrow afternoon after practice.' You've gone through another day of two-a-days, and you're dead tired, and you're thinking, 'What if I get hurt? Hell, I get paid nothing.' So it was a deal that I really disliked, and at the end of the '72 season I told him, 'Tex, we're going to get together. I'm not waiting until late to negotiate this deal.' So I called him in February, and we got together one time. I kind of surveyed the linebackers around the league, and the top ones were making $150,000, and I was making $40,000, and I told him what I was expecting to make, and it wasn't what Butkus or Ray Nitschke were making, it was well below them, but it kind of fit in with some of the players I could fit in with.

"And he was absolutely horrified that I thought I was worth that. He started by saying, 'You're getting up in age. I don't know how much longer you're going to be able to play.' And that's the way he negotiated. It was disappointing. We didn't have agents back then, and we should have, no matter how much we were making.

"And so we negotiated a couple more times, and all of a sudden it was June, and I said, 'Damn, Tex. Let's get this thing done.' He said, 'Well, Lee Roy, we're a long ways apart.' I hadn't come down much, and he hadn't come up *any*. So finally in my last meeting with him, I said, 'Well, Tex, I don't think we're going to be able to do anything. I'll just have to play out my option.'

"He kind of gave me the backhand. He said, 'Go ahead and play out your option, son. It doesn't matter to me.'

"And so I went to training camp, had the best training camp I ever had. I was smoking everyone. And not another word was said about the contract. We got down to it, and they made the last cut of the year before the regular season started, cut the last backup middle linebacker. So the next day I just don't show up for practice. Jerry Tubbs called and wanted to know what was wrong. I said, 'Jerry, I'm not going to be there until I get a contract. I don't have a contract. I'm not playing out my option. And I'm not going to play somewhere else next year. I'm going to finish out my career in Dallas.'

"Then Coach Landry and Tex called me. Finally, we got together in the next day or so, because the starting right linebacker was D. D. Lewis, and he was going to have to replace me at middle linebacker, and his back-up was going to have to replace him at right linebacker.

"And so it worked out that I got some increase. I got right at $100,000, but a lot of it had to be in bonus clauses, 'cause Tex couldn't let me make any more than $75,000 salary. He said, 'Roger isn't making much more than that and Coach Landry isn't making that much, so . . .' I said, 'If you want to give me some of Coach Landry's stock . . .' And that stopped that talk in a hurry.

"And Tex didn't like me ever again after that. I don't know whether he even respected me. It really doesn't matter. I've got my opinion of him, and he has his opinion of me. I just didn't think he was fair to people, and you can do what's fair. I didn't think we were treated that way."

Two players—Tody Smith and Billy Parks—who were unhappy with the way they were being treated by the Cowboys, also asked to be traded. Both players were members of the New Breed. They resented Tom Landry's strict regimen, and wanted to be respected as people, not treated like cattle by the coaching staff. But in 1971 Tom Landry hadn't yet understood or come to grips with the changing society, and his response to both players was the same: If you're not happy, we'll be happy to get rid of you. It didn't matter that both had great talent. It didn't matter that they both needed pats on the back, needed Landry to be a father figure. If they couldn't fit into Landry's system, they would be jettisoned.

You couldn't be sensitive and play for Landry. Tody Smith, the team's number one draft choice in 1971, had suffered all his life from being the brother of All-Pro defensive end Bubba Smith. He had gone to Michigan State to follow in his big brother's footsteps, but after an injury and an unsympathetic coaching staff, he transferred to the University of Southern California. He injured his knee in a basketball game just prior to the Cowboy training camp in '72, underwent surgery, and once in camp was ordered to start practicing before he felt his knee was ready. Lacking confidence and feeling depressed, Smith walked out of camp. When he returned a couple of days later, he revealed that what was bothering him more than his knee was his feeling of being unwanted by the Cowboys. He told reporters, "I feel like a stranger here. I don't feel I'm needed."

Smith was too sensitive for pro football. He refused to take part in rookie hazing rituals, alienating him further from the veterans who cared about that sort of thing.

He told reporters, "There's no way I'm leaving again." Then he added a caveat: "But if my mental health becomes a factor, that's different."

Smith replaced an injured Larry Cole at the start of the '72 season. In one interview Landry complimented Smith, saying he was as quick as Bob Lilly. Then Smith contracted mononucleosis late in the season. Before a game with Philadelphia he couldn't get out of bed he was so debilitated, but he played. At the same time the Cowboy doctors were telling Smith it was all in his head.

Said Smith, "Before the Thanksgiving game my parents begged me not to play, but I did. I finally went to an outside doctor and he said my spleen was enlarged, that there was a possibility of killing myself if I played again like that. Yet they [the coaches] said I had a bad attitude."

After the season he spent five weeks in three hospitals including the Mayo Clinic. In the spring of '73 an angry Smith demanded to be traded, saying he didn't want to play for a team as callous as the Cowboys.

Even before he came to Dallas, wide receiver Billy Parks had a history of wrestling with his conscience over whether even to play football. As a rookie with San Diego in 1970, he quit the Chargers early in the campaign and spent the rest of the season working in a bookstore. He returned in '71, and led the AFC in receiving before suffering a broken arm. He walked out again in '72, and then after Charger head coach Sid Gillman joined Landry in Dallas as offensive coordinator, Gillman convinced the Cowboys to trade for him.

Gillman loved Parks's talent. "He has as fine a pair of hands as I've seen since I've been in football," said Gillman.

But Parks was a sensitive West Coast intellectual who didn't even like to *talk* about football. He once said, "How droll to talk about post patterns. There are kids out on the playground running them just as well. How do you deal with that?"

Parks felt that the nation's emphasis on football was untoward. He saw postgame interviews as ridiculous. "It was like somehow the world had changed," he said. "That some significant event had happened. It was absurd there was so much attention."

With the Cowboys in '72 Parks played erratically. That year he caught only 12 passes in 14 games. But more than anything else, Parks was too *different* to be acceptable. After the miraculous playoff win over San Francisco, Parks said he could not answer questions because "I've been advised by the trainers not to speak." After Parks played without spirit in the subsequent playoff loss to Washington, some of the coaches expressed anger at his attitude. Parks told reporters, "We should be able to accept victory and defeat on the same level. They're interchangeable."

He added, "To me, losing isn't like dying. If everyone does his best, how can you be sad?"

If the white players coming out of college in the mid-70s were looking for meaning in their lives, the black players were looking for justice. *Soul on Ice,* by Stokely Carmichael, and the writings of Malcolm X preached to young blacks that they were entitled to being treated like men, that nothing short of that should be acceptable. While Martin Luther King Jr. had counseled patience, the new generation of black leaders was announcing that they wanted their rights, and they wanted them *now*. And as a result, an entire generation of intelligent, outspoken black men arose to claim their rights under the Constitution and the Bill of Rights. And they wanted them *now*. But the society was not about to give them those rights *now*, and as a result, many of these young black men suffered because of their impatience and their frustrations of discovering that getting society to change was a lot harder than they thought.

In 1973 the Cowboys drafted in the seventh round one such young black man, a linebacker from Rice University by the name of Rodrigo Barnes. At Rice, Barnes had starred in football. He also been one of the organizers of the Black Student Union. When the school dragged its feet on the issue of hiring black teachers and a black coach, Barnes threatened that unless Rice acted on their request, he and the other black players would boycott the rest of the football games. Barnes succeeded, but he was reviled for it. Word spread among pro scouts that he was "trouble." Barnes saw his effort on behalf of black students as a benefit to the college. He saw the diversity as something positive. But the college officials saw Rodrigo Barnes the way white America saw Malcolm X. He was big and black and wasn't afraid of them. They, however, were certainly afraid of him. Had Barnes not been such a militant, he would have been drafted much higher than seventh.

When Barnes came to the Cowboys, he was different from most of the rookies. He wasn't afraid of the vets, wasn't afraid of the coach, wasn't afraid of losing his job. The truth was, he wasn't afraid of anything. When he came to camp Tom Landry wanted him to play outside linebacker, but Barnes did not want to replace Chuck Howley, whom he revered. No, Barnes felt he was a better player than middle linebacker Lee Roy Jordan, who at age thirty-two was on the downside of his career. Barnes told the press that the job he intended to take was Jordan's.

When Landry wouldn't hand him the job, even after he'd proved his excellence during exhibition games while Jordan was sitting out during his contract battle with Schramm, Barnes fumed. Warning lights began flashing in Barnes's brain. The same way Duane Thomas saw warning lights when he led the Cowboys to a Super Bowl and then was forced to play the next year at $22,000, so Rodrigo Barnes believed that he was a better player than Jordan but found himself sitting on the Cowboy bench because of what he perceived to be Tom Landry's racism. Barnes knew his Cowboy history. He knew that Landry had had only white players at linebacker since 1960. He knew that the Cowboys had had only two middle linebackers since 1960, Jerry Tubbs and Lee Roy Jordan. He knew that the middle linebacker was one of the captains of the defense. And Rodrigo Barnes became convinced that Tom Landry wouldn't let him play middle linebacker for only one reason: he was black.

Lee Roy Jordan was still a fine performer, and Barnes could not possibly learn the Flex overnight, but that did not keep Barnes from becoming resentful, angry, and then bitter toward Tom Landry and the Cowboys.

RODRIGO BARNES: "I grew up in Waco, Texas, a town about 92 miles south of Dallas. What I remember most about growing up in Waco in the 1950s was segregation. When you're young and a black man, you experience a combination of things. First of all, you discover you're black and there's a difference. Then you discover because you're black, even grownups eliminate you from certain opportunities in life, therefore your dreams are very structured, and creativity is very low when it comes to the future, except what you can do with your own hands to discover your own talents at an early age. It had and has a tremendous impact when you realize that there are things you cannot do, that you will *never* be accepted, that you'll be treated certain ways and that you are to act and respond in certain ways that are not natural.

"I grew up where the majority was black, my high school was 99.9

percent black in Waco, so I didn't have a lot of confrontations, which probably kept me alive.

"I was a B student, a pretty good student. I always had pride in myself, had self-esteem. My mom put that in me at an early age. I kinda kept that. I always wanted to be with the group that was making things happen.

"Football, basketball, and track were my three sports. And the band and the choir. I was a leader in all three sports, made all-district and all-state in football and track. I was all-district in basketball.

"When I graduated from high school, I had a choice of Wichita State University, Prairie View A&M University, and finally Rice University. Later I got an offer from TCU, but I had already signed with Rice. Other schools asked me to come try out, that sort of thing. I also had scholarships from the United Negro Scholarship Fund after taking the tests. I had worked hard to have somewhere to go. I didn't want to go to Vietnam in 1968. I didn't think it was a good war at the time, I still don't, and I'm glad that I didn't go. However, if I would have been drafted, I would have served. But I wasn't asked to.

"In 1965 the federal government ordered all state-supported teams to accept blacks, and to comply some of them accepted black athletes, some of them accepted black students, and some of them accepted black students and athletes.

"And so Rice itself had to accept blacks. When I went to Rice, there were twelve blacks in the whole school my freshman year, and eight of them were freshmen. I was among their first black athletes to enroll: myself, Stavie Vincent, and Mike Tyler in football, and in basketball Leroy Marion.

"I was looking forward to it. It was a challenge for me academically, and a challenge athletically, to be going to a school that had no program, but had a chance to be successful, so it offered a lot of challenges for me, which I needed at that time.

"One thing I found out: in the South, when you're around intelligent, educated people, they seem to act that way. So you don't find blatant racism, that type of treatment, of verbal expression. It's much more subtle. You might not be included, but you won't know anything about it. It will be a private deal where you're not familiar with it. Matter of fact, the students were anything but racist. Students lent me brand-new cars, did a lot of favors for me, a guy coming from the projects, and I tried to take care of the things they let me use.

"There *were* some incidents from professors and students. That happened, and I overcame them, and they didn't get the best of me at that time. But then, too, at Rice not only was I a student and an athlete, I organized the Black Student Union at Rice University. I was the founder of it, and then we had to do some things to try to bring our university up to par, which created some political problems for me.

"You see, when you are an assertive or a radical person, and you bring about change—and I call myself a positive radical person, 'cause I bring about positive change—you're going to have growing pains. That happens when people who have the advantage lose that advantage. To them, you're not going to be the favorite. I could have gone to Rice, been a good boy, got drafted by the Cowboys, been a good soldier, gone along, and I'd probably be a millionaire today. But being comfortable and rich wasn't first in my life. First was being a man. And being black, being a man is very, very important to me, after seeing what black men have had to go through and how difficult it was to even want to stand up and be a man. It was something I've taken pride in, whether I've made the right decisions or not. I tried to do the right thing and I tried to stand up as a man.

"At Rice University I was the sophomore defensive Player of the Year. I was second-team consensus All-America a couple of years, which means I made everybody's poll. I was all–Southwest Conference. I got all the accolades you could get within the conference. But the big deal at Rice was that because of my political stands, my politics overshadowed my athletics in the city of Houston, and I found that because of that some people denounced my athletic ability.

"But as an athlete, any team that played Rice when I played had to focus on dealing with how they were going to stop me. And I feel very good about that. I got hurt, and we lost those games when I did.

"But I felt like I did a lot, did a lot for the university. I did a lot for blacks. I did a lot for students at Rice. Did a lot for the Southwest Conference. However, it wasn't received like that. I wasn't pictured as a person trying to help. I was pictured as a person who was trying to destroy. But yeah, racism, prejudice, and bigotry, yeah, I was trying to destroy that. If that was the situation, they were absolutely right.

"Just like right now, I'm not in Rice's Football Hall of Fame. It doesn't bother me any. I've never asked them to do it. But at the same time, to me, it makes them look bad. It doesn't make me look bad.

"I was drafted in the seventh round by the Cowboys. I didn't want to go to Dallas. I didn't think they were going to let me play. I didn't think they respected my game. I didn't think they wanted what I had to bring to the table. Because of my color, not because of my game. And I was correct.

"Tom Landry wanted somebody who could play *like* me. He probably prayed for a guy who could play with the ability I had. Because I could run a 4.5 40. I would win the 220. I was quick, agile. I could do it all. I could play all the linebackers' positions. I could play strong safety. But Landry wanted a white boy who could do that, not a black boy. And not a black *man* who was assertive. And so they had a big choice to make, because if you were a linebacker on the Dallas Cowboys, you were a leader, and did they want to give that leadership role to me? And the answer was no.

"The linebackers at the time were white boys: Lee Roy Jordan was in the middle, and Dave Edwards and Chuck Howley—who was the best linebacker I had seen at the Cowboys—were outside. I played middle linebacker, and I was going to be *the* star. And they could see it. When I played against the Miami Dolphins I stopped Larry Csonka on the goal line three times in a row. No linebacker did that back then. I played against Kansas City and graded out a ten-plus. No linebacker ever graded out ten-plus on the Cowboys before then. And so I did some things there to let them know I had the game, but Tom Landry did not want me to be the star. And it was because he knew he didn't have control over me. They weren't going to have control, because I got paid to play football. I didn't get paid to be a boy. And I wouldn't be nobody's boy. Because they can keep that other money. I was just there to play football. And I'm not selling myself for no game. That's stupid. The game is just not that big to me. It was something I can do, but it's not *me*.

"Landry *did not* want me to make the team. During the exhibition season the Cowboys would have me practice at outside linebacker, and in the game they played me in the middle. If they practiced me in the middle, in the game they'd put me on the strong side. So that was setting me up to make a mistake. You got cut based on how you played in those games. But I survived because I was a ballhawk and I understood football.

"Lee Roy and I didn't have any problems. I respected Lee Roy. I wanted his job, and I didn't have a lot of patience to wait on it, but I respected him.

"I remember we were getting ready to play Kansas City. I was in the shower after we got through practicing. It was our last defensive practice that week, and the fullback, Walt Garrison, he was in the shower with me and Lee Roy, and Walt said, 'Hey, Lee Roy, man, I sure hate you not playing this week. We're going to get our butts kicked on Sunday. They're going to run right up the middle. So and so, so and so, so and so . . .' I was standing right there taking a shower. Walt knew I was starting. So he was just dissing me right in front of Lee Roy. He didn't care. He wasn't saying to me, 'Have a good game. You can do it.' It was like in your face.

"It may have been them trying to psych me up. I didn't know. And it *did* psych me up. I had no fear. I knew I could handle the situation. And after I had such a great game, it shocked them. Shocked them! They never were the same. Because they knew I was ready. You see? Lee Roy couldn't do anything I couldn't do. I had more speed, quickness. I hit harder. Everything. His day was just up. But Landry wanted to keep him there.

"I should have had the job. Really and truly. Landry tried me and saw I could handle it. When we played against Kansas City, he saw I could do the job. That wasn't the problem. The problem basically was that he did not want the package. The package was the problem."

Two days after the final exhibition game in 1973, one of the Cowboy stars found himself in the headlines after what appeared to be an acid trip that went bad, though this was never confirmed. John Niland had been troubled his whole life. He was orphaned and adopted at a young age by a fifty-year-old woman, and grew up in Amityville, Long Island, in relative poverty. In 1994 in an article in the *Fort Worth Star-Telegram*, he told journalist Christopher Evans that he had been emotionally and sexually abused as a child.

An only child, he lived in an industrial area near the railroad tracks. He had his first job at age ten or eleven, pumping gas for 50¢ a night and a free pizza pie.

Niland grew up to be a large man, weighing 255 pounds, and he was a talented enough football player to earn a scholarship at the University of Iowa, where he became an All-America.

Niland was drafted in 1966 in the first round by the Cowboys, and during a ten-year career, he was picked for six Pro Bowls. He was artistic, and he was popular. Only Roger Staubach attended more high school awards dinners. He was also quick with a quip. One time he attended a press party at a local spaghetti joint and observed that the "only thing Arkansas produces are hookers and football players."

"Wait a minute," said an indignant man in the audience. "My wife is from Arkansas."

"What position does she play?" Niland asked.

During his career and later in his life he abused alcohol, and amphetamines and for a time used LSD, which caused him at times to become involved in violent antisocial behavior.

MEL RENFRO: "I liked John. A nice guy. Whenever he was at the practice field or around us, he was as nice as he could be. But then he'd go out and get crazy with drugs. And he'll admit it to this day."

Niland's life has been plagued with incidents, from fights in bars to a 1988 prison term after he was convicted of trying to obtain a loan by fraudulent means. Niland had signed a document for a friend, a too-common occurrence for naive ex-athletes who allow friends to get them into trouble.

Niland's problems stemmed in part from a failing marriage. In 1967 he married Iree Van Cleve, a Braniff flight attendant. She was preparing to fly Military Aircraft Command planes carrying Vietnam troops to Singapore and the Philippines when they up and eloped.

Unfortunately for Iree, she discovered that Niland had an insatiable appetite for female flesh, alcohol, and drugs. She soon was on to him, and part of their relationship involved her surveillance of him in an attempt to keep him out of the arms of other women. Niland freely admits the infidelity of his former life.

"I was coming out of a bar on Lemmon Avenue with this girl and I saw my wife sitting over there in a car," said Niland. "So what did I do? I brought this girl out, we get in my car, we go 100 miles an hour down Lemmon Avenue, I lose Iree, then finally come home later and deny the whole thing."

For six years, their relationship continued in this vein until Iree finally had enough. They separated in 1973, and she moved to Aspen, Colorado.

She was back in Dallas on the night of September 10, 1973, when she and Niland were invited to the home of a mutual friend to watch the television show *In Concert*. Niland took acid, and he was sitting around with Iree and his friends when, Niland said, he was overcome by an "intense feeling."

"I felt as if I couldn't breathe, as if I was being gassed or something. I had to get out of that house," Niland explained to Frank Taggart of the *Dallas Times-Herald*.

Without saying a word, Niland got out of his chair and walked out the door and away from the house. "But when I got out of the house, I still had that feeling, and I started to run."

Niland said he started running down the middle of the street as fast as he could. He was running so fast, he said, he lost his shoes along the way. "I actually felt like I was going to die."

Meanwhile, back at his friends' house, his wife and friends at first didn't think anything of Niland going outside. They thought he had forgotten something in his car and had gone to get it. It was only when he didn't come back that they became concerned.

After running about a mile from the house, Niland, exhausted and out of breath, slowed down and then stopped. "I said, 'God, if you want me, if I'm going to die, take me.'"

Niland began to hallucinate. All of a sudden, Niland said, he began to see visions. "I saw Landry, Jim Myers, my offensive line coach, Paul Anderson [a former world champion weightlifter turned evangelist], and Pat Boone, among others.

"I still don't understand why I had visions of these people. In fact, I don't even like Pat Boone as a singer," he said.

"Looking back on it, most of the men I saw in the visions were Christians. And I understand that Pat Boone went through a similar experience as I did a long time ago. So maybe that's why I saw him," said Niland.

Continuing the story, Niland said he again had the urge to run, only this time he felt totally different.

"It was as if I had died and had suddenly been reborn. I felt elated. As I picked up momentum, I started to speak in tongues.

"I couldn't control my lips. They kept saying things as if I had no control over them. It was as if God was speaking through my mouth for me."

He said one of the first things he began to mumble were the words "player-coach."

He was asking himself whether he should stay in football, and those were the words that came in reply.

Niland said in the article he still didn't know what it all means.

Then, he said, he started to say, "Find Iree. Find Iree.

"Again, I don't know why I was saying it. But it was as if God was telling me to find my wife and reunite with her.

"All this time I was running and saying, 'Find Iree.'

"But suddenly I stopped in front of a house. And I asked myself, 'Is Iree here?' not really thinking she was back at my friends' house. My mouth kept saying, 'Find Iree. Find Iree.'"

He knocked on the door of the home of a rabbi, who asked Niland if he could help him. Niland asked if he knew where his wife was. Niland said the rabbi directed him to a house across the street. He went there while the rabbi called for an ambulance to pick up an incoherent behemoth flipped out on a bad drug trip and take him to a hospital.

About 2:20 A.M officers were called to a home near Hillcrest and

Royal Lane by a retired business executive. He said Niland was yelling and banging on his door, thinking this was where he would find his wife. The man didn't know Niland and wouldn't let him in. He called the police.

The police came to take Niland home. When the officers arrived, he was not coherent. They said he was not drunk. (They didn't say he was on acid.) Niland said he would go by himself, but the police were concerned for his safety and the safety of everyone else, and they told him they wanted to take him to see a doctor. Niland then went totally bonkers, and it took seven men to subdue him and force him into the patrol car.

Niland was taken to Parkland Hospital, where he was admitted. The Cowboy doctor was summoned to attend to him.

After the effects of the drugs wore off, he was back to normal, and the very next day Niland returned to the team.

John Niland may have been crazy, but not crazy enough to keep him from playing in the season opener.

Several days later Niland explained that he had had a religious experience. "The best way to sum it up is to say that I gave my life to Christ. I became a Christian. Now I have to live the life I foresee coming. I have to fulfill a promise made to God."

Niland told the press that the first thing he asked his wife when he saw her was, "Are you ready to accept Jesus Christ?" She said she was. Niland said they were back together and had found a new meaning to their relationship.

Said Niland, "Coach Landry and I sat down and talked about my experience the Thursday after it happened. He seemed real happy about it.

"But more important, for the first time I understand what Coach Landry has been talking about all these years. I found out what it means to be a Christian."

Niland even got backing for his "born-again" saga from the local rabbi at the home he first visited the night of the incident.

Frank Taggart of the *Times-Herald* interviewed the rabbi, Max Zucker, who said he believed Niland's religious experience to be "genuine."

"There are just too many coincidences that cannot be explained in any other way," said the rabbi. "For instance, of all the homes that Niland could have visited on that night, he went to a rabbi's home. Why did he choose to go to a rabbi's home? I don't know."

Zucker said he had never met Niland and that there was no way Niland could have known he was a rabbi.

However, said Zucker, he was not surprised when Niland showed up at his door that night.

"I've had a number of people, not necessarily Jewish, come knocking on my door at all times of the day and night. I have helped quite a few nonreligious people find God in their own way."

Zucker said he called for an ambulance because he wasn't sure what kind of help Niland needed. "It was the neighbors across the street who became frightened and called the police."

What was not amusing about the incident to the Cowboys was that Niland was injured during the fracas. He had a badly cut elbow and some possible nerve damage in his right hand. Being handcuffed for a long period didn't help things.

In a subsequent game against Chicago, the elbow was hit and became infected. Niland had to play the season one-armed and one-handed.

RODRIGO BARNES: "You have to understand: John didn't go crazy. John used good sense. He saved himself from going to the penitentiary. He kept himself in the league, kept the paychecks coming, and later, when he got worse, he went to a psychiatrist.

"If a black guy had done what Niland did, there's no doubt he'd have gone to jail for ten years, but black people have been taught to live in this country differently than white people. You're told, 'You can't act like that. That's for the white man.' The only problem white folks have is when a black guy gets treated as good as a white person.

"It was like in the '50s and '60s, if you walked down a sidewalk and a white woman walked by, you got off the sidewalk. If she wore a minidress, you better look down at her ankles. And it was that way with the Cowboys. There was a certain way you had to act, and if you didn't act that way, they didn't say nothing about it; they just got rid of you.

"But as black men we expect that treatment. We have seen it over and over. The only thing that is shocking us now is that finally something is being done about it. People are finally getting to, 'Oh, you mean the law is really going to be the law? You mean they are really going to do what they say they are supposed to do?' That's where we are as black people. We are just saying, 'You mean you really are going to do it? Oh, you mean they'll go to jail for beating Rodney King?' We all thought you'd never notice that. 'Oh, you mean you didn't believe cops beat up us black men for the fun of it?' 'Okay, well, we thought ten witnesses was enough.' But now a video camera makes a difference, so now black men are toting video cameras around so we can show you what happens. 'Cause he's a policeman he never lies, huh? Never heard of the code of silence, huh?

"We're not crazy. It's just that we haven't been able to do anything about it. We're stuck. Until society changes. Until white men change.

"The veteran black players told me all the time, 'Boss, I'm scared for you.' I said, 'Scared for me? If you'd taken care of this, I wouldn't have to be dealing with it.' That's why the Cowboy players didn't like me. That's why I didn't get invited to a lot of the parties. I told them, 'Somebody has to do it, because I can't live like you. I can't go to sleep and wake up in fear like that.' That's why a lot of them didn't like me. They thought I was a troublemaker. But my thing was, Hey, I'm not going to be scared. I'm not going to be like that."

48

The Free Agent

While Rodrigo Barnes was fighting for justice, another Cowboy rookie, a little-known free agent receiver by the name of Drew Pearson, scratched for a spot on the Cowboys roster. Pearson, like Barnes, had been a black-rights crusader in college, albeit reluctantly. Pearson had grown up in New Jersey and had experienced no racism until going to college in Oklahoma. At Tulsa University he helped lead an insurgency against the school athletic director, who was forcing the coach to play his son at quarterback. The black players felt that Pearson was the better quarterback, but they realized they could not unseat the A.D.'s son unless they took a stand. After the black players threatened to boycott games, Pearson became the starting quarterback and the team went on to win the Missouri Valley Conference.

Pearson was as practical as he was talented. He realized the only way he was going to make it in the pros was to switch to wide receiver, so his junior year he became an end. When no pro teams drafted him, Pearson was free to sign with whomever he wished. Influenced by the Cowboys' avalanche of propaganda touting their prior success with free agents, he signed with Dallas for a bonus of $150. When he came to camp he was listed as the number-eight receiver on the depth chart. That Drew Pearson would go on to become an All-Pro and a certain future Football Hall of Famer seemed inconceivable at the time.

DREW PEARSON: "I'm from New Jersey, and I grew up in white America. When I was in high school, I was the only black in the senior class. You didn't have many black families in the little town of South River, and it just so happened that the kids from the other families weren't the same age as me.

"I never experienced any true racism. If it was happening, I certainly wasn't aware of it. Because I was successful as an athlete, they accepted me. South River, New Jersey, is a little Polish town, and everybody's last name ended in 'ski' and they used to call me 'Drewski.' They made me one of them.

"It was at Tulsa my freshman year that I experienced racism for the first time. Our campus was situated such that there was a convenience store, U-Totem, only about a quarter mile down the street, and we'd be hungry after dinner, we didn't have much money, so we'd go in there and get what we called the 'Tulsa Steak,' which was a honeybun and a 'Tulsa drink,' which was an R.C. Cola. And we'd come back to the dorm and eat it and bull jive.

"One day one of our black teammates went to the store on his own, and a car full of white guys drove up and started attacking this guy, and they beat him up. He was able to get away, and he ran back to the dorm to try to get help, and we went out there after them to try to chase the guys, and of course, they were gone by then. But from then on there were instances just like that all around campus, where a group of white guys would just chase us, come after us, and it got so bad that we got to the point where we never went to the store or anywhere after dark on campus by ourselves. We had to go in groups, because we were afraid of getting attacked.

"I went to Tulsa for three recruiting visits before I decided to go there. When my father took me down there to enroll and register, he was supposed to stay that day and leave the next morning. But he felt the racial tension so intensely that he decided to stay, stay, stay, and he ended up staying a whole week before he left. He wasn't sure about the place. And the last thing he said—I remember this like it was yesterday, the last thing he said to me as he was getting on that plane to head back to New Jersey was, 'Son, you sure you want to stay here?'

"And I said, 'Yeah, I'm going to stick it out and see how it goes.' That's the type of tension he felt and witnessed in that one week. So that was very much a culture shock for me to experience after being in New Jersey and around whites and thinking maybe I was one of them and not really what I was, a black man, and thinking everywhere was like what I was raised in and grew up in. As I found out later, everywhere certainly *wasn't* like home. So it was a tough experience.

"When I was quarterbacking my sophomore year at Tulsa, I almost beat out the starter, John Dobbs, a senior. John's father, the great Glenn Dobbs, was athletic director, and this was his youngest son, the last one to come through, the last hope of one of his sons being a pro quarterback. It was clear-cut, in spring ball, early preseason practice, that I was better than him, that I should have been the starter. And my teammates saw that, and we lost the first two or three games, and we were having problems on offense, and my teammates, the black ones, rallied around me. They said, 'Drew needs to be the starter.' They saw everything I was doing, but I wasn't getting opportunities in games. And so we decided to stage a boycott, a black player boycott. We had the support of all the black players.

"The coach at that time was Clark Gibson, a former NFL player, played with the Raiders. His nickname was Hoot, and he *was* a hoot. He was only thirty-four years old, and he hadn't sowed all his wild oats yet. He was pretty wild. And he really felt I should have been starting, too.

"Anyway, we planned this boycott. We were going to nix practice however long we had to do it, and we went in and talked to the coach and let him know what we were going to do, and told him the reason why we were going to do it. He never really contested it. He just kind of said, 'Do what you have to do.'

"We were ready to pull out of practice that afternoon, and I went to talk to him, and he told me I was starting that next week. Therefore we didn't have to boycott. We went to practice and went on to win the Missouri Valley Conference title with me at quarterback. I never experienced anything like that. A boycott? Sitting out of practice? Jeopardizing your scholarship? But protests were a big part of society at that time.

"It was effective, and the thing is, it was effective against a guy who was Mr. Tulsa, Glenn Dobbs. He was, in my estimation, pulling the strings on the head coach and telling him who to play. We had to deal with that, but they didn't want that type of issue on their campus, and only after they saw we were serious about it did they succumb to our wishes, which as it turned out was the right thing to do. It was the only winning season we had in the four years I played at Tulsa.

"After that season, I moved to wide receiver. They had recruited about five or six quarterbacks, and four of them were junior college guys,

COWBOYS HAVE ALWAYS BEEN MY HEROES ☆ 537

and they found two they were high on, and that gave them the reason to move me to receiver. I wanted to move because I knew I didn't have the talent to play quarterback in the pros. Actually the only reason I played quarterback in the first place in high school was because I played after Joe Theismann. He left South River, went to Notre Dame, and then they had nobody to play quarterback. I had played my freshman year, played a little JV, and they wanted me to play quarterback so I replaced Joey, and it was okay for high school ball, because you touch the ball all the time. But I knew. I didn't even want to play quarterback in college, and that was one of the reasons I didn't want to go to Nebraska, because I wanted to move to receiver. Which was kind of ironic, because so many blacks *want* to play quarterback, and they are moved to receiver. But I knew I didn't have the necessary skills to be an NFL quarterback, and knew if I was going to make pro ball, it was as a receiver.

"When I wasn't drafted, I was plenty discouraged, but I wasn't beaten. I was hurt. It's like somebody kicked me right in my stomach repeatedly. It was a terrible feeling. It was two days of going through the worst agony other than physical agony. It was the worst mental agony I ever went through in my life.

"I was sitting by the phone waiting anxiously, and the reason I had the hope, and the reason I was waiting, was that scouts had been telling me that I was going to get drafted. The Cowboys had sent scouts to Tulsa regularly. Ron Meyer, the former SMU coach, an NFL coach and CNN broadcaster, was one of the scouts. He told me, 'Oh yeah, you're definitely going to play. You're definitely going to get drafted. You're anywhere from a second- to sixth-round pick. No question.' I thought, 'That's great.'

"So I had those hopes and expectations, so on draft day I was sitting around and waiting. The first day went by, and we had two players drafted in the second round—Ralph McGill went to San Francisco as a defensive back and Arthur Moore went to New England as a defensive lineman—and that was pretty much it for Tulsa that first day of the draft. Of course, I was shocked. They only got to the fourth or fifth round that first day, but I was still shocked and disappointed. But here comes the second day, thinking, 'Okay, this has got to be it.' They went seventeen rounds. I waited around all day again, and it actually got to the point where I couldn't sit there anymore.

"I left my apartment and walked up to the campus and walked around the athletic department just in case they heard something that I didn't hear, and of course, there was no news. F. A. Dry, the former TCU coach, was our coach at that time, and I went and talked with him, and he said, 'Don't get too discouraged, because if you don't get drafted you might be able to sign as a free agent. One advantage you might have as a free agent is that a lot of teams might be interested in you, and you can pick and choose where you want to go.' That was some consolation. That made me feel a little better. I didn't think *all* was lost. But eventually we had a few more players get drafted, and of course, the day ended, and I didn't get drafted.

"Bob Griffin of the Cowboys called me that night. And he wasn't calling long distance either. He was in Tulsa, and he was at the Camelot Hotel, and he asked me if I could come down there to visit with him.

"I went down there thinking, 'What can all this be about?' Bob Griffin gave me the big pitch, 'We're sorry you didn't get drafted. We couldn't believe it. We thought you were draftable material, but we had some other interests and we couldn't believe after the draft was over you were still out there, so that's why I'm here to sign you as a free agent.' I said, 'That's good. I'm excited,' but I was remembering what F. A. Dry told me, that other teams might be interested, and that was the only reason I didn't sign right then and there. Still, I didn't want this guy to leave town without 'Drew Pearson' on a contract. I was thinking, 'He might not come back and give me another opportunity.'

"I didn't sign, and I went back to my apartment, and the next morning I got a call from Pittsburgh and Green Bay, saying they were interested in signing me. Tim Rooney of the Steelers came to Tulsa. I met with him at the Holiday Inn. He made a nice contract offer and said they really wanted me as a wide receiver. They offered ten times what the Cowboys offered in the signing bonus: $1,500. The Cowboys offered $150.

"I sat and talked with Tim Rooney and told him I would have to think about it, make a decision, and I never really did talk to anyone from Green Bay. They talked with F. A. Dry, and F. A. Dry relayed to me that they were very interested.

"I can remember before I came to Dallas, as part of their propaganda the Cowboys made us think everything was rosy in Dallas. Tex and Gil set us up by telling us what a great city Dallas was, what a great team the Cowboys were to play for, a great organization, and back then they used to send out all these materials, brochures, telling the black players how the city of Dallas incorporated the black players, what the black players were doing, pictures of the black players with their houses, pictures of the players by their nice cars, and that kind of gives you a picture that everything is rosy in Dallas, so hell, I was looking forward to going down there. I wanted to be a part of this.

"I went to Dallas so one day I could be in that section of the *Cowboys* magazine that talked about the free agents making the team and how successful they were, and what they had. I wanted to be in that. And that was part of my motivation to make the team and to bust my butt and to work hard and do what you had to do to make the team. At the same time Harvey Martin, who was a rookie with me, who was from Dallas, had a totally, totally different picture of the city.

"We talked, and Harvey would tell me how tough the black and white separation was, how blacks had to sit in the back of the bus, whites in the front. Harvey worked at Joske's in downtown Dallas busing tables and doing these other odd jobs, and he would tell me about the colored rest rooms and white rest rooms in Joske's. And Harvey would tell me some of the problems he had just being a black kid growing up in Dallas. These things had happened only two or three years earlier, and it was kind of scary.

"I signed with Dallas. I took that $14,500 salary and took the $150 bonus. I paid two months rent on my college apartment, and I started getting ready to make the Cowboys football team.

"Back in '73 the draft was in early February. At the end of February the Cowboys invited all the rookies for a minicamp. We came in, had our camp, and then the rookies who were impressive in that minicamp, whether they were drafted or free agents, you got invited to the minicamp with the veterans, which was at the end of the next month. Off-season conditioning wasn't what it is now. Matter of fact, the Cowboys with those minicamps initiated off-season conditioning, now a big part of the process of becoming a professional football player.

"After that rookie minicamp, they invited me back down to the veteran minicamp, and I was shocked, but happy. All of a sudden here I am in the locker room with Roger Staubach, Bob Lilly, and Lee Roy Jordan, Walt Garrison, Bob Hayes, thinking, 'Oh my God, this is great.'

"That was an inspiration to me to really get after it to make this team. I had a pretty good minicamp with the veterans. It was mostly learning and watching and seeing how they did some things I needed to work on, like my strength. When we had the rookie minicamp, the rookie quarterbacks were there, and I was catching everything they threw with no problem.

"And then I went to this veteran minicamp, and you had Roger Staubach, Craig Morton, Jack Concannon. They were throwing the ball, and I was dropping more balls than I ever did in my life. I remember I ran a post pattern, and Roger zipped it in there, and it zipped right through my hands. I just couldn't believe it, because I was always noted for catching. I couldn't believe it, so I knew that I had to go back to Tulsa and get on the weights and strengthen my hands and my upper body so I could hold on to those passes.

"They kept inviting me back with the veterans at the end of these minicamps, and then finally the school year was over at Tulsa. I didn't graduate on time, but at the end of May I decided to pack up everything I owned, took my wife, and we loaded up everything into a Volkswagen Bug and went down to Dallas and moved into an apartment; the Cowboys set it all up. It was right next to the practice field. It was called the Premises. To me it was beautiful, the Taj Mahal. From where I had just moved out of in Tulsa, this was *great*, man. The Cowboys arranged a job for me. I worked at Merchants Van Lines, loading the big 18-wheeler trucks with merchandise. I was making six, seven bucks an hour, which I thought was great. So I was doing that, and I was also working out. The main thing was to be over there at the practice field working out.

"I would work out in the morning, get up early, do distance running, then go to the field and whoever was there, run routes in the morning, and at one o'clock I was supposed to be at work. I'd work from one to seven, and then leave there and go home and run at night, distance running. This was the month of June, and not many Cowboys were there, because that was their time to take vacations with their families, so when I'd go to the practice field, most of the time there'd be no one there. Then Roger Staubach came, and he would always be there, and we just got to running routes. From the minicamps he knew I was a receiver, and he saw a little promise in me, and I mean, we would run routes all morning long, back and forth. He'd say, 'Drew, are you tired?' My tongue would be hanging out down to my cleats, and I'd say, 'No, sir.' He'd say, 'Do you have any more in you?' Even though I was so tired, I'd say, 'Yes, sir.' "

Until Drew Pearson arrived in Dallas in May to begin working out in preparation for training camp in '73, no one had worked as hard as Roger Staubach. Day after day it would be the two workaholics, the famous quarterback and the unknown rookie free agent, running pass pattern after pass pattern. Of course, it wasn't enough that Pearson was dedicated. Staubach soon saw that in addition to his great desire, the skinny kid from New Jersey had good speed and great hands as well.

ROGER STAUBACH: "Some of the veteran receivers hadn't come in yet, and I would throw to whoever was out there, and Drew was out there all the time. Also, he was really good. There were other free agents who were okay. But I could really see that Drew was good. And we kind of clicked. I had a lot of confidence in Drew.

"Drew made it because he worked so hard. He came out and worked, and he was good. If he hadn't been good, it wouldn't have mattered how hard he worked.

"'Cause when he came I didn't know him. All I knew was this guy was out there, and he had a lot of talent. He wasn't the fastest guy in the world, but if you look at film, when he got behind a defender, the guy didn't catch him. Drew was a heck of a football player. He had good instincts, basketball instincts. He knew how to get in position. He'd catch balls. If you threw it to him, you wouldn't get it intercepted. You just felt good about throwing it to him. You knew he was going to be where he was supposed to be and he was going to battle for the ball. Drew had those instincts and intangibles that they didn't recognize in the draft."

DREW PEARSON: "Roger and I would work out and then I'd leave the field and go home and change, get dressed and go to work, and after a while Roger saw that I was getting tired, that I wasn't the same guy in practice as we were working out, and he asked me about it. I told him what I was doing, and he couldn't believe I was going to work after I was leaving those workouts. 'Cause those workouts were work in itself. That was enough to get anyone going. So he went to Gil Brandt and Tex Schramm and told them, 'This guy has some potential. He's been out at the practice field every day. I need him out there. Can you do anything so he doesn't have to work this job every day at the moving company?'

"I got a call one afternoon. I was laying around trying to recover from all these busy days for two straight weeks. Gil Brandt called me in, and said, 'We want to give you a bonus.' I said, 'Fine. What did I do?' He said, 'You've been working real hard, and we think you have a good chance to make this team, so we're going to give you a bonus.' So they gave me a $500 bonus. He said, 'We want you to spend more time at the practice field and continue to work out with Roger.' I'm thinking, 'All right, this is great.' 'Cause I would make $500 working the whole month at the Van Lines, and I was thrilled I didn't have to work there. So this was great. And I also thought, 'Hey, these guys have noticed me. These guys think I have a chance to make this Cowboy football team. So that inspired me to work even harder.

"And I tell you, because Roger went to bat for me, it not only got me that extra money, which I really needed, but because they made an extra investment in me, it gave me a longer look in training camp, because that first week of training camp I stunk up the place. I was so nervous. I said, 'Oh God, they are going to cut me.'

"After I got through the first week of jitters, I was ready to go. My real problem was mental. Physically I could go out and do all the things they wanted me to do, but mentally, I had trouble picking up the assignments and making adjustments as a wide receiver. I had only played wide receiver two years. In college if you were told to run a certain route, you just ran the route no matter what defense you got. In the pros you had to learn keys, learn what to do.

"A big problem for me was that it was Mike Ditka's first year as an assistant coach, and besides that, he was a tight end. He didn't know shit about wide receiver, so all he could teach me, a green wide receiver, somebody looking for guidance, looking for knowledge, were my assignments. 'Here's what you do on this play. And here's what you do on that play.' The person I turned to was Otto Stowe. I would have turned to Bob Hayes, but he was playing the other receiver, so I was never lined up with Bob. I watched Bob in certain drills, but I learned more from Otto Stowe, because I was lined up behind him every day in practice, and he learned the game from Paul Warfield when he was with Miami. He played with Warfield for two or three years. He was the spitting image of Paul Warfield as far as running his routes. So I observed Otto. It wasn't, 'Otto, could you help me?' I just took it upon myself to watch him and learn from him, and that's the only reason I was able to make that team, to gain enough knowledge at that position to get over to make that team.

"When I came to training camp I was way down the depth chart. Otto at the top and Mike Montgomery, and there were a bunch of rookies in front of me. It was a long way to climb to make that team.

"My first exhibition game was against the Rams in the Coliseum. A Cowboy scout, Reed Johnson, who was my freshman coach in college, really pushed me to be a punt and kick returner. He knew that you have to do these kind of things to be versatile enough to make the team, so he really pushed me. So the first game, they stuck me back there on kickoffs and punts. Now kickoff returns weren't bad, even though you really got racked. You saw the ball, you caught it, and you'd have time to do your thing. But on a punt return, it was up there, it was in the lights, and I was thinking, 'How many games at Tulsa did I play under the lights?' None. And then you're thinking, 'Pro ball. Pressure. These guys are bearing down on you.'

"So we went into this first exhibition game against the Rams, and we didn't force them to punt until the second quarter. I was nervous as hell on the sideline. I almost peed on myself I was so nervous.

"They finally punted, and I was back there, and the ball was coming down, and it seemed like it took forever to come down, and it came down and hit me in the chest and went right through me. I fumbled it, and they recovered it, first down. I got up on one knee, and I looked on the sideline, and there was Landry, shaking his head. I came to the sideline expecting to get yanked off this punt return team. I had number 13 on my back. That was the number they gave me to wear. I said, 'This number is jinxing me.'

"We forced them to punt again, and they stuck me back there again, gave me another chance, I don't know why, but they gave me another chance, and I caught this one, and I got around the wall, and I took it 59 yards down the sideline to the one-yard line. And even though it was called back for a clip, it showed them something. It was on film. And that got me another week in training camp.

"When you're a free agent like I was, you go week by week. Actually, first you go day by day, and then you get into the exhibition games, and you try to get in that game to do something on the field to get you another week in camp and get to the next exhibition game in hope you get another game. And I was fortunate in that every time I got a chance to get in a game, I made plays, a pass catch or a block or whatever, a punt return or kickoff return. I was continuing to make plays, and I ended up making the roster."

49

Roger to Drew

DREW PEARSON: "Before I joined the Cowboys in '73, I hated the Cowboys so I didn't follow their history. I was a New York Giant fan, a New York Jet fan. I could tell you all about those teams. But I didn't follow much of the Cowboy history so I didn't know there had been a feud from the Super Bowl between Roger and Craig, and I didn't know of Landry's indecisiveness as far as making the call who should be the starter and who shouldn't, and I didn't even realize all that was part of what Roger was dealing with and what he was going through.

"When I joined the team in '73 Craig was there as well, and it appeared to me they were both vying for the starting job, but there was no question in my mind who was the better quarterback from what I was seeing. Nothing against Craig Morton, who was a good quarterback, but in my opinion when I got a chance to be close to him in '73, Roger was clearly the better quarterback."

ROGER STAUBACH: "Craig took over and played very well in '72. I got a chance to play again at the end of the year. Craig was a heck of a quarterback, and so we had another quarterback controversy going into training camp in '73. I told myself that if I wasn't the starter in '73, I was going to ask to be traded.

"I had been hoping to play, but with Tom you never knew. I still think he had this—that I was not his kind of quarterback. As far as desire and wanting to win I was, but I was a freelance, gambling, change-the-play-and-run guy. Yet we won, so he believed in me, but I think he still felt, deep down, that the reason we won with me in there was that I was executing the system. I felt my leadership aspect was positive, but after that '72 season, I had no idea what he was going to do."

Tom Landry really was in a bind. After the exhibition season, Staubach had the better statistics, but Morton looked in top form. Staubach finally forced the issue. He told Landry, "You need to make a decision and stick by it. If you aren't going to start me, I want to be traded. If I have any choice in the matter I'd prefer you trade me to Atlanta."

Landry told Staubach, "You're going to be the starter."

ROGER STAUBACH: "About that time I found out my mother was dying of cancer. My wife, Mary Anne, was a nurse, so we took care of her here. The good thing was that my mother was very independent. She had been working for General Motors. She would never have come down here if she knew how bad it was, so we didn't tell her the truth until we got her down here. She was tough as could be and never complained. It helped that I was with her every day, but it was a bad deal.

"I was really in a dilemma then, because I had just moved her down to Dallas so I could take care of her. I told my wife, 'I still can't stay here in Dallas if I'm not starting.' If Tom would have said, 'Roger, you're going to be my number two quarterback,' then I would have been sitting there with my mother's situation. But I made up my mind that I would just move with her.

"Tom asked to meet over at the practice field, and I knew it was a meeting to talk about who was going to be the starting quarterback. I really didn't know what he had in mind, because he didn't say, 'Roger, I'm glad you're back healthy again. You're my starting quarterback.' He asked me, 'How do you feel?'

"I said, 'Coach, there are no hard feelings, but obviously if I'm not the starting quarterback for Dallas, I'm not going to be back. It's your decision. I'm not trying to be difficult . . .'

"I don't know if that's when he made his decision or not. I really don't. But it was unusual for him to ask how I felt versus coming out and telling me, and at the end of the conversation he said, 'We're very comfortable that you're our starting quarterback.'

"And that year Craig was very good as our backup quarterback. I was surprised Craig didn't force Tom to trade him. I would have. For the team's sake, it would not have been good for me to have been there. I just could not have handled it. And I'm not saying whether that's right or wrong. I would not have reported. I would have sat out. I would have said, 'That's it,' and they would have been forced to trade me."

In 1973 Roger Staubach led the NFL in passing. That same year Calvin Hill ran for 1,142 yards, but he also led the club in receptions: 32 catches for 290 yards. Those statistics were one indication of the turmoil surrounding the receiving corps.

During the early part of the season the team struggled, in part because of injuries and the inconsistency of the new crop of receivers, including their number one draft choice, tight end Billy Joe DuPree, Otto Stowe, Billy Truax, and rookie Jean Fugett. Another part of the problem was that the Cowboys were trying to force-feed rookie Golden Richards into the system while at the same time attempting to force Bob Hayes out. Richards had speed and he had great PR value. He was a white guy with the name "Golden." How great an attraction would he be if he could become a star? Bob Hayes had not only lost favor with Tom Landry, but his confidence was down so low he was demanding that the Cowboys trade him. Rookies Drew Pearson and Rodrigo Barnes watched the way Landry was treating Hayes and wondered.

Drew Pearson: "I could see very clearly what the Cowboys were trying to do to Bob Hayes, because it was that obvious. Golden Richards came in, a second-round draft choice, and they brought him in as the heir-apparent to Bob. And granted, Bob might have been on the downhill side, but I mean, there is nothing Golden Richards could have done to replace Bob Hayes, unless they *wanted* to replace him. And they really *wanted* to replace Bob. They really pushed Golden. They pushed Golden in practice by giving him more opportunities to catch the ball, sending him deep all the time. They really thought this guy was going to be the heir apparent to Bob Hayes. So I could see that.

"And Bob could see that. Bob and I were good friends. He's one of the guys who took me under his wing. Bob had revolutionized the game, made zone defenses a part of the game.

"It was the Cowboy way. What I mean by that, as long as you're out there producing and being effective, you're great. 'We'll do anything for you.' But when your skills start to diminish and you start on your downhill side, then 'We're getting rid of you. You're going out the door.' And I've seen a lot of players go through that, and the thing about that, it wasn't a black-white thing. It happened to *everybody*. It was a football player thing. Even though Bob may not have been as effective as he used to be, he was still faster than anybody out there. If he had had a little more discipline, a little more direction, if a little more appreciation had been shown to him, respect shown to him for being who he was, I think Bob would have adjusted and dealt with the pressure, instead of succumbing to it, and saying, 'If you guys don't want me, trade me. Get rid of me.' He succumbed to the pressure instead of dealing with it.

"When I saw the kind of pressure they were putting on him, the things they were doing to him, the lack of respect they were showing him, yeah, you could see why he came out and said, 'I want to be traded. I want out of Dallas.' But Golden Richards was their boy. That's the guy they wanted to push, so that's why they were pushing Bob out one door and bringing Golden in another.

"Jean Fugett was there a year ahead of me. Jean was a guy who was ahead of his time. He projected an image that he was a little too smart for his britches. He was a smart guy, came from Amherst, very bright, very sharp, very articulate.

"Jean didn't try to disrupt the system. All he did was question the system. He wanted to know 'why.' And once he got the why, he'd say, 'Why don't we do it like this instead of this?' And he made sense. And Coach Landry didn't react to that very favorably. It was 'How can you question me? This is the way we've been doing it.' You don't come in and question that. But Jean was a little too smart and a little ahead of his time.

"And Rodrigo Barnes. There is no question, he would have been a super, super football player for the Cowboys if they had given him the opportunity. He just was a radical at a time when radicals weren't popular. Today, Rodrigo would fit in nicely with anybody. The things he did, if he did those things nowadays, they wouldn't even be questioned. There wouldn't be any big deal about it. But he came in questioning the system, and you could see the sort of racial undertones that the system was projecting. What conclusions can you draw when you see they are pushing Bob Hayes out, but they were not pushing Lee Roy Jordan out? And Rodrigo couldn't understand that. And I'm telling you this stuff because it's true. I was there.

"Whether the Cowboys think it was that way, I'm sure they will give you another story. Do I have negative feelings against the Cowboys because of this? No. But I'm just telling you what I saw and observed and what was actually happening there while we were being labeled America's Team and everybody thinking everything was rosy down here in Dallas, Texas. And it wasn't. 'Cause if you're a black player observing this, you're wondering when your time is going to come. How are they going to get rid of you? How are they going to push you out of the door? How is the hammer going to come down on you, because eventually it comes down on everybody? And you're wondering how it's going to come down on you, but again, it wasn't so much or all toward blacks, it was the way they did *all* players back then.

"It's like with me, after I made the team I had to compete with Golden about who was going to suit up that week and who was going to be on the taxi squad. And it should have been a no-brainer. I could play both wide receiver positions, I was running back kickoffs, I was running back punts, I was covering kickoffs—my real value was as a special teams guy. Golden wasn't doing any of that. But every Friday I had to go through the anxiety, who was going to go? Thank God, of the fourteen weeks of the regular season I went each and every one of those fourteen weeks, and there were many times when Golden was left at home or didn't suit up for home games. But for what I did in training camp that year, the plays I made, there shouldn't have been any question who was going to go.

"But Golden was the number two draft choice, and I was a free agent, and man, he was the Golden Boy. They wanted him to make it bad. He was going to replace Lance Rentzel, Lance Alworth, Billy Parks. He was *the* guy."

RODRIGO BARNES: "Bob Hayes was a tremendous athlete, speed out of this world. Landry got Golden Richards to get rid of Bob Hayes. He got him just to do that. They changed Bob into the flanker, and let the other guy run the bombs. And it was stupid, because Bob was the clear-out man. But Landry didn't want Bob.

"Landry wanted Hayes to run the flanker routes or the split end routes, and Staubach threw bullets, and so Staubach would be throwing bullets at Bob from ten or fifteen yards, and Bob's hands are just not like that. Bob'll catch the long balls that he can run under, but when Landry moved him, he was moving him to fail."

When the Cowboys opened 4–3 in 1973, part of the reason was that Richards, a rookie, was making rookie mistakes. Also injuries took their toll. Otto Stowe had broken an ankle and had to miss a month of the season, Billy Truax had ulcers from the aspirin he took for pain, Billy Joe DuPree had a sprained right foot, and Jean Fugett had a strained hamstring.

Rookie Mike Montgomery replaced Stowe, but against the New York Giants he suffered a severely pulled groin muscle and had to miss three games. There was only one eligible receiver on the roster: the skinny free agent from Tulsa University, Drew Pearson. Landry disliked starting rookies. But here he was starting a free agent rookie! It was unheard of.

In this case the Cowboys would gain glory from their seeming misfortune. It's possible that had the receivers on the depth chart above him not gotten hurt, Pearson might have rotted on the bench before being given a chance to play. It's also possible he might have sat on the bench for three or four years before breaking into the starting lineup. But because of the spate of injuries during training camp and then the mid-season injuries to Otto Stowe and Mike Montgomery, Drew Pearson got to play his first season and he went on to become one of the greatest receivers in Cowboy history.

Pearson gained notice in his very first game, against the Giants, and then in the 14–7 loss to the Dolphins, he caught seven passes for 71 yards and made another big play when he picked up a Walt Garrison fumble and ran it 28 yards.

Very quickly, everyone began to notice that this free agent rookie could really play the game.

DREW PEARSON: "I was ready to go. I tried to have a great, great week of practice, and I did. I was catching everything. I ran so many routes that week, I wanted to build not only Roger's confidence but Coach Landry's confidence and the rest of my teammates' confidence in this rookie starting in this critical part of season. So I ran a lot of routes in practice and tried to get their confidence. Coach Landry, he's a pretty smart guy. He knew he had all these other weapons. He knew he didn't have to rely on me to win in this game. So he gradually worked me into the game and into the game plan. He threw me that little bone, that little sideline route, just to get me acclimated. And then we played four days later on Thanksgiving Day against the Miami Dolphins, and then he wore me out. He ran me *all* these routes. I ended up catching seven or eight in that game, and they were all inside routes, turning, tough-catch routes.

"And for some reason a quarterback really loves a receiver who will go inside and make those tough catches for him. Even though they might have the greatest receiver to go deep on, he's going to draw an attraction to that receiver. And from that game, Roger started having more and more confidence in me, and you could see it building."

In that loss against the Dolphins, Roger Staubach found himself a big-play go-to receiver. After that same game, Staubach lost the autonomy that Tom Landry had given him at the start of the season.

With the world becoming more and more radical, Tom Landry was fighting for control of the things over which he had influence. At the beginning of the year he had ceded the play-calling to his quarterbacks, but after Staubach called an audible and failed to make a first down against the Dolphins, Landry revoked his quarterbacks' freedom. How Staubach would respond to the challenge posed by Landry's desire to be in control would determine the future fate of the Cowboys.

ROGER STAUBACH: "We won our first three games, and then in the fourth game against Washington, I got a bruised knee, but I finished up the half. We were winning at halftime. But I got banged up, and that was the excuse Tom used to take me out. And I had told him I wasn't hurt. It was a real strange deal. We lost when they stopped Walt Garrison on the goal line.

"There was no quarterback controversy, because Tom said after the game that I hadn't played because I was banged up. So that was a weird deal.

"I wasn't playing particularly well, but we were winning. We were 6–3 going into the Thanksgiving Day game against the Dolphins. Our offense was scoring. We had just put my mother back in the hospital. She was dehydrated, and she had only a matter of a month to live. Against the Dolphins we trailed and we had a third-and-one, I audibled to a running play, a sweep. I felt it was the right audible, but we didn't score.

"We lost, 14–7, and after the game Tom told said to me, 'Your mother's situation, I know how bad it is. You've got too much on your mind. I want you just to worry about formations and reading defenses and not worry about memorizing the game plan. I'm going to call the plays.' That was his reasoning, that I had 'too much on my mind.'

"I told him I'd rather call the plays and said I felt I was able to do it. In training camp during the preseason Craig and I had made a deal with him to allow us to call the plays, and we had had a really good preseason. But his reasoning was that I had too much on my mind, and I should let him worry about the plays. And of course, really, he was reverting back, because he had done it before. That was his deal. Of course, the trend was going that way with coaches trying to see what was going on on the field, recognizing and sending plays in after viewing everything from the press box. We were using a lot of multiple looks, two tight ends, and if you're calling the play, you have to make sure you have the right players in the game, so his thinking was, 'We have too much going on. We can send the play in and the right players for that play.'

"It was about control. For him to be personally calling the plays made it even more a control thing. It should have been the job of the offensive coordinator, but Tom coached both defense *and* offense. When the offense left the field, he was there with Ernie Stautner seeing to the defense. Even during the week he'd spend time with the defense, and then he'd come into offensive meetings. Tom is a brilliant guy. Tom Landry is *brilliant.* But you can get to the point where you are doing too much trying to run the whole show. Who called the plays was somewhat of an issue, but when you're winning, you sure can't complain about it."

With Tom Landry calling the plays, the Cowboys finished the season beating Denver, their hated rivals, the Washington Redskins, and the St. Louis Cardinals to finish 10–4. Staubach's mother had died the week before the Cardinals game, and he returned in time to complete 14 of 19 for 256 yards and three touchdowns. Drew Pearson caught five passes for 140 yards and two of those touchdowns. It was a remarkable performance.

DREW PEARSON: "Roger's mother had died before the Cardinal game. And Roger played a great game. To this day, Roger is a special kind of a guy. Talk about thick skin, there is no question he had that. His parents raised him with a lot of discipline, and so in doing that, he's been taught a lot of the values you really need, and Roger is the type of teammate, even though this tragedy happened in his life, he knew that his mother wanted him to continue to go out there and play. He didn't want his anguish, his grief, his problems to become our problems, and that's just the kind of guy he was. He played that game being mentally injured, because his mother had passed, and you know what you have to go through dealing with that, but he played many games where he was physically injured, and he was always out there, always giving his all, and even though he was injured he never pulled back to try to avoid further injury. I mean, he was just that type of guy, and because he was that type of guy, it made me that type of guy. It made me want to be the same way. And I wasn't the only guy on the team who wanted to be like that. It made me tougher. Not only physically, but mentally as well, and it made me look at life differently, made me respect morals and values. When I made that Cowboy team, I said to myself, 'That's the guy's pocket I need to get in. If I do things like Roger Staubach, I'm going to be okay.' I don't have to be his great buddy, go to his house for dinner every night so his wife has to tell me, 'Drew, it's time to leave.' We never were that kind of friends. But the respect was there, and I *knew* he was the guy you needed to model yourself after.

"The way I came through Dallas trying to project a positive image for myself is what I learned from Roger and what I took from him. I always said to myself, 'If I leave this game without any money, but if I have my name intact, I could do something with that after my playing days are over.' Well, I left this game with no money, and I had to rely on my name after everything was over, and it's paid off for me. Some players even label me 'The black Roger Staubach.' They say that Roger was the guy Landry talked to when he wanted to get to the white players. I was the guy Landry talked to when he wanted to get to the black players.

"Landry would say to me, 'What's going on? What's everybody thinking?' If there was an incident, 'What's happening with this incident?' That kind of thing. If there was a problem the black players were having, I was the guy they went to—I was their mouthpiece to talk to Landry about their problems. And a lot of that stemmed from my role as captain of the team and the fact that Landry looked at me in those eyes, and it wasn't something that just happened, it was something I was very conscious of, something I wanted to happen. I worked to make it happen that I was respected and looked upon in that same light. So Roger and I, because of that, we got along great. Again, a lot of people talk about our relationship. They think it was real tight, but it wasn't 'Do you want to have a beer after practice?' 'Let's go to church together.' But when we got to the locker room, it was there, and it was real.

"I saw how he dealt with the media. I saw how he dealt with his teammates. I saw how he dealt with the coaches. I saw when he made personal appearances how he dealt with the fans, how he dealt with corporate America, people who were hiring us to do certain things. I said, 'I'm going to do it the same way. I'm going to follow that guy. That's the guy I'm going to follow.'

"Roger has a big back. He can carry a lot of people. And he never knew I was on his back. But I rode his back for the eight years I played with him as a teammate, and I continue to ride it. And if he had known, he wouldn't have cared. He would have said, 'Come on.' He would have carried me. He's that kind of person. There is nothing I would or could ever say bad about Roger. If I tried, there wouldn't be anything to say. He's the only player I've played with who everything they say about him is true. People ask me, 'What's that Roger Staubach like?' I'd say, 'What did you read?' They'd tell me, and I'd say, 'It's true. He's the one player everything you read about him is true.'

"Roger set a lot of the foundation for me as an adult. He set a lot of the foundation for me as a parent. He set a lot of the foundation for me as a businessman. I owe a lot to him. If I ever make the Hall of Fame, it's going to be hard to pick and choose a presenter because Tom Landry and Roger Staubach meant so much to my career. They meant *so much* to my career, how could I leave either one of them out?"

It was in that St. Louis Cardinal game that Staubach figured out how to "play" Landry. Late in the game, Landry called a play, but in the huddle Pearson told Staubach he could get open by breaking off his route in the seam of the Cardinal zone. As a result Staubach ran his own play, not Landry's.

The throw, into double coverage, was almost over Pearson's head, but the lithe rookie leaped up and grabbed it. The momentum of the throw bent him backward, and defenders hit him from all sides, but he hung on for the touchdown.

When Staubach came back to the sidelines, Landry did not ask why he had changed the play. Rather, he congratulated him. Staubach made note of that fact.

Landry had insisted on calling the plays for Don Meredith, and Meredith had been so browbeaten and cowed by his domineering coach that he didn't have the nerve to change plays, and as a result Dandy Don had not been able to figure out a way to deal with his deep resentment of Landry. But Staubach would be different. He was not afraid of Landry the way Meredith had been. Staubach became convinced that if he changed a play in a tight situation and was successful, Landry would look the other way. And time after time, especially in crucial, last-minute situations, Roger Staubach would commit civil disobedience toward Tom Landry. And time after time, his improvised plays like the one in the Cardinal game to Drew Pearson would succeed. Handling Landry would turn out to be the true genius of Roger Staubach. And so Roger Staubach would succeed where Don Meredith had failed. Even so, the issue of who would call the plays would remain a sore subject between Roger Staubach and Tom Landry for the next seven years.

The next Sunday, in the first round of the playoffs against the Rams, Pearson and Staubach concocted another improvised play. Ahead 17–16, Landry ordered a deep sideline pass to Bob Hayes. In the huddle Staubach told Pearson to change his turn-in route to a post pattern.

DREW PEARSON: "The Rams had all the momentum, and remember, Roger was taking a chance on a rookie. He had just been sacked, and he told the line to give him maximum protection. I took off on the post and was double-covered by Eddie McMillan and Steve Preece. No way should Roger have thrown it, but here it came. The defensive backs ran into each other, and I was gone for an 83-yard touchdown. Tom was *shocked*. That was the backbreaker."

ROGER STAUBACH: "We had gone ahead of the Rams 14–0, and the Rams came back. The momentum had changed dramatically. The score was 17–16 with under ten minutes left. We lost yardage when Calvin Hill got hit in the backfield on a sweep and fell on his elbow, suffering a crippling injury. It looked bleak. We were third-and-long, and if we didn't do something, we would have had to punt from way back.

"And in that same series we hit a play to Drew Pearson that broke the game wide open. It was an in-route for 83 yards, and we were all excited, and we ended up winning.

"It was a 16 route, a route Drew and I had started to feel real comfortable with. It was a timing play over the middle. He had to get by the linebacker. Most receivers worry about a safety trying to take your head off, but Drew was the type of guy who didn't worry about that.

"When I threw it, I knew we'd score. Sure enough, Drew was coming out of his break, and the safety was coming over to try to coldcock him, and he caught it between the safety and the cornerback, and he took off and went 83 yards.

"My mother had died two weeks earlier, right before the St. Louis game—we had a great game to win the division—and so after the Rams game and that touchdown to Drew, I told everyone, 'My mother threw that one.' "

DREW PEARSON: "We beat the Rams 27–16 in the opening round of the '73 playoffs, and in the game Calvin suffered a crippling injury to his arm.

I had a lot of respect for Calvin. I looked up to a lot of our older black players, Calvin, Cornell, Jethro, Rayfield Wright. I looked at Rayfield as a pillar, a rock of strength, 'cause he was a great player. I could see at the end of his career some of the things he was going through as a Cowboy. They were trying to push him out the door, but he was so strong, he never would let them get to him. They might be able to get to him as an athlete, but they never got to him as a person. I had so much respect for him, for Mel Renfro, Bob [Hayes], Robert Newhouse, and of course, Calvin Hill.

"I saw Calvin one Monday after a game, he was in the locker room, and he had so much fluid on his knee that it had drained all the way down to his ankle, which made everything swollen. It looked like he had elephantiasis, and if you put your finger into his calf, when you pulled it out, you left an indentation in there. That told you there was all fluid inside, and he would have his knee drained, pumped, and everything else, but he always was out there playing. He took a lot of physical beating, because back then the running game was everything with Landry. We ran first, and Calvin Hill *was* the runner. And Calvin Hill took a lot of beating out there, but he never wavered, never complained. And he was always ready on game day. And then come game day, he'd carry the ball 25 to 30 times in a game without practicing all week. I wondered, 'How does the guy stay in shape?' It was amazing. Calvin was an amazing, amazing athlete. He was a lot tougher than a lot of people give him credit for."

The Cowboys played the Minnesota Vikings for the NFC championship and the right to go to the Super Bowl. It was no contest. Led by Fran Tarkenton and running back Chuck Foreman, the Vikings kept the Cowboy defense guessing all day long. Rookie Rodrigo Barnes, his anger growing with each game, placed the blame on the shoulders of Lee Roy Jordan, the Cowboy vet he felt all season long he should have replaced.

RODRIGO BARNES: "I should have started, should have played the game. Jordan had a poor game. A real poor game. They ran right up the middle. It's in Staubach's book. He wrote the book about '73, said that Jordan just had a bad game that day. I don't know what happened to him. And I don't guess he was the only one, but they ran right up the middle, right where he was. They ran right by him. I don't know if Lee Roy was hurt, it was something, and then at halftime I got hurt, so I couldn't even replace him if I wanted to, but Landry should have made the move earlier. He should have played me because you can't get better unless you play. You need a hitter, and the Cowboys didn't have a hitter. You got to have a hitter, and when you have a hitter, you have to make room for a hitter. A hitter is as important as an interception on defense, and when you've got a good hitter, man, you let him play. Well, those guys didn't understand that hitters cause fumbles, that they are going to cause a whole lot of things. They didn't understand that. But that game, our defense was intimidated, and Minnesota beat us. We should have won that game. We should have won the Super Bowl that year.

"We paid the price by not playing the people we needed to play to win. You can't win by playing who you want to have play. You win by playing the guys who can hit and make the plays."

Staubach had a different analysis. He blamed the loss on the injury to Calvin Hill, to bad luck, and to the worst pass he made in his entire career with the Cowboys.

ROGER STAUBACH: "Calvin getting hurt at the time really killed us the next week against the Vikings, because they didn't worry about our running game and went after me the whole game.

"We had two tipped passes for interceptions. It was a miserable game. It was the worst game I had ever been in.

"We had some shots. Golden Richards ran a punt back for a touchdown to make the score 10–7 Vikings. We recovered a fumble, and we had a big play to Billy Joe DuPree. I hit him as he was coming across the middle, but the ball hit off his body instead of him catching it, and it bounced into the hands of Jeff Siemon, one of their linebackers, and that killed us, because we possibly could have gone in and scored.

"And then I threw a pass that was just terrible. It was a motion pass. Bob Hayes was in motion going across the field, and he broke a sideline route, and I tried to throw it across the field, and Bobby Bryant intercepted it and ran it back 63 yards for a touchdown. If I'm not mistaken, it was the only pass in my career that was run back for a touchdown. But Bryant ran it, man. He caught that thing and ran right down the sideline. I had *no* chance to get him. He cut right in front of Hayes. It was probably the worst pass I ever threw. The momentum of that game was going in our direction, but my job was to turn it around, and I didn't turn it around. So I think that was the worst game I ever had. We lost that day, 27–10, and then the Vikings lost to Miami in the Super Bowl."

DREW PEARSON: "I was really sick after losing that game to the Vikings, because the Super Bowl that year was going to be played in Houston, and

I couldn't think of any better climax to my rookie season than playing in the Super Bowl as a rookie, and as a starter at that. We thought we could beat the Vikings. The Vikings are one of those teams, man, they frustrate you so, because they don't do anything fancy. They just come at you and play football. They come out there on the field, and there's no rah rah. They just do their jobs, and they kick your butt, and they leave town. They don't talk no shit, or nothing. They kind of piss you off because they are so businesslike, so professional-like. It all permeated from Bud Grant, wearing the black shoes, those ugly uniforms, and they were out there kicking our butts.

"I was a little upset in that game because I wasn't getting a lot of opportunities. Coming off that Rams game, I thought I'd be that 'go-to' guy in that Viking game, and it didn't turn out that way. It was just very frustrating and devastating. We lost that game on a Sunday, and on a Monday night I caught a plane, and I was in New Jersey. 'Cause it was a long season, and I just felt I needed to be around my family, my mother, my brothers, and sisters. My wife couldn't believe we were leaving so soon after the game, but I just wanted to be there. And actually, that's when I knew I was a star, when I got back home and I saw how people saw me, how they looked at me differently. I went to a party with my brother, and he introduced me, and the women went crazy. So I was saying, 'Oh, I must be something!' 'Cause you get caught up in the season especially as a rookie and you're making plays, but you don't think about being a star, 'cause you're just playing football. You don't think you're doing anything different. And the only reason it's different is that it's getting attention on TV, and everybody sees you doing it, and now everyone wants to associate themselves with you. I was a guy who gave a lot of people encouragement, because my rookie year I was 160 pounds, a rail, certainly looked like anything but a football player, so they would say, 'If he can do it, I can do it.' My buddies back home said, 'If you made the pros . . . I used to kick your ass. If you made the pros, I can make the pros.'

"I said, 'Well, go try.' "

50

Come the (Short) Revolution

Since 1967 the Dallas Cowboys had been the most successful franchise in the NFL, despite Tex Schramm's policy of paying his players about half the going rate. Even when athletes on other teams began mocking the Cowboy players for accepting such low wages, the players would inevitably end up signing and swallowing hard. Schramm knew he could afford to do so in part because there wasn't much his beef on the hoof could do about it, and also because the team was successful. Amazingly, during all the years of Schramm's penury, the success on the field never was affected by it. If a player didn't like what he was being offered, Tex would tell them he could play "somewhere else." But with the excellent chances of going to the Super Bowl almost every year, few wanted to miss being part of that.

Then in 1974 the World Football League was organized, and suddenly there *was* a somewhere else, and for the first time, if Tex wanted to keep his players in Dallas, he would have to pay them the going rate. The Cowboys' first-round draft choice, Ed Jones of Tennessee State College, signed for a reported $400,000 salary for three years, as much as double what he would have gotten had the Detroit Wheels not also been vying for his services.

The same day Jones signed with the Cowboys, the Houston Texans of the WFL proclaimed the league's long-range strategy when it was announced that Craig Morton had signed to play with the Texans starting the following year, in 1975. Morton was said to be getting $300,000 for three years. Calvin Hill revealed he had signed a future contract with the Hawaii team of the WFL, then Mike Montgomery said he had signed a contract with Birmingham to join that team in '75.

Said Montgomery, "They'll certainly have to take a look at the organization to see why folks are leaving them. Maybe this will help them to get a more human-type relationship into the organization."

The next day Tex Schramm retaliated. He got a restraining order from a district court judge to stop the WFL from negotiating with players whose contracts had not expired. Morton, Hill, and Montgomery, moreover, were enjoined from trying to sign other Cowboy players for the new league. The ruling on its face seemed illogical and wrongly decided, but such was Schramm's power in Dallas. On appeal Judge Harold Bateman of the Texas Court of Appeals reversed the decision. As a result, third-round draft choice Danny White, the talented quarterback from Arizona State, signed with the Toronto Northmen. White said his offer was double what Schramm wanted to pay him. White was the first draft pick lost by the Cowboys since E. J. Holub signed with the AFL in 1961.

Schramm, hearing threats from Lee Roy Jordan that he would listen to offers from the WFL, signed Jordan and gave his quarterback, Roger Staubach, a multiyear contract extension. Staubach was never a hard bargainer, which made his teammates upset with him, because Schramm would always say to them, "How can I give you that when Roger only makes this?"

LEE ROY JORDAN: "Roger was making pretty big money in the off-season, so they'd get Roger signed quick, and get him to sign low. After football, after we retired, I told him, 'You're the reason no one else could ever get a raise, 'cause they based all the salaries off yours. We had to be X number of percentage points close to you.' I told Roger, 'You're making $200,000 in the off-season, and I'm making $200. There's a lot of difference in that.' He was embarrassed.

"But it is true. It's *very* true. I think that was just like the deal with Tom and his salary. They kept that down so they could put up to the players, 'Tom is only making $50,000. How could you make more?' I don't know what kind of bonus he'd make, and I know he owned some stock, and that was appreciating very nicely. That was the leverage they had on us, and most of us weren't making enough to split with an agent or an attorney, so we didn't have anybody else involved. And if you brought an attorney, then you *really* got on Tex's bad side."

ROGER STAUBACH: "The one problem I had with some of the players was that I did my own contracts, and they felt I was setting the team's salary level because I was the quarterback. I didn't think of it that way, and looking back on it, I wish I would have done it differently. I didn't think I was affecting somebody else, that there was this food chain.

"But I've never particularly wanted someone trying to represent me, trying to fight for money. I'm the same way today. I have a fee, and that's the fee. I don't negotiate. I had a price, and that was my price.

"I have never been greedy per se, but financially I was in the real estate business, and at the time I was making more money in real estate than I was in football. And I was making money making endorsements. So I was satisfied with my salary. I looked at it all as a total package. I wasn't thinking, 'How was that affecting other players?' Which was a shame. Because I was satisfied. And I thought I was getting a big salary. Looking back, I wish I had done it differently. I would have tried to raise the level for my teammates."

In addition to having to battle the WFL to keep his players, Tex Schramm also had to contend with those players when the NFL Players Association went on strike on July 1 over the issue of free agency. When training camp opened, the veterans refused to report. They wore shirts that proclaimed, "No Freedom, No Football." The College All-Star game had to be canceled.

Four players—Bob Lilly, Lee Roy Jordan, Pat Toomay, and John Fitzgerald—refused to cast a strike vote, and Ralph Neely announced he would not support the strike.

These were men who didn't like Big Government, didn't like unions, didn't like being told what to do or think. Lee Roy Jordan, for one, didn't believe in striking. He didn't think the players who went on strike would ever benefit themselves sufficiently to make up for the money they lost going on strike.

LEE ROY JORDAN: "I thought the free agency deal was not a good plan for us at the time. Maybe it turned out to be great for everybody now, but at the time I felt what we needed more were benefits. Our pension is horrible. The retirement plan they have for NFL players is absolutely horrible. I'm getting mine now, and it was $600 a month, but one of the lawsuits was finalized and they put more money in it, and I'm up to $800 a month, so you can see I'm really knocking them down. And I played fourteen years. Just think of a guy who played five years. He's not going to get a lot. Normally four-point-something years is an average career in the NFL.

"I didn't think they were working to get the retirement plan to what it should be and the medical care after football, preparing guys for a career after football. Those were the things I thought we were so lacking in. Because back then football was not a career that put you in a position to live after football. You had to get prepared to make a living after football, because if you went away with part of your house paid for and a car paid for and a little savings, that was about all you could make out of football. So I felt like the important points were the retirement plan, the medical care after football, those things were very important to me, and I can see a lot more of it now when I see guys having to have knees replaced, hips replaced, and I'll tell you what, even with my own sinus problems, where I got hit in the nose, if I hadn't had my own company and absorbed my expenses and with my own company medical plan, I'd a had a hard time paying for it.

"And I also felt that going on strike never seemed the way to really get anything done, because I don't think anyone ever got back the money they lost from the times they didn't play. I can recall after I had retired and the players were going to have another strike, one of the players was making $31,000 a week, and he called me and asked me what to do, and I said, 'Randy, run through that door if it's locked. Get inside. Don't miss your paycheck. You're not going to make back what it's going to cost you if you miss some paychecks.' That was my attitude. Because what did it get us when we went through that?

"And at the time my difference of opinion with the leadership made some of them pretty angry. Len Hauss was one of the early guys who was for the union up in Washington. He hated my guts because I didn't go along with the deal. I said, 'Hey, Len, that's just the way I am. I don't believe in what you're doing. If you could convince me otherwise, I'd vote for it.' "

In response to the five defectors, some of the black players began to see the strike in racial terms, which only tended to stir up further animosity. Bob Hayes made a veiled threat, saying they would be marked men "looking out of the corner of their eye." Said Hayes, "If they are not going to back us, to hell with them. They can feed them to the fish as far as I'm concerned. I feel this way. If a guy doesn't want to back us, why is he part of it? I just can't see why a guy wouldn't want to be part of something that stands to benefit his family."

MEL RENFRO: "The players who spoke out against them for the most part were the young, strong bucks that were into the power thing—I don't want to say black power—but stand-up-for-your-rights power, and these are rights that will help minority players, and here were some white guys not going along. They were the guys who would speak out. They were the ones who would forge new territory, who would go where others wouldn't go. That was their personality."

Twenty-year-old Jean Fugett was one of the leaders of the strike, and for him it was a crushing experience. Fugett was idealistic and thought the players could win out against the might of the Cowboys' organization if only they could stick together and not give in. What he hadn't anticipated was that Tex Schramm was as tough an opponent as any corporate CEO fighting to keep out a union and that enough of the players were content with the status quo that the strike didn't stand a chance.

By the end of July, there were two types of articles in the local papers, rumors of certain players signing with the WFL, and reports of other players reporting to training camp. In the first wave of camp attendees were the Texans and the guys who needed to have that paycheck coming. Dave Manders and Walt Garrison reported. Said Garrison, "I ran out of rodeos and I figured I might as well report to camp." Golden Richards reported, saying, "Frankly, the Cowboys have given me everything I have, my car, the clothes on my back, everything. And economically, I'm just not prepared to sit this thing out."

RODRIGO BARNES: "The union sold out everybody. Whenever you're going to strike at the beginning of a work week, at the beginning of the season, that's stupid. If you're going to strike, you strike at the end of the season when people have gotten paid. So to my mind, the whole striking was to defeat the players. It wasn't to win. Ed Garvey didn't have any intentions of helping the players. His own thing was to work with the owners. He sold out. That whole thing Ed Garvey did in '74 and '75 was a sellout. That striking at the beginning of the season was a sellout. It was stupid. If you're going to strike, strike at the end of the season, right before the playoffs. So to me, it's real obvious. All of it is obvious to me."

*   *   *

It wasn't long before Schramm began making veiled threats aimed to pierce the vets' feeling of security, as he and Tom Landry pumped up rookies in the papers to make the strikers feel doubtful about their futures, insinuating that if they didn't come back to work soon, they would be replaced. One by one, the players began crossing the picket lines. Roger Staubach reported along with Lee Roy Jordan. Said Jordan, "If they're going to negotiate, they will. My staying out of camp won't affect it." The next day Bob Lilly reported.

Calvin Hill, seeing that the strike was going badly, had harsh words for Tex Schramm. He said, "Duane was run out of town because he was an individual. Supposedly his individuality was bad for the team. Now management is *encouraging* players to be individuals and report to camp. It's hardly consistent. We should all be for the team or should all be individuals."

Hill denied the players were losing the strike. He said, "I think we're right, and if you're supporting something, something you feel is right, you're not losing."

Hill said that once Staubach left the strikers and reported, the practices no longer had organization. "You can't do a lot when the quarterbacks are gone," said Hill.

After Staubach reported to camp, Ed Garvey, the head of the NFLPA, said snidely, "I'd hate to have been at Pearl Harbor with him." The remark finished him with Staubach and some of his teammates.

Staubach bristled, charging that Garvey had mixed reasonable player demands with foolish ones. He accused Garvey of arrogance. "He immediately made the owners mad, which doesn't seem like a good way to me to begin negotiations." Concluded Staubach, "It makes more sense to me if a person stands up for what he believes is right rather than go along with a man who had no more common sense than to make an analogy like that one about Pearl Harbor. I just think this man has done a lot of harm." Bob Lilly called Garvey the "Jimmy Hoffa" of the players' association.

John Niland reported, citing Bible passages including Ephesians 6: 5–9; Colossians 3: 22–25; and Timothy 6: 1–2.

"I am trying to follow God's word by the law and be a servant to my master, but through my love of Christ and wanting to serve God I've decided to report," said Niland. Niland said that because he was a Christian, he was reporting. He said that if he hadn't been a Christian, he would have stayed out, because "my own personal will is one of siding with the players on some of the issues."

Charlie Waters reported August 7, and then the first of the black players, Rodney Wallace and Benny Barnes, came to camp. Then the flood: Drew Pearson reported.

DREW PEARSON: "I supported the strike, but I didn't want to. I supported it because it was the union, and I thought it was the right thing to do. But I certainly couldn't afford to go on strike. After making $14,500 my first year, and my wife was pregnant, getting ready to have a baby in July. And here I am. . . . I needed to go to training camp. I needed that check. My money had run out, even though I worked in the off-season and made some extra money. But I stuck with the team, the majority of the players, and supported their cause. But I didn't know what the hell was going on."

Then Mel Renfro reported, shocking his teammates.

MEL RENFRO: "I was very low-key and benevolent, and I was under the feeling that we would agree to disagree. But these guys didn't want to do it. These other guys did want to do it. These guys don't like that these guys don't want to do it, so what? Let's go find a place to drink beer and go have a good time.

"Once the season began, I didn't think there was any bad blood. Once we hit the field, we put the strike behind us. That's the way I felt."

By August 12, the NFLPA had lost, but to save face it announced a cooling-off period and said the strikers could go and report to camp. In the end there were ten veterans manning the picket lines: Jean Fugett, Calvin Hill, Bob Hayes, Billy Gregory, Otto Stowe, Jethro Pugh, Rayfield Wright, Rodrigo Barnes, and also Blaine Nye and D. D. Lewis.

When eight of the last ten reported, Tom Landry commented, "They'll be treated like everybody else until they prove to me they don't deserve to be treated like everybody else."

With the strike over, Landry extended the training camp two weeks and worked his players like Trojans. Every morning at practice, the players had to run a nearly two-mile course, over rough terrain that the players called the "Ho Chi Minh Trail."

In late August the Cowboys put Otto Stowe on waivers, hoping to trade him. End coach Mike Ditka accused Stowe of "not applying himself."

Said Rayfield Wright, "I hated to see that man go. He could have helped us win the Super Bowl." Cliff Harris and Mel Renfro called Stowe the "best receiver on the team." Said Renfro, "It doesn't surprise me the way things are going. Otto's the best, but Tom has his opinion about what was happening, and he's the boss."

In response, Stowe went to bat for Calvin Hill, accusing the Cowboys of maligning Hill for political reasons and ignoring his accomplishments. "Calvin gained 1,000 yards back-to-back and no other Cowboy has done that," he told the *Dallas Times Herald*. "He signed with the WFL and they said his success was because of the line. He was a good back, but it was the line. Any back could have done the same thing, they said.

"The fact is they've had Duane Thomas, Danny Reeves, and Walt Garrison, good backs who've never gained 1,000 yards. Other players see how they treated Calvin and myself and Mike Montgomery and say, 'Wow, if that could happen to them, then any day it could happen to me.' It's a bad place to be, a bad situation to be in."

DREW PEARSON: "In preseason of '74 the Cowboys pushed Otto Stowe out the door. Otto said his ankle was sore. Landry said he wasn't trying hard enough to get in shape. And Landry and them were listening to doctors as opposed to listening to the player himself. Coach Landry didn't look at Otto Stowe for Otto Stowe. Otto was not the kind of player to slough off. When Otto Stowe says his ankle isn't right, you should take heed to that and say, 'If he's saying his stuff isn't right, it must not be right.'

"And another thing they didn't take into account, Thousand Oaks, California, is a good place to train, 'cause of the weather mostly. But the surface out there, because of the weather being dry, was very hard. The field is very hard, harder than AstroTurf. It would go weeks and weeks without rain out there, and that dry air, that field is very hard, and for somebody to come off an injury and try to run on that, especially on a bad ankle, it's going to be pretty tough. They should have had patience and waited, and gave Otto the time, and Otto would have done the things and eventually rehabilitated himself and gotten back there on the field. But that surface was so hard out there, we had a number of players have back problems every training camp. One training camp I was laid up for almost two weeks with a back problem. I never had a back problem in my life, and when I left training camp, I never had one again. I only had it out there, and the only reason I had it is 'cause of that hard surface, that pounding, that never gave. That's another thing they didn't take into account when dealing with Otto. He couldn't run on that hard surface. A tender ankle, man. That's the worst thing you could do was try to run on that hard concrete-type surface out there."

*   *   *

On October 6, the Cowboys traded Stowe to the Denver Broncos for a draft pick. Ten days later, it was reported that Rodrigo Barnes, the outspoken backup middle linebacker, had quit the team. In addition to wanting more money, Barnes complained that he couldn't stand that everyone wasn't treated alike, and that Landry wanted him off the team because he couldn't stand to have a player who spoke up for what he believed in.

After almost a full month went by, on November 11 Barnes was traded to the New England Patriots. He was too radical for whomever he played for, refused to wait his turn to play, and ultimately ruined a promising career long before it should have been over.

The 1974 Cowboy season was marked by tension and division. Quite a few of the players had signed with the WFL, and their teammates accused some of them of not putting out for fear of sustaining an injury that would hamper them in their new league. Some players continued being upset over low salary and others were angered by the failure of the strike to do much. Injuries were the other factor hampering the Cowboys. Roger Staubach was recovering from a foot operation and was slowed down.

Craig Morton finally got fed up and demanded to be traded. The ten-year Cowboy veteran was dealt to the New York Giants for a first-round draft choice in '75 with barely a "thank you." Morton's replacement, Clint Longley from Abilene Christian, had a great arm but lacked discipline. Clint had little interest in learning the keys. All he wanted to do was throw long. He drove Landry crazy.

The disorganization hurt the Cowboys in the early part of the season. After an impressive 24–0 shutout of the Atlanta Falcons, the Cowboys lost four extremely close games in a row to the Eagles, Giants, Vikings, and Cards. Each loss was more incredible than the last. For the Cowboys, it was as though they were in the Twilight Zone. Once past the 1–4 start that doomed their playoff chances the '74 Cowboys finished out the season 7–2 and at the end played as well as any team. All for naught.

ROGER STAUBACH: "Every off-season I'd work out like gangbusters, but after the '73 season I had problems with my ankle. I had an inflammation of the tendon on my Achilles' heel, and it just killed me. I couldn't set up, couldn't run, so I really couldn't work out. It was very frustrating. I tried acupuncture, tried everything, but when I'd go to work out it would bother me. So I finally had my ankle operated on in June. They scraped my Achilles' tendon.

"A typical dumb guard" is Buddy Dial's assessment of John Niland, the Cowboys' first-round pick in 1966. "But number 76 could play a little football." *(courtesy of the Dallas Cowboys)*

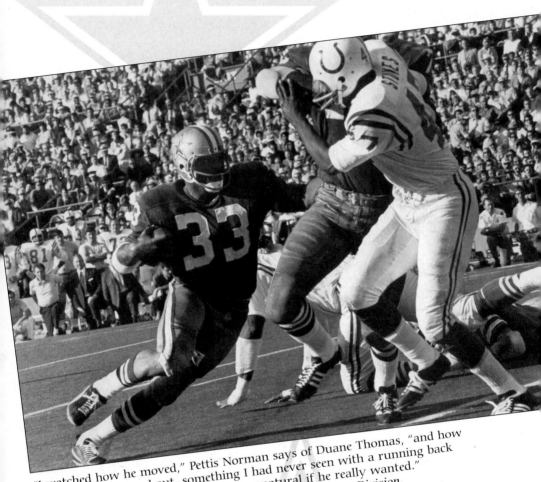

"I watched how he moved," Pettis Norman says of Duane Thomas, "and how he would slide in and out, something I had never seen with a running back before, thinking, this guy could be supernatural if he really wanted." *(from the collection of the Texas/Dallas History and Archive Division, Dallas Public Library)*

"A whole generation of great linemen never got written about because they were playing alongside Bob Lilly," says Lee Roy Jordan; Jethro Pugh comes to mind. *(courtesy of the Dallas Cowboys)*

Randy White was drafted as a linebacker in 1975, "but that wasn't Randy," remembers Drew Pearson. "Too much thinking, too much confinement. He's the kind of guy you need to turn loose and let him wreak havoc." *(courtesy of the Dallas Cowboys)*

Craig Morton never really recovered from a shoulder separation in 1969. "Had he not been injured," Pettis Norman wonders, "had he not had to alter his throwing motion, how good could Craig have been?"
(courtesy of the Dallas Cowboys)

"Chuck Howley is getting old," announced Steve Kiner when he was drafted in 1970, "and I'm here to take his job." Kiner's independent attitude went against the grain and he was traded the following year.
(courtesy of the Dallas Cowboys)

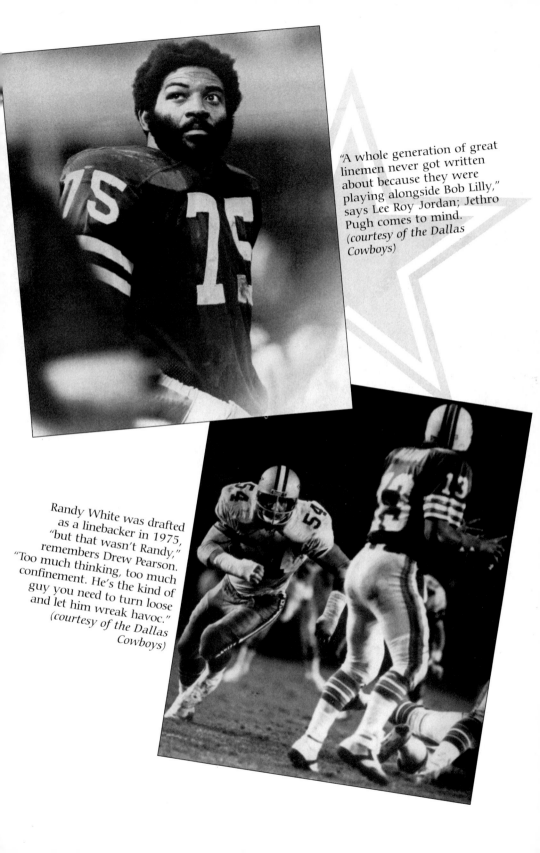

"A whole generation of great linemen never got written about because they were playing alongside Bob Lilly," says Lee Roy Jordan; Jethro Pugh comes to mind. *(courtesy of the Dallas Cowboys)*

Randy White was drafted as a linebacker in 1975, "but that wasn't Randy," remembers Drew Pearson. "Too much thinking, too much confinement. He's the kind of guy you need to turn loose and let him wreak havoc." *(courtesy of the Dallas Cowboys)*

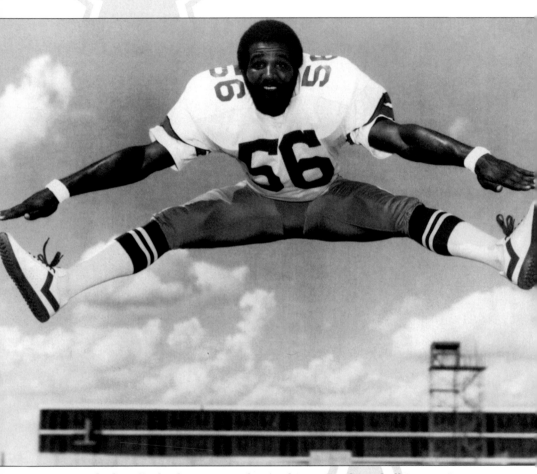

"I was the best linebacker to ever play in the National Football League," says Thomas "Hollywood" Henderson. "Before there was an L.T., there was a T.H." *(courtesy of the Dallas Cowboys)*

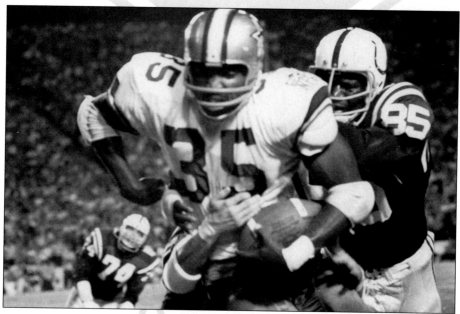

Calvin Hill struggles for yardage. "People don't realize Calvin was 6'4", weighed 235 pounds," says Cornell Green. "He could fall forward for five yards." *(from the collection of the Texas/Dallas History and Archive Division, Dallas Public Library)*

Craig Morton never really recovered from a shoulder separation in 1969. "Had he not been injured," Pettis Norman wonders, "had he not had to alter his throwing motion, how good could Craig have been?" *(courtesy of the Dallas Cowboys)*

"Chuck Howley is getting old," announced Steve Kiner when he was drafted in 1970, "and I'm here to take his job." Kiner's independent attitude went against the grain and he was traded the following year. *(courtesy of the Dallas Cowboys)*

Teammates compared Duane Thomas with Jim Brown. Duane would hit the hole and "he just kept pounding," remembers Steve Kiner. "He didn't look that big, and he didn't look that fast either, but I've never seen a guy take a football and do any more with it than what he did." *(courtesy of the Dallas Cowboys)*

Tom Landry believes his 1975 Cowboys, seen here attempting to block a field goal, were "the best group I've ever had from the standpoint of character, morale, spirit, and teamwork." *(from the collection of the Texas/Dallas History and Archive Division, Dallas Public Library)*

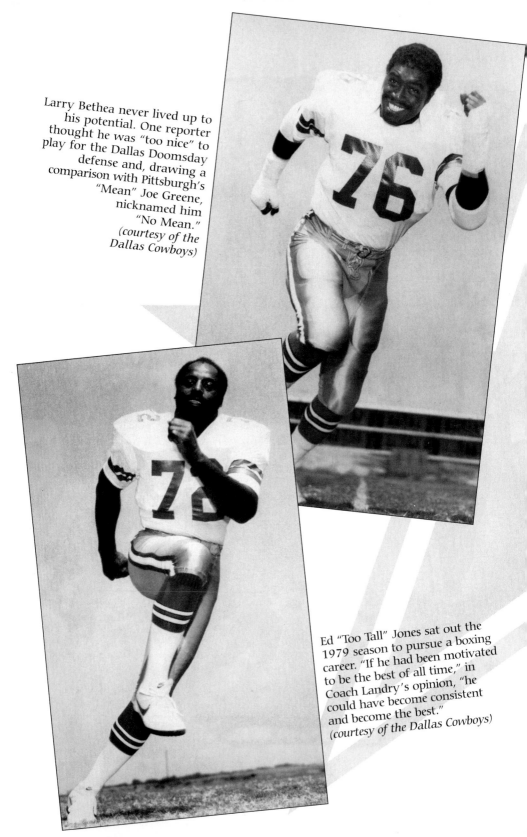

Larry Bethea never lived up to his potential. One reporter thought he was "too nice" to play for the Dallas Doomsday defense and, drawing a comparison with Pittsburgh's "Mean" Joe Greene, nicknamed him "No Mean." *(courtesy of the Dallas Cowboys)*

Ed "Too Tall" Jones sat out the 1979 season to pursue a boxing career. "If he had been motivated to be the best of all time," in Coach Landry's opinion, "he could have become consistent and become the best." *(courtesy of the Dallas Cowboys)*

Backfield mate Walt Garrison considers Roger Staubach "the epitome of what Landry thought a quarterback should be." *(courtesy of the Dallas Cowboys)*

Danny White learned his craft in the shadow of Roger Staubach, and when he stepped into the starting position in 1980, "all he had to do was fit in," says Drew Pearson. "Initially Danny tried to do too much, tried to establish his own identity. He tried to carry the team, and that wasn't necessary." *(courtesy of the Dallas Cowboys)*

Preston Pearson "revolutionized the game" as a third-down specialist, says Drew Pearson. "You run Preston out of the backfield on pass routes, and who's covering him? Linebackers. And he was killing them."
(courtesy of the Dallas Cowboys)

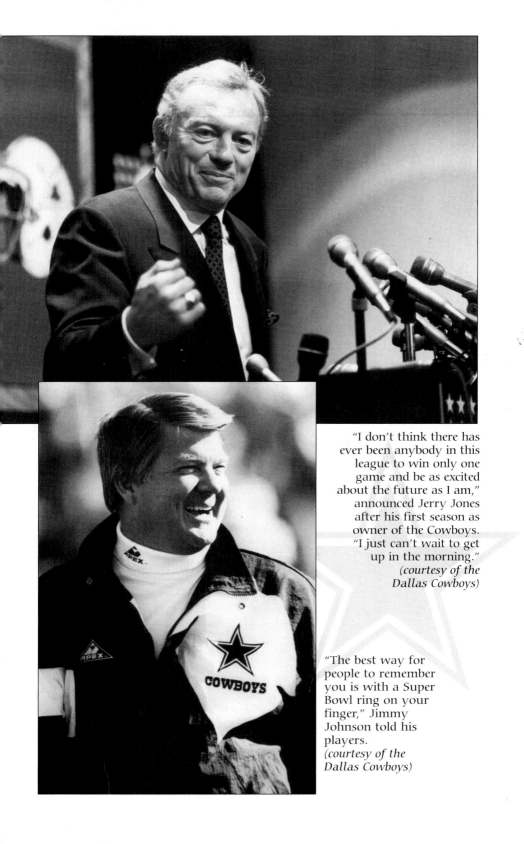

"I don't think there has ever been anybody in this league to win only one game and be as excited about the future as I am," announced Jerry Jones after his first season as owner of the Cowboys. "I just can't wait to get up in the morning."
(courtesy of the Dallas Cowboys)

"The best way for people to remember you is with a Super Bowl ring on your finger," Jimmy Johnson told his players.
(courtesy of the Dallas Cowboys)

"The Cowboys got nothing more than a huge handful of Minnesota smoke," said one columnist after Herschel Walker was traded to the Vikings in 1989. "And who knows if there'll ever be a fire." The fire starters would turn out to include Emmitt Smith, Russell Maryland, and Darren Woodson. (*courtesy of the Dallas Cowboys*)

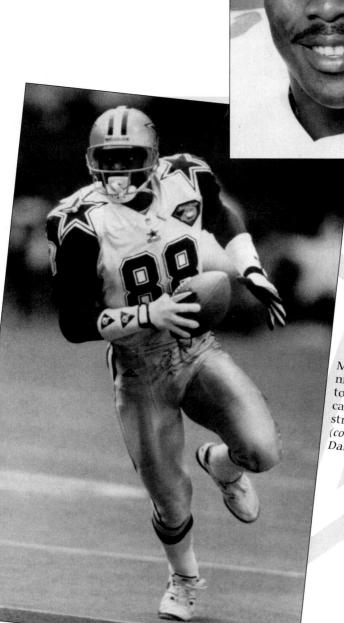

Michael Irvin: "It's a nightmare having to cover me! How can lightning keep striking like this!" (*courtesy of the Dallas Cowboys*)

"Emmitt Smith is like the mailman," says Nate Newton, who opens holes for the running back. "Rain or shine, he always delivers." *(courtesy of the Dallas Cowboys)*

"A quarterback has to win," believes Troy Aikman. "If he doesn't do that, then no matter how well you play or how good you look, the people out there think there's something wrong with you." *(courtesy of the Dallas Cowboys)*

"This could be my last chance in coaching," says Barry Switzer. "I'm going to make it a hell of a run." *(courtesy of the Dallas Cowboys)*

"By the time I got to training camp, I had this open sore that was oozing blood, but my ankle felt good. It was a weird deal. It finally closed, and it was the first time in seven months that I really could run.

"We went into the exhibition season, and I pulled a hamstring, 'cause I really wasn't in shape yet, so I didn't play the exhibition season.

"We opened up against Atlanta, and we had a good game, and then we went into the tank for four straight. The worst streak we ever had. We lost four in a row, and then we were out of it.

"But that streak was unbelievable. We had the Philadelphia Eagles beat. We were up there in Philadelphia. I handed the ball to Doug Dennison across the goal line for the game-winner, and he fumbled. Joe Lavender ran it back 96 yards for a touchdown. If Doug had scored, the game would have been over. In fact, the Eagles were warming up another quarterback to replace Roman Gabriel. So Roman came back into the game and pulled them back. So we ended up losing to the Eagles. I threw an interception at the end of the game.

"Against the Giants we lost 14–6. We couldn't score until right at the end, when I threw a touchdown to Bob Hayes, and then we missed the extra point. I was intercepted three times. I was trapped six times.

"We were playing the Vikings in Texas Stadium, and literally I was miserable against the Vikings, until the fourth quarter, and we came back and had a sensational fourth quarter and went ahead. We were winning. They got the ball at the end of the game, drove down and fumbled, and we should have recovered. The ball bounced near five of our guys, and it bounced back to Chuck Foreman, who had fumbled. It was just a screwed-up deal. So with ten seconds left they kicked a field goal, and their kicker, Fred Cox, booted it and then put his head down, because he thought it was wide, but all the fans in the stands were up cheering and screaming, and the refs called it good. Really, everybody thought it had missed. The kicker thought he missed it.

"Then we played St. Louis and we were tied with them. We kicked off, and they ran the kickoff back to about the 30, and with a minute left Jim Bakken kicked a field goal to beat us. So we lost four games, the freakiest four-game stretch, and then after that we played pretty good.

"We had a game on Thanksgiving Day when Clint Longley came in and beat the Redskins in a game we should have lost. By that time we were out of it, but it hurt the Redskins for the home-field advantage. We ended up 8–6.

"We lost to the Raiders the last game of the season when we should have beaten them. We fumbled on the one. The Raiders won on a touchdown pass by George Blanda. Hell. We played a good game, but we lost. We still could have gotten a wild card spot if the Rams had defeated the Redskins in their final game. But it didn't happen."

The Cowboys failed to make the playoffs for the first time since 1966. Experts were predicting that the Cowboys were getting old and would slip into mediocrity.

The experts would be very wrong. Coming were the Glory Days. Soon the Dallas Cowboys would officially become America's Team.

51

So Long, Bob Hayes

I n the spring of 1975, the NFL Players' Association sued the team owners in federal court in an attempt to gain free agency. To succeed, they had to overturn what was known as the Rozelle Rule, an edict from the commissioner that provided that if another team signed a free agent player, Pete Rozelle would decide what the proper compensation should be.

In court, one of the players who risked his career by testifying was Bob Hayes. The Cowboy star agreed to demonstrate just how duplicitous the NFL was in telling players they were free to leave and play for another team while at the same time relying on a rule that effectively killed any chance a player had of doing just that.

Under oath Hayes testified that in 1969 he was making a salary of $23,000, and in 1970 he asked for $75,000 but was turned down by Tex Schramm. He said he played out his option, taking a 10 percent pay cut, with an eye toward signing with another team at the end of the season.

Hayes said Landry told him before the '70 season, "You are important to our game plan." But, he said, once Tom Landry learned he was playing out his option, the coach sought to make him seem much less attractive to other teams by keeping him on the bench much of the season. According to Landry, Hayes was benched because he wasn't blocking like he should.

Even so, the Washington Redskins approached his agent to sign him for the '71 season. But because of the Rozelle Rule, George Allen was afraid that Rozelle would punish him for not abiding by the hands-off-free-agents understanding by forcing the Redskins to give up younger star receiver Charley Taylor as compensation, and Allen decided against it. Similarly, the Miami Dolphins also wanted Hayes but were afraid Rozelle would rule that compensation would be Paul Warfield.

In '71 Hayes was offered a five-year contract for $55,000 a year, plus a yearly $10,000 bonus, and a deferred payment of $60,677. Schramm was giving him his $75,000 a year. In the hearing in '75 Hayes's attorney, Ed Glennon, said that Hayes was still making that same $55,000 salary and $10,000 bonus.

On July 18, 1975, Bob Hayes was traded to the San Francisco 49ers. Two days later Bob Lilly would retire to mounds of press adulation and torrents of words of praise from Tom Landry. But even though Bob Hayes had revolutionized the game with his blazing speed, catching 365 passes for 7,295 yards and 76 touchdowns during his ten-year Cowboy career, he departed virtually unnoticed. He had fought Schramm and Landry for too long, and with his skills on the wane, they were glad to be rid of him. The reporters followed their lead.

With Rodrigo Barnes traded, Calvin Hill ("I was just a number on the Cowboys, someone who was expendable") jumping to Hawaii in the World Football League, and Hayes now gone, the criticism of Tex Schramm and Tom Landry by the black players quieted considerably. Jean Fugett, the last of the outspoken blacks, would be gone in another year. With the Vietnam War over and with the Black Panther movement dead along with many of the Black Panthers, peace returned to America and to the Cowboys. In early August 1974, President Richard Nixon resigned as president, and his successor, Gerald Ford, gave Nixon a full pardon. He said his act would "spare Nixon and the nation additional grief in this American tragedy."

Another American tragedy concerned what happened to Bob Hayes. To this day some of his teammates have not forgiven the Cowboys for the way they treated Hayes. After so many years of outstanding service to the Cowboys, Bob Hayes was summarily cast aside, unappreciated for all that he did for the Cowboys, they say, because he dared speak up, for himself and for the other black players.

And the other thing they cannot forgive: that the Cowboys did not do more when Hayes found himself the target of a very fishy drug bust.

In April of 1978, Hayes was making his way from sports to the business world as vice president of a telemarketing firm called Dycon International. One of the secretaries at Dycon was dating a Braniff Airlines pilot named Dennis Kelly. Through the secretary, Hayes met Kelly.

Kelly, who worked as a part-time undercover officer for the Addison, Texas, police, says the secretary told him that Hayes was selling prescription drugs at Dycon. He said he became friends with Hayes for the purpose of busting him. It took Kelly three months to succeed.

First Kelly had to get close to Hayes. It was easy. Bob Hayes was the sort of person who loved to make friends and admirers. Always generous, teammates said he would do anything for them. It was this compelling need to be liked by everybody that sealed Hayes's fate.

Hayes and Kelly were friendly enough that they regularly ate lunch together and talked on the phone. To earn his trust, Kelly initiated talks about a deal in which his friend would make Hayes a partner in a restaurant in exchange for the use of his name.

Once the friendship deepened, says Hayes, Kelly asked if he could buy a couple of Quaaludes. Two other times he asked to buy a gram of cocaine. Hayes was faced with the quandary that every person faces who is asked by a friend to get him illegal drugs. If you say no, you're not being a real friend. If you say yes and your friend turns out to be a narc, you face going to jail. It becomes a question of faith and trust. Hayes, who bristled at bigotry, was not himself a bigot. Maybe Hayes would have been better off if he had himself been prejudiced and not trusted Kelly simply because of the long history of hatred of blacks in America by the Irish. But that wasn't Bob Hayes. Hayes could not imagine that his friend was an agent of the government asking him to do favors for the express purpose of putting him behind bars. (Who could? This sort of subterfuge is the closest thing we have in America to the Stalinist form of spying, where the Russian government used to get friends of "subversives" to get their friends to make damaging statements, rat them out, and then the police would go and arrest them.)

Hayes got Kelly both the Quaaludes and the coke from a neighbor by the name of Ben Kimmell, who was given a probated sentence. Sure, Hayes knew the drugs were illegal, but his friend was asking him a favor, and a lot of people in the nightclub circuit were doing drugs at the time, and Hayes was the sort of guy who would go out on a limb for a friend. Hayes took Kelly's money and paid Kimmell for the drugs. (Hayes has an affidavit from Kimmell swearing that Hayes was not a participant in the transactions in question, and that Kelly told Kimmell, "We don't care about you. We want Bob Hayes.")

Kelly then asked Hayes if he could get him a pound of coke and a pound of heroin. This is the point where Bob Hayes should have said to Kelly, "I wouldn't do that for my mother."

Hayes had a serious problem here. He wanted to do this for his friend, but, says a friend who was around when it happened, Hayes didn't have the connections to get that much dope. When Bob Hayes started asking around, the whispering began. Dealers who could have come up with it were told that Hayes was not reliable enough to make a deal with, that he was too much of a rube. They were told, "Stay away from Hayes. He doesn't know what he's doing."

Hayes, persistent, told Kelly he had a friend whom he thought might be able to fill Kelly's order. Hayes—who was *never* a dealer and used cocaine in only small amounts—told Kelly to call the friend. Kelly did. Nothing came of it. A second meeting was scheduled, but this time Hayes backed out.

At three the next morning Hayes was arrested on charges of selling cocaine and Quaaludes. Dennis Kelly was knocking on the door of his Stone Canyon home in North Dallas, leading the arrest team. According to Hayes, he was naked when his "good friend" Kelly walked in and screamed at him, "You fucking nigger, where's that coke?" Kelly, indeed, had been a narc all along.

After Hayes was arrested, his lawyer figured a black client involved with drugs had zero chance of getting off in the all-white Dallas suburb, and so rather than mount a defense, he advised Hayes to plead guilty and then throw himself on the mercy of the court. Unfortunately for Hayes, it was to be a court with very little mercy.

Hayes's lawyer brought in a string of famous character witnesses including Tom Landry, Drew Pearson, Roger Staubach, and Pettis Norman from the Cowboys and a couple of Olympic teammates. All pleaded for the judge to sentence Hayes to probation. Hayes was sentenced to two five-year sentences for two cocaine sales, and to seven years' probation for "selling" the Quaaludes.

Months following his release from prison in February of 1980, the Texas Court of Criminal Appeals reversed his two cocaine convictions, citing improper wording in the indictments. To this day Hayes contends that he has never sold drugs in his entire life, and that the only reason he went to jail was that Dennis Kelly did to him what he could have done just as easily to any other human being in his position.

Dennis Kelly disputes much of what Hayes has to say, but he cannot dispute one naked fact: Hayes would not have found himself behind bars if Kelly hadn't befriended him for the purpose of destroying him.

Robbed of his dignity, Bob Hayes will never be the same man again. The drug convictions ruined all chances Bob Hayes had of surviving in business. He couldn't get loans. Clint Murchison offered him a job in the real estate business, but he could not get a realtor's license because of his record. Roger Staubach hired him to manage some of his properties, but that arrangement ended. Hayes turned to alcoholism, and finally, in the spring of 1985, he entered an alcohol rehabilitation clinic.

He started drinking and doing drugs again. Staubach caught him. Hayes entered another program. Staubach paid for it.

Hayes has returned to his hometown, Jacksonville, where he lives with his relatives.

Bob Hayes's outstanding football career with the Dallas Cowboys has earned him his rightful entry into both the Hall of Fall and the Cowboys' Ring of Honor. He should be elected into both, now.

What saddens Bob Hayes is that he cannot go to each and every Dallas Cowboy fan and tell them, "You have to believe me, I am not a drug dealer." Though he was not wholly innocent, he was not a drug dealer. He was a guy trying too hard to please who became a patsy.

PETE GENT: "Ten years ago I was flying on a Braniff flight, before they went bankrupt. Braniff had been our charter plane when I was playing. I was up in first class, and the guy sitting next to me was a Braniff pilot deadheading back, and he looked familiar. We both finally realized he was the guy who used to fly our charters years back. We got to talking, and the subject came around to Bob Hayes, and I said, 'God, wasn't that tragic.'

"He said, 'Listen, I was involved in that. My co-pilot, Dennis Kelly, was an auxiliary cop in Addison, Texas. His girlfriend worked for the company where Bobby Hayes was working, and Bob thought they were friends. They'd go out drinking all the time, go out for dinner.'

" 'Kelly kept asking Hayes to get him some cocaine, and Bob said, "Cocaine? I don't do cocaine. Forget it." '

"I know Bob didn't do much dope, because we had those conversations. Bob was a boozer. And Bob was the kind of guy who would slough anything off, even stuff he didn't mind doing. But finally the guy nailed him down, and Bob said, 'All right.' And at that time there were a lot of black clubs in South Dallas near the Cotton Bowl. I went to a couple of them with Willie Townes, and there was cocaine around. What Bob did was drive down there, park in the parking lot, go in, and come out with a tinfoil-wrapped gram of cocaine.

"Now the guy got Bob to go back to his apartment and sit in front of a one-way mirror, while the guy wrote Bob a check for the cocaine. And God knows what that really was in the tinfoil wrapper. And Bob took the check, and the guy says, 'Now, can you get me $50,000 worth?' And Bob laughed.

"Bob said, 'I can't get you anything,' and the next morning the guy put him under arrest.

"Bob was no longer playing football. Nobody would help him, except for Roger Staubach. He quickly ran out and got Racehorse Haynes's partner, Phil Burleson. Hayes felt that since he was out of football and no longer had money, Burleson just treated his case like it was another cocaine deal and plea-bargained him out.

"So instead of a defense of entrapment, what Bob ended up with was Landry going down, Staubach going down, several of the players going down and speaking as character references. That was his defense. He was no longer playing for them. He'd gone to San Francisco to play for Dick Nolan for a while. And that was it. That was separate from the Cowboys altogether. That was one of those where once you're out of the game, life kills you."

52

Two Number Ones

After a disappointing 8–6 season in '74, followed by the defection of star running back Calvin Hill to the World Football League, the Cowboys' future looked ever bleaker when in mid-June veteran back Walt Garrison suffered a career-ending leg injury in a rodeo competition in Bozeman, Montana. The thirty-year-old Garrison was competing for the National Intercollegiate Rodeo Association steer wrestling championship when he dropped from his galloping horse onto the steer.

He landed too far forward, and as a result put too much weight on the animal's head, and both rolled onto the arena floor. Garrison did not get up. He underwent an operation to repair a ligament in his left knee. He had been bulldogging since he was twelve, and it was the first time he'd ever gotten hurt doing it.

When contacted, Garrison told reporter Bob St. John, "I'm not going to kill myself. You know, it's a long time till the end of the world."

If there was any good news for the Cowboys, it was that the WFL looked to be folding, as Tex Schramm had predicted all along. Schramm had said that the league didn't have enough millionaire owners, and he bitched that their salary structure was too high. As a result of the WFL's weakness, the NFL could breathe a sigh of relief when in May of 1975, sixty-five NFL players, including Joe Namath, became free agents. Those players knew that because of the Rozelle Rule, no other team would sign them. But with the rumblings that the WFL was on shaky financial footing, few left the NFL. Several Cowboys, including D. D. Lewis and Pat Toomay, had been considering the WFL but were at a crossroad when the new league threatened bankruptcy.

Lewis had signed to play with the Memphis Grizzlies in '75 and Toomay with Birmingham, but when Birmingham announced it was broke, Toomay refused to report.

The day before Lewis was to report to the Memphis Grizzlies, he was paid $5,000 by the Grizzlies to get out of the contract. Had he reported the next day, the Memphis team would have been obligated to pay him another $40,000, the second half of their signing bonus. Said Lewis, "They didn't want to pay my salary. They also wanted to trade me to Philadelphia, but I had a no-trade clause. I didn't want to go."

The Cowboys were delighted.

The joy over retaining D. D. Lewis was short-lived when three outstanding veterans—center Dave Manders, defensive back Cornell Green, and Hall of Fame lineman Bob Lilly—announced they were retiring. The praise for Lilly came in volumes.

Said Tom Landry, "Bob was the best lineman I ever saw. He combined great strength with quickness. It was kind of uncanny the things he did. Two or three men blocking him every play, and he still goes in and traps the passer."

Said Roger Staubach, "He's the only player I ever remember who, when we'd watch our defensive films, other guys would oooh and aaah and talk about what he did."

If the Cowboys were going to improve, they would have to depend on their draft choices. Tex Schramm had once again displayed his brilliance in his trade of quarterback Craig Morton to the New York Giants. The Giants had been slogging along under Norm Snead and wanted better, and they desired Morton, and so Schramm was able to extract from Giant owner Wellington Mara their first pick in the '75 draft. Morton's problem with the Giants was that the New York line was a sieve, and so the immobile Morton spent much of his time on his back as the Giants finished at the bottom of the NFL, along with the Baltimore Colts, a team crashing under the yoke of one of the new breed of pro sport owner-tyrants, Bob Irsay.

Baltimore and New York flipped a coin to see who would get the first pick, and Baltimore won. Baltimore then traded its pick to the Atlanta Fal-

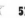

cons so that the Falcons could draft quarterback Steve Bartkowski from California. Because of the Morton deal, the Cowboys had the next pick, and they selected the best defensive player in the draft, Randy White of the University of Maryland. White was large and mobile and was one of the strongest men in the world. He could bench press 475 pounds. He was so strong, his nickname was Manster—half man, half monster. In games he was known for his great intensity, charging hard from the first play to the last, close game or not. The only question was whether White would be better at linebacker, which was Tom Landry's inclination, or at down lineman, which was what line coach Ernie Stautner wanted. Either way, White looked like a solid addition to the Cowboy defense.

LEE ROY JORDAN: "I liked Randy right off. I thought he was going to be a great middle linebacker because you knew he was going to be a great something. He had all the tools and attitude, the work ethic, and toughness, he had all of it. But he had been playing down lineman, and he just couldn't quite get used to the steps from a standing position and that frustrated him, because he wasn't able to compete and play. He played on all the kicking teams, and he probably didn't think he was going to take my job the first year. He thought it would take a year or two, but he was frustrated that he couldn't play more than just the kicking teams and on some special defenses we had put together that had him as a standup linebacker."

In addition to Randy White, the Cowboys still had their own first-round draft choice, and they used it to pick a small-college defensive standout, a tall, powerful, extremely quick linebacker by the name of Thomas Henderson from Langston University, thirty-five miles north of Oklahoma City.

Before he was drafted, few had even heard of Thomas Henderson, but when Henderson reported in July, he grandly announced he was after D. D. Lewis's job. Trumpeted the rookie, "I'll tell you, I'm going to make him that much better a player . . . that is, if he sticks. All I can say is I'm after that job and may the best man win."

Henderson made it clear he would not be like the usual rookie. He was his own man, and he would bow down to no man, not even Tom Landry. Henderson had had to grow up quickly. At twelve he saw his mother gun down and seriously wound his stepfather with a .22 rifle. He saw his best friend die after an accidental shooting. A survivor, he decided to get out of Austin before he, too, was dead. Over his mother's objections, he moved to Oklahoma City to live with his mother's estranged stepmom, found a job, became a high school football star, and even after none of the big universities recruited him, he persevered, walking on at the local all-black college, Langston University, where he became an All-America. He was named NAIA All-America his junior year along with Ed "Too Tall" Jones and Walter Payton.

He had made it. On his own.

THOMAS HENDERSON: "When I was growing up in Austin, all the guys I grew up with are dead or in the penitentiary. One buddy of mine was a year or two older than me. He just always got caught stealing, and he kept going to jail. My experience with him was I never wanted to go with him, and he always ended up in jail. James Sauls was my best friend, and I did run with him. We were little breaking-and-entering guys, and we stole bicycles, and the more we looked forward to stealing, the bigger the items became, including firearms. James and another friend of mine were playing with a .357 Magnum he had found in one of the houses he had robbed, and he was in the school parking lot showing it to a friend who had never held a gun before, and James was accidentally shot in the chest and died instantly. And that changed me. That got my attention.

"It traumatized me. It had always been fun when we were shooting guns, playing, and fighting. One of us would get stabbed or cut every now and then in these little fights. Now they call them gangs. Back then, we were just little friends. But when my friend died it came too close to reality. No one had ever died. I decided to leave Austin and live with my mother's stepmom in Oklahoma City.

"Because of the transfer, they wouldn't let me play junior year, but I was basically into acceptance. 'I can't play this time? Okay.' It was acceptance with hope. 'I can play next year, okay?' And of course, coming out of Austin, I was just glad to be in school talking to a coach. The alternative was the penitentiary in Texas.

"In high school I always found myself running around with older guys, guys with cars, and I always pitched myself to be an older guy, because of my street experience in Austin. And so, yes, I was smoking pot in '69, and I smoked pot from '69 through '83. But I didn't notice it in high school. It was there, we smoked it, but we weren't smoking at school. We smoked in the park. We smoked on the weekends, at night.

"High school was the last time I really enjoyed football, where I *wanted* to play. Because high school football was something you did after school. It wasn't primary. It was secondary to everything I did, and of course, in high school there was no classroom associated with football. There was no studying associated with football. It was all single-minded like, 'Okay, here's what we're going to do.' We never went into the shit the Cowboys talked about, 'Here's what they do, and here's what they *may* do, and here's what they have done . . .' In high school the game was a pure experience for me then.

"I was All-State honorable mention, but no college wanted me. Not Oklahoma or Oklahoma State. I was a flash in the pan. I had no history. I didn't get to play junior year. Only played senior year.

"I was about 6' 2", 190 pounds, but again, nobody knew me, no one saw me come along as a sophomore and a junior, so nobody recruited me, not Barry Switzer or Darrell Royal from Texas or the coach at Oklahoma State. I did have a great year, and I was about a C student, which relatively speaking would have been great grades. But *everybody* missed me. As a matter of fact, Barry Switzer finally came around to saying, 'Everybody missed you. Not only me, everybody did.' I don't blame any of them. I just didn't have any history.

"My biggest disappointment came after I sent articles from the paper, my All-City stuff, along with a letter to Wichita State University. The whole team had been wiped out by a plane crash. I sent them a letter saying I'd like to play football at their school. I got a letter back turning me down. Now you talk about almost getting you to go and do something else. When a school turns you down that doesn't have a team, you feel a *little* suspicious about your talent. I got one offer from a school in Montana. They sent me something to come up there, but I had visions of football players on skis! In my psyche Montana never did ring up.

"I was determined to go to college. To this day I have no idea why that was something that I did. When I talk to my daughter today or anybody who is in school and struggling and trying to work, I say to them simply, 'I spent four years at Langston University, the toughest four years of my life, but I am so glad I hung it out.' There were always the other things coming at me, great oil jobs in the Gulf of Mexico, an opportunity to go to Saudi Arabia and work in the oil fields, women, drug deals, everything you can fathom, women, marriage proposals. I would say, 'But I have to go to school.' Where did that come from? If I were to tell you intuitively down deep, I have no idea, except I've always been a finisher. If I started something I wanted to finish it. Maybe if I can analyze it, it had to do with my pride. I didn't want to quit school. But again, there was no evidence I had that kind of commitment.

"And so after being turned down at Wichita State, and after no one else called me, I approached the coach at Langston University, and he gave me financial aid. Not a scholarship, but financial aid. The coach, Big Daddy Nivens, said he had been interested in me, but he hadn't contacted me because Langston was this little small, black, rinky school with a rinky-dink football program. At that time the coach had coached high school in the Muskogee School District, so he spent a lot of time recruiting football players from Muskogee. I don't remember any great players from Muskogee. There were some with potential, but they never panned out.

"I didn't get the respect I deserved from the coach at Langston that some of the Muskogee guys got, but well, I'm not sure I wanted his respect. I just wanted to be on the team long enough to be drafted by whoever was going to draft me. It didn't matter who. This man kicked me off the team a couple of times. But I had just enough sense to shut up, be humble, be remorseful, and ask for his forgiveness, because I knew I was wrong. Matter of fact, I knew I was wrong when I left campus. It's just like the law. You can only get convicted when they can prove intent. So whenever I've been wrong in my life, that's what I've done.

"When I was drafted in the first round by the Cowboys, well, Coach Nivens wanted all the credit for it, which was natural and normal. And he should get some credit for it, for putting up with my ass. But he put up with me under conditions of my being a great player. He admitted at a roast for me down in Austin a couple of years ago that he would kick me off the team and tell one of the assistant coaches, 'Go get that boy, now.' Just in case I wanted to leave the school.

"And I can remember the day after they drafted me, there was a picture in the paper of Landry shaking hands with Randy White, the other number one. I saw it, and I understood it, and it pissed me off. I understood he was the first player picked, and it was customary for the owner or the head coach take a photograph with the number one draft choice. But in this year they had *two* number one draft choices, so I felt Landry slighted me. Here again, I didn't feel racism. I felt pissed off. I was pissed off that they had traded Craig Morton to the Giants and gotten that second number one pick. Otherwise, I would have been the guy in the picture. Because I was their eighteenth pick that year. If not for the trade, I'd have been *the* guy. So there were several things happening there, but again, it's important that I didn't think racism. I just thought it was unfortunate. And when Landry picked a bunch of guys—white guys— to go to the college All-Star game, but didn't pick me, I understood that, too. Landry was saying, 'Thomas Henderson comes from a small school. He needs to get all the work he can get here.' As a matter of fact, I thought he was smart to do it, because I was not ready or prepared to become a student of football. I just wanted to play.

"I disliked Landry's football system, because it is for disciplined players, and I was not a disciplined player. Whenever there was a concept that I saw that had restraint and that limited my ability to play the position, I balked at it, wouldn't do it.

"Let me tell you what I would do. I *never* scored more than a 60 percent in his game film evaluations after any one game. See, every week Landry graded his football players on who did the right steps, and who had the right angle on your drop, and were you in position and did you read the play right? I never scored very high, but I finally found a way to appease Landry. I would take the initial steps toward what he wanted me to do, and then I would take off to pursue the angle I wanted to pursue. And I made All-Pro. So there was a way to play Landry's deal and get away.

"I always did it that way. They just didn't like to see me doing it. See, intuitively I picked it up, but see, football to me was the snap of the ball, and then the concert of the dance. In other words, I saw the game real quick at the snap of the ball. I couldn't see the game on computer printouts or little round circles and arrows pointing here and there. You could show me a play, but you couldn't show me how to defend it. Because in football, everybody is not always where they are supposed to be, and in football, for me, it's up to me to make the tackle. It's not up to me to depend on inside pursuit or 'This guy is coming and so you contain it.' No. My deal was, 'I gotta make the play. If I don't make the play, nobody is.' And Landry's system was to play in concert, and so I never played like that. As a matter of fact, Landry paid me the highest compliment. It took him four years. He called me a pro. Because he finally saw that I had taken the good from his system and used it to my advantage.

"By my last season with the Cowboys, I contend that I was the hardest working man in the franchise. I was playing defense, third-down defense, kickoffs, kickoff returns, punts, punt returns, field goal rush, field goal block. I was playing *everywhere* except offense. I remember Gil Brandt said to me one time after I asked him for a $250,000 salary, 'We don't even pay Roger Staubach $250,000.' I said, 'He doesn't work as much as I do.'

"There was one thing I liked about Landry. He taught me something. He said, 'When you keep your shoulders parallel to the line of scrimmage, you're the most powerful thing on the field.' So my little skinny 215-

pound ass had to have every possible trick, and that was one of the great ones. And I used to knock 300-pound tackles and guards on their ass by squaring up to the line of scrimmage and just knocking the shit out of them.

"That was the thing he taught me that helped me. As a matter of fact, Landry would come out sometimes and try to give me instructions on how to play linebacker, and I'd say, 'But you never played linebacker, did you? I know how to do this. Why don't you go and talk to those defensive backs.' And the team would just die laughing.

"The other guys, particularly the older guys, were afraid of Landry. Jethro Pugh, Rayfield Wright, Mel Renfro, some of the older black gentlemen on the Cowboys had experienced racism from a powerless point of view. And that doesn't mean that they weren't great men. But when they saw me being free and expressive, they would get all upset. I would even smoke cigarettes in my locker. Shit, those guys would go smoke in their car.

"I fired up in my locker. Why shouldn't I smoke? I was twenty-two years old. There was no rule. But the older guys wouldn't do it. I did. I smoked on the airplane, everywhere. I took smoke breaks.

"When I first became a Dallas Cowboy, Landry was this dictator, this Castro, this Khrushchev, this Saddam Hussein, this Ayatollah. You know. You didn't talk back. It was religious. It was communism. It was all these things you fear, and people marched around like they were in the Red Army. And I was walking around going, 'What the fuck are you all doing around here? Lighten the fuck up. Fuck him. He's just a fucking coach.'

"It never occurred to me to be afraid of Landry. It never occurred to me to take him as seriously as he thought he was.

"The coach I had the best relationship with my first year was Mike Ditka. He was offensive coach and also special teams coach as well. Ditka liked the way I got things done. To this day Ditka will say, 'Thomas Henderson was a good football player.' Then he'll say, 'He's crazy as hell, but he's a good football player.' Because Ditka and Ernie Stautner and all the coaches who ever coached me, the one thing they will tell you: they never saw me back down. That's a statement. You watch films on a player and he'll get hurt and wince and run or dodge. They *never* saw me back down. I don't have that in me. Ditka was a very, very intense man. All he wanted you to do was do your job and do it right. He would tell me to go down the field and do this or that, and I did it, and he liked the way I got things done. An he never saw me back down.

"The first year I got some help from Dave Edwards too. He taught me how to use my hands. In college I was always escaping people, but in the NFL you had people who were your size and as fast as you, so you had to entertain them some. I don't have huge hands, but I saw that Dave Edwards had great big hands. And I just noticed the way he grabbed on to people and held them, and I asked him to show me how he did that. But I added a twist to it. Dave would grab a guy and match the force. If a guy was trying to block him, Dave would shuffle his feet and go down the line. If it was an end sweep, for instance, the guy would be trying to hook him and contain him so the linebacker could get around him. Dave would shuffle his feet side to side and match the force of the blocker, and at some point he might even throw the blocker. If you're pushing a guy and he's pushing you, and all of a sudden you pull him, well then, he'll shoot to the right and you go make the tackle.

"Well, I decided I didn't want to dance with anybody like that. So I would make the initial contact, and I would make little small jolts, a constant jab. I was pushing and yanking him, but little bitty. I'd have the guy fucked up. He didn't know what I was going to do. I was trying to see how the play was going to develop, and then I would see how I was going to dispose of him. It made to where guys couldn't block me. I was just so quick they never knew what I was doing. No one ever knew what I was doing."

53

The Dirty Dozen

I n addition to first-round picks Randy White and Thomas Henderson in the '75 draft, the Cowboys made other excellent choices, including linebacker Bob Breunig, defensive back Randy Hughes, center Kyle Davis, offensive linemen Herb Scott and Pat Donovan, fullback Scott Laidlaw, and punter Mitch Hoopes, all players who would help the team immediately. Of course, for them timing was everything. Any other year they would have had vets like Bob Lilly, Cornell Green, Pat Toomay, Calvin Hill, Bob Hayes, Walt Garrison, and Dave Manders in front of them. This year, Landry had to put aside his reluctance to play rookies. The Cowboys were depleted, and he needed these rookies badly.

In the exhibition season the Cowboys finished 2–4, giving little reason for optimism, but once the season began, the Cowboy defense gave glimpses of greatness, with Ed "Too Tall" Jones and a young lineman named Harvey Martin anchoring the line alongside the talented but little-noticed Larry Cole and the hulking Jethro Pugh, an outstanding player now free from the long shadow of Bob Lilly. Behind them were linebackers Lee Roy Jordan, D. D. Lewis, Dave Edwards, and Randy White. In the backfield were Mel Renfro, Cliff Harris, Charlie Waters, and Mark Washington. Plus the rookies. Thomas Henderson played on all the special teams. He not only ran back kickoffs, he was on the field when the Cowboys kicked off and punted. Wherever he was, Henderson terrorized the other team. Throughout the training camp, he had seemingly refused to learn Landry's system, but his natural talent was immense.

In the season opener against the Los Angeles Rams, the Cowboy defense held the opposition to a lone touchdown in an 18–7 victory. The Rams, led by quarterback James Harris, could neither run nor pass. This new crew of defenders was, in short, awesome.

Said Too Tall Jones, "I thought if we could win this one, that's it. We can win eleven or twelve if not all of them."

DREW PEARSON: "In the eleven years I played with the Cowboys, '74 had been the only year we didn't make the playoffs. We finished 8–6. Then we lost all those players, so we weren't confident that we could get back to the Super Bowl level in '75, but it was still important for us to strive for that. We needed to get back there, and then we found out later that these rookies they brought in were pretty good, and they could help us.

"During training camp immediately I knew Randy White could play. It was pretty obvious. It was a matter of where they wanted to play Randy. They didn't know where they wanted to stick him. He was supposed to be the man at middle linebacker, but that wasn't Randy. Too much thinking, too much confinement. He's the kind of guy you need to turn loose and let him wreak havoc. And that's what they finally did.

"Thomas Henderson showed all the natural abilities, and when Henderson first came in, he was fine. He was no problem. He wanted to make the team just as bad as any other rookie would, so he was no trouble. And they ended up helping us get back to the Super Bowl that year."

LEE ROY JORDAN: "We had a great draft in 1975 and so we had a lot of young guys, people like Randy White, who we knew were going to be players. When we finally put Randy at defensive tackle, after about a day of watching him there, you knew that's where he was going to be.

"Thomas Henderson was brash. He was loud. Thomas was a very talented athlete. I always liked Thomas, admired him and respected him. But he had some other things that didn't fit too well. He didn't have much of a work ethic. His deal was he always had a slight injury. He didn't need to practice. He was one of those guys who had played on teams where he was so good if he was ready to play on game day, the coach was glad to let him play. But our program has always been one that if you didn't practice all week, or even part of the week, you didn't play on game day. Thomas certainly was talented enough to take anyone's place, but he didn't study, didn't learn what to do very well. He just thought it would be automatic that he would take D.D.'s job or my job or anybody else's job. I was always having to tell him what he would have to do to fit into the program as far as working and studying and learning his responsibilities as far as the secondary, as far as the defensive line.

"Those rookies renewed our enthusiasm after being out of the playoffs. We came back with a real committed attitude. We had a great off-season training program, and like myself, I was committed to 'Hey, I can compete for a few more years, and I want to do the best I can,' and the attitude we had with the young guys, Burton Lawless, those guys, eleven or twelve of them, and Randy Hughes on defense, Rolly Woolsey was a defensive back, so we had a number of good players come out of that draft.

"Tom didn't like to start rookies, but that year we didn't have much choice. We had to use these guys. And I think when you plug Randy White into Bob's position, here's a twenty-three-year-old plugged into where Bob was, and who was very similar in his ability to make big plays. And we had a tremendous pass rush from the middle with Larry Cole and Randy, and we had the great pressure from the weak side from Harvey Martin and Ed Jones, who was a tremendous player on the strong side, because he was always in the face of quarterbacks. He was six-nine, had five-foot arms, and if you didn't put the pressure on the guy, he batted down a lot of passes and was real hard to throw around."

ROGER STAUBACH: "In '75 we started with a team that wasn't supposed to do a whole lot. We played the Rams the opening game of the year, and we made some big plays. Fortunately, I was healthy again at the start of the year, and Drew Pearson was in stride, and our defense fought and scratched, and so all of a sudden we were a team. It was the best year we ever had as a team the whole time I was with the Cowboys.

"We had these young guys, we had old guys, and we'd win games any way we could. In that Rams game, for example, I ran for over 100 yards. But it was a real team effort. The defense played well. We scrambled, and that became the way we played all year long. We fought and scratched and clawed together the whole year. Everybody pitched in, and as the year went on you could see the depth of these guys. 'Cause no one was sure what Randy White was going to do. They moved him around, and then all of a sudden he was at defensive tackle, and it became, 'Geez, this guy is something.' Thomas Henderson, Bob Breunig, Randy Hughes, Scott Laidlaw, as the season went on, these rookies got better and better."

*   *   *

The '75 Cowboys won their first four games. Against the St. Louis Cardinals, Thomas Henderson had suffered a serious hip pointer just before halftime, and he could barely walk when special teams coach Mike Ditka told him the Cowboys were going to open the second half with him running a double reverse on the kickoff.

"I don't know if I can," said Henderson.

"Can you go?" asked Coach Jerry Tubbs.

Said Henderson gritting his teeth, "Yeah, I think I can run that sucker."

The Cards kicked deep to rookie Rolly Woolsey. Henderson faked as though he were blocking, then turned and doubled back. Woolsey had fumbled, confusing things further, and finally picked it up as Henderson ran toward him. At the three-yard line, Woolsey made the transfer and ran to his right. Henderson went left and turned upfield. Ditka had set the blockers perfectly, and the Card defenders fell one after the other. Randy White made the final hit, and Henderson completed his 97-yard run for a touchdown. After he crossed the end zone line, he ran under the goalpost and thrilled the Texas Stadium throng by dunking the ball over it.

Against the Giants, starting running back Charles Young badly sprained a toe, forcing Tom Landry to play veteran Preston Pearson, who had been picked up during training camp from the world champion Pittsburgh Steelers on waivers. Pearson had walked the picket line wearing the "No freedom, No football" slogan, angering Steeler coach Chuck Noll so badly that Pearson was the final cut. Preston Pearson would turn out to be the needed piece of Tom Landry's puzzle to turn this mystery team into surprise champions.

ROGER STAUBACH: "Getting Preston Pearson on waivers from the Steelers was a big deal, a great move. That helped us a tremendous amount. Preston really brought a great ability out of the backfield to catch the football. And we really weren't a backfield-type passing team. Our passing game was oriented more downfield because back then you couldn't hit the receivers downfield, so people were going back deeper, and linebackers were going back in support, so you were dumping the ball off a lot. And Preston brought with him the ability to come out of the backfield and catch passes. Also, we went to the shotgun formation where we could use him. And Preston was the sort of receiver who could adjust well to the defense. He'd turn in when he was supposed to, so he really took a lot of pressure off Drew Pearson."

DREW PEARSON: "See, Landry had it in his mind that he wanted Preston to be a third-down specialist. Football was becoming a game where on third-down situations the other teams were taking away the wide receivers, so to be effective on third downs you had to have good inside receivers. The defenses weren't sophisticated enough to put in what nickel defenses are nowadays. The nickel defense back then meant you had four defensive backs, and you brought in one extra, and that was it. Now you take out damn near all your linebackers, and bring in all these defensive backs to cover third-down situations.

"Landry recognized what Preston could bring. First of all, Preston was a consummate pro. He was a pro all the way. He was intense, not only in practice but in meetings. He was taking notes, writing down every word that came out of Landry's mouth. I played with a lot of players, but I only felt three of the ones I played with would end up being coaches one day, Charlie Waters, Dennis Thurman, and Preston Pearson. Just because of the way they approached the game. They wanted to know everything about the intricacies of the game so they could use that later on as coaches.

"But Preston really revolutionized the game as far as third-down coverages, because when he first joined us and Landry first started using him with effectiveness, it was in third-down situations. You had Drew Pearson, Golden Richards, Billy Joe DuPree, so we had some pretty good weapons there, and so now you bring Preston in as a running back, and run him out of the backfield on pass routes, and who's covering him? Linebackers. And he was killing them. And the thing was, Preston turned out to be better than Landry ever, ever imagined he would be at what he did. Because Preston was the type of guy he was, he took it and he studied it and he made it. He worked on his pass routes, and he invented pass routes from that position. His biggest pass route was the sideline route. He took it another step: sideline turn-in. Faking here and going there. Preston made it happen. He was able to set up a defender and kill him with a pass route.

"Landry, of course, saw this, too, and started making adjustments. Instead of having him run a sideline, he had him run a sideline turn-in, or a sideline post. But Preston was the man who made it all effective. There is no question in my mind, he was *more* than the Cowboys ever expected him to be when they brought him in for that year. Preston, being as smart as he was, with common-sense type smarts, he took advantage of it. He knew that was his niche, and he took advantage of it and took it to its highest level. And now he's regarded as one of the greatest to ever play in third-down situations coming out of the backfield."

*   *   *

After a close loss to the Green Bay Packers, the Cowboys played the Philadelphia Eagles in Veterans Stadium. The Eagles hated the Cowboys and punished them physically on every play. It was an important test that the Cowboys passed, 20–17.

DREW PEARSON: "Everybody had it in for us. And the reason they did was because of our arrogance. Not so much the Cowboy players on the field. We respected our opponent to the utmost, but it was what Tex Schramm was projecting for the Cowboys as a team. They saw Coach Landry nicely dressed, wearing a tie, a hat on the sideline, and their coaches are in a coaching shirt, a little ugly green jacket. It was what we projected. We projected class. When we traveled, we wore ties. You don't think people recognized that? Sure they did. And if they recognized it, they were going to write about it, and they were going to tell about it. 'This team is class. They project the image of their coach. They wear ties on the road. And they do it this way, do it that way,' and a lot of people got tired of hearing that crap. They just got tired of hearing it. And our opponents used that to help psych themselves up, help motivate themselves to want to beat us. And that's why every time we played anybody, I don't care who it was, the worst team or the best team, they played us like it was their Super Bowl.

"We had to be ready for each and every opponent, and thank God, we were. Because we as players knew what we were. They saw Landry's system, coming out with the movement, the Flex defense, Drew Pearson running across the backfield back and forth. 'What is all this crap?' They felt all that stuff was unnecessary and they thought we were trying to finesse our opponents and beat them that way, and so everyone labeled us as a 'finesse' team. And everybody we played always tried to intimidate us physically, and they found out that didn't work, because even though we did those type of things, football is not a finesse game. Basketball might be a finesse game, but football is not. And I don't care what you do to try to make you think to get you out of position with all that movement and adjustments and stuff we did, we were still physical. But we were smart enough to take advantage of our physical qualities and try to make it easy for us."

The Eagles were leading 17–10 when Dallas took over on their own 33 with 3:50 remaining. Roger Staubach hit fullback Robert Newhouse coming out of the backfield for 18 yards, and gained 15 more when Eagles defensive back Bill Bradley slugged him late. The Cowboys were down to the Eagle 31. This was the year Staubach and Drew Pearson were getting to know each other, and with time running out, the two were making up plays as they went along.

"What do you have?" asked Roger.

Pearson ran a curl but then altered the route when he saw Bradley and Cliff Brooks in his path. He cut inside and headed for the goal line, where Staubach hit him between the two furious Eagle defenders. The score was tied.

Dallas got the ball back on its own 40 with 35 seconds left. In that short time, somehow Roger Staubach ran seven plays! The biggest was a second-and-10 from the Eagle 45. With seconds left, Staubach lined up in the shotgun. Landry called a pass to a running back. Staubach changed it. He told Pearson to run a deep sideline route. Staubach let fly, and with Brooks and Randy Logan bumping him, Pearson leaped back for the ball, caught it, and stepped out of bounds. The brilliant reception allowed Toni Fritsch to kick the winning field goal.

Said Landry, "I don't know how he got it, and I don't know how he got out of bounds."

After losses to the Washington Redskins and the Kansas City Chiefs, the Cowboys rebounded with wins against the New England Patriots and the Eagles.

The Cowboys were 7–3. In the locker room before the next game against the Giants, Lee Roy Jordan made a short memorable speech to the rest of the team, reminding them that a lot of vets in the league had never gone to a Super Bowl. Erroneously, he cited Preston Pearson as an example. Pearson, in fact, had been there the year before with the Steelers and had been there once before with the Baltimore Colts. No matter. Lee Roy was making a point, and everyone was listening.

LEE ROY JORDAN: "We'd hold team meetings at times during the year—just the team, not the coaches, and this was an opportunity where I felt I needed to impress on these guys that, 'Hey, a lot of guys were here ten, twelve years before we got an opportunity to go to the Super Bowl, and here are a lot of young guys who might get to go there the first time out of the shoot. And so I tried to impress on them how important it was to play hard every play, and the great thing about it, I was always challenging them. 'Hey, who's going to make the play this time?'

"And what I was trying to do was challenge them again this particular time. 'Many teams and many great players have never been to the

Super Bowl. Here we are with a chance to be in the playoffs, an opportunity that we *can* do it this year.' "

DREW PEARSON: "It was the kind of speech Lee Roy made the year they won their first Super Bowl in '70. That year it had looked like the season was lost, and so the players took it upon themselves to do what they could to salvage it, and the next thing you knew, they salvaged themselves a Super Bowl. So it was pretty much the same thing here. Lee Roy recognized some things within the football team, and he was trying to pull everyone together and get everyone to rally.

"Lee Roy was that type of leader. We all respected him. He'd kick your ass if you didn't respect him. And if you didn't like him, he didn't care. And that's why he got respect. He wasn't trying to win friends or be favorites with certain players. He treated everyone the same, and hey, if you were sloughing off, he didn't care if you were the Pope. He'd let you know it. And not just verbally, sometimes physically. If he'd have to jack you in the corridor, throw you up against a locker, he would. And that's the way football was played back then. We were all for one and one for all, and we all had to be together.

"I had a lot respect for Lee Roy. No question. Even today I see him, and it sometimes sends chills down my spine. I want to make sure I'm looking okay. I check, 'Is my tie all right?' I still don't want this guy to get on me, you know?

"When I came Landry motivated us by that fear to perform for him. If you didn't perform, you were out. He prepared us. He got us so prepared that we knew our opponents so well that it gave us a lot of confidence. But he wasn't the motivator. He couldn't give a pregame pep talk. Lee Roy was that guy. He was that kind of leader. I loved that guy."

The Cowboys won the game 14–3. Staubach hit tight end Jean Fugett with a 54-yard touchdown pass right down the middle of the field. It was third-and-ten, and Staubach called a hook-and-go, a surprise play that angered the Giants into calling it a "Mickey Mouse" play. After the game Giant defensive back Jim Steinke fumed, "That's something you might make up in the street." Little did Steinke realize that he had identified Roger Staubach's greatest asset: his ability to improvise at heroic times.

All the scoring came in the first period, and time after time the Cowboy defense stifled Giant quarterback Craig Morton in his attempt to score against Lee Roy Jordan and his team of tormentors. Morton was sacked four times, and he threw three interceptions on this futile afternoon of work.

LEE ROY JORDAN: "Morton never beat the Cowboys, not ever. We always felt we had the pass rush that could get to Craig, and if we didn't have it out of our front four, we would certainly put it into a blitz package. We were not a high-percentage blitz team, but we always looked for an opportunity to blitz a guy and make sure we got to him. And if that meant an all-out blitz, that's what we would do.

"And we sacked him four times. That was a game where we felt we could do that and certainly create some turnovers by speeding up his delivery of the football, if he got rid of it. And so we had three interceptions as well."

After a loss to the Cardinals, the Cowboys won their last two games, against the Washington Redskins and New York Jets. With the 31–10 win over the Redskins, the Cowboys assured themselves of a playoff spot. Said Tom Landry, "A 9–4 record is beyond my imagination."

In the next and final game, Landry's gang of old vets and young kids made it 10–4 with a 31–21 win against the New York Jets behind the quirky Clint Longley, who played to allow Roger Staubach's various injuries to heal before the playoffs. The Jets went out in front 14–0, but Longley brought them back. With the score tied 14–14, Harvey Martin put a hit on Joe Namath that finished Namath and ended any chances of the Jets winning.

54

Hail Mary

The Cowboys entered the '75 playoffs as the Eastern Conference wild card team behind the St. Louis Cards, who had won the division with an 11–3 record. The opening round opponent was the Minnesota Vikings, the Central Division champions. Led by coach Bud Grant, the Vikings had streaked to a 12–2 record and were clear favorites to beat Dallas. Viking quarterback Fran Tarkenton was rated the number one quarterback in the NFL, and fullback Chuck Foreman was one of the top backs in the league.

DREW PEARSON: "When we got into the playoffs as a wild card, we knew we had a chance then, because at that time, even though we had twelve rookies, by that time most of those rookies were pretty educated as to what was going on in the NFL.

"That first wild card game we played the Vikings, in Minnesota, and they were a pretty good football team. I mean, *nobody* was expecting us to win. We went up there, of course confident we could win, but we also knew that this obstacle in front of us was pretty stout."

The Cowboys led in the third quarter by a field goal, but Tarkenton then led a 70-yard drive, capped by a one-yard plunge by back Brent McClanahan.

The score was 14–10 Vikings with 1:51 left in the game and the Cowboys on their own 15. It appeared the Cowboys were going nowhere. With less than a minute left in the game, they had the ball fourth-and-16 on their own 25.

ROGER STAUBACH: "We were doing just what we could do going into that last series. We were in a shotgun formation, and John Fitzgerald got hurt, he hurt his elbow, and Kyle Davis came in. We were fourth-and-16 from our own 25 because of bad snaps in the shotgun. And Drew had not caught a pass the whole game."

DREW PEARSON: "Yeah, I was very frustrated, very disappointed. Even though this Viking team was better than us, no question, we still had played them tough, even though we didn't play that well on offense—our defense played very well that day to hold them to 14 points. But our offense didn't play well at all, and that's where my frustration came, because when we were not playing well that's when I felt most frustrated, especially if I didn't get to contribute. I was thinking that I could make some plays. I was saying to Roger, saying to Landry on the sideline, to the other coaches, 'Call my name. Call my number. I can make something happen.'

"I wasn't getting the ball mainly because of what the Vikings were doing. I found out through the course of my career that as long as Bud Grant was with the Vikings, their defensive philosophy was to take away the strong receiver, to double-cover him. Their reads were there, and those reads were going to take Roger away from me, make Roger go to a back, a tight end, or Golden on the other side. But that was frustrating me more. Even though they were playing this defense and saying, 'Go somewhere else,' I was saying, 'Let's *not* go somewhere else. Let's beat them at what they're doing.' I felt I could get inside of Nate Wright. I felt I could still beat the double coverage. 'So let's go with something *my* way.' "

LEE ROY JORDAN: "It was amazing to look at that sideline. There were a lot of faces that showed they had about given up, but there were a lot of us who had been in games when we had come back before, and that was something about our team as a defense: we always felt we could get the ball back and we knew if we got it back, Roger, given a chance, could do it. He had done it before. So what we were trying to keep up was the attitude that even though they had made some plays against us and moved the ball on us, we could still win.

"With seconds to go we were a long way from scoring a touchdown, but I knew we still had a chance."

Unlike the veteran Jordan, rookie Thomas Henderson was mentally packing his bags and heading for home.

THOMAS HENDERSON: "During that last series I was sitting on the bench. We were so far away I was packing. I was packing out of my apartment. I was going to go back to Oklahoma City. I was sitting on the bench thinking, 'Give up. It's over. Can't wait to get out of this cold mother-fucker . . .' And so I stood up and walked over to the sideline."

LEE ROY JORDAN: "It was fourth-and-16 or so, and this was, 'Hey, the game is over if we don't do something to get a first down.' I kept reminding the guys, 'Hey, we're behind, but this game is never over till the final second.' Even on the sidelines some of us were still talking the game up. 'Hey, let's hang in there, let's hang in there. We got a chance.'

"Drew then ran an 18-yard sideline, and I mean the ball was on a rope when it got there. Roger threw it so straight, and Drew pulled it down just in time to get both feet inbounds. So it set us up about the 50-yard line."

DREW PEARSON: "We had a long way to go, and I don't know why we should have had confidence, because we hadn't moved the ball very well all day. But when we started that last drive I got excited because Roger was asking me, 'What have you got? What can you get open on?'

"We didn't have time to get plays sent in from the sideline. We didn't have time to confer with people in the press box. We had to go *now*. It had to be feeling, gut-type things. So Roger asked me, 'What can you get open on?' Early in the drive we kept running these turn-ins. I had caught one turn-in, then a sideline pass, and then we got bogged down because John Fitzgerald's arm was hurting and he messed up the snap. John snapped the ball, and Roger fumbled it around, and after he recovered it for a loss, we had a fourth-and-16.

"Roger just asked me. He said, 'What can you get open on?' I said, 'I don't know, but we have to get enough for this first down.' So Roger said, 'Why don't you run a post-corner.' And he said, 'Make sure you run a good post to get Nate Wright to bite on that.' And the last thing he said coming out of the huddle was, 'Make sure you get enough for the first down.'

"I took it downfield running a post, and I could feel Nate on my shoulder, which was right where I wanted him. I gave him that little move like I was shifting to that next gear to go deep on a post, and that gave me what I needed to break outside, and Nate kind of swiveled on his turn, and by that time the ball was in the air. Roger threw this ball. This might have been the best pass of his career. I mean, he drilled this ball, and I ended up catching it going out of bounds for 22 yards, got hit as I was going out of bounds, but I still think I could have gotten my feet in if I didn't get hit. But because I was forced out, it was called a good catch. I was sliding across the ice there, and I later found out that a security guard from the Vikings came across and kicked me.

"But anyway, we got 22 yards on the play, got the first down."

ROGER STAUBACH: "After we hit the fourth-and-16 Drew was tired. We were at the 50, and I said to him, 'Hey, what can you do?' He said, 'I'm too tired right now.' So I called a play and threw the ball to Preston Pearson, and he dropped it, which was good, really. We would have probably gotten off another play, but it would have been different. Anyway, he dropped it. There were 26 seconds left in the game."

DREW PEARSON: "We had no timeouts. If Preston had caught it and they had tackled him and held him down, then we'd have eaten up significant time, valuable time off that clock. And we might not have gotten another play off, and even if we had, it would have been a desperation play."

ROGER STAUBACH: "Drew came back to the huddle, and I said, 'Remember against the Redskins how you made that in-route? Why don't you try that move on Nate Wright and go deep?' And that's what he kinda did. We were trying to get him isolated on one guy [Wright] and let him jump for the ball. I wanted him to make that little in-route and hold that one safety [Paul Krause] there and break back out, and then release [go long] and stay right. I'd try to keep Paul Krause away from running over there. I told everyone to block, to give me some time."

DREW PEARSON: "When Preston dropped the ball, the clock stopped. We got back to the huddle, and Roger said, 'What do you got?' I said, 'I don't know, but we have to go *now*.' He said, 'You know, last year against the Redskins, you ran that turn-in and take off.' I said, 'Yeah.' He said, 'Well, run that.'

"Our bread-and-butter play still was the deep turn, the 16 route, so we figured we could get Nate Wright to bite on that. Roger said, 'I'll pump Paul Krause to hold him in the middle,' so when I came out of my break, I'd be man-to-man with Nate Wright."

ROGER STAUBACH: "What I did, I pumped Krause. Krause was the safety in the middle of the field. If he realized I was looking to throw the ball to Drew, he would have been running across the field, and he would have been there. In fact, if you see the film, he got to the play—late—and started to yell at the referee while Drew ran another five yards. But he got there late, so he wouldn't have affected the pass. But he could have made the tackle. That was a weird deal.

"When I threw it, I actually underthrew it a little bit, because I pumped and then I turned to throw. Drew had taken off down the sideline, and he actually came back and caught the thing underneath his arm."

DREW PEARSON: "When I came out of my break, Nate Wright and I were even. He might have had a step ahead of me on the play, but when I looked back to try to find the ball, I saw it was underthrown, and I was able to do the 'swim' move, to come over the top of Nate Wright, and when I was doing so, the ball was there, and it hit my hands, and I thought I had dropped it, but I was bent over, and the ball slithered through my hands and just stuck between my elbow and my hip, stuck right there, and I was as surprised as anybody that I had caught the football.

"Nate Wright fell on the play, and they said I pushed him. You know, there *was* contact. When I brought my arm around, there *was* contact. And that might have been what knocked him off balance. But there was never, ever any deliberate push or anything of that nature. How can you push somebody and make the catch at the same time? I'm not that good. But anyway, I was able to make the play and take it into the end zone for that touchdown."

ROGER STAUBACH: "Drew says he didn't push Nate, that Nate kind of slipped. There is no angle to show he flagrantly pushed him. And to this day Nate Wright doesn't say Drew pushed or shoved him. Though he *did* slip.

"After I threw the pass I got knocked down. It was an away game, and when I didn't hear any screaming, that was good. And then I saw some objects coming on the field. I thought they were flags, but they were oranges the fans threw on the field. The Super Bowl was in the Orange Bowl that year. I guess that's why they had the oranges there. But the place was just stone silent. It was the eeriest feeling I ever had in a stadium.

"So then all of a sudden I realized, 'God, he scored!'

"It got even eerier when a Vikings fan threw a whiskey bottle and hit the referee in the head.

"Here we were, this unknown bunch of new guys. The Vikings were a *really* good team. They thought that this was going to be their best team. And because the Vikings got beat, the Rams thought they had it made. We were just happy to get out of there. We couldn't believe it. It was like ecstasy."

THOMAS HENDERSON: "I was a rookie, twenty-two years old, and Roger threw this long ball to Drew, and I saw Drew catch it and walk into the end zone, and then I saw the official signal touchdown. Well, I started to run toward Drew at full speed, just full speed. I don't think I ran with that intensity on kickoffs."

LEE ROY JORDAN: "It was an unbelievable reaction and feeling on the sideline when we saw Drew in the end zone and the official with his hands up. If he doesn't catch it, we go home. The season is over. And it would have been a great season at that, for this young team. We had been out of the playoffs the year before. We turned it around, came back, would have been a good season anyway. But not nearly as good as going on to the championship game in L.A."

DREW PEARSON: "People ask me about the emotions of doing that. When it happens, you're just being a football player. You're just reacting. You don't realize what you've done until all the media surrounds your locker. You fly back to Dallas, and bam, there's hordes and hordes of people out at Dallas/Fort Worth Airport, and they can't wait to see you. As a matter of fact, my teammates, man, they made me get off the plane first to distract the crowds so they could go the opposite way. 'All they want to do is see you, Drew, so you go up there.' They made me get off the plane first. Everybody swarmed to me, and here I am, a couple years in the league, but I've never done anything like this. So it was nice. I was riding high. I was on cloud nine, very excited, couldn't sleep that night.

"Man, I stayed up all night that night, replaying that play over and over and over and over again in my head. Just charged up. Eventually my wife fell asleep, and I just couldn't go to sleep. A guy blows a play in the World Series or the Super Bowl, and they say, 'He won't sleep tonight.'

Those guys don't sleep, but the guys who make great plays, they don't sleep either. The things you do good to help you make your team win keeps you up just as when you do something bad. But it's good, because all you do is keep rehashing the play, rehashing the circumstances, rehashing the results of all that.

"I had caught some big passes before then, one in a playoff game in my rookie year against the Rams, the next year against the Redskins, and then this one, but none of the reaction was like this one. This was like, 'God,' unbelievable, and it wasn't only in Dallas or in Texas, it was a national reaction. This was *the* play. This was the play that devastated the Minnesota Vikings, the worst loss they ever suffered in their illustrious history, and this was *the* play that sent them on a downward spiral, the play when people talk about it today, twenty years later, they know exactly what they were doing, where they were, and this was the play where I go to autograph sessions, traveling around the country, everybody wants to talk about it still.

"I think the controversy surrounding the play, whether I pushed Nate Wright or not, because of that controversy, it keeps it alive. There never was a final chapter, because they don't think they should close the book on it because there is still discussion about it, so it's kept alive, and it's been exciting for me to be part of that now. It was exciting then, but even twenty years later, it's still exciting, and even though I made a lot of other significant catches throughout my career, that's the one people remember most, the one they want to talk about the most. Even in business speeches, motivational speeches I give, I refer to that story. I refer to two stories actually, my rookie year when I caught that 83-yarder, and how Roger had confidence to go to a rookie in that situation, and then the Hail Mary, how the odds were against us and how if everybody sticks together, pulls together, you have a chance to overcome those odds, not guaranteeing you will, but at least you have a chance, and that's all you want.

"So those are the things. That play is what people associate Drew Pearson with more than anything. That play labeled me as a 'Clutch' receiver, labeled me as 'Mr. Clutch.'"

55

Super Surprise

I n the first preseason game of the '75 campaign, the Los Angeles Rams had defeated the Cowboys in a rout 35–7. Before the rematch for the National Football Conference title, Lee Roy Jordan told reporters, "I bet nobody thought we'd be back for the championship after that." Few experts had given the surprising Cowboys a chance. And now, with a trip to the Super Bowl in the balance, even fewer thought the Cowboys would succeed.

DREW PEARSON: "We went out there to L.A. to play the Rams in the Coliseum. For championship games you have to go out there two days before, and we had to read in the press how we didn't even have a chance, and how the Rams were so prepared, and 'Get your Super Bowl tickets immediately following the game,' and all this kind of crap. We relished that role of being the underdog and not being taken seriously. Here's a team that comes in as a wild card, twelve rookies, we beat a great Viking team but look how we had to beat 'em. Everyone said, 'They're just lucky to be here.' And we could have easily said this was enough. Nobody expected us even to be in L.A. We could have easily rolled over and let them kick our ass. But man, we were on a mission. We wanted to win that football game, and all the negative talk kind of inspired us to go after them."

* * *

The hometown crowd in the Los Angeles Coliseum had little to cheer about. On defense, the Cowboys were spectacular. They didn't allow a single first down. They held star back Lawrence McCutcheon to ten yards on eleven carries and sacked quarterback Ron Jaworski five times for minus-51 yards, as Too Tall Jones, Harvey Martin, Randy White, and Jethro Pugh led a pass rush that never let up all game long. Linebacker D. D. Lewis starred, making two interceptions, and Lee Roy Jordan, the play caller and motivator, orchestrated the Flex, Tom Landry's much-maligned but very effective defense that held the 12–2 Rams to but a single touchdown.

LEE ROY JORDAN: "Drew's catch against the Vikings propelled us into a great frame of mind. Everyone was really high during practice for the game against the Rams. We had a level of confidence that was just unbelievable, and God, we went to that Ram game high. We believed our defense was really going to do a job on their offense—and we did. And we created some plays too, some turnovers that helped us.

"Once we got in a comfort level against someone who believed in the run, once we forced them to pass and they had problems doing it, then we felt awful strong about our chances of winning and what we could do. And that's the way we felt about L.A. and Jaworski, because we felt that once we stopped the run, then our pass rush guys were going to really have a day on him.

"This was the greatest tribute to Landry and the Flex. It proved that he was one of the truly great coaches. No doubt about it. Dick Nolan took the Flex to San Francisco and they became a very dominant team. They were number one in defense one year right ahead of us. So it was a great concept, a great scheme, and once you've got it down, you could really make it work.

"Our team was just playing so well. We were so confident we could control their offense totally, and we did. They didn't get a first down. It could have been the greatest day the Cowboy defense ever had."

Though he was "only" a special teams player, one of the defensive standouts was rookie Thomas Henderson, who punished the Rams with his mouth *and* his body. The play that really set the Rams off took place on the opening kickoff, when Henderson clobbered the Rams kicker, Tom Dempsey. Few would have noticed had it been any other kicker, but Dempsey was born with a withered arm and a deformed foot. Dempsey played with a prosthesis made of metal for his right foot, and with it he once kicked a 63-yard field goal, the longest in NFL history. Special teams coach Mike Ditka wanted to make sure Dempsey wouldn't be a factor. He enlisted Henderson in his quest.

Dempsey dropped his head to look at the ball and kicked off. Henderson raced down the field and hit Dempsey in the chin with his helmet before he had time to look up. Said Henderson, "He went down like he was dead."

LEE ROY JORDAN: "Thomas didn't have mercy on a lot of people. 'Hey, if you're a player, you're a player, man. No matter whether you have short toes or not.' "

Dempsey's later kickoffs were short, and in the third quarter Dempsey lined up to kick a field goal. Henderson yelled for the Rams to hear, "I'm gonna take Dempsey *out*!" He blocked the kick.

On offense, Roger Staubach threw four touchdown passes, the only time he ever did that. Three went to Preston Pearson, who time after time beat Rams linebackers for big gains. Pearson finished the game with seven catches for 123 yards. The running game was good enough. Fullback Robert Newhouse, who ran for 930 yards during an outstanding season, rushed 16 times for 64 yards. Staubach himself ran the ball for 54 yards, running like an experienced halfback. Toni Fritsch had three field goals. In all, the Cowboys rolled up 37 points.

ROGER STAUBACH: "It was the most perfect football game we ever had as Cowboys. Everything we executed worked. We had the shotgun, used the shovel pass, everything I threw seemed to have eyes. I threw three touchdown passes to Preston and one to Golden Richards. It was just one of those games where everything worked perfectly, and the Rams were shocked. They were a *very* good team. We were *big* underdogs. We beat them 37–7."

DREW PEARSON: "They had called our offense 'rinky-dink,' but we blew them out. We beat the Rams 37–7. We kicked their ass, man. At halftime we felt like we were going to the Super Bowl, and that was a damn good feeling.

"We had a great game plan on offense. I wasn't included very much in it, which I expected, and we expected them to pay a lot of attention to me after that Hail Mary, and that's what opened up Preston, and made him the go-to guy in this game. They disparaged our shotgun, but it eventually was that shotgun that blew them away, 'cause they couldn't cover it. They couldn't cover it all day. And they certainly couldn't cover Preston. They stopped some things. We didn't run very well against them, but we really didn't have to. Roger was on, and Preston was on, and that's what we rode, on into the Super Bowl, and we needed that Super Bowl that year because if we don't get there that year, it might have been quite some time before we even got close again. So that was a big victory for us, to get us into that Super Bowl."

The Cowboys' opponent in Super Bowl X was the Pittsburgh Steelers, a powerful defensive team that was back for its second year in a row. Pittsburgh had defeated Minnesota in Super Bowl IX by the score of 16–6. That the Steelers could hold Fran Tarkenton to six points was a testament to the defense's quickness. "Mean" Joe Greene, Ernie Holmes, Dwight White, and L. C. Greenwood were a formidable front line, and middle linebacker Jack Lambert was a wildman in the mold of Dick Butkus.

Upon the urging of special teams coach Mike Ditka, the Cowboy game plan began with a surprise. Though Thomas Henderson was a linebacker, he could run the 40 in 4.5. Against the Cardinals on a reverse he had run a kickoff back 97 yards for a touchdown, and before the game Ditka explained to the rookie that he was to do it again. For one of the few times in his life, Thomas Henderson had butterflies.

THOMAS HENDERSON: "I think Landry didn't want me to. Landry was very, very concerned that a linebacker was handling the ball. I think Ditka had to live with the decision. Someone told me this: Landry didn't want me handling the ball. He liked the results, but he was always nervous about a linebacker handling the ball. Which is a legitimate concern.

"Let me tell you about how I was feeling before that game. You're talking about a guy who was nine years from witnessing his mother shooting his stepfather with a gun, just six years from his best friend getting shot at close range and dying, just a year out of Langston University. I had played that season in the NFL and had run for a touchdown. But to be in the Super Bowl . . .

"And I'd already wrapped up. I got elbow pads on, and all this extra padding, hand pads, got pads everywhere, because I'm going to be kicking butt on these special teams. And Ditka came over to me after we warmed up and came back in and he said, 'If we win the toss, we're going with the reverse.' And of course, I had to take all that shit off. I had to put stickum on. It scared me to death! It was like, 'Geez, you're going to let me handle the fucking ball the first fucking play of the Super Bowl?' I mean, there were times in my life when I've been afraid. This was the first stagefright I ever had. Because of the pressure. Again, I agreed with Landry at that moment. I'm a linebacker. Jesus Christ, give the fucking ball to somebody else. But, on the other hand, 'Give me the fucking ball. Let's go.' 'Cause I was a running back in high school, in my early days. I knew how to run.

"They kicked it off, and I had to fake my little deal and Preston Pearson took it deep, and I had to go around. I was standing on the 30-yard line, and I had to go back to him at about the ten. He started my way, and I went his way. He gave it to me, and I took it the other way, and a wall set up. When I turned the corner, everything looked pretty good, except the Steelers weren't quite as fooled as the Cardinals had been. At some point, I thought I could have cut back. I figured, 'If I cut back, I don't know. . . . '

"I'll tell you what I did: I ran the play the way it was designed. Not freelance and make something happen. Ditka was like that. He didn't like you to go out there and start doing your own tap dance. 'No ad-libbing, Goddamn it.'

"So I ran the play the way it was designed, which was better for me. And they were very pleased. The only Steeler who could have stopped me was the kicker, Roy Gerela, and I was going to see if Gerela could stop me. I was going to see if I could run over him. If I could run *over* him, I could score."

Henderson couldn't run over him, and the two tumbled out of bounds on the Steeler 43-yard line. When Gerela was untangled from the collision, he had broken ribs that affected his kicking the rest of the game. Henderson's 48-yard run was the longest kickoff return in Super Bowl history, and it gave the Cowboys great field position for the first set of downs. A 29-yard touchdown pass from Roger Staubach to Drew Pearson gave the Cowboys a lead they would be able to hold until the final period.

What Cowboy fans remember about that game was the brutality of the Steelers and the refusal of the referees to curb it. The entire game long the Steeler defenders were holding, punching, and elbowing Drew Pearson and Golden Richards, who finally had to leave the game battered and bruised.

DREW PEARSON: "I think they were surprised 'cause we came down our opening drive, and I scored that touchdown coming across the middle.

That woke them up to let them know they were going to be in a football game for this afternoon.

"Their whole M.O. going into the game was to be physical, be intimidating. Again we had to live down that finesse image, not being a physical football team, and that was pretty much the Steelers' style anyway, so they were pretty much playing the way they normally play. They wanted to be extra physical and not take anything from us, and if it was any kind of talk or arguing, they weren't going to stand for that, they were going to put their hand in your face, and try to intimidate you, and little extra stuff after the play.

"Even though they were being physical, they weren't intimidating us. They broke Golden Richards's ribs. They spit on him throughout the game.

"I'm not saying they didn't intimidate *all* of us, because they did intimidate a couple of our players. I wouldn't call any names, but it was very evident that certain guys just didn't want to go out there."

ROGER STAUBACH: "The Steelers were tough. That was probably the best team we ever played. Their defensive team, I think, was the best defense that's ever played in the NFL. And they intimidated us. They kicked Preston Pearson when he was down, and our team didn't react where they should have.

"I screamed at Jack Lambert, calling him every name in the book when I saw Lambert kick Preston. But we didn't retaliate against him. We let him get away with that, so they won the war of intimidation."

LEE ROY JORDAN: "The referees, I don't know what they were thinking about. They could have thrown Jack Lambert out several times during the game. He was clotheslining, forearming guys. On one play we were rushing the extra point, and he tried to kill two of our guys with a karate chop in the area of the throat and head. And after the plays were over, their guys were spiking our guys on the ground, and nothing was being called. There were a lot of late hits, too.

"The officials were a little intimidated by the defensive team of Pittsburgh and were afraid to call them. If you go back and look at the film closely, you'll see a lot of instances where it certainly was a flagrant deal, like when Lambert one time kicked Preston Pearson in the groin while he was on the ground. I think the Steelers felt like we had a team where the best way to beat us was intimidation, and they did that very well.

"I still don't think they beat us because they intimidated us. I feel like we were very competitive with them. As a young football team we just made some mistakes in the secondary, where we had them in a tough position, and we made mistakes and they made big plays."

Despite the Steelers' rough play, the Cowboys led 10–7 going into the final period. Great players win important games, and after a safety on a blocked punt and two Roy Gerela field goals, the Steelers seemingly put the game away when receiver Lynn Swann made a sensational 64-yard touchdown reception on a pass from Terry Bradshaw. That Swann was even in the game was remarkable. Two weeks before he had suffered a concussion playing against the Oakland Raiders. He suffered from bleeding in the brain, and after the bleeding finally stopped his timing was off in workouts and he was dropping passes. In the days before the game Swann was not sure whether his presence in the lineup was a good idea.

But in the final minutes against the Cowboys, Lynn Swann was the difference. His touchdown with 3:02 remaining gave the Steelers a 21–10 lead. Swann finished with 161 yards on the day, a Super Bowl record.

THOMAS HENDERSON: "Lynn Swann was one of the great receivers off the ground. He loved to jump. Because he was a long jumper in college. And it just seemed like he loved to jump, and Bradshaw *loved* to throw it up for him to go get. And he made some great catches. He had great concentration. That catch he made against Mark Washington [in the second quarter, when he went high in the air to grab the ball away from the defensive back], that was something."

The Steelers held their 21–10 margin with only three minutes left in the game.

DREW PEARSON: "We almost came back to win. We got behind and then we started to open things up. That's what we should have been doing the whole game. 'Cause if you become conservative against that Steeler defense, you're playing right into their hands. But if you play like you're in a frenzy, then you got a chance to beat those guys, because maybe they'll make a mistake somewhere along the line. They were so seasoned and so well schooled in their defense, had such an understanding of the personnel around them on both offense and defense, they very seldom made mistakes, and even if they made one, someone was there to cover up. They had a *great* team. There is no question going into that game, we knew they were the better team, but we felt we were the team of destiny that year, and we felt because of that, it gave us a lot of confidence that we could beat them."

ROGER STAUBACH: "We started on the 20. We had a tight end offense going into that game, which really hurt us, too, because in the second quarter Jean Fugett pulled up lame, and that was a big factor in that game as far as what we were trying to do. The Steelers had a double coverage type deal on Drew and Golden.

"We were trying to figure out a way to get Drew and Golden open. They were a big, physical team. They had big cornerbacks who hit our backs downfield, and if a receiver went inside, the rule was you could hit him as long as the ball wasn't in the air. You could hit him 20 yards downfield. Mel Blount and Glen Edwards were really killing our wide receivers, to the point where they hurt Drew and seriously hurt Golden Richards. His ribs were banged up, so Percy Howard had to come in. And I finished the drive with a 34-yard touchdown to the Bird. That's what we called Percy. It was the only pass Percy ever caught with the Cowboys."

THOMAS HENDERSON: "Percy was a great-looking athlete, 6' 4", 210, just solid muscle. And later in the game there was another pass play to Percy that he almost caught for another touchdown. He could have been the man. He could have been the Super Bowl hero."

ROGER STAUBACH: "After we got the ball back again there were twelve seconds left in the game when I threw Percy a pass that would have won the game—he went down the right side and he was jumping to catch the ball—he was a big basketball player—but he was interfered with in the end zone, but the refs just weren't going to call it. The Steelers didn't have a single penalty called against them in that game. The defensive back just pulled him down by his shoulders. And the ball was right there. He could have had another one, and it would have been one of the most *unbelievable* stories of football. Percy could have had two touchdown passes to win the Super Bowl, the only two passes he ever caught! We came very close, but it wasn't to be.

"And even at the end we had a shot to win it. We played a very good football game against a really very great football team. That Super Bowl was a tough one, but we did have a shot."

DREW PEARSON: "The last play of the game was another Hail Mary to me. Roger threw it up as far as he could, and I ran down the field as fast as I could. I wanted to go up between the three guys who were back there, who eventually converged on the football, and my first thought was to go up and try to outleap them and come away with the football, but if that didn't happen, then I was going to try to make a reaction off the football once it was hit up, try to find it and make the catch. But there wasn't any Hail Mary in that script.

"They were looking for me on that play. They were laying back already for that. Glen Edwards picked that one off."

The Cowboys had lost 21–17 in what was billed as the most exciting Super Bowl game ever.

DREW PEARSON: "Turnovers cost us that football game. It wasn't anything else. Turnovers, and a couple of great catches by that other number 88, Lynn Swann. He was well covered on a couple of plays, and he just made fantastic Super Bowl–type catches, the kind of catches you dream about making in a Super Bowl. So he made them, and that hurt us more than anything. That and the turnovers. But other than that, I thought we played them head up."

Said Tom Landry about this Cowboy team, "This was the best group I've had from the standpoint of character, morale, spirit, and teamwork. They're the type who give you your greatest reward from coaching, who really make it enjoyable."

56

Roger's Ordeal

uarterback Clint Longley thought of himself as an outlaw. Born in Wichita Falls, Texas, on July 28, 1952, Longley was the son of a career IRS executive. After his family moved to a small town in Colorado, he had a desultory high school career because the coach featured a running game, but Longley returned to Texas to attend Abilene Christian College, where he became a small college All-America. His senior year he threw 28 touchdown passes and gained 3,167 yards leading his team to an undefeated season and an NAIA championship.

He became known as the "Mad Bomber" because he loved to throw long. He had talent, but some wondered about his common sense. One time Clint went out into the Abilene brush and with a forked stick captured a bucketful of rattlesnakes. He interrupted a meeting of his coaches when he walked in and dumped them out on the floor. Clint thought it uproarious as the coaches scrambled to tabletops to avoid the snakes.

After Clint joined the Cowboys he continued to see himself as a rebel. He told reporter Bob St. John, "I like the Western movies and things like that. I like guns, the six-shooters. My uncle was Bill Longley. He was an outlaw who ran around with John Wesley Hardin. Only he didn't live very long. They hanged him for stealing a horse. I wouldn't have liked that part."

Longley also pictured himself as an NFL star. During the few times Coach Landry had let him play, he had been electrifying, throwing long touchdown passes in Cowboy victories. But Landry demanded his players be disciplined, that they do things his way and not freelance. Landry wanted team players, not outlaws, and by 1976 the difference between Clint Longley's dreams and reality began to take a toll on his psyche.

At the start of the '76 training camp, Longley announced, "I'm going for number one." But by the end of the 1976 training camp not only wasn't Longley number one, he wasn't sure he was even number two. The Cowboys had signed Danny White, formerly a star at Arizona State and a refugee from the World Football League, and White, like Staubach, was a highly disciplined athlete, the kind favored by Landry. White didn't have as strong an arm as Longley, but he showed he could move the offense. Longley might have been as talented as Danny White, but he became the odd man out, and his resentments built.

DREW PEARSON: "Clint Longley was a very good quarterback, and I think he could have been a very good quarterback in the National Football League if he had done everything right. But he let outside things get in the way of what he was personally trying to accomplish as an NFL quarterback.

"But I would not say Danny White had better skills than Clint Longley.

"Clint's real problems came after the '75 season when we brought in Danny White. Clint was second-string, Roger was first, and Danny was third, so he was feeling it coming from both ends, and here was Landry who was much like Roger and Danny in their beliefs and the things they liked, and Clint out of that group was the renegade, the outcast. And to add fuel to that fire, he made it worse by separating himself from the group and trying to be different. If we were going to do it this way, Clint wanted to do it that way. If we were going to throw everything to the right, Clint wanted to throw everything to the left. He just tried to be different, to show he was smart enough and he could do things his own way. And eventually that rebellious-type attitude got him in trouble.

"You could see the tension between Clint and Roger. Roger tried to get to know Clint and bring him around, but Clint was very much against that, and I think Roger had a problem with that, because I don't think he ever had a teammate who didn't like him. But Clint didn't like him. Clint didn't like Danny. Clint didn't like Coach Landry. He didn't like those guys. That's just the way it was. They were just different from him, and they tried to make him change, and because of that, he didn't like them, and so Clint always was doing things the opposite of what should have been done.

"This one day we were working out in training camp after practice. I must have run a hundred routes all through practice in the two and a half to three hours we were out there. Now we had to run more, so I was a little pissed off anyway, and Clint was pissed off because he had to be out there, and I ran a quick out, five yards and out, and Clint threw it over my head. He did it on purpose.

"I said something to him. 'I'm not going to run any more routes for you if you're not going to throw the ball right.' And Roger said something to him and that ignited it. When I said something back at Clint, Clint said something derogatory toward me, like 'Screw you'—for lack of a better word—'you skinny-leg mother huh huh,' and Roger heard it, and he said, 'What? You're the one who's wrong.' Clint wanted to fight right there, but Roger said, 'I'll fight you down the hill.' And they went down the hill. They walked over there, and we were standing there watching. And the next thing you know, I saw Clint's feet up in the air, and Roger slamming him to the ground. And the fight was over.

"It was so funny, man. Clint's feet were straight up in the air. I don't know what Roger did. He put one of them Vietnam holds on him, that kung fu fighting. Next thing you know, Clint was down and his feet were up in the air.

"Roger came back, but he wasn't going to brag about nothing like that. He was more embarrassed about that than anything. But the media saw it. They jumped all over that, and so the next day in the paper it said 'Roger Staubach Wins Round One.' And Clint Longley didn't think he had lost the fight so he was furious. He was going to get back at Roger.

"The next day when Clint decided to get revenge on Roger, it was a beautiful day, another day in paradise in Thousand Oaks. Another day you regretted having to go to practice because it was so beautiful. We were preparing for the afternoon practice, and everything was going as normal. What was abnormal was finding Clint sitting in the locker room. The quarterbacks and kickers and punters are usually the first ones to hit the practice field, so it was unusual for Clint to be there. That was a very unusual day, a very eerie situation because Clint was there, sitting in the locker room, waiting. He had his pants on, no socks, a little half T-shirt, and he was sitting there kind of bent over, his foot on the brace of the chair flicking up and down nervously, and he was supposed to be out on the field. That was kind of strange to see him just sitting there and not really talking to anybody, just staring straight ahead. I came by and said, 'Clint, you need to go out there.' He didn't say anything, didn't respond.

"Roger wasn't there yet, because he had an engagement in town, but we did not notice that as anything unusual because since we didn't see him, we thought he was already out on the practice field. When Roger arrived, he was late getting to practice, so he was rushing and hurrying, and he had put on his pants real fast, and he started to put his shoulder pads on, and I didn't see him because I had gone to the back part of the locker room, but I heard the rumbling, the tremendous commotion, and then I ran in to see what was happening, and I saw Roger and Clint really going at it on the concrete floor of the locker room, and there was blood all around, and I found out later the blood was the result of Clint's initial attack on Roger. When Roger got his pads over his head, he couldn't use his arms, and that's when Clint decked him. Roger was caught off-balance and went flying back onto the scale that was there for us to weigh in and weigh out before and after each practice, and he was falling backward, and he turned, and as he turned, his head hit the scale, and blood went gushing everywhere. These two guys were grappling in the middle of the locker room floor, and the space was limited.

"Everybody was trying to separate them and nobody could. They were grappling on the floor, and blood was just flying everywhere. It was a gusher coming out of Roger's head. Randy White went in there, and he was the one who separated them. He grabbed one and grabbed the other and pulled them apart. Roger was still very upset and was really trying to get back at Clint, and once Randy let Clint go, he grabbed his stuff out of his locker, and was gone.

"Clint took off to the dorm, because apparently this was all premeditated, and he knew what the consequences were going to be, and he was packed up ready to go. I went outside to watch Clint, to make sure of what he was up to, make sure he didn't go get a gun, make sure he really was gone. Because in training camp Clint had guns. From his dorm window he used to shoot at rabbits and anything else that came near the dorm all night long. He was crazy. You'd be sleeping and hear, 'Boom, boom, boom.' You'd think, 'That's just Clint.'

"As Clint was going out, Tom Landry was coming in. Clint walked past Landry and didn't say anything, and Landry could see Clint was all red, had blood on him, and I was the first person Landry came in contact with. He said, 'What happened?' I said, 'Clint jumped Roger, and Roger's in the training room.'

"The trainer came in and stopped the bleeding, and Roger said, 'I'm okay. I'm all right.' The guys were holding him back, and the trainer was holding a bandage to his head, and Roger said, 'I'm okay. I'm all right. Everything's fine.' So Randy let him go, the other guys let him go, and Roger, zoooom, he took off. He started running toward the dorm to go get Clint. We had to damn near tackle Roger to stop him from going back over there.

"Landry of course couldn't believe what was going on, and of course that was the end of Clint Longley."

ROGER STAUBACH: "In 1974, his rookie year, Clint didn't care that I was the starting quarterback ahead of him. He sat with me on all the team planes that year. He was like my buddy.

"And then in '76 Danny White came, and he went to the third team, and then he quit talking to us. And I confronted him on that, and we got into a little skirmish in practice, and the next day he took the cowardly route out.

"If he really wanted to fight like a man, he could have come into my room and said, 'Hey, let's finish up what we started on the field.' Which he didn't want to do. The thing the team understood was that he was a chickenshit guy.

"The thing about Clint, he really wasn't into learning the system. Danny White came in, and he knew the system better than Clint did. Danny was a good player, and Danny took his job as backup quarterback, and when Clint didn't play in the last exhibition game in '76, that's when Clint really went weird.

"And I've never seen him since."

After Longley's departure, Danny White stepped in for Staubach as needed, and the Cowboys didn't miss a beat in winning their first six games. The offense scored consistently, despite a subpar running game, and the Doomsday defense was solid, behind the front wall of Ed Jones, Harvey Martin, Jethro Pugh, and Larry Cole.

After a loss to the Cards, the team flew to Chicago to play the Bears. Early in the second quarter Roger Staubach ran four yards for a touchdown. As he reached the end zone, defensive back Virgil Livers's helmet collided with Staubach's right hand which held the ball. Staubach played the rest of the second quarter, but the hand began to swell and hurt. X rays at halftime revealed a fractured hand. Danny White came in and threw two touchdown passes in a 31–21 win. The team's record ran to 6–1.

Staubach returned against Washington and had his passing hand stepped on, which led to a sore arm. Staubach could not pass effectively the rest of the year. Before the injury he was passing at 70 percent. After it, it was under 50 percent. With both Robert Newhouse and Preston Pearson hobbled by injury, the offense had to struggle the rest of the season.

After beating the Buffalo Bills 17–10, the team record stood at 9–1, but there was considerable dissension on the team. Coach Landry had praise only for O. J. Simpson, the outstanding Bills running back. Blaine Nye complained about the performance of the offensive line. Ralph Neely complained about the running game.

DREW PEARSON: "Our standards of performance were always, I think, too high. But that's okay. Because we always worked to try to strive for that. Expectations were high. The year before we were in the Super Bowl, and of course, when we blew everybody away at the start of the season, and then Roger hurt his hand, that's when we started having trouble offensively, because all you have to do is look at the numbers. We scored only 17 points on Buffalo, and then we lost to Atlanta, scoring 10, had only 19 points in a win over St. Louis, scored 26 to beat Philly, oooof, we really did have a rough hoe. We lost the final game to Washington to finish 11–3, but that was a tough year for us, no doubt."

ROGER STAUBACH: "In '76 we started out winning on big plays. I was having the best year I ever had. The passing game was just going crazy. But we were relying on it. Robert Newhouse was banged up a little bit, Preston pulled a stomach muscle. And then I broke my finger against the Bears, and after I was hurt, the passing game faltered, and we limped into the playoffs and lost to the Rams."

The opening playoff game was against the Los Angeles Rams. The Cowboys led 10–7 going into the fourth quarter. A last minute touchdown plunge by Lawrence McCutcheon beat them.

DREW PEARSON: "We were at home. Everything was in our favor. We should have beat them. We were just having a bad time. We were not able to come out of a negative December and turn it into a positive through the playoffs. We struggled through the second half of the season, and when the playoffs hit, we didn't have that momentum going in. The Rams were a team we should have beat. It was just disappointing, because the Rams were looking for a measure of revenge, because we had beaten them in a championship game the year before. They came in fired up, but still, losing 14–12, to give only 14 points and lose . . . the defense was playing very well. The offense . . .ʺ

ROGER STAUBACH: ʺI was so frustrated by the first-round loss to the Rams, I went to Landry to suggest a trade. I felt personally responsible for the team getting beat. And all because of that little finger of mine. I was in a highly emotional state.

ʺLandry told me, 'That's crazy. The team had problems with its running game and you were injured. You played well under the circumstances. We just didn't have much support in other areas.' ʺ

THOMAS HENDERSON: ʺRoger Staubach was an incredible talent. He exemplified the spirit of a gladiator football player. Roger Staubach was and *is* one of my idols. The point of the matter is this: You may grow up wanting to be like a lot of people, but if you're lucky in your life, you will be in the presence of somebody who is exactly what you'd like to be, but you don't even know it.

ʺRoger was a Dr. Jekyll and Mr. Hyde kind of a guy. This man with impeccable ethics, this man with impeccable family ethics, faithful to his wife, a Christian, but then he was this crazy fucking football player, this guy with the drive to just whip your ass, this competitive thing.

ʺBut it wasn't Roger's fault we lost. Late in the game Lee Roy and I stopped Lawrence McCutcheon at the goal line six inches short. I squared him up. He was *not* in the end zone. But the referee gave it to him anyway. It was horrible.ʺ

HARVEY MARTIN: ʺWe simply had no running game, and being forced into passing on every down rendered Roger less effective.

ʺOne player, I moaned to myself, just one running back, and we'd be the best damn team God ever gave breath to.ʺ

57

TD

On February 18, 1977, the NFL entered a new age as the league and the players signed to a new basic agreement that increased the likelihood of free agency and much higher salaries. Under the five-year pact, the Rozelle Rule was officially dead. The only compensation for signing a free agent could be a draft pick or two.

A month later Tex Schramm and Gil Brandt again proved their ability to keep the Cowboy franchise well armed when they traded four draft choices to the Seattle Seahawks for the second pick of the draft, University of Pittsburgh running back Tony Dorsett, a three-time college All-America. Dorsett had led Pitt to a 12–0 record and, after becoming the first college runner ever to run for over 6,000 yards, was awarded the Heisman Trophy.

The first pick in the draft, selected by the Tampa Bay Buccaneers, one of the worst franchises in the history of the NFL, was Ricky Bell. The trade with Seattle had been contingent on Tampa Bay taking Bell, not Dorsett.

Shortly after the Bucs announced their choice of Bell, Tex Schramm marched hard into the press room of the Cowboy offices on the eleventh-floor of Expressway Towers by the Central Expressway with a blue and white jersey tucked under his arm.

"Gentlemen," he announced to the fifty or so reporters in the room, "I don't have our draft choice here with me, but I do have his jersey."

He drew it across the back of a chair. The shiny blue letters read D-O-R-S-E-T-T above the number 33. A few reporters chuckled, figuring it was a joke Tex was playing, an indication of his wistfulness. Soon it was clear he was serious.

The Cowboys had traded their first pick and three second-round picks for Dorsett. One of the picks had been obtained when they exiled Pat Toomay, another when they discarded Clint Longley. The Seattle draft picks turned into guard Steve August, tackle Tom Lynch, linebacker Terry Beeson, and, after making other trades, center Geoff Reese and receiver Duke Fergerson.

Seattle general manager John Thompson said he was pleased with the deal. Sure he was. He wasn't going to have to give his top draft choice a million dollars, as Dallas did. The year before Seattle could have had Chuck Muncie but instead let New Orleans pay the freight. It settled on Steve Niehaus, a defensive tackle, instead.

A grinning Tex Schramm immediately praised Seattle for stocking its fine team and then returned to the truth when he crowed that Dorsett was the best running back to come along since O. J. Simpson. He was, in fact, the most dangerous Cowboy offensive threat since Bob Hayes.

Said a furious Bud Grant, coach of the Minnesota Vikings, "Dallas and Seattle must be sleeping together. I don't understand it at all." Said an insightful Baltimore Colt general manager Ernie Accorsi, "The Cowboys got themselves a Hall of Famer for four draft choices."

Tony Dorsett, the Cowboys' first million-dollar player, grew up in Pennsylvania mill country. Like Mike Ditka and Joe Namath, football for Dorsett was a way out of the mills. His father had worked for Jones & Laughlin Steel, and he didn't want his son following in his footsteps. As a kid Dorsett had had a lot of fears: the dark, the dead, sleeping alone, even playing football. He outgrew all his fears but one: he was very fearful of failing his parents, whom he worked so hard to please. He was accepted on scholarship at the University of Pittsburgh, though he almost left school before his first game when his steady girlfriend became pregnant. The day he intended to quit, he called his mom, who told him, "You're supposed to be a grown man now. You only get this one chance once in a lifetime." Dorsett called Pitt coach Jackie Sherrill, who helped calm him and who persuaded him to stay.

On the day of his first varsity game his girlfriend gave birth to his first child. The relationship broke up before his senior year, and the girl-friend moved to West Virginia along with his son. That day, though a freshman saddled with worries, he started at halfback against Georgia Tech and ran for 101 yards. From the first Dorsett was a sensational player, a once-in-a-lifetime performer. Of course, his fame also brought negative publicity. When he was cited for $1,200 in parking tickets his freshman year at Pitt, newspapers as far away as Tokyo wrote about it.

When Dorsett arrived at the Dallas camp, the other players saw his flair. He drove a midnight-black Porsche and wore a full-length mink. He gravitated to the North Dallas night spots, looking for pretty girls, white or black, and he wasn't in town a week when he learned something about being black in southern society. At the Number 3 Lift, a disco bar, the bouncer, unhappy that this well-dressed black man wearing sunglasses was seeking entry, began baiting him. He was stopped and carded. He produced plenty of identification, but no ID satisfied the bouncer. The bouncer told Dorsett he didn't like the fact he was wearing sunglasses at night. After the bouncer finished getting his jollies at Dorsett's expense, he finally allowed him inside.

Once there, the bartender continued the race-baiting. It was Ladies' Night, and Dorsett wanted to dance with white women, and the bartender told him straight out that he didn't want him coming around on Ladies' Night.

The bartender then accused Dorsett of not paying for the drink that sat in front of him. He had, in fact, paid, but Dorsett realized that what the bartender was insinuating was that because he was black, he was stealing something, and it made him furious.

The bartender then asked him to leave the bar area, saying he was in the way of the waitresses. The guy was quoted as saying, "Well, we don't want you standing here anyway. Get away right now." Tony Dorsett indignantly refused to budge. The bartender then picked up his drink and walked it to the other end of the bar.

"I couldn't understand why he was telling me this," said Dorsett. Finally, Dorsett told him, "If you want me to move, you'll have to come over and move me."

The bartender then came around the bar to get him. Dorsett slugged him. The bartender began calling him foul names, including racial epithets.

The cops came, and Dorsett was charged with assault, though the charges were later dropped.

It had not been this way in Pittsburgh. In that city, where he was more famous than the mayor, he was accepted anywhere, including the ethnic neighborhoods. He found it hard to adjust to the racism and to a mindset bent on keeping the two races apart.

Despite the incident, Dorsett talked about how happy he was to be living in Dallas. Dorsett told Mary Elson, "I've been recognized everywhere. Supermarkets, gas stations, restaurants. The people down here in Dallas are so friendly it's unbelievable. They all come up and say they're so happy I'm here. But let me tell you, they're no more happier than I am to be here."

That was his public face. In private, Dorsett was unhappy not to be as free as he had been in the city of Pittsburgh.

MEL RENFRO: "He came out of the East Coast, from Pittsburgh, where he had lived by a different set of rules. In Pittsburgh, *everybody* loved him. In Dallas and the South, although the blacks were treated okay, he couldn't do what he did back home, and so Tony had a bitterness. He resented that even though he was such a good athlete, even though he was popular in the sense that the people liked his football performances, he still couldn't live the way he was used to living.

"I know when he bought his home in Dallas, he bought it way out where he brought all the activity to himself. And when he did go out, he went out with a limo and a driver so he would not be put in a position where he was by himself or where he was someplace he was not wanted. He was always surrounded by people and always had someone to drive him around and so he was somewhat isolated.

"After a couple of incidents, most of his activities were at his home, where he had his parties, where he had his friends come out to him."

What Dorsett found equally hard to take at first were Tom Landry's military-like practices. At Pitt, football had been fun. Not in Dallas. Like most rookies, he was having difficulty learning the system. The veterans chided him for not being more serious.

Then in preseason he was injured and missed most of the exhibition games. He felt animosity and envy coming from some of the vets. Not only had he won the Heisman and Walter Camp awards, but his paycheck was much bigger than theirs, and some of them weren't happy about that. When the season began, Coach Landry used Dorsett in a spot role. Preston Pearson continued as the starter, and for the first three games, he carried a total of 21 times. He was uncomfortable and unhappy with the limited duty.

DREW PEARSON: "Tony Dorsett came in with a truckload of credentials from his college career, and what was impressive among all those credentials was the fact he was durable and tough, because when you look at the guy, his physical presence wasn't that overwhelming. He was short, 5' 9", 5' 10". He says he's 5' 10", but he's 5' 9". He weighed 185, 190 pounds at the most, so he wasn't that big, and here was a guy we had traded all these draft picks for, the guy we had picked number one to come in and pretty much ride his back to a Super Bowl. So we knew his credentials, but as teammates we really didn't know how much Tony was going to help us that rookie year.

"We knew going into training camp in '77 that if we stayed healthy, we could have a special season. We felt coming off an 11–3 the year before and losing that first round in the playoffs, we were possessed, committed to making it a good season. We knew going in that we were going to have a special type of year if a lot of things fell into place, and for the whole year, it really did. Tony Dorsett was one of the pieces that had to fit, and once he hit the practice field, boy, you could see the talent, the quickness, the speed, and this was one thing he never got enough credit for: his acceleration. He could start from zero and be at 60 miles an hour in no time flat. That's what made Tony Dorsett what he was all through his career, his ability to accelerate so quickly.

"So once he hit the field, you could see his talent. You could see he was everything as advertised. And Coach Landry was the type of coach, he was not going to put too much pressure on a rookie initially, not even a Heisman Trophy winner, not even a guy who just won a national college championship, not even a Tony Dorsett. He wanted to make sure he brought Tony along gradually, and for a long time through that '77 season, Preston Pearson continued as a starting running back, but we all knew as teammates in our mind that Tony was the man and that eventually, if we were going to go to the Super Bowl and win it, we had to ride his back. With all due respect to Preston, because he certainly was very valuable through the course of that season, he wasn't Tony Dorsett. And it was only so long Coach Landry could keep Tony Dorsett on the bench.

"Coach Landry was very calculated as to when Dorsett would become an integral part of our offense.

"When we put Tony in our offense on a full-time basis, he just created so much havoc and problems for the defense, because we had a lot of weapons. Roger, Billy Joe, Tony Hill was a rookie that year, and we had Preston, good weapons, and then with Tony back there it just made us that much better. It gave us that game-breaking offensive weapon we needed.

"Tony was the first Cowboy player to get $1 million. That didn't bother me at all. Tony was a Heisman Trophy winner from a national champion Pittsburgh Panthers, and he was the number two pick in the draft. So that warranted a certain salary level, and back then draft choices were getting more money than the veteran players. It was something understood. What it did, it created a new salary scale for us to go by. There was no resentment there, because players better than anybody understand the finances of the NFL. They know when you have your opportunity to get your money, you got to get it, whether you're a rookie or a ten-year veteran, you might only get one opportunity, and you gotta get it while you can.

"And quickly, Tony showed us he was special. That year we were 12–2 in the regular season. We scored over 340 points. We were a machine, and Tony was the game-breaking piece that we needed in our offense. He could turn a game around at any point on the field at any time in the game with just one quick hit up the middle. Preston started in our opening win against the Vikings, and then in the second game of the season when we beat up on the Giants, Tony ran seven times and scored two touchdowns."

In the third game, a solid 23–7 defeat of Ricky Bell and Tampa Bay, Dorsett ran 10 times for 72 yards. After the game he showed himself to be a harsher critic of himself than even Tom Landry could have been. After the game he told reporters, "Mentally I just collapsed . . . totally. I stopped two drives with my mistakes. I lined up wrong once and we had to call timeout because of that.

"Another time I didn't block the right man. I had a misunderstanding of who I was supposed to block." He concluded, "I still have a long way to go."

DREW PEARSON: "I was friendly with Tony. We hung out a little bit. I didn't hang out with too many players. I went out and ran into players, but I never was the kind of guy to call up a guy and say, 'Let's go out,' to Tony or anybody else. At that time Harvey Martin was probably my closest friend on the team. I never even did that with him, but I was close to Tony. Even though I had been in the league a few years and he came in as a rookie, I had a lot of respect for Tony for what he accomplished and the way he accomplished it at Pitt. He was the Man at Pitt. He carried 40 times a game and would take some tremendous licks and come back to the huddle and never seem to complain, but when they lined up again, he was ready to go, so I had a lot of respect for Tony when he came in.

"A lot of people thought he was aloof because of his personality and his demeanor, but once you got to know him, you found out that's just the way he was, and you accepted that.

"The next game was against the St. Louis Cardinals, who we beat 30–24, and against the Cards Tony ran only 14 times but he ran for 141 yards, including a 77-yard touchdown run.

"We had everything going for us. Against the Redskins, Roger hit me with a 59-yard touchdown pass. He threw for over 250 yards and two touchdowns, and he had his old form back. Roger was having a great year. He was throwing the ball. We had had an excellent off-season of work. We had an excellent preseason, and it was carrying right over into the season. Roger was the key, the igniter, and he made us go. He was having a great year.

"We beat the Eagles, and then we shut out the Detroit Lions, 37–0, then beat the Giants big to go 8–0, the best in our history."

ROGER STAUBACH: "Tony Dorsett made a *big* difference when he came in '77. Getting Dorsett was a real shot in the arm. This guy was a sensational player. He had speed, and he was tough, could run inside. He took a lot of the pressure off me. With him we had a very balanced game. That year Tony Hill also came, and when you have Tony and Drew and Tony, we were one heck of an offense.

"Tony Hill was a good guy, yet he was very outgoing, very precocious, and he could drive you crazy. I think I had better control of Tony than anybody. I was able to control him, and he really made a lot of great plays, made them for Danny White too, won *a lot* of big games. But Drew was a Hall of Fame receiver, and Tony got lost in his shadow. When we hit the field offensively, we were *really good*."

The question was whether the Cowboys could go undefeated. Tom Landry said he didn't think they could. What was required was for Roger Staubach to stay healthy. In the next game, against the Cardinals, the Cowboys were leading by a touchdown with nine minutes left when Staubach sprained the thumb on his passing hand. As a result, he was ineffective at the end and Card quarterback Jim Hart threw two touchdowns, one to Mel Gray, the other to Jackie Smith, to break the streak.

After the one loss, the Dallas writers were wondering in print whether the Cowboys were going to choke. Tony Dorsett, patient no longer, now told

Landry he wanted to start. Landry called the rookie into his office and told him how unhappy he was with the progress he was making. Dorsett, who was not afraid of the coach, told Landry he was bored and dissatisfied with the way he was being used.

"We've been expecting you to be starting for us," Landry said. "But the way you've been going, I have my doubts about all that."

"Coach," said Dorsett, "I have my doubts that I would ever be starting this season. It is not my favorite thing to do—to come into a game, to come out of a game."

"Well," Landry said, "if you showed some intensity in practice, some more hard work, it might be different."

Dorsett told Landry, "Coach, with not starting and not feeling a part of things, I was getting ready to write it off and get ready for training camp next year and try to win me a job."

Landry told him, "That's not the correct attitude. We have big plans for you right now. But you've got to get more into things."

"Well, I guess what we have is more a problem of miscommunication than anything," said Dorsett. "I admit I could have applied myself a little more. But if you'd told me in training camp that later on I would be starting for the Cowboys, I would have busted my butt more."

"It's not too late," said the coach.

That week Dorsett worked especially hard in practice, and Landry started him against the Pittsburgh Steelers, replacing an angry Preston Pearson, who felt he was being made a scapegoat.

Said Landry, "The move has nothing to do with Preston. We felt Tony had been running very hard and we wanted to see how he looked starting."

Though the Cowboys didn't win the game, a second loss in a row, Dorsett looked just fine. He ran 17 times for 73 yards, including one 13-yard touchdown run, as he fought to learn the Cowboys' complicated Multiple Offense system.

DREW PEARSON: "The loss to St. Louis was disappointing, but we were right in that football game right up to the end. Then we came back and lost to Pittsburgh up there. That was the most disappointing loss, 'cause we wanted to beat the Steelers, and wanted to beat them at a time when it really counted. The only time we ever beat them was in the preseason exhibition games. We went up to Pittsburgh to win that football game. Roger got knocked out in that game, and they whipped our butts again. We didn't think there was any real concern for our football team. We knew we could get it back together."

In the next game, against the Washington Redskins, Tony Dorsett ran for 64 yards, most of them in the second half, and scored the winning touchdown in a close 14–7 slugfest.

DREW PEARSON: "It was a very physical football game. The Redskins had some great players. I do remember Tony Dorsett staggering back to the huddle after one hit by Chris Hanburger or somebody—I don't know whether it was Hanburger or Neal Olkewicz or this other guy who got killed out on a highway fixing a flat, the middle linebacker, Harold Mc-Clinton. He was an unsung hero on that defense, but he was a sledgehammer. He could knock your head off. But Tony staggered back to the huddle after one lick on the sideline. I was straightening his shoulder pads out. I asked him, 'Tony, are you all right?' He said, 'Yeah, but these guys are *men.*' That's when he realized he was in the NFL and it was a little different, because these other defenses were very strong and very tough, but Washington got more up to play us and kicked Tony's ass.

"And then against the Philadelphia Eagles, Tony ran for 206 yards, breaking Calvin's record for one game by 53 yards! Tony was a great player, man. He could hit that daylight and the next thing you knew, he was gone in the defensive secondary.

"I always remember before Tony joined our football team, Landry had always stressed blocking for the wide receivers, but when Tony joined our football team, he made it a point to say that, 'Hey, if you're a wide receiver and you don't block, you don't play. We got a Tony Dorsett back here that could break it on any play. We don't want you to be the reason that he's not going long distance.' There were a lot of games I made five or six catches, caught touchdowns, but Coach Landry would jump on me or whoever 'cause we missed a block that could have sprung Tony. In film sessions he would always show that in front of the whole team, so you could feel like a small piece of shit as he was going over and critiquing it. So what you wanted to do, every time Tony got his play called in the huddle, you were downfield hustling trying to throw a block, not just because of what Coach Landry said but because you knew that this guy had the ability to go all the way, so you were down the field hustling, working.

"And I can remember against the Vikings a little later in his career, a Monday night football game, and we had ten men on the field, and we were backed up on our own one-yard line. They called a dive Double H up the middle, and our center Tom Rafferty got a great block on the nose tackle, and Tony came flying through there, and I slipped back, saw Tony bust into the secondary, and I started hustling and running, trying to lead some interference downfield. The next thing you know, he was way off, and I'm trying to throw this last block so he can go 99 yards and I can be in the Hall of Fame highlight film with him.

"I ended up throwing it about the Minnesota 30, and Tony went around that block and took it all the way. That's an example of the game-breaking speed and abilities that he had.

"And with Tony breaking Calvin Hill's rookie record, we finished the regular season 12–2 and had to face the Bears in the opening game of the playoffs.

"We were confident. We had beaten a very good Denver Bronco team that last game of the season in a very physical game. I remember so clearly getting racked up by Billy Thompson coming across the middle on a play. It was a physical game, but we won, and we felt we had momentum going, and we knew Chicago would have a hard time beating us. For them to beat us, we would have to beat ourselves, and we certainly didn't do it. We were clicking. We beat them 37–7, and then we beat the Vikings 23–6, another tough team, and a playoff nemesis, a team that always gave us a lot of trouble in the playoffs, but again, we had Doomsday. We talk about our offense, but Doomsday was being mighty effective, too, and the Vikings had some very good offensive weapons still, but we shut them down pretty good. We were rolling right on into that Super Bowl."

Super Bowl XII pitted the Cowboys against the Denver Broncos, a team led by former Dallas quarterback Craig Morton. Craig had toiled a half dozen years for the New York Giants before coming to Denver, and not once had Morton been able to defeat the Cowboys. The Morton Factor, as much as anything else, gave the Cowboy players added confidence going into the game.

MEL RENFRO: "In our first game against the Giants when Craig played quarterback, I picked him off. He never once beat the Cowboys, because we knew how to get to him. We knew what to do. We pressured him. Blitzed him. Went after him. Didn't give him time. If you give him time, he'll throw the ball pretty well. So you don't give him time. He wasn't able to scramble because of his knees. We knew he wasn't mobile, and that's what happened in Super Bowl XII. We knew he didn't have good mobility, and if we didn't give him time, we could pretty much shut him down. We had Harvey Martin and Randy White plus Ed Jones, so we had the line where we could do it."

DREW PEARSON: "We blitzed in a lot of situations throughout that football game, and we just kept constant pressure on Craig Morton. Even though the final score was 27–10, for a long time it was close, a tough game, but when the Denver Broncos started having success moving the football, it was when Craig left the game and they brought in Norris Weese, and he started scrambling around back there trying to avoid the rush, and that's when Denver started moving the football."

The star of the game offensively was running back Robert Newhouse, who not only threw a 29-yard touchdown pass to Golden Richards but ran 14 times for 55 yards, filling in for Dorsett after the rookie star sprained his knee and didn't play the second half.

DREW PEARSON: "Robert's role was mainly short yardage, goal line, the lead back to block for Tony. Newhouse was a role player throughout his career with the Cowboys. There is no question he had the ability to be a starter and to start for a long time, but for some reason Landry never gave him—I don't want to say he didn't give him opportunities to start, but Landry never really saw him as the starter. There always seemed to be somebody else, Walt Garrison, Scott Laidlaw, Timmy Newsome, who would seem to end up getting more playing time than Newhouse. But Newhouse was never one to complain. He was the consummate team player, and whatever role Landry wanted him to play, Newhouse was willing to play it and not just play it, but play it well."

ROGER STAUBACH: "We had played Denver the last game of the season and really fought like crazy to beat them 14–6. Denver had a great defense. The Orange Crush. We knew their defense was tough, and this Super Bowl, *our* defense made it easy for us. If their offense had been on and playing well, it would have been a heck of a game, but once we saw our defense was in control, we became very conservative.

"We hit this play to Butch Johnson, which was kind of a made-up kind of deal, but other than that, we were conservative because the defense dominated.

"We'd been watching film, and I saw that Bernard Jackson, their weak safety, liked to gamble a lot. He wouldn't get back into coverage. He'd be looking for things over the middle. So the play was sent in, a strongside play to the fullback or to Billy Joe DuPree, our tight end. Butch, who brought in the play from Coach Landry, was supposed to run an in-route.

"I told Butch, 'You run a real strong post.'

"He said, 'No, I'm supposed to run an in-route.'

"I said, 'Butch, you just run a good post route, and I will throw it to you if Jackson is not back in his coverage.'

"If I had called '83-Y post' in the huddle, everybody would have said, 'Roger's going against the coach.'

"Butch ran a great post route. Steve Foley was playing to the outside a little bit. He should have prevented anything to the corner or the outside. And Jackson was the guy who should have made the play. Well, Jackson was cheating, so I threw it over his head, and I actually thought I threw it too far, and Butch Johnson made a sensational catch. It was controversial, because Denver said he didn't have control as he crossed the goal line, but when you see the film, you could see he had possession. It was just a great catch. Butch had a flair for making those kinds of catches.

"That really put the game away. We led, 20–3.

"But our defense just totally dominated the game. They could have had Jim Thorpe at quarterback for Denver, and he would have been in trouble. So it wasn't Craig Morton's fault. Craig Morton didn't have a shot in that game. Craig had a great season for Denver that year. They beat the Raiders in the playoffs. Craig had a great year. In fact, Craig was MVP in the AFC."

DREW PEARSON: "We were pretty happy, elated. I was kind of hurting, just drained, dehydrated, and cramping up quite a bit. Winning the Super Bowl was kind of anticlimactic that year. Because we felt we *should* have won it. Landry put it in perspective by saying it was the 'challenge of the chase' that gave us our real satisfactions, all the things we had to overcome to get to the Super Bowl and win it was what was really satisfying to us, not necessarily just winning that one game, but just winning all season long and finishing 12–2 in the regular season, 15–2 overall. We knew we had accomplished a lot.

"So we were happy and elated and having a good time, but it was also businesslike. It was something we expected to do."

58

The Assassin

A fter the 1977 Super Bowl XII victory, Harvey Martin and Randy White were awarded the co-MVP trophies and given cars. Martin had four tackles, two of them quarterback sacks. White had five tackles and a sack. But it could certainly have been argued that the Most Valuable Player on the team had been a part-time defender who starred on the special teams and at linebacker on third downs. His name was Thomas "Hollywood" Henderson.

THOMAS HENDERSON: "In '76 I had a major role in the Cowboys' defense. I was the hardest-working man on the Dallas Cowboys. I played on third-down defense, and every special team, and that year Gene Stallings entrusted to me the best receiver out of the backfield. On third downs I'd come in, and shut down the receiver out of the backfield. It became one of my marquee traits. Didn't matter if the receiver was a running back or a wide receiver. His ass was not going to catch a pass. If you ran a draw play, I was going to tackle him.

"I was really one of the first linebackers to ever do that job. Most teams will go to a strong safety or a free safety or a backup defensive back to do what I used to do. So if there was anything in '76 that Thomas Henderson became known for it was, 'That damn linebacker can cover out of the backfield.'

"Sometimes it could get pretty scary, man. A couple of the scariest moments was having to cover Terry Metcalf four plays in a row with seconds on the clock on our 20-yard line. That's when I came into my own, when Landry realized that even if I made what he called 'mental errors' that he had to have me on the field. Although they continued to play their own games that sometimes affected me, most of the time they didn't.

"It was Lee Roy's last season, but Lee Roy had basically held the Cowboys ransom, saying if they didn't give him his payday he would walk, so there was no fanfare for Lee Roy. Not that I gave a fuck what was going on with Lee Roy, because I believe *everybody* ought to get paid fairly, but toward the end of that season Landry started Bob Breunig at middle linebacker some games instead of me. Breunig started purely because Landry trusted his studiousness. He trusted his playbook knowledge. He trusted his work ethic in the books. But when third down came, he'd say, 'Hey, Breunig, come on out of there. Henderson, get in there and take care of what's important.'

"And then in '77 Landry announced that Randy White would start on the outside, with Breunig in the middle and D.D. on the other side. They hadn't had a black linebacker in that Cowboy corps ever. Landry made it clear it was Randy's job. But to keep it interesting, he made me a contender.

"The Cowboys came real close to losing me that year. They don't even know it. I had talked to real close friends of mine. I was close to leaving. If Landry thought I was going to play second fiddle my third year, he had lost his fucking mind. And I almost walked out of camp on another occasion, because what I did was embarrass Randy White at strongside linebacker. Randy White owes me some fucking money for my getting his big ass on the line where he was supposed to be, 'cause in training camp I took my little turn—Jerry Tubbs would call out the starting group, and they would go out there, and after a couple of plays I would go out, and I would intercept a pass. I would be in the right zone. I'd intercept balls. I would cover the backs out of the backfield, intercept the ball, take it back for a touchdown. Well, Randy White looked like Andre the Giant trying to fall back in a fucking 12-yard drop. There was no grace in this eight-to-12-yard drop, no grace in his break on the ball. There was *nothing*. Randy White had no business in the secondary, ever, except to visit.

"Randy could run. Randy was powerful, and I think Landry dreamed of him never letting the tight end get off the line of scrimmage. So there were some points. Randy White could probably play the run. But a strong-side linebacker has many more responsibilities than that. So Randy could probably play half of that position, which wouldn't be fair to the team or to the position. Because I worked out every day with these guys. They would watch me in wonder. To see me back up ten yards and break on the ball was a thing of poetry. To see them do it was like golf. Randy White dropping into a zone was like seeing golf divots.

"To get Landry to see the light, I just played my ass off. I watched them. I wondered, 'What are they doing? They have Breunig, D. D. Lewis, and Randy White.' And here was my evaluation, without taking anything from those guys. I was the best fucking player of the group. Period. No apology. Best all-around player of the group. I wondered, 'Why am I the sixth man?'

"And I had made a decision in my own mind. I didn't know nothing, wasn't sure anybody else wanted me, but if I hadn't become a starter in my third year, I was leaving. I was out of there. I didn't know where I was going. I was just going to quit. One morning I wasn't going to show up. I wasn't going to go to practice. I didn't know what was going to happen. But if Randy White would have become the starting linebacker for the Cowboys in my third season, I was *not* coming back.

"I even told Gil Brandt. I was *very* upset. 'Cause they were giving me the runaround. And then, heh, heh, heh, heh, instead of Landry saying, 'Thomas Henderson has proven to me that I have made a fucking error trying to play Randy White at strongside linebacker,' instead of him doing that, he said he was moving Randy White to the line. All this time I had been competing with Randy White. Then Landry says, 'And Thomas Henderson and Mike Hegman will compete for the starting job at strongside linebacker.' Which was the worst slap in the face that Landry ever did to me. He *really* hurt my feelings. He hurt everything about me.

"And from that point on I hated his fucking ass. I hated the bald-headed motherfucker. I *hated* him. I remember the day.

"So I went on with my job. I was a professional, kicking ass, taking names, with Hegman trying to take my job, and I remember the day Landry announced his starting lineup for that season on defense, his starters. Jerry Tubbs, the linebacker coach, came to me and said, 'I don't know. It's pretty close.' I said, 'You know what, Jerry. Real close is me leaving this motherfucker. That's what's close.' That was my statement to him. 'What's real close is me leaving, you motherfucker, with all these games you all are playing.'

"And Landry in his wisdom announced me as the starter. And that began my starting with the Dallas Cowboys.

"Let me tell you something. The '77 Cowboy defense was one of the greatest defenses of all time, if anybody would ever study the caliber of players, the speed, the experience, the quickness. You go down that lineup, with Thomas Henderson, Too Tall Jones, Jethro Pugh, or Bill Gregory, Randy White, Harvey Martin, D. D. Lewis, Breunig in the middle, Benny Barnes, Mel Renfro, then Charlie Waters and Cliff Harris. What an ensemble! Jethro was this steel-worker. He came in with the beatup lunch pail. Him and Larry Cole were the unsung heroes of the Dallas Cowboys.

"Me and Too Tall made the same NAIA All-America team in 1973. Maybe he *was* too tall. Too Tall was a great player, but people always expected more out of him. I found him to be a great football player.

"That year I intercepted a pass against Tarkenton in the Minnesota game, and against Tampa Bay I intercepted a pass and returned it 79 yards. Then I dunked the ball over the crossbars. Yeah. I'm different, man. See, Landry didn't like that. I antagonized Tom Landry. To get Landry's praise it took me whopping Russ Francis's ass in Texas Stadium in '78 after the papers had said 'Russ Francis is the best tight end in the world ever, and if you don't think so, watch him drag Hollywood around Texas Stadium.' And I flat whipped his ass for four quarters.

"To start the game I punched Francis in the mouth. Fucking knocked him out. Just bam. I whupped him so bad it hurt my back. That's how bad it was, and Landry came into the meeting room that Monday and took a moment, the first time in my career, and he said, 'I want to say something here. Thomas Henderson had a great challenge.' He said, 'Men who step up to those challenges are men who I like. I want to say this. Thomas Henderson is a pro.'

"Tom Landry called me a pro, and I never heard him call anybody else a pro. I played there five years and never heard Landry call anybody a pro. All the years he coached football, there were some people he looked at and said, 'That's a pro.' I know he thought Roger Staubach was a pro. But I don't think he thought everybody was a pro. I would like someday to find out what he meant by that. I never have confirmed what he meant by 'Thomas Henderson is a pro,' but I knew it was the highest compliment, had to be because I never heard him call anybody else that since then.

"And that same year I had to cover Terry Metcalf. For those who don't know, if you look at his son, Eric, his son was not as good as his dad. So anybody who watches Eric Metcalf these days knows his father was outstanding. At one point that year his father led in rushing, punt returns, kickoff returns, and receiving! He led in every offensive category.

"Jerry Tubbs called him a rabbit. Which is a good description. Have you ever seen a rabbit running on cactus through the brush? And I stopped him.

"I've said it before. I was the best linebacker to ever play in the National Football League. And I didn't play long. But I was the best there was. Before there was an L.T., there was a T.H. I made 56 the glamorous number that it is today. Everybody thinks it started with L.T., Lawrence Taylor. Lawrence Taylor wore 56 because I wore it. So when I say that, historians will say, 'Yeah, the son of a bitch was good.' I never had anybody argue with me when I say I was the best all-around linebacker. What I mean by that, I could play the run. I played the strong side as a 210-pound linebacker. I played the run, I played the pass excellently. I could blitz.

"The year Landry fired me [1979] I had 12 quarterback sacks. And Landry loved me blitzing because he knew when he called a Sara 33 or a blitz for me that I was going to get to the quarterback. I picked the lines that were effective to get things done.

"People can talk about Jack Ham and all the other linebackers, but I would put my game-to-game film against any linebacker in history. I played the run perfect. You couldn't block me. I could control with power. I could escape. I caused major problems. I understood *how* to fuck up a play.

"My philosophy was to do my job, and then I went to help. 'Okay, Landry, you want me to do this little shit of yours, okay.' 'Take this step, okay, Landry, how you like that?' Because he was watching me on Monday. He had to watch the whole team on Sunday. He would sit and criticize on Monday. So I would go and take my little step for Landry. 'Here, Landry, one-two,' and then I would take off. That's how I became an All-Pro in Landry's system.

"That's also what Roger did. Yeah. Roger got results. And Landry, in spite of his wanting you to do it his way, he liked the results. Landry would finally say something to me like this: 'Okay, Thomas. You made a mistake right there, but with your speed . . .' He was compensating for me even in defensive sessions. In my third and fourth year, the two best years of my career, and part of my fifth year until I got too fucked up on coke, we'd be in the middle of something, and he would be explaining something to me, and he'd say, 'Well, with your speed, you'll handle it. You'll instinctively know how to react to that.' He would acknowledge my instincts as a football player.

"I remember in Super Bowl XII playing one of my finest games. Mike Ditka, the consummate competitor, said to me, 'Thomas'—and he knew I loved doing shit like this—'on the first punt, if you get a shot at Rick Upchurch, take the penalty. Just take him out. Not hurt him, but get his attention. Make sure he's going to be looking for you the rest of the day.' 'Cause we were afraid of him. We felt that Rick Upchurch could beat us returning kickoffs and punts.

"I flew down the field with my mission orders, and I took a 15-yard penalty. I just creamed Upchurch. I came to the sideline, and Ditka had moved away, and I had to see Landry. I basically said, 'Well fuck, Ditka told me to do that.' And Landry turned to look for Ditka and couldn't even find him!

"Another play in that game, I was on the kickoff return team, and I was over there on the sideline bullshitting with the Denver coach, Red Miller, saying stuff like, 'Hey, Red, we're gonna whip you'all's ass today. You ain't got a fucking chance to win, buddy.' I said, 'Watch this,' and I don't even remember the player—I was supposed to block the third guy from the end. That's the way we set those plays up. And I did something I learned at Langston, which was to take not a forearm, but more of an elbow to the head. And this guy came running down the field doing 22.6 miles an hour, and I clocked him just right upside the head with an elbow, just flat out knocked him out. And Red was hollering at the officials, 'Fifty-six, you can't do that.' I said, 'But I already did it. What do you mean I can't do it? It's already done.' The guy was lying out on the ground, and Red was telling me I couldn't do that! I said, 'What do you mean I can't do that? You should have told me that ten minutes ago.'

"I played against Riley Odoms, who was the tight end who rated himself far better than he was. He was basically whipped and noneffective. He didn't do shit. But he talked the whole day as if he was doing something, and to this day, and the history of Super Bowl XII, it was like he wasn't even there.

"In '77 I felt, and do to this day, that was the finest football team ever to be assembled. We just couldn't be beat. We had too many ways to hold you, too many ways to beat you. We had a great chemistry. It was a great team."

59

Hollywood

In 1978 the Cowboys started slowly, compiling a 6–4 record and all the while putting up with the antics and carryings-on of Thomas Henderson. When the fleet middle linebacker arrived as a rookie in 1975, he was called "Thomas." But after that season he discovered *the big time,* a new lifestyle introduced to him by the Hollywood entertainment crowd. He began a romance with one of the Pointer Sisters, and he also started his love affair with cocaine. One of his druggie partners was comedian Richard Pryor, another victim of the cocaine epidemic of the late '70s.

When he came to camp in 1978, gone was Thomas Henderson. In his place was a larger-than-life in-your-face character named Hollywood Henderson. For two short years, supernova Hollywood Henderson became the mouth of the South, the outrageous, braggadocian public persona of the Dallas Cowboys.

THOMAS HENDERSON: "America discovered cocaine for the first time in the mid-'70s. Back then, cocaine was the drug you heard about. It was Donna Summer and Barry White and disco music and limousines and Hollywooooood. And if you wanted to be hip, slick, *and* cool, you eventually moved toward it. The reason I ended up with a severe drug problem was that I *liked* cocaine, I *loved* it. I savored it, I worshiped it. I had a relationship with it. I had sex on it. I had sex with it. I had parking-lot sex. I had sex in clubs.

"I've been sober since 1983, and I remember telling someone recently, 'You know, back in the '70s, it would be about 4:15 in the morning when I'd get laid, and have these ménage-à-trois and these orgies.' I said, 'Today I'm asleep at eleven o'clock.' So if I was going to have sex these days, I'd be shit out of luck, because I can't be awake at 4:15 to do *anything*.

"How prevalent was it on the Cowboys? Let me break it down like this. Five whites and seven blacks I knew of, including myself, who were using marijuana, pills, cocaine, and other mind-altering substances.

"It was sometimes a secret and sometimes you made a love connection. I would get some for some friends, and they would get me marijuana, or they would provide me with pills. It was not a loud thing. It was a very covert operation.

"It was like the first time I discovered there was someone in the locker room passing out pills. I just noticed a guy walking around. He had a bottle, and the top shelf of those lockers is normally about 6'2", not eye-level, because there's a bench, and then there's the shelf when you look into a Texas Stadium locker. You really couldn't see over the edge of the shelf. And he would put whatever they wanted. Like a Percodan, a Black Molly, right over the top of the shelf. When you stood and looked in the locker, you couldn't see the pills. But if you stood on the bench, you could see them.

"So I noticed him doing that. I think he did it in front of me because he knew what I was doing. And so then I said, 'Hey man, what is that? What are you doing?' And he said, 'This here is for pain, and this here is to get you up for the game . . .' And there was born my little pill relationship.

"I also did THC, but that kept getting me in trouble. It was such a potent drug, it would completely incapacitate me if I got the wrong dose in me. It was something me and one other white teammate got into pretty good.

"I was a free spirit. I rarely had any philosophical conversations with anybody because if someone asked me something, they were going to get the truth very loud. 'What did you do last night, Tom?'

" 'Last night I had these two ho's freakin'.' I mean, I was crazy. I wasn't insane crazy. I was a free spirit with no shame about it. It scared them, because they thought it might rub off. They didn't treat me like a leper, but they didn't come ask me too much either.

"When I came to training camp in '78, I had a deviated septum from doing so much coke, but it didn't affect me on the field. I was vicious. I was 215 pounds of assassin, explosive, physical, terminator. I was rude. And physically and in strength and explosion and power, you couldn't match up with me. So it didn't matter that I was fucked up on drugs. I was twenty-five years old. I was in the middle of the prime of this physical superiority.

"The only problem I had was that I had contracted hepatitis. It was real bad, because I didn't know I had it. I kept waking up trying to feel better, 'cause I've often thought that the body can heal itself. But that hepatitis had my weight down from 210 to 185 pounds.

"I went to work one day, and the trainer, who had served in the military, looked at me and said, 'Goddamn, Henderson.' My eyes were yellow. By the time they put me in the hospital what I had had killed Elvis Presley's mom. The degree, my blood levels, all the readers, it had killed her. And here I was smoking marijuana, drinking white lightning, and snorting and smoking cocaine.

"The one thing Landry knew was, if I didn't start, I really hated it. I liked being introduced. I liked the publicity of it. I was the best fucking player he had, so why the fuck wouldn't I want to be a starter? Why is he going to put some fucking slugs on the field? Out of your fifty guys, I'm the best fucking guy here.

"And after a point it didn't matter I was sick. What mattered was that Landry took personally what Thomas Henderson did. And he shouldn't have.

"In the second game of the season against the Giants, I was really hurt. I took Larry Csonka on a Near G.O., which means the tight end blocks down and the fullback blocks the linebacker. I stepped across to take on Csonka, and I had great position. I had taken on this type of block many times, but I didn't have my back foot on the ground by the time Csonka and I collided.

"My collision with Csonka went from the top of my head out my ankle, all the force going back down to the ankle. I was putting the foot down, so by the time the force got down there, I just snapped. I remember laying in the training room a few days after that and saying to my coach, Jerry Tubbs, 'I'll be back next week.' And I had every intention of coming back, but my ankle was about 25 inches around.

"I think I broke it, but they didn't tell me that. I ended up missing five weeks. I became depressed. I was putting my foot in ice and getting gloomy. I was coming off an All-Pro year, and I asked our equipment man,

Buck Buchanan, 'Buck, I need some high-tops.' He got me a pair. I went across the street to the Tom Thumb grocery store and bought six or seven tins of black shoe polish, and I went to my locker, sat there with ice on my ankle, and I painted these white high-tops black. And I did a horrible job. I got black on the soles, and they were just ugly looking, just the worst paint job. Like if you let me spraypaint your car. It just looked horrible. And when I returned in a game against the Philadelphia Eagles, I wore the black high-tops.

"First thing, I wore them to practice. I was trying to limp a little bit out there, and they were ugly! To see Thomas Henderson, who always wore the white socks rolled down and the nice feet . . . So I wore them when we played the Eagles, and I had a good game. It was my first game back. My ankle was sore. I had had a little injection in there for the pain, and I did a good job. And all Landry could say was that he didn't like my shoes. You know? Of all the things a coach could be doing, thinking about, contemplating, planning, this man called me into his office and said, 'Thomas, I don't want you to wear the black shoes any more.'

"I told him, 'Have you lost your fucking mind? What does wearing black shoes have to do with me playing football?' I said, 'You're out of line.'

"And I continued to wear my black shoes, until they became obnoxious to me, and I finally just threw them away. I wore them a couple more weeks just because he asked me not to. What kind of deal is that? I'm sure he wouldn't want to take that to the people: 'I'm benching Henderson because he won't take off those black shoes.' I mean, he had a bad position, and I knew it. I mean, Landry was a guy who grew up in the '40s when they all wore black shoes! He *came* from black shoes.

"We finished the regular season 12–4. We beat the Falcons in the first playoff game when Danny White came in after Roger was knocked out. Then we played the L.A. Rams. Before the game I said that the Rams didn't have enough class to go to the Super Bowl, and they proved it when they tried to hurt me during the game. One of the things I did pretty good was block field goals. I used to jump that gap and get through there and block the ball on the kick, and the Rams knew that I did that, and when I said they had no class and didn't have enough class to go to the Super Bowl, I think they just decided to hurt me.

"When a guy goes to block a field goal, he gets around that corner and in the gap and lays out with his hands extended trying to block the ball as the guy goes to kick it, and in that position you're vulnerable, because you're not expecting anything. The worst thing you can do is run into some tackle. So the Rams designed a play for the linebacker on the other side, instead of him blocking his responsibility, he turned and like a pulling guard came to hurt me. The Rams appointed a linebacker, number 50, Kevin McLain, to hurt me on this play. And what happened, I jumped the gap and laid out, and I saw Kevin coming and I was surprised. 'Why the fuck is he coming?' But he missed me. And the Rams missed the field goal. But that was one of the most chickenshit designed plays I've ever seen or heard of in my life.

"I went after Rams coach Ray Malavasi after that, called him a 'fat fucking drunk.' Oh yeah. I told him, 'I'm going to singlehandedly beat your fat ass today.' And I did it. I ran back an interception 68 yards to add insult to injury.

"Jim Jodat, a running back, ran a ten-yard out pattern. If Ferragamo would have thrown the ball on the break, he might have completed it, but he gave me time to come out of the break and get going. I saw him release the ball, and part of being the athlete I was, like Deion Sanders, there is another gear. There's fast, and then there's another gear. I don't know how to explain it, but I could be running, and then if I needed more, I could get it. And on that play, I decided to floor it, and when I floored it, I closed the gap and closed on the ball, and people who know me know I don't have the greatest hands, but that ball stuck in my hand like I had on two tons of superglue. I tucked it under my arm, and it was over. I took all angles away with pure speed.

"It was too wet in the Coliseum to dunk the ball over the goal post, so I did a George Gervin finger roll. We were going back to the Super Bowl.

"And when I made the cover of *Newsweek* magazine, the first thing I did was to look to see whether there was any cocaine showing in my nose. I knew it was there. I told reporters, 'I'm more famous than the Shah of Iran.' And I was. When I arrived in Miami before our game with the Steelers, I told the reporters, 'Bradshaw is so dumb, he couldn't spell *cat* if you spotted him the *c* and the *a*.'

"I was concerned before the game. Remember when Fred Williamson was the Hammer, and the Green Bay Packers ran a sweep around him in Super Bowl I after he ran his mouth, left him out there standing at attention laying down? You're *always* concerned. Also, at the time I had a nose problem. It was always stopped up or bleeding, but no one knew I was shoveling cocaine into it. My problem was that I couldn't get flaky cocaine in my nose any more. I had to put it in a liquid, and so it became a part of my addiction, but more so, a part of maintenance, because once your nose gets as fucked up as my nose was, you need cocaine just to keep your eyes from watering. Without the cocaine, it would hurt my physically. I needed it. Cocaine became a maintenance thing.

"But in Super Bowl XIII, like Elvis's voice, my legs never failed me. If I could get there, I was going to do the job. So that day I played the finest football game of my career. Anybody who wants to get the special teams reel, the defense reel, the third-down reel, go get that film and look at the performance of Thomas Henderson. You won't see a better performance of a football player."

60

A Crushing Defeat

T he game against the Pittsburgh Steelers—Super Bowl XIII—was for the title Team of the Decade. The game has been called the best in Super Bowl history. The winner would become the first NFL team to win three Super Bowls.

ROGER STAUBACH: "At the beginning of the year, we lost a couple games, lagged at the start of the season, and then we got our act together, and we won eight in a row going into that Super Bowl.

"The Steelers were tough, too, but we had them. At the end of the half it was 14–14, and Tony Dorsett ran out of bounds around their 25-yard line, and a guy hit him late, and the ref threw the flag, and as Tony was coming back onto the field, he shoved the ball in the guy's face. So instead of having a 15-yard penalty, there were offsetting penalties.

"We had a play-action pass called to Drew Pearson past Jack Lambert, the linebacker. Lambert was the one I was worrying about. I threw it past Lambert, and Mel Blount made a great play and intercepted. Blount should not have been where he was. But he saw the motion, came off his coverage and intercepted, and as he caught the ball, Billy Joe made a great tackle, and the refs gave him a 15-yard penalty for roughing, and on the

640

last play of the half, Rocky Bleier scored, and the Steelers went ahead 21–14. It was a real crime.

"We dominated the whole third quarter, should have tied the game. We missed a play to tight end Jackie Smith that could have been a touchdown.

"The play was a brand-new goal line play put in a couple days before the game. It was a play with three tight ends. One of the tackles was the third tight end.

"On the play I was to look for Billy Joe, the tight end on the other side, to go to the corner, and I was to come back looking for the fullback out of the flat. The fullback was there strictly as an outlet receiver. What Jackie was supposed to do was get into the back of the end zone.

"We were on the 11-yard line. It was a third-and-one, and Landry sent in this play. I realized he was sending in a goal line play, but I noticed we didn't have the right receivers in the game, so I had to call timeout.

"There was no time left on the [play] clock, so I went off to the side and I said, 'Coach, that's a goal line play.' He said, 'Well, you're right.'

"We had been practicing that from the one- or two-yard line. Jackie was to go to the back of the end zone and stand there and wait for the ball. But in this case we were on the 11.

"Landry said, 'Run it anyway, because they'll be in a goal-line type defense.' And he was right. It was not a bad play. Landry said, 'Look for your keys and make sure we get the first down.' In other words, he wanted me to hit the fullback out in the flat for a first down.

"I called the play in the huddle. I said, 'We're going to run the goal line play.' And sure enough Mel Blount went with Billy Joe to the left, so he was out of the play. The fullback went into the flat and took a defender with him. And Jack Lambert blitzed up the middle, and as he was coming in, Scott Laidlaw just cleaned him, actually knocked the wind out of him. Lambert had to leave the game after that.

"And no one was near Jackie Smith, who was running to the back of the end zone, where he was supposed to go. Now if he would have just stopped at the goal line, it would have been perfect. But that's not what he was told. He knew his job was to get to the back of the end zone, which was 21 yards instead of 11 or 12. So he was running into the end zone, and I saw him wide open. I was seeing the whole thing. I'm saying, 'Oh my God, there is no one near Jackie Smith.' No one is even close to him. They let him run free.

"I released the ball, and I took something off it, because Jackie was not totally turned. He was just starting to turn when I was throwing the ball. And I think it surprised him that the ball got to him that fast. I really do. And I threw it a little bit low, and he kind of slipped.

"And the thing was, he really hadn't run that play. If he would have stopped at the goal line, he would have been standing there waiting. And it would have been real easy to hit him, and he would have caught it.

"But see, he was running to the back of the end zone, and I was getting blitzed, so I'm throwing it, and he just ran too deep. 'Cause the play was perfect. It was a great call, a great play if Pittsburgh blitzed, and they loved to blitz deep in their territory, so it worked like a charm.

"But Jackie was surprised, and the ball hit him in the chest, and he couldn't catch it. We had to settle for a field goal so it was 21–17 Pittsburgh instead of a tie.

"Even so, we were still in charge. The Steelers didn't have a first down in the third quarter. We got the ball back, and we should have scored, but we had to punt, and they got the ball back with just a few minutes left in the third quarter, and Terry Bradshaw threw the ball up for grabs to Lynn Swann, and the officials made the worst call in the history of football. I mean, the back judge was right there, swinging his arms to indicate the pass was incomplete, when from the middle of the field Fred Swearington, who was not the referee, was just the field judge, threw his flag. He said that Benny Barnes had interfered with Swann. He shouldn't have made that call. Back then, even if you threw a flag, it didn't matter. You didn't overrule the call of the referee.

"But on this play that's what they did even though Swearington saw the play differently from every other person in the Orange Bowl. And because of that penalty, they went in and scored on a run by Franco Harris after the referee ran into Charlie Waters, who would have stopped him.

"And the bad thing about it, they kicked off, and Roy Gerela slipped and squibbed the ball to Randy White, who had a broken hand, and Randy tried to run the thing back, and he fumbled on our own 18. On the next play Bradshaw threw for another touchdown. So they made fourteen points in a matter of two minutes, and they hadn't even had a first down!

"It's not an excuse, but let me tell you, that's a big swing in that game. 'Cause I really believe we had them confused. We were moving the football, and of course, we continued to do that, but we didn't have enough time.

"With six minutes left we trailed 35–17. We moved the ball and scored twice. Billy Joe DuPree caught a touchdown pass, and then Butch Johnson caught one to make the score 35–31, and we had the ball again when we tried an onside kick, and the Steelers recovered the ball. Unfortunately, we should have done that in the third quarter. And that's why it was so unfair to blame Jackie. He got hammered on the deal, which was so unjust. There were so many plays in that game that made a difference. I threw an interception, Randy White fumbled, the flag on the bogus interference call, and who got the hammer? Jackie, which was so unfair. It was a tragedy for him.

"This was the most disappointing game I ever played in, because we had this great team. Breaks were going to determine that game. No one dominated the other. To me, the '78 team was the best team we *ever* had in Dallas."

DREW PEARSON: "We should have won Super Bowl XIII. We felt going into that game that we were a better team than the Pittsburgh Steelers, and we were devastated by that loss, really. It took a lot out of us. We wanted to be regarded as one of those unique teams that won back-to-back Super Bowls, but we just made too many mistakes in that game, just didn't have enough time at the end to beat the Steelers, but we should have beat them.

"Everyone blamed Jackie Smith for dropping that pass, and when it happened it was a disappointment, but no more a disappointment than the fumble on the exchange that I had with Tony Dorsett on our first drive on a reverse pass we had set up where Billy Joe was wide open, which would have led to a touchdown on our first drive. It's no different than the disappointment we felt when Randy White tried to run a squib kick back with a cast on his wrist. And the other mistakes we made were disappointing, as were the bad calls that went against us. Jackie's play was only one play in a series of plays that led us to lose that football game.

"We lost 35–31, and when it was over I was more disappointed in losing that game than any other. It was a tough loss to take. We had done so much and overcame so many obstacles and we wanted it so bad. We wanted the back-to-back Super Bowls so badly that we could taste it, we could feel it, we lived it. We were a committed team, the players, the coaches, the organization, and nothing less than winning the Super Bowl was acceptable. There was no joy unless we could have won it all, and we didn't, and so it was sad and disappointing. It took a lot out of myself and a lot of players. It was really tough to take, but we dealt with it as professionals and gave credit where credit was due."

61

America's Team

t the end of the '78 season Bob Ryan of NFL Films called Cowboy public relations director Doug Todd to suggest a possible title for the Cowboys' highlight film: *Champions Die Hard.*

"I don't like that," said Todd. "We're not dead or dying."

"Then how 'bout something that projects the Cowboys as a national team? We've got all this footage of people in stadiums all over the league waving Cowboy pennants. How 'bout calling it *America's Team*?"

"I like that," said Todd. "That sounds good."

The title America's Team was hated by the Cowboy players, because it smacked of that same arrogance that for years the Cowboys had been accused of displaying. Tom Landry didn't care for it, because it gave opposing teams one more thing for which to hate the Cowboys. "It gives the appearance that we are saying that we are the best team in the country," said Landry.

Tex Schramm, the marketing whiz, loved it.

By the late 1970s, no sports team in America was as popular as the Cowboys, not even the New York Yankees. The Cowboys had 225 radio stations in their network, including 16 in Spanish. The *Dallas Cowboy Weekly* had 95,000 subscribers, more even than *Pro Football Weekly.* A full 30 percent of apparel sold by NFL Properties had the Cowboys name on it, much of it with Roger Staubach's number 12 on the back. (The Pittsburgh Steelers were second, with 8 percent of the market.) The Cheerleaders sold over a million posters. Their made-for-TV miniseries drew bigger ratings even than *Roots* or *Jesus of Nazareth*. In every town where the Cowboys played, there were significant numbers of Cowboy fans. America was Cowboy crazy.

Art Spander of the *San Francisco Examiner* made this analysis of the phenomenon: "These are difficult, complex times in America. Inflation, court-ordered busing, oil crises, lack of leadership. People seek a simpler life, a hero. That would be the cowboy—small *c*—and the Old West.

"Levi's, boots, 10-gallon hats are now worn as often in the East and Pacific Coasts as they are in the Southwest.

"And what's in Texas? Not much, really. Flat land, tall steel buildings, oil wells, and yes, with a capital *C,* the Cowboys, the most stable entity in America. In their twenty seasons of operation, they have had one owner, Clint Murchison, one president, GM Tex Schramm, one head coach, Tom Landry, one personnel director, Gil Brandt.

"Our best cars are from Europe. Our best electronic equipment and cameras are from Japan. What happened to the Great American Dream of working harder, producing better? It's alive and living in Texas Stadium."

DREW PEARSON: "By 1978 we could tell how much the Cowboys had become a part of America's culture. We could feel it. Everywhere we went people wanted to be part of the Cowboys, people wanted to identify with the Cowboys. When we went out of town to play away games, airports, hotel lobbies were always packed with Cowboy fans, and it had been that way in previous years, but it was really peaking, really out there. We knew from the type of endorsements some of the players were getting, the type of appearances players were getting, we knew by the reaction of this city, anywhere we went we were known, and we were treated as special individuals.

"Our popularity was at an all-time peak, and it wasn't just in Dallas. It was on a national basis. I was running the Cowboy basketball team at that time, and we would go all over and sell out not just gyms but arenas. We played the Pittsburgh Steelers up in Pittsburgh, and 9,000 people came. We played a group of All-Stars in San Antonio in the HemisFair Arena, and 10,000 people were there for that game. So we understood our popularity and what success and winning had brought to us, and we liked it. We wanted to keep it going."

*   *   *

But for America's Team to continue winning, it had to stay intact, and in 1979 it lost several of its key pieces, including Jethro Pugh, who retired, and its entire strongside trio of Ed "Too Tall" Jones, Charlie Waters, and Hollywood Henderson.

Before that happened, there were smaller tremors. On June 8, 1979, Gigi Clayton, Tony Dorsett's eighteen-year-old girlfriend, died mysteriously. She had been a child actress, an honors student, and they were going to be married. Out of the blue, she had become paralyzed. Doctors could not find the cause. A week later she died. Then on June 14 John Murchison, Clint's brother, died suddenly in mid-June while addressing a dinner of Boy Scout volunteers.

A week after that Ed "Too Tall" Jones shocked everyone when he announced that he was quitting the Cowboys to become a professional boxer. Jones had played out his option in '78 and become a free agent, and he was asking for $250,000 from Tex Schramm. When Schramm wouldn't give it to him and no other NFL team contacted him, Jones retired to go into boxing. Because Jones was 6'9", the media scoffed, but when Jones was growing up in Tennessee, he had won the state Golden Gloves championship. Boxing was his true love. Jones was training with Murphy Griffith, the uncle of boxing champ Emile Griffith.

Losing the 6'9" defensive end was a huge loss for the Cowboys. Jones, whose Tennessee State teams lost just two games in the four years he was there, could run the 40 in 4.75 and high-jump 6'10".

When Jones announced his resignation, Tom Landry told reporters, "Too Tall had great ability but limited desire. If he had been motivated to be the best of all time, he could have become consistent and become the best." His teammates disagreed. Said Thomas Henderson at the time, "The Cowboys are saying he had a motivational problem, but he was motivated every game. He made the big tackles. He was hurt because he didn't get the recognition."

With first Jethro Pugh in retirement and now Jones, Tom Landry was glumly realistic. "Their loss has weakened us considerably," he said.

July was quiet, but then in August it was reported that Tony Dorsett had suffered a broken toe after he dropped a heavy mirror on it. Two days later Danny White broke his thumb, Thomas Henderson was hospitalized with a hiatal hernia, and in an exhibition game against the Seattle Seahawks, defensive back Charlie Waters suffered a serious knee injury, underwent an operation for torn ligaments, and was lost for the season.

Despite all this and Thomas Henderson's increased friction with head coach Tom Landry, the Cowboy machine rolled on. In '79 Tom Landry let

Staubach loose, and he began having monster days and Tony Dorsett continued his climb toward greatness.

ROGER STAUBACH: "In '75, '77, and '79 I played football as well as I ever did as far as what I had to do. Seventy-nine was the first time Landry opened up the passing game. Today you see quarterbacks throw for 350 yards—in '79 we were that type of team. Drew and Tony Hill both went over 1,000 yards, and we were a big-play team. We would hit the key third downs.

"Third down was the measurement. We got them, and we would score. The question always is: how do you get the ball into the end zone? When we got down there, we could use Dorsett, could use Drew, could use Tony. That's where I felt my strength was. I could figure out how to score. That was my job. No matter how you cut it, the quarterback has got to get his team in the end zone. Guys can have great statistics and not get it in. The thing was, we had the people, and different people. We also had Billy Joe DuPree, a big tight end. He made a lot of key plays. So we really had a lot of good players."

The Cowboys were 7–1, but in a 14–3 loss to the Pittsburgh Steelers, who taunted them for being America's Team, L. C. Greenwood tackled Roger Staubach as he tried to scramble and sent him backward hard to the ground, knocking him out. No one knew it at the time, but Greenwood's hit would later change the course of Cowboy history.

DREW PEARSON: "It was a very physical game. As a matter of fact, I got my bell rung twice in that football game. I was knocked out twice—once in the first quarter by Dennis Winston, who was playing middle linebacker in place of Jack Lambert, who was hurt, and the other time was in the fourth quarter, just before Roger got hurt on the same pass pattern, by the same guy, Dennis Winston.

"But I remember Roger scrambling around. We were trying to run a pass pattern. He was scrambling around, and I was actually coming back to him, coming back to the ball, and L.C. caught up to him, and it wasn't a vicious hit. L.C. led with his head, and he caught Roger in the midsection, pulled him down with his legs, but when Roger was going back, the force, the momentum, was so great that his head hit that hard turf in Three Rivers Stadium, and you could actually see his head bounce, like L.C. was dribbling his head on the turf. I knew it was a severe hit. Of course, Roger was out. He was totally out. He didn't know what hit him, what happened.

And as a matter of fact, he didn't become coherent until we were on the airplane flying back to Dallas after that football game. We used to sit across from each other, and I could tell when he snapped to.

"He was conscious—you're conscious when you get your bell rung. These concussions, I've had almost one a year throughout my whole career. I had a concussion, got my bell rung in the first quarter against the Tampa Bay Buccaneers one game in Texas Stadium, and played the whole half of the game unconscious, but conscious. Caught a couple passes and everything. When I finally came to, I couldn't believe we were in the locker room in halftime. What had happened to the first half? How did we score? So it was the same thing with Roger. He just came to on the plane, and he asked what happened, and I told him, 'L.C. gave you one of those great hits.' But it was tough. Not even Roger Staubach could sustain that one."

Despite the concussion, Staubach didn't miss a game, and the next week against the New York Giants he pulled the game out in the final minute on a 36-yard touchdown pass to Drew Pearson, followed by a Rafael Septien field goal, as the Cowboys won 16–14. Then came two losses, to the Philadelphia Eagles and the Washington Redskins. In the third period of the Redskin game, the cameras caught Thomas Henderson mugging and fooling around. Linebacker coach Jerry Tubbs caught Henderson's act and was angry and upset. He told Tom Landry. The next day Landry kicked Henderson off the team, saying that Henderson would never play in Dallas again. In all the reporting there was not a single mention of Henderson's cocaine addiction.

DREW PEARSON: "I was surprised that Thomas had let it get to that point. But he had become a disruptive force within our football team. And then when I found out he was doing cocaine on the sidelines during that game then hey, I wanted to kick his butt. Here we are playing a big football game, and everything's on the line, and you're doing cocaine while we're out here risking our lives? You're playing high? It was a disappointment to me. We didn't deserve to win if we had one player on our team doing something like that, we didn't deserve to win, 'cause you can't condone that. You can't do those things and expect to win, and we shouldn't have won.

"The guy had more ability than anybody who ever played defense for the Cowboys. He could have been the greatest player ever to play for the Cowboys. But he had another agenda. He wanted to be the greatest partyer, the greatest womanizer in Cowboy history, and he won that. He got that title. 'Cause he had women lined up, and he partied. And many times I partied with him. I'm not trying to say I acted like a saint. Many times I partied with him. Even though I was married at the time, many times I left his house early in the morning and went right to practice the next day with the same clothes I had on the night before. But we partied hard, and he was the hardest of the partyers. He was an All-Pro at partying."

In '79 Thomas Henderson's downward spiral continued. The year began when he went to the Bahamas to participate in the Super Stars competition and he was almost busted by local authorities. His season—and, with it, his Cowboy career—ended on November 18. It was not until 1983 that he was able to put his life back on track.

THOMAS HENDERSON: "They should have busted me in the Bahamas. It might have changed the course of history. I had an ounce of cocaine, some marijuana, and the customs inspector took my bag off my shoulder, opened it up, looked in my bag, opened up my drug compartment, looked at me, looked back at my bag, looked at me, and in a Bahamian accent, he said, 'Have a good time, Hollywood.'

"I was so fucking arrogant and so fucked up, I'm not sure I was even scared. I was just nuts. I was world-famous. I had just done that commercial for 7-Up, 'America's Turning 7-Up.' This was all basically done on the self-promotion of Thomas Henderson. The great PR guy Tex Schramm never fucking promoted me, only the people he wanted to promote, so everything Thomas Henderson received in the perks department was his own doing. And it was one of those deals. But I *played* myself into that 7-Up commercial, too. You know, I wish I had kept drinking that shit instead of drinking booze.

"I arrived in training camp in a limo and announced I wanted my contract renegotiated. I was underpaid. I was going to make $90,000 or $100,000, and it had gotten to the point where my performance and my work didn't match my money. I was so nuts that I pulled up at the training facility at Thousand Oaks and had the limousine driver drive the car up on the field and sit there on the shoulder. And it pretty much disrupted practice, because as they were practicing, they kept wanting to know who was in the limo, and I was in the limo snorting coke, smoking marijuana, and drinking champagne. After I held them in suspense for forty minutes, I got out of the car with cowboy boots, shorts, cowboy hat, sunglasses, and I walked out on the field, and Landry knew I was going to come right over and shake his hand, and he shook my hand like George Bush would shake Saddam Hussein's hand, with no firmness, no look in the eyes.

"And then in August, right before the Seattle exhibition game, I had a freaky thing called a hiatal hernia. You can look it up. The symptoms of it are very similar to a heart attack. It's where the flap on your esophagus doesn't function properly, and the flap stays down, which causes you to have gas on the chest, and it really mimics a heart attack.

"And even though I had that, Landry wanted me to travel. If Staubach would have had a hiatal hernia, Landry would not have asked him to get on an airplane to fly to Seattle for a preseason game. But because my name is Thomas Henderson, and because I don't like to practice and I don't like his meetings and I don't like him, even with a team of doctors standing over me with scalpels, his only decision is out of some prejudice against me, and so he said he wanted me to travel, and I told Landry, 'I ain't flying to no motherfucking Seattle to stand up and watch no fucking game.'

"Well, his punishment to me was, 'If you're not going to Seattle with us, go to Dallas to the hospital.' So they sent me to Dallas. Of course, Landry didn't want to leave me at Thousand Oaks. He figured I'd go up and get some pussy when he was gone.

"The hernia hung around for longer than normal. I don't know how many days or weeks it's supposed to last but this thing got on me and stayed a couple of weeks.

"It is something you operate on if that flap doesn't open up. The scar is from the middle of your back all the way around. They crack your ass like a coconut and look in there and fix stuff.

"I flew to Dallas, and they put me in Baylor Hospital and I felt a lot better when I got to Baylor. That's when I started feeling better, because they had me sleeping in almost a standing position. With a hiatal hernia, they put your feet down and your head up. They have you sleeping at an angle. They put a policeman by my door. And I climbed out the window.

"I recovered, and against Houston in a preseason game, I stopped Earl Campbell all by myself on the goal line. It was one of the greatest hits in football, but see because of Tex Schramm—if D. D. Lewis would have made that play, it would have been on NFL films for the history of the game. If Bob Breunig would have made that tackle, same thing. But shit, I had to go *find* that fucking play on the game films. Damn right. I found it by calling the Cowboys after Jerry Jones took over. So I now have it.

"When Landry first was aware of Thomas Henderson, when he looked at me in training camp, when I was twenty-two years old, Jerry

Tubbs and him put me on goal line defense, because they wanted to check out the linebackers who will run through the hole, because when you're on the goal line, there is no time for hesitation. You just have to go in there and put your head in, and so the first time Landry ever saw me play on a goal line play, Jerry Tubbs explained to me, 'Thomas, if the halfback goes this way, you run through that hole. If he goes that way, you run through this hole.' Well, on several occasions after those instructions, I'd knock people out, 'cause I ran through the hole with reckless abandon and hit whatever the fuck was in the hole. Well, that same philosophy is what I hit Earl Campbell with. Earl was running the play away from me, and his cutback cut back to me. Let me tell you, you have to think in football. I had about two seconds to decide what to do with this Earl Campbell. And my decision was to hit him in his fucking mouth. If I'd a hit him low, he'd a run over me. It would have been, 'Goddamn, well he ran over Henderson, didn't he?' But the way I hit him, it didn't mean he was going to go down, but he was going to remember that I smacked his ass. And so to Earl's surprise—a guy like him is always surprised when someone hits him in the face—and I had just big enough cojones to go hit him in the face, and I was successful.

"Matter of fact, real fans of the Cowboys and of me, whenever I'm in Texas or around the country, will come up to me, and they'll go, 'Man, let me tell you something. I saw you hit Earl Campbell. The damnedest hit I ever saw in my life.' I still get those comments.

"The Cowboys had a 7–1 record, and we were going to play the Steelers when Landry came up to me and said, 'You know what our deal is.' Right then, I knew Landry'd lost his mind. He had started focusing so much on discipline with me that he lost all reason with Thomas Henderson. He started treating me differently. He started treating me a little like Duane Thomas, and I wasn't going to have that. I had been sick. I had just come off hepatitis. I had the hiatal hernia, so I did not have a good summer. I was legitimately sick, and I had the flu, man. I mean, I had the flu bad, and the doctor and the trainer told me to take off a couple of days. I'm talking about nose stopped up, snot rags, headaches, weak, chills, just sick, but Landry, of course, made up these rules that said to me in effect, 'If you don't practice every day, you don't start on Sunday.' 'Hey, you're the boss. Make up whatever fucking rules you want.'

"But you have to have a waiver on illness. He came over to me, and he said, 'You know what our deal is, Thomas. Hegman is going to start. You missed practice.' Well. Bob Breunig was sitting there, and he could see me, a black man, turn red. He was going to start Mike Hegman, play him a series, and then put me in. 'Cause he knew who his horse was. And I said, 'Fuck that.'

"I got up and went over to Landry's breakfast table in front of Stallings, Stautner, Tubbs, the whole crew, and I tapped him on the shoulder. Landry looked around, and I said, 'Let me just tell you this. If I don't start, I ain't playing today. Now, you handle that.'

"I guess nobody in his life had ever done that to him. I went over to the stadium, and my uniform stayed in the locker. I didn't tape my ankles. I just sat in my locker, and at some point Landry came over to me and said, 'I talked to the trainer,' as if he didn't know, and he backed off, said I was starting. And one more time my teammates saw something they had never seen before. They saw somebody challenge Landry. And it was probably the only time in my life I was right and he was wrong.

"There were other guys trying to have their own personalities, trying to be flamboyant, but trust me, I was the only one challenging Landry at the time. The guys would run in the corner and sniggle about what I was doing! They would say things like, 'Do you believe that motherfucker would do that?'

"But my days as a Cowboy were coming to an end. I was even losing Mike Ditka, who had always championed me on his special teams. The one thing between Ditka and me, I always knew that Ditka was a great football player, and Ditka knew I was a great football player. So we had a common knowledge of each other, and although he was coaching, I always knew that if I ever played against Mike Ditka, I'd a had a full day's work. But Ditka finally came to me one day and said, 'You know, Thomas, Buffalo Bill was a Cowboy.' And it wasn't long after that that I was released. Ditka knew something was in the works. Landry had probably said to him, 'I don't know how much longer I'm going to put up with this fucking Henderson.'

"So we played the Redskins in Washington, and I was still sick. I was ill that year. The tight end, he just owned me that day. And that doesn't mean he abused me. I just couldn't get around him. I had no strength. I just couldn't play. I was weak, but no excuses. I played. I remember one time I blitzed, and I hit John Riggins, and bam, I just slid down to the ground and he took off. So it just wasn't a good day. Wasn't the worst day, but it was not a good game for me.

"And after the game somebody came up to me and said something like, 'You shouldn't have been looking at the camera.' I said, 'Aw fuck you. What do you mean?' I just went ballistic on whoever said it to me, and then on the airplane going home, I basically got drunk and walked up to first class, and said, 'You all can kiss my ass,' 'cause Jerry Tubbs had come to me and said, 'Thomas, you shouldn't have been looking in the camera.' Well, fuck you. They put the camera in my face. What do you want me to do, stick my head in my ass? But the camera incident was the culmination of a lot of things, not *the* thing. The next day Landry called me in to say he was letting me go. And I told him, flat out, 'Landry, you're never going to win another Super Bowl.' 'Cause I had been telling Gil Brandt and Tex Schramm that all along. I said, 'I am you'all's main ingredient on this fucking team. I fucking block punts, I cover your fucking punts, I cover your kickoffs, shut down all these great-ass return men.'

"I believe this: I wasn't the only weapon, but I was a very efficient weapon for the Dallas Cowboys. I contributed to the key areas of success of the Dallas Cowboys. From the time I was a rookie, playing on every special team, I was an impact player. And when Landry didn't have me on the defense, Mike Hegman went back to being Dave Edwards, a boring-ass linebacker on the strong side. So Landry lost that component. He lost me on third down, lost me on punt coverage, lost me on kickoff returns, he lost one of the best players in the National Football League.

"He had Staubach, Dorsett, Charlie Waters, but I *was the difference.* I made a difference. I always made something happen. I caused a turnover. I made a touchdown. I blocked a punt. I tackled the best fucking punt return guy in the league. I did all those things that average players don't do.

"He should have showed me some respect. He could have got a lot of miles out of me with some respect. I always felt that Landry looked down on me, I know that Landry is not a racist, but he acted like one. If it was not that he didn't act like a racist, he acted holier-than-thou, it was just that he was better. That was his persona. That is all not true, but that's the way he did it. I never had a conversation about anything normal with Tom Landry until *long* after my career was over.

"You know what Landry should have done? Landry claims they knew about my cocaine addiction. See, I think Tex Schramm knew and Gil Brandt knew that I had drug problems. I'm not sure they told Landry. And that's the kind of way the Cowboys were run in those days. They insulated and protected Landry from that sort of thing. I don't know that Landry could have done anything else because I was the drug addict, the alcoholic, the crazy motherfucker. If anything, when it came time for him to get rid of me, if he knew that I had a drug problem, if he loved me, if he cared about me, 'Okay, I've been a bad boy.' But if you know why, if you know 'You've been a bad boy because you've been on drugs,' then if he says he knew, if he *knew* that, why didn't he send me to treatment? Say,

'Thomas, either you're going to a clinic for the drugs you're on or I'm going to release you.'

"In response to Landry releasing me, I announced my retirement. Yeah, it was one of those drunk-defying moments, like growling at the bartender. 'Ah, ah ah ah ah. They can't fire me. I quit.'

"But the Cowboys never did get back to the Super Bowl without me. They missed Thomas Henderson."

62

Casualties

When Ed "Too Tall" Jones embarked on his boxing career in 1979, the player slated to replace him as the strongside defensive end was the Cowboys' number one draft pick of 1978, Larry Bethea. A defensive tackle out of Michigan State, the 6'5", 250-pound Bethea could run the 40 in 4.8 seconds and bench-press 390 pounds. In 1977 he was named the Big Ten's MVP, the first lineman to be so honored since Dick Butkus in 1963. His senior year he had 45 solo and 44 assisted tackles. He finished his college career with a school record 43 sacks.

When the Cowboys drafted Bethea first in '78, Gil Brandt told reporters, "He's no gamble at all."

During his rookie season, Bethea showed great ability but little heart for the game. Thomas Henderson, who was always very good at reading people, called him "Papa Bear." After one play during practice, he wanted to rest. He would refuse to play with minor ailments, not caring that competing players were taking his place for the few extra plays, something unheard of when you're trying to beat out others for a job.

During training camp in '79, Bethea didn't show the necessary aggressiveness to play left end, which required him to charge from a left-handed stance into the teeth of the other team's attack. How, Bethea wondered, could he be mean while having to think about so much?

Tom Landry moved him inside to left tackle. Larry Cole was shifted to end. Skip Bayless reported that Bethea was "too nice" and nicknamed him No Mean Bethea, a takeoff on the nickname of "Mean" Joe Greene, the Steeler behemoth.

Bethea had turned down offers to go to Harvard and Yale so that he could play football at Michigan State. By his second training camp, he was decrying his choice. "I'd be in law school by now," he said. Bethea told Bayless that because he was so big, everyone expected him to play football.

"Yeah, when I was back in high school I had more forethought than most. Everybody else was into stars and heroes, and I had bigger plans. My coaches and counselors all wanted me to go into premed and prelaw, but they just didn't mix with football. I was athlete of the year in Virginia, and everybody just *expected* me to . . ."

Now, Bethea discovered, he couldn't devote himself to the game the way Tom Landry's system demanded. He also could not adjust to the brutality of the pro game. He would watch Randy White maul opposing players in practice and ask him, "What turns you on?" White answered, "Wearing the uniform turns me on."

Bethea responded the way he figured Coach Landry would want him to: "Come Saturday," he said, "I'll show all those nice folks out there I can be a crazy SOB. Yes, sir, ole number 76 will show 'em." The words, however, were hollow. Like a lot of players, Bethea also had great difficulty grasping the Flex. He would ask teammates and reporters, "Man, am I just not good enough?"

By the end of his second training camp, Gil Brandt was singing a different tune. "I just wish there was a way to stick a needle in a guy's arm and find out whether he wants to play or not. That will be the next breakthrough in scouting."

When Ed Jones returned for the 1980 season, Larry Bethea's opportunity to start for the Cowboys was over. He began snorting cocaine, an addiction that captured him for the rest of his too-short life.

THOMAS HENDERSON: "In terms of pro football players, Larry Bethea was not a good football player. He was a mistake. Whenever you pick a guy number one he should end up as a starter. The Cowboys have had some of those guys throughout their history, like Bill Thomas, Aaron Kyle, Billy Cannon Jr., and so Larry was a decent football player, but Larry was *not* a number one draft choice. And I'm not sure what the criteria was for picking him. It was probably his ability to run. He could run a 4.8 40. But

Larry was a good little soul, but here he was playing behind Too Tall Jones and Harvey Martin, and he didn't measure up.

"Larry and I never talked about our cocaine habits. I never had those conversations. But by the time I was talking to Larry, we couldn't even talk. We'd look at each other, and our lips wouldn't move. We were smoking that cocaine. The only conversation we were having was how we could get some more dope."

Bethea continued as a backup through 1983 when his name was mentioned by Tex Schramm in connection with a federal cocaine investigation along with four other Cowboy players. No charges were ever filed. When the Cowboys offered him only a small raise and no bonus to re-sign in '84, he signed a three-year contract for $550,000 with the Michigan Panthers of the USFL. When he left Dallas, he was bitter, complaining that Tom Landry had never given him much of a chance to be a starter.

He went from the Michigan Panthers to the Oakland Invaders, then to the Houston Gamblers, and when the USFL folded, so did Bethea's football career. His life after football was a steady spiral downward.

In July of 1985 he was arrested for setting three fires in Mount Rainier National Park in Washington state. He pleaded guilty and was ordered to pay a $1,000 fine and undergo psychiatric evaluation. A few months later he asked Gil Brandt for his severance pay but didn't give a return address because he was homeless, living on the streets of Seattle.

In mid-1986 Bethea returned to live with his mother in Newport News, Virginia. According to Johnny Yu, a convenience store owner who knew him in Newport News, no local businessman would give him a job.

In August of 1986, Bethea was arrested for stealing his mother's life savings of $64,000 from the attic safe. When he was brought in, he had $61,375, mostly in twenty-dollar bills, in his pockets. That day he had gone to the home of his estranged wife and bloodied her lip and scratched her arm in a scuffle. Adding to the confusion, Bethea's wife claimed half ownership of his mother's money, saying she was entitled to it under a divorce petition. Bethea was sentenced to four years in jail, but the judge suspended the sentence and ordered him to pay back his mother.

Ed Jones ran into Bethea not long after the incident with his mother. He was hoping Bethea was getting help, but he could see that he wasn't straight.

In March of 1987 Bethea applied for a job at a local 7-Eleven Store. He was a regular customer there. He didn't get the job. At the time he was living on biweekly checks of $332 for retirement benefits from the Houston Gamblers. According to Yu, Bethea spent most of the money on ciga-rettes, beer, and cocaine.

On April 23, 1987, Bethea went to Yu to cash his final paycheck. He was depressed because it was for half the usual amount. He told Yu he had to get out of town. He cashed the check and went out and bought cocaine.

Bethea stole a gun from a parked car and robbed two convenience stores that evening. The stores were near his mother's home, and he was recognized as the robber in both instances. One of the stores was the 7-Eleven where he had applied for a job.

A few hours later he was found in the backyard of a run-down board-ing house where a childhood friend had been staying. The friend, Tony McNight, had not been seen for a week. His brother, Jason, told Susie Woodhams of the *Dallas Times-Herald* that he thought Bethea had gone there to be in a familiar atmosphere.

When police found Bethea by the side of the boarding house, a bul-let from the gun used in the robberies had ripped through his right temple. He had killed himself. He was thirty years old.

Jason McNight, who had himself been arrested and convicted of drug use, blamed himself for Bethea's death. "If I'd been there," McNight said, "I could have taken the gun and sent him home."

No one in Dallas could believe what had happened to him. Bethea had been so intelligent, so sensitive, so together. His motto had been "A man is only as good as his word." But he had been unable to control his drug habit, and the cocaine made him an animal, a creature forced to do terrible things so he could buy drugs he apparently no longer could stand doing. Hating himself for his drug habit and his twilight zone existence, Larry Bethea put himself out of his misery.

THOMAS HENDERSON: "My heart always goes out to those afflicted by the disease of alcoholism and drug addiction. He shot himself in the head after he robbed a store of people he knew. And I understand where Larry had been."

Thomas Henderson had been fired from the Cowboys in the middle of the 1979 season. Petulantly, Henderson announced he had retired, a big mis-take, because now the Cowboys still owned his contract. Had he allowed them to put him on waivers, he could have cut a rich deal with whoever picked him up. He ran off to Las Vegas. When he returned to Dallas, his cocaine habit had reached $400 a day. No longer a Cowboy, his safety net was gone. After twelve federal agents raided his hotel room, he flew to

California to play for the San Francisco 49ers. The cocaine, however, made it almost impossible for him to function. He fell asleep at meetings, even at practice. He told the team doctor about his addiction and asked for help, but none was forthcoming. Henderson wore out his welcome in San Francisco when he did coke with one of the 49er secretaries, who was busted and was asked to tell what she knew about Henderson. Meanwhile, Henderson's wife, Wyetta, called 49er coach Bill Walsh and told him about his cocaine habit. That evening he was put on waivers.

Said Henderson, "I had asked for help, but instead of trying to heal me, the 49ers were letting me go."

Next stop was the Houston Oilers under Bum Phillips. Henderson had just about broken his neck in San Francisco, and in his third week in Houston, a hamstring popped. His heretofore perfect body was cracking under the strain of the drug habit, which by now had climbed to a one-day record of $2,100. He began freebasing, the ultimate high. In nine weeks, Henderson spent $110,000.

He moved out on his wife. "Thomas" Henderson was no longer in his body. In his place was a madman. He was paranoid. One night he packed his paraphernalia, sure he was going to be busted, and walked fifteen blocks from his room in the Marriot Hotel to the Astrodome, certain he would be safe there. He sat down in the middle of the parking lot. He was sure the cops were watching him. He pulled his coat over his head—and smoked his cocaine.

He started screaming at the rustling bushes at the edge of the parking lot. "I know you cops are there." He shouted that if they came after him, he would break his pipe on the macadam and throw the coke all over the parking lot.

He sat under his coat for forty-five minutes, peeking out and screaming. Only after the pipe clogged was he able to stop and stand up.

He flung the pipe across the parking lot. It smashed into shards.

"I threw the coke away," he yelled. "I don't have any drugs on me. I'm going back home now."

He walked back to his hotel room. He was holding more rocks of coke in his hand.

Amazingly, his hamstring healed, and he returned to football. He had missed seven games. Football didn't matter. There was only cocaine. He was put on waivers and then reinstated at the end of the season in the final game against the Vikings. Incredibly, Henderson made the interception that saved the game for the Oilers. In the playoffs, they lost to the Oakland Raiders. Henderson was having blackouts, and he couldn't remember much of the game. He was drooling.

He flew back to Dallas. In three weeks he went through $15,000 in cash and another $5,000 he had borrowed. A girlfriend asked him, "Where, in this sickness, lives this man?"

Henderson couldn't say a word. He was running, and he couldn't stop. He thought to himself, "I am going to die."

Not knowing where to turn, Henderson was watching Super Bowl XV on TV when he saw Charlie Jackson, the head of NFL security. He called Jackson in New Orleans and told him he was freebasing and needed help. "It's ruining my life. I'm spending all my money. I'm going crazy," he said.

Jackson gave him the name of a psychiatrist and said he would help get him into a drug rehab center. But when the psychiatrist asked Henderson about his children, he exploded and ran off.

Henderson was sent to Camelback Hospital in Scottsdale, Arizona, the first NFL player ever to admit to drug addiction. While in the clinic, his wife served him divorce papers. He got drunk that night. He was put in psychiatric lockup.

Even after sixty days of treatment, his cravings for cocaine were very strong. Any time he drank a beer or smoked marijuana, the craving returned. He flew back to Dallas, and he returned to freebasing.

Henderson wanted to play football again, and he called Don Shula, who said he could try out for the Miami Dolphins in May of '81. To pay for his coke, Henderson sold his dream house in North Dallas.

At camp he was heavy, but he could still run. He scrimmaged with the rookies, and Shula personally accompanied him to AA meetings. But one of the rookies was freebasing, and Henderson could not say no.

In the last preseason game he took off his neck protector. In the second quarter against the Kansas City Chiefs, running back Joe Delaney hit him so hard he felt he had been hit with a sledgehammer. He blacked out. The tingling wouldn't stop. He started to feel numb. On the next snap, he ran *away* from the play. This time his neck was broken. He lay in the clubhouse the rest of the second half until the game was over.

Instead of being sent to the hospital, he was sent home, where he couldn't sit, couldn't lie down. The next day he could not get out of bed. His arms and legs didn't work. He started screaming. There was no one to hear him. He screamed from 4 A.M. until almost 8:30 in the morning. "Please, help me!" Finally, a maid heard him. She went and got help.

The doctor came and said he had a pinched nerve. Henderson told him he was sure his neck was broken. A CAT scan proved him right. His football career was over.

Henderson moved back to Dallas and found a new coke connection. He was getting a check for $6,000 every week based on a $125,000-a-year salary with the Dolphins, but the money was going to buy cocaine. Nothing else mattered to him but the pipe.

By December 1981 Thomas Henderson was broke. His money was gone. His house had been sold. He had no possessions. He pawned his Super Bowl rings and smoked that money. All he had left were his Mercedes and his clothes.

For over a year Henderson lived with singer B. J. Thomas, who supported him that whole time.

He got a job in an executive recruitment firm. He started to get into the nuances of drinking lunch. He began having blackouts. From beer at breakfast, he became a full-blown alcoholic. Now he had a double addiction. Then he began having seizures.

B. J. Thomas had to finally ask him to leave. To rent an apartment he had to borrow money. As collateral, he put up his precious car. In February 1983, he stopped paying rent and lost the car.

On his thirtieth birthday, March 1, 1983, he was dead broke. He owed everyone in Texas money, so he fled to California in the car he was supposed to turn over to his ex-employer.

Speeding across Texas and Arizona, his only thought was: I really want to die.

Then on November 2, 1983, Henderson and two underage girls shared some coke and had sex. The cops were at his door. His arrest, of course, made national headlines. He freebased heavy, hoping to die. Said Henderson later, "I wanted to stick a gun in my mouth and blow my brains out, but the police had my gun."

Four days later he checked into another treatment center. He met people as sick as he was. When he was finally able to admit he was an alcoholic, his life began to change. He finally recognized that if he didn't change, he would die, that if he freebased, he would die.

He was sentenced to four years and eight months for statutory rape. He was seven months and three days sober when he went to prison.

He got out on October 15, 1986. He was sober, which he has remained to this day. Now living in Austin, Thomas (no longer Hollywood) Henderson has become one of the preeminent spokesmen on alcohol and cocaine addictions.

In a way, Thomas Henderson has become a symbol of the excesses of the 1970s, a professional football player who threw away a certain niche in the Hall of Fame because of drugs. But really, the symbol should have been Larry Bethea, who had been unlucky enough to be holding a gun at the same time his drug habit had defeated him. When Henderson wanted to die, he was unarmed. As a result, Bethea is dead, Henderson alive.

"I'm the most famous ex-cocaine addict in the world," he states as a matter of record. And that is true, but what Thomas Henderson is most proud of is that he has been sober since 1983 and since that time he has been able to help hundreds of other addicts who were where he had once been. And that, in the end, should be Thomas Henderson's legacy.

63

Roger in Mothballs

wo weeks after Thomas Henderson's dismissal in mid-season of '79, the Cowboys suffered another serious setback when Drew Pearson was injured. He had just caught his second touchdown catch of the day against the New York Giants when he attempted to spike the ball. In doing so, he took a misstep, twisted an ankle, and severely damaged his knee. He returned to catch yet another touchdown pass, but it was to be his last game of the season.

DREW PEARSON: "I caught three touchdowns in the December 2 game against the Giants. That game I had three touchdowns, and I was all fired up because it was against Terry Jackson, who was a nemesis of mine. We just had an ongoing war. When he came in as a rookie, I had been in the league a few years. I had known his brother, Monte Jackson of the Raiders, real well, and Monte was the type of guy you could do anything to, and he would never say anything throughout the whole game. You could spit on him, kick him, cut him, hold him, and he wouldn't say a thing. Push him. Nothing. So I thought Terry was the same way. When we played the Giants in the first game we played against him, I went right at Terry Jackson. I was going to knock the shit out of this guy and have him scared the whole game. And I went after him, but the only thing, Terry wasn't intimidated. It made him mad as hell, and he came back fighting like hell. So from then on, we had a feud.

"We were friendly and respectful after the game, but during the game he was trying to kill me and I was trying to kill him back. It was whoever got to whom first, so I scored early in that football game on Terry, and then scored another one on him, and I got so excited on the second one, I jumped up and didn't know whether I wanted to throw the ball in the stands or spike the ball, and I decided to throw it in the stands, but by that time I was on my way down and landed wrong. My ankle turned, but my knee hyperextended, and I went down like someone had shot me from the stands. The knee was hurting. It swelled up immediately, but I was embarrassed and didn't want Landry to be too upset with me so I went back out there on our next series, and I caught a 44-yard touchdown pass, this time on Ray Rhodes, who was playing cornerback at the time for the Giants. I limped through this pass route, I mean, literally limped through it. But I had to go back out there to save face and I ended up catching it for 44 yards, but then I had to come out of the game after that, and the next day my knee just blew up.

"That was my 100th straight game, and I couldn't play my next one, against Philly, and that was a big game, for the title. We beat them when Butch Johnson came in and caught the winning touchdown pass, and then we came back against the Redskins in Texas Stadium, where we were losing 17–0 and came back and won. John Riggins burst down the sideline for 66 yards to make the score 34–21, and it looked like the game was lost, and then we came back. Roger hit Tony Hill going away in the end zone over Lemar Parrish and we won that game. I remember that game well because I started that game but I couldn't finish, because of my leg. But we came back and won that game, 35–34, one of the best games in Texas Stadium, and it not only won us a division title, got us into the playoffs, but it knocked the Redskins out of the playoffs as well.

"Then in the opening round of the playoffs against the L.A. Rams, we lost 21–19, with two minutes left on a 50-yard bomb to Billy Waddy.

"We fell flat on our face. We didn't play worth a damn. I don't know. I think we went in with a big head full of ourselves, and the Rams came in and surprised us. That was a disappointing loss. That loss hurt very bad, 'cause we felt we had a good team. We could have been in our third straight Super Bowl, should have been.

"We had one last chance to win at the end. I don't know what happened. We just didn't move the ball. You gotta give guys like Jack Youngblood and Fred Dryer and Larry Brooks credit because they kept pressure on Roger all day, and that was Roger's last NFL game, and to let you know what kind of day it was, his last completed pass went to Herb Scott, an offensive lineman. Roger was scrambling around, and just threw it. It was illegal, and we got a penalty and gave up the ball on the play. But that was Roger's last pass. To Herb Scott."

In 1979 Roger Staubach had suffered five concussions, the worst from the hard hit by the Steelers' L. C. Greenwood, and at the end of the year he announced his retirement. A long and glorious era had ended. Since he began playing in Dallas in 1969, Roger Staubach had become the heart and soul of America's Team. He was a military veteran, a football hero, a poster boy for decency and Christian brotherhood, yet as fierce a competitor as ever put on shoulder pads. Twenty-three times, the last being the great 35–34 victory against the Washington Redskins, Staubach led the Cowboys to come-from-behind wins, fourteen times in the last two minutes. Most of these occurred on national television. As long as there was time, Roger Staubach believed the Cowboys could win, and because of this competitive confidence, so did his teammates. Part of the surprise about his retirement was that no one thought he would step down after failing in the opening round of the playoffs to the Rams. Everyone thought he'd come back for at least one more year to try to take the team back to the Super Bowl.

ROGER STAUBACH: "I did a lot of soul-searching before I decided to retire. I was thirty-eight. In the '79 season I had three concussions where I had to leave the game and couldn't return. And against the Rams in the playoffs, Jack Reynolds grabbed me and drove me into the ground. I was dazed, really wasn't totally with it at the end of the game.

"It really bothered me the way we ended the game. I was thinking to myself, 'Hey, I'm thirty-eight, I really want to make this decision on my own.'

"After a total exam, Dr. Fred Plumb in New York told me I definitely should retire. He saw a difference in reactions between my right and left sides. They were very minimal, but he said it could be the beginning of scar tissue syndrome.

"Dr. Paul Williams here in Dallas didn't feel that way. He said he didn't see any difference. But Dr. Williams said there had been enough concussions that retiring was probably not a bad idea. So it was part of the factor.

"If I had been thirty-four, I would not have retired. But being thirty-eight, I told myself it was time. We had been in three Super Bowls in four years, and Danny White was definitely ready to play. So I wasn't abandoning a good team. It was a *very* good team, and I would have had fun with that team. I wish I would have had more years with Drew and Dorsett. We could have won a lot of Super Bowls.

"And Danny White did one hell of a job, really. They just lost some tough games. But it still was a very good team for three or four years.

"I wish I were still playing. But I never second-guessed that I retired. I did miss it a lot more than I would have thought. Maybe if I had known that, knew how much I'd miss it, known that Ed Jones would come back, that Charlie Waters would come back, maybe . . . 'cause see, '79 was a tough year. We played pretty well that year, but Jones wasn't there, Charlie tore up his knee in the exhibition season, Randy White hurt *both* his insteps, Benny Barnes had a bad knee, so we kind of limped through the year. And then everyone came back healthy in '80, and I would have enjoyed quarterbacking that '80 team, that '81 team.

"But Danny quarterbacked them very well. They scored. The big mistake Landry made was giving Gary Hogeboom a chance, not that Gary wasn't a fine athlete, but he wasn't Danny White. That hurt Tom, and when Danny came back he started playing well again, and then Tom tried Pelluer, who was another fine athlete, but Pelluer couldn't handle the deal emotionally. He had to call three timeouts in the first quarter of one game. So there were games that were lost that could have been won.

"I think losing Mike Ditka and Dan Reeves as coaches hurt, too, because they were that link to the players, and Tom listened to both those guys, and then all of a sudden Tom surrounded himself with yes-people. And Ditka and Reeves weren't like that. He needed their influence, because the league was becoming decentralized. You couldn't do it all yourself. I don't know if he would have made the Herschel Walker trade, but if he had had Troy Aikman, he would have won again.

"We were a great team. We had a better '70s than the Steelers. The Steelers won four Super Bowls, but we had nine winning, great seasons. We won so many games, but you are graded on whether you win the Super Bowl. We were the only NFC team to win a Super Bowl in the '70s. But we were very competitive in all of them. In '75 the Steelers were *the* team. I think we overachieved that game. We played a great game that day, and we still could have pulled it off. And we should have won both the Colt games and the second Steeler game. Those were the tough ones. I don't want to sound greedy. It's just that I hate to lose."

DREW PEARSON: "During the season Roger had mentioned retirement a few times, because he had so many concussions. He had that severe one against Pittsburgh. But I never thought he would quit, because nobody likes to go out with a loss, and Roger Staubach certainly was like that. We just felt he would be back. It was something he had to deal with during the off-season. He made a calculated decision.

"The story is if Coach Landry would have let him call his own plays, or if he would have given him more leniency in calling his plays, he would have continued to play, but Coach Landry wouldn't let him do that. I had a lot of influence on Roger as a teammate, and being his receiver, I could have probably begged him or coaxed him to come back, but I didn't. I pulled back. In that type of situation you have to let the player make his own decision. It's got to be him and his family. He has enough pressure from outside influences to try to get him to continue to play. So I never pressured him, or went over to his house and talked to him and said, 'Hey, if you retire, then I'm going to retire,' or threatened stuff like that. I wish I had, because nothing against Danny White, but Roger still had some years left in him in his body and some good games. We all go through the concussion thing. I had just as many, maybe more than Roger had, and you have to be concerned about that, but despite that, I knew Roger had a lot of games left in him, and I didn't want to see him go. And it really was disappointing to me. I never even expressed it to Roger, because I had to accept his decision. If I wasn't willing to come up and persuade him otherwise then I should be willing to accept it when the final decision was made.

"I couldn't even go to his press conference, because I didn't want the whole world to see me crying and broken up. I did watch it on TV, and I watched it with nothing but tears in my eyes and sadness in my heart, because I didn't want to see him go. It was tough to take, but as always in life, it goes on and you have to keep moving."

64

Close, but No Cigar

A t the time he announced his retirement in mid-March 1980, Roger
Staubach was rated the number two passer of all time in the NFL
behind Otto Graham. Third was Sonny Jurgensen, with Lenny
Dawson fourth. The retirement of Staubach was a shock, but it was
blunted some when Ed "Too Tall" Jones announced he would abandon
his boxing career and return to the Cowboys. Jones had earned $300,000
boxing, but he learned that he didn't have the overhand right to get him
to the top of the boxing game. Jones would star for Dallas from 1980
through the 1989 season, becoming one of the most durable players in
franchise history.

The year before, Tex Schramm had liberated talented defensive line-
man John Dutton from a deteriorating situation in Baltimore under owner
Robert Irsay, and so in 1980 the starting defensive front four was Ed
Jones, Harvey Martin, Randy White, and Dutton.

On offense the only change was Danny White for Roger Staubach. It
took a while for White to understand that it was more important for him
to fit into the team than the other way around.

DREW PEARSON: "We had a pretty good year in 1980, finished 12–4. We
overcame a lot. Our offense was high-powered, scored a lot of points.

Danny did a nice job. The thing is, all he had to do was fit in. We took the driver out and put a new driver in. All the other pieces to that puzzle were still in place. Initially, Danny tried to do too much, tried to establish his own identity. And he tried to carry the team, and that wasn't necessary. All he had to do was fit in.

"It took him about halfway through the season to understand that. But you see what we had back. That's why I'm saying Roger was very tough to lose. He could have played that next year. You see the success we had with Danny, and not to slight him any, but, you know, if Roger was there, would could have had that same success. We were in position to go to another Super Bowl."

After the Cowboys thumped the L.A. Rams in the opening round of the playoffs, White engineered a tremendous victory over the Atlanta Falcons with a winning touchdown pass to Drew Pearson with 49 seconds left, but in the NFC title game against the Philadelphia Eagles and their star receiver Wilbert Montgomery, the Cowboys were only able to score a lone touchdown and lost 20–7. White had a poor day, and Tony Hill was criticized for not playing hard.

In '81 the Cowboys, led by Tony Dorsett's 1,646 yards rushing, again finished 12–4, the sixteenth winning season in a row for the Cowboys under Coach Landry. In the playoffs they seemed invincible, shutting out Tampa Bay, 38–0. Then against the San Francisco 49ers, Dallas led 27–21 and was getting close to field goal range, but Danny White misfired on a pass to Doug Donley, and the Cowboys had to punt with only minutes remaining.

Behind young quarterback Joe Montana, the 49ers drove the length of the field and scored when Dwight Clark made an acrobatic catch in the end zone to give the 49ers the 28–27 lead with less than a minute left.

The Cowboys had one more chance. White connected with Drew Pearson, who would have scored, but Eric Wright pulled him down by his uniform shirt. Then with seconds remaining, White dropped back to pass to Tony Hill, but he tripped, fell, fumbled, and the 49ers recovered. It was possibly the most disappointing loss in Cowboy history. It also prevented Danny White from getting the acclaim he deserved. Had the Cowboys won that game and gone on to the Super Bowl, Danny White would have had a far more esteemed place in Cowboy history. The loss to the 49ers, though, was so devastating, it caused everyone to forget all the games played up to then and forced everyone to focus on the defeat.

DREW PEARSON: "I was stunned. It was just so disappointing. We had done what we had to do to get that lead, and heck, if we were going to turn the game over to anybody, why not our Doomsday defense, because they had played well all season long? We expected them to be able to stop the 49ers. We never expected the 49ers to be able to drive it like they did, 90-something yards, and to win the game. I thought somewhere along the line we'd stop them and make them punt and work to get the ball back or they'd kick a field goal and try to cut the lead that way. For them to come all the way down the field was devastating.

"We came back after that. Danny hit me on a play over the middle for big yardage, and I thought I was gone actually. I got caught from behind. I never saw the guy, Eric Wright. He just reached out and was able to grab my jersey. He was able to enforce it by grabbing the shoulder pads, and he yanked me down. But still, that was one play in that drive. We could have come back. I came back to the huddle, and I wanted Danny White to line me up on the other side and instead of my going inside this time, wanted him to send me out and bring it. That would have given us another 20 yards, but Danny called Tony's number, and Tony took a little longer than normal to get downfield trying to avoid coverages, and Danny waited on him instead of looking away and going to the other side, and waited and waited, and he finally got hit and fumbled, and that was the end of that game."

In 1982 everyone expected that this was the year the Cowboys would return to the Super Bowl, but a crippling player strike temporarily changed everyone's plans. The issue was severance pay, and the strike caused seven games to be cancelled. What hurt the Cowboys as much as anything was the anger directed at Danny White, who met with Tex Schramm and tried to end the strike behind the backs of the other players. White had taken a pro-management stance, and afterward the sentiment was that the team didn't want White as their quarterback anymore, but preferred instead backup Gary Hogeboom.

DREW PEARSON: "Nobody wanted to strike. Taking eight games off your career, that's hard to get back. You can get the money back, but you can't get those eight games back. 'Cause time waits on no one.

"I was player rep at that time going through all that, and here was Danny White going behind our backs, trying to solve the strike by meeting with Tex Schramm. We didn't take too kindly to that. It might have been different if he had discussed it with us, and we blessed it—we all wanted to end the strike. We were disappointed Danny took that approach. I think he meant well in what he was trying to do, but his approach got him in trouble, and that's when the feud between him and Gary Hogeboom started brewing. The players resented Danny for doing that, and they started getting on Hogeboom's bandwagon.

"Hogeboom didn't turn out to be the quarterback he was cracked up to be. Hogeboom had us all infatuated, including Coach Landry. I think Gary Hogeboom would have turned out to be a pretty good quarterback, but there was one game after I retired, we were playing the New York Giants, and Hogeboom was having a pretty good year, but Lawrence Taylor steamrolled him on a blitz, and looking at Hogeboom's stats from then on, he was never the same player. He took a devastating hit, and he never recovered from that hit, and he became happy feet back there from then on, and then he became a journeyman. He went from potentially the next great quarterback for the Cowboys to a journeyman.

"In 1984 it was announced that Clint Murchison was putting the team up for sale. I realized there would probably be some changes because Clint, from all we saw, was the ideal owner. He let football people run football business. It was Tex's deal. Tex paraded himself as the owner, and rightfully so, because he was perceived that way, because Clint gave him that type of clout. It was perceived as Tex's team. When the sale happened, you wondered how things were going to shake out, and who was going to get caught up into the transition.

"Around that same time in the winter of '84, I was going through a divorce, and then I fell asleep at the wheel after driving home from a basketball game and rammed the back of a semi that was parked on the shoulder, and that was it for me. When I announced my retirement in August, I had a huge hole in my liver. There was no way I could play again.

"I had planned on playing another three or four more years. I was on the verge of signing a new contract. Actually it was the first time I played out a contract with the Dallas Cowboys, 'cause I kept renegotiating all the time, trying to make up the loss I had coming in as a free agent at such a low salary. So I was on the verge of signing a big lucrative contract in the $500,000-a-year range, so I was looking forward to continuing to play. But because of the accident everything was gone, so I had to scramble around to find out what I was going to do. When the Cowboys made it clear my current contract and their financial obligation to me ran out in August, I said, 'Oh Lord, I have to find something to do.' Because I had gotten divorced in February, and in that divorce I gave up just about everything I had because I wanted it to be a smooth transition, not only for my ex-wife but for my kids. I felt I had a lot of earning power, and I was willing to give that up as long as I could go forward with everything else in place and that being mine.

"When it was announced a few weeks after the accident that I was going to retire, a few people in the TV business were interested, NBC and CBS, and they both offered me opportunities to join their broadcasting teams as a color analyst, and I ended up signing with CBS. I enjoyed that, did seven NFL games that first year. Rudy Martzke's *USA Today* voted me Rookie of the Year, and I enjoyed the work and was looking forward to another season after a year of learning. My agent, David Falk, approached CBS about renewing the contract, and CBS decided, 'Hey, we don't want the guy.' Yeah, well. 'We want to go in another direction.' So I was really really shocked, didn't know what I was going to do, and that's when I started talking about a comeback. 'If they are not going to let me talk about the game, then I will give them something to talk about.' So I was going to go back out there and play.

"After almost a year of being out, the liver regenerated itself and the hole closed up and went from the size of a softball to a silver dollar, so I asked my doctor if I could play again, and he said yes. So I was working to make a comeback and called Tex Schramm and asked his feelings, and he was elated, ecstatic, but the last thing he said, 'Of course, we want our doctors to check you.'

"So I told Coach Landry how I was working out and how I had my weight up and felt good, and some of the guys saw me at the practice field and said I looked like Drew of old, maybe even a little quicker, but they sent my X rays up to the University of Pittsburgh to Dr. Stargell, who's the leading liver specialist in the world, and he said I could play again, but he would not give me 100 percent clearance. He gave me 99, and Coach Landry and I discussed that and we came to the conclusion that if we were going to do this, it had to be 100 percent okay. We were both in accordance with that. I said, 'If I had in the back of my mind that something could happen,' and even Dr. Stargell said if something does happen, if you get hit, you'd have to get hit squarely on that spot, and even if it did start hemorrhaging, which was the biggest fear, that you could probably stop or control it before it became life-threatening. But having that in the back of my mind, I knew I'd have trouble being the same type of player that I was, that fearless guy going over the middle, and so Coach Landry and I concluded over the phone, he said it was probably in the Cowboys' and my best interest not to pursue it.

"And after we decided I wasn't going to play anymore, he offered me an opportunity to come out to training camp to work with the new wide receivers, to coach them in training camp, to help them develop and get them ready. So I did that for five weeks, and I kind of enjoyed it. It was good because they had two rookies, Leon Gonzales and Karl Pow, small-college receivers, had ability but were very green, very raw, who ended up making the team, and the big reason they made it was my guidance and coaching. The other two receivers were Mike Renfro and Tony Hill, so those two guys were set in their ways. My main concern was those two young guys. Since these two guys were on the team, Coach Landry needed them to continue to learn and progress, so he asked me if I wanted to stay on as a part-time, full-time assistant. It was only part-time in pay, but full-time in hours. Doing that for a year, I found out that coaching wasn't for me, and so I got out and had some opportunities as a sports-caster down in San Antonio, doing the weekend sports, did that for six months, and there were a lot of things I tried, had my hand in, but the real deal was after I quit the Cowboys, I had already started this business, and I knew that was going to be my security. I found out that TV was like foot-ball, here today, gone tomorrow.

"While I was still playing I started a company that intended to make sports caps using the logos of the various professional sports teams. The problem was that we were not able to get licensing agreements from any of the pro leagues. We had our struggles, no question. We were no differ-ent than anybody else. These licensing agreements, arrangements, are commodities and very difficult to get. It wasn't anything personal. It was just a business decision these leagues were making. They wouldn't give us the opportunity to do business. This is true of any black entrepreneurs trying to break into the white establishment, which was why we didn't take it personally. It's tough for anybody, let alone if you're a minority, to try to get those opportunities. And even beyond that, it was tough just being an ex-football player. They don't take you seriously. 'You were a good wide receiver, but what the hell do you know about business?' And at that time I didn't know much about business, but I was eager and com-mitted and willing to learn, and I tried to surround myself with business partners who had the expertise I didn't have so I could learn. It was a tough road, but I understand what the NFL and the other leagues were doing.

"Our first agreement was with the United States Olympic Commit-tee. They saw a need to hire a minority vendor in connection with the '88 Olympic Games, and we were the vendor that they hired for headwear, and when we got that, we didn't know what we were doing, so we hooked up with another headwear company who had been bidding for the opportunity, but lost out, and we rode their financial strength, their sourcing capabilities, and their overall marketing expertise during that first year. They did a decent job with the Olympic headwear, but we ended up losing money on the program. But in the meantime, it gave us a lot of credibility in the market, and all of a sudden, 'Who are these guys?' and, 'How did they get an Olympic license?' And so it gave us credibility. We had some nice products.

"And then in '87 Al Campanis made those negative statements about blacks and minorities, about why they aren't fit to be in coaching positions and front-office positions, that they don't have the 'necessities,' the mental capacity, and then Jesse Jackson jumped all over that, and he started the 'Fairness in Sports' committee, and I joined that committee.

"They had their first meeting in Chicago in connection with the Rainbow Coalition conference, and I went up there without an appointment but with an agenda, and my whole agenda was to try to get in front of Reverend Jackson to let him know there is another issue that needed to be put on the table and brought to light, that these sports leagues don't do business with any minorities either. And so that was like, 'Oooh, really?' And so they had this big national press conference, and everybody spoke on the discrimination against minorities in sports, coaching, management, but Reverend Jackson gave me the opportunity to speak on the discrepancies in minorities doing business with these entities, and from there Major League Baseball contacted us, and they were willing to give us an opportunity, a chance, and after I left that meeting in Chicago, I came back to Dallas and went right to a meeting I had scheduled with Tex Schramm.

"My whole point in the meeting with Tex was to make him aware of an opportunity they could take advantage of 'right now' to try to ease this negative situation, and that was to get us a license to do business with them, to publicize that, and get the name Drew Pearson out, and it would go a long way. I explained it would take a long time to hire coaches and the same thing in office positions, so he will continue to have this pressure, so I said, 'This is something you can do immediately and release some pressure.' He saw the value of doing that.

"It just so happened that weekend the NFL owners were getting together in San Diego, and Tex promised me he would talk to Pete Rozelle at that meeting, and that meeting happened, and on Monday we got a call in our office, 'When can you come to New York to meet with Robert Caray, the president of NFL Properties.' So we went up there to meet with them, and they gave us kind of a token-type category, the golf cap category, where you can use all the teams' logos, but it has to be on a golf-style hat, which means it has to have the braid in front and a leather strap in the back, so we said, 'Fine. We'll take that and develop that.' It was a way to get in, and eventually they found out they really didn't want to give us that, so they called us back into New York, and we had them pretty much over a barrel, because by giving us that category, they stepped on some toes of other licensees, and they were putting pressure on them. Robert Caray admitted he was reneging on what they had promised us. So we said, 'Fine.'

"We knew we were in a pretty good position, because they didn't want this to get out, and they were willing to work with us. We asked them, 'If you take this back, what can you give us?' So they gave us the low-end market on headwear, which at that time was no market. But we took it, and we developed it and made it work, and now we are one of their top licensees, in the million-dollar club, which means for the last three years we've been paying NFL Properties over a million dollars in royalties off the hats we sell.

"One of the biggest thrills for me was at one of the NFL awards dinners one evening, the first year we made the million-dollar club. It was a big thrill for me to go up there to the stage to be called and accept this trophy, which is in our lobby for our recognition for reaching that million-dollar club. And standing up there in front of all those licensees who were out there, guys who gave us a hard time—and they know they gave us a hard time negatively talking about us and trying to run us out of the business—knowing we had overcome that, knowing we did it right and that we had made a significant contribution to NFL Properties, more so than a lot of people sitting out there who tried to keep us from doing it, it was a tremendous feeling of satisfaction.

"It was as much fun as winning the Super Bowl. It gave me the same satisfaction."

65

Clint Goes Under

The beginning of the end for Clint Murchison, Tom Landry, Tex Schramm, and Gil Brandt came on June 14, 1979, when John Murchison, a partner so silent that few knew he owned half interest in the Dallas Cowboys, died shortly after speaking at a fund-raising dinner for a group of Boy Scout volunteers.

John Murchison was visiting the home of Governor William P. Clements. In the middle of an informal talk, John began coughing, and he excused himself. A highway patrolman drove John to the hospital, and on the way John's breathing became labored. The trooper driving the car loosened John's tie.

The driver sped up, and at the intersection of Avondale and Oak Lawn around nine o'clock, as the vehicle raced through a red light, another car ran into it broadside. John had a heart attack. He was transferred to a fire department ambulance and taken to the hospital, but he died an hour later. The medical examiner said the collision had nothing to do with his death.

John, though an equal partner, had little interest or enthusiasm for football and so John had received none of the prestige from the Cowboys, nor did he desire any. John's wife may have resented Clint's fame and attention as a result of his ownership of the Cowboys, but John never did.

In the news about his death, it did not even mention that John Murchison co-owned the Cowboys with his brother.

John, in fact, in many ways was disgusted by his older brother's behavior. Clint, though quiet and demure in appearance, was a swinger. He lived to party. During his marriage to his wife, Jane, Clint enjoyed stepping out. He liked the chase, thrilled to the challenge of getting a young woman into bed. For personal thrills, Clint bought a penthouse apartment at the southeast corner of Park Avenue and 57th Street in Manhattan, an aid to an obsessive quest for an unending string of young female conquests. To enhance his ability to lure beautiful young women into his circle in Dallas, in 1972 the Cowboys officially added sex to their image. Clint and Tex Schramm hired eighteen beautiful young women, had them don short shorts, halter tops, pushup bras, and white go-go boots and had them wildly shake their breasts and their comely rear ends to the suggestive beat of rock and roll in front of the Dallas fans during breaks in the action on the field. These magnificent, scantily clad women were named the Dallas Cowboy Cheerleaders, but they led no cheers, except for the libidinous reaction from the male fans every time they went into their routine. The "cheerleaders" only served to enhance Dallas's image as a town that both hates and loves sin, sometimes at the same time. As the owner of the team, Clint Murchison made personal forays, romancing a cheerleader when the spirit moved him, until the cheerleaders got so famous by 1977 that he decided he was in too much danger of suffering from adverse publicity and backed off.

In 1972 his wife, Jane, divorced him. After the divorce Murchison admitted that his womanizing wasn't as much fun.

By the mid-1970s Clint found he was having some difficulty making love to his lady of the night, so he added cocaine to his vices when he discovered its power to aid him in lovemaking. Like some of his players who were chastised for their drug use, by the mid-1970s Clint Murchison also was acting erratically. He had tongues wagging when he started seeing Anne Farrell Brandt, the wife of his chief scout, Gil Brandt, and the tongue ran faster when Anne divorced Gil and in June of 1975 Anne and Clint announced they would marry. Clint became Anne's fourth husband. And though Gil lost his wife, he didn't lose his job.

After the marriage Clint had little time for Anne, who devoted herself to charity work and to religion. By the middle of the next decade, Anne would sit by and watch as Clint turned a billion-dollar family fortune into dust.

*   *   *

At the height of their success in the mid-1960s Clint and John Murchison owned 100 thriving companies with a value of more than $1.25 billion. But the Murchison brothers had an Achilles' heel, which was that Clint Murchison had a self-destructive streak that he worked to hide from his more conservative and responsible brother. Where most people seek out wealth, Clint already had it. He wanted more out of life than mere wealth: He craved excitement like a gambler who can't stay away from the roulette wheel, but who insists on putting a tall pile of chips down on the number with the longest odds.

Without telling John what he was doing, Clint began risking everything the brothers had worked for on increasingly risky investments, beginning with a string of real estate deals in California. He began building single-family apartment complexes and residential developments up and down the West Coast.

Then Clint got involved with an Australian named Richard Baker, a man with *big* plans who fascinated him. The first deal was the purchase of a 46-acre estate near Washington D.C. Baker paid $4.5 million too much for the land. Clint didn't care.

Beginning in 1973 Clint let himself be taken in by another wheeler-dealer, Lou Farris Jr., who involved him in ten real estate projects, eight of which lost money because the deals involved little cash flow. Refusing to listen to his associates, Clint argued that real estate values would always climb, and contended he was satisfied merely to own the properties.

He continued his plunging. One venture was supposed to turn cow manure into natural gas. Clint, who in his own quiet, intellectual way was as much a rogue as his dad, named the company Calorific Reclamation Anaerobic Process, or CRAP. Clint wasted $10 million before the process proved the accuracy of its acronym.

By the mid-1970s Clint appeared intent on sabotaging his empire. It seemed that the less likely the success of a project, the more he wanted to invest. The worst thing an adviser could tell him was, "Clint, that will *never* work." Once that was uttered, chances are he would invest. As an example, Clint spent millions financing a ski resort in Iran.

From 1975 through the end of his life, Clint made borrowing more and more money an obsession. Clint sometimes even gave his personal guarantee on a loan, a step considered folly even in sure-thing deals.

While his brother John became more and more conservative in his dealings, borrowing less and less, Clint, without the knowledge of his brother, was running up a gigantic debt. When John finally learned the extent of Clint's borrowing, he ordered his brother to consult him before running up more debts, but Clint ignored his warning.

By the end of the 1970s, inflation had jumped as high as 18 percent, and sales of real estate had come to a standstill. With little cash flow, the bank notes on Clint's loans kept coming due. By the late 1970s, Murchison was borrowing money to pay existing debts. At this point Clint was no longer addicted to women or coke. His new addiction was borrowing money.

Finally in 1978 John had enough, and the brothers agreed to dissolve the partnership no later than October 1981. Unfortunately for John and his family, untangling the complex maze of corporations to determine who owned what seemed almost impossible. They were still entwined when John died in June of 1979.

With the passing of John Murchison, his son Dabney, who preferred to be called John Jr., began looking into his father's affairs and discovered that Clint had borrowed heavily against his $30 million trust. Afraid he would never see the estate left to him by his father, in 1980 John Jr. sent his uncle a memo demanding the trusts be dissolved and paid out. Clint, as was his habit, ignored the memo. But John's son didn't tolerate Clint's arrogance the way his father had. As co-executor of the estate, John Jr. was on a mission to save Murchison Brothers from the reckless, self-destructive Clint. He continued writing memos, demanding accountability. Clint kept ignoring them. A frustrated John Jr., fearful that Clint would bankrupt everybody, then sued for a final dissolution of the partnership.

In self-defense a proud Clint Murchison lied to his brother's widow, Lupe, that their financial problems were being caused not by him but by John Jr., whom Clint disparagingly referred to as the "Punk." Clint was so persuasive that he managed to get Lupe and her three daughters to sue John Jr. to remove him as co-executor of his father's estate. The trial was scheduled for April of 1981.

A few weeks before the trial, Lupe and a date returned to her mansion after having dinner. Two gunmen were waiting for them. The gunmen blindfolded the date, threw him in the back of her Mercedes, and threw Lupe in the trunk. When the youngest daughter, Barbara Jeanne, arrived home with two friends, the intruders tied them up. Four hours later the gunmen left with a few pieces of jewelry. No one was hurt. The intruders were never caught.

Rumors abounded that Clint had planned the robbery, hoping Lupe would think John Jr. had set it up. It was a "prank" reminiscent of Clint's seeding of RFK Stadium with chicken feed prior to the release of hundreds of chickens or another of his anti–George Preston Marshall schemes whereby Clint hired helicopters to hover above RFK Stadium and release ten thousand silver and blue Ping-Pong balls, only to be foiled at the last moment by the FAA.

At the trial, John Jr. was vilified. Lupe's attorneys portrayed him as a "vicious and ungrateful son." That night John Jr. caved in to the pressure. He resigned as co-executor, and in exchange, his mother agreed to loan him $3 million at an 18 percent interest rate to be adjusted annually.

John Jr. had lost a battle, but he was determined to win the war, and now he had the funds to wage it against Uncle Clint. In February 1981 John Jr. sued Clint and his four children claiming Clint had used funds from his trust and demanded $30 million and an injunction forcing Clint to segregate John Jr.'s assets from the family trusts.

At the same time the value of oil and real estate was dropping steadily as interest rates were climbing. Clint had a flood of debt and little cash to pay it off. Banks were calling Clint every day for money. He had to scramble each day to keep the doors of Murchison Brothers ajar.

The very wealthy tend to believe they are too smart for things to go terribly wrong, and as late as 1982 Clint still believed interest rates would fall and save him.

But that was the year the Arab oil-supplying nations began fighting among themselves, and as the warring countries began glutting the market with oil, the world price of oil dropped sharply, causing Texas real estate values also to crash. By 1982 interest rates were at almost 20 percent, and Clint was paying $80 million just to service the interest on his notes. He could only pay a fraction of that amount.

Clint's fortune was built on a house of cards, and once John Jr.'s suit revealed the shakiness of his position, Clint was doomed to bankruptcy. Under the terms of John's lawsuit, Clint was forced to take the liens off some of his properties so that John's trust fund would be unencumbered.

Against his brother's orders, Clint had invested heavily in a computer company called OSI, and in October 1981 John Jr. forced Clint to release his assets from all debts connected with OSI. Clint still had another $24 million of encumbered trust funds to go. Making Clint's life harder was a temporary injunction obtained by John Jr. stopping Clint and his children from refinancing any debts on assets in the trusts. Around this time John Jr. also began threatening Clint with going to the press to reveal the extent of his uncle's indebtedness.

In December of 1981, Clint might have survived the crisis had he acted reasonably and fairly toward John Jr. But he was the great Clint

Murchison, and so when John Jr. offered to give up his interest in two companies in the trust with assets of $4 million and forget the damages if Clint would pay out the remainder of his trust, Clint laughed at him. But unable to bluff any longer, in April of 1983 Clint finally removed the debts from the remainder of John Jr.'s assets and turned them over to him.

By this time the other five Murchison children were becoming nervous that Clint was on a course that would leave them penniless. Around this time Lupe finally figured out that of the two combatants, John Jr. had right on his side. The family met to force the liquidation of Murchison Brothers. Lupe took some assets, and the children took their trusts, leaving Clint with a mound of debts.

In early 1983, with Clint's ship about to sink, his law firm announced it would no longer represent him, despite the fact that it had been Clint Sr. who had made the firm what it was. Around this time the Dallas banks, who for years had been reticent to force Clint to pay up, started turning the screws. Many had figured that because Clint owned the Dallas Cowboys, he would be good for any debts, but as the rumors began to spread through the banking community about Clint's precarious financial position, the nervous bankers began to panic, and the cry for payment became a chorus. Those who screamed loudest got paid first but Clint didn't have nearly enough money to pay everyone.

Adding to Clint's accumulation of crushing problems was the diagnosis in 1983 that he was suffering from an extremely rare degenerative nerve disease, similar to Lou Gehrig's disease and just as deadly. In the spring of 1983 Clint invited Tex Schramm to his home and asked him to find a buyer for the Cowboys.

Clint knew he would have to give up his most precious asset, but before he did so, he made sure that his two most loyal employees, Tex Schramm and Tom Landry, were well taken care of. Murchison gave Schramm a $2.5 million bonus and raised his salary to $400,000 a year. He gave Tom Landry a $2 million bonus and raised his salary to $650,000 a year. Gil Brandt's salary was raised to $225,000.

In late 1983 Tex Schramm found a buyer, Dallas businessman Harvey R. "Bum" Bright, who paid $63 million for the team and $20 million for the stadium. (To demonstrate Clint Murchison's bad timing, after the market turned around Bright sold the team and stadium in 1989 for close to $150 million.)

Large portions of the proceeds from the sale were used to pay off Clint Murchison's most boisterous creditors. After the sale was announced, the remaining creditors panicked big time and lawsuits against him came in an avalanche. By this time Clint was wheelchair ridden, as the disease continued to get worse.

Two months after selling the team, the suits totalled $75.7 million, most of the debt coming from bad real estate deals. Clint, weak and unable to go to the office, sought to hold off creditors by telling everyone that they would be paid in full when the oil business turned around. But by the summer of 1984 creditors demanded payment.

That year he began losing lawsuits. By the end of the year his judgments amounted to $100 million. Sixteen banks held liens on his home and property. Complicating matters was that Clint had often borrowed money or made investments without putting anything down on paper, and because of his disease he was losing his ability to communicate. By January 1985 the claims against him had reached $185 million.

When three creditors summoned the courage to force the almost-paralyzed man into bankruptcy, more creditors stepped forward, until the demands totalled $560 million! By the time his assets were distributed, his creditors ended up with between 10¢ and 30¢ on the dollar.

In the fall of 1986 Clint and Anne had to sell their mansion, and they moved across the street into an ordinary middle-class development home where Clint spent his last days in a tiny room, alone much of the time, relying on his wife and a nurse to aid him. In mid-March 1987 he contracted pneumonia and was hospitalized. On March 29 his ex-wife, Jane, came to see him, as did John Jr. The following day Clint became unconscious, and in the evening the sixty-three-year-old founder of the Dallas Cowboys passed away.

At the service there were four eulogies, including one given by Tom Landry. Some of Clint's closest friends were appalled at the Christian Fundamentalist nature of the service. Others were embarrassed by it. They knew Clint was antireligion, and they blamed his wife, Anne, who was born again and deeply religious. But still others realized the hypocrisy of the moment, and they laughed it off as "Clint's last prank."

In a tribute, Tex Schramm said about Murchison, "He's what kept the whole thing here together. He was the glue. Our twenty-five-year record is a tribute to him. I don't think he ever got the credit he deserved."

Schramm said that what made the Cowboys was not that Murchison was absent, but that he was so supportive.

"It was his support of all those people that made it possible. You can stay out and not contribute, but his whole thing was he gave the support and backbone to the organization that allowed people to have the confidence to perform their jobs."

* * *

Clint Murchison was not the only one to lose everything, only one of the first. In 1988 alone, 113 Texas banks failed, more than half of the two hundred banks that failed around the country. Among those to lose big were the Hunt brothers, William, Nelson, and Lamar. Nelson would later be involved in a scheme to corner the silver market. Another who lost big was former Texas governor John Connolly, who had invested heavily in Texas real estate and lost most of what he had, including his home.

Clint Murchison Jr. had lacked so many of his father's traits, especially shrewd judgment and common sense, as well as the father's uncanny ability to adapt to changing circumstances. But after his father had thrust Clint Jr., a man who had wanted to become a teacher, into a position of economic importance he really hadn't ever wanted, perhaps the son's exercise in frittering away his huge fortune had been part of an unspoken plan to make sure he wouldn't do to his kids what his father had done to him. By not leaving his kids money, they would have to be resourceful and make it on their own in an occupation of their choosing. Perhaps that's what Clint had intended by his recklessness. If that had been the case, then in that he succeeded Texas-style.

In the end Clint Jr.'s children not only didn't get their trusts, neither did they receive any inheritance. Clint had made repeated promises to pay them, but he never did, even though he could have at any time, and after his death in 1987, they were left bitter and angry at their father's betrayal.

Clint had taken a company worth $1.25 billion and in less than a decade created a debt of more than $500 million. As pranks go, that's one that's very hard to top.

66

Bum Bright

On November 13, 1983, word leaked to the press that Clint Murchison had put Tex Schramm in charge of selling the Dallas Cowboys. By then, Murchison's problems had grown so serious that he had no choice. The Cowboys had been Texas's darlings, the premier franchise in the National Football League. They had been in five Super Bowls, winning twice, and in the last eighteen years had been in the playoffs seventeen times. This was a *very* desirable property.

Tex Schramm knew he had to be very careful finding a buyer, lest he lose his job. Murchison was leaning toward selling the team to a syndicate headed by Vance Miller, a former business partner, and W. O. Bankston, a Dallas car dealer and oilman.

In the early '80s Miller had involved Murchison in a deal in which he didn't have to put a cent down. The deal netted Murchison $8 million. They were close friends.

For the playoff game against the Rams the previous December, Miller and Bankston had plunked down $550,000 for the remaining available tickets so the local TV blackout would be lifted. They gave the tickets away. Miller and Bankston were offering Murchison about $90 million, but Tex Schramm kept putting them off. Tex wanted assurances that his job was safe, and he wasn't getting them, and so Schramm steered Murchison toward a deal with another old friend of Clint's, H. R. "Bum" Bright, an acquaintance since they were boys. (He got his nickname as an infant because his father thought he looked like a hobo when bundled up in blankets.)

As early as 1983 Tex Schramm had been in contact with Bright, who as a boy had been a roughneck in the Oklahoma oil fields. After graduating from Texas A&M in 1942, at the age of twenty-seven, he became a petroleum engineer. He had twelve bucks in his bank account, and he and his partner ate peanut butter sandwiches for lunch. Four years later he was a millionaire. Folksy, persistent, and ruthless, he began trading oil leases, and after fifteen years proved a wizard at it. One time he persuaded one woman to lock her recalcitrant husband out of their bedroom until he signed over an oil lease on his property. Another time he strapped a pen to a hospital patient to get him to sign over a contract. He acquired a trucking company by warning the aging owner that he'd drive him to his grave and then buy the firm from his relatives at a discount.

"I play to win," said Bright. "I don't care if it's checkers or gin rummy or the oil and gas business. You play the game to win."

He branched out into real estate in the early 1950s, and then became involved in trucking, insurance, and providing mortgages, and he was successful in them all. His advertising slogan: "The future is Bright."

When the Arab oil embargo forced the price of oil from $3 to nearly $40 a barrel, Bright was amassing a fortune. Natural gas prices also rose from less than $1 per thousand cubic feet to nearly $5.50, and by 1984 Bright was producing and selling $60 million cubic feet of it every day. Construction boomed. Real estate prices soared, and by 1984 Bum Bright was one of the fifty richest men in the world, worth an estimated $600 million. The AP had named him one of the ten most powerful Texans.

Bright was a workaholic who once said the fear of poverty, the memories of being poor as a boy, drove him to work long days. His passion for making money drove him to drive hard bargains.

As an example of Bright's dislike of sloth, in 1972 he agreed to let his secretary marry, but he gave her only an hour and a half off work to prepare for the ceremony.

Another time he had to have his gallbladder taken out. One doctor told him he would have to stay in the hospital for ten days. Bright found a new doctor, refused to be put to sleep, talked through the operation, and checked out that night. Two days later he was back at work managing Bright & Co., a company whose assets were estimated at $500 million in 1982.

Bright was also renowned for his penuriousness. He was so frugal he tacked his wife, Peggy's, beauty parlor bills to his office wall. He told

Robert Tomsho of the *Wall Street Journal,* "It costs me 16.5 cents an hour to keep Peggy's hair, hands, and feet." Once, the story goes, he walked out of a cafeteria because the coffee cost 85¢. He was known for wearing shoes until they fell apart. He watched TV on a beat-up lounge chair whose springs had sprung.

During negotiations to buy the Cowboys, one of the brokers ran out of cigarettes, and Bright sold him individual smokes for $1 a piece.

Newspaper accounts also reported his eccentricities. He was said to organize his bills in his wallet by serial number. His real estate companies were named after pasta (fettuccine, manicotti, lasagna), minerals, and seas (Java, Malacca). As for superstitions, he was said to favor the numbers 1, 3, 7, 11, 33, and 55. He drank his milk at breakfast in seven gulps. When he pulled into the driveway at night each evening, he honked his horn eleven times. He never closed a deal on Friday the thirteenth, and every morning he put his right shoe on first, then his left.

Bright had a special affection for dogs. During the invasion of Normandy in World War II he rescued an injured great dane and, using his whiskey rations, bribed a doctor to make a cast for its broken foreleg. Bright built a wheeled cart to carry around the animal and eventually brought it back to Texas, where it lived for several years more.

Years later Bright took another dog to Texas A&M's animal hospital for throat surgery. Bright was so impressed that he asked the doctors if they needed any equipment. They suggested a color-flow ultrasound machine that detects heart murmurs in animals. Bright wrote them a check for $125,000.

A devoted family man with four children, Bright and his family sat down for a formal dinner every Sunday night. Like most oilmen, Bright's politics were very conservative. Like most right-wingers, he distrusted the federal government.

"I have no use for government meddling in private affairs," he said. He raised large sums of money for Barry Goldwater and George Bush.

Bright had never been a raging Cowboy fan. His energy and money had been directed toward the football program of Texas A&M, where he was chairman of the Board of Regents. But once Bright assured Schramm that if he bought the team, he would have no interest in running it, Schramm did all the arm-twisting he could to make sure Bright ended up as owner of the Cowboys, even if one of the arms Schramm had to twist belonged to Bright himself.

When in 1983 Schramm initially told Bright that Murchison wanted him to buy the Cowboys, Bright said he wasn't interested. Two days before the purchase Bright had had Sunday dinner with his family and hadn't even mentioned it. What changed Bright's mind was a phone call from Charles Pistor, chairman of the board of Republic Bank. Bright was also on the Republic board. Murchison owed the Republic Bank money. Pistor told Bright the bank would benefit greatly if Bright bought the Cowboys and as an inducement offered Bright a very favorable loan if he would buy the team from Murchison. Bright was making $8 million a month in his oil business. In 1983 the Cowboys had made a stated profit of $600,000. But Republic was making it painless to buy the team. Bright finally thought, "Aw, it'll be fun."

Bright, along with minority investors (including Schramm at 3 percent), agreed to buy the Cowboys and the 30-acre tract of land in Valley Ranch where the new team headquarters were being constructed for $60 million, and to buy the remaining sixty-five years on the Texas Stadium lease for about $20 million. The total price was $84.5 million. Bright's participation was only 17 percent, despite an NFL policy that it preferred one investor to own a majority of the stock. But Schramm believed that his best chance of remaining with the Cowboys for the rest of his life rested on the shoulders of Bum Bright, and Schramm got NFL Commissioner Pete Rozelle, his former Ram employee, to help push through the sale regardless.

The sale transferring the Dallas Cowboys from Clint Murchison to Bum Bright took place on March 19, 1984. Though the sale price was $84.5 million, not a penny went to Clint Murchison. It all went to his creditors and to lawyers.

BUM BRIGHT: "[The sale] had to be at 7 A.M. because a Saudi bank needed a [Murchison] note paid by 2 P.M. There were eleven different lawyers [mostly representing members of the Murchison family, who wanted their rightful shares]. There was a lot of hostility and maneuvering. When everyone got paid, there was $365,000 left. But Henry Gilchrist [Murchison's lawyer] said, 'Conditional precent to closing: legal fees!'

"I said, 'Aw, Henry, send him a bill.' But Henry said, 'I've been sending the son of a bitch a bill for two years . . .'

"So in the end poor old Clint got not a penny."

As part of the deal, Bright officially named Tex Schramm "designated managing partner," giving him authority to run the team. Schramm stated publicly that he had been looking for another Clint Murchison, someone who would sit in the background and take a low-profile, hands-off approach. For the time being, the jobs of Schramm and Coach Landry seemed safe.

Schramm had planned wisely, because only a few months later the $130 million Key West Resort development, a 200-acre resort planned by Tex Schramm and two partners and financed by Clint Murchison, went under. The plan called for 597 condominiums to be built around a championship golf course. With Murchison's financial and personal health failing, Schramm needed to keep his day job.

A month later Bum Bright, through a holding company he controlled called Texas Federal, bought the Texas Federal Financial Corp. and merged with Trinity Banc Savings Association. Bright predicted he would turn the thrift into a "financial juggernaut." He began buying up other savings and loans and investing heavily in commercial real estate. The savings-and-loan craze was on. Ronald Reagan's go-go hands-off government of the '80s was in full swing.

When the Cowboys opened their 1984 season, seven of their veterans were no longer on the team. Harvey Martin, Billy Joe DuPree, and Pat Donovan retired, Larry Bethea, Glenn Carano, and Bruce Huther signed with the United States Football League, and Butch Johnson was traded to the Houston Oilers. When Drew Pearson was injured in a car crash during training camp and had to retire, he became number eight.

Tom Landry opted to see if backup QB Gary Hogeboom could do a better job than Danny White, and it turned out he couldn't. The team started strong, with Hogeboom throwing for 343 yards in a win against the L.A. Rams, but by the heart of the season he lost to a winless Buffalo Bill team, prompting Frank Luksa of the *Dallas Times-Herald* to ask, "Who ruined the Cowboys?" It was about this time that reporters, including Luksa, began questioning whether Tom Landry was too old, whether his ideas were passé. When the Cowboys lost to the Miami Dolphins, 28–21, after Dan Marino threw three touchdown passes to Mark Clayton in the last game of the season, the 9–7 Cowboys were eliminated from the playoffs for the first time in ten years. "Three against America's Team," Clayton shouted in the locker room after the game.

In 1985 Tom Landry did one of his best coaching jobs, leading a mediocre team back to the NFC East title. Bob Breunig retired, and the linebacking corps was mediocre at best. Without dominant linebackers, Tom Landry's Flex was looking very solvable.

Some of the losses were brutal: 44–0 to the Chicago Bears, 50–24 to Cincinnati, 31–16 to San Francisco. But a patched-up defensive backfield, called "Thurman's Thieves" by Danny White, captured the public's imagination. The group of low draft picks and free agents—Dextor Clinkscale,

Mike Downs, Everson Walls, Bill Bates, Ricky Easmon, and Dennis Thurman—intercepted 33 passes, all in key situations. Only the Chicago Bears, the Super Bowl winners, had more, with 34.

By the end of the season defensive coach Gene Stallings instructed his defensive backs to abandon the Flex. They began playing a "46," blitzing on almost every down.

Before their Monday night game in St. Louis, the Thieves went to Union Station and bought Indiana Jones fedoras, like Tom Landry's hat, only with more flash. But while Landry looked astute, the Thieves looked like gangsters.

An hour and a half before kickoff, Dallas TV station WFAA did a live remote from St. Louis. It was a quickie interview staged outside the locker room. The Thieves showed up wearing their new hats.

A couple of the white players, Randy White and John Dutton, resented what this group of black defensive backs (plus Bill Bates) were doing, seemingly making fun of Landry, cutting up, showing off. Jim Jeffcoat, who is black, didn't like it either.

In the third quarter of the game, Thurman told linebacker Jeff Rohrer and end Jim Jeffcoat, who had just blown a play, that they had to communicate better.

A furious Randy White interceded. "What the fuck are you talking about?" he asked. Thurman told White he wasn't talking to him. White pushed him, forcing Thurman into a confrontation. Players had to break them up.

When Landry asked the Thieves to stop wearing the hats, they refused. When the Thieves appeared on a popular poster wearing the hats, the other faction was not pleased.

Nevertheless, without Dennis Thurman and his Thieves, the '85 Cowboys would have been far less successful.

In the first round of the playoffs, against the Los Angeles Rams, the Thieves did a number on quarterback Dieter Brock, but Eric Dickerson ran for 248 yards in a 20–0 Ram victory.

This was the year Tom Landry should have retired. But Landry hated to leave the team when it was on the way down. And when Tex Schramm asked Landry to train younger coaches, Landry said he would, though he was constitutionally unable to do so. It had always been Tom Landry's way or no way, and it would be that way to the end.

67

The Fall of the Cowboys

I n an article dated January 31, 1973, in the *Fort Worth Press,* Tex
Schramm bemoaned the fact that the rest of the NFL teams had caught
up with the Cowboys' scouting technique. Before '73 other teams
would ignore or not be aware of great players from small colleges, who
the Cowboys would take in late rounds. No longer.

"They have caught up with us, I'm afraid. Every guy drafted through
the first two rounds was just about the way we had them rated. Our scouts
have seen it coming. They say it's like a jungle out there. Every place they
go to look at a player they run over half a dozen scouts from other teams."

The Cowboys had struck gold in '75 with their Dirty Dozen, and the
team made the NFC playoff almost every year after that. Meanwhile the
NFL had exploded in size, adding Minnesota in '61, Atlanta in '66, New
Orleans in '67, and ten American Football League teams in '70; Tampa
Bay and Seattle were added in '76. All of which meant that when it came
time for the Cowboys to take their first player, by 1977 they were getting
the 28th pick of the draft, the equivalent of the last second-round pick ten
years earlier. The Cowboys had been able to get Tony Dorsett that year
after Schramm hoodwinked the Seattle Seahawks by swapping four draft
choices for him. But after that heist, the Cowboys' well virtually ran dry
when the ground rules changed. In 1978 the other teams organized a

league-wide scouting combine, bought computers, and added software that would lead to better player selection, and the draft was moved from late January to late April, giving everyone more time to scout the college kids.

Once the scouting reports of opposing teams matched theirs, the Cowboys found themselves cut off from being able to draft impact players, and so rather than choose the obvious players, guys rated as solid but not outstanding, Tex Schramm, Gil Brandt, and Tom Landry decided to take chances on players with athletic ability who may have been missing something else.

"Because we had great success and our only goal had been to reach the Super Bowl, our whole goal was trying to find players that would be stars on a Super Bowl team," said Tex Schramm. "But when you draft late, you have to take people who haven't demonstrated that kind of talent but have the potential.

"We felt you had to take a gamble, and if he hits . . ."

Usually their gambles failed. Beginning in '76 with Aaron Kyle, a string of Cowboy first-rounders provided little production. Larry Bethea didn't have the requisite toughness or desire. Robert Shaw didn't make it, and neither did Howard Richards nor Rod Hill, a little-known cornerback from Kentucky State who was traded a year later for a sixth-round draft pick, or Billy Cannon Jr., a player with a marquee name who was badly injured early on. Jim Jeffcoat, the first pick in '83, became a fine defensive lineman, but all in all by 1986 the Cowboys were old, and they had few young studs to fill in for the creaky veterans.

It was in 1985 that observers began to crucify Gil Brandt, chiding him for an alarmingly poor draft record over the past eight years. In '85 only fourteen picks from those eight drafts were still on the Cowboys' roster. In the last five drafts, only six players had made the team. Only one first-round pick, Jim Jeffcoat, had become a regular. Six years later critics would recall that in 1979 Joe Montana had been available, but the Cowboys took Doug Cosbie instead. Of course, at the time Roger Staubach was months from retirement, and in addition to Staubach, the Cowboys had Danny White and Glenn Carano, but years later Tex Schramm would say that not picking Joe Montana was one of the worst mistakes the Cowboys ever made.

Then in 1983, with White and Gary Hogeboom on the roster, the Cowboys passed on Dan Marino and took Jim Jeffcoat instead. But four other QBs had been taken before Marino in that draft. Who knew?

Said Ernie Stautner in '85, "Gil Brandt should have been let go ten years ago. I'd suggest defensive linemen, but they wouldn't listen to me."

Mel Renfro, who was working on the Cowboys scouting staff, said the same thing.

"I saw it coming," said Renfro. "In '77 I told Gil, 'If you guys don't start preparing to replace these old guys, we're going to be in trouble. You have to get some guys to shore up these positions.' They had draft picks who were not going to be able to carry the team. But they wouldn't listen to me.

"I showed them guys," said Renfro. "I said, 'These guys will help you.' Gil would say, 'We don't want them.' Why? Because Gil didn't discover them. I scouted for the Cowboys almost a year, and I went out and saw guys who could play, and they would show up on other teams as stars. Just because I said, 'This is the guy you need,' Gil disregarded it. Gil was the one.

"They didn't know what they were doing. They were reading statistics. They could no more go out and watch a guy . . . Even when I was playing they would bring guys to me and say, 'Mel, work him out and write a report on him.' And this was *after* they paid him money and brought him in. I said, 'Why are you asking me to do this? You already gave him all that money, and he's here.'

"And oh man, they brought people in there, and I'd say to myself, 'What's going on here? This guy can't play.' They would send these guys over to me and say, 'Mel, what do you think?' I'd say, 'You've got to be kidding. Give me a little bit of that money.' They had the nerve to ask my opinion after the fact."

One of the first indications that things were changing on the Cowboys came in April of 1986 when Gil Brandt lost half his job. In the past Brandt had been in sole charge of personnel. He had been the scouting genius. Now that genius was coming into question.

To bolster their front office, Tex Schramm hired Bobby Ackles, a man whose job it was to know intimately every opposing player in the NFL so that when the Cowboys sat down to trade, they would be more knowledgeable.

"He can bring a new dimension to us, and that's what I want him to do," said Schramm.

During training camp in '86 Tom Landry upset his vets when he released the two ringleaders of Thurman's Thieves, Dennis Thurman and Dextor Clinkscale. They had had their picture taken with machine guns. They were pretending to be "bad dudes," and when Landry sent Thurman and Clinkscale packing, there was outrage among the black players. Said Everson Walls, "This is a terrible blow for this team."

The year before the Cowboys had made 33 interceptions. This year the number would drop to 17.

Landry would also begin a simmering feud with Bum Bright. The new owner had told Tex Schramm he would be silent like Clint Murchison, but only Murchison was so idiosyncratic that he would own a $90 million corporation and not be interested in having input into the way it was run. Every man who watches football on TV thinks he knows as much as the coach, and in this respect Bum Bright was no different. Despite the fact that the Cowboys had led the league in passing yardage in '85, the next year Bright wanted it changed. He wanted it more imaginative, more open, more exciting, regardless of whether Tom Landry wanted it that way or not.

Bright had first met Tom Landry after Bear Bryant left Texas A&M for Alabama after the 1957 season. Bright was helping to conduct the search for Bryant's replacement, and Landry contacted him. According to Bright, he interviewed Landry for the job and was "singularly unimpressed."

Bright may have even been looking for a sometime-down-the-line replacement for Landry when he asked Texas A&M offensive coordinator R. C. Slocum to name someone to rejuvenate the Cowboy offense, and Slocum in good faith recommended a young coach by the name of Paul Hackett. Hackett was a guy who had a history of making good quarterbacks better. Hackett had developed Steve Bartkowski and Joe Roth at California and Vince Evans and Paul McDonald at the University of Southern California. He helped Brian Sipe become MVP with the Cleveland Browns in '80. Hackett had worked under Bill Walsh in San Francisco, and Joe Montana raved about him.

When Hackett joined the Cowboys, sportswriter Skip Bayless warned him that he would not be able to work with Landry. Said Bayless, "You might feel you'd gone from the funny farm to solitary confinement. Landry runs everything."

When Landry met Hackett, he didn't know a whole lot about him. When they sat down to talk, it turned out that Hackett's offensive philosophy was diametrically opposed to Landry's. Hackett came from the Don "Air" Coryell–Bill Walsh school of offense. His philosophy was that you ran certain plays no matter what the other team was using. If the primary receiver is covered, you throw to the secondary guy. If he's covered, you go to number three. If no one is open, the receivers have to adjust and try to get open. To Tom Landry, this was heresy.

But Tom Landry was also a good soldier, and he knew Paul Hackett was there on orders from Bum Bright and Tex Schramm. Landry told reporters he believed that the offense could integrate Hackett's system, because he had Danny White, an intelligent, experienced quarterback. White thus would be able to employ both systems, using Hackett's systems while continuing to read Landry's keys. Under Hackett, Danny White would become the leading passer in the NFL.

If there was any controversy in training camp in '86, it came from star running back Tony Dorsett. Dorsett's agents had helped get him in terrible financial trouble with some unwise investments. Each month the IRS was taking his check. He also had borrowed $500,000 from the Cowboys and had three years left on a contract that specifically forbade him from renegotiating it. Dorsett pleaded for Schramm to help him.

Tex did. Schramm restructured the contract so he could pay the IRS, draw a decent salary, and have an annuity of $50,000 a year for five years. Schramm had saved him.

And then Schramm signed former USFL star Herschel Walker, giving him a $5 million bonus to play for the Cowboys. Landry knew that the Cowboys' future would be the twenty-five-year-old Walker. Walker, moreover, was a coach's dream. He was a rare individual, a star with humility who was always eager to learn. In meetings he always sat in the front, pencil in hand. All-Pro Dorsett, at thirty-three and running out of time, was pleased with the acquisition of Walker, until he found out the Cowboys had given him $5 million as a signing bonus. Once he learned that, Dorsett bolted training camp.

"I'm not playing second fiddle to anyone," he said. Dorsett threatened to become a "very disruptive force on the team."

Dorsett did return, and he started, and Landry used Herschel Walker to advantage in spot situations.

Everything started out swimmingly. Paul Hackett was dismayed at how weak the offensive line was. "But we'll trick 'em," said Hackett. In the Monday night opener against the New York Giants, the Cowboys gained 378 yards and scored 31 points against the team that would finish with the best defensive statistics in the NFL. During the game Hackett suggested the plays, and usually Landry went with them.

By midseason the Cowboys were 6–2. Their two losses were to the Atlanta Falcons and Denver, the latter when Danny White was injured and couldn't play. White came back, but against the New York Giants, Carl Banks blitzed and no one blocked him. After White extended his arm to pass, Banks crashed his helmet or shoulder pad into it, fracturing White's wrist and ending his—and the Cowboys'—season. The injured wrist would plague White—and Tom Landry—the rest of their careers.

White was replaced by Steve Pelluer. With three minutes to go, the Cowboys trailed, 17–14. Pelluer dumped a screen to Tony Dorsett, who ran 30 yards to the Giant six. But tackle Phil Pozderac, who had already been caught holding twice in the game, got nailed again, and the play was called back. Then Pelluer hit Timmy Newsome for another 30 yard gain inside the Giant ten. This time Pozderac, who could not hear the snap count, was suckered offside by Giant end George Martin.

Hackett did not blame Pozderac. He blamed Landry and Schramm and Gil Brandt. "We cannot win in this league with the tackles we have," he said. "It is staggering how poorly this team has drafted for the last eight years. You compare this team to the 49ers, man for man, two deep, and it's a joke."

The great irony was that when Hackett was with the 49ers, Bill Walsh had sent him to the University of Washington to scout Pelluer. Hackett reported back that he wasn't impressed. Now Pelluer was all he had.

The end came the following week against the Los Angeles Raiders. Dallas dominated but only led 13–3 at the half. A touchdown was called back on a hold by Glen Titensor, and the Raiders went on to win when Jim Plunkett lofted a 40-yard touchdown pass that Dobie Williams caught in the end zone above three Cowboy defenders.

During the game it was apparent that Herschel Walker's ankle hurt him badly and would limit his play. Walker would run for 737 yards and set a Cowboys record with 75 receptions. Moreover, Tony Dorsett's knees were limiting his ability. He had to miss three games, breaking his streak of 94 games started consecutively. He ran for 748 yards, the first season he failed to reach the 1,000 mark in a brilliant career.

Pelluer was hit so much, he became confused when he was urged to stay in the pocket. By the end of the year he was punch drunk. In one game alone, he was sacked 11 times. Said Hackett, "I'm not sure any quarterback has ever taken a worse beating for a longer period and kept getting up."

In the season finale held in Texas Stadium, head coach Mike Ditka of the 14–2 Chicago Bears took pity on the Cowboys during a 24–10 win. Quarterback Doug Flutie threw only eight passes in the second half, scoring but a field goal, as Ditka fought to hold the score down against his mentor. The Cowboys looked so inept that after the game the Bears players were sympathizing with Tom Landry. The Dallas fans, of course, were less sympathetic. There was a banner that read, "Remember the Alamo; Remember the Cowboys." Several fans wore paper bags over their heads.

Dallas finished the second half 1–7, 7–9 on the season. A string of twenty straight winning seasons had come to an end; the last time the Cowboys had not enjoyed a winning season was 1965, when they finished 7–7. (To show how remarkable that is, at the time the team that was second in consecutive winning seasons was the Miami Dolphins, which had six.)

The last three weeks of the season Tom Landry took away all of Paul Hackett's authority. He went back to calling the plays for Pelluer.

At the end of the '86 season Tom Landry said, "No, I won't be retiring, unless someone decides to fire me, and that could be a possibility. We will try to bring this thing back up where it belongs. That will be a tough job."

In the spring of 1987 Paul Hackett was offered the head coaching job at the University of Southern California. Hackett told Schramm, who asked Hackett to be patient just a little longer. Hackett turned down the USC job, a terrible mistake.

It was clear that Hackett was Bum Bright's choice to replace Landry, but Tex Schramm was more loyal to Landry than he was to Bright. Landry, his job no longer as secure under Bright as it had been under Clint Murchison, told Schramm he wanted a three-year contract at $1 million a year, a figure comparable to what was being paid to Bill Walsh, Joe Gibbs, Don Shula, and Chuck Noll.

Bright told Schramm to give Landry three contracts at $800,000, $900,000, and $1 million. But Bright also ordered him to be sure to give him three one-year contracts, not three guaranteed years. Bright would not find out for several weeks that Schramm had ignored his orders and given Landry the three years guaranteed.

Once Tom Landry had his three years guaranteed, Paul Hackett became persona non grata. And under new coach Larry Smith, USC went to three consecutive Rose Bowls.

Training camp began and ended disastrously in '87. It started with accusations against Rafael Septien, the best place kicker the Cowboys ever had. Septien was accused of having sex with the ten-year-old daughter of a friend. Landry needed Septien and wanted Schramm to give him another chance. Schramm refused. Landry then released star receiver Tony Hill, a starter since 1978 and one of the great receivers in Cowboy history, saying he was overweight and could no longer make the grade. The year before Hill had been on schedule to catch 1,000 yards worth of passes, but halfway through the season Landry stopped calling his number, as Mike Sherrard became the team's go-to pass catcher. Hill needed 11 catches to break Drew Pearson's record of 490 receptions by a Cowboy receiver. When in '87 Landry cut him in training camp, Tony Hill never got that chance. Sherrard would be penciled in to be the Cowboys' new game-breaker.

Then in a seven-on-seven passing scrimmage against the San Diego Chargers, Sherrard, the top draft choice in '86 and the best receiver on the team, ran a simple pass pattern and was knocked off balance by Charger defender Carl Brazley. One cleat hit the opposite shin, freakishly shattering it. Teammates said they could hear the *cur-rack* from 20 yards away.

"From the way it sounded, it was like two helmets had collided," said receiver Mike Renfro. Sherrard's bone protruded through the skin, and he was lost for the season. Danny White was so heartsick, he left the field saying he couldn't continue.

As Sherrard was carried to an ambulance, Paul Hackett cried.

Wrote sportswriter Jim Dent, "Tony Hill doesn't look that overweight now."

Then came the players' demand for free agency, followed by the threat of a strike if they didn't get it. In his negotiations with the players' association, Tex Schramm, who was a member of the owners' negotiating team, told union president Gene Upshaw that "there will never be free agency even if the players remained on the team for thirty years."

Recalled Upshaw, "He said the players are like cattle and the owners are ranchers and the owners can always get more cattle."

The cattle went on strike. It was the most bitter players' strike in NFL history. After three regular season games were cancelled, Tex Schramm and the other owners hired scabs to replace striking athletes. The first three games of the '87 season were played with a team consisting of replacement players and stars whom Schramm strong-armed into participating.

The reason the Cowboy vets played is that Schramm had boxed them into a corner so they had no choice. Anticipating a strike, Schramm had inserted clauses in contracts of some of his top players that if the player missed a game or practice for any reason other than injury, he would lose a large annuity built into his pay. Schramm, smart and ruthless, forced Danny White, Randy White, Too Tall Jones, Tony Dorsett, Doug Cosbie, and Everson Walls to face the decision whether to cross the picket line or stick with their teammates and lose hundreds of thousands of dollars.

Randy White crossed the first day, telling reporters, "I just can't walk away from the money I'm earning now." Striking would cost White $45,000 a week. Many of White's teammates were furious, because in 1984 he had held out for more money, and they had supported him, going so far as to wear number 54 on their jerseys. Tony Dorsett labeled him "Captain Scab." A few days later a sheepish Dorsett (nicknamed Captain Stab by the strikebreakers) joined White when Schramm pointed out that if he didn't play, he stood to lose $6.4 million in annuities. All but Cosbie and Walls crossed the line and played with the replacement players. Dorsett played while hating every minute of it.

The venom toward Randy White was nothing compared to how the players reacted when Danny White crossed the line. Danny White also cited the clauses in his contract. At the time Danny White was facing a federal investigation for mail fraud in connection with a used truck parts company he owned. He admitted to owing creditors $230,000 but said he was innocent of committing fraud.

But Danny White had an ulterior motive for crossing the picket line, said several of his teammates, who charged that Tex Schramm had given him a $300,00 salary advance to solve his financial problems in exchange for playing. The strikers were furious, with both White and Schramm. Only the Cowboys were forcing their veterans on the field with the strikebreakers. Other owners even called Schramm to ask him not to play them. Schramm refused, and the Cowboys became a marked team.

Said veteran tackle John Dutton, who was waived in midseason, "Tex Schramm made a marked team out of us." Added a disgusted Everson Walls, "People used to hate us out of respect. Now they hate us out of disrespect."

Tom Landry, to his credit, didn't play Danny White, Tony Dorsett, or Mike Renfro, who also crossed the picket line. He played the replacement players, and in their first game, played before 12,000 in the Meadowlands against the Replacement Jets, quarterback Kevin Sweeney led the Replacement Cowboys to a 38–24 win.

Tex Schramm had anticipated the Cowboys having to use replacement players, and he hired an excellent replacement team, led by Sweeney. Sweeney had set passing records at Fresno State and had been drafted by the Cowboys in the seventh round. But Paul Hackett was convinced Sweeney was too small at 5'11" and too slow to do much but throw deep. Schramm loved the kid, but Hackett had cut him. As the strike loomed, Schramm wooed Sweeney into coming back and playing for the ersatz Cowboys.

In a poll conducted by the *Dallas Times-Herald,* 82 percent of the 6,000 people polled said that they supported the owners in the strike. Clearly, Texans extended their antiunion stance to football. Those Texans, moreover, were more enthusiastic about their replacement players than they had been toward their veterans.

By the second replacement game, Kevin Sweeney was the new Texas hero. The second replacement game took place before 40,000 fans in Texas Stadium. As the Replacement Cowboys met the Replacement Eagles, one sign read, "White's a Weenie. We Want Sweeney." The Replacement Eagles were a bad team because coach Buddy Ryan refused to give legitimacy to these games. Tom Landry, however, played it like it was the real thing. On the first play Landry called a reverse that split end Kevin Edwards took 62 yards for a touchdown. After the Replacement Cowboys won the game 41–22, Ryan called Landry "a hypocrite and a phony."

In the final strike game against the Washington Redskins, 60,612 Cowboy rooters came to Texas Stadium to watch "Kevin from Heaven," as reporter Skip Bayless called him. There was a fierce debate over whether the Cowboy quarterback should be Danny White or Kevin Sweeney. Bum Bright wanted Sweeney in there because the fans loved him so.

But rather than start Sweeney, Landry went with Danny White. Some fans even asked for their money back. White did not play very well as Washington won, 13–7. Once the strike was settled, Landry returned Danny White to his starting role and put Kevin Sweeney in mothballs.

Landry also set in motion the end of Tony Dorsett's Cowboy career. Against New England in mid-November, Landry started Herschel Walker at halfback. Dorsett sat on the bench all but six plays. By the three-quarter mark in the season, Dorsett had disappeared.

"It was pure meanness," said Dorsett, who told Tex Schramm and Tom Landry he wanted to be traded.

"Tom Landry didn't run me out of town," said Dorsett. "Tex Schramm didn't run me out of town. Not playing me ran me out of town. They chose not to use me and that was something I wouldn't stand for."

There was an aura of bitterness that lingered long after the strike had ended that almost resulted in Tom Landry's dismissal. In part because Landry had played Danny White instead of Kevin Sweeney and in part because Bum Bright resented what he called Tom Landry's "unapproachable arrogance," Bright had a burning desire to fire Landry.

Bright told Tex Schramm, "Tex, it's a goddamn business. Call Landry, and let's fire him."

"No, we can't do that just yet."

"Okay, call him, and I'll fire the son of a bitch."

"No, let me handle it my way."

It was during that conversation that Tex Schramm informed Bum Bright that he had just signed Landry to a three-year guaranteed deal that would cost Bright $1.9 million if he fired Landry then and there. Bright was furious. Schramm apologized, telling Bright "he didn't remember" Bright telling him not to guarantee the three years.

There was a time when Bright might have forfeited the $1.9 million just to get rid of Landry, but Landry had luck on his side because by this time Bright's empire had shrunk by $200 million, and Bright wasn't willing to toss away more money.

As the owner, however, Bright could, and did, make things rough on Tom Landry. Once the regular players returned, it became clear that the Cowboys were fielding a lackluster losing team. They lost to the Eagles badly when a vengeful Buddy Ryan ran up the score. They lost 44–38 to Minnesota, three weeks after a loss to Detroit, which had won but one game. After the game Tex Schramm said on his regular Monday night radio program, "I'm not sure it's all on the players. There's an old saying, 'If the teacher doesn't teach, the students don't learn.' "

Then after the Cowboys lost to another bad team, the Atlanta Falcons, Bum Bright unleashed a withering attack on Tom Landry. He told one reporter, "I get horrified sometimes at our play calling. I've heard we're not using certain players because they haven't been brought along yet. Maybe the problem is we can't utilize the talent of certain guys because we don't have anybody to direct how to use them. It doesn't seem we have anybody in charge that knows what they're doing."

Tex Schramm, who was also unhappy with the poor performance of the team, told another reporter that the Falcon game was "the absolute low point of my years with the Cowboys."

Tex's remark hurt Landry far worse than Bright's. Said Landry, "It was easier to discount Bright's comments because he knew nothing about football."

Landry, who wasn't used to this sort of criticism—disparaging comments losing coaches had heard in cities all across America since the days of Red Grange and Bronko Nagurski—defended himself.

"We have a quarterback with a bad wrist, an offensive line that keeps getting banged up—and we lost our best receiver before the season even started.

"Oh, nobody is ever really fair when it comes to coaches, but that's just the nature of the business."

The season ended 7–8. In the final game Landry installed Steve Pelluer at quarterback. Using his tried-and-true multiple offense with Pelluer at the commands, Landry proved the worth of his system, as Dallas beat two playoff contenders, the Los Angeles Rams (29–21) and the St. Louis Cardinals (21–16). Herschel Walker ran for over 100 yards in each game.

Everyone had hope going into 1988. But it was to be false hope. Tom Landry's hourglass had run out of sand.

68

Bum Bright's Payback

The Dallas Cowboys had the eleventh pick in the '88 player draft, and with it they selected Michael Irvin, a wide receiver from the University of Miami. "This will speed our return to the living," said Tex Schramm.

When Irvin arrived at the Cowboys training camp the other players couldn't help but notice that he wore enough jewelry to be a Hollywood movie producer. He had on an earring, gilt-edged sunglasses, a designer watch, and flashy rings, and he was driving a brand-new BMW. Irvin had specifically told the dealer *not* to tint the windows because he wanted to be recognized inside.

In practice, he never allowed the defenders to forget he was there, taunting and talking trash to the defenders he beat: "It's a nightmare having to cover me, isn't it? How can lightning keep striking like this?"

But at the same time on the field he worked harder than anyone, and he made catches that didn't seem possible for a runner lacking the blazing speed possessed by others. What struck others most was his seeming desperation to become a bona fide star.

What drove him, like so many others from dire straits, were the circumstances of his youth. He had little privacy and less to call his own. Irvin grew up on 27th Avenue in Fort Lauderdale, the fifteenth of seventeen children born to Walter and Pearl Irvin. First came Willie Pearl, then Alice, Willie James, Walter Jr., Ray, Sheila, Janet, Rosalind, twins Vaughn and Don, Sharon, Laverne, Lisa, Patricia, Michael, Brenda, and finally Derrick. The house had two bedrooms, until Pop Irvin closed in a porch and a garage to add bedrooms. Michael didn't sleep in bed alone until he went to college. Many Christmases there was nothing under the tree. Irvin recalled Christmases when he would stay inside all day, so he wouldn't have to discuss the things he didn't get. Sometimes he ate mayonnaise or ketchup sandwiches. He enjoyed going to school because he got a free lunch that filled his stomach. "Lunch was my primary goal in school."

All the Irvin children worked. As soon as he was strong enough, Michael joined his father in the roofing business. It was a twelve-hour-a-day job, and at thirteen Michael was taking buckets of wet roofing cement atop roofs under the blistering Florida summer sun. His father paid him, then took some of the money for rent and food. Sitting on those hot roofs, Michael Irvin decided football would be his way out.

Michael was trained by his brother Willie. He ran several miles each day and as a sophomore, he became a starter on the Piper High School football team. At Piper, there was racial tension. The whites in the public school, including some teachers, harbored prejudice that enraged him.

Said Irvin, "They didn't have time to slow down and catch me up. They didn't care, and if they didn't care, why should I?" He added, "When you're young they just think you're a dumb black kid who doesn't know any better. But as you get older it's, 'Oh, no, he should have learned by now, so we need to throw him in jail.' "

Michael saw for the first time that other kids had things he didn't, and he became envious. He has admitted to embarking on a short career of stealing but has never discussed details except to say that once he got fired from working at Burger King for stealing food. Moreover, he says, "When I went to Piper, me and my friends used to do a lot of wrong things." He was suspended his sophomore year in high school but refuses to say why.

His father sent Michael to private school. He enrolled at St. Thomas Aquinas Catholic school, so angering the Piper High coaching staff that they sought an injunction, charging recruiting violations. "They said I was too damn dumb to make those decisions on my own," Irvin told sportswriter Ed Werder. When Piper refused to sign the waiver to allow Irvin to transfer, he was forced to sit out his junior year.

But that year St. Thomas changed Irvin's outlook. He saw students with educational plans. Teachers and administrators worked with and encouraged him to read and write and study. And at St. Thomas, Michael met whites who weren't hostile, but on the contrary, were helpful and generous with their time and friendships.

That year, too, his father developed cancer, and Michael watched his father's optimism in the face of so much pain. Walter would laugh, and Michael adopted his dad's bright front. Walter Irvin never wanted anyone to see his weakness, and Michael learned from that.

One day he came home from school to learn his father had died. He ran from the house as fast as he could the five miles to school, where he sobbed in the arms of a priest. Michael blamed his dad's death not on the cancer, but on working himself to death, and he swore that when he grew up, no one in his family would have to work that hard.

Sure enough, when Michael signed a $1.8 million contract, he bought his mother a four-bedroom house with a swimming pool. He bought a satellite dish so she could watch the Cowboys on TV. He gave her a credit card, which she didn't know how to use: She had never seen a credit card before. When a family member needed help, he was always there. His one request in return: The children must attend St. Thomas Aquinas.

From the beginning of his college career, his coach at the University of Miami, Jimmy Johnson, recognized his toughness. In the fall of 1984 Johnson was starting his first season, and Irvin was a freshman. A few days into the fall semester Johnson was called into the cafeteria after Irvin had gotten into a fistfight with senior tackle Mike Moore, a 245-pounder, after Moore had cut in front of him in the serving line. Johnson was afraid that Irvin had taken a beating, but when he arrived to mediate he discovered that Irvin had pounded Moore pretty badly.

Irvin told Sally Jenkins of *Sports Illustrated,* "My problem is when I take my football energy off the field. If someone challenges me, I can get in altercations."

In 1987 Irvin, a junior, helped Miami to an undefeated season. Miami was losing to Florida State 19–3 late in the third quarter when Irvin grabbed the headphones connected to the assistant coaches and ordered them, "Get me the fucking ball!" In the fourth quarter he caught touchdowns of 26 and 73 yards as Miami pulled out the victory en route to a national championship.

Taking Irvin would turn out to be the highlight of a dismal season that would feature a starting lineup without either of the Whites, Danny or Randy, both hobbled with injuries. Danny would appear in but two games before a knee injury put him out for good. Two defensive starters, linebackers Jeff Rohrer and Mike Hegman, would go down before the season even began. Top draft pick Ken Norton had to go on injured reserve. A free agent, Garry Cobb, turned out to be the team's best linebacker.

Tom Landry decided he would take total control of the offense. Landry decided that if the ship (or plane) was going to go down, it was going to do down his way. For twenty years his teams had won using his tried-and-true Multiple Offense system. Paul Hackett wasn't going to tell him what to do. Neither would Tex Schramm nor Bum Bright. He was going to go with what he knew best. Landry planned a simpler, more basic offense that he felt would be better suited to a young team and an inexperienced quarterback, Steve Pelluer. Herschel Walker would be the main weapon in the offense. Landry knew the team was green, but he was optimistic.

The season opener set the tone for the season. Trailing by three points late in the game, the Cowboys had a third-and-two at the Steelers' four-yard line.

Landry called a play that was supposed to result in a touchdown to tight end Doug Cosbie. Steve Pelluer was supposed to fake, roll out, and pass to Cosbie in the right corner of the end zone. If Cosbie was not open, he was to throw the ball out of bounds. But Pelluer got mixed up, and he ran the wrong play. He threw the ball in the direction of three Steelers, the ball was intercepted, and the Cowboys lost.

In another game, the Cowboys lost by two points to the Giants when the referees mistakenly gave the Giants a safety. In yet another game, against the New Orleans Saints, they lost when end Thornton Chandler dropped a pass in the end zone.

Against Philadelphia, the Cowboys had a 20–0 lead with only seconds remaining in the first half. They were on the Eagles' 23, close enough to kick a field goal, but Tom Landry wanted to get the ball closer because he was wary of the reliability of kicker Roger Ruzek, who had missed all of training camp in a contract dispute. He had Herschel Walker to go to, but instead called for a rollout by Pelluer.

On the play Pelluer was cornered, and instead of eating the ball, he threw it away. After Pelluer was penalized for intentional grounding, the Cowboys lost 12 yards and were out of field goal range. They had to punt.

The Eagles won 24–23 when Randall Cunningham led his team on an 85-yard drive, throwing a two-yard touchdown pass with two seconds left in the game. Tom Landry took a roasting for losing that one, as the Cowboy record sank to 2 and 6.

After the game Landry was asked about the play. He said, "I hadn't been comfortable with the ball on the 30." Of course, the reporters knew that the ball had been on the 23, not the 30.

On TV that night one of the commentators accused Landry of a memory lapse. For the first time came the kiss-of-death accusation for any coach: he's too old. The next day in the Dallas papers, the mantra was picked up.

Landry tried to defend himself, saying he didn't care whether the ball was on the 23 or the 30, he still didn't want a field goal at that time. He had wanted a first down, regardless.

This was one time that Tom Landry needed an ally. He needed an assistant coach or Tex Schramm or the owner to back him. But Landry's loyal lieutenants had left for head coaching jobs with other NFL teams: Mike Ditka was in Chicago, Dan Reeves in Denver, Raymond Berry in New England, John Mackovic in Kansas City, and Gene Stallings in Phoenix.

For years Landry had panicked in high-pressure situations late in the game, but in the past he had had veteran quarterbacks—Don Meredith, then Roger Staubach, then Danny White—who usually pulled him out of the fire because they were exceptional and because his system had given them the tools to do so. This time he had a quarterback with little experience, Steve Pelluer. And his offensive coordinator, Paul Hackett, would not cover for him. Hackett felt he had been betrayed by Landry. Why should he show loyalty to a man who had showed him none? When the reporters ran to Hackett, Hackett told them the truth: Landry messed up and was blaming his quarterback for his mistake.

"Tom just lost it," he told Skip Bayless. "Completely lost it. It was total chaos on the sideline. Steve Pelluer played his heart out, and now he'll be the goat again. I just don't know how much more of this I can bear to watch."

This was nothing new. Landry had always panicked at the end of close games. And he had always made his quarterback the scapegoat for his mistakes. But this time, for the first time, Landry was unprotected, on his own. The wolves were at the door, and it was turning out to be a screen door. The reporters keening for Landry's head roared louder.

Bum Bright had wanted Landry out, and in interviews he was not supporting his coach. Even Tex Schramm was talking openly of replacing Landry with Jimmy Johnson, Michael Irvin's old coach at the University of Miami. Schramm even contacted Johnson when he heard the Philadelphia Eagles were after him. But Schramm was hesitant to broach the subject with Tom Landry. In Dallas, Tom Landry was still God.

The losses mounted. The Cowboys led the Phoenix Cardinals 10–0 but lost 16–10. They led against Houston 17–10 in the third quarter and lost when Cornell Burbage fumbled a kickoff with 4:32 left.

Bum Bright had not lost his affection for Kevin Sweeney, and in part to boost fan interest, Tex Schramm persuaded Landry to start Sweeney against the New York Giants. Paul Hackett, knowing how small, slow, and brittle Sweeney was, prayed he didn't get hurt. But against the Giants, Sweeney was terrific, throwing for three touchdown passes as Hackett called the plays for him. The Giants still won, however, 29–21.

Landry started Sweeney against the Minnesota Vikings. In that game Sweeney threw four interceptions and was sacked in the end zone for a safety in a 43–3 shellacking.

Steve Pelluer went back to quarterback against the Cleveland Browns, and Tom Landry went back to calling the plays. The team lost 24–21 when two field goals were nullified by penalties.

Late in the game, trailing by three, Pelluer had the Cowboys within scoring distance. With a third-and-four on the Cleveland 22, Landry called a play in a way it had not been practiced before. Herschel Walker, who had split out right, didn't understand the call. Neither did Kelvin Martin, also spread right. Before calling signals, Pelluer had to reroute them.

Pelluer's pass to Martin fell incomplete, and the Cowboys lost. After this game Skip Bayless in the *Dallas Morning News* called Landry "Mount Senility."

The Cowboys lost ten games in a row. During that stretch they had lost five of seven games in the final minute. Interceptions on the goal line by the opposition cost them three of the ballgames.

Unlike the reporters, who saw gloom and doom and were looking to hang those responsible at high noon, Tom Landry saw an inexperienced team that couldn't make the big play to hold a lead. He saw immaturity. But he also saw character and potential. Throughout the year, the players worked hard. No one gave up. No one stopped giving his all.

"The team's reaction to adversity gave me real reason for hope for the future," said Landry.

In the next-to-last game the Cowboys defeated the Super Bowl champion Washington Redskins, 24–17. Pelluer was 21 of 36 for 333 yards and threw three spectacular touchdown passes to the Cowboys' newest hopeful, Michael Irvin.

There was great celebration after the victory. The win had eliminated the hated Redskins from the playoffs. The party was as raucous as after Super Bowl victories.

In the clubhouse after the game, lineman Tom Rafferty, who was one of only four players remaining from the Cowboys' 1975 Super Bowl team, stood up before the team to award Tom Landry the dirt-caked game ball.

"This is for the guy who stuck by us when we were 2–12," said Rafferty, tears streaming down his cheeks. "He's taken a lot of shit. And he's the guy who's going to get us back on top." Rafferty handed Landry the ball, who also stood with tears in his eyes as his players chanted, "T.L., T.L., T.L., T.L."

Said Randy White about Landry after the game, "He deserves a game ball each week. If you're on the inside, you know this is one of the best coaching jobs he's ever done here. We've lost twelve games but nobody's quit. That comes from the top. He's still out there coaching every position. If they leave Tom Landry alone, he'll turn this team around. This guy's one of the greatest coaches who ever coached anything. And he still is."

It was one of Tom Landry's most memorable wins. And it would be his last.

In the season finale, Buddy Ryan and the Philadelphia Eagles clobbered the Cowboys 23–7. The team finished 3–13, worst in the league, worst since Landry's inaugural season in '60, when they were 0–11–1.

Said Tex Schramm, "I honestly never thought the day would come when I would be having a press conference on the last game of the season for being the poorest team in the league. It's nothing we're proud of. But now I guess it's a reality." On the up side, the loss assured the Cowboys the first pick in the draft.

The day after the final game Tom Landry went on his regular radio program and said that '88 was the most difficult season he had ever coached.

"Next year we're going to be a much better team coming out of training camp because we now have a higher experience level. Then we can start thinking about going back to the playoffs." It was not what Bum Bright and Tex Schramm wanted to hear.

After the season Landry took steps to strengthen his position on the team. He demoted Paul Hackett to special projects, assuring that Hackett's influence had ended. When Hackett applied for several college head coach jobs and a couple in the pros, he was turned down every time. Desperate, he took a job as offensive coordinator for the University of Pittsburgh.

Jerry Rhome, an old Landry favorite, replaced Hackett.

"I'm a soldier," said Rhome. "He's the general."

But for Tex Schramm to okay the firing of Hackett, Landry had to do something for Tex in return. That "something" was the abandonment of his beloved 4–3 Flex, a defense that opposing teams had seemingly solved. Tex wanted a change, and Landry agreed to replace it with a 3–4 defense in '89.

To oversee the change it was announced that the Cowboys were sacking Ernie Stautner, who had worked under Landry for 23 seasons. Stautner was being put in charge of those same "special projects" that Paul Hackett was supposed to be running.

Replacing Stautner would be George Hill, an expert in the 3–4 who had been unfairly fired in Indianapolis by Bob Irsay.

Stautner did not see Schramm's hand in his firing. Rather, he saw himself as Landry's scapegoat. When he left the Cowboys, like most everyone else before him, he did so feeling bitter and unappreciated.

Tom Landry went off on a Caribbean cruise, and when he returned he told reporters at Valley Ranch that he "definitely" planned to coach in 1989.

"I might even coach into the '90s," he said.

But for the first time since Tom Landry began as coach of the Cowboys, there was a real question about that. Said Tex Schramm enigmatically, "If [Landry returning] is in the best interests of the Cowboys, I'm for it. If it isn't, then there will be a change."

In the fall of 1988, Bum Bright's financial empire, like Clint Murchison's before him, was crumbling. Bright had begun his banking empire by buying the Trinity Savings and Loan for $15 million. In 1984, right after buying the Cowboys, he bought Texas Federal Savings and Loan for $71 million and merged it with Trinity Savings and Loan. A year later he added Dallas Federal Savings and Loan for $107 million, making him the seventh largest privately held mortgage broker. These were top-of-the-market prices, though of course Bright could not have known that at the time. The other thing Bright didn't know was that many of the loans made by Texas Federal Savings and Loan were shaky at best with collateral on real estate projects that would never be completed.

Bright could not have anticipated what would happen to him, because he could not foresee that economic quagmire that lay ahead. He had fallen into the same trap of all the other get-very-rich-quick investors who saw the value of their real estate investments double and were counting on these investments to continue their precipitous climb. Through the 1980s, investors schemed to buy land, then overvalued its worth even more in order to borrow money to buy more land from friendly banks glad to pocket the commissions. It was like the Emperor's New Clothes. Everyone knew the land was worth 20¢ on the dollar. But as long as no one would admit it, the game could continue.

Then in 1988 the house of cards holding up the investors and their banks collapsed. The price of real estate dropped so steeply that the real estate holdings became albatrosses to the title holders. And when the owners couldn't sell the land at inflated prices, they couldn't pay back the money borrowed to buy the land. Banks all over America were forced to declare bankruptcy.

At the same time oil prices were falling fast, dropping to $26 a barrel, as a result of global overproduction. By February 1986 the price of a barrel of West Texas Intermediate Crude fell below $10 and put the Texas economy in the toilet.

Bright Banc was one of those S&Ls in free fall. Billions had been loaned against wells that were being capped and against real estate projects that were being abandoned.

The irony was that the federal government, hated so deeply by Bright and under the presidency of his own George Bush, moved in to shove him off the board of the First Republic Bank Corp. just before the once-mighty bank-holding company collapsed. Federal regulators then seized his tottering $4.7 billion savings and loan association and began serving as conservators.

Before the government could step in and clean up the disaster, the Bright Banc alone would cost taxpayers $1.4 billion. Several years later the government accused Bright and his son-in-law James "Boots" Reeder of fraud, negligence, making misrepresentations to federal bank regulators, and breaking their duties to the thrift and its depositors. The government sought damages of $160 million.

Bright called it an "unprincipled witchhunt." He added, "This suit is nothing more than another suit in a recent string of cases against honest men and women to extort money from them."

Bright accused the government of causing his downfall, arguing that the Tax Reform Act of 1986 took away investors' depreciation advantages. "That was why the banks and most savings and loans started to fail," said Bright.

Bright had built 118 luxury suites in Texas Stadium, but more than 100 remained unsold because the fans were unwilling to shell out so much money for a facility they could only use ten times a year.

When word of Bright's problems began bubbling, Bright's desire to sell the Cowboys was also made known. Several potential buyers surfaced. One group, a consortium of Japanese businessmen, told Bright to name his price. But Bright still had not forgiven the Japanese for Pearl Harbor and World War II, and he turned them down.

Another potential buyer, Don Carter, the owner of the Dallas Mavericks, wanted the Cowboys but not Texas Stadium. Carter was also a great admirer of Tom Landry. But Bright needed to sell the stadium as well as the team, and he also wanted to make sure Landry would get what he felt he deserved, and so Carter was dismissed as a potential buyer.

The third candidate was an Arkansas oil driller by the name of Jerry Jones. While fishing with his son in Cabo San Lucas, Mexico, he noticed an item in the *Wall Street Journal* that Bum Bright had retained Solomon Brothers to find a buyer for the Cowboys. From Mexico, Jones called Solomon Brothers, who had put him in touch with Bright.

Jones had played football at the University of Arkansas. He had been a teammate and at times a roommate of Jimmy Johnson, the head coach of the University of Miami. Jones satisfied Bright that he had enough money, and in their first meeting Jones had said the magic words. He told Bright that if he bought the team, he would fire Tom Landry and Jimmy Johnson would be his new coach.

In fact, during talks with Bright, Jones would bring Johnson along with him. The negotiations dragged on through the winter of 1989. Bum Bright was demanding almost $150 million, and Jerry Jones was looking at the negatives and arguing that Bright's asking price was too high. For one, the value of NFL franchises had stopped rising along with that of the condos and shopping centers. For another, because more and more players were becoming free agents, the payrolls were rising swiftly. And Jones could certainly argue that a 3–13 Cowboy team had far less value than one fighting for a playoff berth.

Jones, meanwhile, dragged his feet, hoping to get Bright to lower his price as his financial problems mounted. In the battle of two tough hombres, Bright held firm.

For four days straight the two men negotiated, getting no sleep. The final impediment to closing the deal was a disagreement over $300,000 in closing fees. Bright suggested a coin flip to settle the issue. "Winner take all." Jones agreed.

Bright produced a quarter. Jones called tails. It came up heads. Jones paid full price. Bright had the coin mounted and a week later presented it to Jones.

When the deal to sell the Dallas Cowboys to Jerry Jones was completed in February of '89, Bum Bright had not only managed to extricate himself from a difficult financial situation, he had also gotten his revenge: the firing of Tom Landry. And even better, Bum Bright wouldn't even be blamed for it. Jerry Jones would take the heat for that.

When Jerry Jones was introduced as the new Cowboy owner, Bum Bright told the crowd, "What we have here is a new generation, someone with the competence and intelligence to help make the Cowboys what they once were."

Few paid attention at the time, but Bum Bright was setting into motion events that would cause great upheaval for the Cowboys and their fans, though in the end, his words would prove prophetic.

69

End of an Era

om Landry and his staff were preparing for the upcoming draft.
UCLA's Troy Aikman, the best quarterback to come along since John
Elway, would bring the Cowboys back, Landry was certain.
Schramm and Landry were excited.

Tom Landry had settled the quarterback situation in his own mind.
He felt good about Steve Pelluer, and he thought the team would be better served if Troy Aikman learned behind him. In '89 Landry decided he
would return to the basic passing game he had used for so many years.
With Hackett gone and his former quarterback Jerry Rhome to replace
him, he would also return to calling the plays for the quarterback and not
leave it to an assistant. Tom Landry would rebuild the Cowboys his way.

Then on Thursday, February 23, 1989, there was a report from KXTV
channel 5 on the ten o'clock news that the sale of the Cowboys was immi-
nent. Neither Tex Schramm nor Tom Landry knew anything about it. The
next day Schramm called Bum Bright, who told him to meet with him the
next day. Meanwhile Don Shula, the head coach of the Miami Dolphins,
called Schramm to tell him that Jimmy Johnson had asked his son, David,
if he wanted to join him in Dallas as an assistant coach.

At Tom Landry's home a string of reporters called wanting to know
whether he was going to be fired.

Late on Friday Schramm and Landry met. Schramm told his coach of twenty-nine years, "Tom, I think it's over." Landry shrugged and took a breath. There was nothing either of them could do about it.

Landry and Schramm didn't know it for sure, but the reports in the newspaper that the buyer, Jerry Jones, had flown University of Miami coach Jimmy Johnson into Dallas in his private plane were accurate. The draft was coming up soon, and Jones wanted to talk to Johnson about his coaching staff.

With entire sports staffs of newspapers searching high and low in the high-rent Dallas hotels for Jimmy Johnson, on Friday, February 24, Jones and Johnson were holed up in two rooms at the Embassy Suites Hotel trying to stay out of sight. That night, they got hungry for Mexican food. Fearing that Jimmy Johnson would be recognized, Jones asked the bellman to recommend an "out-of-the-way little place." He sent them to Mia's, a local Tex-Mex place on Lemmon Avenue. The two out-of-towners figured it would be a quiet dinner, that no one would see them.

But they couldn't have known that Mia's was not only Tom Landry's favorite Tex-Mex restaurant but a shrine to him as well, with photos of Landry all over the walls. Jones, Johnson, and their wives entered and sat down in a small opening next to the cash register to wait for a table. Ivan Maisel, a college football reporter with the *Dallas Morning News,* looked up from his nachos to discover he had the scoop of the year. Maisel had spent the afternoon staking out the Mansion, hoping to ask Jimmy Johnson if he was replacing Tom Landry. And here were Jimmy Johnson and Jerry Jones ordering a round of beers. Maisel walked behind Johnson and tapped him on the shoulder.

"Oh, shit. What are *you* doing here?"

"I live a block from here," said Maisel. "What are *you* doing here?"

Johnson answered vaguely, and Maisel snuck off to look for a telephone. He exited through the kitchen, jogged to a nearby Chinese restaurant, and called the paper to request a photographer pronto. When the cameraman arrived, he asked Jones, Johnson, and their wives to smile for the birdie.

Said Johnson, "No, no, no, we don't need this! Jerry, dammit, tell him we don't need this!"

Jones wasn't concerned. "Aw, go ahead and shoot. This is a done deal."

Their picture, prominently featuring beer cans on the table, appeared in the paper the next morning. The picture said it all: Here they sat in Tom Landry's favorite restaurant grinning and seeming so jubilant! The Dallas faithful, who months earlier were calling for Landry's head, fumed at the way these "furriners" were now treating him.

According to Bum Bright, that Friday Tex Schramm had told Landry to stay close to Valley Ranch so Bright and Jones could talk to him about his dismissal, but instead of waiting around, the next day, a Saturday, Tom Landry got out of Dodge, piloting his Cessna 210 to his weekend retreat in Lakeway, just west of Austin. His children, Kitty, Lisa, and Tom Jr., met him there. While Bum Bright was trying to get in touch with him at his home, calling in the morning every thirty minutes for three hours, Tom Landry was out of town on the golf course, whistling in the wind, making believe that Jerry Jones's guillotine was not made of tempered steel. For almost thirty years countless players had tried to run and hide from Tom Landry's Turk. Now it was his turn, and he would be no more successful than his former players had been.

Though it was Tex Schramm's job to fire Landry, Tex wouldn't—or couldn't—bring himself to do it, not for Bum Bright, and not for Jerry Jones. Schramm told Jones that the honorable thing for him to do was to dismiss Landry face to face, not do it over the telephone. He said to Jones, "Before you have any press conferences or make any announcements you need to talk to Tom, and I strongly suggest you do it in person." Jones naively agreed. Schramm was setting up Jones to be the bad guy in the scenario. Schramm was Iago, Jones Othello, and the Cowboys were Desdemona. When the negative reviews flooded in, Jones didn't know what hit him.

That Saturday morning Schramm met with Jones, Bright, and Johnson to defend the team's policies to the new owner. After the meeting Schramm interrupted Landry's golf game to tell him things didn't look good. Schramm said they were flying to Austin to meet with him. Landry finished the round as though nothing had happened.

Jerry Jones and Tex Schramm boarded the Learjet with the Cowboys blue star insignia for the short flight from Dallas to Austin. Jones and Landry shook hands. Landry told the new owners, "If you're just coming down here for a publicity stunt, you need not have bothered."

Jones told him, "Oh, Tex insisted I talk to you. He felt we should meet face to face. I'm here now and so is Jimmy."

The meeting lasted forty minutes. In the end, Landry was no longer head coach after twenty-nine years with the Dallas Cowboys. Landry's 270 wins were third-most in NFL history, behind Don Shula, who had been so successful with Baltimore and Miami, and George Halas, who had owned and coached the Chicago Bears for 40 years.

After the meeting Landry went back to the golf course, where he had dinner with his family. Never one to worry about things he couldn't control, Landry carried on, stoic as ever.

At 8 P.M. that Saturday night Tex Schramm scheduled a press conference to announce what everyone knew: Jerry Jones was the new owner, Jimmy Johnson the new coach, and Tom Landry was out.

At the press conference Jerry Jones was introduced. At what reporters perceived as a wake for Landry, Jerry Jones pounded the podium like Nikita Khrushchev once did at the UN and talked only of the (Landryless) future. "This is like Christmas for me . . ."

Jones began extolling the virtues of his friend, Jimmy Johnson, whom Jones called "the best coach in America." Reporters rolled their eyes as Jones began praising the new king without first holding the requisite tribute for the old one. When his remarks appeared in the morning newspapers, every Dallas Cowboy fan who loved and cherished Tom Landry hated Jerry Jones.

Summing up his years with the Cowboys, Tom Landry told reporters, "I don't know if any team in professional football will ever duplicate what happened. The success of that era is something of which all of us who were a part are very proud. It was a great accomplishment."

On Monday Landry spoke to his players.

"This will be our last meeting together," he began. He told the players not to worry about him, that he was going on with his life.

"We will all go on," he said. "You . . . you'll . . . forget me . . . in a couple of weeks."

Tears came to his eyes. The players lowered their heads, embarrassed for him. He continued, "The way you react to adversity is the key to success. Right now . . . the situation around here is in turmoil and how . . . we react will be important . . . important in how the season goes next . . . year. I . . . don't want anyone to concern themselves with what has happened to me but to . . . to look . . . forward to playing football in September . . ."

Tears fell from his face. He asked the players to do all they could do to make the Cowboys an elite team again.

"That's . . . important for . . . you know, to know that you didn't quit, that . . . we didn't quit."

He broke down and couldn't go on for a while. The room was quiet.

Finally, "The things . . . I'm going to miss the most . . . are the coaches and you . . . the players."

As Tom Landry sobbed, many of the players cried, too.

Landry recovered. He said, "I'll be with you in spirit, always. I love you guys. God bless you and your families."

The players gave him a standing ovation.

After posing for pictures with the staff, Tom Landry got into his car with his son Tom Jr. and drove away. Cowboy players and staff stood on the steps outside the main building or looked through their office windows and watched him drive away.

Not long after his firing, "Landry for Governor" bumper stickers started to circulate. One billboard read, "Tom Landry. Thanks for 29 Great Years." Then in April 1989 came his "Hats Off to Tom Landry Parade."

On April 22, 1989, more than 50,000 people turned out for Tom Landry Day. Volunteers raised $90,000 to pay for the celebration. When Roger Staubach first asked Landry about it, his response was, "Why would anyone want to hold such a thing for me?"

People were lined up six and seven deep for a mile along the streets of downtown Dallas. The governor of Texas and mayor of Dallas were there, and Staubach read telegrams from George Bush and Billy Graham. Bob Hope called to congratulate him.

The parade was held partly in response to his firing by new owner Jerry Jones. Before he had been a hero. Now he was a martyr.

When he saw the huge turnout, Jones, a decent man who had been placed in the role of villain, was happy for Landry. "I would have been more concerned if there had been apathy," said Jones.

There were eighty-six floats in the parade. Roger Staubach rode on one, as did Herschel Walker, Tony Dorsett, Drew Pearson, Ralph Neely, and Walt Garrison. Then a 1954 Buick carried the Landry family.

"I don't deserve this," said Landry, "but I am so thankful for it."

Tom waved as the fans shouted, "We love you, Coach."

With his firing, Landry became a martyr. The next year he was enshrined in the Pro Football Hall of Fame where thousands gave him a thundering standing ovation.

Fans fondly recall his 270–178–6 lifetime record with the Cowboys, the twenty consecutive seasons making the playoffs, the five Super Bowl appearances. Cowboy fans see the calm Tom Landry standing on the sidelines wearing his famous cloth hat, impassive, concentrating, and they smile at the memory. In retrospect, for many fans, Tom Landry *was* the Cowboys. His players for the most part have forgiven him his shortcomings, and the fans have forgotten the final years of futility and recall only the good times.

Tom Landry today lives in Dallas, comfortable and relaxed at home with his wife, Alicia. He spends his time managing his considerable portfolio of real estate and security investments and speaking to Christian groups, and he remains Texas's only living saint.

TOM LANDRY: "We started tough, no draft, no players. Don Meredith and Don Perkins were the only two players who were considered draftable. We had hoped to turn it around in three years, but when we didn't get any draft choices, it became obvious it would be hard to build that fast. I had developed the 4–3 defense back when I was with the Giants, and everybody started using it, so when I became the Dallas coach, I had to come up with an offense that could beat my defense, and so we put in multiple sets, shifting up and down, moving our players around at the last moment, so the defense couldn't determine what was going to happen before the snap of the ball. At the beginning we didn't have good enough players to make the system work, and at the same time the players had to believe in me, believe in my ability to do it. If they didn't adhere to what we were doing, they wouldn't be there. And we struggled those early years. And yet in 1962 our offense tied with New York and Green Bay. We scored more than 400 points that year, even with the players we had. We slipped in '63, but I never changed my theory, and we were very fortunate to have a great draft in '64, and that was the thing that enabled us to turn the corner. It wasn't until 1965 that we won as many as we lost. And from then on, we kicked off.

"I really was always very confident in what we were doing, and in the players we had to play for us. We were very fortunate to have players like Don Meredith in his beginning. Don was a good quarterback in a tough era. When you had to play in the '60s with the Cowboys with what we had—the punishment—Don was probably the toughest player that I had. He played hurt. He was kind of a happy-go-lucky guy, but he was really intent on doing the job. We were always at odds a little bit, because he wasn't Roger Staubach, who was my type of quarterback. But Don was a good guy. He was just kind of like a chip on your shoulder. When you worked with him, he didn't particularly want to be like I was, very disciplined. He didn't want to be that way. He was a funny guy. I remember an exhibition against the New York Giants one season, he came out of the huddle and looked at the defense, and he couldn't read it, and he said a four-letter word, you know, and he turned around and walked back to the huddle. And he was frustrated by it. But he was that kind of guy.

"We had some great teams with Don. The 1966–67 teams were great teams. And then Roger took over at quarterback. I didn't think Roger would ever play. I remember he was still in the service when he came out to training camp, and we'd give him a playbook, and Pete Gent used to say to him, 'Don't worry about it, Roger. They all get killed in the end.' 'Cause that playbook was so thick. And I never paid much attention to him. He would be out there throwing, and I'd be working getting ready for the year, and he'd be out passing and trying to work out. I never thought he would stay, and then when he came to us and played that great game against the 49ers, a fantastic football game, for him to come off the bench and win a football game like that against an excellent football team, was really an amazing eye-opener for us. And then I had to make a tough decision.

"Craig Morton was signed as quarterback. And I enjoyed working with Craig. He was really a fine person, and you had to make that decision. I had those two quarterbacks. We were very fortunate we were able to have that kind of caliber player at quarterback through those years and even into Danny White. If Danny hadn't been hurt against New York that time, we would have gone to another Super Bowl or two, just because of his ability, because he was an excellent quarterback. And so, that's kind of where it ended, as we went into the '80s, and we were fighting to try to stay up, because we were drafting so late for so long, and we were very fortunate. If we hadn't drafted Too Tall or Dorsett or Randy White—those were all first-round choices we traded for—without them, we'd have been nosediving long before then.

"As far as personal satisfaction, looking back, you have to be extremely proud of your first Super Bowl win, mainly because it meant so much to a team that couldn't win the big one for four years. Before we went to our first Super Bowl, I'll never forget, we played St. Louis on a Monday night game, Howard Cosell was up there and Meredith, and we were behind by two games and this was a very important game, and we got beat 38–0. Well, we lost everybody, including my old buddies in the press box, Gifford and all the rest of them. But the next day when we went into our meeting there, boy, they were down. Their heads were down. They were just defeated, and finally they had a little talk, and when I came in, 'Fellas, let's go out and play touch football.' And so they went out and played touch football and got real relaxed and we went on to win all the rest of our games, got beat in the Super Bowl on a field goal at the end.

That was a great turnaround. But that only happens when you have character. If you have character, you can turn a club around. If your team doesn't have the character, then they'll fall. They won't come back. But that team had character.

"It was almost five years before we won the Big One. And that was very satisfying. As we were getting ready for the game, I remember Dave Edwards came up to me. 'Hey Coach, if we're not ready, we're never going to be ready.' They were so confident that they could beat the Dolphins at that time. There wasn't any doubt in their minds. I don't get that feeling as a coach. I can't say before the game, 'We're going to win regardless.' It's very hard for me to say that, because I've seen it turn around so many times. But those players for that game, they really knew they could win. And they went out and won.

"I think the most enjoyable and most satisfying season was the season we went to the Hail Mary pass in 1975. Because that year we had a lot of people retiring. We had twelve rookies, and nobody expected us to go anyplace, and we were almost defeated in Minnesota when the Hail Mary pass came.

"You know, on that field, the old field, it wasn't the Dome, and therefore you're on a baseball field, and both teams were on the same side, and we were down on our own 20-yard line, and that's where we took over the ball. We had to go all the way. And I really couldn't hardly see the play when Drew caught it, because we were blocked off by the Minnesota team, and so I didn't recognize it. And I tell you, I was almost in shock, when you think about it, that he did catch it, he did score. It was amazing because this was one of Minnesota's best football teams. Of all of Bud Grant's teams, this one was really a good one, because of their defense, and to pull this off really was a miracle.

"They said when Roger came off the field after that, he sat down by Doc Knight, and they sat there for a while, and Roger turned to Knight and said, 'Can you believe that?' He was in doubt. Everybody was. The thing that was so amazing about that drive was that Preston Pearson was in there on a third-down play, and we didn't go to him because we were out of timeouts. So we were down about the 30-yard line, and Roger, instead of downing the ball, threw it to Preston. If Preston catches it, the game is over with. Time runs out. And Preston dropped it. And he never dropped it. And then came a fourth-down play, which was to Drew on a sideline, and one of the funniest things that happened on that thing, the guard who was walking up and down the sideline to keep people off, he was right there where Drew caught the ball, and Drew hit the ice and fell and slid, and the guard came up and kicked him in the ribs! We didn't see that until we saw the film the next day. But that was an amazing drive, a greater miracle than the one against the 49ers out in San Francisco that time.

"Duane Thomas was one of the great football players. If Duane Thomas would have stayed with us and Calvin Hill, too, if they would have stayed with us, if we had had the strength of those two players, we would have competed very strongly against Pittsburgh in the '70s. But it was very difficult. In Duane Thomas's case, it was a shame. He came to us kind of surly. But he was okay that first year. We ended up going to the Super Bowl against Baltimore. And the next off-season, he went to California, went to Los Angeles. He got into the drug scene there, and it was really a shame.

"Really, in those days, football coaches had no idea about drugs. I had never seen drugs. I wouldn't have any idea about drugs. And so we didn't know how to handle it. We were negative in the way we faced it, because we just didn't understand it. But when he came into training camp the next year, he was a Dr. Jekyll and Mr. Hyde. That next year we went to the Super Bowl again and won it, you remember he wouldn't talk to anyone, and he was amazing, and the next year I had to get rid of him because he was just so disruptive. So that was the era we were in.

"Nothing would have corrected Duane. No. Regardless of what Tex had offered him. After he went to L.A., and after he came back again and went to that Super Bowl we won, there was no turning back with him. Yet, I spoke a couple years ago out at Albuquerque. He and his wife came over from Las Cruzas, they came down and visited at the banquet for the Fellowship of Christian Athletes. He was very friendly. And he tried. I don't know where Duane is now. He was trying hard. But boy, when you're on drugs . . . What a great team we'd a had had he stayed.

"Thomas Henderson was a good guy. He was so unusual. I remember we sent a scout out to see him down in Oklahoma where he went to school, and the scout came in and was on the sideline and Thomas Henderson was in street clothes. They were out there scrimmaging. And he was in street clothes. He said to our scout, 'Would you like to see me play?' And so he goes in and changes clothes, puts on his uniform, comes out and puts himself into the scrimmage, plays for a while in there, and then he came over and said, 'Have you seen enough?' And so he went in and put on his clothes again. That's the lack of discipline of that era. You know? There was *no* discipline. And that's what happened from the late '60s well into the '70s. There just wasn't any discipline at all.

"I was very fortunate. I spent two careers with two great teams, New York and Dallas, and it was something you really enjoyed, being in Dallas and being a part of what took place. I love Dallas.

"The way the people responded to me personally, the Tom Landry Day after I was released, was really special. That's something you don't realize will happen, with the parade and all the things that took place there. They were wonderful times for us, and most people thought I should be bitter. I wasn't bitter. I wasn't bitter at all.

"When I left football, I just left it completely. I have been to Texas Stadium twice, never been at the practice field, never invited. None of us were.

"The Ring of Honor was one time I was there, and I went for Randy and Dorsett. Those were the only times. And it's a shame. I kind of feel sorry the way things have worked out with them. It's a new era, the hot-dogging and all that, the big salaries, people like Deion. It's just not football as we knew it.

"People say, 'Can you coach today?' Well, I probably could. I might not enjoy it, but I could."

70

The Devil and Mr. Jones

In any morality play there must be bad guys as well as good guys. Who would have heard of the Lone Ranger had there not been bank robbers, land swindlers, and other low-down varmints? And so in the Cowboy morality play that followed the sacking of Tom Landry, there had to be a bad guy, and what better bad guy could have come along than a carpet-bagger from "Soooey Pig" Arkansas, for Landry's sake. And this dirt farmer hired a coach who also came from Arkansas, for Landry's sake.

To Texans, Arkansans were created by Al Capp, residents of Dog-patch. Rich Arkansans like Jerry Jones are likened to Jed Clampett and his kinfolk in the sixties TV show *The Beverly Hillbillies*. A Texan might snap up Ellie Mae in a heartbeat. But the rest of them hog sloppers, forget it. In fact, two days after Jerry Jones bought the Cowboys, linebacker Jeff Rohrer was lifting weights in the team strength room when a TV crew from channel 8 came over for an interview. Rohrer, whose degree from Yale suggested he should have known better, looked into the camera and sang the following words to the theme song of *The Beverly Hillbillies:*

The first thing you know ol' Jer's a millionaire.
The kinfolks said, Jer, move away from here!

They said, Dallas, Texas, is the place you wanna be!
So he hopped in his Lear and bought America's team.

After Rohrer's stellar performance, the Dallas fans began referring to Jerry Jones as "Jethro," Jed's lovable but dumb-as-a-post nephew. (Six months later, the Cowboys cut Jeff Rohrer. Jerry and Jimmy Johnson made it clear they didn't want any smartasses around.)

Texans probably feel the way they do about Arkansans because of college football. For many years in the Southeast Conference, the only non-Texas school was the University of Arkansas with its rabid rooters who wore red hats in the shape of razorbacks, the wild oinkers with big snouts, all screaming, "Wooooo, pig, sooooo-ieeee." A Texas assistant coach once said that playing a game in Fayetteville, Arkansas, was like "parachuting into Russia." Before one game there a local minister posted a sign meant for UT coach Darrell Royal: "Darrell Royal—Do Not Cast Your Steers Before Swine."

And so it wasn't bad enough that a newcomer had come in and defiled Cowboy tradition by firing Tom Landry. That newcomer had turned out to be Boss Hawg himself.

Jerral Wayne Jones was born on October 13, 1942, in Los Angeles. During World War II his father, Pat, had moved there from Arkansas to escape the Depression by getting work in an aircraft manufacturing plant. Two years later, Pat and his wife, Arminta, moved back to Rose City, Arkansas, North Little Rock really, where Pat opened a drive-in fruit stand that stood along the four-lane England Highway.

Business boomed, and Pat Jones added a bakery and a meat market. The store became Pat's Supermarket. Pat began hosting live radio shows from the store with country-and-western acts performing in front of large audiences. The radio broadcasts beamed into fifteen counties. Listeners wondered what it was like shopping at Pat's Supermarket, and his business increased dramatically.

Pat, meanwhile, never stopped working hard. He would never forget the Depression. Nor would he allow his son Jerry to forget it. Jerry worked in that store every day, and he became adept at selling. Jerry would stand at the door and ask, "Help you find somethin', ma'am?"

Pat's Supermarket wasn't far from Dixie Street, where the blacks lived. Though segregation was strict, blacks and whites mixed easily at Pat's. Many of Jerry's friends were black, though when he went to school, he says, "my black buddies disappeared."

"Looking back on it," says Jones, "it makes me feel bad that I didn't at least ask, 'What is going on here?' "

Jerry Jones channeled his aggressiveness into football. He was a quarterback his freshman and sophomore years, and he switched to fullback junior year. On defense he played "Monster Man," part linebacker, part safety. His job was to head for the action and make the tackle. By senior year he was team captain, and that year he caught the winning touchdown to beat the perennial state champs, Little Rock Central High.

In 1960 Jerry Jones was recruited by the new coach at the University of Arkansas, Frank Broyles, because he was quick, technically sound, and, most important, fought hard. A Broyles team usually gave away twenty pounds, but it would win with finesse, versatility, better conditioning, and what he called "carektuh."

At 6' and 190 pounds, Jones came to Arkansas as a running back, but Broyles and freshman coach Barry Switzer soon turned him into a guard. Conditioning was brutal. Jones says it was a "living hell." But Jones and Switzer soon became friends, and they shared their passion for football, coeds, and cold beer. Also helping Jones get through his freshman year was a budding romance with Eugenia "Gene" Chambers, voted the statewide Poultry Princess and a future Miss Arkansas USA. Gene, the daughter of a banker, was dating Jerry, the son of the owner of a fruit stand. Gene's father called a banking friend of his in Little Rock to check up on Jones. Said the friend, "Jerry is a very smart boy. Look at it this way, John Ed. He's smart enough to want to marry the banker's daughter, isn't he?" By the end of their sophomore year they were married. They have been together ever since.

Jones was redshirted through the entire '61 season, didn't play in '62, and played two games in '63; sitting on the bench behind a stocky guard named Jimmy Johnson, he almost quit. In '64 Johnson moved to defense and Jones moved into the starting lineup at offensive right guard as a senior.

In Jones's senior year the Razorbacks started winning football games, and they climbed in the national ranking, especially after a stunning 14–13 win over Texas, the national champs the year before. In their last five games opponents didn't score a single point against them.

Arkansas played Nebraska in the Cotton Bowl. Nebraska led most of the game 7–3 and would have scored more if it weren't for the play of Jimmy Johnson. A last-minute touchdown by Arkansas gave them the win, 10–7. At the same time Texas defeated Joe Namath and top-ranked Alabama in the Orange Bowl. Arkansas was thus the nation's only unbeaten team, and the Football Writers of America voted the Razorbacks the Grantland Rice Trophy.

It was Jones's fifth year, and in addition to taking six hours of graduate courses and playing football, Jones began his entrepreneurial life. After practice Jones put on a suit and threw his suitcase into his Cadillac Eldorado to recruit salesmen for his father's life insurance company. He was already on the road to success while his teammates were worried about passing final exams.

After leaving Arkansas in 1965 with both undergrad and graduate degrees, Jones joined his father in the insurance business full-time in Springfield, Missouri. Using borrowed money, he invested in McDonald's, Kentucky Fried Chicken, and in a soon-to-fail pizza chain called Shakey's. He also invested in Tyson Foods, which would not take off for another decade. He borrowed money to buy real estate, almost going broke in the mid-'60s when he overextended himself. Jones tells a story how his first year out of college he was paying out $125,000 in interest against a yearly salary of $25,000. He was so unnerved, he says, his hands would shake when he picked up a glass.

Jones entertained the notion of heading a syndicate to buy the San Diego Chargers for $5.5 million in 1966 but was talked out of it by his father, who thought the debt too great for a twenty-three-year-old boy. Two months later the AFL and the NFL merged. Four months after that, the Chargers were sold for $11 million. His father would later admit he had made a mistake.

In 1970 Pat Jones sold the insurance company for millions of dollars and moved with his family back to Little Rock, where his intention was to enter the oil business, at a time when the big oil companies were laying off exploration departments.

When Pat told relatives of his intention, he was put in touch with a geologist named Bill Sparks. Sparks had developed an interesting theory about finding oil and gas wells. Sparks's idea was to drill between the dry holes that marked the Red Fork Channel Sands in the Arkoma Basin on the plains of Oklahoma. Sparks had studied and mapped hundreds of these wells. He noticed that a productive well would be found, and right next to it the well would be dry. His theory was that oil moved in a meandering stream and that the dry wells marked the edges of the channel. If you could find two dry wells, then that would mark the two edges of the channel, and a productive well ought to be found between them at a depth of about 7,000 feet.

Sparks's problem was that the execs at Monsanto, the company he worked for, thought he was nuts. The idea that there was oil at 7,000 feet seemed unlikely if not absurd, and when Sparks persisted, Monsanto fired him.

Sparks had great faith in his theory, but he didn't have the capital to drill. Then in walked Pat and Jerry Jones. Pat was skeptical, but his son was impressed both with Sparks's vision and also with the possibility of great riches. For the rest of his life Jerry Jones would become immensely wealthy by putting his money down on the right people. Jones's plunges would also be marked by initial snickers, followed by incredible success. Those who got to know him would find out a basic truth about Jerry Jones: This is a very smart man who should never be underestimated.

Jones told Bill Sparks he would back his plan to drill under the Red Fork Channel Sands. Jones and a partner were selling mobile homes at the time they heard of Sparks's scheme, and immediately agreed to pony up the dough to see if Sparks's theory was right. Jones raised $200,000 without going to a bank, and Sparks identified and selected a drill site. When Jones and Sparks started drilling on the dusty, desolate land, competitors laughed, sure that Jones was throwing his money down a rat hole.

Said Sparks, "Right off the bat, Jerry believed in me. Why, I don't completely know, other than the fact that he was hungry to get rich. But there was one other thing. All he could talk about was that he wanted to make enough money to buy a football team."

The first well hit for $4 million. Now they had enough money to go to a bank, borrow money, and keep drilling. Sparks's theory was no more complicated than merely connecting the dots on his map, and it was more valuable than one of those pirates' treasure maps as the group hit the second well, and the third, and the first fifteen attempted. Between 1971 and 1980 the group drilled 2,000 wells and hit 700. Jerry Jones made more than $50 million.

Then in 1981, at a time when competitors were plunging in the oil business, amid predictions that the price of a barrel of oil would soar from $40 to $100 per barrel, Jones got out of the oil-drilling business. His timing (or luck) was impeccable. Following the Shah's downfall in Iran (1978–1979), the price of oil dropped to less than $10 a barrel.

In 1981 Jones made the switch from oil to gas when he met Mike McCoy, who was in the natural gas business. McCoy had wanted to drill in the San Joaquin Basin near San Francisco. He drew a large circle on a map to show Jones "the largest natural gas field in northern California."

As he had with Bill Sparks, Jerry Jones decided that Mike McCoy was someone worth backing. McCoy was smart, and he was sure of himself. The two bought the lease on an asparagus farm north of San Francisco for $250,000. They also drilled a well selected by McCoy in southeastern Oklahoma.

After spending $500,000 preparing the Oklahoma hole, an employee negligently filled it with cement, ruining it. Another man in that situation might have freaked out and given up. But there was another aspect of Jerry Jones that would contribute to his success: He kept the faith once he made up his mind to attempt a venture.

Though he was out $500,000 because one of McCoy's trusted employees had goofed, Jerry Jones didn't blink. His confidence in McCoy was unshaken, and he financed another hole. The distraught employee, moreover, kept his job. They drilled again, and though the first reports were not encouraging, eight hours later they were rich. The natural gas well was worth $40 million. Then the California well hit, and they had made another $40 million strike. Jerry Jones was a rich man. The question for all rich men during the 1980s was whether he would be able to escape the Texas real estate holocaust that had ruined Clint Murchison and almost sank Bum Bright.

Jones was not immune. He got caught up in the cycle of borrow, buy land, borrow more based on the value of that land, buy more land, borrow even more money—when the crash came.

Jones found himself in deep financial trouble after borrowing a pot of money from the Penn Square Bank to buy real estate that turned out to be unsellable when the price of oil dropped.

Jones, though, was luckier than Murchison, who had invested his in banks. Jones returned from the brink of disaster when in 1983 he was able to find a bank to buy up the loan. Also at that time Jones made a deal with his close friend, business partner, and neighbor Sheffield Nelson that was so profitable for him that the howls could be heard from the halls of the statehouse in Little Rock all the way to Washington.

Before Jones and Nelson made their big score, together they had owned a television station, a farm, a race horse, and a condo. They had also been partners of Jim McDougal (Bill and Hillary Clinton's partner in the Whitewater land deal) in a land investment on Campobello Island, located between Nova Scotia and New Brunswick.

What Jerry Jones obtained was a 50 percent interest in the oil and gas rights to 28,000 acres in the Arkoma Basin of eastern Oklahoma for $15 million from Nelson's company, Arkansas-Louisiana Gas Inc. (ArkLa), a public utility that supplied natural gas to customers in Arkansas. Nelson, the president and CEO, slipped the deal past the noses of the other board members.

Under the terms of the contract structured by Nelson, Jones's Arkoma Inc. only had to put up $3,750,000. Nelson lent Jones the rest at 10 percent interest. For his part Jones agreed to spend $30 million drilling wells, a sum to be matched by ArkLa. In return any gas recovered from the property would be sold by Jones to ArkLa.

The deal didn't seem extraordinary except for one fact: ArkLa didn't need to spread the risk of drilling because there was no risk. Nelson said the deal would help spread the costs of developing the field. But in the context it made *no* sense. The Arkoma Basin was a gas bonanza for ArkLa. Prior to the deal with Jones, ArkLa had hit on the first fifty-nine wells in a row. Why give Jones a 50 percent interest in a sure thing?

Years later, after Jerry Jones cleared more than $300 million from his deal with ArkLa, the howls still reverberate among Arkansans stung by the notion that he had somehow gotten very rich because the wolves had somehow gotten into the henhouse.

And because ArkLa was paying Jones more than it was paying other suppliers because of that same contract, Jones was accused of making his fortune at the expense of citizens of Arkansas. The state of Arkansas even investigated the deal, but found no wrongdoing.

Nelson, of course, also became rich, though not megarich like Jones. By the time Nelson retired as president and CEO of ArkLa, Jones was on the board, and it was Jones who led the move to shower on Nelson a bonus said to be in the millions. In addition, Nelson exercised stock options that earned him $3.6 million.

By 1986 the deal was threatening the financial health of the utility because ArkLa was paying Jones $40 million a year for gas it didn't need. To get out of the deal, ArkLa paid Jones $49 million for Arkoma, and Jones was allowed to drill for two years after the settlement. During those two years Arkoma opened sixty-five new wells. In all, Jones and McCoy had drilled two hundred wells in the Arkoma Basin. One was dry. One hundred and ninety-nine were producers!

By 1989 Arkoma had made $300 million, and this was right at the time when Bum Bright decided to sell the Cowboys. Though Jerry Jones says he could have bought the Cowboys without the ArkLa deal, the Arkoma millions ensured that Jones would be able to run the team without having to worry whether he could afford the rising salaries of his players. It would not be long before the poorer millionaires would find themselves squeezed by Jones to keep afloat.

Had the Texans known the Jerry Jones saga from the first, they would have marveled at this man, his guts, his rogue nature, his determination to play by his own rules. He played the game the Texas way, the same way Clint Murchison Sr., the Hunts, Sid Richardson, and the earlier oil barons had played it. No rules. Only results.

But Jones's Texas-style success story wasn't found on the sports pages of the Dallas newspapers when he took over the team in 1989. The press and the fans focused only on their bitterness over the firing of Tom Landry. And as in the past, Jerry Jones would be ridiculed and underestimated.

From the first Jones made it clear that he would be the guiding hand of the Dallas Cowboys.

"There's no way in the world that with my enthusiasm and love for what I'm getting ready to do, and the kind of price I'm paying, that I can look in the mirror if I don't plan to be a part of everything. I want to understand that everyone associated with it is giving it everything that they can do.

"I'll be a part of every decision. I won't leave anything to the football people." He made it clear he would make the draft-day decisions. He told everyone he was setting up shop at Valley Ranch.

"My entire office and my entire business will be at this complex. I intend to know and have an understanding of the complete situation. An understanding of the player situation, the jocks and socks, the TV."

The snickering was universal. Jones had played football at Arkansas, but did that make him an expert? He was compared with Brad Corbett, a maker of plastic piping, who bought the Texas Rangers baseball team thinking he knew as much about baseball as he did pipes. His manager, Billy Martin, had the team in contention when Corbett bought the team, but when Corbett began interfering, he alienated and then fired Martin, and the team sank precipitously.

In his speech, Jerry Jones made everyone understand that he was going to be the boss, and others thought immediately of George Steinbrenner, the Mad Hatter of baseball owners. Everyone was well aware of how Steinbrenner had taken the proud Yankees and reduced them to laughingstock status, trading players willy-nilly, firing managers and coaches at his whim, deriding his players in the newspapers.

Others conjured up images of Bob Irsay, who ruined the Baltimore Colts franchise, then offended the entire city by moving the Colts to Indianapolis in the middle of the night.

Brad Corbett, George Steinbrenner, Bob Irsay, and now Jerry Jones. The fans called him Boss Hawg Jones. And because of Jones's reference to "socks and jocks" in his opening remarks, the reporters began referring to him as "Socks and Jocks" Jones. And boy, would they all turn out to be mistaken.

In three short years Jerry Jones would turn out to be the premier owner in the NFL, a mover and shaker who would make Dallas proud. Jones would not be a Corbett or a Steinbrenner. Instead, he would turn out to be more in the vein of George Halas or Paul Brown, one of the rare historical figures in sports. He wouldn't make the fans forget about Tom Landry, but he would continue the Cowboy legacy of greatness and once again make the Cowboys the number one franchise in all of sports.

71

Scar Head

L ike Landry, Jimmy Johnson was a Texan, from the southeast coastal
Texas oil town of Port Arthur, the home of the singing Cowboy, Tex
Ritter, Olympic star Babe Didrickson Zaharias, J. R. Richardson
(known as the Big Bopper), and rock legend Janice Joplin.

Jimmy Johnson was actually a former classmate of Joplin's at
Thomas Jefferson High School in Port Arthur. Johnson, a jock, and Joplin,
a hippie with a burning desire to escape Port Arthur, despised each other.
She called him Scar Head. He called her Beat Weeds: Beat, because of her
shaggy, disheveled appearance, and Weeds, a reference to her vagina.
When Joplin became a star, Johnson was amazed. He didn't even know
she could sing.

But in a funny way they were very much alike: Each abhorred prejudice and respected diversity. Janice loved black rhythm and blues, making it her trademark. Jimmy Johnson appreciated the friendship of his
black friends, a quality that would serve him as a football coach as much
or more than any other attribute.

Janice and Jimmy were both controlling, very smart, and driven to
fame and fortune. But Janice, the sensitive girl scorned and shunned in
Port Arthur, had a death wish that eventually killed her at the age of
twenty-seven. Jimmy Johnson, the football hero, had a dedication to him-

self that saw only the next rung of a very tall ladder. Jimmy Johnson needed to be in charge, needed to finish on top, and he needed everyone to know he deserved all the credit for being there. At all three he was very successful.

Johnson's father, C.W., was from Clarksville, Arkansas, and he and his wife and their first son, Wayne, moved to Port Arthur in 1942 with the oil boom. C.W. went to work at Gulf Refinery. Jimmy was born on July 16, 1943, and when he was six, his father went to work at the Townsend Dairy supervising milk packaging and ice-cream making.

Growing up, Jimmy Johnson's closest friends were black, boys with names like Baby Joe and I.E. They played pickup football games together on the grassy medium separating the lanes of DeQueen Boulevard in front of his house. When Jimmy went to work at the dairy, he worked with Mexicans and Cajuns, and by the time he reached high-school age, he would snap at anyone who made racial remarks.

Jimmy Johnson was a rogue as a boy. He was a good student, but from his early teen years, he was a Bobby Layne–Don Meredith Texan, a pursuer of good beer and better women. From the age of fourteen on, he and his friend Jimmy Maxfield loved to go to the whorehouses near the docks of Port Arthur and hang out with the girls and drink beer. On weekends they would cross the Neches and Sabine Rivers and party in Louisiana, where the drinking age was lower.

Johnson began playing football at Jefferson High for legendary coach Clarence "Buckshot" Underwood, a disciple of Bear Bryant. Underwood, who for six years had been Bryant's line coach at Kentucky, worked his players hard. "I work them hard so they won't be out on the streets getting in trouble," he would say. He believed in smash-mouth football—three yards and a cloud of dust—and one season his team didn't throw a single pass.

Underwood's modus operandi was to teach intimidation. He had drills to teach his linemen to strike the opposition with a forearm to the face. Johnson became a menace, going around town hitting immovable objects with his meaty forearms, especially after he had had too much to drink.

On the field Johnson became an honorable mention All-State lineman. He was recruited by the air force, Texas A&M, TCU, and even Alabama's Bryant. But all his life Johnson's father had told him about the University of Arkansas, and when Arkansas offered him a scholarship, he went to Fayetteville, sight unseen.

At Arkansas he played under Frank Broyles on the same team with

Jerry Jones, who was a year ahead of him but, since he had been red-shirted, had the same amount of football eligibility left.

Like Jones, Johnson fell in love with a campus beauty queen. His was Linda Kay Cooper, a sorority sister of Jones's wife, Gene. Jimmy and Linda Kay were married by the end of his freshman year. Linda Kay went to work as a schoolteacher, and he would work summers in the Port Arthur shipyards. Jones and Johnson roomed together during road trips but were not close; social class separated them. Unlike Jones, whose family was wealthy, Johnson always had to scrape for money, winning $40 to $50 hustling cards—bridge, not poker—from eggheads who thought they were smarter than the chubby-cheeked jock. After college Johnson would cross paths with Jones several times, and over the years they stayed aware of each other.

Johnson was all–Southeast Conference his senior year, but he was too small to be considered by the NFL, so his plan was to major in psychology, graduate, and go to work for a company as an industrial psychologist.

That plan changed toward the end of his senior year when coaching staffs from around the country descended on Frank Broyles and his defensive coordinator, Jim MacKenzie, to learn the "Arkansas Monster Slide Defense." At one of these meetings, MacKenzie asked Johnson to go to the blackboard to explain the defense to the visiting coaches. In detail and with great clarity, Johnson explained the defense and the role of every player in it, including the defensive backs. After the meeting, Johnson thought nothing of it.

He returned to Port Arthur for the summer and worked as a welder's helper at a shipyard, making money in preparation for going to graduate school. Jim MacKenzie called, asking Johnson if he would be interested in coaching at Louisiana Tech. The head coach, Joe Aillet, had liked the way he handled himself; the defensive coordinator had had a heart attack, and they needed someone to fill in for the season.

Louisiana Tech offered $1,000 a month for three months, the use of a car, and an apartment free. In 1965 that was a lot of money. Johnson accepted, gladly, and in Ruston, Louisiana, he discovered that he was blessed with an ability to coach.

The next year he returned to Fayetteville as a graduate assistant and looked for a full-time coaching job. Bill Petersen promised him a job at Florida State, but just as the season was about to begin, he hired someone else. Stuck, Johnson took a job coaching high school football in Picayune, Mississippi. When Jimmy arrived, he discovered that the year before the

Maroon Tide hadn't won a game. Segregation had turned Mississippi football upside down, as many of the best white players fled the public school system to attend makeshift private schools to escape having to go to school with blacks. Once again, the Picayune team lost all ten games. At the end of the season Barry Switzer, who had coached him at Arkansas, called to say that Wichita State needed a defensive line coach. Larry Lacewell, Switzer's best friend, was the defensive coordinator at Wichita State. After one semester, Johnson rented a U-Haul and moved his family to Wichita, Kansas.

The next step was Ames, Iowa, where he worked for Johnny Majors as defensive coordinator in 1968 for $12,000. Hootie Ingram, the head coach of Clemson, called. He was offering $14,500. Iowa State matched it. But South Carolina was warmer than Iowa, and off went the Johnson family.

Johnson stayed at Clemson six weeks. Larry Lacewell had been hired as defensive coordinator at the University of Oklahoma, and he called to say that head coach Chuck Fairbanks wanted him as defensive line coach there. Johnson turned the offer down, afraid that snubbing Clemson so soon after arriving might hurt his career.

But Fairbanks would not give up. He offered Johnson a $2,000 bonus above the money he was offering. Johnson would be making more money than Lacewell. Johnson went to both Ingram and the athletic director, Frank Howard; both told him to go with their blessing.

When Johnson arrived in Norman, Oklahoma, he discovered that the year before the Oklahoma defense had given up the most points in the history of the school. As a result, the defensive coordinator resigned, and Lacewell took his place. That enabled Lacewell to hire Johnson. The two fought furiously. Johnson wanted his defensive linemen to be more offensive. Johnson called it "upfield pressure." He didn't want his linemen reading blocks. He wanted them charging into the backfield. (In that respect, Jimmy Johnson couldn't have been more unlike Tom Landry.) His theory was that by being aggressive at the snap of the ball, his defensive linemen would plug the gaps if there was a running play and nail the quarterback if there wasn't. Let the linebackers wait around and see what transpires.

It was an innovative theory, and it was very effective. His first year Johnson had three linemen who became stars. Lucious Selmon became an All-America, as did Derland Moore, who would shine with the New Orleans Saints, and Sugar Bear Hamilton went on to have a great career with the New England Patriots.

In Johnson's final season at Oklahoma in 1973, the Sooners shut out five opponents. Jimmy Johnson would get a great deal of the credit. At the end of the season Frank Broyles at Arkansas called for Jimmy to come home to be his defensive coordinator. In his own mind he was coming back to Fayetteville to stay forever. In '75 Arkansas won the Southeast Conference, and the thirty-two-year-old Johnson had aspirations of replacing Broyles as head coach when he retired.

But when Broyles retired in '76 to take the job of athletic director, he didn't pick Johnson to replace him. Instead, he told his coaches that he was going to hire a big-name coach from outside the program. The coach he brought in was Lou Holtz. Johnson, sorely disappointed, resigned.

Around that time Jackie Sherrill, who had once worked for Johnson, became head coach at the University of Pittsburgh, and that was Jimmy Johnson's next stop. One of his players was Hugh Green, who would star in the NFL at Miami and Tampa Bay. Hugh had been raised by an aunt, and Johnson and Linda Kay almost went so far as to adopt him legally, but by then he was grown, and they didn't go through with it. After two seasons at Pitt, Johnson was finally offered a head coaching job: at Oklahoma State.

The position was open because Jim Stanley got canned because of NCAA irregularities. Jerry Jones was friendly with Kevin Leonard, who was on the selection committee, and on his recommendation Leonard called Johnson.

Johnson, concerned about an NCAA investigation while Oklahoma State was on probation, turned him down. Then Jerry Jones called Johnson, and Leonard called him a second time.

Johnson relented and took the job. Rather than clean out his locker at Pitt right then and there, Johnson stayed on for the Tangerine Bowl. It was one of his few mistakes in judgment.

His acceptance at Oklahoma State caused a rift with Pitt head coach Jackie Sherrill, who became angry because so many of the other assistants wanted to go to Oklahoma State with Johnson. Even Hugh Green wanted to transfer and go to Stillwater to join him. The loyalty of the other assistant coaches and of Hugh Green was an early indication of Johnson's strength as a coach: They loved the guy.

Johnson began his first year at Oklahoma State in 1979 with fifty-five scholarship players, about forty fewer than Oklahoma and Nebraska. Johnson decided to turn this negative into a positive, and he invited anyone who wished to try out. It was a move that made the entire student body feel closer to the football program. One year two hundred kids tried out, so many they didn't have enough uniforms to fit them all. Johnson got to use the extra bodies as human tackling dummies. For their part, they got to brag they had been on the football team.

That first year Jimmy Johnson won seven games! Only because the team was on probation did they not go to a bowl game. The next season the record dropped to 3–7–1, then jumped back to 7–4 and an Independence Bowl bid. Nineteen eighty-two was sub-.500, but in '83 Oklahoma State won eight games and went to the Bluebonnet Bowl in Houston. Johnson was able to recruit running back Thurman Thomas, and he had dreams of beating Nebraska, if not the University of Oklahoma, the next year.

Frank Broyles then called to see if Johnson wanted to take over at Arkansas. Lou Holtz had been fired/quit and went to coach at the University of Minnesota. Johnson said he was interested, though he had qualms about leaving Thomas and the rest of his recruits behind. Ken Hatfield, who was a member of the Fellowship of Christian Athletes, was being considered for the job, but Jerry Jones, for one, wanted Johnson because he felt Johnson would appeal to *all* the kids, not just the religious ones. Johnson went for an interview, but halfway through he was sent home. He was outraged and embarrassed when he found out Hatfield had been offered and accepted the job *before* Johnson was interviewed for it. Apparently Frank Broyles hadn't the guts to tell him. And as a result, Jimmy Johnson has had little to do with his alma mater since.

In the spring of 1984 Johnson attended the national coaches' convention in Dallas. He was approached by the athletic director of the University of Miami, Sam Jankovich, to replace Howard Schnellenberger, who had developed a national power. After 9–3, 9–2, and 7–4 records, in '83 Schnellenberger led Miami to a national championship, completing an 11–1 season with a raucous 31–30 victory over Nebraska, but then resigned to go into the United States Football League.

The one catch, Jankovich told Johnson, was that he would have to retain Schnellenberger's old staff. He couldn't bring his own assistants until the assistants quit on their own. Johnson tried to talk Jankovich out of that, arguing the importance of the bond among coaches on a staff. Jankovich, who was being loyal to his assistant coaches, wasn't moved. If Johnson wanted the job, Schnellenberger's assistants would have to remain for at least one season.

Johnson asked about a dozen friends, including Gil Brandt of the Cowboys, whether he should take the job under those circumstances. Nine defensive starters were graduating at Miami. All told him to turn it down.

Larry Lacewell was the one friend who told him to take it. He said, "Jimmy, you can't win a national championship at Oklahoma State. But you can win one at Miami. It's been proven. It's been done. I think you ought to go." Lacewell told him he'd be able to straighten out the coaching situation before long.

The next day Johnson took the job. When he arrived in Miami he discovered that three of the Miami assistants had applied for the job of head coach, and all were bitter they had lost out to Johnson. Defensive coordinator Tom Olivadotti as much as told Johnson he thought he was an inferior coach, and he quit immediately. Two of the other assistants quit in the middle of the season. As for the Miami fans and the media, everyone was furious that Howard Schnellenberger was no longer the coach, and that in his place was this other guy, Jimmy Johnson. They were cool to Johnson for another reason: They had heard Johnson was connected to the black community, and there was concern that Johnson would bring in too many black players.

There was really only one group of people that first year in Miami who readily accepted Johnson: the players. Johnson made a smooth transition when at their first meeting he told the players, "It's a lot easier for one guy to change than for one hundred guys to change. I'll change. You guys don't have to."

Johnson kept the offense the way Schnellenberger had set it up. He had Bernie Kosar at quarterback, Alonzo Highsmith at fullback, and wide receivers Eddie Brown and the freshman Michael Irvin.

The first year he left the 3–4 defense alone. When Olivadotti quit, Johnson promoted his line coach to defensive coordinator and brought Butch Davis from Oklahoma State to be line coach. Davis was an ally, as was another coach, Hubbard Alexander. (It would not be too many years before the coaches who snubbed Johnson discovered that they had made a very foolish career move.)

The first two games Miami beat Auburn with Bo Jackson and nationally ranked Florida. There was a loss to Michigan, and a win over Purdue, but then Florida State beat Miami badly, 38–3. (It was the only time Johnson lost to FSU.) After a big win in South Bend, the team was 8–2 with two games to go.

After leading Maryland 31–0 at the half, Highsmith got hurt, and Miami lost 42–40. All conversations with his assistant coaches on the defense ceased. Then came the season finale against Boston College. The day before the game Johnson's defensive coordinator, Bill Trout, told him he was quitting after the game. Miami was ahead until the final play when

BC's Doug Flutie threw a Hail Mary pass that wide receiver Gerald Phelan caught on his back for a touchdown at the gun.

In the Fiesta Bowl in Phoenix against high-powered UCLA, Miami lost 39–37. Feeling his coaches had hurt the team badly on defense, Johnson eagerly called a press conference to announce his new staff. He brought in his friends, talented coaches with whom he had worked in the past, guys he could trust. Among them were Gary Stevens and Tony Wise on offense and Paul Jett as defensive coordinator.

Johnson finally had his unity. It would be his show. He needed to be in control, and now he was. Jimmy Johnson inculcated his coaches with his revolutionary defensive philosophy: attack, attack, attack. Rolling up the score never bothered him. His attitude: I can't help it if you have a bad football team. In a blowout he'd put in substitutes, but he would never tell his players to do less than their best. No matter what the score, Johnson, a perfectionist, wanted the game played right. If the defense blitzed, Johnson had his quarterback throwing. It was the proper move, and if his team scored six more with a 40-point lead, it wasn't his fault. They shouldn't have been blitzing.

Jimmy Johnson was a purist. He wanted the best players, no matter what color they were. He wanted them to graduate. He wanted them to practice hard, play hard, and win. From the beginning he promised that if they did things his way, they *would* win. That's how sure of himself Jimmy Johnson had been.

And under Johnson's aegis, in the next four years the Miami Hurricanes would win 44 games and lose only four. Their record of 36-straight regular season wins would be the fifth-longest in NCAA history.

In the first game of his second season, in 1985, Miami proved the effectiveness of Johnson's attack defense. His boys broke the leg of Oklahoma quarterback Troy Aikman en route to a 27–14 win over Barry Switzer's Sooners. Though the team had only one senior starter, the Hurricanes were 9–1 and in contention for the national championship, with only Notre Dame remaining on the regular schedule.

When the Fighting Irish players arrived in South Florida, they celebrated when they heard that the long-sought resignation of head coach Gerry Faust had come to pass. The players thought Faust inept and bristled when he asked them to pray in crucial situations. They needed a coach, not a priest, and when it was announced that Faust would be fired after the Miami game, they took out their joy by partying right up to gametime. Before a national TV audience, Notre Dame played poorly, and Johnson's hard-charging Hurricanes ran over the hungover Irish 58–7.

In the TV booth sat Ara Parseghian, the former Notre Dame coach, whining that Johnson lacked compassion for the poor kids from South Bend. (This from the same guy who routinely ran up scores: in 1966 Parseghian beat Duke, 64–0; in 1958 it was 58–8 over Illinois; in 1970 56–7 over Navy, and in 1973 it was 44–0 over Miami. Ruthlessness, moreover, had long been part of the Notre Dame tradition. Knute Rockne once beat Kalamazoo 74–0.)

Johnson was disgusted when he learned of Parseghian's comments. Said Johnson, "I learned way back on DeQueen Boulevard in Port Arthur, Texas, that nobody cries louder and more pitifully than a bully who's just had the shit stomped out of him."

But on that day Saint Ara Parseghian made Jimmy Johnson out to be a bad guy on national television, and in large part that contributed to Johnson's image of being something of a rogue. Not that he cared, for one of Jimmy Johnson's great strengths—as well as weaknesses—is that he never once cared what anyone ever thought of him.

Miami, now the Team America Loved to Hate, was invited to play Johnny Majors's University of Tennessee in the Sugar Bowl. The Volunteers took advantage of the din made by their fans in the Superdome in New Orleans and beat Miami, 35–7. Johnson vowed to do better in '86.

In the high-powered club of Florida college football, the two teams Johnson had to compete with were Florida and Florida State, teams with huge alumni organizations. Miami is a small private school, like Notre Dame, and Johnson set out to make it, like Notre Dame, the team for the public. Part of Johnson's strategy was to recruit players who would mirror the ethnic diversity of the Miami area. He signed black and Latino players, and he encouraged them to be demonstrative and theatrical on the field. Michael Irvin, for instance, was a dazzling receiver who would run up to the lower end zone seats after catching a touchdown pass and point to the fans in the stands amid a wild celebration. George Mira Jr., the son of the great quarterback, was a flamboyant linebacker. The presence of Johnson's show-offy, cocky black players gave Miami an Oakland Raider-like aura that the area fans loved. As a result not only was Jimmy Johnson winning games, he was also filling the Orange Bowl, something not even Howard Schnellenberger had done.

In 1986 Miami was undefeated during the regular season, but its reputation as a college for renegades grew when before the fourth game against number-one rated Oklahoma, outspoken Sooner linebacker Brian Bosworth labeled Johnson's team the "University of San Quentin." It was one more badge for the Miami Hurricanes to wear. The final score was 28–16. It wasn't even close.

Miami elected to play against number-two ranked Penn State, coached by Joe Paterno, a media favorite. They could have played them in the Citrus Bowl in Orlando. Instead they opted for the Fiesta Bowl in Phoenix. During this time the television show *Miami Vice,* starring Don Johnson and Philip Michael Thomas, was all the rage, and when the black stars of the Miami team trooped off the airplane and into the terminal scowling and wearing combat fatigues, there was an uproar in Barry Goldwater–conservative Phoenix. What sort of image was Johnson perpetrating?

Miami lost the game, 14–10, after quarterback Vinny Testaverde threw five interceptions. Testaverde had injured himself in a motor scooter accident, missed the final regular season game, and wasn't sharp against the talented Nittany Lions. Johnson calls it "the most devastating loss I've had."

Johnson flew to Tokyo to coach in an all-star game, and when he returned to Miami, he discovered that because of all the negative publicity, university president Tad Foote was reneging on his announcement that he was extending Johnson's contract. Foote called a press conference so Johnson could apologize for the actions of his players in Phoenix. Johnson, who despises public relations, thought Foote wrong for siding against his players before talking to him. Johnson almost quit. He considered blasting Foote and leaving town. But he didn't. Johnson knew what he had there and couldn't walk away. At the press conference Foote did most of the apologizing, and Johnson blasted the media for the skewed public perception of his players.

Johnson was angry because he had a firm belief in his program and a devotion to his players. And not only were they winners, but three quarters of them graduated in four years. Not a lot of college programs could say that.

Johnson hired two academic counselors and instituted mandatory study hall and class attendance. He knew many of his players were disadvantaged, so he continued their scholarships during the summer so they could stay on campus and continue pursuit of their degrees. His players had a 75 percent graduation rate, far better than the general college population. Why didn't anyone write about that?

It was a good thing for Johnson that he held his tongue and stayed. He had assembled one of the finest college football teams in the history of the sport, and in 1987 he finished the season undefeated behind sophomore quarterback Steve Walsh. Irvin and Brian Blades were his receivers. Melvin Bratton was the star back.

Miami beat Florida 31–7, crushed Arkansas 51–7 as Johnson got payback and the game ball from his adoring players, knocked off Florida State and Deion Sanders, 26–25, and shut out Notre Dame, now under Lou Holtz, 24–0.

Miami finished the season 11–0 and was ranked second in the nation behind Barry Switzer's Oklahoma team. They met in the Orange Bowl. Miami won the game 20–14. Jimmy Johnson was on top of his world. His team was undefeated and ranked number one. Said Johnson, "We had taken on a world of bullshit, and Florida, and Florida State, and Arkansas, and Notre Dame, and Oklahoma, and Edward Thaddeus Foote II. And we had kicked their collective ass."

And in 1988 they were even better. Miami started by drubbing a very talented Florida State team, 31–0. After two more wins, there was a re-match with Notre Dame, whose fans wore shorts that read "Catholics vs. Convicts." Before the game in the tunnel leading to the field, the two teams began pushing, shoving, and even fighting. Notre Dame led through most of the game. Miami scored a final touchdown, trailed by one, went for the two points, and didn't make it. The final was 31–30, the last of the four games the Hurricanes lost in the final four years of the Jimmy Johnson regime.

Undefeated Notre Dame was named national champions that '88 season, and Miami finished 11–1, including an easy 23–3 Orange Bowl win over Nebraska. When NBC commentator Bob Trumpy accused Johnson of running up the score, Johnson fumed over what he called "all the trappings and the baggage and bullshit."

The week before Johnson had gotten a phone call from Jerry Jones in Dallas.

"I'm still working on this other thing," said Jones.

Johnson didn't pay much attention because until the day the deal was done there was a real question whether Jones would end up owning the Cowboys. But after the Orange Bowl game, Jones called him again. It's time, Jones told him.

Jones had never asked Johnson if he would coach the Cowboys once he bought the team. Both men just assumed that would be the case. The next day Johnson flew to Dallas and met with Jones. That night Johnson told Linda Kay, his wife of many years, he wanted a divorce.

"Is this something you want to do?" she asked.

"It's something I *have* to do," he said.

In Miami there had been alumni functions to attend with his wife ("silly-ass alumni sitdown dinners listening to people's small talk"). In Dallas, no parties were necessary, only the business of football. There was no longer a need for him to be married. ("No image-conscious pretenses.") He intended to devote all his considerable energy to the Dallas Cowboys.

At his initial press conference he told the public, "I have deep feelings for the Dallas Cowboys. For me to want to hurt that is completely asinine. I think Tom Landry is one of the finest individuals and finest coaches I could ever hope to know. And it hurts me when someone says I did something out of disrespect of Tom Landry.

"If I did, I'm deeply sorry. I never claimed to know everything. But I really did want to become coach of the Dallas Cowboys."

Johnson reminded everyone that he was a Texan, too. "I don't expect to replace Tom Landry," he said. "All I can ask is just let me do my thing, let me work, let me show my enthusiasm and judge me by what happens later."

72

The Depths Revisited

W hat happened "later" was a 1–15 record in the Cowboys' first season under the regime of Jones and Johnson. For both men, winners all their lives, the year 1989 was a nightmare. Before the season's end, Jimmy Johnson would be distraught, and Jerry Jones would begin to suffer from an irregular heartbeat. Both would have trouble sleeping and would drink too much. By the winter of '89, Jerry Jones was looking ten years older; Jimmy Johnson was feeling that way.

Five days after buying the Cowboys, Jerry Jones called the department heads for a meeting. They sat around a large conference table in Jones's office. Tex Schramm introduced them to Jones.

Jones told them there would not be any more changes. "I need all of you," he said.

But Jones, who, like Johnson, demanded complete loyalty from his employees, was uncomfortable working with strangers, especially since so many Cowboy employees had expressed their outrage over Landry's firing and their contempt for him. Seven weeks later, six of the eleven were gone, fired by Jones. PR director Doug Todd was one of the first, fired before the league had even approved the new ownership.

Jones had planned on keeping Tex Schramm in his job, but Schramm had his own loyalties, and those loyalties were stronger than the one to Jones. Schramm could not stand that Jones was firing his people left and right. Even Tommy Loy, who for twenty-two years had played the "Star Spangled Banner" on the trumpet before home games, was replaced by a trumpet quartet. Schramm was able to stop Jones from firing assistant trainer Don Cochran, a twenty-four-year veteran, but barely. When Jones fired one of the assistant ticket managers for no apparent reason, Schramm flew into a rage.

At the initial press conference, Schramm had to stand when minority owner Ed Smith boorishly swiped his chair. When a reporter asked Jones where Schramm stood in the new regime, Jones looked back at Tex and said, "Well, he's standing a little behind me now."

When Jerry Jones later let slip that he had signed Jimmy Johnson to a ten-year contract, Tex Schramm hadn't even known about it. At the signing Jones told the press, "I'm the owner and general manager, and Jimmy is the coach and general manager. No one will be between us."

Schramm knew that under Jerry Jones he was going to be a third fiddle. No longer would he run the Cowboys. Tex, who, until Jones took over the team, was the second-most-powerful man in the NFL behind Commissioner Pete Rozelle, no longer had any responsibilities to carry out or decisions to make. Jerry Jones and Jimmy Johnson were making the decisions now. To keep the paychecks coming he could stay in his office, play with his paper clips, and keep quiet, but Tex was not the sort of person to do that.

Schramm, a man too proud and talented to stay on when he was no longer needed or wanted, resigned. Vice President Joe Bailey quit, and personnel director Bob Ackles quit before Jones fired him.

Gil Brandt, the third member of the twenty-nine-year Schramm-Landry-Brandt Cowboy brain trust, was one of the last of the old guard to go. Jones wanted to keep Brandt around for the college draft. On draft day, Jimmy Johnson had one room, Brandt another. But Jones and Johnson made all the decisions.

Brandt thought his job was safe because he and Jimmy Johnson had known each other since the time Johnson began as an assistant coach. Brandt thought they were friends, but he was wrong. Brandt would learn what others had found out: Jimmy Johnson is a lone wolf who has very few, if any, real friends.

When rumors surfaced that Brandt might become a player agent, Johnson and Jones feared he might use classified draft information to help him launch a new career. Soon after the draft, Jones met with Brandt in the scouting library and told him the Cowboys no longer needed his services.

Brandt couldn't have been more dazed if Mike Tyson had hit him in the face. The career Cowboy personnel man had no other job plans and could not conceive of doing anything else but what he had been doing the past three decades. He could not bring himself to leave. Brandt didn't clean out his desk, and he continued playing raquetball at the Valley Ranch complex.

One day Brandt arrived at the Valley Ranch complex to discover the lock had been changed to the door of his office. His belongings had been boxed and stored in a shed. The security guards were instructed not to let him back in the building.

The experts thought he was nuts, but Jerry Jones was not fazed that after firing so many experienced football people he was on his own.

"As far as I'm concerned, it's good to walk into a room and see some blank walls. It makes you think imaginatively."

Out on the field Jimmy Johnson was doing with his players the same thing Jerry Jones had done with the front office. He cleaned house. Johnson, an absolute control freak, didn't want Tom Landry's players around him, comparing him to Landry, talking about the way things used to be done. So he got rid of them. Jones and Johnson realized that if he kept his current players, the Cowboys could finish with a .500 season. They didn't want that, preferring to start from scratch, even if it meant a winless season in '89.

During training camp Johnson made the players undergo weeks of physical contact, making some of them whisper that he was nothing but a "Joe College" coach. But Johnson only wanted players willing to do things his way. The bitchers—seen as Tom Landry's boys—he discarded wholesale.

The biggest names among the Tom Landry Cowboys—Danny White, a Cowboy since 1976, and Randy White, a fourteen-year vet—were told to retire. Johnson cut regulars Jeff Rohrer and Mike Downs and shipped out Steve Pelluer. Ed "Too Tall" Jones remained to anchor a shaky defense.

Johnson decided he would make a very un-Landry move: start a rookie at quarterback. Johnson had tried to recruit Troy Aikman when he was coaching at Oklahoma State, and after he left to coach Miami, he again sought to sign up the big quarterback after Aikman announced he was transferring from Oklahoma his sophomore year. That time UCLA got him.

After Jones and his business partner Mike McCoy signed Aikman to a four-year, $11 million contract, Johnson announced that Aikman would be the new QB.

When the Cowboys drafted him, the fans all thought they were getting a flamboyant California quarterback, a flashy performer like John Elway, because Aikman had lived in Cerritos, California, until he was twelve and had graduated from UCLA. But in fact, Aikman was far closer to the image of the Oklahoma plowboy, tough, durable, stoic, and hardworking. Some writers made him out to be a cowboy, but Aikman never rode a horse in his life.

All his life he had struggled. The youngest of three children, Aikman was born with a deformity of both feet. Between the ages of eight months and fourteen months, his feet were entombed in casts. Until he was three he wore orthopedic shoes. His mother strapped the heels of his shoes together to keep his feet straight.

When Aikman turned twelve in 1979, his family moved from California to a ranch near Henryetta, Oklahoma, population 6,000, where the Aikmans lived on a 172-acre ranch and raised cattle, pigs, and chickens. Troy starred for the Henryetta Hens beginning his sophomore year and then went to the University of Oklahoma to play for Barry Switzer. Switzer had promised Aikman, who was a classic drop-back passer in the mold of Craig Morton, that if Aikman came to Norman, he would abandon his wishbone offense and its running game and make Aikman's passing the focus. But after halfback Marcus Dupree, the star who was going to make the new I formation sing, left Oklahoma and went back home, Switzer stayed with the wishbone. ("He lied to me, plain and simple," Aikman told Randy Galloway of the *Dallas Morning News*. "He tells me he's going to a passing game, and four days into workouts, he's back to the wishbone." Aikman says he liked Switzer anyway.)

So there was Aikman, the pure passer, stuck behind a sievelike wishbone line, and his sophomore year against the University of Miami, Jerome Brown and John McVeigh smashed him to the ground and broke his leg. Jimmy Johnson tried to get Aikman to transfer to Miami, but his father was living in California, so he transferred to play for coach Terry Donohue at UCLA, where he could use his strong arm, intelligence, and competitiveness to become a candidate for the Heisman Trophy.

Backing up Aikman would be another rookie, Johnson's former University of Miami quarterback Steve Walsh. At the time no one said it, but the Walsh pick was brilliantly conceived. The Cowboys had Walsh in reserve if Aikman got hurt, and at the end of the year if another team was desperate for a top-rated quarterback, Jones and Johnson could trade him for a group of choice draft picks. (And that's how it would play out.)

Once Johnson had completed his housecleaning, the Cowboys were left with one certifiable superstar, running back Herschel Walker. Unlike Tony Dorsett, who periodically garnered negative headlines, Walker was a PR man's dream, a role model for kids who said and did all the right things.

Walker would tell the story of how he asked his high school track coach how he could improve as an athlete, and the coach told him to do push-ups and sit-ups and run sprints. Every morning throughout his football career, Walker would get up at five in the morning and do 1,500 sit ups and several hundred push-ups, sometimes with one hand behind his back.

While Dorsett always seemed to be clashing with management and making wrong-place, wrong-time headlines away from football, Walker expressed his strong Christian faith, danced with the Fort Worth ballet, and conducted clinics for kids. Walker said he one day wanted to work for the FBI.

Walker was first noticed at Johnson County High School in Wrightsville, Georgia, where in 1979 he rushed for 3,167 yards and scored 45 touchdowns! He won the Heisman Trophy at the University of Georgia in 1982. He left college prior to his senior year to join the New Jersey Generals in the United States Football League, later owned by Donald Trump. His contract paid him $4 million a year for three years, and Adidas added another million as an incentive to join the pros in exchange for his wearing their clothing. In 1985 he rushed for 2,411 yards, a record, and was named the league's MVP. Through it all, Walker never acted like a celebrity. He worked with charities and signed autographs for hours. He even built a new house for his parents.

In 1985 Tex Schramm drafted Walker—who at 6'1", 225 pounds had the physique of a bodybuilder but could run the 100 in 9.1—in the event the USFL folded, which it soon did, and the next year the Cowboys gave Walker a $5 million contract for five years, angering Dorsett, who refused to work alongside the newcomer. For two years Walker played behind Dorsett, and then in 1987 Walker was given the starting job.

In 1987 Walker rushed for over 700 yards and had another 700 yards of receiving yardage, and the following year, the 3–13 disaster, he was even better, as he rushed for 1,514 yards and caught 53 passes for another

505 yards. His combined 2,019 yards made him only the tenth player in NFL history to reach the 2,000 mark in one season.

But once the losses started, everyone began wailing. After just two losses, Jim Reeves of the *Fort Worth Star-Telegram* was the first to suggest that the Cowboys would be terrible, with or without Herschel Walker, and that Jones should trade him for a bucket of draft picks. "Think about what a windfall like that could do for the Cowboys!"

Walker must have been thinking along the same lines when, after a 28–0 loss in New Orleans, Walker told Johnson he wanted the ball more. Walker wanted the team rebuilt all right, but he wanted it built around him, not Aikman. The move, in retrospect, was a challenge to Johnson, who wasn't that enamored of the big back to begin with.

According to scout guru John Wooten, Johnson, a superior judge of talent, saw that "Walker didn't have what the great backs had—the vision, running skills, the ability to make you miss. Jimmy saw a guy who ran straight up."

By the third loss, a 30–7 drubbing by the Washington Redskins in the Texas Stadium opener, Cowboy fans were holding up signs that read "We Miss Tom," and Jerry Jones was forced to admit, "We're not a very good football team. This is not complaining. It's just assessing and going forward."

In the fourth loss, against the New York Giants, Troy Aikman broke his finger and had to miss five weeks of play. After the game an angry Johnson got rid of four of Landry's old players.

"We just need to start over," he said.

And start over they did when, on October 12, 1989, Jones and Johnson traded Herschel Walker to the Minnesota Vikings in a deal that shook up the entire NFL.

The transaction had been set in motion late in September after Cleveland lost running back Kevin Mack for the season with a knee injury. Browns owner Art Modell called Jones to see if Walker was available. Jones asked Johnson whether he was willing to trade Walker. "In a New York minute." Johnson then had personnel director Bob Ackles call around the league to see if anyone else wanted Walker and for what price. Figuring that the Minnesota Vikings were a big back away from being a Super Bowl contender, Ackles called Viking general manager Mike Lynn.

When Lynn heard Walker was available, visions of a Super Bowl appearance began to dance in his head. Ackles told Lynn he would have to act fast, because the Browns had made a terrific offer. Four hours later, Mike Lynn faxed the Cowboys a deal memo.

Johnson showed the fax to Jones. Johnson could not contain his excitement.

For Walker, the Vikings would give up eight draft choices—a first, second, and sixth in 1990, a first and second in '91, and a first, second, and third in '92.

In addition, they would trade to the Cowboys linebacker Jesse Solomon, defensive tackle Alex Stewart, running back Darrin Nelson, linebacker David Howard, and cornerback Issiac Holt.

Lynn really expected the Cowboys to keep these five, because the success of the deal for the Vikings hinged on this clause: for every one of the five players Johnson kept, the Cowboys would have to return a draft choice.

(Just before the February 1 deadline, Lynn learned that the Cowboys intended to drop all three of the remaining players and keep all of the draft choices. Lynn was so stunned and disgusted with himself that he told Johnson to keep the three remaining players in the deal as well.)

In all, the Cowboys would trade Herschel Walker for seven high draft choices and two sixth-rounders acquired when the Cowboys traded Nelson and Solomon. Johnson liked Issiac Holt, and he played four years for the Cowboys. (Among the Cowboys drafted as a result of the Walker heist were Emmitt Smith, Russell Maryland, corner Kevin Smith, safety Darren Woodson, and corner Clayton Holmes.)

But first Jones had to get Herschel Walker to agree to leave his beloved Dallas. Walker had a no-trade clause, which put him in a strong bargaining position. He was making more than $1 million outside of football from his TV show, a radio show, a newspaper column in the *Dallas Morning News,* and from endorsements. It would cost Walker a lot of money to leave, and so to complete the deal, Jerry Jones made Herschel Walker whole, paying him $1.2 million in cash, plus a car, a condo in Minneapolis, and twenty round-trip tickets between Dallas and Minneapolis. Walker left town, grateful to be leaving a loser and going to a contender.

Ironically, at the time of the trade Mike Lynn was being praised for the deal by those writers who were blasting the Cowboys. But Walker never did bring Minnesota a Super Bowl. Walker played there for two seasons, and after the '91 season, Minnesota cut him. The Eagles signed him and cut him. Then in 1995 he returned home to the city of his greatest triumphs with the New Jersey Generals when he signed with the Giants. And after one season with the Giants, he returned to the Cowboys for the 1996 season.

After the Walker trade, the mood of despair and foreboding lifted at Valley Ranch. Suddenly, despite the Cowboys' 0–5 record, Jimmy Johnson stopped being distraught. According to John Wooten, the Walker trade "saved" Johnson, giving him a ray of hope. "He'd just sit back and look at that list [of draft choices]," he said.

And what was truly surprising was that despite the fear Jerry Jones felt that he would be criticized and made fun of for trading his star running back, the reaction was not strong. The team was so bad, there wasn't much Jones and Johnson could have done that would have upset the fans further.

JERRY JONES: "Still, I was concerned about the reaction we would get. We had made a lot of changes already and we go and trade the only Pro Bowler we had. I think we finished that trade at about 1:30 A.M. on a Friday, and when I walked out of the session I didn't know what might happen when the people in Dallas woke up in the morning and found out we had traded Herschel Walker. I thought they might run me out of town.

"But there was not the negative response I would have expected."

Columnist Randy Galloway reflected the consternation after the trade. "The Cowboys got nothing more than a huge handful of Minnesota smoke. And who knows if there'll ever be a fire."

But there also was praise. *Dallas Times-Herald* columnist Skip Bayless, who could wield the sharpest rapier, responded to the Walker trade by writing, "I'd prefer to moan through 0–16. How much face would be saved if Johnson won one or two with a Herschel whose heart isn't in the new pass-oriented scheme?"

Even so, Bayless concluded, "How does he keep from getting run out of town before Christmas Eve?"

Tim Cowlishaw of the *Dallas Morning News* was more upbeat. "There is hope," wrote Cowlishaw, "because Walker's departure represents eight players to be added the next three years. If Johnson hits on more than half of those picks, then it won't matter whether Walker takes the Vikings to the Super Bowl or not. His exit from Dallas will have been more than justified."

The '89 Cowboys would lose their first eight games in a row, giving Cowboy fans an opportunity to try out their wittiest jokes and routines. These are some of them:

- Tom Landry bought a sky box at Texas Stadium because he wanted to get as far away as possible from professional football.
- What's the difference between SMU, TCU, and the Cowboys? SMU and TCU have basketball seasons to look forward to.
- A lady takes her three children to the Cowboy games and they get lost. Later, someone from the stadium calls her and says, "Ma'am, could you come get your kids. They're beating the Cowboys 14–3."
- A guy discovers that his car has been broken into, and he thinks, "Goddamn, I hope they didn't take my Cowboy season tickets." When he checks the car, he finds that the thief has left an extra set of tickets.
- There's a new television show called *thirtysomething, Cowboys-nothing.*
- The Dallas Cowboys are thinking of changing their name to the Dallas Tampons. They're good for only one period, and they don't have a second string.
- Ever notice those people in the stands holding Bible verses: John 3:16? Well, I got even with them. I went to a service at the World of Faith Church and held up a sign that said: "Tom Landry sure got screwed over."

And then there were the Jerry Jones jokes:

- Jerry Jones recently went to a black-tie function with only one shoe on. Someone said, "Jerry, you lost a shoe." Jerry said, "No, I found one."
- Jerry Jones removed the "No Shirts, No Shoes, No Service" signs from Texas Stadium so that his relatives from Arkansas could come to the games.
- Did you hear that Jerry Jones is trying to buy the Southland Corporation? He's going to change the name of 7-Eleven to 0–11.

Then on November 5, the Cowboys defeated the Redskins 13–3 in Washington, behind Steve Walsh, who was 10 for 30 but didn't throw an interception. Bill Bates presented Johnson with the game ball. Johnson said he was happy to have the win but warned the fans that "the rocky days are not over for the Cowboys." As soon as the game ended everyone wondered whether Johnson would start Walsh at quarterback or Troy Aikman, whose broken wrist had healed.

Aikman got his job back. He had been away five weeks, and when he returned, most everyone around him had changed. Herschel Walker was gone, replaced by Paul Palmer. Michael Irvin had suffered a season-ending injury, a terrible blow to the offense, and he was replaced by Derrick Shepard. Wide receivers James Dixon and Bernard Ford were also new. Under Aikman, the Cowboys proceeded to lose the rest of their games. The game QB took a pounding all the way to the end. But there were sparks of hope. Against the Phoenix Cardinals, Aikman set an NFL record for yards passing by a rookie quarterback, when he threw a spectacular 379 yards. On the other end of his passes, Dixon caught 203 yards worth of passes, a Cowboy record. But in the final two minutes, Aikman was tackled by linebacker Anthony Bell and he had to be carried off the field with blood dripping from his ear. He had suffered a concussion. The Cowboys lost the game 24–20, on a long touchdown pass with 58 seconds remaining. Aikman thought to himself: "We will not win another game." And he was right. Still, the Cowboys were improving.

Wrote Jim Reeves in the *Fort Worth Star-Telegram,* "For the first time this season, the Cowboys looked like the old Cowboys. By that, I mean the 1988 version. Now there was a Cowboys team that could disappoint with the best of them."

They lost to the first-place Miami Dolphins 17–14 when Luis Zendejas missed a 53-yard field goal with six seconds left in the game. Aikman completed 25 of 33 passes for 261 yards and drew comparisons to Dan Marino.

The Cowboys led the Rams 31–21 and lost. In his eighth NFL start, Aikman threw four touchdown passes, a feat the legendary Roger Staubach only accomplished one time in his long career.

In a season of dismal results, there was one bright ray of hope: Troy Aikman. Four times Aikman's team had lost by a touchdown or less. Twice Aikman had the Cowboys ahead, only to see the defense blow it in the final two minutes.

But Aikman never whined. He never pointed fingers at his teammates, though he knew some weren't giving sufficient effort. Mostly, he blamed himself.

"A quarterback has to win," Aikman said. "If he doesn't do that, then no matter how well you play or how good you look, the people out there think there's something wrong with you. Look at Pelluer or Testaverde. People start thinking you're weak or stupid, or both.

"The knock on me used to be that I couldn't win the big ones. Heck, I can't win any games."

The best thing to happen to Aikman was breaking his finger and missing the five games, which enabled him to put the team in proper perspective. He could stop blaming himself.

By season's end Troy Aikman's effectiveness as a quarterback was on a par with the league's best, Dan Marino, John Elway, and Randall Cunningham.

Nevertheless, the thin-on-talent Cowboys finished the season 1–15. The final game was a loss to Green Bay in which the Texas Stadium toilets froze. Jimmy Johnson was taken by the symbolism until he arrived home after the game, only to discover that all the toilets in his home also were frozen.

Despite all the adversity, what was marvelous to witness was the resilience and the unflappable nature of Jimmy Johnson and Jerry Jones.

Johnson told reporters, "I think with a year behind us, I think realistically—and this may sound crazy—that in itself gives us the chance to get to the point of being .500.

"The toughest thing is not being .500. The toughest thing is taking that next step. I think we can get to .500. The difficult thing is making the playoffs."

Said Jones, "I can sit here today and honestly say I don't think there has ever been anybody in this league to win only one game and be as excited about the future as I am. Even though we're sitting here at 1–15, I don't believe there are too many people in this league that don't believe the Dallas Cowboys can be a championship football team again."

The February following the 1–15 disaster, Susie Woodhams of the *Dallas Times-Herald* went to Jerry Jones to interview him about the trials and tribulations of owning a team unable to win.

"It was very emotional, and very stressful," Jones explained. Then he thought a second and blurted out, "It was the best year of my life."

Woodhams asked Jones about the future.

"I just can't wait to get up in the morning," he said.

73

Emmitt

When Jimmy Johnson predicted that the 1990 Cowboys would be a .500 team, there was no reason to put much faith in his statement. While Jerry Jones had impressed the media with his ability to take vicious criticism and come back with a smile and a handshake, Jimmy Johnson had alienated a lot of those same reporters by sometimes evading questions and other times showing them contempt. Johnson had gained a reputation at the University of Miami for his penchant for portraying reporters to his players as the enemy, and the writers were wary of him from the start. A private man to begin with, Johnson made few friends among the sportswriters, and so after a 1–15 season, his prediction of an 8–8 season held very little credence for them. Plenty of hotshot collegiate coaches like Tommy Prothro, John McKay, and Darryl Rogers had flopped in the pros. Johnson, they felt, could go either way.

What the Dallas writers and by extension the fans could not anticipate was that Jimmy Johnson was not only an instinctive, unerring judge of talent, as John Wooten had said, but that he also had an incredible determination to strengthen his football team. Johnson was *driven* to succeed. And he had the talent to organize a coaching staff of great teachers. All he needed were better players.

That he was able to get them was a credit to his talent-judging ability, Jerry Jones's willingness to spend whatever it took, and fortuitous timing. Two rule changes were introduced to the NFL in 1990. Johnson would take advantage of the new limited free agency, and for the first time he could draft college underclassmen who wished to enter the NFL draft.

Thus the first wave of moves made by Johnson (with Jerry Jones's money and backing) was an unprecedented foray into the world of free agency. Under the NFL's Plan B, negotiated as part of a new bargaining agreement, teams were allowed to protect thirty-seven players. All others were free until April 1 to sign with any other team—and this is the crucial part—without any compensation.

These weren't the star players, of course. They were second stringers, but on some teams the backup guys were better than what the Cowboys were starting in '88.

That winter 43 Plan B free agents were selected by the 28 teams. The New York Jets signed 4 of them, second most. The Cowboys took the most with 14. Though Jones had lost somewhere between $5 million and $10 million in '88, he nevertheless proved his willingness to spend what it took to develop a winner when he pledged to spend $1 million on these Plan B free agents. It was to be a forecast of things to come when free agency became even more widespread. The other owners had to be furious. Johnson predicted that 8 of the Plan B signees would start for the Cowboys in '90.

One of the fourteen picks was Phoenix Cardinals tight end Jay Novacek, who had caught 81 passes for 1,048 yards the previous three seasons. Another was Chicago Bears wide receiver Dennis McKinnon, signed because of Michael Irvin's knee surgery. In a game against San Francisco early in the season, the Cowboys' first-round pick had torn an anterior cruciate ligament in his right knee, and no one, not even Irvin himself, knew whether the talented rookie would be able to play again. McKinnon was insurance in case Irvin's recovery was slowed.

Then came the draft of college players. Johnson and Jones would begin reaping the benefits of the Herschel Walker trade. The Cowboys might have had the very first pick, but they had forfeited it for the right to sign quarterback Steve Walsh, and so they had to wait for the twenty-first player in the draft, the first-round Viking pick from the Walker trade.

Johnson's intent was to select a linebacker in the first round of what experts called the deepest NFL draft ever, bolstered by the addition of thirty-eight college underclassmen desirous of playing pro ball. Johnson had determined that to win in the NFL, a team must have a top quarterback and a ferocious pass rush. The Cowboys already had Troy Aikman.

Their greatest need was to replenish the defense. But everyone else seemed to have the same needs, and twelve of the first sixteen teams picked defensive players, including tackle Cortez Kennedy, end Ray Agnew, and linebacker Lamar Lathon, all players Johnson would have loved. Johnson had made a deal with the Kansas City Chiefs to get the Chiefs' pick, the thirteenth of the draft, in order to draft James Francis of Baylor to play linebacker, but the Cincinnati Bengals had the twelfth pick and took Francis, ending that possibility.

As defender after defender was snapped up, Jimmy Johnson switched gears. It arguably would be the most important decision he would make as coach of the Cowboys.

He had signed Plan B free agent running back Keith Jones and traded his second-round draft pick to the San Francisco 49ers for tailback Terrence Flagler. Johnson was so pleased about getting Flagler that he gave everyone the impression that Flagler was better than any back available in the draft. But once the quality defenders were taken, Johnson's new object of affection became University of Florida running back Emmitt Smith.

Smith was available because of the turmoil in the University of Florida football program. His offensive coach had been Whitey Jordan, who had come over from SMU, where he had helped make Eric Dickerson a star. Jordan gave Smith the ball often, and the back thrived. But five games into the season, head coach Galen Hall quit, amid rumors that he had been fired. Hall's recruiting no-nos were made public. A year after Hall left, the team was put on probation. When Steve Spurrier came in as head coach, Smith felt the new coach was "cool" to him. And when Spurrier fired Whitey Jordan, Smith decided it was time to test his value in the pro game.

The knock on Smith was that he was too slow for the pros—the New York Giants had timed him at only 4.70 in the 40, but Jimmy Johnson had timed the two-time All-America who had started as a freshman at Florida, and he wasn't *that* slow—4.45—and Johnson wondered how slow could he have been considering that in three years competing for the University of Florida Smith had run for 3,928 yards and scored 37 touchdowns. Even better, Smith was an accomplished pass catcher, an important asset in Johnson's offense.

Johnson held the twenty-first pick, but he knew he needed to climb several rungs higher to get Smith, and the gods were with him when the Pittsburgh Steelers, who didn't need another running back, traded Dallas its pick for Dallas's twenty-first pick and one of its third-round picks as well.

Johnson and his scouting staff had rated Emmitt Smith the fourth-best player in the entire draft. Only Blair Thomas of Penn State, chosen number two by the New York Jets, was rated a better back. Dick Mansberger, the Cowboys' director of scouting, called Smith the "Bob Hayes of the '90s." Smith was given uniform number 22, Hayes's old number (and also the number Smith wore in college). Scout Walt Yowarsky called Smith the "Tony Dorsett of the new Cowboys organization." Dorsett held the Cowboy record for touchdowns scored, with 72; Hayes was second, with 71. Skeptics wondered whether the Cowboy PR machine was blowing hot air. Many wondered why, if Smith was so great, he had only been the seventeenth pick. But teams not only suspected his lack of speed, they were also afraid of his agent, Richard Howell, who had his clients hold out if he didn't get the money he wanted. Johnson wasn't fooled by his lack of speed, and Jerry Jones wasn't afraid of any agent. Like Johnson, all Jones wanted was talent.

After the draft Johnson and Jones were ecstatic. That night Jones went on the radio and bragged how the Cowboys had stolen Smith, crowed that they had ranked Smith the fourth-best player in the draft. Jones's remarks were relayed to Smith, who relayed them to his agent, who would make Jones pay.

The defense would still need help but on offense the Cowboys had a combination of outstanding players at the three key spots: quarterback, running back, and receiver. Not since the days of Roger Staubach, Tony Dorsett, and Drew Pearson had the Cowboys featured a threesome as potent as Troy Aikman, Emmitt Smith, and Michael Irvin, though it would take the better part of the '90 season for Johnson, Dallas, and the rest of the NFL to finally discover this.

In addition to Smith, the Cowboys in '90 drafted speedburning Auburn wide receiver Alexander Wright and defensive tackle Jimmie Jones, one of Johnson's former players at the University of Miami. Jones was available because he had dropped out of school to take a job in a restaurant and lost his job to Cortez Kennedy. But Johnson knew how good Jones could be, and he, too, became a Cowboy.

When he drafted Emmitt Smith number one, Johnson knew a lot about him. Smith had grown up in the inner city of Pensacola, Florida, the second of six children, and until he was eight his family lived in a government housing project and had to eat government cheese and powdered milk. But Emmitt had an advantage many of the other ghetto kids didn't. His parents had not split up, and he grew up in a loving, caring environment, where his parents taught him the values of hard work and keeping a level head.

Smith's father had himself been a high school football star who had had a couple of college offers, but he also had two bad knees that had to be drained constantly. So instead of going to college, he went right to work after high school driving a city bus.

When Emmitt was twelve, his father took a job at the Magnolia Nursing Home, where his mother worked in the office. He pushed around elderly patients in wheelchairs. He preached to Emmitt the values of an honest day's work.

By the end of his rookie year, Emmitt Smith would become a significant force, and before long he would easily break Tony Dorsett's Cowboy career touchdown record. His teammates would nod their heads knowingly when, after each touchdown he scored, Emmitt Smith clutched the football to his chest and toted it back to the bench, where it would be placed inside a trunk for safekeeping. His purpose: when he retires he's going to auction them off, more than 100 in all.

His skill was able to lift the Cowboys to glory, but his loyalty was to himself, and in just a few years he would become the epitome of the modern athlete: intensely private, independent, wealthy, and as famous as any television or movie star.

After the Cowboys drafted him in 1990, Emmitt Smith held out for forty-nine days, as he let the Cowboys stew until he got every penny of the money he was demanding. As predicted, agent Richard Howell turned out to be a royal pain for Jerry Jones and his partner, Mike McCoy. Howell refused to negotiate on the telephone, insisting they exchange faxes. Days went by between faxes. Two weeks before the start of the season Smith upped the pressure on Jones when he reenrolled at the University of Florida. Said the practical Smith, "When I could be in school, why sit home and wait for something that might not materialize?"

Less than a week before the start of the season Smith signed a contract for a $1 million signing bonus and a four year, $4 million salary.

Partly as a result of Smith's late signing, which prevented the coaching staff from appreciating the gem they had in him, the Cowboys began the season 3–7. Except for an opening day squeaker over San Diego that ended a fourteen-game home losing streak, and two four-point wins over the perennially inept Tampa Bay Buccaneers, 1990 wasn't turning out much better than 1989. As the losses mounted and the writers talked of the team's "youthful ineptitude," Jimmy Johnson's talk of a .500 season was ridiculed.

Emmitt Smith began his pro career in the third game, against the Washington Redskins. He gained two yards. In the following game, against the New York Giants, linebacker Lawrence Taylor punched him in the face as a welcome. He carried all but six times, and the Cowboys lost badly. By the sixth game, Emmitt Smith was feuding with offensive coordinator David Shula.

Shula was basing the offense on Troy Aikman and his wide receivers, augmenting their contributions with passes dumped to the backs, with a small mixture of runs to keep everyone honest. It's what Shula, Don's son, had done in Miami with Dan Marino, and it's what he had done the year before.

But Emmitt Smith refused to be anyone's afterthought. Since his high school days, when he ran for 8,560 yards and 103 touchdowns, through his college years when he was one of the few freshmen to finish in the top ten of the Heisman voting, Emmitt Smith was the catalyst. On the Cowboys, Smith was frustrated because he felt that David Shula didn't see it that way, didn't appreciate his talent sufficiently.

After two straight drubbings by the New York Jets and the undefeated San Francisco 49ers in games in which the backs carried only a dozen times, Smith told running back coach Joe Brodsky, "You give the running backs fifteen carries. That's too much pressure on Troy, and it's not enough work for us."

The next Sunday, against the defensively weak Los Angeles Rams, the Cowboys let Emmitt Smith carry 21 times, and he made 54 tough yards on the ground while catching 117 yards worth of passes. On that day Aikman threw for three touchdowns to beat the Rams. Michael Irvin caught two touchdown passes, of 61 and 10 yards. It was the first time since 1988 that a Cowboy receiver had caught more than one touchdown in a game.

It was the beginning of the new beginning.

The next Thursday, Thanksgiving Day, the Cowboys hosted the powerful Washington Redskins before 60,355 hometown fans in a game broadcast halfway around the world to the Saudi desert for the Desert Storm troops.

The first time the teams met the Redskins had beaten Troy Aikman to a pulp, sacking him eight times and intercepting twice. Midway through the third quarter of this game, the Redskins led 17–13.

But in this game Aikman's line jelled, and in the final fifteen minutes the big Oklahoman completed seven of eight passes for 107 yards and two touchdowns. Emmitt Smith carried for a career-high 132 yards.

The first drive was highlighted by a series of passes to Kelvin Martin and Jay Novacek that set up a touchdown to make the score 20–17. On the second drive Emmitt Smith took a handoff from the Redskins 48, went off right guard behind John Gesek, cut sharply to his left and found himself in a footrace with Darrell Green, one of the fastest defensive backs in the league. Smith, the runner with the suspect speed, faked out Green at the 30 on a stop-and-go move and beat him for the touchdown, the first of more than 100 he has scored as a Cowboy. His score closed out the 27–17 Cowboy victory.

"This is the victory of all victories," said Michael Irvin, and for the second-year receiver, it was. Nothing the Johnson-led Cowboys had done had come even close to it.

Asked an incredulous Frank Luksa in the *Dallas Times-Herald,* "Who are those guys and where did they come from?" Luksa reflected the feelings of all Cowboy fans when he added, "Who knows? Who cares, now that they're here."

After the game the players gave the game ball to Jerry Jones. Said defensive tackle Dean Hamel, "When you look at how far this franchise has come in two years, you've got to look at Jerry Jones. This is his team. He assembled it. He paid money to bring some talent in here.

"You could have given the ball to Emmitt, or to Troy, but you don't have those kind of players unless the people up top make the commitment."

The columnists, however, saved their praise for Jimmy Johnson. Wrote Gil LeBreton in the *Fort Worth Star-Telegram,* "The time has come to throw some palms at the little general's feet," wrote LeBreton. "He has raised the *Titanic.* He has rebuilt Rome. He has brought the entire Metroplex cheering to its feet.

"The reasons for the Cowboys' resurrection aren't so elementary. Johnson's obstinacy, his hands-on influence and patience with the offense, his decision to mostly ignore the waiver wire, good karma—whatever, they have all helped the Cowboys clear a mighty hump in one great whoosh.

"Just as we blamed Jimmy Johnson, we should applaud him. If he weren't here, he probably would be in some other NFL port, being ornery. And building a respectable winner, as he always has."

Jim Reeves, another *Star-Telegram* columnist, was equally effusive. Reeves, who during training camp was certain the Cowboys would be as terrible as they had been the year before, wrote, "Forget Jimmy Johnson as National Football League coach of the year. Don't even think of stopping there. Johnson should be coach of the year *and* co-NFL executive of the year with owner Jerry Jones. Period. No arguments. No excuses."

But he also wrote, "Give Johnson credit. *All* the credit." In dismissing Jerry Jones's role in the resurgence of the team, Reeves then discussed how Johnson had reached an uneasy peace with Troy Aikman and went on to praise him for the trades, the draft picks, and the Plan B free agent signings.

Reeves summed up, "Whatever you or I may think about Johnson, whether it's love, hate or something lower on the scale, give him credit. He has brought the Cowboys a long way, and he deserves to be recognized for it."

The next week the Cowboys continued their streak as they beat New Orleans 17–13 in an inspiring win, followed by a 41–10 blowout of the Phoenix Cardinals, a team that had defeated Dallas 20–3 earlier in the season.

Against Phoenix, the Troy Aikman to Michael Irvin combination was devastating. And Emmitt Smith ran the ball 24 times for 103 yards and scored four touchdowns. On one 11-yard touchdown jaunt, Smith eluded six tacklers, ducked, weaved, improvised, and stayed on his feet to score, a spectacular, exhilarating effort. On one short-yardage plunge, Smith carried three defenders with him into paydirt.

Linebacker Eugene Lockhart, who had had to spend much of the time on the field early in the season because of the ineptitude of the offense, asked no one in particular when Smith was scoring his third touchdown, "Is this the same football team?"

The Cowboys could have made the playoffs as a wild card team had they won just one more game. But against the Philadelphia Eagles, a team of bruisers, Aikman was knocked out of the game with a separated shoulder before the end of the first quarter ("The Fall of Troy"), and the Cowboys had no one to take his place. When the New Orleans Saints lost starting quarterback Bobby Hebert, they had been desperate for a quarterback, and so Johnson and Jones had traded them backup Steve Walsh for some great draft choices, and at the time the move was hailed by everyone, but now with Aikman disabled—he could not raise his right arm as a result of the injury—their losing gamble on a healthy Aikman would cost them dearly. Leaving Aikman as the sole veteran QB was a mistake Johnson and Jones would not make again. Babe Laufenberg wasn't talented enough to lead the Cowboys into the end zone, and after a 17–3 loss to Philly, the Atlanta Falcons successfully blitzed a shaky Laufenberg and keyed on Emmitt Smith. It turned into a 26–7 loss.

Even with the two losses, the Cowboys still had a chance to make the playoffs if the Rams could beat the Saints in the final game of the NFL regular season.

Unfortunately for the Cowboys, the Steve Walsh trade came back to haunt the Cowboys both ways. The Cowboys didn't have Walsh for the last two games, and the Saints did have him as they faced the Rams. Michael Irvin, who was Walsh's teammate at the University of Miami, knew that Walsh would win it. "Why am I here?" Irvin asked. "I've known this man for years. I know he's not going to lose this game."

And he didn't. Walsh led the Saints to a 20–17 win over the Rams, passing the Saints down the field for Morten Anderson to kick the winning field goal with two seconds left in the game. The Saints finished 8–8 and took the 7–9 Cowboys' spot in the playoffs.

The only consolation for Jimmy Johnson and Jerry Jones was that the second-round draft choice the Cowboys got for Walsh would turn into a first-round pick should the Saints reach the NFL championship.

Emmitt Smith was named offensive Rookie of the Year on the strength of his 937 yards gained, best among rookies and tenth among all backs. But Smith still was not happy because he had only carried 241 times. He wanted David Shula gone, and one week after the end of the '90 season Jimmy Johnson demoted David Shula and gave the job of offensive coordinator to Norv Turner, who would turn out to be another catalyst to Cowboy greatness. Johnson was named Coach of the Year.

The Cowboys were back, just like Jerry Jones had said. And now Jerry Jones would become the biggest story of them all, bigger than Troy Aikman or Michael Irvin or Emmitt Smith, or even Jimmy Johnson. Jerry Jones was the owner of what soon would be the most visible franchise in all of American sports, and it would not be long before he would be transformed into a media darling.

And Jerry Jones, along with his coach, Jimmy Johnson, would shortly perform a miracle.

74

All the Way Back

In 1990 the success of the Aikman-Irvin-Smith threesome proved that the Cowboys could compete on offense, and then in the spring of 1991 Jerry Jones and Jimmy Johnson made several moves that would bring excellence to the Cowboys defense.

The New England Patriots had first pick in the entire draft, but when Notre Dame kick and punt returner and pass receiver Raghib "Rocket" Ismail asked the Pats for $17.5 million, the Pats traded the pick to the Cowboys for the number 11 pick, the number 41 pick, and a couple of players.

Jerry Jones, who had had to sit through training camp biting his nails when Emmitt Smith held out for forty-nine days, decided that this year if a player wouldn't agree to sign *before* he was drafted, he would not take him.

So when Ismail, who would have made the Cowboy offense as potent as any in the history of the game, wouldn't budge from his salary demand of $17.5, Jerry Jones and Jimmy Johnson switched objects of desire and pursued 6'1", 280-pound defensive tackle Russell Maryland, who had played for Jimmy Johnson in Miami and had won the Outland Trophy as the top college lineman of 1990.

At Miami, Maryland was known as the "Conscience." Said Cowboys defensive line coach Butch Davis, who coached under Jimmy Johnson and had Maryland at Miami, "He was the guy who went to other kids' dorm rooms, got them out of their bed, made them go to class, made them go watch film, made them work out.

"He would father-figure some of the younger guys, pick up some of the guys who were struggling with the same things he did: long ways from home, little overweight, don't know your role on the team."

In addition to getting Maryland, a pass rusher of extraordinary ability, the Cowboys were also able to cash in on the trades of Herschel Walker to Minnesota and Steve Walsh to New Orleans the year before. The draft picks they got in exchange turned out to be linebacker Dixon Edwards, defensive end Tony Hill, and on offense the Cowboys got Erik Williams, a big, talented tackle, and wide receiver Jimmy Smith. Johnson also held out high hopes for rookie cornerback Larry Brown of TCU.

Completing the draft bonanza was the acquisition of Alvin Harper, an explosive wide receiver from the University of Tennessee.

If that had been all Jones and Johnson would have accomplished, it would have been a ton, but two days later Jones and Johnson made another major coup when they traded two 1992 draft picks to Atlanta for disgruntled defensive standout Tony Casillas. Casillas, perhaps the strongest man in professional football, was feuding with Falcons coach Jerry Glanville, and it was Casillas himself who started the ball rolling when after the 1990 season finale against Dallas he personally told defensive coordinator Dave Wannstedt about the problems he was having with Glanville. "Hey, if there's any way I could get an opportunity to play for you guys . . ."

Johnson had tried to recruit the 6'3", 280-pound Casillas when he was a coach at Oklahoma State, but the big nose tackle went to play for Barry Switzer at Oklahoma instead. As he did with Troy Aikman, Johnson was given a second chance to make good with a star player who had once evaded his grasp, and he wasn't going to blow it again.

Training camp was brutal. During the heat of the summer, in one stretch the players practiced nineteen days in a row. On offense, the new coordinator, Norv Turner, was making friends and influencing people, and on defense the Cowboys without warning were turning into a solid unit, with Tony Casillas, Jim Jeffcoat, Tony Tolbert, and Danny Noonan up front, with Jimmy Jones and Russell Maryland in reserve, and a linebacking corps of Jesse Solomon, Jack Del Rio, and Vinson Smith, with Ken Norton Jr., the son of the heavyweight boxer, behind them.

Before the season began Jimmy Johnson boldly predicted, "Not only will we make the playoffs, but we will have success in the playoffs."

Jim Reeves, for one, thought Johnson was nuts and predicted a 6–10 season. "They're just not going to get there," wrote Reeves, who was seriously underestimating the rebuilding job of Jones and Johnson. Norm Hitzges hedged his bet when he opined that the "team could win nine or it could win four." Hitzges said that if the Cowboys won four, there would be a feeding frenzy for Johnson's scalp.

After starting the season with a win over the Browns and two tough losses, the Cowboys defeated the Phoenix Cards 17–9 in a game in which Emmitt Smith carried 23 times for 182 yards and two stunning touchdowns of 12 and 60 yards. They then went up against Lawrence Taylor and the New York Giants, a team they hadn't even had a *lead* against in four years. The game was a Texas Stadium brass-knuckles slugfest. The Giants led 16–14 with six minutes left in the game, when Troy Aikman started a drive from his own 16-yard line.

He completed passes to Alexander Wright, Michael Irvin, and Jay Novacek to put them at the New York 21. Emmitt Smith tried the line but was thrown back. It was second-and-twelve with three minutes left. The Giants anticipated that the Cowboys would try the middle, pile up, and go for the field goal. But Michael Irvin saw that the Giants had abandoned their double coverage, and he wanted the ball.

Aikman went back to pass and saw that Irvin was covered only by Mark Collins. Aikman threw it up, and Irvin caught it in the end zone for the score. Irvin finished the day with six catches for 91 yards.

"He (Collins) went for tackling the football instead of me," said Irvin. "I grabbed it in. I think he was trying to strip the ball. I was thinking touchdown."

Said Troy Aikman, who was 20 of 27 for 277 yards, "It's the biggest win since I've been here, that's easy to say."

Added Jimmy Johnson, "We took a big step as a team, as a franchise today. It was a *very* big step."

Jerry Jones agreed. "We all know what we did," he said. "We beat Mike Tyson." It was a landmark victory for the Cowboys, the first over the defending Super Bowl champion Giants after six straight losses.

After the game Michael Irvin praised his teammates, especially Alexander Wright and Alvin Harper. Linebacker Steve DeOssie voiced that everyone had seen that quarterback Troy Aikman was no longer a rube. He had learned to read defenses and was ready to become one of the star quarterbacks in the NFL.

All praised Jimmy Johnson for hanging with them, for being honest with them, for creating such a strong bond among the Cowboys.

* * *

In 1991 the Cowboys would finish 11–5, including a 24–21 victory over the previously undefeated Washington Redskins in RFK Stadium. (Said Emmitt Smith: "We shocked the world.") Troy Aikman had thrived under Norv Turner's new system, leading the league in passing yards and completions before suffering a sprained lateral collateral ligament (knee) injury after a vicious tackle by the Redskins Wilber Marshall. For the third year in a row Aikman would be disabled at the end of the season. In the 35 games he had played with the Cowboys, he had been sacked 91 times!

But this year Jones and Johnson had a contingency in the event Aikman went down. Backup Steve Beuerlein had been a starter for Phoenix and had won, and in the second-to-last game of the regular season Beuerlein led the Cowboys to a 25–13 win over a fierce Eagles team to put the Cowboys in the NFL playoffs for the first time since 1985.

As the game was winding down, Jerry Jones called over his publicity director, Rich Dalrymple. He asked Dalrymple if a win over the Eagles put the Cowboys in the playoffs.

Dalrymple didn't know, so he called over his assistant, Dave Pelletier, who told the owner that there were six playoff spots and that five teams were ahead of the Cowboys. Two other teams, the Eagles and 49ers, he said, were also in contention but neither could catch the Cowboys.

"So, does that mean we're in?" asked Jones.

Pelletier nodded.

Who would have believed that Jerry Jones and Jimmy Johnson could have rebuilt the Cowboy franchise in such a short period of time?

Said an ecstatic Jerry Jones after the game, "Three years ago I just couldn't imagine it."

The season finale was the team's fifth win in a row, a 31–27 win over the Atlanta Falcons before a sellout crowd at Texas Stadium. Emmitt Smith rushed for 160 yards to become the first Cowboy ever to win the NFL rushing title. Smith's 1,583 yards surpassed the 1,548 yards of Detroit's Barry Sanders and the 1,407 of Buffalo's Thurman Thomas.

Michael Irvin caught a career-high 10 passes for 169 yards, including a 58-yard touchdown pass.

Then in the opening wild card playoff game, Steve Beuerlein led the Cowboys to a stunning 17–13 win against Mike Ditka's Chicago Bears. But in the second round, against the Detroit Lions, the Cowboys keyed on Barry Sanders; unfortunately, while they were doing that they were picked apart by Lion quarterback Erik Kramer. On offense Jimmy Johnson gave up on Steve Beuerlein quickly, only to see the Lion defenders swamp over a gimpy, rusty Aikman. The final score was 38–6.

Said Nate Newton, a tackle who was developing into a fine offensive lineman and an equally adept spokesman, "This loss won't tear down our meat house. Our meat house is packed."

After the game Jimmy Johnson praised his players, saying that the loss did not take away from an outstanding season. But as Johnson sat immobile and in isolation in his seat on the bus while the players dressed and got ready to leave Detroit, his body language spoke of his deep disappointment. Jimmy Johnson was not the sort of man who could sit still after a loss like that. He would make sure it would never happen again. His Miami team had won a national championship. He would do whatever was necessary to take the '92 Cowboys to the Super Bowl.

75

How 'Bout Them Cowboys

For the second year in a row, it was announced that Jerry Jones had continued his practice of refusing to draft a player unless he agreed to a contract first. Jones had been burned in 1990 when Emmitt Smith and Alexander Wright held out the entire training camp. As a result, said Jones, it took Smith an extra two months to fit into the Cowboy offense, and Wright never attained his potential. By signing players before drafting them, Jones was only making sure this would never happen again.

Jones's practice brought a howl from the other team owners. What if Jones makes a player an offer, they said, and the player turns it down? Now we have to negotiate with him. What if our offer is lower? The player will say, "The Cowboys offered me *this* much."

There was an even bigger concern. Paul Tagliabue, the NFL commissioner, had argued that the draft had been set up not to keep salaries down, but to make sure there was competitive balance within the league. But Jones's signing policy suggested the opposite. Should the players ever challenge the draft, Jones was giving them very strong evidence.

As always, Jones dismissed the criticism out of hand.

"Everything we've done in this area is not only a benefit to the organization, the team and our fans, but to the player. We are giving everybody a better chance to succeed."

Jerry Jones may have grown up in Arkansas, but the oil and gas mogul was becoming very Texas. No one was going to tell him how to run his business, not the federal government or the NFL, or Paul Tagliabue, or the other NFL owners, whose business practices Jones was coming to view as behind the times. Jones had paid close to $150 million for the Cowboys, and he was determined to run his team *his* way. His signing policy would not be the last time he would butt heads with the other teams in the league.

What was most remarkable about Jones and Johnson as a unit was that although the Cowboys had come within two games of going back to the Super Bowl in '91, neither man considered the huge strides made by the team to be sufficient. Both had but one standard: to be Super Bowl champions. That both of them were willing to improve the team further after the miraculous jump the year before was testimony to the dynamism of their partnership. Jerry Jones certainly could not have rebuilt the team without the expertise of Jimmy Johnson, and Jimmy Johnson could not have done it without the financial and emotional backing of Jerry Jones. That two men possessing great egos could work so closely together without squabbling spoke volumes of their dedication to their sole task: bringing the Super Bowl trophy back to Dallas.

To that end Jones and Johnson took steps to remedy the pass-rush deficiency of the year before by acquiring two potential All-Pro defensive linemen. In '91 the Cowboys had only had 23 quarterback sacks, and with the signing of Chad Hennings and Charles Haley, Jones and Johnson both knew that '92 would be a different story.

The credit for signing Hennings went to neither Johnson nor Jones. Hennings was a gift from the U.S. and Russian governments. At 6'6", 270 pounds, the man-mountain was a farmboy from Elberon, Iowa, who in his senior year at the Air Force Academy had won the Outland Trophy for being the best collegiate interior lineman. The All-America had been drafted by the Cowboys in the eleventh round back in 1988 under the Tex Schramm-Gil Brandt-Tom Landry regime. He had served for four years overseas in the Air Force as America's beefiest fighter pilot, a member of the exclusive Euro-NATO pilot program.

Hennings had signed for an eight-year stint to fly jets in defense of his country, something he had always dreamed of doing. Between April and June of '91 he flew 45 missions, piloting A-10 tank blasters above the rocky terrain of northern Iraq, protecting the C-130 aircraft planes that were dropping supplies to the fleeing Kurds.

When Jerry Jones bought the Cowboys, one of his first calls was to Robert Strauss, the U.S. Ambassador to Russia, to ask Strauss what could be done to get Hennings released from his service commitment. Strauss spoke to defense department officials and could get nowhere.

World events then conspired to make him eligible to depart the armed services early. After the dismantling of the Berlin Wall and the crumbling of communism, the military began cutting back its international forces and offered early releases. Hennings thus had the opportunity to fulfill a second dream, playing pro football.

Despite his size, Hennings could run the 40 in 4.8 seconds. The Denver Broncos had expressed interest in trading for Hennings, but at a Cowboy minicamp, Jimmy Johnson watched Hennings warm up before running the 40-yard dash, and he was impressed with Hennings's smooth stride. He turned to Jerry Jones and said, "Forget about trading this guy."

When Johnson put the twenty-six-year-old Hennings through a pass-rush drill, he scored better than Georgia Tech defensive end Marco Coleman, who was taken as the twelfth pick by the Miami Dolphins.

"I don't think I've lost anything," said Hennings, who bench-pressed 450 pounds.

Hennings returned to England, where he was discharged June 14. The next day he reported to the Dallas rookie camp. As an indication of how times had changed, when Schramm signed Hennings in 1988, he gave the gentle giant a $25,000 bonus, then signed him to a first-year contract worth $300,000 with incentives. Back then it was big money. By 1992, it was low pay. Gloated the retired Tex Schramm, "The Cowboys are going to find themselves with an excellent player for virtually nothing."

Good old Tex.

The second All-Pro acquisition came about because of Jimmy Johnson's ability to get along with idiosyncratic black ballplayers. By 1992 all teams were drafting as many, or more, black players as white. In fact, there were even black head coaches in the NFL by 1992. But some white coaches were still intolerant of black players with an attitude, and Charles Haley had challenged 49er coach George Seifert, telling him, "I'm not going to stop doing my thing."

Charles Haley was the premier pass rusher in the league. He had charm, intellect, and wit, but he was as sensitive and volatile as sulfuric acid, and when he went "off," he could become one large black dude with a giant-sized attitude. As a result, the San Francisco 49ers chose to trade him to the Cowboys rather than put up with his bursts of antisocial behavior. Haley respected those who could take his relentless barbs. You had to have thick skin to be Haley's friend. Not everyone had it. Twice Haley had made racial remarks to Jim Burt, leading to fights. Another time he taunted a teammate about his alcoholism, starting a row. Reporters were standing targets. Once he berated and harassed a female reporter. Then there was the time Haley didn't like the way a male reporter was looking at him in the locker room. An undressed Haley started screaming at him, "You're looking at me weird," and then accused him publicly of being a homosexual.

Jimmy Johnson didn't like malcontents, but he'd heard another story that told him Haley was the kind of competitor he valued. Haley, who had led the 49er defense to two Super Bowls, had become so upset after a loss to former teammate Ronnie Lott and the Los Angeles Raiders that he fell apart in the locker room after the game. He began berating quarterback Steve Young and cursing the coaching staff for playing Young. Haley had worked himself to such a frenzy, then crashed in a fit of melancholia, that he was curled up against the wall. The coaching staff had to bring Lott over from the Raider dressing room to soothe Haley's feelings. This was the kind of player Jimmy Johnson wanted by his side. No one practiced or played harder or with more intensity than Charles Haley. Johnson wanted that, and he'd put up with the occasional outburst to get it. Haley was also a risk because in March he had undergone arthroscopic surgery on the rotator cuff of his right shoulder and two weeks earlier had had his right knee scoped. Jones and Johnson wanted him anyway.

Jerry Jones arranged to swap San Francisco president Carmen Policy a second-round pick in '93 and a third-rounder in '94 for Haley. Jones also wagered Policy that the Cowboys would finish higher than the 49ers. If they didn't, Jones said, the Cowboys would swap places with the 49ers in the first and third rounds of the '93 draft.

Jones agreed to pay Haley $1.4 million, more than what Troy Aikman was making. When Haley flew into Dallas, Jerry Jones personally picked up the big lineman at the airport.

Jones did something else few noticed. After signing Haley, he sent holdout lineman Danny Noonan to Green Bay, dumping his $650,000 salary on the Packers and cutting the cost of the Haley deal considerably. He was getting a Ferrari Testarossa for the price of a Mercedes-Benz.

The only negative through the preseason were holdouts by Michael Irvin and center Mark Stepnoski. But four days before the season opener, Irvin dropped his $3 million-a-year demand and signed for an annual

$1.25 million plus incentives for three years. Said Irvin, "Now I can take care of my mother. Now I can take care of my people. They are about to arrive at the Promised Land, just like Martin Luther King used to talk about."

Two days later Stepnoski signed for $600,000. The Cowboys were whole. Let the season begin.

The season opener was the most important game of the Jones-Johnson regime. The Washington Redskins had won the Super Bowl in '91, and Jerry Johnson knew that the winner of the game would have the inside track to Pasadena. The contest was televised nationally on *Monday Night Football.* All through the preseason Jimmy Johnson had pointed toward this game. He knew that Washington's no-huddle offense had been very effective against his team, and in this game he was determined to give Redskin coach Joe Gibbs a surprise of his own: Johnson had devised a scheme for signaling his players what defense to set up without a huddle of their own. The week before the game, Jimmy Johnson not only told them they were going to win, but he let them know exactly how they were going to do it.

The Redskins started the game with no huddle, as expected, and on the first play, Johnson sent linebacker Vinson Smith on a blitz that threw Washington quarterback Mark Rypien for a big loss. On the second play, a run was stopped for a three-yard loss. An incompletion left the Redskins reeling. The Cowboys won 23–10.

The day after the Redskin game Jerry Jones's partner, Mike McCoy, told Jones he thought the Cowboys still had a weakness at safety. McCoy said he didn't think Ray Horton or James Washington were up to the task. Jones did not disagree, and in a subsequent conversation with Pittsburgh Steelers owner Dan Rooney, Jones learned that the Steelers were about to cut safety Thomas Everett, who was a contract holdout. The Steelers were offering a three-year, $1.75 million deal to Everett, an All-Pro who hit so hard he would injure himself on plays. A Baylor grad, Everett had built a home in far North Dallas and wanted to play for the Cowboys.

Jones gave Rooney a fifth-round draft choice in '93 for Everett and signed him for less money than the Steelers were offering. Everett would play an important role with the Cowboys.

The next week the Cowboys proved the Washington win wasn't a fluke when they outdueled Lawrence Taylor, Phil Simms, and the New York Giants, 34–28, and for the rest of the season, the Cowboys were the talk of the league. There were a few bumps in the road. In the middle of the second half in a game against the Chicago Bears, Jerry Jones brought

Prince Bandar bin Sultan, the Saudi Arabian ambassador to the United States, and six of his bodyguards to the sidelines to shake hands with some of the players. Bandar, one of the richest men in the world, was a Cowboy fanatic who had tapes of Cowboy games flown back to him on the *Concorde*. Bandar was also Washington's most important contact in the Middle East. Jones would contribute heavily to the campaign of soon-to-be-elected President Clinton, and he felt it important to show Bandar as much Texas courtesy as he could muster.

During that second half, reserve running back Curvin Richards fumbled twice in a row and Johnson, who deeply hated turnovers, cut Richards after the game, shocking everyone.

Said Johnson, who was also angry at Curvin for not taking notes during meetings, "I couldn't depend on him for the playoffs. It was the right thing to do."

Seething, Johnson also confronted Jones about bringing Bandar and his men to the sidelines, shouting obscenities at the owner for breaking everyone's concentration. Jones himself did some seething after Johnson's tongue-lashing.

Some of the players wondered whether Johnson, who seemed to be always on edge despite the success of the team, had "lost it." Others wondered whether he would quit. He seemed manic-depressive, with a very dark side when angry.

After the Bears game, Jones told a reporter, "Of course, the one thing I would not want to see is for Jimmy to wind up in a mental institution."

With Johnson finally cooled off, Jones explained to his coach why he had brought Bandar on to the field.

The players may have been leery of their coach after the Richards firing, but the move had a positive effect on the players. From then on when Johnson would tell them, "There are no second chances," they believed him and played accordingly.

The Cowboys were playing the best football in the NFL, and they stormed to the NFC championship, first clobbering the Philadelphia Eagles, 34–10; Jones said, "Our guys just became men." Then they survived the muddy sod of Candlestick Park by outlasting the San Francisco 49ers, with Joe Montana and Jerry Rice, 30–20. Emmitt Smith ran 24 times for 114 yards and Troy Aikman surgically took the 49ers apart, completing 24 of 34 passes for 322 yards and two touchdowns. (He was 13 of 16 for 208 yards in the second half!)

Ahead by only 24–20 with four minutes to go, Aikman dumped a short pass to Alvin Harper, who raced 70 yards to set up the clinching score. The win put the Cowboys in the Super Bowl for the first time in fourteen long years.

After the game Jimmy Johnson praised Aikman effusively. "Troy's come a long way," said the joyful coach, "and he's brought me with him." Johnson later shouted at the television cameras, "How 'bout them Cowboys! Not just today. Not just this week. This started four years ago. I know everybody in this league works hard. But I can't imagine anyone working harder than the group we have. The coaching staff, time and again we demanded more and more, to the point where the players might not have been able to give. But they responded in a positive way, and now we're one game away from where we want to be."

All season long Johnson had been telling his players and the media that the "best game of the season that we play will be the last one," and that game was to be the Big One against the AFL champion Buffalo Bills, losers in the last two Super Bowls.

The Bills' gimmick, like that of the Washington Redskins, was the no-huddle offense led by quarterback Jim Kelly. As for their defense, Johnson was certain the Bills could be beaten deep.

The night before the Super Bowl, without telling anyone where he was going, Johnson bused the team to a different hotel. There were no distractions, no phone calls in or out. Johnson knew that assistant coaches Dave Wannstedt and Tony Wise would be leaving after the game for Chicago, where Wannstedt would take over as head coach of the Chicago Bears.

Johnson's eyes welled as he told his players, "The best way for those people to remember you and remember this game is with a Super Bowl ring on their finger, remembering the feeling of the win."

Johnson was certain the Cowboys would win.

"It was just a matter of how much. We held a royal flush. It was just a matter of dropping the cards."

Johnson saw that the Bills had a weakness: turnovers. "Patience," he admonished. "Patience and they will crack."

Super Bowl XXVII was played in the Rose Bowl before 98,374 fans and millions more on TV. The Bills scored first, on a Thurman Thomas run, but then late in the first quarter after Charles Haley smacked Jim Kelly on the two-yard line, the quarterback fumbled, and Jimmie Jones recovered to give the Cowboys the lead. Ahead 14–7, the defense was smelling blood. Ken Norton Jr. tackled Kelly and knocked him out of the game. His replacement, Frank Reich, wasn't up to the task, and for the rest of the game the Bills made turnover after turnover—nine in all—just as

Jimmy Johnson had predicted. Aikman alternated completions among Michael Irvin, who caught six passes for 114 yards and two touchdowns, Jay Novacek, and Alvin Harper, who each had one, while Emmitt Smith ran wild for 108 yards and a score. Norton completed a spectacular day with a fumble recovery and touchdown run, and the final score was Cowboys 52, Bills 17. Troy Aikman, who gained his place in pro football history with a 22-for-30 273-yard, four-touchdown explosion, was named the MVP of the game and was awarded a Buick Park Avenue Ultra in addition to the $36,000 winner's share.

The Cowboys would have had seven more points for a Super Bowl record, except that defensive lineman Leon Lett recovered a fumble on his own 35, ran hard for most of the way, slowed at about the Bills ten, and as he was hotdogging, doing the boogaloo, a Bills defender caught up to him and knocked the ball from his hands before he crossed the goal line. The play, a classic for the look on Lett's face after Don Beebe's hustle deprived him of what should have been a touchdown, will be replayed before every future Super Bowl for eternity.

It was a good thing for Lett that the game was a blowout. Even Johnson was laughing as the big lineman sheepishly trotted back to the bench.

As the clock was ticking down Emmitt Smith hollered, "Mess it up! Mess up the hair!" He finally took it upon himself to muss the always immaculate coif of the world's most fastidious coach. Said Smith, "At that moment in his life, nobody could deny the magic he had performed: He'd taken the Dallas Cowboys from 1–15 to Super Bowl champs in four years."

After the game, Jerry Jones wandered around the Rose Bowl field repeating the phrase, "Dallas Cowboys, world champions." He was saying it when he and Jimmy Johnson met. He said to Johnson, "It feels great to be the best in the world."

In the dressing room Johnson told his stunned players, "The feeling you have at this very moment is one of the best things you will ever have in this life . . ." The tears began to flow. "Especially the feeling you have for one another, more than the event itself, the feeling of accomplishment with a teammate, more than the actual winning of the Super Bowl."

For Jerry Jones, the coaching staff, the players, and the fans, it was a moment few would ever forget.

"How 'bout them Cowboys!"

76

The Rift

hree weeks after the Super Bowl, Jerry Jones announced that he had raised Jimmy Johnson's salary from $550,000 to more than $1 million a year. Jones also gave the assistant coaches raises. At the same time Jones enraged many employees by refusing to give the cash bonuses traditionally given to them after winning Super Bowls.

"I'm ecstatic," Johnson told the press after Jones announced the raises. But their smiles were a mask. There was trouble between the two former Arkansas teammates that had begun in 1992 after it was clear the team was going to contend for the championship. The issue: credit. Two important Cowboy trades for Charles Haley and Thomas Everett had helped lift the team to the title. Jerry Jones, who had been getting counsel from Al Davis of the Oakland Raiders without Jimmy Johnson's knowledge, had played important roles in both the trades, and Johnson was upset that some reporters were saying that they were Jones's deals. In turn, Johnson began dumping on Jones's ability as a judge of personnel. With a grimace Johnson was telling anyone who would listen that Jones "didn't know shit" about football talent. His remarks were getting back to Jerry Jones.

Johnson's assistant coaches wondered, "Why should Jimmy really care what Jerry is telling his friends about how much he had to do with a trade?"

One assistant coach told a member of the Cowboys' PR department, "Jimmy never gave Jerry any credit. I'm not saying Jimmy didn't deserve to get butt-fucked by a billy goat . . ." (Translation: Jimmy did deserve it.)

These events of the '92 season were revealed in *Sports Illustrated* in an article by Skip Bayless, who quoted Jimmy Johnson as saying, "My girlfriend knows more football than Jerry."

In response, Johnson backpedaled furiously to keep the peace. It's what people do when they are quoted correctly saying antagonistic things about people with more power than they have. He told the *Dallas Morning News,* "Not only did I never say that, but he misspelled her name."

But even though Bayless had misspelled a name, the reporter had his other facts straight as a string, and in '93 the issue of who was responsible for the brilliant Cowboy personnel decisions continued.

Beginning his first year, Johnson deeply resented that Jerry Jones asked for credit Johnson didn't feel he deserved for rebuilding *his* team. When in mid-'93 tight end Jim Price broke his foot, Johnson asked Jones to find a replacement. When Jones didn't move fast enough for Johnson, the coach called his scouting department, got a list of five free agent tight ends, and from the list it was Johnson who selected Scott Galbraith, an important player down the stretch in '93.

The carbuncle on the flesh of the Jerry Jones–Jimmy Johnson relationship opened up and began to fester and ooze at the end of a long holdout staged by Emmitt Smith, who had won the last two rushing titles. Smith had begun his negotiation right after the '92 Super Bowl win, when he declared that he would leave the Cowboys if he had to in order to make more money. Under the new player agreement, the Cowboys could either match any offer from another team or else offer him $800,000, and if he then left, the Cowboys would get a first- and third-round draft pick for him.

After Smith declared his willingness to leave Dallas, Jerry Jones announced that Smith would never play for another team. Smith had made $465,000 in '92. In two seasons Smith had rushed for 3,276 yards, scored 30 touchdowns, and won a Super Bowl championship, and in '93 he was demanding the $4.4 million that Dan Marino earned with the Dolphins.

Then on July 21, Buffalo Bills star running back Thurman Thomas signed for $13.5 million for four years. Smith's agent told reporters Smith was worth more than Thomas, more than Marino, even more than Steve Young, who was getting $5.35 million a year from the San Francisco 49ers.

Jones parried. He called the agent for disgruntled running back Cleveland Gary to see if he would be interested in playing for the Cowboys.

The Emmitt Smith–Jerry Jones negotiation was as taut and interesting as a Muhammad Ali–Joe Frazier heavyweight fight or a Spassky–Kasparov chess match. Each move was well thought out and potentially lethal. But with every move, the other side would make a countermove of equally breathtaking suavity. The stakes were high, and the difference between what Emmitt Smith wanted ($17 million for four years) and what Jerry Jones was offering ($9 million for four years) seemed gaping. The contract brawl was followed closely by all Cowboy fans.

Jones, a master negotiator, figured he would appeal to Smith's loyalty to his teammates. He argued he had very little room to budge because of the new salary cap that would take effect in '94. But in Emmitt Smith, Jones was not dealing with a softie like Michael Irvin, who had held out during the training camp the year before and signed because he couldn't stand that the Cowboys were playing without him. Smith was in the game for the money. He would feel no guilt about missing training camp or even sitting out regular season games. Said observer Skip Bayless, "Smith has Jones's back to the goal line. Jones now faces a Smith and Wesson."

Jones didn't blink. He told reporters, "If he has to miss a few games, so be it."

Charles Haley, for one, wondered why Jerry Jones was so quick to sign Troy Aikman and pay him in line with other top players but had refused to accord Emmitt Smith the same respect. Nate Newton, continuing the dialogue, was quick to say that racism had nothing to do with it. "I think every player wonders why Emmitt has to go through this, but truthfully, it probably gets to the black players a little more. If Mr. Jones just walks in and signs Troy after all this with Emmitt, then it's not going to look good in the locker room."

Jimmy Johnson, whose record would depend on how soon the two men could come to an agreement, was not sympathetic to Jones's salary worries. He had another Super Bowl to win, and he wanted Smith back. When the season started and Smith continued to sit out, Johnson fumed. The Cowboys lost their first two games, against Washington and Buffalo, without Smith. In his place was Derrick Lassic, a rookie from Alabama who showed a lot of talent but was crushed under the spotlight and the pressure of being expected to play as well as the best running back in football. Against Washington, the Redskin defenders taunted Michael Irvin, "Hey, boy, you're out here by yourself tonight. Your boy is back at home. What you gonna do now?" The loss to Buffalo was the result of two Lassic fumbles. ("I'm a rookie, but I don't have time to be a rookie," lamented Lassic.) Before the Texas Stadium faithful Troy Aikman had a chance to win the Bills game with four seconds left, but he threw an interception.

"I'm tired of talking about Emmitt Smith," said Jimmy Johnson after the game. In the locker room the volatile Charles Haley threw his helmet against the wall. While walking near Lassic's locker he raged, "We're never going to win with this rookie running back."

The day after the Bills game, the Israelis and the PLO signed a peace accord at Camp David. When Dallas radio station WLIF asked listeners for their opinion about the historic breakthrough, all the callers wanted to talk about was the absence of Emmitt Smith.

Jimmy Johnson would only say that the team was having an identity crisis. Smith's absence was creating a poison throughout the team, he said. Even Troy Aikman was criticizing Jerry Jones.

There was a real question whether the Cowboy players were trying their hardest against the Bills. In an article written by Peter King in *Sports Illustrated,* one Cowboy said, "As crazy as it sounds, we knew the only way we could get our team back was to lose. We weren't trying to lose, but we knew if we won a game, Jerry would figure we could get along without Emmitt. And we know we're not the Dallas Cowboys without Emmitt."

With the two losses, something had to give. Jerry Jones upped his offer to $13.6 million for four years, a salary greater than that of Thurman Thomas. Smith admitted to Mike Fisher of the *Fort Worth Star-Telegram* that he would accept that much. The problem was that Jones and Smith weren't talking to each other. Smith's public statement was that now he wanted $15.1 million for four years. Jones felt betrayed.

A journalist isn't supposed to become part of the story, but Mike Fisher, who was as big a Cowboy fan as anyone, knew what no one else knew: Smith would take the $13.6 million. And after Fisher relayed that information to Jerry Jones, magically the standoff ended and Emmitt Smith signed.

No team had ever gone on to win a Super Bowl after losing the first two games, but when Emmitt Smith returned, the team immediately started to win again. And convincingly. Phoenix, Green Bay, Indianapolis, and San Francisco fell big. Against Philadelphia, Emmitt Smith carried 30 times and gained 237 yards. On his final carry Smith took a draw up the middle, cleared the linebackers, then outran the secondary for a 62-yard touchdown.

Said Nate Newton, "Emmitt Smith is like the mailman. Rain or shine, he always delivers."

It was the best performance in Cowboy history, breaking Tony Dorsett's record of 206 yards. The win returned the Cowboys to first place in the NFC East.

Against the Giants, Troy Aikman left the game with a strained left hamstring. He was replaced by Jason Garrett of Princeton and the World League of American Football. Garrett led two scoring drives in the 31–9 blowout.

To back up Aikman, Jerry Jones signed Jimmy Johnson's former University of Miami quarterback Bernie Kosar for $1 million. Kosar had been released by the Cleveland Browns after eight and a half seasons. Johnson wanted him. Jones put up the money. It was also a brilliant move for Jones in his salary wrangle with Aikman.

Before the season Jones had promised his star QB he would renegotiate his contract, but Jones took his sweet time about it. He had heard what Nate Newton had said about what the players would think if he signed Aikman quickly. It took Jones eleven and a half months in 1993 to come through. Aikman steamed about it, until Jones gave him a whopping $50 million for eight years, including an $11 million signing bonus. Then it was Emmitt Smith's turn to stew. "What happened to the doggone salary cap Jerry griped about for weeks on end?" Smith wanted to know.

But Jones now had Aikman and Smith wrapped up, he had Kosar in reserve, and man-for-man his Cowboys were perhaps the greatest football team to play the game since the Dallas Cowboys of 1978.

The winning streak continued through seven games, then the team suffered two defeats, to Atlanta and Miami. The latter was a Thanksgiving Day game they should have won, except in the final minutes a blocked field goal attempt touched Leon Lett's leg, making it a free ball. The Dolphins recovered on the one and kicked a field goal to win the game.

This time it was Jim Jeffcoat who made the hole in the wall. Said Kevin Smith, "If you work at a chemical plant, you have to know the chemicals."

The Cowboys didn't lose another game all season. But there were hints that all was not milk and cookies on the team. In an interview on ESPN, Jimmy Johnson told the sports world how intrigued he would be if the expansion Jacksonville Jaguars were to offer him the twin jobs of general manager and coach. When asked about it, Jerry Jones told Mike Fisher that the whole thing was frivolous. "I'm assuming it was some sort of good-natured joke," said Jones. Said Johnson, "I didn't think it would be such a big deal. . . . I was in a philosophical mood, so I decided to say that yes, anything is possible."

But when Jaguars owner Wayne Weaver called Johnson to ask him who he would suggest for the job, Johnson told Weaver the same thing: I just might be interested. Now it wasn't so frivolous, and when Jerry Jones found out, he was furious at Johnson's blatant disloyalty. Jones told Weaver if he signed Johnson, Weaver would have to pay him two first-found draft choices and more. Weaver backed off, leaving Johnson and Jones in an uncomfortable situation.

The Cowboys had also suffered a scare the final week of the season in a 16–13 overtime win against the New York Giants, when Emmitt Smith separated his shoulder after he was wrestled down following a 46-yard run. He had never been hurt before, and at halftime he wept. Then he returned to the game, carrying nine times for 59 yards and catching four passes.

Said Smith, "I've always heard about guys playing in pain. I wanted to show my teammates I could do it, too." Smith finished the season with 1,486 yards and won his third straight rushing title, one of only four players in the history of the NFL to accomplish that feat. (Jim Brown, Earl Campbell, and Steve Van Buren were the others.) And Smith had missed the first two games. Smith was named MVP of 1993, the first Cowboy ever to earn that honor. Said Smith not unreasonably, "How come I had to go out and break my shoulder to receive this kind of recognition?" (He didn't know it, but the voting took place before the Giant game.)

Jerry Jones paid Smith the highest compliment for not looking back once the contract dispute was settled. "He was totally positive, and that started in the first game against Phoenix," said Jones.

The Cowboys whizzed through their playoff games, against Green Bay and San Francisco. The Packers were a 27–17 laugher, though perfectionist Jimmy Johnson complained about the team not being "sharp." The Thursday night before the 49ers game, Johnson was sitting at home listening in to radio station WBAP/820 AM's *Sports at Six*. Dan Reeves, the New York Giant head coach and former Cowboy running back, was the guest, and Reeves predicted that the Cowboys would win the game. Johnson called in and, like the true Texan he was, with great braggadocio predicted that the Cowboys would beat San Francisco for the right to represent the NFC in the Super Bowl.

Said Johnson, "We *will* win the ballgame, and you can put it in three-inch headlines." He added, "We will beat their rear end and go to the Super Bowl. That's my personal opinion."

Johnson, under the influence of a Heineken or two, had been brazen, but his prediction was modest. He had said the game would be close through three quarters, and the Cowboys would win in the final period. Instead, it was a blowout from the opening whistle. The Cowboys took charge and never let up in a 38–21 win. Johnson said later that he made the prediction because he "wanted his players to respond to the challenge." Said Johnson, "We were not going to have any excuses. The bottom line was win and we go to the Super Bowl."

Troy Aikman was almost perfect against the 49ers, 14 of 18 for 177 yards and two touchdowns in the first half alone. Then after Aikman suffered a concussion on the second play of the second half when 290-pound lineman Dennis Brown kneed his head, Bernie Kosar proved the value of the Cowboys' investment in him when on a blitz, he hit Alvin Harper on a slant breaking from his right. Two 49ers went for the ball, Harper made a leaping catch, spun, and with no one to stop him, sprinted for the end zone to cap a 38–21 win. It was the second time in two years that Harper had ruined the 49ers.

Charles Haley had a superb day against his old teammates—perhaps his best day—with a sack, a forced fumble, a batted pass, and constant pressure.

Said Haley, "This was my Super Bowl. We play Buffalo in the Super Bowl, and it's just another game for me. The only thing that can happen is we get overconfident and get beat, but I think Coach Johnson will keep us in check." The Dallas Cowboys were going to a record seventh Super Bowl.

As Emmitt Smith and Jimmy Johnson were walking off the field together at Texas Stadium, Jimmy wrapped his arms around Emmitt's neck. Shouting above the noise, Johnson said, "I love you."

"I love you too," Smith replied.

"You mean a lot to me, you know," said Johnson.

"I know, Jimmy. I know," said Smith.

After the game the hottest-selling items were T-shirts with Jimmy Johnson's "We will win" prediction emblazoned on them.

They would be going to Atlanta to play in Super Bowl XXVIII against the Buffalo Bills, a team traveling to the game for the fourth year in a row. The Bills were a talented, deep football team, but in pro football, going to the Super Bowl has little cache unless you win it at least once. Having lost three times in a row, no one gave them any credit or a chance this time. And when the Cowboys beat up on them for the second year in a row, everyone was happy, but no one was ecstatic. Ho hum, we beat the Bills again.

Jim Kelly and Co. gave Dallas a game for one half and led 13–6 at the break. Matter-of-factly, Jimmy Johnson predicted to his players that the Cowboys would win the fourth quarter. He told them to be patient and not to panic, and he asked the defense to attack in the second half. They obliged. Leon Lett caused Thurman Thomas to fumble, then safety James Washington recovered and ran 46 yards for a touchdown. Behind the inspired running of Emmitt Smith, who during halftime pleaded with offensive coordinator Norv Turner to give him the ball more often ("Just put the ball in my hands." "How would you like it, throwing it to you or handing it?" "It doesn't matter."), the Cowboys dominated in the second half, scoring 24 points and allowing none.

Dallas for the second straight year defeated the Buffalo Bills in a Super Bowl, this time by 30–13. In doing so they won a record-tying (with Pittsburgh and San Francisco) fourth Super Bowl. Emmitt Smith was named Super Bowl MVP on 30 carries for 132 yards, including touchdown runs of one and 15 yards.

Said President Bill Clinton, bursting with pride at the success of his supporter and fellow Hawg, "I think the country, in some respects, is even more impressed with this Super Bowl victory than the first one."

Frank Luksa tuned into the Jerry and Jimmy postgame show, wondering if something dramatic would happen. Luksa wondered whether Johnson would announce that he was retiring to raise tropical fish on a small atoll near Bermuda. He was only half joking, and he was disappointed when he heard Jerry say that Jimmy had done it all and heard Jimmy say that he couldn't have done it without Jerry.

The citizens of Dallas and all the Cowboy fans across the country were celebrating the magic of Jerry Jones and Jimmy Johnson when on February 23, 1994, an article in the *Fort Worth Star-Telegram* gave pause. Emmitt Smith had been in Philadelphia to receive the Bert Bell Award as the league's MVP. He was talking to Mike Fisher about the surgery on his right shoulder, then made a vague revelation that sounded ominous if true.

Said Smith: "It's not as happy as a lot of people may think it is. Things stay with players and that's why I think you'll see a number of our players trying to get out of Dallas right now. They won two Super Bowl rings, and they're probably fed up with certain situations down there and are probably looking forward to moving on elsewhere, where people respect them."

In the article Smith specifically mentioned his coach, Jimmy Johnson. "I think that Jimmy has done everything that he wants to do in Dallas, and he's looking forward to going elsewhere and doing some other things elsewhere."

A month went by. All was quiet on the Cowboy front. Then in March of '94 as the NFL held its winter meetings in Orlando, Jimmy Johnson and Jerry Jones captured everyone's attention by publicly showing that the Jones-Johnson partnership was a volatile relationship, which Skip Bayless compared to that of Olympic teammates Tonya Harding and Nancy Kerrigan.

Booze was the fuel that fanned the flames. Since the new age of the Independent Athlete, beginning with Duane Thomas, Thomas Henderson, and Butch Johnson, and going right through to Michael Irvin and Charles Haley, coaches had to bite their lips and accept fits of rage, had to listen to players questioning their coaching abilities, had to turn the other cheek over and over again in order to keep the talent in the lineup and the players productive. For the first time a Cowboy coach was acting in this manner toward the team owner, and the big question was: Would Jerry Jones want to keep Jimmy Johnson badly enough to turn the other cheek?

On the night of March 22, 1994, at Walt Disney's Pleasure Island theme park in Orlando, Jimmy Johnson and three former assistants—Dave Wannstedt of the Bears, Norv Turner of the Redskins, and Bob Ackles of the Phoenix Cardinals—sat around a table while Johnson rehashed one of his Jerry Jones stories. It seems that the day before the 1992 NFL draft, Dallas offered the Cleveland Browns a trade, and that afternoon Cleveland coach Bill Belichick called back to accept the deal. The next day the Cowboys announced the trade to the media. Jones, who had not been told of it, was upset.

Jones met with Johnson until about five minutes before the start of the draft and said to him, "You know the ESPN camera is in the draft room today. So whenever we're about to make a pick, you look at me, like we're talking about it." Jones did not want the public to think that he was just a spectator.

At that request, Johnson headed for his office instead of the draft room. He told Dave Wannstedt, "Let Jerry handle the draft. He knows all about it."

Johnson put enough of his anger away to attend the draft, but he boiled all day over Jones's request.

Johnson had just finished recounting this story when Jerry Jones himself approached the table.

Jones, who bubbles with great emotion when he is feeling happy, wanted to share his happiness with these men to whom he felt a deep sense of gratitude. He raised his glass to propose a toast to their contributions to the Cowboys' back-to-back Super Bowl victories.

Sheepish about having almost been caught talking about the boss behind his back, their response was halfhearted. In comparison to Jones's buoyancy, their tepid response was a signal that Jones was not standing on friendly turf. What Jerry Jones didn't realize—and perhaps Jimmy Johnson didn't realize it himself—was that Jimmy Johnson no longer wanted to coach the Cowboys. He was burned out. He hated that Jones was getting equal credit for the success of the Cowboys. But how do you quit a team that you have just led to two Super Bowl wins? Jimmy Johnson knew just what he was doing when he responded to Jones's toast halfheartedly. The coaches raised their glasses almost reluctantly, and then when Jones was finished toasting Johnson and his assistants, no one said anything more. Jimmy Johnson could have stood and said, "I wish to offer a toast to Jerry Jones, the finest owner in the history of sports." He could have said "Thank you."

When Jones got in return a dull, distant silence, and when Johnson didn't invite the Cowboy owner to sit down with them, Jones knew he was being slighted, if not downright insulted. Nothing grates on a proud man worse than being excluded from a group he so badly wishes to join.

Jones, a proud man, angrily told Jimmy Johnson, "You can go back to your fucking party now," and left them. Wannstedt, for one, defended Johnson, saying that the Cowboy coach hadn't said a word. But that was exactly why Jones was furious. Johnson's silence expressed a palpable contempt for his boss.

Seething, Jerry Jones returned to the Hyatt Regency Hotel, where he sat at the bar with friends within earshot of at least four reporters. An angry Jones told his friends loudly, "I should have fired him and brought in Barry Switzer. There are 500 coaches who could have won the Super Bowl with our team." Jones had never forgiven Johnson for saying that his girlfriend knew more football than Jones. This was payback.

The reporters said Jones repeated his intention to fire Johnson eight or nine times. It's what Jerry Jones really wanted to do. But how does it look to fire a coach who has just won two Super Bowls? Jones, one of the smartest men on the planet, had it figured out all the way.

It didn't take the reporters long to find Jimmy Johnson and tell him what Jones had said. Johnson said he was "stunned" when he heard that Jones had threatened to fire him. Said Johnson, "I am really dumbfounded for the simple reason I don't know what I did." Yeah, right.

Johnson responded by leaving Orlando and flying back home to Dallas, where he met with Jones the next day. At the meeting Jerry Jones told Johnson he could keep his job but refused to apologize for his remarks.

Said Jimmy Johnson in a statement, "I'm deeply hurt that after five years of total commitment to the rebuilding of the Cowboys, and after two consecutive Super Bowl championships, that I have been treated in this way. I will be in my office Monday morning, doing my job."

Logic dictated to both of them that the status quo should remain. Johnson had led the Cowboys to a 36–8 record over the past two seasons. Johnson had the players' confidence, as well as the confidence of the media and the fans. Jimmy Johnson was in position to lead the Cowboys to an unprecedented three straight Super Bowl wins. Why screw up a good thing?

Jones didn't want to take any more of Johnson's insults. Johnson didn't want to have to listen to Jones talk about his contributions to the Cowboys.

The problem Jimmy Johnson had was that his contract called for him to make more than $1 million a year. He couldn't just quit and jeopardize all that money. He needed another job that would pay him that kind of dough before he could quit.

Ed Goren, the executive sports producer for the Fox Television Network, put in a call to Jimmy Johnson to ask him if he wanted to join Fox's studio analysis team.

Goren knew that Johnson, personable, opinionated, and well known, was a natural for TV. "He'd be tremendous," said Goren.

Johnson had often stated his goal was to replace Don Shula, the head coach of the Miami Dolphins. Fox was the perfect interim gig until Shula finally stepped down.

Once Fox made its pitch, Johnson didn't need Jerry Jones any more.

At the same time Jerry Jones was making sure he had a replacement for Jimmy Johnson should Johnson be fired or quit. Jones called Barry Switzer, the former University of Oklahoma coach who had been the freshman coach and dormitory supervisor at Arkansas when Jones and Johnson were there. Jones told his former coach he hoped he hadn't embarrassed him by bringing up his name during his outburst in Orlando. "Are you kidding?" said Switzer. "You have honored me and you have complimented me." Jones asked him two questions: "Do you still want to coach?" and "Would you like to think about coaching the Dallas Cowboys?" Switzer said he was interested. "Call me if you need me," said Switzer. Jones now had a fallback position.

When Jones and Johnson met the next day, Jones said the meeting was productive. Johnson called it "ugly." The players and fans, meanwhile, waited for the other shoe to fall. "It's like the Branch Davidians, Day One," said one macabre Cowboys front-office official.

On March 28, Jerry Jones gave Jimmy Johnson an ultimatum: commit himself to the Cowboys for five more years, or quit.

On March 29, 1994, Jimmy Johnson chose the latter. "It finally hit me that 'Hey, it's time,' " said Johnson. "I decided I couldn't give 100 percent. I didn't want to give 75 percent, because it would hurt the team more than help."

To the end, Jones and Johnson did all they could to display their civility toward each other. They both agreed that future conflicts would jeopardize the team's ability to win. At a final news conference together, they smiled, even hugged briefly, and praised each other.

"We're going through a little transition here," said Johnson. "Well, maybe a big transition. This is in the best interests of the Dallas Cowboys."

Jimmy Johnson, whose contributions to the Dallas Cowboys became an important part of their history, left the team with what he acknowledged was a more than generous $2 million buyout and flew to Miami to spend some time on his boat, *Three Rings*.

Everyone agreed that Jimmy Johnson had brilliantly extricated himself from having to work for Jones. Said Troy Aikman, "He wanted out, saw a crack, and he took it. He got a ton of money, and he got everyone to feel sorry for him."

And with the abrupt, even shocking departure of his two-time Super Bowl coach, Jerry Jones was thrown back into the same situation he had been in immediately after buying the team from Bum Bright: Jethro lives.

Outside the Valley Ranch complex, two discontented fans carried a placard that read: "When hillbillies have hangovers, this is what happens." Said another sign: "Jerry, Call Betty at the Clinic: 1-800-Charter," a reference to the Betty Ford Clinic and to Charter Hospital, both of which administer to victims of alcohol and drug abuse.

The din against him grew worse when Jones announced he was hiring former University of Oklahoma coach Barry Switzer, as he had threatened earlier. Switzer's reputation had been sullied after a series of criminal accusations against his players at Oklahoma. Switzer's recruiting skills were known, but he wasn't considered to be half the coach that Jimmy Johnson was.

Peter King in *Sports Illustrated* quoted an unnamed AFC general manager, who told him, "I can't wait until Jones and Switzer start looking at the waiver wire together."

For his part, Jerry Jones was unapologetic. As far as he was concerned, the Cowboys would win under Barry Switzer just as he had with Jimmy Johnson.

He told *SI*'s King, "Remember, in 1989 when I bought this team, the same kind of things were said. The system is still in place, and Barry Switzer, believe me, knows a football player when he sees one.

"People can say I've positioned myself for a fall, that if we don't go to the Super Bowl, I'm going to get the blame. Fine. What we have is a challenge we didn't have before. Maybe that challenge is just the thing we need for a third straight Super Bowl victory."

77

Bootlegger's Boy

For more than fifteen years Barry Switzer, the Cowboys' new head coach, was one of the most hated men in Texas. The reason was simple: During the years he was head coach of the University of Oklahoma, his teams beat up on UT's Longhorns, and just about everyone else as well, with regularity, at the same time bad-mouthing the Longhorns' revered head coach, Darrell Royal. One time Switzer infuriated the whole state of Texas after he blasted Royal for supporting a proposal that sought to limit the number of visits a coach could make to a prospect. Royal was the president of the Football Coaches Association of America at the time, and Switzer was convinced the rule was being proposed specifically to stop him from signing so many Texas players for OU.

Said Switzer without mentioning any names, "Some coaches don't want to coach anymore. They would rather sit home and listen to guitar pickers." Royal was a close friend of Willie Nelson and Waylon Jennings, and when Royal read the remarks, he went into orbit. Royal called Switzer unethical and demanded Switzer take a lie detector test to allay suspicion that Switzer was paying his players to come to OU. But paying players wasn't the reason OU was beating Texas, Switzer knew. Racism was.

Darrell Royal had won a national championship at the University of Texas in 1969 with an all-white team, but with the advent of desegregation, it would no longer be possible to win championships without recruiting blacks, as Royal would discover. UT did begin signing blacks— Roosevelt Leaks was one of the first and Earl Campbell followed—but Switzer was signing an *entire team* of black stars, and Switzer continued beating the University of Texas as great black Texas players, including Billy Sims, Greg Pruitt, Billy Brooks, Thomas Lott, and Mike Thomas, all came from Texas and starred for OU.

When Royal and his UT followers whispered that the only reason the black Texas players went to Oklahoma was that Switzer was paying them, Switzer finally took the lie detector test Royal was demanding he take, and he passed it.

Says Switzer, "That was the simple, easy, and stupid way to explain why Texas lost those players. Bullshit. They came to us for the same reason the whites did—to be winners, to be champions. And more important, they wanted to be part of our family."

Even after Switzer passed the polygraph test Royal bad-mouthed him. And in the four times the two coaches met, Switzer was gleefully beating Royal's brains out. (OU was the *only* team the great Texas coach didn't beat regularly.) His first season in 1973, Switzer's team beat Texas 52–13, gaining 508 yards in total offense.

For sixteen years Texans muttered while Switzer fashioned an eye-popping 157–29–4 record. He won a dozen Big Eight titles and national championships in 1974, 1975, and 1985. Six times his teams were ranked at number three. And he did it with a lot of inner-city black kids.

Upsetting the Deep South enough with his heavy recruitment of blacks, Switzer then did the unthinkable. He made those black kids the *leaders* of the Sooner team, even playing them at quarterback and linebacker, positions heretofore reserved for the white players. When a delegation of his own OU supporters warned him against starting J. C. Watts at quarterback, Switzer told them he was the one who would make that decision, and that was the end of it. Watts, who is black, ran Switzer's wishbone between 1978 and 1980.

All the while Switzer scoffed at the antiquated, self-serving, often stupid, NCAA rules, calling them unrealistic and against the interests of the athletes. His players were poor, and if they were homesick or if a relative died and they didn't have the money to get home, he would pay to fly them home for a visit, or he would buy them clothing or dinner. He saw his acts as generosity. The NCAA saw them as violations. But Switzer didn't care about the NCAA and he didn't get caught. He only cared about his kids.

As a result, to outsiders, Barry Switzer was seen as a brash, arrogant, Hell's Angel rulebreaker. But to his players, Barry Switzer was family.

Barry Switzer was born on October 5, 1937, during the worst part of the Depression. His father, Frank, operated a toll bridge over the Ouachita River near Crossett, Arkansas. After the Japanese bombed Pearl Harbor, Switzer's dad fled to California to find work in a shipyard. Switzer and his mother, Mary, joined his dad in Long Beach. His mom opened a cafe called Arkies.

When the war ended, the shipyard shut down and his father returned to Crossett, where he failed in a series of business ventures. He then got involved in the one business he was good at: bootlegging.

His mother didn't like the fact his dad was a bootlegger, but there wasn't much she could do about it. His dad's workers were all black, and as Barry grew up, most of his close friends also were black.

When Barry was in the fifth grade, his mother left his father and moved to another town, where she opened a cafe. Two years later she moved back. Because he was a bootlegger's boy, many of the white families in town ostracized them, so he hung out with the black kids. From the time he was in the ninth grade, his dad took him on bootlegging trips. His mom stayed behind. She had few friends. Her sole companions were her books. There was no television.

Barry didn't know it, but his mother was drinking heavily and started taking barbiturates. His father was also a drinker who downed a fifth of whiskey every night.

One afternoon his senior year his father was sent to the Arkansas State Penitentiary. That year Barry Switzer was named the outstanding lineman in the state. His father didn't see a single game.

In 1955 Switzer was recruited for the University of Arkansas by head coach Bowden Wyatt. He could have gone to the Naval Academy, but he didn't have enough self-confidence to spend a year attending prep school to bring up his grades. But Wyatt quit to go to the University of Tennessee before Switzer signed his papers, and Jack Mitchell took over and signed him up. He redshirted his sophomore year and made the dean's list.

That year his dad got out of prison, but life at home was hell. His father drank and ran around on his mother, and his mother drank and suffered. One night she got a call that her husband was out on the town with another woman. Distraught and drunk, she grabbed a .38, jumped in their Jeep, and drove off to kill her husband and his girlfriend, Jewel. Fortunately, the Jeep broke down before she got to town.

From that day on, Frank wouldn't let Mary talk on the phone unless he knew first who was calling. She fell into fits of deep depression. She'd drink, take barbiturates, and read her novels. Son Barry suffered seeing her that way.

On the night of August 26, 1959, Barry saw his mother sitting on his bed glassy-eyed, loaded on booze and downers. Barry said to her, "Mother, I would rather not ever see you again and know you are safe and well taken care of, than to see you like this all the time."

She bent over in her drunkenness to kiss him. He turned away. She went to a closet, got out a pistol, and before Barry could react, she walked out onto the back porch, put the gun to her head, and pulled the trigger. For the rest of his life Barry was convinced his words had caused her death. For twenty years he could not talk to his brother about that night.

After helping his team win the Southwest Conference championship, Switzer graduated from Arkansas in 1960. He hoped to go into coaching, but if he didn't get a chance, then he would go to law school or into business in Little Rock.

Switzer had enlisted in the reserves for six months in the summer of 1960, when he was asked if he wanted to return to Arkansas as an assistant coach under Frank Broyles. His girlfriend's father had influential contacts, and to get out of the reserves early, he wrote to them. He was discharged just in time for the start of practice in '61.

Almost immediately, Switzer had success recruiting, and several of his boys from West Texas helped Arkansas win twenty-two in a row in '64 and '65. Among the players on that team were Jerry Jones and Jimmy Johnson. When Arkansas defensive coordinator Jim MacKenzie was offered the head coaching job at the University of Oklahoma in 1966, MacKenzie offered Switzer a spot on the staff. Switzer accepted, and he and his wife, Kay, flew to Norman, where he would reside for the next twenty-three years.

MacKenzie was head coach for one season. Switzer was his offensive coordinator. The Sooners were 6–4, though three of the losses were by seven points or less. Under MacKenzie, the Sooners for the first time recruited blacks at Oklahoma, great players including Greg Pruett, Joe Washington, and Billy Sims.

Jim MacKenzie suffered a massive heart attack and died on April 26, 1967. The university hired Chuck Fairbanks to replace him as head coach. He made Switzer an offensive coach, putting him in charge of the backs. That year Oklahoma finished 10–1 and beat Tennessee in the Orange Bowl. After two less-than-great seasons, in 1970 the Sooners lost to an inferior Oregon State team, and Switzer, unhappy with the two-back offense he was using called the Veer, decided the offense would be more potent if he were to copy the triple-option offense used by Darrell Royal at UT, called the wishbone. Fairbanks gave Switzer his blessing.

The first game using the wishbone resulted in a 41–9 drubbing by Texas. The alumni were calling for their scalps. Switzer figured that since the staff was going to get canned, he'd throw a party for the other assistant coaches, Jimmy Johnson, Larry Lacewell, and Gene Hochevar. They got roaring drunk, dressed in their wives' clothing, and went over and woke Chuck Fairbanks in the middle of the night. Fairbanks joined them. That Saturday they beat a very good Colorado team. By the end of the season Oklahoma was named national champions in at least one poll. After tying Alabama in the Bluebonnet Bowl, Bear Bryant also switched to the wishbone. Oklahoma and Alabama were the only two teams to win over 100 games in the 1970s.

In the middle of the 1972 season Switzer's father was murdered. Back home in Crossett, Arkansas, he had started a prosperous business as a money lender to black neighbors. He lived alone, or sometimes with Lula Mae, his (black) girlfriend, and he kept a lot of cash around the house, and Barry feared for his father's safety. But it wasn't someone's greed that killed him. It was the jealousy of another woman.

Lula Mae returned to Frank's home unexpectedly, and she discovered he had another girlfriend. She took a .38 from her glove compartment, and when he told her she couldn't come in the house, she shot him in the chest.

He tried to call for an ambulance, but it was a party line and someone else was on the phone. Lula Mae took him to the hospital to try to save his life, but she was driving too fast, skidded, and hit a pole. The car exploded into flames and both Frank Switzer and Lula Mae were burned to death. When Barry arrived at his father's house, he discovered that someone had dug up all his money. It had been stolen.

At the end of the 1972 season, Chuck Fairbanks decided to move up to the pros, taking a job as head coach of the New England Patriots. Switzer asked Fairbanks if he would recommend him for the head coaching job. He said he would. The regents were hesitant because he had never been a head coach before. They gave him a one-year contract, though Switzer made them announce it was for four years, so his recruits wouldn't be nervous about him getting canned. He was thirty-five years old. As soon as he heard the news, the first thing Switzer did was to get on the telephone and personally call every recruit on his list.

Before Switzer could settle into the job, the NCAA learned that two of Chuck Fairbanks's players were eligible for OU only because their high school grades had been tampered with. One of the players was suspended, and OU was forced to forfeit three games and go on probation for four years. Switzer was bitter, but he told the alums, "Nothing is going to stop our team."

And nothing did for almost sixteen years, until a handful of his black ballplayers went too far.

One of Switzer's main strengths led to his downfall. Switzer had always insisted that his players should have the freedom to be themselves, but in 1989 several of his players ran amok, and his loose reign was seen by the administration as part of the reason why.

Defensive lineman Jerry Parks shot a teammate, and eight days later two of Switzer's players raped a white coed (both were sentenced to ten years in prison). When star quarterback Charles Thompson was convicted of selling cocaine to an undercover police officer, the university needed a scapegoat and chose Switzer.

In his own defense Switzer told Barry Horn in the *Dallas Morning News,* "Every player I recruited, Notre Dame recruited and Michigan recruited and Southern California recruited. Where did my kids come from, Devil High School? I beat them. I got them. The thing that infuriates me is I have to defend great kids.

"All this because of a handful of dopin', rapin', shootin' kids."

In June 1989 Switzer resigned under pressure from OU, and for five and a half years he remained in Norman, Oklahoma, in semiretirement, hunting, fishing, undergoing psychoanalysis to rid himself of the demons of a violent childhood, and writing his memoirs.

It's hard to imagine that the Dallas press and fans would have accepted *any* coach to replace a man who had just won two Super Bowls. But most of the pundits accused Jones of making a *really* bad pick in Switzer. The man hadn't coached since 1988. He was coming to a strange coaching staff. He had employed the wishbone offense at Oklahoma, and he wouldn't be able to make the change to a passing offense in Dallas. These reasons were smokescreens. The real bottom line: Nobody wanted Jimmy Johnson to leave, and if they couldn't have Jimmy Johnson, they didn't want anyone.

The hue and cry, moreover, wasn't only over coaching. Jimmy Johnson had convinced a number of reporters that he and only he was capable of keeping the Cowboys on top with his player evaluations and his trades, and Johnson suggested—not subtlely—that with him out of the picture, no one on the Cowboys would be capable of making the crucial personnel decisions.

Johnson's replacements in the personnel decision-making were Jerry Jones and his son, Steven, and most of the reporters decided that they were going to screw up royally, resulting in disarray and despair for the Cowboys.

Jones, for one, bristled at the notion he was merely a pretender, a bumbler, an inept empty suit whose role was that of a meddler.

He said, "I do resent the fact that because I'm here every day, because I'm involved in day-to-day operations, that that is being called 'meddling.' When you get to where I've gotten by working as hard as I have, only to have it called 'meddling,' that would get you defensive. I'm tired of being defensive." He challenged the reporters: "Just keep on going. It motivates me."

Jones predicted that the Cowboys would maintain their lofty position in the NFL under the fifty-six-year-old Switzer, to whom he was giving a five-year $5 million contract. Switzer promised the same thing.

"Nothing is going to change," was one of Switzer's first comments to the media. "Get ready to watch the Dallas Cowboys be the best in the NFL. We got a job to do and we're going to do it, baby."

When asked about his relationship with Jerry Jones, Switzer told reporters, "I give Jerry my commitment of loyalty. I promise you I don't have an ego that allows me to put myself in position to damage the relationship.

"I'm not attacking Jimmy here, but when it comes to getting credit, what the hell difference does it make?"

Switzer said his immediate goal was to convince the Cowboy free agents to stay in Dallas, and almost immediately, the players threw their support behind their new coach. Jimmy Johnson had been like family, and now he was gone. But this was pro football, and the players knew they would have to make an adjustment, and they seemed to make it easily. Free agent Daryl Johnston said he would not leave Dallas because of the coaching change. Troy Aikman and Emmitt Smith both expressed their support for the new coach, and Michael Irvin, who had played for Johnson at Miami and was least amenable to the change in coaches, also came around after a few angry explosions when reporters asked him how he felt about Johnson's departure and Switzer's arrival.

The assistant coaches, too, looked forward to Switzer's arrival. In his news conference, he said of the holdover coaches, "I want them to give *me* a chance." Switzer had always had a reputation for delegating authority and for taking advice. Scouting director Larry Lacewell had worked with Switzer before at Oklahoma—until Switzer had an affair with Lacewell's wife. The two men patched up their differences many years later, and Lacewell told reporters, "Barry's like any other good football coach: He just wants to do what works."

A minority of the observers also concluded that under Switzer the Cowboys would do just fine. Said Skip Bayless, writing for a highly respected publication called the *Insider,* "Once again, believe it or not, 'Jethro' Jones has moved quickly, decisively, and logically. Congrats, Jerry Jones. You got the right guy."

The litmus test of any football coach besides the won–lost record, is what his former players think of him. On that test Switzer scored the highest of marks. When he was hired to coach the Cowboys, his former players were happy for him. Many had been upset when OU fired him, and they had worried about him during his hibernation. Now that he was back in the spotlight, they cheered.

Once Switzer was hired by the Cowboys, reporters scoured the country interviewing his former players to learn about their coach. To a man, his players praised his caring nature. Brig Owens described how when his dad died, when he arrived at the cemetery he was surprised to find Barry Switzer standing there.

Jack Mildren, the lieutenant governor of Oklahoma, was one such former player. He said of Switzer, "At those times in your life when things look darkest, that's when Barry will show up.

"His former players . . . we all kind of worry about him. It's kind of a paternal thing."

Said Switzer about his appointment as head coach of the Cowboys, "Maybe I made a lot of mistakes growing up. And some people mature later in life than others. I'm reaching the point now, I understand.

"This could be my last chance in coaching. I'm going to make it a hell of a run."

78

Jerry versus the NFL

To prepare for the 1994 NFL player draft, rookie coach Barry Switzer rolled up his sleeves and spent ten hours a day for nine straight days evaluating four hundred players with his assistant coaches, scouts, and film graders. Above all, what everyone noticed about Switzer was that he had unlimited enthusiasm for the job. They also discovered he had a fine mind for football. He knew the game, even if he had never coached in the pros before.

"I can look at film and tell you whether a guy can play at this level," Switzer told Frank Luksa. "The defense the Cowboys play is like the one we had at Oklahoma. Look, you have only eleven players. Seven to force and four in the secondary. The talent level is what's different.

"The Dallas talent level is the best. My job is to see I don't screw it up."

Nor did he. Rarely had a newcomer come to pro coaching with so many critical eyes on him. In this case it was the eyes of Texas. Unlike Missouri, whose motto is "Show Me," the Texas motto is "Win the Super Bowl or Else." Would Barry Switzer from the other side of the Red River ride into Dallas County like the Lone Ranger and start shooting up the place, letting his players know he and not Jimmy Johnson was now the boss? Would Switzer try to change the team chemistry, never mind the team uniforms? Would Troy Aikman be running the wishbone? Would the laws that the former marshal put in place be revoked (which would have been the natural tendency of most new bosses coming into a hostile environment)? Players hate change, and the Dallas athletes were wary.

When the Cowboys took the practice field to get ready for the 1994 season, Barry Switzer kept a remarkably low profile. He didn't try to force himself on anyone—not on his coaches, nor his stars. Instead, he pursued a strategy of doing just what his predecessor, Jimmy Johnson, had been doing successfully the last two years. In fact, he *ordered* his coaches, men loyal to Johnson, not to deviate. Barry Switzer quickly earned the respect of both the coaches and the players.

He impressed upon his players that their primary goal—to win the Super Bowl—had not changed. He told several second-string players that he wanted them to "step up" their game so this team could return to the championship level.

If Switzer acted to make one change, it was to let Troy Aikman know that he intended to make the quarterback the coach on the field when it came to the offense. Switzer told Aikman he needed to work closely with him, and it wasn't long before Aikman reported, "Everything's fine with Barry."

Early on Switzer called defensive end Charles Haley and fullback Daryl Johnston into his office and told them how much he needed their leadership contributions. Both told him they had never been in the office of the head coach before.

Even Michael Irvin, who hated the idea of losing Jimmy Johnson, who'd been his coach in college, was smiling after one week of practice, happy with his new coach. "We don't look damn bad on the football field," he said.

Announced defensive star Russell Maryland, "Amongst us, everything has been resolved."

As for his relationship with Jerry Jones, Switzer made it clear he was not in competition with his boss. He said he was happy for the Cowboys owner to go wherever he pleased and do whatever he wanted to do; whenever Jones wanted an update as to what was going on, Switzer said he was only too happy to give it to him. Moreover, in the tricky area of the salary cap, Switzer was quick to see that Jones and especially his son, Stephen Jones, were proving to both agents and players that Dallas had become expert at the fine art of staffing the team with the biggest bang for the buck.

The salary cap had come to the NFL after the owners and players agreed on a contract in January 1993. The plan allowed players with more than five years of experience to become free agents. A salary cap was put into effect, which limited players' salaries to 67 percent of the team's expected revenue the following year. The end result was that while a team could limit its total salary expenditure, individual players who became free agents could skyrocket their salaries. It would cost Jerry Jones at least a million a year for each free agent he wished to keep. In 1994 the salary budget for each team was pegged at $34.6 million.

With Troy Aikman, Emmitt Smith, and Michael Irvin signed to megadeals, Jerry Jones knew he would have to let some of his players go in order to keep salary costs under the cap. For '94 the Cowboys signed free agents center Mark Stepnoski, fullback Daryl Johnston, and guard Nate Newton, three players critical to the continuity of the offense. Throughout their history, the Cowboys had always been a poor-paying franchise; Tex Schramm had fought against free agency for thirty years. But now Tex was gone, free agency was in, and players would finally get the money justly due them. In 1993, for instance, Daryl Johnston had played for a salary of $700,000, less than the market value. But with the new free agency and cap in place and the Washington Redskins pursuing the Pro Bowler, the Cowboys offered him a 1994 salary that called for him to make $1.7 million.

Because of the new cap rules Jones could not keep all his players, and at the end of the '93 season he said goodbye to defensive tackle Tony Casillas, linebacker Ken Norton, defensive tackle Jimmie Jones, guards John Gesek and Kevin Gogan, and safety Thomas Everett. To replace these men, the Cowboys would have to have a successful draft, and when Switzer and Jones went after beef in 1994, it was prime. The Cowboys' first-round choice was a defensive end from Arizona State, Shante Carver. And to further anchor the offensive line, they signed the 325-pound guard Larry Allen from Sonoma State and the even larger 355-pound George Hegamin from North Carolina State.

For Switzer, Allen turned out to be the pick of the litter. A second-round selection, he received $1.7 million to sign. Big as a house and fast as a defensive back, Allen grew up in the inner city of Compton, California, where at the age of ten he was stabbed twelve times in the head and neck by a twelve-year-old neighbor. As a teen he joined a gang for one day, but, after he and a friend traded their jackets to a crack dealer for rock cocaine, they learned that street life was not for them when they had to abandon the drugs to escape the police. Allen swore right then and there that he wanted nothing to do with being part of a gang.

When his parents broke up, Allen and his mother moved constantly.

He attended four different high schools in four years. His grades were not good enough for him to go to Clemson or USC, two teams that wanted him, and instead he went to Butte Junior College in Oroville, California, and then to Sonoma State, where for two years he was a roman candle amid firecrackers.

With Barry Switzer motivating his players and the ghost of Jimmy Johnson fading by the day, the '94 Cowboys started out strong, jumping out to a 6–1 record. Then talented offensive right tackle Erik Williams caused Dallas fans angst when he had a few drinks and drove too fast in his Mercedes 600 SL. Skidding out of control, he struck a guardrail, plowed across a grassy area head-on into a retaining wall, and nearly killed himself; he suffered a broken rib, two torn ligaments in a knee, a torn ligament in his right thumb, a sprained wrist, and facial cuts and was lost the rest of the season. (That same night Shante Carver, under suspicious circumstances, overturned his truck, though without serious injury. Was this a return of Barry Switzer's Renegade U? the press asked.)

But Larry Allen stepped in for Williams and played beautifully, and the team kept winning, finishing with a 12–4 regular season record. Of the four losses, three were by less than a touchdown. The San Francisco 49ers won a key divisional matchup, 21–14, as Steve Young threw two touchdowns and ran for a third. That's how close Barry Switzer's Cowboys came to an undefeated season in 1994.

In the playoff opener, the Cowboys manhandled the Green Bay Packers, 35–9, in a game featuring a 94-yard touchdown pass from Troy Aikman to Alvin Harper, the longest pass in NFL playoff history. The following week, however, the San Francisco 49ers, led by Jerry Rice and the always-exciting Deion Sanders, beat the Cowboys for the NFC championship, 38–28, crushing everyone's hopes for a third-straight Super Bowl win.

The disappointment of the Dallas press and fans was so great it was almost as though the Cowboys hadn't won a game all season. Barry Switzer had taken the Cowboys to within one game of the Super Bowl— an amazing accomplishment if one wanted to be rational and objective about it, though few were. Many Dallas fans considered the '94 season a failure.

The fault was laid at the doorstep of Switzer and Jerry Jones, who decided that for the Cowboys to go back to the Super Bowl, they needed a player who could take the pizzazz quotient up a notch. The player was Deion Sanders, the NFL's Defensive Player of the Year in '94, and what made the signing of the peripatetic free agent superstar even more special was that Sanders had been a key operative on the 49ers, the only team that could stop the Cowboys from reaching their Super Bowl goal.

Before signing Sanders for $35 million for seven years, including a $12 million bonus, Jerry Jones consulted his Big Three: Troy Aikman, Emmitt Smith, and Michael Irvin. All were enthusiastic. Though Sanders missed several games at the start of the '95 season because of ankle surgery, he made an impact immediately. That Deion Sanders was instrumental in helping the Cowboys to a 27–17 victory over the Pittsburgh Steelers in Super Bowl XXX on January 28, 1996, was to the everlasting credit of Barry Switzer and Jerry Jones, who has become the most visible and powerful owner in the NFL.

There was only one bump on the road to the top in '95. After racing to a 10–2 record, the Cowboys lost consecutive games to Washington and Philadelphia. Against the Eagles, Barry Switzer became the focus of attention when he twice ordered his offense to run the ball on fourth and one rather than punt. Both times Emmitt Smith ran into the line, and both times he was stopped. The decision to go for the first down helped the Eagles to victory, and after the game and for the next two weeks, all the media seemed to write about was Switzer's ill-conceived play-calling.

The player who stood up for Switzer the loudest was Sanders, who berated the Dallas media for its negativism. "When you win around here, it's not good enough because you didn't win big enough," he said. "And when you lose it sure isn't good enough. How can we win the Super Bowl when you try not to even let us get there? You are trying to tear us apart. We won't let that happen.

"Barry Switzer hasn't lost any games, including [at] Philadelphia. Barry Switzer doesn't make the plays. He doesn't cover a Jerry Rice. The last time I saw a coach on the field was Woody Hayes. But every day you try to make Barry Switzer an issue. It's constant shots at our coaches and my teammates. I'm sick of it."

Getting Deion Sanders for the Cowboys was a rare coup. Not only was Neon Deion an incredible presence on the field, but, along with Michael Jordan and Shaquille O'Neal, he was one of the three most famous athletes in America. To sign Sanders, according to Jones, a number of the other Cowboy players allowed him to restructure their contracts. As it was, the NFL invalidated the contract and sued Jones for going $1.39 million over the cap. The suit did not stop Sanders from playing, however, and Jones eventually agreed to charge an added $1.6 million a year over the next four years to his salary structure for signing Sanders.

When Jones signed Sanders, he knew exactly what he was getting: a

Cowboys publicity and advertising machine. Every kid in America wanted to be Deion Sanders, who sold millions of dollars worth of Nike shoes and cheese-crust pizzas for Pizza Hut. Jerry Jones himself appeared in the pizza ad with his star defensive back.

"Do you want to play defense or offense?"

"Both."

"Do you want regular crust pizza or cheeze lovers' pizza?"

"Both."

"Do you want ten million or twenty million?"

"Both."

In the ad Deion and Jones laugh uproariously, though one might suspect that Deion's laughter was more genuine.

The signing and marketing of Deion Sanders was part of a nationwide publicity drive that Jerry Jones had launched in the summer of 1994, when he announced his intention to lure national corporations into the orbit of the Dallas Cowboys. Just one month later he stood the NFL on its ear when he revealed that Pepsi Cola/Dr. Pepper would pay him $25 million for the exclusive right to pour its soda in Texas Stadium for the next ten years. Ordinarily no one would care which soda Dallas fans drank, except that under a longtime system begun by former NFL commissioner Pete Rozelle, sponsorships were sold leaguewide by NFL Properties, its marketing arm, and not by individual teams.

But deep in the heart of Texas, Jerry Jones was decrying a socialistic system in which the successful franchises supported those less profitable. Declaring his championing of free enterprise, in September of 1995 Jones again thumbed his nose at the NFL brotherhood when he announced he had signed a deal with Nike in which, for $2.5 million a year through the year 2001, he would allow the company to paint its trademark "swoosh" logo on Texas Stadium, install a theme park there, and outfit all Cowboy coaches and other sidelines personnel in Nike-manufactured apparel. For years, Nike's efforts to become an NFL sponsor had been rebuffed because the official NFL apparel sponsor has been Reebok. Nike's slogan is "Just Do It," and that's exactly what Jerry Jones did. He announced the deal with Nike on a Monday-night national telecast, with a press release that trumpeted: "Cowboys Owner Bucks NFL Again."

Jones called for the end of NFL Properties in much the same way that Clint Murchison Sr. had once called for the end of federal regulation of the oil industry.

"You don't have to be a rocket scientist to do better than they did," Jones said. "You wake up in the middle of the night thinking of ideas." At the same time, he said he had done nothing wrong because these deals were Texas Stadium deals, not Dallas Cowboys deals.

Meanwhile, the owners of teams that don't own their own stadium (everyone else but Wayne Huizinga in Miami and Robert Kraft in New England) could only sit by and swear at or envy Jones. Jones has been called a rogue on a par with Oakland/LA/Oakland Raiders owner Al Davis, who has supported Jones from the time he took over the Dallas franchise in 1989.

"I like the way he does business," said Davis. "He's a winner."

The league sued Jerry Jones for $300 million, and Jones countered in another suit, asking the NFL for a billion dollars. Two weeks after Jones was served with the lawsuit, he announced he had made another deal, this time with American Express, which would become the official credit card of Texas Stadium. If you want to use a credit card to buy Dallas Cowboys season tickets, you must use American Express. Don't leave home without it.

At the same time that Jones was announcing his deal with American Express, Art Modell, the owner of the Cleveland Browns, announced he was uprooting his team after forty-five years in the City on the Lake and carpetbagging it to Baltimore. Unhappy with his lot in life, Modell wanted a new stadium, wanted to be able to sell luxury boxes like Jerry Jones, wanted more side income like Jerry Jones. Suddenly Jerry Jones was being accused of bringing about the downfall of the NFL.

In his defense, Jerry Jones says that the disharmony he has created will make for a stronger NFL. Until and unless the NFL figures out a way to stop him, Jones will continue to mastermind a successful, contending franchise.

Meanwhile, the combination of Troy Aikman, Emmitt Smith, and Michael Irvin, perhaps the greatest scoring combo in the history of the NFL, continued to work their magic. Explained Michael Irvin, "We're unique for a couple of reasons. Not just because of the numbers we've put up or the wins. It's because of the relationship we share. Not once do we bicker. We don't care about the fame, the money, the spotlight. We all understand winning is the ultimate judge."

Super Bowl XXX was played in Phoenix, Arizona, only after a bitter struggle. Arizona governor Bruce Babbitt had declared Martin Luther King Day a state holiday but his successor, Evan Mecham, appealed to the lowest common denominator and rescinded the holiday. The protest was so great that the state lost an estimated $256 million in tourist dollars.

In March 1990 the NFL had awarded Tempe the 1993 Super Bowl, but a number of team owners swore the game would not be played there unless the holiday was reinstated. In Arizona a lot of people said they didn't want to observe Martin Luther King Day because King was a Communist. When a referendum failed and the measure lost, the game was played elsewhere. When Tempe was awarded the 1996 game, black ministers and politicians began a campaign to educate Arizonans about Dr. King's nonviolence and his message that all men are created equal. In November 1992, 62 percent of Arizona voters passed the measure, removing the stigma of racial intolerance from the state. Dr. King's widow, Coretta Scott King, attended a prayer breakfast before Super Bowl XXX.

As for the racial situation in Dallas and the country, great strides have been made since the Dallas Cowboys came into existence in 1960. Blacks must no longer ride in the back of the bus. In fact, many black Cowboy players ride in a Mercedes-Benz or limousine. Blacks can eat wherever they want, go to any restaurant including country and western bars, and they can live in any part of the city, thanks to the courage of people like Lyndon Johnson and Mel Renfro.

Bigotry does remain entrenched in certain quarters in Dallas. Roger Staubach continues to shun joining the country club across the street from his home because of its policy excluding blacks and Jews, and he is criticized for believing in affirmative action in his hiring practices. But Staubach and other men of conscience realize that steps must be taken to improve the lot of blacks in Dallas. He realizes that, given the embedded racist culture of the South, the black community has not been afforded equal economic opportunity. This was made evident after rioting during the Cowboy victory parade of 1992, when black youths went on a rampage in downtown Dallas.

Despite the disparity, both societies, white and black, are beginning to understand that prejudice and bigotry hurt not only the object of exclusion but all of us. There is now a huge black middle class, possible because for the first time whites have accorded blacks an equal opportunity for education. The next step will be to allow blacks a fair shot at a good job.

At the forefront of helping to spread understanding and reconciliation among the races are our athletes. Can a young white boy bearing the image of Emmitt Smith on his shirt or rooting for Deion Sanders hate others who have the same skin color as these great athletes? It's not so easy. Perhaps one day white society will be as tolerant of Emmitt Smith's brother or cousin or friend as it is of him. Our children may make it so. By the millions they continue to buy and wear clothing bearing the likenesses of such great stars and heros as Michael Jordan and Shaq and Ken Griffey Jr. and Frank Thomas and Barry Bonds and Scottie Pippin and David Robinson and Grant Hill and Jason Kidd and Jerry Rice and the Dallas trio of Emmitt Smith, Michael Irvin, and Deion Sanders, who has been a star in not one but two major league sports.

On the other hand, accusations made against high-profile black players for drug-related and violent crimes tend to make even tolerant whites scornful of black society. The stereotype of white bigots is that blacks are by nature violent and lawless. It's why whites have always moved out of neighborhoods when blacks begin to move in. And over the last few years, some of the black players on the Cowboys have fueled that stereotype, having been accused of drug abuse, rape, and other antisocial behaviors.

Erik Williams, who had nearly killed himself in a car accident in 1994, was accused of the attempted rape of a topless dancer. Star lineman Leon Lett was suspended for a year for testing positive for drugs a second time. Michael Irvin was suspended for the first five games of the 1996 season after he was found in a hotel room with two self-employed models and a plate of coke. The man who blew the whistle, a hotel employee, first said he called the police because of complaints about noise in Irvin's room. Later it turned out the desk clerk had lied and that there had been no complaints. To some legal experts, there was a real question whether the arrest was tainted, because no legitimate probable cause had existed for the police to arrest Irvin in the first place. Adding to the murkiness of the case was the arrest of Dallas police officer Johnny Hernandez, who reportedly lived with one of the women. Hernandez, who had been subpoenaed to testify at the trail, drove to the parking lot of a Dallas mall and reportedly paid a federal DEA undercover officer posing as a hit man big bucks to kill Irvin.

When the first jury panel was polled in the Irvin case, only four of fifty-seven prospective jurors said they could put aside their feelings for the Cowboys and the team's star receiver.

"I'm a Cowboys fan, and that's all there is to it," said one of them. Another woman admitted her daughter was "infatuated" with Irvin. Whether Irvin's wife will remain a big fan is another story.

After Irvin was arrested, a former Cowboys employee by the name of Dennis Pedini accused former wide receiver Alvin Harper of leasing a house near the practice field in which Harper, Irvin, and other Cowboys used drugs and had group sex. The house, which the players called the

White House, had been managed by Pedini. Speculation quickly arose as to the identities of those unnamed Cowboys who had frequented this lair.

In the end the prosecutors let Irvin off the hook for the same reason O. J. Simpson walked: Irvin's defense attorneys made the local police force look inept. On the stand officers contradicted each other about what happened the night of the arrest. After a week of testimony about topless dancers, coke use, charges of witness intimidation, and other lines of inquiry that left Irvin's good-guy reputation sullied, the talented wide receiver decided to cut bait, took a deal, and head off to training camp. Michael Irvin pleaded guilty to cocaine-possession charges in exchange for not having to serve any jail time. He was placed on four years probation and fined $10,000. If he could stay clean, his slate would be wiped clean.

Without Irvin for the first five games of '96, the Cowboys seemed listless. When Irvin returned, the team played well enough to win the NFC Eastern Division championship and then soundly defeated the Minnesota Vikings in the opening round of the playoffs.

Then on December 30, early in the week before their second-round playoff game with the upstart Carolina Panthers, Irvin's reputation plummeted anew when a young woman accused him of holding a gun to her head while teammate Erik Williams and a third man raped her in Williams's home. Police reports leaked to the press revealed that there was a videotape of the incident. Tom Landry went on *Nightline* to say that the fault lay with Jerry Jones, though he did admit it was hard to control players who made as much money as modern athletes. Pundits called for the immediate suspension of both Irvin and Williams. Barry Switzer was quick to defend his players.

Michael Irvin was contemptuous of the allegations, saying he hadn't even been at Williams's home that night. Williams, who in 1995 made an out-of-court settlement with a seventeen-year-old topless dancer who'd accused him of sexual assault, also denied he had done anything wrong. He had made videotapes of this and other sexual encounters he said, so he could protect himself against lovers who sought to accuse him of a rape. Peyton Place had been Sunday school compared to this.

Fans and teammates, meanwhile, were becoming weary of the almost constant controversy surrounding the Dallas players. Some felt that the taint of scandal was removing the luster of being a Dallas Cowboy. "For a guy who his whole life wanted to play for the Dallas Cowboys, you know at times it really makes you sick to your stomach," said Bill Bates, a fourteen-year veteran.

808 ★ PETER GOLENBOCK

Although Irvin and Williams were ultimately cleared of all wrong-doing, in the end, the '96 Cowboys were defeated not by scandal but by injuries. Irvin dislocated his shoulder in the first series of plays against the indomitable Panthers, leaving the offensive burden on the shoulders of Troy Aikman, who was heroic, and a subpar Emmitt Smith, who had not been his all-world self for much of the season due to some kind of unreported injury. When Deion Sanders suffered a broken bone above his eye late in the second half, the Cowboys just didn't have enough weapons left in their arsenal to bring down Carolina.

After the 26–17 loss, someone asked Emmitt whether he was feeling okay. "Pretty much," he said, summing up the season, "except for a broken heart."

The morning of the big game, in a reminder that today's Cowboys do not exist in a vacuum, Thomas Henderson, the player formerly known as "Hollywood," wrote a letter in the *Dallas Morning News* to Cowboys fans everywhere apologizing for his cocaine addiction and his subsequent legal problems in the early 1980s. He admitted that he had been under the spell of the drugs to the extent that he had considered suicide. He asked forgiveness.

The hint of sex and drugs, the aura of violence, the skill of gridiron warriors, and the power of television are the components that make many millions of Americans fascinated by NFL football. But the one ingredient that makes them *care* about a team is that team's ability to win, something the Dallas Cowboys have been doing since 1966.

As a result, the Cowboy Nation continues to fascinate. Jerry Jones and Barry Switzer have both been painted as buffoons, even though one has made a sheik's fortune in oil and the other was one of the most successful coaches in the history of college football. With Switzer as coach of the Cowboys, all they did was win the Super Bowl. And yet in the papers the naysayers continue to chirp, blaming Switzer for losses and making dire predictions about how the salary cap will negatively affect the Cowboys in the future. The predictions of Jones's failures have been broadcast since 1989. You would think his four Super Bowl victories would allow him some sort of a brief respite from the criticism.

If nothing else, things are rarely dull around One Cowboys Parkway as controversies continue to swirl around celebrated players who are as renowned as movie stars and richer than all but the oilmen. But all that goes with the territory. The Cowboys have long since stopped being just a franchise, or a sports team. They are headline news, and as every player who has ever donned a Cowboys helmet will tell you, there's something unique about wearing the silver and blue. Something that makes them stand apart from all the rest. Something that makes them distinctive, proud of their football heritage and eager to leave a legacy. And that goes a long way toward explaining why, love them or hate them, the Dallas Cowboys have been, and shall continue to be, America's Team.

Notes

1. The Two Clints

3 *just a fun thing*   Wolfe, *Murchisons,* p. 239.

4 *if the railroad could do it*   *Ibid.,* p. 20.

5 *a very unethical approach*   *Ibid.,* pps. 32–33.

6 *nine million vehicles*   Priestley, *Saga of Wealth,* p. 101.

7 *give them a dollar*   O'Connor, *Oil Barons,* p. 127.

7 *cash makes a man careless*   Wolfe, *Murchisons,* p. 118.

7 *owe more than you can pay*   *Ibid.,* p. 61.

8 *American Liberty pipeline so hot*   Priestley, *Saga of Wealth,* p. 173.

11 *just the shyest little boy*   Wolfe, *Murchisons,* p. 65.

12 *have at it*   *Ibid.,* p. 160.

12 *I saw him yesterday*   *Ibid.,* p. 285.

14 *afford to go broke once*   *Ibid.,* p. 168.

14 *feared that Clint Jr. was unbalanced*   It was almost thirty years before Murchison Sr.'s instincts would be proven correct.

2. Growing Pains

Interviews with Mark Goodman and Tex Schramm. See also Don Kowet, *Rich Who Own Sports.*

18 *tell him to go to hell* Wolfe, *Murchisons,* p. 29.

23 *football is no place for soft people* Wismer, *Public Calls It Sport,* p. 30.

23 *he knew he was wrong Ibid.,* p. 60.

24 *you couldn't make that sort of basic boo boo* "Bobby Baker Talks to Texas Journalist Larry King," *Playboy,* June 1973.

3. Tex

Interviews with Byron Bradfute, Don Perkins, and Tex Schramm.

36 *something I never could be* Bud Shrake, "A Cowboy Named Dandy Don," *Sports Illustrated,* September 16, 1968.

4. The Bombardier

40 *wasn't a prettier smelling place on earth* Landry, *Autobiography,* p. 1.

42 *wondered how much greater he might have been Ibid.,* p. 74.

44 *acute hatred for receivers Ibid.,* p. 100.

45 *chased me all the way to our bench Denver Post,* September 14, 1986.

53 *only one man who could have done this* St. John, *Man Inside,* p. 87.

5. The Expendables

Interviews with Dick Bielski, Bob Fry, Don McIlhenny, and Jack Patera.

56 *such a big challenge intrigued me* St. John, *Man Inside,* p. 93.

6. The Disgruntled

Interviews with Gene Cronin, John Gonzaga, Ray Mathews, and Jerry Tubbs.

7. Mr. Nice

Interviews with Frank Clarke and Tex Schramm. See also Leslie, *Dallas City Limit,* and Payne, *Big D.*

8. Little Eddie

Interview with Eddie LeBaron.

9. The First Herd

Interviews with Gene Babb, Dick Bielski, Byron Bradfute, Frank Clarke, Fred Cone, Bob Fry, John Gonzaga, Eddie LeBaron, Don McIlhenny, Jack Patera, and Jerry Tubbs.

98 *Cross gave the boy a pan* Stowers, *Journey to Triumph,* pps. 15–16.

10. 0-11-1

Interviews with Gene Babb, Dick Bielski, Byron Bradfute, Frank Clarke, Gene Cronin, Bob Fry, Eddie LeBaron, Don McIlhenny, Don Perkins, Tex Schramm, and Jerry Tubbs.

109 *I never even had aspirations* Stowers, *Journey to Triumph,* p. 27.
117 *playing against Bob Gain* Ibid., p. 35.

11. The Righteous and the Sinners

Interviews with Gene Babb, Dick Bielski, Byron Bradfute, Frank Clarke, Fred Cone, Gene Cronin, Bob Fry, John Gonzaga, Eddie LeBaron, and Jerry Tubbs.

123 *unequal relations between the races* Nolan, *Negro's Image,* p. 18.
132 *Eddie had been playing well* Stowers, *Journey to Triumph,* p. 31.

12. Big Bob and Hogmeat

Interviews with Gene Babb, Byron Bradfute, Frank Clarke, Bob Fry, John Gonzaga, Chuck Howley, Eddie LeBaron, Bob Lilly, Don Perkins, Tex Schramm, and Jerry Tubbs.

138 *he was like some damn animal* Garrison, *Once a Cowboy,* p. 91.
150 *I had definitely not had a good day* Stowers, *Journey to Triumph,* p. 36.
152 *all along Tom knew what he wanted* *Dallas Morning News,* June 6, 1968.

13. Pettis and Cornell

Interviews with Cornell Green, Pettis Norman, and Tex Schramm.

14. Inconsistent D

Interviews with Byron Bradfute, Chuck Howley, Bob Lilly, and Dick Nolan.

15. Clarke Star

Interview with Frank Clarke.

16. A Season Dies with a President

Interviews with Frank Clarke, Bob Fry, Cornell Green, Chuck Howley, Lee Roy Jordan, Tom Landry, Eddie LeBaron, Bob Lilly, Dick Nolan, Pettis Norman, and Tex Schramm.

184 *gravy* Landry, *Autobiography,* p. 146.
185 *look sharp, men* Ibid., p. 148.

191 *get off Caroline's tricycle* Payne, *Big D,* p. 309.

192 *go out and raise money* *Ibid.,* p. 314.

199 *start thinking about life after football* Landry, *Autobiography,* p. 147.

17. Mel and Maury

Interviews with Mel Renfro, Tex Schramm, and Maury Youmans.

207 *one of our first team meetings* Stowers, *Journey to Triumph,* pps. 104–105.

18. Buddy and Don

Interviews with Frank Clarke, Buddy Dial, and Pettis Norman.

212 *we were in a team meeting* Stowers, *Journey to Triumph,* pps. 87–88.

218 *the most courageous and gutsy season* Landry, *Autobiography,* p. 149.

220 *wasn't really a matter of courage* Bud Shrake, "A Cowboy Named Dandy Don," *Sports Illustrated,* September 16, 1968.

19. Pete

Interview with Pete Gent.

20. Bob Lilly and the Flex

Interviews with Lee Roy Jordan, Bob Lilly, Dick Nolan, and Maury Youmans.

21. Varmint

Interview with Pete Gent.

22. Turmoil and Dandy Don

Interviews with Frank Clarke, Buddy Dial, Pete Gent, Lee Roy Jordan, Bob Lilly, and Pettis Norman.

264 *completed an embarrassing 38 percent* Landry, *Autobiography,* p. 159.

265 *finally I called Meredith into my office* *Ibid.,* p. 159.

23. Iconoclasts

Interviews with Buddy Dial, Pete Gent, Bob Lilly, Dick Nolan, and John Wilbur.

287 *don't bother reading it, kid* St. John, *Man Inside,* p. 119.

24. Success–At Last

Interviews with Frank Clarke, Pete Gent, Bob Hayes, and Bob Lilly.

291 *the guy has shown me a lot* Stowers, *Journey to Triumph,* p. 133.

295 *Dallas will be the world champion* *Dallas Morning News,* October 22, 1966.

298 *what if I'd missed it* *Dallas Morning News,* November 14, 1966.

298 *this team loves that guy* *Ibid.*

25. Two Feet Away

Interviews with Frank Clarke, Buddy Dial, Pete Gent, and Lee Roy Jordan.

26. Lance on the Flank

Interviews with Frank Clarke and Pete Gent.

321 *I can't tell the difference* St. John, *Man Inside,* p. 129.

27. Agony

Interviews with Frank Clarke, Pete Gent, Cornell Green, Chuck Howley, Bob Lilly, and John Wilbur.

28. The Ice Bowl

Interviews with Frank Clarke, Pete Gent, Cornell Green, Chuck Howley, Lee Roy Jordan, Bob Lilly, Jerry Tubbs, and John Wilbur.

335 *like standing in a pot of ice* *New York Times,* January 14, 1996.

337 *quarterback sneak by Bart Starr* Garrison, *Once a Cowboy,* pps. 185–186.

29. Uncivil War

Interviews with Pete Gent, Pettis Norman, Mel Renfro, and John Wilbur.

30. Jordan versus Gent

Interviews with Pete Gent, Cornell Green, Lee Roy Jordan, Pettis Norman, Mel Renfro, and John Wilbur.

31. Trials and Tribulations

Interviews with Pete Gent, Cornell Green, Lee Roy Jordan, and John Wilbur.

362 *me and Meredith went out drinking* Garrison, *Once a Cowboy,* pps. 75–76.

39. Rentzel's Compulsion

Interviews with Pete Gent, Steve Kiner, Bob Lilly, Pettis Norman, and Mel Renfro.

40. The Mountaintop

Interviews with Margene Adkins, Pete Gent, Cornell Green, Lee Roy Jordan, Steve Kiner, Pettis Norman, Mel Renfro, and Roger Staubach.

41. Almost Super

Interviews with Lee Roy Jordan, Craig Morton, Pettis Norman, Mel Renfro, and Roger Staubach.

461 *I know [Manders] recovered it*   Stowers, *Journey to Triumph*, p. 167.

461 *I looked across the room*   *Ibid.*

464 *I'm not taking any shit about this game*   Toomay, *Crunch*, p. 61.

42. Duane versus the Plastic Man

Interviews with Margene Adkins, Pete Gent, Cornell Green, Lee Roy Jordan, Steve Kiner, Pettis Norman, and Mel Renfro. See also the Duane Thomas interview with Will Grimsley in the *Dallas Times-Herald*, March 15, 1972.

468 *if we discriminated against them*   Wolfe, *Murchisons*, p. 307.

468 *so that God can see His team play*   *Ibid.*, p. 368.

472 *when I saw Bob Lilly and Jethro Pugh*   Thomas, *Fall of America's Team*, pps. 95–96.

472 *I don't think Tom ever understood*   *Ibid.*, p. 95.

474 *a rumor going around camp*   *Ibid.*, p. 80.

481 *Duane Thomas was a big factor in us winning*   Ditka, *Autobiography*, p. 118.

482 *how did you and Duane get along*   Garrison, *Once a Cowboy*, pps. 69–70.

483 *time for the defense to practice*   *Ibid.*, pps. 70–71.

483 *worst anguish Tom ever went through*   Ditka, *Autobiography*, pps. 117–118.

484 *Duane ran us right into the Super Bowl*   Garrison, *Once a Cowboy*, pps. 70–71.

43. Roger Takes the Helm

Interviews with Lee Roy Jordan and Mel Renfro.

487 *Landry's responsibility to pick a quarterback* St. John, *Man Inside,* pps. 167–168.

489 *a group of the Cowboys started riding motorcycles* Garrison, *Once a Cowboy,* pps. 102–104.

44. Super

Interviews with Margene Adkins, Cornell Green, Chuck Howley, Lee Roy Jordan, Mel Renfro, and Roger Staubach.

45. Duane Thomas's Legacy

Interviews with Pete Gent and Roger Staubach.

503 *you have paved the way* Bayless, *God's Coach,* p. 109.

46. Craig Fills In

Interviews with Lee Roy Jordan and Roger Staubach.

512 *I don't understand it* *Dallas Morning News,* November 24, 1972.

47. A Study in Black and White

Interviews with Rodrigo Barnes, Lee Roy Jordan, and Mel Renfro. See also Frank Taggart's 1973 *Dallas Times* interviews with John Niland (September 11) and Rabbi Max Zucker (October 2).

528 *what position does she play* *Dallas Times-Herald,* October 10, 1973.

529 *I was coming out of a bar on Lemmon Avenue* *Fort Worth Star-Telegram,* July 31, 1994.

48. The Free Agent

Interviews with Drew Pearson and Roger Staubach.

49. Roger to Drew

Interviews with Rodrigo Barnes, Drew Pearson, and Roger Staubach.

554 *Tom was shocked* Bayless, *God's Coach,* p. 126.

50. Come the (Short) Revolution

Interviews with Rodrigo Barnes, Cornell Green, Lee Roy Jordan, Drew Pearson, Mel Renfro, and Roger Staubach.

565 *a bad place to be* Frank Luksa, *Dallas Times-Herald,* August 21, 1974.

51. So Long, Bob Hayes

Interview with Pete Gent. On Bob Hayes's drug bust, see Carlton Stowers, "Tarnished Star," *Dallas Observer,* September 26, 1991. See also *Austin American-Statesman,* August 21, 1991.

52. Two Number Ones

Interviews with Thomas Henderson and Lee Roy Jordan.

53. The Dirty Dozen

Interviews with Lee Roy Jordan, Drew Pearson, and Roger Staubach.

54. Hail Mary

Interviews with Thomas Henderson, Lee Roy Jordan, Drew Pearson, and Roger Staubach.

55. Super Surprise

Interviews with Thomas Henderson, Lee Roy Jordan, Drew Pearson, and Roger Staubach.

608 *the best group I've had from the standpoint of character* St. John, *Man Inside,* p. 215.

56. Roger's Ordeal

Interviews with Thomas Henderson, Drew Pearson, and Roger Staubach.

609 *I like the Western movies* *Dallas Morning News,* July 20, 1975.

615 *we simply had no running game* Martin, *Texas Thunder,* p. 92.

57. TD

Interviews with Drew Pearson, Mel Renfro, and Roger Staubach. See also Dorsett, *Running Tough.*

619 *I've been recognized everywhere* *Dallas Times-Herald,* July 10, 1977.

58. The Assassin

Interview with Thomas Henderson.

59. Hollywood

Interview with Thomas Henderson.

60. A Crushing Defeat

Interviews with Thomas Henderson, Drew Pearson, and Roger Staubach.

COWBOYS HAVE ALWAYS BEEN MY HEROES ★ 819

61. America's Team
Interviews with Thomas Henderson, Drew Pearson, and Roger Staubach.

645 *it's alive and living in Texas Stadium* San Francisco Examiner, September 9, 1979.

62. Casualties
Interview with Thomas Henderson.

63. Roger in Mothballs
Interviews with Drew Pearson and Roger Staubach.

64. Close, but No Cigar
Interview with Drew Pearson.

65. Clint Goes Under
See Wolfe, *Murchisons.*

66. Bum Bright
687 *poor old Clint got not a penny* Bayless, *God's Coach,* p. 217.

67. The Fall of the Cowboys
Interview with Mel Renfro.

693 *singularly unimpressed* Bayless, *God's Coach,* p. 51.

699 *they chose not to use me* Dorsett, *Running Tough,* p. 173.

701 *that's just the nature of the business* St. John, *Landry Legend,* p. 70.

68. Bum Bright's Payback
706 *I just don't know how much more of this I can bear* Bayless, *God's Coach,* p. 270.

69. End of an Era
716 *I don't know if any team will duplicate what happened* St. John, *Landry Legend,* p. 24.

717 *God bless you and your families* Ibid., p. 35.

70. The Devil and Mr. Jones
727 *he wanted to buy a football team* Dent, *King of the Cowboys,* pps. 67–68.

71. Scar Head

738 *you can win one at Miami* Johnson, *Turning the Thing Around,* p. 105.

740 *nobody cries louder than a bully* Ibid., pps. 125–126.

742 *a world of bullshit* Ibid., p. 153.

72. The Depths Revisited

749 *Walker didn't have what the great backs had* Bayless, *The Boys,* p. 132.

751 *sit back and look at that list* Ibid., p. 132.

751 *still, I was concerned* Ibid., p. xx.

73. Emmitt

See Smith, *Emmitt Zone.*

74. All the Way Back

765 *an opportunity to play for you guys* Johnson, *Turning the Thing Around,* p. 186.

75. How 'Bout Them Cowboys

774 *Jimmy to wind up in a mental institution* Bayless, *The Boys,* p. 10.

775 *just a matter of how much* Johnson, *Turning the Thing Around,* p. 254.

776 *nobody could deny the magic* Smith, *Emmitt Zone,* p. 204.

76. The Rift

777 *why should Jimmy really care* Bayless, *The Boys,* p. 13.

782 *heard about guys playing in pain* Ibid., p. xiv.

77. Bootlegger's Boy

791 *explain why Texas lost those players* Switzer, *Bootlegger's Boy,* p. 99.

Bibliography

Anderson, Terry. *The Movement and the Sixties.* New York: Oxford University Press, 1995.

Bahas, Dr. Gabriel. *Keep Off the Grass.* Pleasantville, N.Y.: Readers Digest Press, 1976.

Bayless, Skip. *The Boys: Jones vs. Johnson and the Feud that Rocked America's Team.* New York: Pocket Books, 1994.

———. *God's Coach.* New York: Simon & Schuster, 1990.

Blair, Sam. *Dallas Cowboys: Pro or Con?* New York: Doubleday, 1970.

Dent, Jim. *King of the Cowboys: The Life and Times of Jerry Jones.* Holbrook, Mass.: Adams Publishing, 1995.

Ditka, Mike, with Don Pierson. *Ditka: An Autobiography.* Chicago: Bonus Books, 1986.

Dorsett, Tony, with Harvey Frommer. *Running Tough.* New York: Doubleday, 1989.

Garrison, Walt, and John Tullius. *Once a Cowboy.* New York: Random House, 1988.

Gent, Pete. *North Dallas Forty.* New York: William Morrow, 1973.

Harris, David. *The League: The Rise and Decline of the NFL.* New York: Bantam Books, 1986.

Henderson, Thomas "Hollywood," and Peter Knobler, *Out of Control: Confessions of an NFL Casualty.* New York: G. P. Putnam & Sons, 1987.

Johnson, Jimmy, as told to Ed Hinton. *Turning the Thing Around.* New York: Hyperion, 1993.

Kowat, Don. *The Rich Who Own Sports.* New York: Random House, 1977.

Landry, Tom, with Gregg Lewis. *Tom Landry: An Autobiography.* New York: Zondervan Publishing, 1990.

Leslie, Warren. *Dallas City Limit.* New York: Grossman Publishers, 1964.

Martin, Harvey. *Texas Thunder.* Rawson Associates, 1986.

Nolen, Claude H. *The Negro's Image in the South: The Anatomy of White Supremacy.* Louisville: University of Kentucky Press, 1967.

O'Connor, Richard. *The Oil Barons: Men of Greed and Grandeur.* Boston: Little, Brown, 1971.

Payne, Darwin. *Big D: Triumphs and Troubles of an American Supercity in the 20th Century.* Dallas: Three Forks Press, 1994.

Powledge, Fred. *Black Power and White Resistance.* World Publishing Co., 1967.

Priestley, James. *A Saga of Wealth.* New York: G. P. Putnam & Sons, 1978.

Rentzel, Lance. *When All the Laughter Died in Sorrow.* Saturday Review Press, 1972.

St. John, Bob. *The Landry Legend.* Dallas: Word Books, 1989.

———. *Landry: The Man Inside.* Dallas: Word Books, 1979.

———. *Tex!: The Man Who Built the Cowboys.* New York: Prentice Hall, 1988.

Schapp, Dick. *Quarterbacks Have All the Fun.* Chicago: Playboy Press, 1974.

Smith, Emmitt, with Steve Delsohn. *The Emmitt Zone.* New York: Crown, 1994.

Staubach, Roger, with Frank Luksa. *Time Enough to Win.* Waco, Tex.: Word Incorporated, 1980.

Stowers, Carlton. *Journey to Triumph.* Dallas: Taylor Publishing, 1982.

Switzer, Barry, with Bud Shrake. *Bootlegger's Boy.* New York: William Morrow, 1990.

Thomas, Duane, and Paul Zimmerman. *Duane Thomas and the Fall of America's Team.* New York: Warner Books, 1988.

Toomay, Pat. *The Crunch.* New York: W. W. Norton, 1975.

Wiley, Ralph. *Why Black People Tend to Shout.* New York: Birch Lane Press, 1991.

Wismer, Harry. *The Public Calls It Sport.* New York: Prentice Hall, 1965.

Wolfe, Jane. *The Murchisons: The Rise and Fall of a Texas Dynasty.* New York: St. Martin's Press, 1989.

Index